NUTRITION IN
INFANCY AND CHILDHOOD

NUTRITION IN INFANCY AND CHILDHOOD

Edited by

PEGGY L. PIPES, R.D., M.P.H.
Assistant Chief,
Nutrition Section, Clinical Training Unit,
Child Development and Mental Retardation Center;
Lecturer, Parent and Child Nursing, School of Nursing,
University of Washington,
Seattle, Washington

CRISTINE M. TRAHMS, M.S., R.D.
Teaching Associate, Division of Pediatric Genetics,
Department of Pediatrics, School of Medicine;
Director, Nutrition Services,
PKU and Biochemical Genetics Clinic,
Child Development and Mental Retardation Center,
University of Washington,
Seattle, Washington

FIFTH EDITION

With 107 illustrations

 Mosby

St. Louis Baltimore Boston Chicago London Philadelphia Sydney Toronto

Dedicated to Publishing Excellence

Editor-in-Chief: James M. Smith
Acquisitions Editor: Victoria E. Malinee
Developmental Editor: Gina Gay Chan
Project Manager: Patricia Tannian
Production Editor: Suzanne C. Fannin
Designer: Gail Morey Hudson
Cover illustration: Molly Babich

Fifth Edition

Mosby–Year Book, Inc.
11830 Westline Industrial Drive, St. Louis, Missouri 63146

Library of Congress Cataloging in Publication Data
Pipes, Peggy L.
    Nutrition in infancy and childhood/Peggy L. Pipes, Cristine M.
Trahms. -- 5th ed.
      p. cm.
    Includes bibliographical references and index.
    ISBN 0-8016-6567-1
    1. Children--Nutrition. 2. Infants--Nutrition. I. Trahms,
Cristine M. II. Title.
    [DNLM: 1. Child Nutrition. 2. Infant Nutrition. 3. Nutrition--in
adolescence.   WS 115 P665n]
RJ206.P56 1993
613.2'083--dc20
DNLM/DLC
for Library of Congress

93 94 95 96 97 CL/MY 9 8 7 6 5 4 3 2 1

Contributors

JUDITH BUMBALO, PH.D.

School of Nursing,
University of Wisconsin, Milwaukee, Wisconsin

MIRIAM E. LOWENBERG, PH.D.

Professor Emerita, Pennsylvania State University,
University Park, Pennsylvania;
Consultant, Seattle, Washington

BETTY LUCAS, M.P.H.

Lecturer, Parent and Child Nursing, School of Nursing;
Nutritionist, Child Development and Mental Retardation Center,
University of Washington, Seattle, Washington

MARY J. O'LEARY, PH.D.

Nutrition Consultant, Private Practice,
Albuquerque, New Mexico

SALLY M. O'NEIL, PH.D.

Behavioral Psychologist, Private Practice,
Seattle, Washington

ROBIN PRITKIN GLASS, M.S., O.T.R.

Occupational Therapist,
Children's Hospital and Medical Center, Seattle, Washington

JANE MITCHELL REES, M.S.

Teaching Associate, Division of Adolescent Medicine,
Department of Pediatrics, School of Medicine;
Director, Nutrition and Education Services, Adolescent Clinic,
Child Development and Mental Retardation Center,
University of Washington, Seattle, Washington

JOAN ZERZAN, M.S., R.D.

Neonatal Nutritionist,
University of Washington Medical Center, Seattle, Washington

TO
Marion Miller
a friend and supportive colleague

with love to
Anna, Peter, and Paul,
and to
Lunette

Preface

Nutrition in Infancy and Childhood has, from the first edition, been prepared to offer information for students and health care professionals who provide or plan to provide clinical services to infants and children and their parents. The fifth edition has been reorganized and expanded to better meet this objective. Two chapters have been eliminated and the information from them has been integrated into existing and new chapters that address current concerns of nutrition and children. The fact that nutrition plays a major role in the prevention of disease has been made known to most parents through the media. Most parents are vitally interested in providing the best possible diet for their children. Many have questions about what to feed their children, and others who know what foods provide the needed nutrients or diet modifications for their children do not know how to create the environment in which children will consume these foods. Answers to these questions are provided in each chapter.

CONTENT FEATURES

The book presents information on growth and development, nutrient needs of infants and children, and the clinical approach to collecting and assessing food intake information before the discussions on infancy, preschool-age, school-age, and adolescent children. Two chapters focus on the development of food patterns; one of these is written by one of the pioneers in child feeding—Miriam Lowenberg, Ph.D., and the other addresses current research and practice. These discussions are followed by chapters that present the application of nutrition in special circumstances; the child who is a vegetarian, children with special health care needs, and the prevention of chronic diseases. The final discussion focuses on parent and child interactions as they influence food patterns and the use of behavior modification techniques to achieve the acceptance of new foods and teach feeding skills to young children.

Two new chapters will be found in this edition; one on the school-age child, and another on nutrition intervention in special circumstances in adolescence. The chapter on the developmentally delayed child has been expanded to include a greater number of conditions that affect children with special health care needs. Review questions have been added to aid the student in reviewing information in the chapters. Developmental and behavioral parameters have been integrated into each of the discussions. The clinical application has been presented in each chapter to guide students as they apply nutrition information for individual clients. Suggested learning activities continue to be included to provide suggested approaches on learning the clinical use of the information presented in the chapters. The glossary has been significantly expanded to aid the reader in defining unfamiliar words in the chapters.

The implementation of many nutrition plans for children, especially those with special health care needs, and when medical or psychosocial factors play a role in the etiology of the nutrition concern, requires an interdisciplinary assessment and management model. Therefore the interdisciplinary approach has been emphasized. In fact, an interdisciplinary group of professionals including an occupational therapist and a nurse with expertise in behavior management techniques, as well as nutritionists known for their skills in nutrition intervention for specific age groups and conditions, contributed to the book. A variety of students and health care professionals will find the book useful, especially those in nutrition/dietetics, maternal and child nursing, occupational therapy, and physical therapy.

ACKNOWLEDGMENTS

In the preparation of any manuscript, many make significant contributions. Our clients at the Child Development and Mental Retardation Center have willingly discussed their nutrition concerns and provided detailed information on what their children ate and factors that influenced their acceptance of foods and food plans. They have helped us to develop the approach to nutrition services we present in this book. The Nutrition Fellowship students have asked many probing questions that have influenced our approach to the subject matter. The contributors have developed their chapters under considerable stress because of busy schedules. The faculty and administrators at the Child Development Center have been most supportive and understanding when timelines had to be met.

The editors at Mosby including Gina Chan and Suzanne Fannin have made the book a reality. At the same time, they have been patient and pleasant as they tried to keep us on their timeline. We appreciate their understanding and support.

We are also grateful to the reviewers who gave of their time and expertise to help us develop a useful text.

Finally, we thank our family members who gave us the time away and the support we needed to complete our task. To Anna and Peter—who had a mother away from home on many weekends, and Paul—their father who understood, and to Lunette—the mother who waited at home, we are grateful for your understanding and support and we express our gratitude.

Peggy L. Pipes
Cristine M. Trahms

Contents

5 The Preschool-Age Child, 121

Peggy L. Pipes
Cristine M. Trahms

6 Nutrition and the School-Age Child, 142

Betty Lucas

1

Nutrition: Growth and Development

Peggy L. Pipes
Cristine M. Trahms

Objectives

✦✦✦

After studying this chapter, the student should:

✔ *Understand the effect of nutrition on physical growth and development.*

✔ *Understand characteristics of cell growth and the concept of critical stages of growth and development.*

✔ *Recognize appropriate equipment necessary to secure accurate measurements of height, weight, and skinfolds.*

✔ *Recognize if anthropometric parameters are secured in a manner that provides accurate data.*

✔ *Be able to interpret growth data on individual children in relation to norms.*

A normal, healthy child grows at a genetically predetermined rate that can be compromised or accelerated by undernutrition, imbalanced nutrient intake, or overnutrition. Progress in physical growth is one of the criteria used to assess the nutritional status of populations and of individual children. It is therefore important that persons concerned with nutrition and feeding of infants and children be familiar with the process and parameters of growth, as well as the charts used to assess it.

Although every aspect and component of growth is thought to be influenced by nutrition, this discussion focuses on those parameters dealt with by persons concerned with children's food intake: increases in linear growth and weight, changes in body composition, how to secure accurate measurements of growth, and how to interpret physical growth patterns of normal children. Patterns of catch-up growth after an episode of wasting (when there is a greater deficit in weight than length) and stunting (when deficits of both height and weight are present) are discussed.

1

TABLE 1-1   *Guidelines for Assessment of Growth*

	Length/Height	Weight	Head Circumference
Normal growth	In channel*	In channel	In channel
Energy deprivation	In channel	Depressed	In channel
Protein-energy malnutrition	Depressed	Depressed	In channel
Severe malnutrition	Depressed	Depressed	Depressed
Various disease states	Depressed	Depressed	Often depressed
Recovery or catch-up growth	Accelerated	Accelerated	Accelerated

In channel is defined as the usual growth pattern of the child between the 10th and 75th percentiles.

NUTRITION AND PHYSICAL GROWTH

Children who are undernourished are shorter and weigh less than their well-nourished peers. The rate of gain in weight is affected more than is the rate of gain in height, but if the nutritional deficit is severe enough and continues long enough, linear growth will be retarded or may cease and pubertal maturation and **epiphyseal closure** may be delayed. Linear growth is delayed when energy intake is adequate but protein intake is deficient. Weight is affected when energy intake is deficient, and linear growth will eventually be retarded (Table 1-1). Overnutrition results in taller, heavier, more mature children.

Children from low-income families consume less food and therefore less energy and total nutrients than children from families with greater financial resources. Nutritional status studies have shown that children from these families are shorter and weigh less than children whose families are more affluent. Differences in stature are greater than those in weight. In fact, several studies have found that children who live under conditions of marginal food supplies are shorter yet appear fatter than those who have an abundant supply of food available. Results of studies to determine the effect of nutritional supplementation during the third trimester of pregnancy through the third year of life on impoverished children in Colombia, South America, who were at risk for malnutrition show that children who received supplements were taller and heavier than those in the nonsupplemented control group at 18 and 36 months of age. They, however, remained smaller than Colombian children from higher socioeconomic families who probably had more food available.[1] Infants and children at nutritional risk who have received the Special Supplemental Food Program for Women, Infants, and Children (WIC) supplemental food packages that include iron-fortified cereal, iron-fortified infant formula, or milk, cheese, eggs, and fruit and vegetable juices have experienced increased rates of growth in height and weight compared with children who have not received these supplements.[2]

Growth patterns of children of racial groups whose members have been believed to be genetically small have been found to increase under conditions of improved nutrition. Especially striking was the change in the growth pattern of Japanese children born in the post–World War II period compared with those institutionalized during the prewar period. In 1962 boys at 14 years of age were found to be 7.6 cm taller and girls at 11 years of age 6.6 cm taller than prewar children of the same ages. The change in growth patterns has been credited to an increase in the intake of animal protein.[3] A 1960 survey of children in Japanese orphanages whose food budgets were limited found heights to be significantly less than those of the national averages for children of the same age and sex. Adolescents were shorter as compared with their age-group average than were younger children.[3] During the subsequent 10 years the provision of 180 gm milk and one egg per day, as well as increases in food budgets resulted in improvements in the quality and quantity of protein, as well as in the total amount of nutrients consumed. Increases in average stature were greater than expected. A 1970 survey found that only teenage boys were significantly below the national averages for height.[4]

The long-term effects of malnutrition on physical growth during infancy and early childhood have been studied in children in Barbados who suffered a nutritional insult early in life and were then rehabilitated.[5] Growth deficits were noted at ages 5 to 11 years and 9 to 15 years in both boys and girls compared with healthy children. These findings were most prominent in girls. At ages 11 to 18 years, catch-up growth in height and weight had occurred in the boys. No differences were noted between the study males and control males or in ratings of sexual maturity. The girls who had been malnourished continued to be smaller, however they had experienced an accelerated growth velocity and the differences in height and weight were smaller than had been noted previously. The age at menarche was significantly delayed for girls with histories of marasmus (which had occurred in the first year of life) but not for girls with histories of kwashiorkor (which had most often occurred in the second year of life). It appears that the genetically predetermined growth can be reached even after a nutritional insult if nutritional rehabilitation is effected. However, there may be critical periods in early infancy when a nutritional insult can compromise final stature in females.

CHARACTERISTICS OF GROWTH

Growth may be defined as an increase in the physical size of the body as a whole or as an increase in any of its parts associated with an increase in cell number or cell size. Development is defined as the acquisition of function associated with **cell differentiation and maturation of individual organ systems** or as a change from a lower to a more advanced stage of complexity for greater facility in functioning. Growth and development are affected by genetic, hormonal,

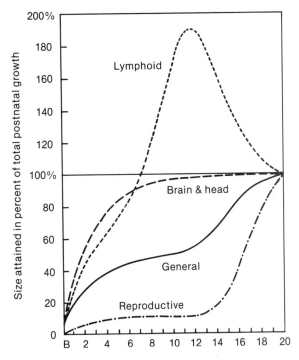

FIG. 1-1   Growth of four types of body tissue as percent of adult size.

(From Scammon RE: Measurement of the body in childhood. In *The measurement of man*, Minneapolis, 1930, University of Minnesota Press.)

environmental, and behavioral factors that interact to determine an individual's growth pattern.

Individual children have their own genetically predetermined growth patterns. Growth and development, however, proceed in an orderly and predictable sequence. Each organ and organ system has its own period of rapid growth marked by rapid cell differentiation, changes in form, and susceptibility to physical and environmental influences. Growth is the composite of many tissues that are growing at different rates. Skeletal muscle growth approximates whole body growth. The brain, lymphoid, adrenal, and reproductive tissue follow different patterns as shown in Figure 1-1. The head reaches 90% of its adult size by 6 years of age, whereas growth of the reproductive system proceeds slowly until puberty when sexual maturation occurs. The lymph tissue grows rapidly until puberty and then reduces in size.

PERIODS OF GROWTH

Increases in physical size are achieved by increases in both the number and the size of cells. Cell growth in any organ proceeds in three stages: **hyperplasia,** in which an increase occurs in cell number; **hypertrophy** and hyperplasia, in which increases occur in both the size and the number of cells; and hypertrophy, in which only the size of the cells increases. Growth in both the number and the size of cells can be assessed by calculation of the rates of weight to deoxyribonucleic acid (DNA) or the rates of protein to DNA.

Enesco and Leblond[6] determined the number of cells in each organ of the rat at different ages throughout growth by measuring the DNA content of the organ. Knowing the weight of the organ, they then estimated the size of the cells. Winick and Noble[7] using the same method for rat studies, found that there is a time when cell division stops before the organ attains its full size. There is a phase when cell number is not increasing but cell size is. Some tissues, like the brain, reach a full adult complement of DNA sometime in the second year, whereas other tissues, such as muscle, continue to increase in DNA throughout adolescence.

Winick and Noble[8] found that rats malnourished by restriction of total food intake during the period of increase in cell number but given normal diets during later growth had a reduction in the number of brain cells, whereas those malnourished later in life and rehabilitated had normal numbers and sizes of cells. Elliott and Cheek[9] in studies of muscle and liver cells of rats, found that restriction of kcalories resulted in fewer cells, whereas restriction of protein and kcalories resulted in a decrease in both cell size and number. Winick and Noble[10] have also found that overnutrition during hyperplasia resulted in larger animals with a larger number of cells in the organs. The period of hyperplasia, the time when cell numbers are increasing, is

the time when the organ is most vulnerable to compromised nutrition and can be considered critical to an individual's acquisition of a normal complement of cells.

GROWTH IN HEIGHT AND WEIGHT

The birth weight is determined by the length of gestation, the mother's prepregnancy weight, and weight gain during pregnancy. The average weight of the normal full-term newborn is approximately 3500 gm. However, about 7% of infants born in the United States are low birth weight (LBW), weighing less than 2500 gm, or are very low birth weight (VLBW) infants, weighing less than 1500 gm.[11] Infants may be LBW because of a premature delivery or because of a retarded rate of growth in utero. A small for gestational age infant whose intrauterine weight gain was poor but whose linear and head growth is appropriate for gestational age has experienced **asymmetric** intrauterine growth retardation. A small for gestational age infant whose length and head circumference are also below the 10th percentile is said to be symmetrically growth retarded. The symmetrical type of growth retardation reflecting early and prolonged intrauterine nutritional deficit is more detrimental to later growth and development.

After birth, genetic influences are target seeking (looking for their genetically determined growth channel). A period of catch-up or lag-down growth may occur.[12] The majority of infants who are genetically determined to be longer shift channels (percentile ratings) of growth during the first 3 to 6 months. However, many infants born at or below the 10th percentile who are determined to be of average height may not achieve a new channel until 1 year of age. Larger infants whose genotypes are for smaller sizes grow at their fetal rates for several months before the lag-down in growth becomes evident. Often a new channel is not apparent until the child is 13 months of age.[12]

Immediately after birth there is a weight loss

resulting from a loss of fluid and some catabolism of tissue. The loss averages 6% of body weight but occasionally exceeds 10%. Thereafter, weight gain in infancy proceeds at a rapid but decelerating rate. Average weight gains for the first 4 months of age are 20 to 25 gm/day and during the last 8 months, 15 gm/day.

By 4 months of age most infants' birth weights have doubled, and by 12 months of age their birth weights have usually tripled. Males double their birth weight earlier than do females, and smaller newborns double their birth weights sooner than do heavier infants. The weight increment during the second year is slightly less than the birth weight. The normal newborn infant who weighs 3.5 kg at birth, for example, can be expected to weigh 7 kg at 4 to 6 months of age, 10.5 kg at 1 year of age, and 13 kg at 2 years of age. Thereafter, the yearly increments in weight proceed at a slower but constant rate averaging 2.3 kg/year until the ninth or tenth year, when the rate of gain shows a steady increase. This rate continues until adolescence, when a rapid increase in rate of gain occurs.

Height, like weight, increases at a rapid but decelerating rate until adolescence when the adolescent growth spurt occurs (Figure 1-2). Infants usually increase their lengths by 50% by 1 year of age, double them by 4 years of age, and triple them by 13 years of age. The average length of an infant at birth is 50 cm. This figure increases to 74 to 76 cm at 1 year of age, 100 to 105 cm at 4 years of age, and 150 to 155 cm in the preadolescent years. Between 6 years of age and puberty sex differences can be noted. At age 6 years boys are taller and heavier than girls. By 9 years of age the height of the average girl is the same height as the 9-year-old boy and her weight is greater.

The range of chronological ages at which children of either sex enter adolescence and at which specific events occur is wide. Females enter prepubescence at a younger age than do males. Males have a more intense growth spurt that lasts longer. Typically girls become taller than boys shortly after the age of 11 years because of their growth spurt. However, by 14.5 years of age boys experience their growth spurt and are taller than the average girl. At approximately 9 years of age, girls become heavier than boys and remain so until approximately 14.5 years of age when boys surpass them in weight (Figure 1-2).

Growth during adolescence is under the control of androgens and growth hormones. Testosterone, other androgens, and estrogen exert an effect on linear growth and accelerate skeletal maturation. Growth hormone, thyroid hormone, and sex hormones are all necessary for proper growth.

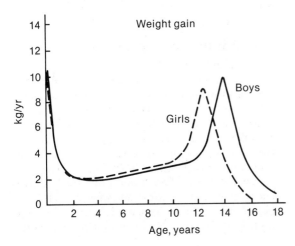

FIG. 1-2 Mean weight gain for age of males and females between infancy and 18 years of age.

(From Hamill PVV, Johnston FE, Lemeshow S: *Heights and weights of youths 12-17 years,* United States, 1966-1970. Vital and Health Statistics, Series II, No 124. DHEW Pub No [HSM] 73-1606, Washington, DC, 1973, Government Printing Office.)

Maturational Stages

Although adolescents enter and complete the stages of growth and maturation at different chronological ages, the events tend to follow a similar pattern. The stages of maturation as described in Chapter 9 are used to describe the current stage of maturation of an individual and to predict future events.

Although no physical maturation is evident in early puberty, there is an increase in the release of gonadotropins and sex steroids that occurs during sleep. Levels of adrenal sex steroids also increase. In early puberty the concentration of these hormones continues to increase. The secretion of growth hormone and thyroid function also increases. Physical changes can be noted.

In females there is breast budding, enlargement of the ovaries, and estrogenization of the vaginal mucosa in early puberty. The uterus begins to enlarge and the distribution of body fat begins to change. During midpuberty the ovaries enlarge and there is separation of breast and areolar tissue. The uterus increases in size and pubic hair appears. Most girls attain peak height velocity at this stage before menarche. In late puberty breast enlargement continues. The areola remains separate from the breast. The vagina elongates and the uterus assumes adult size and shape. Menarche occurs if it has not already begun. Growth slows and is complete in most females within 2 years after menarche.

In early puberty the testicular volume of males increases and the scrotum begins to redden and change in texture. The seminal vesicles, prostate gland, and testes enlarge. By midpuberty males experience enlargement of penile length. Pigmented straight pubic hair appears around the base of the penis. Facial hair appears on the upper lip. The testes and scrotum enlarge and the voice begins to change. The growth spurt may begin toward the end of middle puberty. In late puberty the penis continues to enlarge in length and breadth. The testes, prostate gland, and seminal vesicles continue to enlarge, and scrotal skin becomes pigmented. Muscle mass increases, and peak velocity occurs if it has not occurred in middle puberty. Auxiliary hair develops. Facial hair begins to grow on the upper part of the cheek and midline below the lower lip.

Pubertal Changes in Body Composition

During puberty the percentage of body fat increases in females and decreases in males. Females have a greater percentage of fat before puberty and sustain this fat throughout adolescence and adulthood. Males gain some fat in early adolescence, only to lose it later for gains in muscle. The fat deposition reaches a negative velocity. The result is a body composition of a higher percentage of fat in females than in males.

Both males and females experience an increase in muscle and strength during adolescence. The somewhat earlier increase in girls means that females have more muscle for a short while. Ultimately, the muscle mass increase is greater in males than in females. Increases in muscle size result in increases in strength.

The greatest difference in growth between males and females at puberty occurs in the shoulder and hip. This difference is caused by the specific response of females to estrogen in the hip joint cartilage and the response of males to testosterone in the shoulder joint cartilage. The pelvic outlet in a female, which is already wider than the male, widens further. This, along with increased width, provides room for prenatal growth should there be a pregnancy.

Racial Influences on Growth

Racial differences have been noted in rates of growth. American black infants are smaller than American white infants at birth. American black infants grow more rapidly during the first 2 years, and from that age through adolescence are taller than American white boys and girls of the same age groups. The Hispanic Health and Nutrition Examination Survey conducted between 1982 and 1984 found only minor differences in height of Mexican-American children before adolescence compared with white children in the second National Health and Nutri-

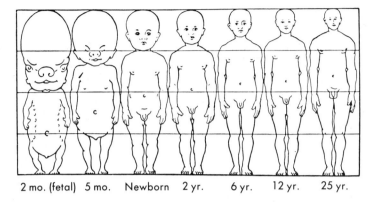

2 mo. (fetal) 5 mo. Newborn 2 yr. 6 yr. 12 yr. 25 yr.

FIG. 1-3 Changes in body proportions from second fetal month to adulthood.
(From Robbins WJ and others: *Growth,* New Haven, Conn, 1928, Yale University Press.)

tion Examination Survey. The differences noted could be attributed to poverty. However, differences increased during adolescence. Mexican-American teenagers were shorter than white teenagers.[13] Asian children tend to be smaller than black children and white children. However, growth status of refugee East Asian children has increased between 1978 and 1989 and is now similar to or approaching that of other ethnic groups in the United States. The researchers at the Center for Disease Control suggest that these studies may indicate that children of different ethnic origins have similar growth potentials.[13a]

CHANGES IN BODY PROPORTIONS

Increases in height and weight are accompanied by changes in body proportions. The head at birth accounts for approximately one fourth of the total body length; however, the head is one eighth of the body length by the time growth has ceased. Brain growth is 75% complete by the end of the second year, and the brain is 100% of adult size by age 6 to 10 years. Leg length increases from approximately three eighths to one half of total body length between birth and adulthood (Figure 1-3).

BODY COMPOSITION

Changes occur not only in height and weight during growth but also in the components of the tissues. Increases in height and weight and skeletal maturation are accompanied by changes in body composition—in adiposity, lean body mass, and hydration. Estimates of the changes in body composition have been made from chemical analysis of human bodies and of individual tissues, from indirect measurements of water and electrolyte levels, from excretions of **creatinine** and **hydroxyproline,** and from estimates of fatness. Indirect measurements of body fat have been attempted by several methods, including measurement of the density of the whole body, measurements of total body weight minus lean body mass, use of fat-soluble gases, measurement of the thickness of fat by **roentgenographic studies,** and measurements of subcutaneous fat layers. Although there is much yet to be learned about body composition, there is an important body of data that can be related to physical growth and nutrient needs.

Determinations of total body water alone or in combination with other measurements such as density or potassium have been used as a basis for estimations of lean body mass. Total body water as a percentage of body weight decreases throughout infancy from approximately

70% at birth to 60% at 1 year of age. Reduction of body water is almost entirely extracellular. Extracellular water decreases from 42% of body weight at birth to 32% of body weight at 1 year of age. This change results from decreases in the water content of adipose tissue, increases in adipose tissue, and relative increases in lean body mass.[14] The percentage of weight of water in lean body mass at any age is relatively stable. In other words, there is a direct relationship between total body water and lean body mass. Water is estimated to be responsible for 80% of the weight of fat-free mass at birth and 72% to 73% of the weight of fat-free mass of an adult. Fomon and others[14] estimated the percentage of water in fat-free mass of the male reference as 77.9% at 4 months, 79% at 12 months, 77.5% at 3 years, and 75.1% at 10 years of age. They estimated the percentage of water in fat-free mass of the reference female to be 79.7% at 4 months, 78.8% at 12 months, 77.9% at 3 years, and 76.9% at 10 years of age. Adipose tissue contains about 15% water.

Anderson and Langham[15] found that the potassium concentration (grams per kilogram of body weight) increases from the first year of life, reaches a maximum at 8 or 9 years of age, and then declines sharply. After this, sex differences become apparent. The decline continues in females, but an increase is noted in males between 14 and 16 years of age, followed by another decline.

Using data on total body water and total body potassium, knowledge of the concentration of potassium in extracellular and cellular water, and the mineral content of the body, Fomon and others[14] have estimated the body composition of children between birth and 10 years of age.

Forbes,[16] in studies of persons 7.5 to 10.5 years of age, with a K^{40} counter (a chamber used to measure body composition), found a linear relationship between height and lean body mass at any age and an exponential relationship between lean body mass, height, and age groups. Sex differences in lean body mass and height ratios were noted in the earlier years, although they were not great enough to be significant. Males had greater amounts of lean body mass per centimeter of height than did females. After 12.5 years of age the lean body mass/height ratio increased rapidly in the male, whereas the increase was more gradual in the female. The female's lean body mass/height ratio maximum, which was about two thirds that of the male maximum value, appeared to be attained at 16 years of age, 3 years earlier than in the male. At 20 years of age males had one and a half times more lean body mass per centimeter of height than did females.

Fat is found in adipose tissue, in sites in the bone marrow, in phospholipids in the brains and the nervous system, and as a part of cells. It is the component of the body in which the greatest differences between children, age groups, and sexes are seen. The fat content of the body increases slowly during early fetal development, then increases rapidly in the last trimester. Widdowson and Spray[17] found total body fat of the newborn infant to have a mean value of 16%. Fat accumulates rapidly during infancy until approximately 9 months of age.

Between 2 and 6 months of age the increase in adipose tissue is more than twice as great as the increase in the volume of muscle. Sex-related differences appear in infancy, with the female depositing a greater percentage of weight as fat than the male.

During childhood the yearly increments for fat show a steady decrease. In many children a prepubertal fat spurt occurs before the true growth spurt. When growth proceeds most rapidly in height, adipose tissue increases least rapidly in the female. In the male there is an actual decrease and loss of fat during high velocity periods of growth.

EXAMPLES OF GROWTH IN SPECIAL SYSTEMS

Brain and adipose cellular development have been intensively studied in relation to nutrition and nutrient intake. Although the long-term physiological and behavioral effects have yet to be clarified, many investigators think that events during early growth of these two systems are important to an individual's growth and development.

Brain Growth

The most rapid and critical period of brain growth in humans begins 9 months before birth and during the first months of postnatal life. During this time there is rapid cell multiplication and increasing differentiation. Thereafter, there is an increase only in cell size with a resulting increase in mass.

Severe malnutrition early in development typically results in spontaneous abortion. Moderate malnutrition throughout pregnancy or severe malnutrition in later pregnancy generally allows continuous fetal development but results in changes in the growth of the placenta and fetus. Animal studies indicate that inadequate maternal energy and protein intakes are associated with LBW infants who have decreased brain weight and decreased numbers of neurons and glial cells. There is also insufficient myelination and impairment of the dendritic development. These changes cannot be reversed by later nutritional rehabilitation.

Postnatal malnutrition is associated with a permanent reduction in the number of glial cells but not with a reduction in the number of neurons. Synaptogenesis and myelination of axons may be inhibited. Some degree of recovery will occur if adequate nutrition is provided.[18]

There have been few studies of cellular growth of the brain in humans. A study comparing brain growth of marasmic and normal infants who died in the first year of life demonstrated significant reductions in wet weight, dry weight, total protein content, and total DNA in the cerebrum, cerebellum, and brainstems of marasmic infants compared with normal infants. The brainstem was less affected.[19] Brains of children thought to be adequately fed in the first year of life but malnourished at an older age have been found to have a normal complement of DNA but reduced brain weight. This indicates a normal cell number but reduced cell size, further defining the critical period of increase in cell number of the brain.[20]

Brasel and Gruen[21] have concluded that most neuronal cell division, at least in the cerebrum, occurs prenatally during the second trimester. They believe that glial cell division is a postnatal event that peaks at 3 months of age. Growth in DNA in the total brain and its two major regions continues into the second year of postnatal life, probably reaching a plateau at approximately 18 months of age.

The rapid increase in brain mass is accompanied by rapid increases in head circumference. The head grows rapidly prenatally and during the first year of life. Head circumference achieves two thirds of its postnatal growth by 24 months of age. Head circumferences of malnourished children have been found to be smaller than those of their well-nourished peers.

Studies of the long-term effects of malnutrition on behavior in humans are difficult to interpret because malnutrition rarely can be isolated as the sole cause of functional deficits. Malnourished children usually live in deprived environments because of a very low family income. Often these families are unable to provide adequate housing, stimulation, or medical care. Also, malnutrition is associated with symptoms of behavior that may functionally isolate children from their environment and delay behavioral development. Children with **marasmus** are typically irritable and apathetic; those with **kwashiorkor** display apathy, withdrawal, and irritability.

Early studies found that children malnourished in early infancy, even when they had been nutritionally rehabilitated, performed less well on a variety of intelligence tests than did normal control subjects. However, subsequent studies recognizing that environments that produce malnourished infants and children are depressed and unstimulating have suggested social and environmental factors as more important variables. Children subjected to malnutrition prenatally because of war-induced famine or during infancy because of disease or anomalies, and who have been discharged to families that provided sufficient food and stimulation, have been able to make up any nutritionally induced deficit.[22,23] Malnourished children adopted by middle-class families have been able to catch up in mental development.[24]

Current research has focused on the mental development of the symmetrically versus the asymmetrically growth-retarded infant. The symmetrically growth-retarded infant presents a uniform retardation in body size with reduction in all organs. The asymmetrically growth-retarded infant has a lower body weight than length with a normal size head for gestational age. Most deficits are related to cell size rather than number.

One study from a community in Guatemala in which chronic undernutrition is endemic found that 3-year-old symmetrically growth-retarded children received lower scores on tests evaluating perceptual performance, problem solving performance, memory, facility, and verbal facility than did asymmetrically growth-retarded infants, who performed as well as normal control subjects. Differences in performance were not noted until 24 months and at that age were not yet significant.[25]

Postnatal growth and cognition. Data from populations in which malnutrition is endemic indicate a relationship between growth retardation of infants and young children and low performance on tests of mental development. Of special interest is the follow-up study of all children in Barbados who were given a diagnosis of marasmus or kwashiorkor in early life as compared to a matched group of adequately nourished children. Those children who were malnourished in infancy and tested at 5 to 11 years of age performed less well academically than did well-nourished control subjects, an effect mediated by deficits in classroom behavior (e.g., lack of attention, poor memory, poor motivation, and easy distractibility).[26] At 8 to 15 years of age the same children performed less well on the Purdue Pegboard test than did controls, an effect thought to be mediated by a lower IQ.[27] Testing of the same children at 11 to 18 years of age found that the generalized deficits in cognitive functioning persisted into adolescence. The IQ scores of children malnourished in early childhood remained lower than those of children who had not suffered a nutritional insult.[28,29] Performance on the Purdue Pegboard test remained impaired. The presence of soft neurological signs measured earlier was again found in the same children and was significantly correlated with pegboard function, implying that early malnutrition has effects on the nervous system function evident through 18 years.[28,29]

In the United States two large-scale studies

disclosed small but significant relationships between anthropometric determiniations and cognitive performance. Investigators associated with the Collaborative Perinatal Project of the National Institute of Neurological Diseases and Blindness[30] followed 37,945 children from before birth until almost 10 years of age. Anthropometric variables (e.g., weight and head circumference) explained a small but statistically significant portion of the variance in IQ at 4 years of age for both black and white males and females when other prenatal and postnatal variables were considered. The U.S. National Health Survey of 7119 noninstitutionalized children ages 6 to 11 years demonstrated a positive and statistically significant correlation between height and test scores.[31]

Adipose Cell Size and Number

The study of the development of adiposity has suffered for several reasons. The number and size of fat cells is estimated by biopsy of surgical specimens. Cell size is estimated by microscopic examination of tissue sections or after collagenase digestion, precipitation of stromal tissue, and osmium fixation of free adipose cells. Cell number is defined by determining the weight of lipid in the average cell and estimating how many cells are in the weight of body.

Adipose tissue is distributed throughout the body. However, cell size varies within a site and the range of cell size varies from one site to another. Estimates of fat, number, or size of cells based on a single biopsy may not be representative of body fat. The method of Hirsch and Gallian[31a] requires a given amount of lipid in the cell to make it float. Only cells with that amount of lipid can be identified. Those that are depleted cannot be identified and counted.

Studies of obesity in adults have shown that obesity may be associated with an increase in both adipose cell number and cell size or with only an increase in the size of the cell. Weight reduction in adults results only in a decrease in the size of adipose cells, not a reduction in the number of adipose cells. Studies of 21-year-old obese subjects who had a history of childhood obesity before and after weight reduction showed a larger number of adipose cells as compared with nonobese adults. Reduction in weight of the subjects was associated with a reduction only in cell size, not in cell number.[32]

Brook[33] found that the number of adipose cells in children who became obese in the first year of life was higher than the number of adipose cells in children who became obese in later childhood. He also found that children who were light for their age and who suffered an insult to growth in infancy had a profound deficit in adipose cell number. He noted, in older nonobese children, little change in cell size during childhood and hypothesized that the increase in body fat during childhood must be a result of a gradual increase in number of adipose cells and that variations in body fatness must be caused by differences in cell size.[32] He believes that the adipose organ grows by increases in both cell size and number during childhood and that increases in cell number do not occur after puberty.

Whether an increased adipose cell number at any age predisposes a child to later obesity or has an influence on the prognosis for weight reduction and maintenance of normal weight remains unknown. There is, however, evidence that obesity in school-age years is likely to continue into adolescence and adulthood and that early-onset obesity is much more resistant to therapy than onset of obesity in later life.[34] The accumulation of excessive numbers of adipose cells or larger cells is to be discouraged at any age.

METHODS OF ASSESSMENT

It is important that persons concerned with a child's nutrient intake be aware of how growth progresses. Assessments are made by periodic determinations of height, weight, and head circumference. The measurements must be determined accurately, and they must be interpreted in relation to the child's current stage of growth. Individual children whose growth does not appear to be proceeding normally may require additional methods of assessment, such as bone-age and skinfold measurements.

Growth Charts

Growth charts for height, weight, and head circumference make it possible to visualize how a child's growth is proceeding. Normative data for bone age permit an estimate of physiological maturity. Skinfold and arm circumference charts provide a basis for determining whether a child is lean, normal, overweight with greater than average muscle and average fat, or obese.

Height, weight, and head circumference. Charts for expected growth have been devised from studies in which large numbers of healthy, normal children of the same race and socioeconomic group were carefully measured at various ages and the data ranked in percentiles. The number in the percentile indicates the position that a measurement would hold in a series of 100.[35] Data from these studies have been presented in tables, charts, and graphs. Growth curves and charts have been designed to measure how far the child has grown (distance curves) or how fast the child has grown (velocity curves). These growth charts are used in health evaluation to give some indication of how a child is growing and are often used in the assessment of nutritional status.

The charts are prepared so that age values lie along the axis and height or weight values or changes in height or weight values are plotted along the abscissa. Height and weight values plotted for one age give information as to how children rank in size in relation to other children of the same sex and age, and information pertaining to the relationship of weight and height as compared with other children. Several measurements of height and weight at different ages plotted on the charts enable the practitioner to visualize if the child's growth is progressing as might be expected. Most children stay in approximately the same percentile during infancy and childhood. Growth, however, does not proceed in a smooth curve as the charts might indicate. Children grow in spurts, and changes may not adhere to the normal curve. A child may have no gain one month but considerable gain the next. During adolescence the growth patterns of many individuals change in percentile, with the early maturer moving to a higher percentile and the later maturer moving to a lower percentile. Both patterns usually re-

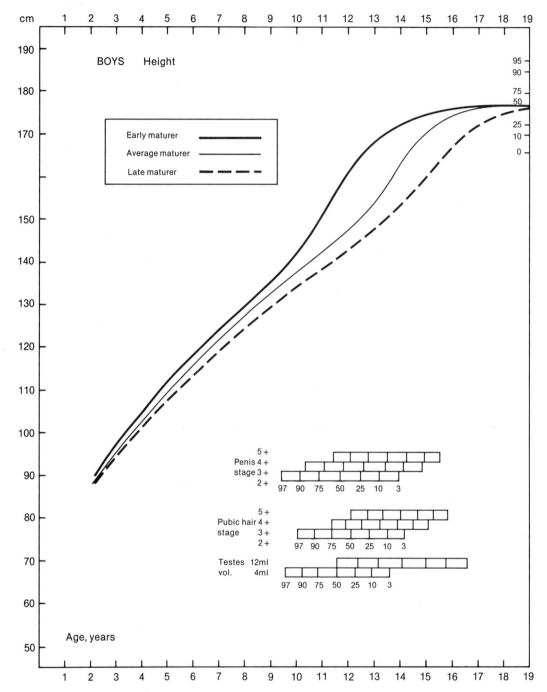

FIG. 1-4   Height attained for American boys *(thin, solid line)*, 50th percentile *(thick, solid line)*, and 95th percentile *(dashed line)* for boys 2 SD of tempo early; 50th percentile *(thin, solid line)*, and 5th percentile *(dashed line)* for boys 2 SD of tempo late.

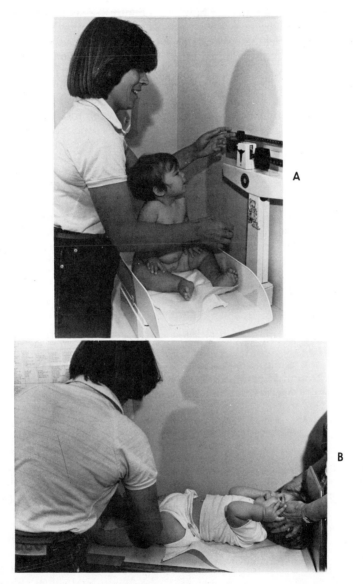

FIG. 1-5 **A,** Infant is weighed unclothed on calibrated beam balance scale. **B,** Recumbent length is measured with suitable measuring board.

turn to the original percentiles by the time growth is complete. It is for this reason that the maturational stages become important in adolescence.

Velocity charts provide an indication of how fast a child is growing.[36] Children tend not to stay nearly as close to a given velocity percentile as they do to a distance percentile. However, change in percentile rating does signal an important acceleration or deceleration. These charts are particularly useful in adolescence when children and parents often become concerned about height and weight in relation to peers and about final stature (Figure 1-4).

The most commonly used growth charts in North America are those prepared by an expert committee for the National Center for Health Statistics (NCHS).[35] Data from the Fels Research Institute were used to determine the percentiles for children from birth to 36 months of age. These data included only bottle-fed infants. The committee used data from the Health Examination Surveys and the Health Nutrition Examination Survey to prepare charts for children from 2 to 18 years of age.

Tanner has prepared both distance and velocity growth charts from the same data for children from 2 to 19 years of age.[36] The distance linear growth chart for adolescent males is shown in Figure 1-4. Note that percentile standards for sexual maturity are graphed on the bottom of the chart.

If the clinician is concerned about the physical growth of a child whose parents are very short or very tall, a correction using mid–parent height can be made using data collected at the Fels Institute.[37]

In addition to graphs that reflect gains in weight and height, the committee constructed body weight for length or stature graphs that are appropriate for plotting values for prepubescent boys and girls.

Appropriate use of these charts requires that measurements be made in the same manner in which the reference data were secured. Weight values for the child less than 36 months of age should be obtained while the child is unclothed, using calibrated beam balance scales. Length values should be of recumbent length, not of upright height (Figure 1-5). The charts for children 2 to 18 years of age use measurements of children in stocking feet and standard examination clothing (Figure 1-6).

Figure 1-7 shows the effect of undernutrition on a female infant subjected to inadequate kcalorie intake because of a dilute formula. The mother of this infant was concerned because the baby was spitting up. A neighbor suggested that she add additional water. When the baby continued to spit up, the mother diluted the formula even more. When a nutritional evaluation was requested at 10 weeks of age, it was found that the child had gained only 460 gm since birth. Her weight was increasing at a very slow rate, dropping from the 10th to the 5th percentile. Her linear growth continued in the 50th percentile. She was consuming an incredible amount of formula but only 190 to 225 kcal/day, approximately 50 kcal/kg. A change to a concentrated formula that provided 24 kcal/oz resulted in a gain of 500 gm the first week and 240 gm the second week. The rapid rate of gain continued until she reached the 25th percentile, where she has remained.

Figures 1-8 and 1-9 show the effect of a restriction in food intake on the growth of a preschool boy because of a sudden change in income and the parents' inability to buy the quantity of food they had previously provided. Catch-up growth occurred when the family applied for and received food stamps and the child was given his normal ration of food.

Growth charts for premature and LBW infants have been prepared by Gairdner and Pearson[38] (Figure 1-10). These charts use the concept of conceptual age, that is, chronological age as corrected to the expected date of delivery.

Measurements of head circumference are made in health examinations by passing a metal, cloth, or paper tape measure over the most prominent part of the occiput and just above the supraorbital ridges (Figure 1-11).

The NCHS growth charts include data on changes in head circumference from birth to 36 months of age in percentiles. Nellhaus prepared

Text continued on p. 21.

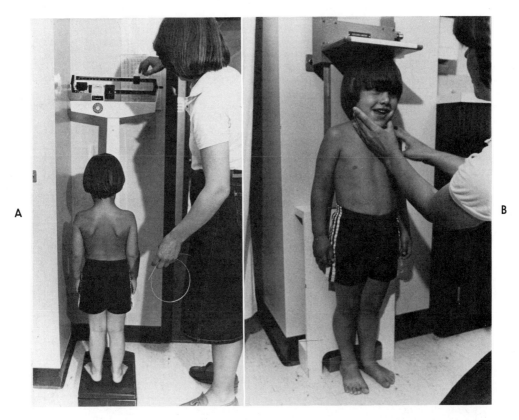

A
B

FIG. 1-6 **A,** Four-year-old is weighed on beam scale. **B,** The child is measured with heels, buttocks, shoulders, and head touching wall.

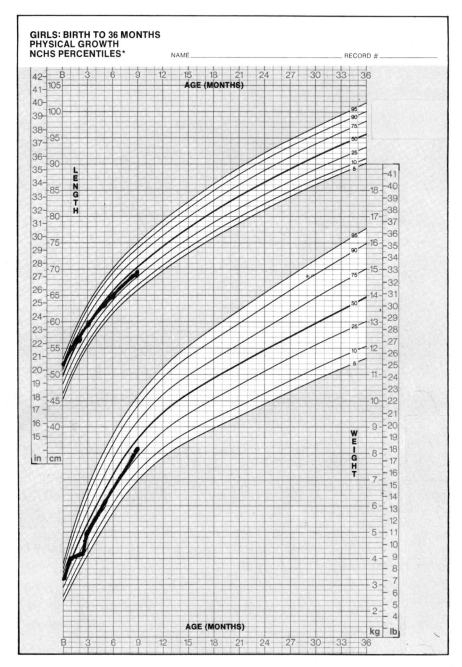

FIG. 1-7 Growth chart for infant girls.

(Courtesy Ross Laboratories.)

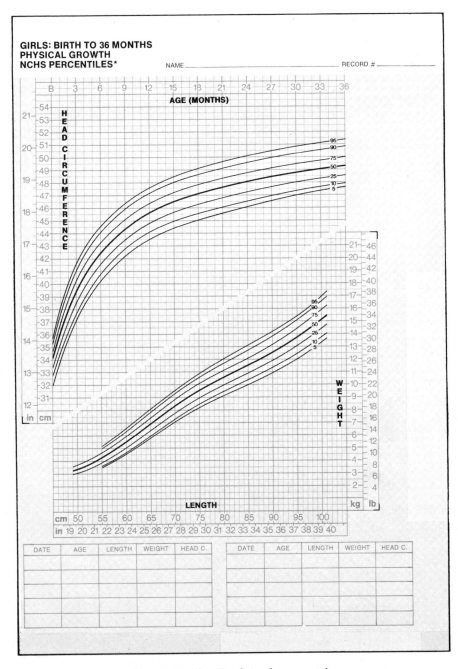

GIRLS: BIRTH TO 36 MONTHS
PHYSICAL GROWTH
NCHS PERCENTILES*

FIG. 1-7, cont'd. For legend see opposite page.

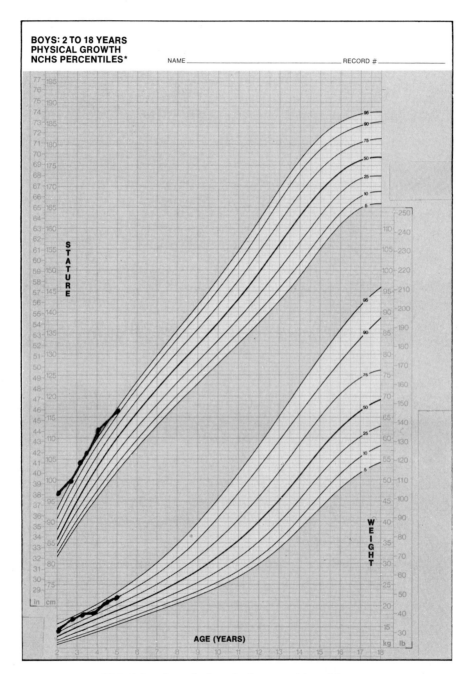

FIG. 1-8   Growth chart for boys aged 2 to 18 years.
(Courtesy Ross Laboratories.)

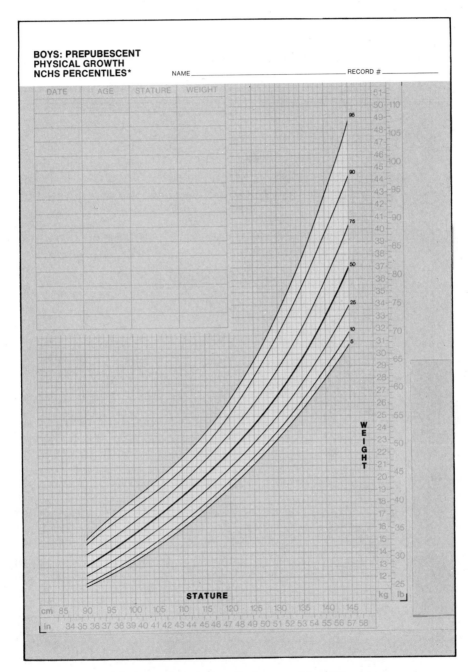

FIG. 1-9 Growth chart for boys aged 2 to 18 years.

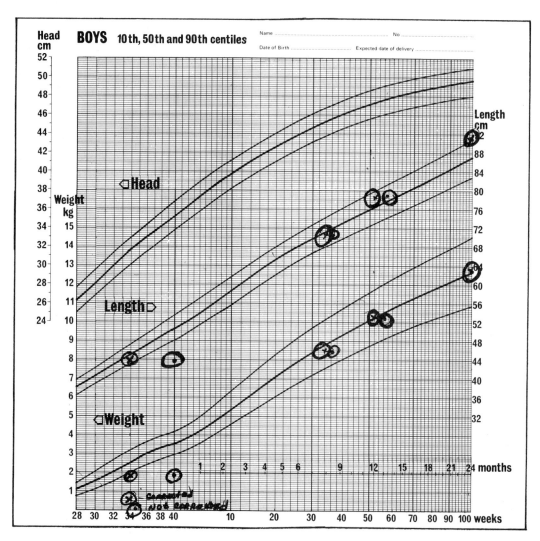

FIG. 1-10 Heights and weights of male infant born at 34 weeks' gestation. ⊗ Denotes plottings when corrected for gestational age. ⊙ Denotes plottings by chronological age. The infant caught up to 95th percentile by age 24 months.

(From Gairdner D, Pearson J: A growth chart for premature and other infants, *Arch Dis Child* 46:783, 1971.)

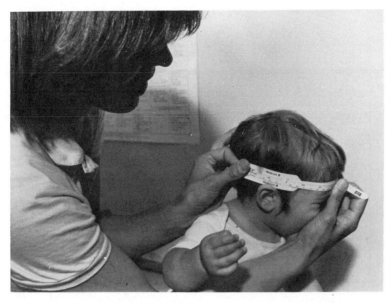

FIG. 1-11 Head circumference is measured over most prominent part of occiput and just above supraorbital ridges.

a graph of head circumference measurements from birth to 18 years of age.[42] His graph reflects weighted averages of variance from records of 14 reports in the world's literature and shows standard deviations.

Most clinics use the NCHS head circumference chart for children less than 36 months of age and the Nellhaus chart for children over 3 years of age. Sequential measurements plotted on these charts can be used to identify children whose cranial growth is deviating from normal. A rapid increase in the rate of growth may indicate hydrocephalus. A slowdown or arrest in the rate of growth may indicate a condition that can cause developmental delays. Such slowdowns and arrests have been noted in children who were subjected to severe undernutrition.

INCREMENTAL GROWTH

Assessment of growth increments is a valuable adjunct to evaluation of growth, especially for children in whom adequate growth attainment has been a problem and intervention strategies have been implemented. The change in growth velocity is more evident when increments of growth are plotted. The growth increments reflect the impact of malnutrition and rehabilitation more readily than the longitudinal charts, which reflect linear growth.

Incremental changes in length or height and weight are ideally plotted at 6-month intervals on the age- and gender-specific charts[39,40] and should be used in conjunction with the NCHS longitudinal charts. For infants the interval is 1 month.[41] Children who remain at the upper or lower percentiles for incremental growth for long periods are of most concern. Increments in the higher percentiles on charts are expected when a child is being rehabilitated and increments in the lower percentiles during periods of restriction of energy intake.

A weight gain increment of 50% to 75% is within normal limits (Figure 1-12).

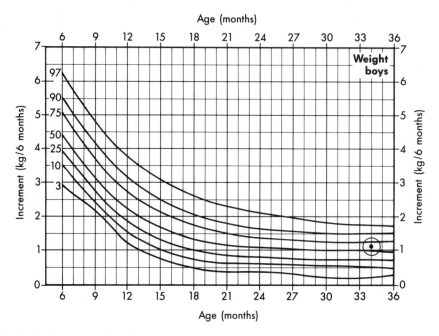

FIG. 1-12 Incremental weight gain of boys between 27 and 34 months of age. Weight at 27 months is 14 kg; weight at 34 months is 15 kg. Weight increment is 1.4 kg. To calculate interval, calculate remaining days in year (12/10 − 12/31 = 21 days). Divide weight increment by total days (217) and multiply by days in 6 months' interval (182 days). A weight gain increment at 50th to 75th percentile is within normal limits for age. Incremental Growth Charts.

(Courtesy Ross Laboratories.)

Skeletal Maturation

Fusion of the epiphyses and the appearance of ossification centers occur first in one bone and then in others in a predictable order. As a result, skeletal maturation can be assessed by observation of the various centers of ossification and the fusion of the epiphyses on roentgenographic studies. Standards of bone age have been devised from longitudinal roentgenographic studies of hands and wrists of children. The most commonly used standards are those of Greulich and Pyle, which were based on 100 hand films of children who were examined periodically from birth to 18 years of age.[43]

Bone age is often used to assess the physiological maturity of a child whose linear growth appears to be proceeding at a very slow or very rapid rate. It is an especially useful tool in adolescence when parents or children or both become concerned about late and early maturation. Bone age correlates with secondary sex characteristics and with mature height.

Undernutrition retards skeletal ossification. Insufficient caloric intake slows bone growth and delays calcification of the ossification centers. Also, the bone appears normal but often is thinner. Protein malnutrition, caused by an insufficient intake of protein, an intake of poor quality protein, or both, results not only in a reduction in bone growth but also in delays in the appearance of ossification centers and possible alterations in the sequence of ossification.[43] Obese children have been found to have advanced skeletal ages.

FIG. 1-13 Triceps fatfold measurements are taken midway between the acromion and olecranon processes.

Skinfold Thickness

Since approximately half of the total body fat is deposited in subcutaneous adipose tissue, the fatness of an individual can be estimated by measuring the thickness of the skinfold at selected sites with special calipers that have been calibrated to provide a constant tension. It is important that proper calipers be used. Plastic calipers are generally not adequate.[44,45] In general, one truncal (subscapular) measurement and one limb (triceps) measurement are advised. If only one measurement is to be used, measurement of the triceps is preferred. The triceps is the easiest site to measure and is representative of body fatness (Figure 1-13).

The triceps measurement is taken midway between the acromion and olecranon processes. The client stands with the back to the measurer, arm relaxed with palm facing the lateral thigh. The tips of the acromial and olecranon processes are palpated, and a point halfway between is marked on the skin. The skinfold is picked up over the posterior surface on the tri-

ceps muscle 1 cm above the mark on the vertical line, and the jaws of the caliper are applied to the marked level.[46] The jaws of the caliper are permitted to exert full pressure as the trigger level of the caliper is released. The dial is read to the nearest 0.5 mm. Measurement error can be minimized by averaging three measurements.

Percentiles for triceps skinfold measurement have been published.[47] Triceps skinfold measurements have been compiled from a cross-sectional study of white subjects from 1 to 75 years of age and are included in the Health and Nutrition Examination Survey I (1971-1974) (Table 1-2).[47] Such measurements are useful as a complement to standard growth charts in the evaluation of children's growth and in the decision as to the necessity to modify kcalorie or nutrient intake. Athletic, muscular children may appear overweight or obese if only height and weight are used as criteria for judgment. On the other hand, handicapped children with poor muscle tone often plot in a lower percentile for

TABLE 1-2 *Percentiles for Triceps Skinfold (mm²) for Whites of the United States: Health and Nutrition Examination Survey I of 1971 to 1974*

Age Group (Years)	Males								Females							
	n	5	10	25	50	75	90	95	n	5	10	25	50	75	90	95
1-1.9	228	6	7	8	10	12	14	16	204	6	7	8	10	12	14	16
2-2.9	223	6	7	8	10	12	14	15	208	6	8	9	10	12	15	16
3-3.9	220	6	7	8	10	11	14	15	208	7	8	9	11	12	14	15
4-4.9	230	6	6	8	9	11	12	14	208	7	8	8	10	12	14	16
5-5.9	214	6	6	8	9	11	14	15	219	6	7	8	10	12	15	18
6-6.9	117	5	6	7	8	10	13	16	118	6	6	8	10	12	14	16
7-7.9	122	5	6	7	9	12	15	17	126	6	7	9	11	13	16	18
8-8.9	117	5	6	7	8	10	13	16	118	6	8	9	12	15	18	24
9-9.9	121	6	6	7	10	13	17	18	125	8	8	10	13	16	20	22
10-10.9	146	6	6	8	10	14	18	21	152	7	8	10	12	17	23	27
11-11.9	122	6	6	8	11	16	20	24	117	7	8	10	13	18	24	28
12-12.9	153	6	6	8	11	14	22	28	129	8	9	11	14	18	23	27
13-13.9	134	5	5	7	10	14	22	26	151	8	8	12	15	21	26	30
14-14.9	131	4	5	7	9	14	21	24	141	9	10	13	16	21	26	28
15-15.9	128	4	5	6	8	11	18	24	117	8	10	12	17	21	25	32
16-16.9	131	4	5	6	8	12	16	22	142	10	12	15	18	22	26	31
17-17.9	133	5	5	6	8	12	16	19	114	10	12	13	19	24	30	37
18-18.9	91	4	5	6	9	13	20	24	109	10	12	15	18	22	26	30
19-24.9	531	4	5	7	10	15	20	22	1060	10	11	14	18	24	30	34

From Frisancho AR: *Am J Clin Nutr* 34:2540, 1981.

weight than height even though they have an adequate amount of adipose tissue.

It must be noted that all data in these norms are derived from white children. Racial differences have been noted in measured fat thickness. Puerto Ricans have greater fat measurements than do North American whites and blacks. Black children have a greater deposition of adipose tissue from infancy through 4 years of age than do their white peers. After 4 years of age the differences are reversed.[48] Group norms and genetic differences must be considered in interpreting skinfold measurements.

Mid–Upper Arm Circumference

Measurement of mid–upper arm circumference combined with triceps skinfold is one method used to estimate muscle and fat bulk. The measurement, like the triceps skinfold, is made at the midpoint of the upper part of the left arm. A paper insertion tape is used most often (Figure 1-14). The subject is positioned with the left arm completely relaxed and extended by the side. A mark is drawn on the lateral side of the arm midway between the acromion and the olecranon. The tape is passed around the arm so that it is touching the skin but not compressing the tissue. It is important to ensure that the tape is on a plane perpendicular to the long axis of the arm.[45] Arm circumference is measured to the nearest 0.1 cm. Arm muscle diameter may be estimated by the following formula:

$$\text{Arm muscle diameter (mm)} = \frac{\text{Arm circumference (mm)}}{\pi} - \text{Triceps skinfold (mm)}$$

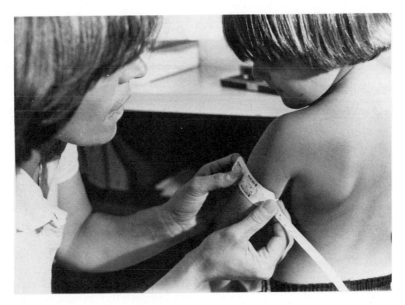

FIG. 1-14 Mid–upper arm circumference is measured with paper insertion tape that touches skin but does not compress tissue.

Normative data for arm muscle diameter and arm circumference have been derived from the Health and Nutrition Examination Survey I.[47]

Some researchers have developed weight-height indexes of relative body weight. Several that are reliable for adults are not applicable for children. Durant and Linder[48] found that the weight-length index calculated by the following formula was the most appropriate for children:

$$WLI = \frac{A}{B} \times 100$$

where

$$A = \frac{\text{Actual weight (kg)}}{\text{Actual height (cm)}}$$

$$B = \frac{\text{50th percentile expected weight (kg) for age}}{\text{50th percentile expected height (cm) for age}}$$

The normal range for children is between 90 and 109. Those who score below 89 can be considered lean; those over 110, overweight; and those over 120, obese. The method does classify muscular children as overweight. How-ever, skinfold measures can validate or negate the assumption.[48]

Body Mass Index

Body mass index (BMI) has been used as a noninvasive clinically convenient manner of assessing chronic energy deficiency and overweight in children over 1 year of age. BMI is expressed as a ratio of weight in kg to height in cm^2.[51]

$$BMI = \frac{\text{Weight (kg)}}{\text{Height (cm}^2)} \times 100$$

The resulting percentage can be used to grade the degree of impact of inadequate or excessive nourishment. If accurate length and height measures are obtained regularly in the clinical setting, the calculation of BMI adds a useful dimension in the assessment of body composition. This index of weight relative to length or stature can be used to monitor relative changes in BMI over time as well as a comparison to the recently developed percentile curves for BMI and the NCHS gender- and age-specific growth charts.

Bioelectric impedance. Much research effort has been expended to determine more precise measurements and determination of body composition. Recently this effort has focused on measurements of the components of body compartments electronically. It appears that measurement of resistance of the trunk is a predictor of the percentage of body fat in 6- to 18-year-old boys and adults.[52,53]

Although bioelectric impedance measures are a relatively accurate measure of the percentage of body fat, especially when used in conjunction with stature, weight, and skinfold thickness, they are difficult to perform because of the technology and difficult to interpret because of the lack of normative data on infants and children.

FAILURE TO THRIVE

If any infant or child fails to grow at the expected rate over a period of several months, a diagnosis of failure to thrive will be made. In one fourth to one third of such children the growth delay is caused by nonorganic environmental factors, including nutrition.[54] The children may be offered inadequate food because of poverty and lack of food, poor feeding techniques, or child neglect. Abnormal mother-child interactions may lead to a child who refuses to eat sufficient food or a mother who does not offer appropriate foods. This often results from inadequate bonding or psychosocial deprivation.

The first step in the evaluation of children with failure to thrive is to evaluate the adequacy of nutrients and energy provided by the food offered and of the food consumed. Observations of a feeding time during the evaluation can give important information when appropriate foods are offered but not consumed (see Chapter 3). If failure to thrive is suspected to result from neurological problems, observations of oral motor skills to assess the child's ability to suck, chew with rotary movements, and self-feed will give information needed to plan intervention (see Chapters 3 and 14).

If a disturbance of mother-child interaction is suspected, the mother's feelings about her child and her expectations about appropriate feeding patterns for the child need to be explored. Such children are often viewed as having had feeding problems in infancy and difficulty in accepting semisolid foods. They frequently consume more food when it is offered by their fathers rather than their mothers. When placed in an environment that provides adequate mothering and stimulation, such as a foster home, they consume large quantities of food; they catch up. Therapy for this failure to thrive must be directed to correction of the psychosocial difficulties that caused the disturbed mother-child relationship.

CATCH-UP GROWTH

During recovery from malnutrition or illness that has ceased or depressed growth, the child grows at a rate above that expected for his or her age. As the more rapid growth proceeds, the child catches up with his or her growth curve. Gain in weight proceeds rapidly until the child reaches the correct weight for height, then proceeds at a slower rate as height and weight increase together. During the second phase, growth proceeds at a height-expected rather than age-expected rate.

The range and magnitude of growth deficits vary with the condition and severity of the disorder that caused the growth retardation. Catch-up growth is, however, possible in all situations, even when growth retardation has been severe and prolonged, provided the epiphyses have not closed and the condition that caused the deficit has been remedied.

It is not unusual for children recovering from malnutrition, who were both wasted and stunted, to gain weight at rates 20 times faster than those of normal healthy age group peers until their weight is appropriate for their length; then, the rate of gain approximates that of children who were only wasted. The average catch-up rate of weight gain for children who are only stunted is approximately three times faster than would be expected for chronological age.[55]

Children who have experienced growth retardation because of malnutrition and continue to live with marginal or insufficient food may have little opportunity for catch-up growth. For these children, pubertal development is delayed. In some cases catch-up growth occurs because of prolongation of the growth period. In other instances children severely malnourished in early childhood who continue to live with a marginal food intake do not catch up in growth even though pubertal development may be delayed 2 years.[55]

Summary

Children grow at their individual predictable rates; the range of growth rates at any age is large. When plotted on growth charts, measurements of growth provide information as to whether children are expressing their genetic potential for growth. Skinfold measurements taken with calibrated instruments provide important information when children are suspected to be undernourished or overnourished. If children are not growing as expected, the adequacy of their energy and nutrient intake should be investigated.

As physical growth proceeds, changes in body composition occur. During adolescence, the deposition of lean body mass per inch of height is greater in the male than in the female. At maturity, males have one and a half times the lean body mass of females.

There are critical stages of development during cell growth when the number of cells in an organism is increasing and an organ is most vulnerable to deprivation. Even so, catch-up growth appears possible if rehabilitation occurs and if sufficient foods and stimulation are provided.

REVIEW QUESTIONS

1. Describe the long-term effects of malnutrition in infancy and early childhood on physical growth and mental development.
2. Why do health care professionals plot heights, weights, and head circumferences on growth charts?
3. When is it appropriate to use an incremental growth chart?
4. Which measurements of body composition are clinically useful?
5. What is catch-up growth?
6. How does one interpret growth data plotted on the NCHS growth chart for non-Caucasians?

SUGGESTED LEARNING ACTIVITIES

1. Obtain heights and weights of a child over several years from a school health record or medical chart, plot them on a growth chart, and interpret the curves on the chart.
2. Describe how you would interpret, to a school-age boy and his parents, the physical growth of a child growing at the 10th percentile whose neighbor of the same age and sex is growing at the 95th percentile.
3. Calculate the weight-height index of a child suspected to be a growth failure.
4. Describe measuring devices and scales that provide valid information.
5. Demonstrate how to correctly measure mid–upper arm circumference and triceps skinfold thickness.

Terms and Concepts

Provided here for your review is a listing of terms and concepts within this chapter. The definitions for terms can be found in the glossary, which begins on page 413. To aid your understanding of the terms' and concepts' application within this text, the page number designating the first mention of each term or concept within the chapter is given.

asymmetry, 4
cell differentiation, 3
creatinine, 8
epiphyseal closure, 23
hydroxyproline, 8
hyperplasia, 4
hypertrophy, 4
kwashiorkor, 10
marasmus, 10
maturation of individual organ systems, 3
roentgenographic studies, 8

REFERENCES

1. Mora JD and others: The effects of nutritional supplementation on physical growth of children at risk of malnutrition, *Am J Clin Nutr* 34:1885, 1981.
2. U.S. Department of Agriculture: *The savings in medicaid costs for newborns and their mothers from prenatal participation in the WIC program,* Washington, DC, 1990, US Department of Agriculture, Food and Nutrition Service.

3. Mitchell HS: Nutrition in relation to stature, *J Am Diet Assoc* 40:521, 1962.

4. Mitchell HS, Santo S: Nutritional improvement in Nokkaido orphanage children—1960-1970, *J Am Diet Assoc* 72:506, 1978.

5. Galler JR and others: Long-term effects of early kwashiorkor compared with marasmus. I. Physical growth and sexual maturation, *J Pediatr Gastroenterol* 6:841, 1987.

6. Enesco M, Leblond CP: Increase in cell numbers as a factor in the growth of the organs of the young male rat, *J Embryol Exp Morphol* 10:530, 1962.

7. Winick M, Noble A: Quantitative changes in DNA, RNA, and protein during prenatal and postnatal growth in the rat, *Dev Biol* 12:451, 1965.

8. Winick M, Noble A: Cellular growth in rats during malnutrition at various ages, *J Nutr* 89:300, 1966.

9. Elliott DA, Cheek DB: Muscle and liver cell growth in rats with hypoxia and reduced nutrition. In Cheek DB, editor: *Human growth, body composition, cell growth, energy, and intelligence,* Philadelphia, 1968, Lea & Febiger.

10. Winick M, Noble A: Cellular response with increased feeding in neonatal rats, *J Nutr* 91:179, 1967.

11. Johnson K, Rosenbaum S, Simons J: *The data book: the nation, states and cities,* Washington, DC, 1985, Children's Defense Fund.

12. Smith D and others: Shifting linear growth during infancy: illustration of genetic factors in growth from fetal life through infancy, *J Pediatr* 89:225, 1976.

13. Martorell R and others: Genetic and environmental determinants of growth in Mexican-Americans, *Pediatrics* 84:864, 1989.

13a. Yip R, Scanion K, Trowbridge F: Improved growth status of Asian refugee children in the United States, *JAMA* 127:937, 1992.

14. Fomon SF and others: Body composition of reference children from birth to 10 years, *Am J Clin Nutr* 35:1169, 1982.

15. Anderson EC, Langham WH: Average potassium concentration of the human body as a function of age, *Science* 130:713, 1959.

16. Forbes GB: Relation of lean body mass to height in children and adolescents, *Pediatr Res* 6:32, 1972.

17. Widdowson EM, Spray CM: Chemical development in utero, *Arch Dis Child* 26:205, 1951.

18. Kanarek RB, Marks-Kaufman RM: *Nutrition and behavior,* New York, 1991, Van Nostrand Reinhold.

19. Winick M, Rosso P, Waterlow J: Cellular growth of cerebrum, cerebellum, and brain stem in normal and marasmic children, *Exp Neurol* 26:393, 1970.

20. Winick M: Nutrition and nerve cell growth, *Fed Proc* 29:1510, 1970.

21. Brasel JA, Gruen RK: Cellular growth of brain, liver, muscle, and lung. In Falkner F, Tanner JM, editors: *Human growth,* vol 2, New York, 1978, Plenum Publishing.

22. Stein Z and others: Nutrition and mental performance, *Science* 178:708, 1972.

23. Beardslee WR and others: The effect of infantile malnutrition on behavioral development, a follow-up study, *Am J Clin Nutr* 35:1437, 1982.

24. Graham GG, Adrianzen TB: Late "catch-up" growth after severe infantile malnutrition, *Johns Hopkins Med J* 131:204, 1972.

25. Villar J and others: Heterogenous growth and mental development of intrauterine growth-retarded infants during the first three years of life, *Pediatrics* 74:783, 1984.

26. Galler JR, Ramsey F, Solimano G: The influence of early malnutrition on subsequent development. III. Learning disabilities as a sequel to malnutrition, *Pediatr Res* 18:309, 1984.

27. Galler JR, Ramsey F, Solemano G: A follow-up study of the effects of early malnutrition on subsequent development. II. Fine motor skills in adolescence, *Pediatr Res* 19:524, 1985.

28. Galler JR and others: Long-term effects of early kwashiorkor compared with marasmus. II. Intellectual performance, *J Pediatr Gastroenterol Nutr* 6:847, 1987.

29. Galler JR and others: Long-term effect of early kwashiorkor compared with marasmus. III. Fine motor skills, *J Pediatr* 6:855, 1987.

30. Bromsan SH, Nichols PL, Kennedy WA: *Preschool I.Q.: prenatal and early developmental correlates,* New York, 1975, John Wiley & Sons.

31. Edwards LN, Grossman M: The relationship between children's health and intellectual development: what is it worth? In Muskin S, editor: *Measures of health benefits,* New York, 1980, Pergamon Press.

31a. Hirsch J, Gallian E: Methods for the determination of adipose cell size in man and animals, *J Lipid Res* 9:110, 1968.

32. Brook CGD: Cellular growth: adipose tissue. In Falkner F, Tanner JM, editors: *Human growth,* vol 2, New York, 1978, Plenum Publishing.

33. Brook CGD: Cell growth in man, *Am Heart J* 86:571, 1973.
34. Committee on Nutrition, American Academy of Pediatrics: Nutritional aspects of obesity in infancy and childhood, *Pediatrics* 68:880, 1981.
35. National Center for Health Statistics: NCHS growth charts, 1976, *Monthly Vital Statistics Report,* vol 25, no 3, Suppl (HRA)76-1120, Rockville, Md, 1976, Health Resources Administration.
36. Tanner JM, Davies PSW: Clinical longitudinal standards for height and weight velocity for North American children, *Pediatrics* 107:317, 1985.
37. Himes JH and others: Parent-specific adjustments for evaluation of recumbent length and stature of children, *Pediatrics* 75:304, 1985.
38. Gairdner D, Pearson J: A growth chart for premature and other infants, *Arch Dis Child* 46:783, 1971.
39. Roche AF, Himes JH: Incremental growth charts, *Am J Clin Nutr* 33:2041, 1980.
40. Incremental growth charts—boys and incremental growth charts—girls. Ross Growth and Development Program, Columbus, Ohio, 1981, Ross Laboratories.
41. Guo S and others: Reference data on gains in weight and length during the first two years of life, *J Pediatr* 119:355, 1991.
42. Nellhaus G: Head circumference from birth to 18 years, *Pediatrics* 41:106, 1968.
43. Greulich WW, Pyle PI: *Radiographic atlas of skeletal development of the hand and wrist,* Stanford, Calif, 1959, Stanford University Press.
44. Gray GE, Gray LK: Anthropometric measurements and their interpretation: principles, practices, and problems, *J Am Diet Assoc* 77:534, 1980.
45. Lohman TG, Roche AF, Martorell R, editors: *Anthropometric standardization reference manual,* Champaign, Ill, 1988, Human Kinetics Books.
46. Cameron N: *The methods of auxological anthropometry.* In Falkner F, Tanner JM, editors: *Human growth,* vol 2, New York, 1978, Plenum Publishing.
47. Frisancho AR: New norms of upper limb fat and muscle areas for assessment of nutritional status, *Am J Clin Nutr* 34:2540, 1981.
48. Durant RN, Linder CW: An evaluation of five indexes of relative body weight for use with children, *J Am Diet Assoc* 78:35, 1981.
49. Garn SM, Clark DC, Guire KE: Growth, body composition, and development of obese and lean children. In Winick M, editor: *Childhood obesity,* New York, 1975, John Wiley & Sons.
50. Behnke AR, Wilmore JH: Evaluation and regulation of body build and composition, Englewood Cliffs, NJ, 1974, Prentice-Hall.
51. Cronk CE, Roche AF: Race- and sex-specific reference data for triceps and subscapular skinfolds and weight stature, *Am J Clin Nutr* 35:347, 1982.
52. Baumgartner RN, Chumlea WC, Roche AF: Bioelectric impedance phase angle and body composition, *Am J Clin Nutr* 48:16, 1988.
53. Chumlea WC, Baumgartner RN, Roche AF: Specific gravity used to estimate fat-free mass from segmental body measures of bioelectric impedance, *Am J Clin Nutr* 48:7, 1988.
54. Rallison ML: *Growth disorders in infants, children and adolescents,* New York, 1986, John Wiley & Sons.
55. Ashworth A, Millward DJ: Catch-up growth in children, *Nutr Rev* 44:157, 1986.

2

Nutrient Needs of Infants and Children

Peggy L. Pipes
Cristine M. Trahms

Objectives

✦✦✦

After studying this chapter, the student should:

✔ *Understand the rationale for recommended intakes of nutrients and energy in infancy and childhood.*

✔ *Recognize appropriate foods as sources of nutrients and energy for infants and children.*

✔ *Be aware of the reasons for the wide range of acceptable energy intakes in infancy and childhood.*

✔ *Be able to make appropriate recommendations for the use of nutrient supplements in infancy and childhood.*

✔ *Understand factors that affect the bioavailability of nutrients.*

Children must consume sufficient high-quality proteins, vitamins, minerals, and energy if acceptable growth is to occur. Energy generated from the metabolism of fats, carbohydrates, and proteins provides the fuel that supports the maintenance of body functions and provides for activity and growth. Protein supplies amino acids for the synthesis of new tissues and nitrogen for the maturation of existing tissues in early childhood.

Vitamins function in a variety of metabolic processes that make protein synthesis and energy metabolism possible. Their requirements are therefore determined by intakes of energy, protein, and other nutrients. Minerals are essential components of body tissue. Their requirements are influenced by rates of growth and the interrelationships they share with other nutrients.

A wide range of opinions exists as to optimal intakes of nutrients for individuals at all ages. The most recent edition of the Recommended Dietary Allowances (RDA), 1989,[1] was controversial at its introduction. In its recommendations the Food and Nutrition Board attempts to include the most recent data from nutrient balance studies, biochemical measurements of tissue saturation, nutrient intake data, epidemiological observations, and when appropriate, extrapolation from animal studies. The recommendations for significant nutrients are shown in Table 2-1.

It is important to remember that the RDAs are recommendations for planning food supplies to meet the needs of populations and for designing public nutrition intervention and education programs. They are not designed to define individual requirements or to assess the adequacy of an individual's intake. If, however, one is knowledgeable about the data used to establish the guidelines and the safety factors added, one can use this knowledge to identify infants and children at risk and to plan diets for infants and children. Combined with growth data and a knowledge of foods as sources of nutrients, such information can be used to identify a need for change in the dietary intake of an individual infant or child.

NUTRIENT NEEDS

Many factors determine an individual's needs for nutrients, including body size, rate of growth, physical activity, basal energy expenditure, and reserves acquired in utero by the fetus or from dietary intake by the infant and older child.

Energy

Total energy requirements reflect that expended for basal metabolism, specific dynamic action, activity, and growth. Because of wide variations in all of the parameters at any age, ranges of recommended intake have been suggested. The recommended energy intakes are shown in Table 2-2.

The energy requirement is very high per unit of body size in a child's first few months of life but declines as the rate of growth decreases. A higher basal metabolic demand in infancy is thought to be caused by a larger loss of heat because of a relatively greater body surface and by a larger proportion of metabolic tissue. Males expend greater amounts of basal energy than do

females. The differences are small during the preadolescent years but become pronounced during adolescence.

Maintenance requirements approximate 1.5 times the basal metabolic expenditure, since some movement occurs even during sleep, and the specific dynamic action is estimated to be 7%-8% of ingested energy for infants and about 5% for older children. Energy costs of growth have been estimated to approximate 4.4 to 5.7 kcal/gm of tissue gained or 15 to 25 kcal/kg/day.[4] Decreasing rates of growth result in decreasing requirements for energy per unit of size (kcal/kg). In other words, as children grow older, they need greater numbers of kcalories because of larger body sizes but their need for energy per unit of size decreases.

The contribution of physical activity to total energy expenditure is variable among children and in individual children from day to day. At all ages, activity patterns among children show wide ranges in both the time spent in the various activities and the intensity of the activities. Some infants, for example, may be quiet, cuddly, and satisfied to explore their environment with their eyes, but others may expend more energy in crying, kicking, and physical movement to see the world around them. Some older children engage in such sedentary activities as looking at books or watching television, whereas their peers may be engaged in physical activities that demand running, jumping, and general body movements.

Spady[5] estimated the energy expenditure of activity of fourth and fifth grade schoolchildren to be 31.2% and 25.3% of total energy expenditure for males and females, respectively.

Energy requirements, which are greatest per unit of size in infancy, decline until adolescent growth is complete. During adolescence the energy requirement is a reflection of the adolescent growth spurt. Since adolescents enter the growth spurt at different ages, recommendations established for a given age must be applied with caution.

During a period of catch-up growth after illness or malnutrition, the requirement for energy and nutrients is greatly increased. Total intakes of 150 to 250 kcal/kg of body weight have been recommended for children of pre-

TABLE 2-1 *Food and Nutrition Board, National Academy of Sciences—National Research Designed for the Maintenance of Good Nutrition of Practically All Healthy People*

Category	Age (Years)	Weight[b] (kg)	Weight[b] (lb)	Height[b] (cm)	Height[b] (in)	Protein (g)	Fat-Soluble Vitamins Vitamin A (µg RE)[c]	Vitamin D (µg)[d]	Vitamin E (mg α-TE)[e]	Vitamin K (µg)
Infants	0.0-0.5	6	13	60	24	13	375	7.5	3	5
	0.5-1.0	9	20	71	28	14	375	10.0	4	10
Children	1-3	13	29	90	35	16	400	10.0	6	15
	4-6	20	44	112	44	24	500	10.0	7	20
	7-10	28	62	132	52	28	700	10.0	7	30
Males	11-14	45	99	157	62	45	1000	10.0	10	45
	15-18	66	145	176	69	59	1000	10.0	10	65
Females	11-14	46	101	157	62	46	800	10.0	8	45
	15-18	55	120	163	64	44	800	10.0	8	55

Modified from *Recommended dietary allowances,* ed 10, National Research Council, Washington, DC, 1989, National Academy Press.

[a]The allowances, expressed as average daily intakes over time, are intended to provide for individual variations among most normal persons as they live in the United States under usual environmental stresses. Diets should be based on a variety of common foods in order to provide other nutrients for which human requirements have been less well defined.

[b]The median weights and heights were taken from Hamill and others (1979).[2] The use of these figures does not imply that the height-to-weight ratios are ideal.

[c]Retinol equivalents. 1 retinol equivalent = 1 µg retinol or 6 µg β-carotene.

[d]As cholecalciferol. 10 µg cholecalciferol = 400 IU of vitamin D.

[e]α-Tocopherol equivalents. 1 mg d-α tocopherol = 1 α-TE.

[f]1 NE (niacin equivalent) is equal to 1 mg of niacin or 60 mg of dietary tryptophan.

school age with 50 to 80 kcal/kg supporting the increased growth. An intake of 200 kcal/kg/day should produce a weight gain of 20 gm/kg/day.[4]

The energy needs of individual children of the same size, age, and gender vary. Reasons for these differences remain unexplained. Differences in physical activity, in the metabolic cost of minimal and excessive protein intakes at equivalent levels of energy intake, and in the efficiency with which individuals utilize energy have all been hypothesized to exert an influence. Recent studies suggest that infants and children are consuming less energy than recommended. Butte and others[6] found that intakes of exclusively breast-fed infants declined from 110 ± 24 kcal/day at 1 month of age to 71 ± 17 kcal/day at 4 months of age. Adair[7] found that the intake of a formula-fed infant during the first year was never more than 90% of the 1980 dietary allowances. Six- to eleven-year-old children have been reported to consume more than 20% less than the suggested intake.[8] Spady[5] found that although the total energy expenditures of fourth and fifth grade boys approximated the recommended allowances, girls expended only 80% of the 1974 recommended allowances.

It should be noted that the most recent recommended allowances (1989) for energy are not directly comparable to previous recommendations because of change in reference weights. In general, the allowances for infants and children 7 to 10 years of age are lower than previous recommendations. This changed recommendation is based on observed intakes that

Council Recommended Dietary Allowances,ᵃ Revised 1989 in the United States

	Water-Soluble Vitamins						Minerals					
Vita-min C (mg)	Thia-min (mg)	Ribo-flavin (mg)	Niacin (mg NE)ᶠ	Vita-min B₆ (mg)	Fo-late (μg)	Vitamin B₁₂ (μg)	Cal-cium (mg)	Phos-phorus (mg)	Mag-nesium (mg)	Iron (mg)	Zinc (mg)	Iodine (μg)
30	0.3	0.4	5	0.3	25	0.3	400	300	40	6	5	40
35	0.4	0.5	6	0.6	35	0.5	600	500	60	10	5	50
40	0.7	0.8	9	1.0	50	0.7	800	800	80	10	10	70
45	0.9	1.1	12	1.1	75	1.0	800	800	120	10	10	90
45	1.0	1.2	13	1.4	100	1.4	800	800	170	10	10	120
50	1.3	1.5	17	1.7	150	2.0	1200	1200	270	12	15	150
60	1.5	1.8	20	2.0	200	2.0	1200	1200	400	12	15	150
50	1.1	1.3	15	1.4	150	2.0	1200	1200	280	15	12	150
60	1.1	1.3	15	1.5	180	2.0	1200	1200	300	15	12	150

TABLE 2-2   Recommended Energy Intake

		Weight		Height			Average Energy Allowance (kcal)†		
Category	Age (Years)	kg	lb	cm	in	REE* (kcal/day)	Multiples of REE	Per kg	Per day‡
Infants	0.0-0.5	6	13	60	24	320		108	650
	0.5-1.0	9	20	71	28	500		98	850
Children	1-3	13	29	90	35	740		102	1300
	4-6	20	44	112	44	950		90	1800
	7-10	28	62	132	52	1130		70	2000
Males	11-14	45	99	157	62	1440	1.70	55	2500
	15-18	66	145	176	69	1760	1.67	45	3000
Females	11-14	46	101	157	62	1310	1.67	47	2200
	15-18	55	120	163	64	1370	1.60	40	2200

Modified from *Recommended dietary allowances,* ed 10, National Research Council, Washington, DC, 1989, National Academy Press.

*Calculation based on WHO equations, then rounded.[3] *REE,* Resting energy expenditure.

†In the range of light to moderate activity, the coefficient of variation is ±20%.

‡Figure is rounded.

support normal growth in developed countries.

In 1930 an expert committee, after reviewing energy intake data in relation to physical parameters, stated that height appeared to be the most appropriate criterion on which to base studies of energy needs.[9] The observation was never used. In estimating energy needs of children, body surface area or weight has continued to be used as a reference for suggested energy intakes of children. Energy per centimeter of height has proved clinically, however, to be a useful reference in estimating energy needs and designing diets for individual children. It is an especially useful reference for children who are genetically short. For example, preschool children with **Prader-Willi syndrome** maintain their weight in the growth channel by consuming 10 to 11 kcal/cm of height as compared with 14.7 to 15.4 kcal/cm of height, the 50th percentile of intake of normal males, and 12.9 to 13.8 kcal/cm of height, the 50th percentile of intake of normal females of the same age.

The best evaluation of the adequacy of infant's and children's energy intake is the adequacy of their growth rates in length and weight. If upward or downward changes in weight percentiles occur without changes in length percentiles, undernutrition or overnutrition should be suspected.

The recommended energy allowances from

TABLE 2-3   *Selected Foods as Sources of Energy for Infants*

Food	Energy kcal/oz	kcal/T
Milk		
Human milk	22	11
Commercially available infant formula	20	10
Whole cow's milk	19	9
Commercially available infant foods (average value)		
Dry infant cereals	129	14
Strained and junior fruits	16	8
Strained and junior vegetables	12	5
Strained and junior meats	34	14
Strained egg yolks	65	28
Strained and junior dinners		
Vegetables with meat	22	9
Lean meat dinners	22	9
Strained and junior desserts	25	11

From Nutritionist III: *N-squared computing,* Salem, Ore, 1990; and *Nutrient values,* Fremont, Mich, 1991, Gerber Products.

TABLE 2-4   *Selected Foods as Sources of Energy for Children*

Food	Portion Size	Average kcal
2% milk with nonfat milk solids	$\frac{1}{2}$ c	69
Meat, poultry, or fish	1 oz	72
Egg	1 medium	75
Peanut butter	1 T	94
Cheese	$\frac{1}{2}$ oz	57
Legumes, cooked	$\frac{1}{4}$ c	58
Enriched bread	$\frac{1}{2}$ slice	33
Ready-to-eat cereals (not sugar-coated)	$\frac{3}{4}$ c	67
Cooked cereal	$\frac{1}{2}$ c	73
Saltine crackers	1	12
Rice, macaroni, spaghetti, cooked	$\frac{1}{4}$ c	66
Potato (boiled)	$\frac{1}{2}$ medium	58
Potato chips	5	52
Green beans	$\frac{1}{4}$ c	9
Carrots		
Cooked	$\frac{1}{4}$ c	17
Raw	2 medium sticks	14
Apple	1 small	81
Banana	1 medium	105
Orange	1 small	62
Orange juice	$\frac{1}{2}$ c	56
Sugar	1 t	15
Jam or jelly	1 t	17
Butter, margarine, oil, mayonnaise	1 t	33
Cookies, assorted	1	50-60
Ice cream	$\frac{1}{4}$ c	67

From Nutritionist III: *N-squared computing,* Salem, Ore, 1990.

the newest RDAs represent the average needs of individuals at various ages. The new recommendations also reflect a change in the weight categories. The weights are now actual median weights from NCHS data[2] and not arbitrary ideal weights. From birth to 6 months the recommendation is 108 kcal/kg/day and from 6 months to 1 year it is 98 kcal/kg/day. As shown in Table 2-2 the recommended energy allow-ances are those reported by the World Health Organization (WHO).[3]

Food sources. Energy values of foods commonly consumed in infancy and childhood are given in Tables 2-3 and 2-4. To demonstrate food intakes that support appropriate energy intakes for several age groups, data for 2-month-old, 6-month-old, 10-month-old, and 4-year-old children are given in Table 2-5.

TABLE 2-5   *Foods That Provide Appropriate Energy for Various Age Groups*

Age	Weight (kg)	Energy Needs (kcal)	Examples of Foods That Provide Appropriate Energy Intakes
2 months	6	650	28-32 oz human milk or infant formula
6 months	7.5	750	28 oz human milk or infant formula 4 T dry infant cereal 4 oz fruit juice 5 T strained fruit
10 months	9	850	24 oz infant formula 8 T dry infant cereal 14 T junior fruit 8 T junior vegetable 4 T junior meat $\frac{1}{2}$ slice toast 1 oz chopped chicken 1 T mashed green beans 1 small banana 2 T ice cream 1 graham cracker
4 years	20	1800	24 oz milk 6-8 oz fruit juice 3 slices bread $\frac{1}{2}$ to $\frac{3}{4}$ c dry cereal 2 T peanut butter 1 t jelly 2 oz lean hamburger patty $\frac{1}{4}$ c macaroni and cheese $\frac{1}{4}$ c green beans $\frac{1}{3}$ c ice cream 1 graham cracker 1 medium apple 1 small banana

TABLE 2-6   Estimates of Amino Acid Requirements

Amino Acid	Requirements, mg/kg/day, by Age Group		
	Infants, Age 3-4 mo*	Children, Age ~2 yr†	Children, Age 10-12 yr‡
Histidine	28	?	?
Isoleucine	70	31	28
Leucine	161	73	42
Lysine	103	64	44
Methionine plus cystine	58	27	22
Phenylalanine plus ty- rosine	125	69	22
Threonine	87	37	28
Tryptophan	17	12.5	3.3
Valine	93	38	25
Total without histidine	714	352	214

Modified from *Recommended dietary allowances,* ed 10, National Research Council, Washington, DC, 1989, National Academy Press.

*Based on amounts of amino acids in human milk or cow's milk formulas fed at levels that supported good growth. Data from Fomon and Filer (1967).[13]

†Based on achievement of nitrogen balance sufficient to support adequate lean tissue gain (16 mg N/kg/day). Data from Pineda and others (1981).[14]

‡Based on upper range of requirement for positive nitrogen balance. Recalculated by Williams and others (1974)[15] from data of Nakagawa and others (1964).[16]

Protein and Amino Acid Requirements

Protein provides kcalories but also serves a more important and complex function. Protein is the basic component of the protoplasm in cells; therefore an adequate intake of protein is essential if normal growth is to occur. Increases in body protein average 3.5 gm/day for the first 4 months and 3.1 gm/day for the next 8 months, with the body protein increasing from 11% to 14.6% in the first year.[10]

Amino acid requirements of infants have been estimated from studies in which pure amino acids were supplied in proportions of amino acids of human milk.[11] The requirement of an amino acid was defined as the least amount required to maintain satisfactory nitrogen retention and weight gain when nitrogen levels and other amino acids were held constant. Fomon and others[12], as well as Fomon and Filer[13], have estimated amino acid requirements from intakes of infants between 8 and 112 days of age who were fed whole protein in cow's milk formulas and soy formulas. Satisfactory linear growth and weight gain, nitrogen balance, and serum concentrations of albumin equivalent to those of normal breast-fed infants were used as criteria of adequacy.

The current estimates of amino acid requirements for infants and children are based on composite data from several studies. The criteria of growth and nitrogen accumulation were used for infants and the amount of intake needed to maintain positive nitrogen balance was used as the criterion for children (Table 2-6).

Investigators have found amino acid requirements for 10- to 12-year-old children to be two to three times greater than those for adults. Requirements of males in all cases exceeded those of females.[16] Histidine is essential in infancy but not in the older child.

Protein needs for growth (expressed as percentages of requirement) decrease as rates of growth decline. Of the protein requirement, 50% is used for growth in the first 2 months of life. This declines to 11% at 2 to 3 years of age

TABLE 2-7 *Recommended Allowances of Reference Protein and U.S. Dietary Protein*

Category	Age (Years)	Weight (kg)	Derived Allowance of Reference Protein (gm/kg)	Recommended Dietary Allowance gm/kg*	Recommended Dietary Allowance gm/day
Both sexes	0-0.5	6	2.20†	2.2	13
	0.5-1	9	1.56	1.6	14
	1-3	13	1.14	1.2	16
	4-6	20	1.03	1.1	24
	7-10	28	1.00	1.0	28
Males	11-14	45	0.98	1.0	45
	15-18	66	0.86	0.9	59
Females	11-14	46	0.94	1.0	46
	15-18	55	0.81	0.8	44

Modified from *Recommended dietary allowances,* ed 10, National Research Council, Washington, DC, 1989, National Academy Press.
*Amino acid score of typical U.S. diet is 100 for all age groups, except young infants.
Digestibility is equal to reference proteins. Values have been rounded upward to 0.1 gm/kg.
†For infants 0 to 3 months of age, breastfeeding that meets energy needs also meets protein needs. Formula substitutes should have the same amount and amino acid composition as human milk, corrected for digestibility if appropriate.

and is gradually reduced to zero after an increase during the adolescent growth spurt. Amino acids required for growth differ from those required for maintenance.

Recommended intakes. The recommendations for daily protein intakes for infants and children have assumed an adequate intake of energy. These recommendations are based on ingestion of milk protein in infancy and a mixed diet that provides protein that has an efficiency of utilization of 75% in older children.[1] Table 2-7 shows the recommended protein intakes by age.

Foman and others[12] have suggested that during infancy, amino acid and protein requirements expressed per unit of kcalories consumed (reflecting both size and rate of growth) are more meaningful than expressions of requirements on the basis of body weight alone. They estimate the protein requirement to be 1.6 gm/ 100 kcal for children 1 to 4 months of age and 1.4 gm/100 kcal for children 8 to 12 months of age.

More recently Fomon[17] has proposed a factorial method of estimating the protein requirement for infants. The requirement for growth plus the requirement of replacement of losses in urine, feces, and skin yielded an estimate of 1.98 gm/kg/day (or 1.65 gm/100 kcal) for the first month of life. This requirement decreased to 1.18 gm/kg/day (or 1.31 gm/100 kcal) by 5 months of age and then remained stable to about 12 months of age. The recommended intake of protein is greater than the requirement calculated by this approach. The Recommended Dietary Intake (RDI) proposed by this group at 1 month is 2.6 gm/kg/day (2.2 gm/100 kcal) and by 5 months it is 1.4 gm/kg/day (1.69 gm/ 100 kcal); this recommendation is stable for the remainder of the first year of life. However, the 1989 Recommended Dietary Allowances suggest an average protein intake of 1.68 gm/kg/ day between birth and 3 months with the reference protein as human milk.[1]

Based on nitrogen balance studies, it was concluded that an appropriate protein allowance for 7- to 10-year-old children would be 45 gm or more per day.[18] Reported protein intakes of children in the United States have shown actual protein intakes to be 10% to 15% of kcalories consumed. During periods of catch-up growth, protein requirements increase.

TABLE 2-8 *Approximate Protein Contents of Various Milks and Foods Fed to Infants*

Food	Protein (gm/oz)
Human milk	0.3
Commercial formulas	0.5
Homogenized milk	1.0
Evaporated milk, prepared	1.1
Infant cereals, high protein, dry	12.2
Infant cereals, rice	2.8
Strained chicken noodle dinners	0.6
Strained vegetable and meat dinners	0.6-0.8
Strained beef and vegetable dinners	2.0
Strained turkey and vegetable dinners	1.9
Strained egg yolk	2.8
Strained beef	3.9
Strained veal	3.8

From Nutritionist III: *N-squared computing,* Salem, Ore, 1990; and *Nutrient values,* Fremont, Mich, 1991, Gerber Products.

Milk protein intakes of 3.2 gm/kg when energy intakes are adequate have been suggested to support catch-up growth for infants.[4]

The Committee on Nutrition of the American Academy of Pediatrics[19] has set minimum protein standards for infant formula of 1.8 gm/100 kcal or 7.2% of kcal with a protein efficiency ratio to that of **casein.**

The protein requirement for any child depends on the rate of growth and the quality of protein in the diet. This implies that evaluation of a child's protein intake must be approached on the basis of the adequacy of the rate of growth, the quality of protein in the foods ingested, the combinations of foods that provide amino acids consumed together, and the adequacy of those nutrients (minerals and vitamins) and energy that are necessary for protein synthesis.

Food sources. Protein of high quality is available to most infants in developed countries as human milk and modified cow's milk formula.

TABLE 2-9 *Selected Foods as Sources of Protein for Preschool Children*

Food	Portion Size	Protein (gm)
Yogurt, made from whole milk	$\frac{1}{2}$ c	3.9
Cheddar cheese	1 oz	7.1
Hamburger patty, lean	2 oz	14.0
Chicken drumstick	1	13.2
Peanut butter	1 T	4.5
Egg	1 large	6.2
Tuna	$\frac{1}{4}$ c	11.5
Nonfat milk solids, dry	1 T	1.5
Milk	$\frac{1}{2}$ c	4.9

From Nutritionist III: *N-squared computing,* Salem, Ore, 1990.

Infants whose parents are unwilling to feed them cow's milk formulas or infants who have allergic reactions to cow's milk are often fed formulas prepared from water-soluble soy isolates.

As discussed in Chapter 4, commercially prepared formulas are manufactured so that all nutrients are provided in the appropriate amounts if consumed in recommended quantities. Home preparation of soy formulas is discouraged because parents may not be careful to heat the soy milk sufficiently to achieve inactivation of the trypsin inhibitor and may discard the residue of soy material from which the milk was made. In so doing, much of the protein and many of the other essential nutrients are discarded.

Table 2-8 lists foods commonly consumed in infancy that contribute protein.

As children grow older and accept table food, they receive additional foods that provide high-quality protein. Examples of foods acceptable to preschoolers that provide high-quality protein are given in Table 2-9.

Examples of combinations of foods that meet the recommended intakes for protein for 2-month-old, 6-month-old, 10-month-old, and 4-year-old children are given in Table 2-10. The examples given include much less protein than most children consume. In fact, it would

TABLE 2-10   *Foods That Provide Appropriate Protein Intakes for Children*

Age	Weight (kg)	Protein Intake (gm)	Examples of Foods That Meet Protein Needs
2 months	6	11	38 oz human milk *or* 26 oz commercially manufactured infant formula
10 months	9	14	24 oz commercially manufactured infant formula 3 oz lowfat yogurt
4 years	20	23	16 oz milk 1 T peanut butter 1 medium egg 4 oz lowfat yogurt

be difficult to provide sufficient energy in the diet if protein intakes were restricted to the recommended amounts. For example, 4-year-old children who consume the food listed receive approximately 500 kcal/day from these sources, leaving 1300 kcal that needs to be met totally from vegetables, fruits, fat, and sweets without protein from meats, breads, nuts, other cereal grains, or cheese (Table 2-10).

The protein intakes of some children are a matter of concern. **Kwashiorkor** (severe protein deficiency) has been reported in infants whose parents purposely withheld milk after episodes of vomiting or diarrhea and who were treated with clear liquids and in children from families who live in extreme poverty where there was marked restriction of protein intake.[20,21] Children with multiple allergies often learn to control their feeding environment by refusing all protein-rich foods. Often they demonstrate catch-up growth when encouraged through reinforcement techniques to accept meats and other protein-rich foods to which they had no allergic reactions. Children who are hypersensitive in the oral area frequently refuse meat, eggs, milk, and dairy products if unlimited amounts of carbohydrates such as starches and sugars are available to them. Limited financial resources restrict the amounts of high-quality protein parents can purchase for their children. Without careful planning the quality of a child's protein intake may be compromised. However, peanut butter and whole wheat bread sandwiches, beans and rice, eggs, and powdered milk are inexpensive high-quality protein sources.

Fat

Fat, the most kcalorically concentrated nutrient, supplies between 40% and 50% of the energy consumed in infancy and approximately 40% of the energy consumed after infancy by individuals in developed countries. Because it is kcalorically concentrated, it may be very important in the diet of children who are lean and physically active and have a small appetite or in the diet of children with oral motor problems who can consume only a limited volume of food. However, chunky, passive children should limit the quantity of fat they consume to keep from gaining weight too rapidly.

Essential fatty acids. Polyunsaturated **linoleic acid** has been conclusively proven to be an essential nutrient for both children and adults. Although arachidonic acid performs some of the same functions, it is considered to be an essential fatty acid only when linoleic acid deficiency exists.

Some investigators consider linolenic acid also essential, although no specific deficiency of linolenic acid has been reported in humans.

One of the earliest manifestations of fatty acid deficiency recognized in animals was an increased basal metabolic rate. Infants who are fed formulas low in the essential fatty acid consume greater numbers of kcalories than do those who consume adequate quantities of linoleic acid to maintain normal growth. Kcaloric utilization has been reported to vary with intakes of linoleate up to 4% to 5% of total kcalories. It has been suggested that the ratio of triene/tetraene fatty acids in the blood serum can be used in assessing nutritional status of linoleic acid. A triene/tetraene ratio of 0.4 or less is considered indicative of normal fatty acid status, and a ratio greater than 0.4 is indicative of an insufficient intake of essential fatty acid.[22] Such biochemical evidence of deficiency appears when linoleic acid is less than 1% of the total kcalories. On this basis the minimal requirements for linoleic acid are considered to be approximately 1% of the kcalories consumed, and an optimal intake is thought to be 4% to 5% of the kcalories consumed.[23]

Recommended intakes. If less than 30% of energy intakes are derived from fat, a dry and unpalatable diet may result.

Recommended intakes of fat are controversial, especially in view of the recent work on blood lipid levels and future disease. However, the Healthy People 2000: Nutrition Objectives[24] list a reduction of dietary fat to an average of 30% of energy or less and an average saturated fat intake to less than 10% of energy intake for people 2 years and older.

Fomon[10] suggests that diets that provide less than 30% of total kcalories or greater than 50% of total kcalories as fat should be avoided for infants and young children.

Food sources. Human milk, cow's milk, and commercially available infant formulas provide approximately 50% of kcalories as fat. Approximately 4% of the total kcalories in human milk and 1% of the kcalories in cow's milk are pro-

vided by linoleic acid. Commercially available infant formulas contain blends of vegetable oils and contribute greater amounts of linoleic acid.

The Committee on Nutrition of the American Academy of Pediatrics[19] has recommended that infant formulas contain a minimum of 300 mg of 18:2 fatty acids/100 kcal (2.7% of the energy content).

Prepared infant foods are relatively low in fat as compared with foods consumed by older children. Tables 2-11 and 2-12 list the amounts of fat provided by foods commonly consumed by infants and preschool children.

Carbohydrates

Carbohydrates are the principal sources of dietary energy and supply between 40% and 50% of the energy consumed by most infants and children in North America. Sugars and complex carbohydrates are the most important dietary carbohydrate sources.

Recommended intakes. Since glucose can be synthesized from amino acids and the glycerol moiety of fat, no specific recommendations for intake have been made. The Food and Nutrition Board of the National Research Council suggests that more than half the energy requirement beyond infancy be provided by carbohy-

TABLE 2-11 *Foods as Sources of Fat for Infants*

Food	Fat (gm/oz)
Infant cereal, dry (9 T/oz)	0.9-1.8
Vegetable and meat dinners	0.06-0.1
Meat and vegetable dinners	0.2
Strained and junior meats	0.2-0.5
Strained egg yolks	4.9

From *Nutrient values*, Fremont, Mich, 1991, Gerber Products.

TABLE 2-12 *Foods as Sources of Fat for Preschool Children*

Food	Portion Size	Fat (gm)
Cooking fat	1 T	12.8
Mayonnaise	1 T	4.9
Butter	1 t	3.8
Cheddar cheese	1 oz	9.3
Peanut butter	1 T	8.1
Frankfurter, 5" by $\frac{3}{4}$"	1	16.6
Broiled hamburger patty	2 oz	10.4
Chicken drumstick	1	6.7
Egg	1 medium	4.9
Tuna, drained	$\frac{1}{4}$ c	3.3
Ice cream	$\frac{1}{4}$ c	3.5
Potato chips	10	7.0

From Nutritionist III: *N-squared computing*, Salem, Ore, 1990.

drates with an emphasis on complex carbohydrates rather than sugars. They recommend minimum intakes of 50 to 100 gm/day.

Dietary fiber plays a role in prevention of many diseases. The Committee on Nutrition of the American Academy of Pediatrics[25] has stated that more work must be done on the effect of a high-fiber diet on mineral status before firm recommendations can be made. However, the committee recommends a substantial amount of fiber to ensure normal laxation. As much fiber as 170 to 300 mg/kg may be desirable.[26] The inclusion of whole grain cereals, breads, fruits, and vegetables in the diet of preschool, school-age, and adolescent children is important.

Food sources. The predominant carbohydrate in the young infant's diet is lactose, found in human milk and cow's milk. It has become a common practice for parents to add starch (in the form of prepared cereals and ingredients of commercially prepared infant foods) and sucrose (which is added to fruits and some vegetables) to the infant's diet at 4 to 6 months of age (Table 2-13).

Some foods contain carbohydrates and few other nutrients, whereas others contribute carbohydrates and other essential nutrients. Candy, cookies, and potato chips, for example, provide primarily kcalories, whereas cereal grains are important sources of the B vitamins; potatoes contribute vitamin C; and legumes offer amino acids, iron, and B vitamins as well as carbohydrates. Therefore careful attention to the nutrients carried by the carbohydrate-containing foods is important in planning diets for children.

Most children prefer sweet foods. In fact, infants at birth appear to distinguish sugar water from plain water. They accept larger quantities of sugar-sweetened solutions than unsweetened mixtures.[27] Indiscriminate consumption of candy, cookies, carbonated beverages, and other sweetened drinks dulls the appetite for nutrient-rich foods, contributes to overweight, dental caries, and general poor nourishment, and should be discouraged. The impact of these sucrose-containing foods on the incidence of dental caries is discussed in Chapter 6.

Water

Even more essential to the body than food is water. It functions as an essential component of body structure and as a solvent for minerals and other physiologically important compounds. It transports nutrients to and waste products from the cells and helps to regulate body temperature.

The percentage of body weight provided by water decreases from approximately 75% at birth to 60% at 1 year of age (see Chapter 1). After 1 year of age intracellular water accounts for approximately 60% and extracellular water for 40% of total body water. The usual daily turnover of water for infants is about 15% of total body weight.

Recommended intakes. Water is lost by evaporation through the skin and respiratory tract (**insensible water loss**), through perspiration when the environmental temperature is elevated, and by elimination in the feces and the urine. During growth a positive water balance is necessary since additional water is obligated as a constituent of tissue and for increases in the volume of body fluids. The amount of water required for growth, however, is very small at all ages.

TABLE 2-13 **Carbohydrates in Foods for Infants**

Food	Carbohydrate (gm/oz)
Human milk	2.1
Prepared infant formulas	2.1
Homogenized milk	1.5
Infant cereals, dry	14.8-26.2
Strained and junior desserts	5.3-6.7
Strained and junior vegetable and meat dinners	2.5-3.2
Strained and junior meat and vegetable dinners	2.2-2.5
Strained and junior fruits	3.7-5.9
Strained and junior vegetables	1.9-4.7

From Nutritionist III: *N-squared computing,* Salem, Ore, 1990; and *Nutrient values,* Fremont, Mich, 1991, Gerber Products.

Water lost by evaporation in infancy and early childhood accounts for more than 60% of that needed to maintain homeostasis, as compared with 40% to 50% in the adult. At all ages approximately 24% of the basal heat loss is by evaporation of water through the skin and respiratory tract.[28] This amounts to 45 ml of insensible water loss per 100 kcal expended. Fomon[10] estimates evaporative water loss at 1 month of age to average 210 ml/day and at 1 year of age, 500 ml/day. Evaporative losses increase with fever and higher environmental temperature. Increases in humidity decrease respiratory loss. Loss of water in the feces averages 10 ml/kg/day in infancy.[29]

The volume of urine, in general, reflects fluid intake. It includes both water required to concentrate the solutes presented to the kidney for excretion and water in excess of the individual's need. The renal water requirement is determined by the diet and by the concentrating power of the kidney.

Ziegler and Fomon[29] have developed a method for estimating the renal solute load by calculating the amount of dietary sodium, chloride, potassium, and urea (estimated to be 4 mOsm/gm of protein). The urinary water requirement can then be estimated from the sum of these values and has been estimated at 1.5 ml/kcal of energy expenditure for infants. Balance studies of 5-year-old children showed intakes of 1100 ml/day; metabolic water contributed an additional 200 ml/day. Water intakes averaged 0.7 ml/kcal/day.[30] Ranges of average water requirements of infants and children are given in Table 2-14.

Food sources. Fluid in liquids and food consumed are the primary source of water. In addition, metabolic water is created from the metabolism of protein, fat, and carbohydrate: 1 gm protein produces 4.1 ml water, 1 gm carbohydrate produces 5.5 ml water, and 1 gm fat produces 1.07 ml water. Table 2-15 gives the

TABLE 2-14 *Water Requirements of Infants and Children*

Age	Water Requirement (ml/kg/day)
3 days	80-100
10 days	125-150
3 months	140-160
6 months	130-155
1 year	120-135
2 years	115-125
6 years	90-100
10 years	70-85
14 years	50-60

From Barness LA: *Nutrition and nutritional disorders.* In Berman RE, Kliegman, RM: *Nelson textbook of Pediatrics,* ed 14, Philadelphia, 1992, WB Saunders.

TABLE 2-15 *Percentage of Water in Selected Foods*

Food	Water (%)	Food	Water (%)
Human milk	85.2	Strained carrots	92.3
Cow's milk	87.4	Hamburger patty	68.3
Infant cereals, high protein	6.1	Chicken, cooked, dark meat	64.4
Infant cereals, rice	6.7	Egg, hard boiled	73.7
Strained macaroni and cheese	87.1	Oatmeal, cooked	83.6
Strained chicken with vegetables	90.0	Bread, white, enriched	35.6
Strained beef with vegetables	85.4	Carrots, cooked	91.2
Strained applesauce	88.6	Peas, canned	81.5
Strained peaches	80.1	Banana	75.7
Strained beef	80.6	Pears, canned	91.1
Strained peas	87.5		

From Gebhardt SE, Cutrufelli R, Matthews RH: *Composition of foods, baby foods, raw processed, prepared,* Agriculture Handbook No 8-3, Washington, DC, 1978, US Department of Agriculture.

water content of representative foods consumed in infancy and early childhood. When milk is boiled the liquid evaporates and protein and electrolytes are concentrated. Boiled milk is an inappropriate food for infants.

Because of a relatively greater demand for insensible water and a renal concentrating capacity that may be less than that of the adult, the infant is vulnerable to water imbalance. Under normal environmental conditions infants do not need additional water.

Difficulties arise when formulas are improperly prepared (see Chapter 4), when infants ingest limited volumes of milk during illness, and when renal losses are greater than usual, such as during episodes of vomiting and diarrhea.[10] To ensure adequate water intakes, infant formula should not be concentrated to more than 100 kcal/100 ml (30 kcal/oz).

As children grow older, the concentrating power of the kidney increases. Children learn to communicate and ask for water when they become thirsty. For older children difficulties in achieving water balance are unlikely in the absence of vomiting or diarrhea.

Minerals

Although minerals contribute only 3% to 4% of body weight, they play important roles in the regulation of body fluids, acid-base balance, and metabolic processes.

Calcium and phosphorus. Calcium and phosphorus occur in three systems in the body. In general, the calcium content of the body is about 2% of body weight and bone contains 99% of body calcium; the remaining 1% is found in body fluids and striated muscle. Bone contains 80% of body phosphorus; the remaining 20% is found in striated muscle and blood serum. Plasma calcium and phosphorus levels are higher in children than in adults. Serum concentrations of the minerals are highest during early childhood, then decrease, paralleling decreases in the parathyroid hormone. The levels stabilize between 6 and 12 years of age and decline to adult values during adolescence.[31]

The calcium content of the body reflects both gender and stature. The amount of calcium accumulated during growth depends on the rate of growth and final stature attained. It has been estimated that the fetus acquires an average cal-

cium intake of 97 mg/day.[32] Shaw estimates the placental transfer at term to be 150 mg/kg/day.[33] The body of the full-term newborn infant has been estimated to contain approximately 27 gm of calcium.

Skeletal requirements for calcium and phosphorus depend on body size and rates of growth. Requirements are greatest for taller, more rapidly growing children at any age.

From roentgenographic studies an average skeletal calcium and phosphorus retention in males of 90 mg/day and 43 mg/day, respectively, in the first year of life was estimated.[34] Skeletal calcium increments during the same period to averaging 150 mg/day have also been reported.[35] A decline in skeletal retentions of the minerals between the first and fourth years is expected, after which the skeletal retentions gradually increase. During the adolescent growth spurt males are estimated to retain calcium at an average of 275 mg/day and phosphorus at an average of 132 mg/day.[34] It has also been suggested that between 15 and 17 years of age, skeletal requirements for calcium average 375 to 400 mg/day.[35] The Committee on Nutrition of the American Academy of Pediatrics[32] estimates a calcium retention of 290 to 400 mg/day in males and 210 to 240 mg/day in females during their peak growth spurts. Skeletal retentions of the two minerals are less in females than in males except between the tenth and twelfth years, when rates of growth of females are greater than those of males.

Recommended intakes. Attempts to establish recommended intakes of calcium have caused considerable controversy for many years. Populations that have adapted to intakes of 200 to 400 mg/day without adverse effects have been identified, yet calcium accretion may be at that level during the pubertal growth spurt.[34] The recommended intake of 400 mg/day for the first 6 months of life has been planned to meet the needs of formula-fed infants who retain 25% to 30% of the calcium consumed in cow's milk. Although breast-fed infants ingest less calcium, estimated at 240 mg calcium from 750 ml of human milk, they retain approximately two thirds of intake. Children may need two to four times as much calcium as adults since they are growing; thus 600 mg/day is recommended for the last half of the first year and 800 mg/day for

TABLE 2-16 *Calcium in Milk and Dairy Products*

Food	Household Measure	Calcium (mg)
Human milk	4 oz	40
Cow's milk	4 oz	176
Powdered milk, nonfat, instant dry	$\frac{1}{3}$ c	276
Cheddar cheese	1 oz	204
Yogurt	$\frac{1}{2}$ c	207
Custard, baked	$\frac{1}{2}$ c	149
Chocolate pudding, cooked with milk	$\frac{1}{2}$ c	133
Chocolate pudding, instant	$\frac{1}{2}$ c	187
Ice cream	$\frac{1}{2}$ c	88

From Nutritionist III: *N-squared computing,* Salem, Ore, 1990.

1 to 10 years of age. The need for higher intakes during the preadolescent years and puberty should provide for maximum calcium retention.

Food sources. Milk and dairy products are the richest sources of calcium in the North American diet. Table 2-16 shows the calcium contribution of selected milk and dairy products. Most dark green leafy vegetables also contribute appreciable amounts of calcium. Absorption of calcium fluctuates from 30% to 60% of intake and may be as high as 75% during rapid growth. Lactase increases absorption. Phytic and oxalic acid reduce absorption while vitamin D promotes calcium absorption. Protein and phosphorus intake may affect the metabolism of calcium but generally have little effect on calcium balance if calcium is ingested at recommended levels. Calcium absorption from carbonate, acetate, gluconate, citrate salts of calcium, and whole milk are similar.[36]

Phosphorus is found in combination with calcium in dairy products but also occurs in foods that contain little calcium. It occurs in most protein-rich foods such as meats, eggs, nuts, and legumes and is found in grains. Phos-

phate-containing additives are ingredients of many carbonated beverages, processed meats, cheese, and refrigerated bakery goods.

In a recent survey, calcium intakes of children whose food patterns included cow's milk were an average of 790 mg/day, calcium intakes of children who received milk substitutes were an average of 415 mg/day and calcium intakes of children receiving neither were an average of 200 mg/day.[37]

Neonatal hypocalcemia. Plasma concentrations of calcium and phosphorus are greater in cord blood than in maternal blood. During the first 2 to 3 days of life the levels of calcium fall significantly.[38] In normal, full-term infants the decline is greatest in those who are formula-fed and least in those who receive human milk. The fall in plasma calcium levels is accompanied by a rise in plasma inorganic phosphorus levels.

After the initial decline, plasma calcium levels stabilize and tend to rise by the tenth day of life, the level being dependent on the phosphorus content or the calcium/phosphorus ratio of milk. Serum calcium concentrations in breast-fed infants are greater than those in formula-fed infants. Serum concentrations of phosphorus reflect the phosphorus content of the milk consumed, being significantly less in breast-fed infants than in formula-fed infants. Breast-fed infants generally show an increase in serum calcium concentration by 5 to 7 days of age.

One of the striking differences between human milk and cow's milk is the content of calcium and phosphorus. Cow's milk contains more than three times as much calcium and six times as much phosphorus as does human milk. There is less calcium relative to phosphorus in cow's milk than in human milk.

Manufacturers of infant formulas have reduced the quantity of phosphorus in cow's milk formulas. The current recommendation for infant formulas is a 1.5 : 1.0 calcium to phosphorus ratio in early infancy and a 1.0 : 1.0 ratio after 1 year of age. Monitoring the amount of phosphorus consumed by infants in the early neonatal period continues to be important.[38]

Magnesium. Approximately 50% of the body's magnesium is deposited with calcium and phosphorus in bone, 25% is in muscle, and the remainder is found in soft tissue. Magnesium is the fourth most abundant mineral in the body and the second most abundant intercellular cation.

Recommended intakes. Although the data on magnesium requirements are sparse, Harris and Wilkinson[39] state that the newborn infant needs to retain 10.2 mg/day of magnesium to satisfy the requirement for growth. Fomon[10] estimates the requirement to be 16.5 mg/day during the first 4 months and suggests an intake of 25 mg/day. The average intake in early infancy is 30 mg/day, and the allowance is set at 40 mg/day for young infants and 60 mg/day for older infants. An intake of 6 mg/kg is the recommended for ages 1 to 15 years.

Food sources. Magnesium is found in many foods. Nuts, soybeans, whole grains, and legumes are excellent sources. Magnesium also exists in all green plants as a component of chlorophyll. The magnesium content of human milk and cow's milk is approximately 4 mg/100 ml and 12 mg/100 ml, respectively.

Iron. Iron is the most abundant trace mineral in the body, accounting for approximately 75 mg/kg of the newborn infant.

The concentration of **hemoglobin** at birth averages 17 to 19 gm/100 ml of blood. During the first 6 to 8 weeks of life it decreases to approximately 10 to 11 gm/100 ml because of a shortened life span of the fetal cell and decreased **erythropoiesis.** After this age there is a gradual increase in hemoglobin concentration to 13 gm/100 ml at 2 years of age. During adolescence a sharp increase occurs in males at the time of the growth spurt. Infants, children, and adolescents need iron not only to maintain hemoglobin but also to increase the iron mass related to growth increases in body size.

Iron deficiency is the most common nutritional deficiency in North America. It occurs most frequently in 12- to 36-month-old children, in adolescent males, and in females during their childbearing years.[40] It may result from inadequate iron intakes, impaired absorption, or blood loss.

Iron deficiency. Iron deficiency results when body iron is diminished. There are three stages of depletion. The first is a decrease in iron status represented by a drop in plasma **ferritin.** The second is normocytic-iron deficient erythropoiesis, in which red blood cell protoporphyrin is elevated and transferrin saturation is reduced. The third stage is iron deficiency anemia, when red blood cells are **microcytic** and hypochromic and hemoglobin levels are reduced. Iron deficiency anemia is diagnosed when **transferrin** saturation falls below 16%; anemia is diagnosed when hemoglobin concentrations fall below 11 gm/100 ml and **hematocrit values** fall below 33%.

Recommended intakes. Iron requirements of individual children vary with rates of growth, increasing blood volumes, iron stores, variations in menstrual losses of iron of adolescent females, and the timing of growth spurts of adolescents. Larger, more rapidly growing children have the greatest requirement for iron at any age.

Because of stored iron the normal newborn can maintain satisfactory hemoglobin levels solely from human milk for 3 months, but beginning at age 3 months and continuing to age 3 years, a daily intake of 1 mg/kg to a maximum of 15 mg/day is usually considered appropriate. The RDA for 6 months to 3 years is set at 10 mg/day and considered adequate for most healthy children. Iron loss during menstruation varies widely among females but is consistent from month to month in individuals. Average losses of blood of 15-year-old girls in a Swedish study were 33.8 ml per period, equivalent to an iron loss of approximately 0.5 mg/day.[41] To attain stores of 300 mg for both sexes by age 20 to 25 years, an intake of 10 mg/day is recommended for children. An additional 2 mg/day intake is recommended for males during the pubertal growth spurt and 5 mg/day for females starting with the pubertal growth spurt and menstruation and continuing through the menstrual years.[42]

Food sources. Diets in North America have been estimated to provide iron amounts of 6 mg/1000 kcal. Muscle meats provide the richest and most usable sources. Other food sources include nuts, green vegetables, whole wheat flour, bread, and fortified cereal products.

Of the iron in pork, liver, and fish, 30% to 40% is in the form of heme iron, and of the iron in beef, lamb, and chicken, 50% to 60% is in the form of heme iron. These foods are sources of nonheme iron also, as are greens, vegetables, grains, legumes, and eggs. The iron content of human milk and cow's milk is 0.5 to

TABLE 2-17 *Selected Food Sources of Iron*

Food	Household Measure	Iron (mg)
Iron-fortified formula	8 oz	2.9
Infant cereals, high protein	1 T	1.7
Infant cereals, rice	1 T	1.7
Strained vegetables with ham	2 T	0.1
Strained chicken with vegetables	2 T	0.1
Strained beef with vegetables	2 T	0.1
Strained beef	2 T	0.5
Hamburger, cooked	2 oz	1.2
Chicken, dark meat	1 oz	1.2
Frankfurter, 5" by $\frac{3}{4}$"	1	0.7
Egg	1 medium	0.7
Pork and beans	$\frac{1}{4}$ c	1.1
Peanut butter	1 T	0.3
Bread, enriched white	1 slice	0.7
Macaroni, enriched, cooked	$\frac{1}{4}$ c	0.5
Carrots, cooked	$\frac{1}{4}$ c	0.2
Orange	1 medium	0.1
Canned pears	$\frac{1}{4}$ c	0.1

From Nutritionist III: *N-squared computing,* Salem, Ore, 1990; and *Nutrient values,* Fremont, Mich, 1991, Gerber Products.

1.0 mg/L. During infancy, iron-fortified formulas and cereals fortified with reduced iron are primary food sources. Table 2-17 lists representative sources of iron for infants and children.

Iron absorption from food. The percentage of iron absorbed from food depends on the presence of heme iron or nonheme iron, the combinations of food consumed together, and the iron reserves of the individual. Individuals with inadequate iron stores absorb approximately 35%; those with adequate iron stores absorb 25% of heme iron consumed. Individuals with deficient iron reserves may absorb as much as 20% of nonheme iron, whereas iron-replete individuals may absorb as little as 2%.[43] The presence of meat, which offers heme iron and and the addition of ascorbic acid, increases the absorption of nonheme iron. Absorption is decreased by the inclusion of phytate and bran in the foods consumed at the same time. Absorption of nonheme iron varies widely depending on the composition of the meal. Overall, about 50% of the iron in human milk, 10% of the iron in cow's milk. and 4% of the iron in iron-fortified formula is absorbed. The addition of strained vegetables to the infant's diet significantly reduces the availability of iron from human milk.[44]

Many foods are fortified with iron salts. Of particular importance to persons concerned with the iron intakes of infants and children are those iron salts used to fortify the commercially prepared infant formulas, cereal grains, and cereals consumed so abundantly by children. Iron-fortified formulas contain 12 mg of iron as ferrous sulfate. Cereals and baked products may be fortified with reduced iron, sodium iron pyrophosphate, or ferric orthophosphate.

Ferrous sulfate is the most bioavailable of the iron salts, but it is seldom used to fortify food because of difficulties in manufacturing. The percentage of absorption of reduced iron depends on the particle size, surface area, and porosity of the salts, which in turn determine the extent to which the particles dissolve in the acid of the stomach. One study in humans indicated absorption is about 5% of that of ferrous sulfate. Fomon[40] feels this iron salt is not a reliable source of iron for infants.

Some pediatricians believe it may be advantageous for infants over 6 months of age to receive one feeding that includes not milk but iron-fortified cereal, vegetables, and fruit or fruit juice containing vitamin C.

A desirable iron status can be compromised by a low-kcalorie diet, poor selection of foods, or any dietary extremes. Assuming that a well-chosen diet contains iron intakes of approximately 6 mg/1000 kcal, adolescents dieting to lose weight will be receiving minimal iron intakes. In addition to this, the common practice of choosing foods such as yogurt and cottage cheese as primary protein foods in a reducing diet results in an even lower dietary iron intake plus reducing absorption.

Ideally, regular monitoring of iron status should be provided for infants and adolescents, especially those with limited high-iron foods or those practicing various dietary extremes or restrictions.

The addition of iron to infant formulas has been controversial because of a belief that additional iron causes gastrointestinal distress. In reviewing the lack of evidence for gastrointestinal change caused by iron fortification of infant formulas and the positive effect fortification has had on the decrease of iron deficiency anemia in young children, the American Academy of Pediatrics has recommended that iron-fortified infant formulas be used for all formula-fed infants.[45] This view is supported by the general improvement of iron status as a result of increased iron intake from fortified formulas by those infants and young children enrolled in the Special Supplemental Food Program for Women, Infants, and Children (WIC).[46] Long-term follow-up of iron- and non–iron-supplemented children indicates a developmental advantage for those children who did not suffer from anemia.[47]

Iodine. Of the iodine in the human adult, 70% to 80% is concentrated in the thyroid gland, which synthesizes its only functional compounds, thyroxine and triiodothyronine. The remaining iodine in the body is distributed in the blood, skin, and other tissues.

Recommended intakes. The breast-fed infant has an iodine intake of 10 to 20 μg/100 kcal from an adequately fed lactating mother. The current recommendations are 40 and 50 μg for younger and older infants. This recommendation increases from 70 to 150 μg/day throughout childhood. It has been suggested that requirements for 8- to 16-year-old children may not be much greater than 56 μg/day.[10] Average intakes of iodine in the United States are five to ten times the recommended amounts. However, wide variations in iodine intakes may be experienced by individuals, depending on sources of food and geographical locations.

Food sources. Iodized salt, bread made with iodate as a dough conditioner, milk, and seafood are excellent sources of dietary iodine. The fact that the iodine content of food is determined by the soil in which it is grown is no longer significant in the etiology of iodine deficiency. Food consumed in one area is often transported from another. The iodine content of milk and dairy products depends on whether the cattle have been given iodine-supplemented feed or iodized salt blocks. Milk iodine levels may be as high as 450 μg/L.

The amounts of iodine absorbed from environments polluted by the combustion of fossil fuels and organic matter can be significant.

Zinc. Zinc is distributed throughout all cells and tissues. The fetus contains approximately 20 mg/kg. During infancy, serum zinc levels are determined primarily by the zinc content of the milk consumed.[48]

Hambidge and others[49] reported low concentrations of zinc in hair in 10 of 132 children over 4 years of age from middle-income and upper-income families that were studied in Denver. The children had histories of poor appetite, consumed small amounts of meat, and had diminished taste acuity. Nine of the ten children had heights that plotted at or below the 10th percentile. Supplements of zinc sulfate providing a zinc content of 0.2 mg/kg resulted in improvements in growth, taste, and appetite.

It appears that many preschool and school-age children from low-income and middle-income families may be ingesting inadequate amounts of zinc. Studies in Denver of Head-start children 3.5 to 6 years of age whose heights were less than the 3rd percentile revealed that 69% had low plasma and hair zinc concentrations. Improvement was noted by increasing daily zinc intake from 0.4 to 0.8 mg/kg/day.[50]

Recommended intakes. Recommendations for intake have been made from studies of zinc intakes of apparently well-nourished individuals and from studies of zinc balance. Growth velocity is the main determinant of the zinc requirement in childhood. The infant is born without zinc stores and rapidly becomes dependent on an adequate supply of biologically available zinc.

Variations in plasma zinc concentrations during growth reflect the continual utilization and depletion of body stores of zinc. Declines occur during periods of most rapid growth. Calculations indicated that the requirement at 4 to 6 months of age is 50% less than at 1 month.[48] Breast-fed infants receive an average of 2 mg/day during the first month and show no signs of depletion because of the high bioavailability of zinc in breast milk.[51] The recommendation for infants is 5 mg/day during the first year of life and 10 mg/day during childhood. Intakes of children 1 to 3 years of age have been estimated to average 5 mg/day; those of children 3 to 5 years of age, 5 to 7 mg/day; and those of adolescents, 13 mg/day.[52]

Food sources. Seafoods and meats are rich sources of bioavailable zinc. Cereals and legumes also contain significant amounts, but refining processes destroy much zinc. Frequently zinc is added back to foods, especially breakfast cereals. Fiber and phytate in plants tend to bind zinc and decrease absorption. The bioavailability ranges from 20% to 30%. Estimates of zinc in human milk and cow's milk range from 3 to 5 mg/L. Picciano and Guthrie[53] found ranges of 0.14 to 3.95 mg/L in milk of 50 lactating women. Colostrum contains 20 mg/L, three to five times as much as later milk. Levels of zinc in human milk decline after 2 months of lactation and may fall below 1 mg/L. Infant formulas are supplemented with zinc and contain 3 to 4 mg/L. Table 2-18 gives the zinc content of representative foods consumed by infants and children.

Fluoride. Fluoride in the body is concentrated in the bones and teeth. The concentration in bones increases linearly with increased intakes.

The role of fluoride as an essential trace mineral lies in its ability to reduce the incidence of dental caries. It has not been proved essential to survival. Epidemiological studies have repeatedly proved that there is a close relationship between tooth decay and the amount of fluoride ingested during tooth development.[54] When the fluoride content of community drinking water has been adjusted to a level of 1 ppm (1 mg/L), the incidence of dental caries has been reduced 40% to 60%. Although the effect is especially important during tooth development, fluoride has also been shown to be beneficial to adults.

Recommended intakes. The Committee on Nutrition of the American Academy of Pediatrics[55] recommends that supplemental fluoride dosages be adjusted to the fluoride content of the water supply (Table 2-19). In communities with a fluoride content less than 0.7 mg/L in the water supply, fluoride supplements of 0.25 mg/day are recommended from 2 weeks to 2 years of age, 0.5 mg/day between 2 and 3 years of age, and 1 mg/day after 3 years of age. It is suggested that children whose drinking water contains between 0.3 and 0.7 mg of fluoride

TABLE 2-18 *Selected Food Sources of Zinc*

Food	Household Measure	Zinc (mg)
Cow's milk	4 oz	0.5
Ground beef, cooked	2 oz	3.0
Chicken drumstick	1	1.4
Egg	1 large	0.5
Oatmeal, cooked	$\frac{1}{2}$ c	0.6
Bread, white	1 slice	0.2
Bread, whole wheat	1 slice	0.5
Green beans, canned	$\frac{1}{4}$ c	0.2
Spinach	$\frac{1}{2}$ c	0.7
Banana	$\frac{1}{2}$ medium	0.1
Orange	1 medium	0.1

From Nutritionist III: *N-squared computing*, Salem, Ore, 1990.

TABLE 2-19 *Supplemental Fluoride Dosage Schedule (mg/day)**

Age	Concentration of Fluoride in Drinking Water (ppm)		
	<0.3	**0.3-0.7**	**>0.7**
2 weeks to 2 years	0.25	0	0
2 to 3 years	0.50	0.25	0
3 to 16 years	1.00	0.50	0

From Committee on Nutrition: *Pediatrics* 63:150, 1979.
*2.2 mg of sodium fluoride contains 1 mg of fluoride.

ppm receive 0.25 mg between 2 and 3 years of age and 0.5 mg between 3 and 16 years of age.

Food sources. All foods and water contain very small amounts of fluoride. Seafood contains greater amounts. Food produced and prepared in areas in which the water is fluoridated reflect the fluoride content of the water. Cow's milk has a fluoride content of about 20 µg/L[56] and human milk contains 5 to 25 µg/L and reflects maternal intake.[57] Average intakes of 15- to 19-year-old males are estimated to be 1.85 mg/day in areas with fluoridated water supplies and 0.86 mg/day in those with nonfluoridated water. Beverages and water contributed approximately 75% of intake.[58]

The recommendation of a safe intake of fluoride for younger children is set at a maximum of 2.5 mg to avoid tooth mottling. Suggested safe ranges of intake are 0.5 to 1.0 mg for the first year and 0.5 to 1.5 mg until 3 years of age. Infants who ingest low levels of fluoride, that is, those who receive human milk or formulas prepared with nonfluoridated water, should receive fluoride supplements of 0.25 mg/day until 2 years of age.

There is an increasing concentration of fluoride in the food chain. Processing food with fluoridated water significantly increases its fluoride content. The fluoride content of ready-to-drink fruit juices increases five to twenty times when fluoridated water is used in processing. The fluoride content of infant cereals is influenced by the fluoride content of the water in which they were produced. Mechanically deboning meat increases the fluoride content of the end products because bone chips are incorporated during processing. Infant formula is no longer manufactured with fluoridated water.

Mottling and fluorosis of tooth enamel. When the fluoride concentrations of drinking water increase above 2 ppm, mottling (a brown stain on the teeth) during tooth development occurs. The incidence and severity of the manifestation increase as the fluoride content of the water increases. At levels of 8 ppm almost all individuals who consumed the water during tooth development have extensively mottled teeth.[59] In areas with a high natural concentration of fluoride, it has become a practice to dilute fluoride in water supply to no more than 1.2 ppm.

Fluorosis, usually manifested as opaque spots or streaks on the enamel of permanent teeth and not discernible by the lay person, has been noted in 63% of children by the time they were 7 to 12 years of age in a community without fluoridated water when the use of fluoride supplements was common.[59] Leverett suggests that the definition of the optimum concentration of fluoride in community water supplies needs to be reassessed.

Selenium. It is difficult to assess both selenium intake and status because humans apparently have the capability to adjust homeostasis over a wide range of intakes, thus invalidating balance studies. Little is known about the selenium requirements of children, so the recommendations have been extrapolated from adult values plus a generous factor for growth. The recommendations are for 10 to 15 µg/day selenium for the first year of life and 20 to 30 µg/day during childhood.

Seafood, kidney, and liver are primary food sources of selenium. Other meats and grains are lesser sources of this nutrient.

Remaining Trace Elements

The fact that only safe and adequate intakes have been recommended for the remaining trace minerals—copper, manganese, chromium, and molybdenum—indicates the lack of information necessary to define specific needs during the life cycle. These estimated safe values are shown in Table 2-20.

Less than adequate intake during infancy and childhood may occur in cases of generalized malnutrition or in infants maintained on nutrient-deficient formulas. Infants and children who consume a variety of foods are likely to consume appropriate quantities of these nutrients.

Copper. Although copper deficiency is rare in humans, it has been demonstrated in severely malnourished children. About half of the copper that accumulates during gestation is in the fetal liver and offers some protection against early deficiency. Again efficient homeostatic mechanisms rule out determination of requirements by the use of balance studies.

Breast-fed infants have thrived on a copper intake of about 40 to 60 µg/kg/day[60]; thus the estimation for an intake of 0.4 to 0.6 mg/day. Infant formulas are supplemented with copper

TABLE 2-20   *Estimated Safe and Adequate Daily Dietary Intakes of Selected Vitamins and Minerals**

Category	Age (Years)	Vitamins	
		Biotin (μg)	Pantothenic Acid (mg)
Infants	0-0.5	10	2
	0.5-1	15	3
Children and adolescents	1-3	20	3
	4-6	25	3-4
	7-10	30	4-5
	11+	30-100	4-7

Category	Age (Years)	Trace Elements†				
		Copper (mg)	Manganese (mg)	Fluoride (mg)	Chromium (μg)	Molybdenum (μg)
Infants	0-0.5	0.4-0.6	0.3-0.6	0.1-0.5	10-40	15-30
	0.5-1	0.6-0.7	0.6-1.0	0.2-1.0	20-60	20-40
Children and adolescents	1-3	0.7-1.0	1.0-1.5	0.5-1.5	20-80	25-50
	4-6	1.0-1.5	1.5-2.0	1.0-2.5	30-120	30-75
	7-10	1.0-2.0	2.0-3.0	1.5-2.5	50-200	50-150
	11+	1.5-2.5	2.0-5.0	1.5-2.5	50-200	75-250

From *Recommended dietary allowances,* ed 10, National Research Council, Washington, DC, 1989, National Academy Press.
*Because there is less information on which to base allowances, these figures are not given in the main table of RDA and are provided here in the form of ranges of recommended intakes.
†Since the toxic levels for many trace elements may be only several times usual intakes, the upper levels for the trace elements given in this table should not be habitually exceeded.

to the level of 60 μg/100 kcal of energy. The relatively stable need for copper of 40 μg/kg/day is demonstrated in the estimation of 1 to 2 mg/day in childhood.[23]

Manganese. Manganese status is difficult to assess. Little is known about the manganese requirement of infants, and manganese deficiency has not been demonstrated in infants. The estimated safe intake for infants and children is derived and set at 0.3 to 1.0 mg in the first year and 1 to 3 mg/day in childhood.

Chromium. The difficulty in assessing chromium status and requirement has led to extrapolation of safe intakes based on expected food intake. This is made more difficult by the limited data on chromium content of foods. These factors have led to the wide range of estimated safe intakes of 10 to 60 μg/day in infancy and 20 to 200 μg/day in childhood.

Molybdenum. Human milk contains small amounts of molybdenum. Little is known about bioavailability. Because deficiency has not been easily demonstrated, it is assumed that the requirement is small and that it can be met with usual intakes of food.

Vitamins

Because of vitamins' functions in metabolic processes, the amounts required are determined by intakes of energy, protein, and fats. Exact needs are difficult to define.

Most vitamins cross the placenta and accumulate in the fetus at greater concentrations than in the mother. Maternal hypovitaminemia will be reflected in the fetus.

Vitamins A and E and beta-carotene concentrations are lower in the newborn infant's blood than in the mother's. The concentration of water-soluble vitamins in the blood of the neonate is higher than in that of the mother.[61]

Fat-soluble vitamins in excess of need are not excreted but are stored. Reserves can be accumulated. The **toxicity** of excessive intakes of vitamins A and D is well documented.

In contrast to vitamins A, D, E, and K, the water-soluble vitamins are stored in small amounts and deficiencies can be expected to occur in a relatively short period if the nutrient is absent from dietary intake.

Fat-soluble vitamins

Vitamin A. The term "vitamin A" is used for a group of compounds needed for vision and growth, as well as the immune system. Vitamin A needs can be met by dietary intake of (1) preformed retinoids with vitamin A activity from animal products or (2) carotenoid precursors of vitamin A such as β-carotene and α-carotene from plant foods. The vitamin A activity in foods is currently expressed as retinol equivalents (RE). The definition of 1 RE is 1 μg of all-trans-retinol, 6 μg of all-trans-β-carotene or 12 μg of other provitamin α-carotenoids.

The recommendation for vitamin A intake for infants is based on the composition of human milk and the usual intake of healthy infants. Human milk contains 40 to 70 μg/dl of retinol and 20 to 40 μg/dl of carotenoids. Therefore the recommendation is set at 375 RE/day. The range of intake that supports normal growth is wide because infants have shown no signs of deficiency on one third of the recommended amount. After the first year of life vitamin A recommendations for children are extrapolated on adult needs and body weight. The recommended vitamin A intake is 400 RE at age 1 and increases to 700 RE by age 10 years. Intakes of greater than 10 times the RDA for age over time can cause toxicity.

Food sources. Preformed retinol is most abundant in liver and fish liver oils; significant amounts are also found in whole and fortified milk and in eggs. Active carotenoids are present in carrots and dark, leafy, green vegetables. Foods fortified with vitamin A such as milk and margarine are also reasonable sources. Absorption of vitamin A is positively affected by dietary fat, protein, and vitamin E and negatively affected by oxidizing agents in food.

Recommended intakes. Recommendations for intakes of vitamin A are interpolated from infant and adult needs even though children under age 5 are at greatest risk for vitamin A deficiency and this deficiency is most commonly due to a deficient dietary intake.[62]

Vitamin D. Vitamin D (calciferol) is essential for skeletal formation. Ultraviolet light on skin is required to synthesize vitamin D_3 (cholecalciferol) from less active forms.

Humans can meet their vitamin D requirement from skin exposure to sunlight. Variables that affect the amount of vitamin D synthesized are amount of skin exposed; higher melanin content of skin, which requires a longer exposure; the angle of the sun; and the age of the individual.

Recommended intakes. It is difficult to establish a recommended intake, since an individual can meet vitamin D needs through sun exposure alone. However, since many individuals require a dietary source to have adequate vitamin D, the recommendation is based on a level that will meet needs without sunlight. Since human milk has a questionable ability to meet the vitamin D needs of the infant without another dietary source, it is recommended that breast-fed infants who are not regularly exposed to sunlight receive vitamin D supplements of 5 to 7.5 μg/day. This appropriate nature of this recommendation is borne out in recent reports of rickets in infants who are exclusively breast-fed and whose mothers have a marginal nutritional status.[63] The recommendation for infants who receive formula is 7.5 μg/day. From 6 months of age through adulthood, that is, until peak bone mass is acquired, 10 μg vitamin D has been set as the recommendation. Intakes of five times the RDA have demonstrated toxicity.

Although 2.5 μg/day cholecalciferol prevents rickets and ensures adequate absorption of calcium and normal mineralization of bone in the infant, better calcium absorption and some increase in growth have been noted with intakes of 10 μg cholecalciferol. Vitamin D can be formed by the action of sunlight on the skin. The amount formed depends on several variables, and amounts formed cannot be readily measured.

Food sources. Eggs, butter, and fortified margarine are recognized sources of vitamin D.

Milk is supplemented with cholecalciferol to a level of 10 μg/qt as are infant formulas. The cholecalciferol content in breast milk is 0.63 to 1.25 μg/L.[64]

Vitamin E. The most biologically active form of vitamin E is α-tocopherol, which is relatively inefficiently absorbed at 20% to 80%. The recommendation for infants is 3 mg. The remaining recommendations are increased with increasing body size. Thus the recommendation is 4 mg for the remainder of the first year to 10 mg in childhood.

Defining appropriate intakes for vitamin E is complicated by large variations in the susceptibility to peroxidation of fatty acids in the diet and tissues. Also, large losses occur in producing products that provide vitamin E.[65] Requirements are related to the polyunsaturated fatty acid content of cellular structures. An assumption is made that requirements increase with body weight until maturity. An intake of 5 IU at 9 kg increasing to 12 IU at 40 kg of body weight should be satisfactory in diets providing 4% to 7% of kilocalories as linoleic acid.

Newborns have low stores of vitamin E. If an adequate supply is not provided, a deficiency characterized by hemolytic anemia will occur. Newborns' diets should include a tocopherol content of 1 mg/gm of polyunsaturated fatty acids.[65]

Food sources. Vegetable oils provide tocopherol as do wheat germ and nuts. Vitamin E is vulnerable to loss in food processing, storage, and preparation.

Water-soluble vitamins

Thiamin. The requirement for thiamin is related to energy intake. Studies of thiamin requirements of infants are sparse. Those available suggest that the minimum requirement of infants is approximately 0.17 mg/day. For preadolescent children, 3 mg/1000 kcal was demonstrated as adequate.[66] Another study of 14- to 17-year-old males indicated that 0.4 mg/1000 kcal meets their minimum requirement.[67] An intake of 0.3 to 0.4 mg of thiamin has been suggested for infants, and an intake of 0.5 mg/1000 kcal or 0.7 to 1.5 mg/day has been suggested as appropriate for children.

Thiamin is abundant in whole grains, brewer's yeast, pork, legumes, and nuts. Enriched bread and cereal products are also reasonable sources of this nutrient.

Riboflavin. Although signs of riboflavin deficiency are unusual, very low riboflavin intakes may interfere with growth. A breast-fed infant is estimated to consume riboflavin at 0.26 to 0.48 mg/1000 kcal of energy/day. It is believed that riboflavin at 0.6 mg/1000 kcal of energy should be taken to meet the needs of all humans. The increase in body size translates into a recommendation of riboflavin at 0.4 to 0.5 mg/day for infants and 0.8 to 1.8 mg/day for children.

Urinary excretion of riboflavin is low in adults and in children maintained on diets containing up to 0.5 mg/1000 kcal; it increases as riboflavin intakes increase. The minimum requirement is thought to be 0.85 mg/day.[65]

Riboflavin is found abundantly in dairy products, meat, poultry, and fish.

Niacin. The fact that tryptophan is converted to niacin makes basic requirements for niacin difficult to determine. Sixty milligrams of tryptophan is equivalent to 1 mg of niacin and thus considered to be 1 niacin equivalent (NE). Minimum requirements appear to be 4.4 mg/1000 kcal.[65]

The niacin and tryptophan content in human milk is 1.5 mg/L and 210 mg/L, respectively, and the NE content is about 7 mg/1000 kcal. Little is known about the NE requirements of infants and children; therefore the recommendations are based on the adult level of 6.6 mg/1000 kcal. This translates to 5 to 6 mg/day in infancy and increases from 9 to 20 mg/day with increasing age and body size.

Meat contains both niacin and tryptophan and is a good source of the nutrient. In general, protein is about 1% tryptophan.

Vitamin B$_6$. Since vitamin B$_6$ functions in amino acid metabolism, the requirement increases with increasing protein intake. The recommended intake of vitamin B$_6$ for infants is based on experience with proprietary formulas and an intake of 0.015 mg/gm protein or 0.4 mg/1000 kcal. An intake of 1.4 gm of vitamin B$_6$ with an intake of 60 gm of protein should be adequate. A generous intake for adolescents would be 2 gm/day.[65] The recommendation for infants is 0.3 to 0.6 mg/day and the recommendation from age 1 through childhood is 0.02

mg/gm of protein or 1 to 2 gm/day based on age and body size.

Folate. The requirement for folacin in infancy has been estimated to be 5 μg/kg of body weight.[68] For older children and adults, folacin needs are extrapolated from those of infants. Herbert believes 3.6 μg/kg to be an adequate intake from birth to 1 year, and 3 μg/kg is adequate for older children and adolescents.[68]

The folate content of human milk is used as the basis of the recommendation for folate intake for infants for the first year of life. The recommendation is for 3.6 μg/kg/day or 25 to 35 μg. The recommendation for children is interpolated from adult data and set at 50 to 200 μg based on size.

Vitamin B$_{12}$. The vitamin B$_{12}$ allowance for infants is based on the content in the milk of lactating women with adequate vitamin B$_{12}$ and a margin of safety, that is, 0.3 μg/day or 0.05 μg/kg body weight. For formula-fed infants the Committee on Nutrition of the American Academy of Pediatrics[69] recommends an intake of 0.15 μg/100 kcal. Herbert recommends an intake of 0.3 to 0.5 μg/day in infancy with gradual increases based on body size to 2 μg/day in adolescents.[70] The current RDAs are similar with a recommendation of 0.05 μg/kg body weight or a total intake of 0.7 to 2.0 μg/day.

Animal products are the primary source of vitamin B$_{12}$ in diets.

Vitamin C. An intake of 10 mg/day of vitamin C is adequate to prevent and cure scurvy in humans. It does not, however, provide for acceptable reserves. Breast-fed infants consuming 7 to 12 mg of vitamin C have been protected from scurvy. An intake of 25 mg/day should provide an adequate margin of safety.[71] However, the RDA for infants is set at 30 to 35 mg/day. In relation to body weight, the vitamin C requirement of older children is higher than that of adults; thus the recommendation increases from 40 to 60 mg/day over time.

Fruits and vegetables are the primary sources of vitamin C in food patterns.

Biotin. Biotin is essential for protein metabolism. However, there are no definitive data on biotin requirements; therefore the estimated safe levels of intake (10 to 15 μg/day in in-

fancy) are based on observation and the content of human milk. The biotin in human milk, which is readily bioavailable, has been reported at levels up to 20 μg/L.[72] Estimated safe levels for children are gradually increased with age from 20 to 100 μg/day.

Biotin is available from whole grains, liver, and yeast.

Pantothenic acid. Although pantothenic acid has been demonstrated as metabolically important, it has not been clinically recognized in humans. Again, the provisional recommendation for safe intake is based on observation and measurements from human milk. Thus the safe intake has been set at 2 to 3 mg/day for infants and gradually increases from 3 to 7 mg/day with age.

Meats, whole grains, and legumes are primary sources of pantothenic acid.

TABLE 2-21 *Selected Food Sources of Vitamin A*

Food	Household Measure	Vitamin A (RE)
Cow's milk, 2%	8 oz	150
Human milk	8 oz	178
Cheddar cheese	1 oz	89.9
Egg	1 large	95.2
Liver, beef	1 oz	3074
Butter	1 t	35
Apricots, canned	$\frac{1}{4}$ c	79.2
Orange	1 medium	26.9
Peach	1 medium	46.5
Watermelon, diced	$\frac{1}{2}$ c	29.2
Carrots	$\frac{1}{4}$ c	958
Acorn squash, baked, mashed	$\frac{1}{4}$ c	21.9
Sweet potatoes, mashed	$\frac{1}{4}$ c	1398
Green peas	$\frac{1}{4}$ c	26.7
Spinach, cooked	$\frac{1}{4}$ c	399
Tomatoes, canned	$\frac{1}{4}$ c	36.2

From Nutritionist III: *N-squared computing,* Salem, Ore, 1990.

TABLE 2-22   *Selected Food Sources of Vitamin C*

Food	Household Measure	Vitamin C (mg)
Human milk	8 oz	12.3
Cow's milk	8 oz	2.7
Broccoli	1 spear	22
Brussels sprouts	$\frac{1}{4}$ c	18
Cabbage, raw, chopped	$\frac{1}{4}$ c	11
Cabbage, cooked, wedge	$\frac{1}{4}$ c	9
Cantaloupe, diced	$\frac{1}{2}$ c	34
Grapefruit	$\frac{1}{2}$	39
Orange	1 medium	70
Orange juice	$\frac{1}{2}$ c	48
Potato, boiled ($2\frac{1}{2}$ inch)	$\frac{1}{2}$	5
Strawberries	1 c	85
Tomato, raw, ($2\frac{1}{8}$ inch)	1	22
Tomatoes, canned	$\frac{1}{2}$ c	18
Tomato juice	$\frac{1}{2}$ c	22

From Nutritionist III: *N-squared computing*, Salem, Ore, 1990.

TABLE 2-23   *Selected Food Sources of Riboflavin*

Food	Household Measure	Riboflavin (mg)
Human milk	8 oz	0.09
Cow's milk	8 oz	0.48
Prepared infant formula	8 oz	0.16-0.24
Cheddar cheese	1 oz	0.11
Infant cereals, high protein	1 T	0.06
Infant cereals, rice	1 T	0.06
Farina	$\frac{1}{2}$ c	0.06
Oatmeal	$\frac{1}{2}$ c	0.03
Macaroni, enriched	$\frac{1}{4}$ c	0.03
Broccoli	1 spear	0.03
Green peas	$\frac{1}{4}$ c	0.04
Spinach	$\frac{1}{4}$ c	0.09

From Nutritionist III: *N-squared computing*, Salem, Ore, 1990.

Food sources. Vitamins reported to be most often consumed in less than appropriate amounts by preschool and school-age children are riboflavin and vitamins A, C, and B[6].[73] Food sources of these vitamins are given in Tables 2-21 through 2-24. Because goat's milk is folate deficient, attention must be given to that vitamin if infants are fed goat's milk.

Vitamin supplements

Vitamin K. Since vitamin K functions in prothrombin formation, a prophylactic intramuscular dose of 0.5 to 1 mg of vitamin K is usually given to infants at birth as a protection against hemorrhagic disease of the newborn.[74,75] After receiving this dose, human beings are able to synthesize vitamin K from the bacteria in their gut. Infant formulas contain 4 μg/100 kcal. Since little is known about the vitamin K requirement, the RDA is set at 1 μg/kg/day or 5 to 65 μg/day depending on size. Vitamin K supplement is needed only for children who malabsorb fat.

Other vitamins. The importance of appropriate vitamin supplementation of breast-fed infants is discussed in Chapter 4. After infancy the percentage of children who are given vitamin supplements declines; however, over half of preschool and school-age children receive multivitamin-mineral preparations.[76]

Because Cook and Payne[76] found that the use of vitamin supplements significantly increased the percentage of second and sixth grade children who meet 67% of the RDA compared with nonsupplemented children, they consider vitamin supplementation advisable.

Farris and others[77] studied 158 10- to 13-year-old children and found that 50% to 75% of the children had never taken vitamin supplements. At age 13 years, 12% of the children were taking supplements. Children who could

TABLE 2-24 *Selected Food Sources of Vitamin B₆*

Food	Household Measure	Vitamin B6 (mg)
Cow's milk	1 c	0.1
Human milk	1 c	0.03
Infant cereals, high protein	1 T	0.02
Infant cereals, rice	1 T	0.01
Infant dinners, vegetable and bacon	1 T	0.01
Infant dinners, vegetable and chicken	1 T	0.01
Strained beef	1 T	0.01
Strained chicken	1 T	0.03
Beef	3½ oz	0.27
Chicken	3½ oz	0.47
Peanut butter	1 T	0.06
Egg	1 large	0.07
Whole wheat bread	1 slice	0.05
White bread	1 slice	0.01
Green peas, canned	¼ c	0.03
Tomatoes, canned	¼ c	0.05
Squash, frozen	¼ c	0.04
Banana	1 medium	0.71
Orange juice	½ c	0.05
Strawberries	½ c	0.04

From Nutritionist III: *N-squared computing,* Salem, Ore, 1990; and *Nutrient values,* Fremont, Mich, 1991, Gerber Products.

benefit most from supplements were not taking them. Those taking supplements often had dietary intakes that met the RDA from food alone. Breskin and others[78] noted no significant differences in biochemical indices with the exception of red blood cell folate of children who consumed supplements compared with those who did not, even though mean intakes of vitamin B₆ of the nonsupplemented group were 30% below the RDA. Many of the nonsupplemented children did not ingest two thirds of the RDA of folate. All laboratory values were in the normal range of accepted standards.

The Committee on Nutrition of the American Academy of Pediatrics[74] has defined four groups of children who are at particular risk and for whom vitamin supplementation may be appropriate: children from deprived families, especially those who suffer from parental neglect or abuse; children who have **anorexia,** poor and capricious appetites, or poor eating habits or who are on regimens to manage obesity; pregnant teenagers; and children who consume **vegan** diets.

Vitamin supplementation of diets of older children should be recommended only after careful evaluation of food intake. Diets of children who restrict their intake of milk because of real or imagined allergies, lactose intolerance, or psychosocial reasons should be monitored for riboflavin, vitamin D, calcium, and iron. Diets of infants and children receiving goat's milk should be carefully monitored for food sources of folacin. Diets of children who consume limited amounts of fruits and vegetables should be checked for sources of vitamins A and C.

Vitamin supplements, especially those that are colored and sugar coated, should be stored in places inaccessible to young children so they are not confused with candy and ingested inappropriately.

Summary

The nutrient needs of individual children vary at any age depending on body size, patterns of activity, interaction of nutrients, and rates of growth. They are greatest per unit of body size in infancy and decline with age.

The recommended dietary intakes during childhood are extrapolated from needs of infants and adult males or are calculated on the basis of presumed energy or protein intake. Intakes of individual children should be evaluated not in relation to the total amounts listed on the RDA recommendations, but on the same basis the RDA was calculated.

Studies indicate that intakes of protein are generally adequate in North America. Nutrients most likely to be consumed in low or deficient amounts are calcium, iron, and vitamins A and C.

Children at risk for nutrient inadequacies are those from the following groups: deprived families; those who have an excessive appetite, poor eating habits, anorexia, or those on regimens to manage obesity; pregnant teenagers; and those who consume vegan diets.

REVIEW QUESTIONS

1. Why is there such a wide range of acceptable energy intakes for infants and young children?
2. Why are the guidelines for protein, energy, vitamins, and minerals described as recommended intakes rather than requirements?
3. Under what circumstances are vitamin and mineral supplements appropriately recommended for infants? For young children?
4. Which factors most effect the bioavailability of absorption of iron?

SUGGESTED LEARNING ACTIVITIES

1. Calculate the energy intake of two children of the same age and gender whose heights are in the 10th and 90th percentile. Compare this with the RDA on the basis of total energy intake, kcalories per kilogram, and kcalories per centimeter.
2. Calculate the grams of protein provided by a preschool and a school lunch. What percentage of the RDA does this provide?
3. Discuss the bioavailability of iron and zinc in foods acceptable to preschool children. How can one ensure an adequate intake?
4. Compare the content of a popular children's vitamin-mineral supplement with an adult vitamin-mineral supplement.
5. Compare the costs of the vitamins available in drug stores, health food stores, or sold door-to-door by individuals.
6. Compare the costs of meeting the RDA for vitamins with food or with vitamin-mineral supplementation.

Terms and Concepts

Provided here for your review is a listing of terms and concepts within this chapter. The definitions for terms can be found in the glossary, which begins on page 413. To aid your understanding of the terms' and concepts' application within this text, the page number designating the first mention of each term or concept within the chapter is given.

REFERENCES

1. Food and Nutrition Board: Recommended dietary allowances, ed 10, National Research Council, Washington, DC, 1989, National Academy Press.
2. Hamill PVV and others: Physical growth: National Center for Health Statistics percentiles, *Am J Clin Nutr* 32:607, 1979.
3. Report of a joint FAO/WHO/UNU expert consultation: *energy and protein requirements,* Technical Report Series No 724, Geneva, 1973, World Health Organization.
4. Ashworth A, Millward DJ: Catch-up growth in children, *Nutr Rev* 44:157, 1986.
5. Spady DW: Total daily energy expenditure of healthy, free-ranging school children, *Am J Clin Nutr* 33:766, 1980.
6. Butte NF and others: Human milk intake and growth in exclusively breast-fed infants, 104:187, 1984.
7. Adair LI: The infant's ability to self-regulate calorie intake: a case study, *J Am Diet Assoc* 85:543, 1987.
8. Food and nutrient intakes of individuals in 1 day in the United States, Spring, 1977, U.S.D.A. Nationwide Food Consumption Survey, 1977-1978, Preliminary Rep. No 2, Washington, DC, 1980, Science and Education Administration.
9. White House Conference on Child Health and Protection: Growth and development of the

child. III. Nutrition. Report of the Committee on Growth and Development, New York, 1932, Century House.

10. Fomon SJ: *Infant nutrition,* ed 2, Philadelphia, 1974, WB Saunders.

11. Holt LE, Jr, Snyderman SE: The amino acid requirements of infants, *JAMA* 175:100, 1961.

12. Fomon SJ and others: Requirements for protein and essential amino acids in early infancy, *Acta Paediatr Scand* 62:33, 1973.

13. Fomon SJ, Filer LJ: *Amino acid requirements for normal growth.* In Nythan WL, editor: *Amino acid metabolism and genetic variations,* New York, 1967, McGraw-Hill.

14. Pineda OB and others: *Protein quality in relation to estimates of essential amino acid requirements.* In Bodwell CE and others, editors: *Protein quality in humans: assessment and in vitro estimation,* Westport, Conn, 1981, AVI Publishing.

15. Williams HH and others: *Nitrogen and amino acid requirements.* In *Improvements in protein nutriture,* Report of the Committee on Amino Acids, Food and Nutrition Board, National Academy of Sciences, Washington, DC, 1974.

16. Nakagawa I and others: Amino acid requirements of children: nitrogen balance at the minimal level of essential amino acids, *J Nutr* 83:115, 1964.

17. Fomon SJ: Requirements of recommended dietary intakes of protein during infancy *Pediatr Res* 30:391, 1991.

18. Abernathy RP, Ritchey SJ: Position paper on RDA for protein for children, *Adv Med Biol* 105:1, 1978.

19. Committee on Nutrition, American Academy of Pediatrics: Commentary on breastfeeding and infant formula, *Pediatrics* 57:278, 1976.

20. John TJ and others: Kwashiorkor not associated with poverty, *Pediatrics* 90:730, 1977.

21. Chase HP and others: Kwashiorkor in the United States, *Pediatrics* 66:972, 1980.

22. Holman RJ, Caster WO, Weise HF: The essential fatty acid requirement of infants and the assessment of their dietary intake of linoleate by serum fatty acid analysis, *Am J Clin Nutr* 14:70, 1964.

23. Fomon SJ: Requirements of recommended dietary intakes of protein during infancy, *Pediatr Res* 30:391, 1991.

24. Healthy People 2000: Nutrition objectives, *J Am Diet Assoc* 91:1515, 1991.

25. Committee on Nutrition, American Academy of Pediatrics: Plant fiber intake in the pediatric diet, *Pediatrics* 67:572, 1981.

26. Barness LA: *Nutrition and nutritional disorders.* In Behrman RE, Kliegman RM editors: *Nelson's textbook of pediatrics,* ed 14, Philadelphia, 1992, WB Saunders.

27. Maller O, Desor JA: *Effect of taste on ingestion by human newborns.* In Bosma JF editor: *Oral sensation and perception,* Pub No (NIH) 73-546, Bethesda, Md, 1973, Department of Health, Education and Welfare.

28. Hey EN, Katz G: Evaporative water loss in the newborn baby, *J Physiol* 200:605, 1969.

29. Ziegler EE, Fomon SJ: Fluid intake, renal solute load, and water balance in infancy, *J Pediatr* 78:561, 1971.

30. Stolley H, Schlage C: Water balance and water requirement of preschool children, *Nutr Metab* 21(suppl 1):15-17, 1977.

31. Arnaud SB and others: Serum parathyroid hormone and blood minerals: interrelationships in normal children, *Pediatr Res* 7:485, 1973.

32. Committee on Nutrition, American Academy of Pediatrics: Calcium requirements in infancy and childhood, *Pediatrics* 62:826, 1978.

33. Shaw JCL: Evidence for defective skeletal mineralization in low birth weight infants: the absorption of calcium and fat, *Pediatrics* 57:16, 1976.

34. Christiansen C, Rodbro D, Neilsen CT: Bone mineral content and estimated total body calcium in normal children and adolescents, *Scand J Clin Lab Invest* 35:507, 1975.

35. Leitch L, Aitken FC: The estimation of calcium requirements: a re-examination, *Nutr Abstr Rev* 29:393, 1959.

36. Sheikh MS and others: Gastrointestinal absorption of calcium from milk and calcium salts, *N Engl J Med* 317:532, 1987.

37. Devlin J and others: Calcium intake and cow's milk free diets, *Arch Dis Child* 64:1183, 1989.

38. David L, Anast CS: Calcium metabolism in newborn infants, the interrelationship of parathyroid function and calcium, magnesium, and phosphorus metabolism in normal, "sick," and hypocalcemic newborns, *J Clin Invest* 54:287, 1974.

39. Harris L, Wilkinson AW: Magnesium depletion in children, *Lancet* 2:735, 1971.

40. Fomon SJ: Reflections on infant feeding in the 1970s and 1980s, *Am J Clin Nutr* 46:171, 1987.

41. Hallberg L and others: Menstrual blood loss—a population study, *Acta Obstet Gynecol Scand* 45:320, 1966.

42. Herbert V: Recommended dietary intakes (RDI) of iron in humans, *Am J Clin Nutr* 45:679, 1987.

43. Monsen ER and others: Estimation of available dietary iron, *Am J Clin Nutr* 31:134, 1978.

44. McMillan JA: Iron absorption from human milk, simulated human milk, and proprietary formulas, *Pediatrics* 60:896, 1977.

45. Committee on Nutrition, American Academy of Pediatrics: Iron-fortified infant formulas, *Pediatrics* 84:1114, 1989.

46. Dallman PR, Yip R: Changing characteristics of childhood anemia, *J Pediatr* 114:161, 1989.

47. Lozoff B and others: Long-term developmental outcome of infants with iron deficiency, *N Engl J Med* 325:687, 1991.

48. Krebs NF, Hambidge KM: Zinc requirements and zinc intakes of breast-fed infants, *Am J Clin Nutr* 43:288, 1986.

49. Hambidge KM and others: Low levels of zinc in hair, anorexia, poor growth, and hypogeusia in children, *Pediatr Res* 6:868, 1972.

50. Hambidge KM and others: Zinc nutrition of preschool children in the Denver Headstart Program, *Am J Clin Nutr* 29:734, 1976.

51. Casey CE and others: Studies in human lactation: zinc, copper, manganese, and chromium in human milk in the first month of lactation, *Am J Clin Nutr* 41:1193, 1985.

52. Schlage C, Wortberg B: Zinc in the diet of healthy preschool and school children, *Acta Paediatr Scand* 61:421, 1972.

53. Picciano MF, Guthrie HA: Copper, iron, and zinc contents of mature human milk, *Am J Clin Nutr* 29:242, 1976.

54. Burt BA: The epidemiological basis for water fluoridation in the prevention of dental caries, *J Public Health Policy* 3:391, 1982.

55. Committee on Nutrition, American Academy of Pediatrics: Flouride supplementation: revised dosage schedule, *Pediatrics* 63:150, 1979.

56. Taves DR: Dietary intake of fluoride ashed (total fluoride) v. unashed (inorganic fluoride) analysis of individual foods, *Br J Nutr* 49:295, 1983.

57. Krishnamachari, KAVR: *Fluorine.* In Mertz W, editor: *Trace elements in human and animal nutrition,* vol 1, San Diego, 1987, Academic Press.

58. Singer L, Ophaug RH, Harland BF: Dietary fluoride intakes of 15 to 19 year old males residing in the United States, *J Dent Res* 64:1302, 1985.

59. Leverett DH: Fluorides and the changing prevalance of dental caries, *Science* 217:26, 1982.

60. Butte NF and others: Macro- and trace-mineral intakes of exclusively breast-fed infants, *Am J Clin Nutr* 45:42, 1987.

61. Baker H and others: Vitamin profile of 174 mothers and newborns at parturition, *Am J Clin Nutr* 28:59, 1975.

62. Olson JA: Recommended dietary intakes of vitamin A in humans, *Am J Clin Nutr* 45:704, 1987.

63. Feldman K and others: Inner-city babies susceptible to rickets, *Northwest Medicine* 7:28, 1991.

64. Tsang RC: The quandary of vitamin D in the newborn infant, *Lancet* 1:1370, 1983.

65. Horwitt MK: Interpretations of requirements for thiamin, riboflavin, niacin, tryptophan, and vitamin E plus comments on balance studies and vitamin B_6, *Am J Clin Nutr* 44:973, 1986.

66. Boyden RF, Erikson SE: Metabolic patterns of preadolescent children: thiamine utilization in relation to nitrogen intake, *Am J Clin Nutr* 19:398, 1966.

67. Dick EC and others: Thiamine requirement of eight adolescent boys, as estimated from urinary thiamine excretion, *J Nutr* 66:173, 1958.

68. Herbert V: Recommended dietary intakes (RDI) of folate in humans, *Am J Clin Nutr* 45:661, 1987.

69. Committee on Nutrition, American Academy of Pediatrics: Commentary on breast-feeding and infant formulas, including proposed standards for formulas, *Pediatrics* 57:279, 1976.

70. Herbert V: Recommended dietary intakes (RDI) of vitamin B_{12} in humans, *Am J Clin Nutr* 45:671, 1987.

71. Olson JA, Hodges RE: Recommended dietary intakes (RDI) of vitamin C in humans, *Am J Clin Nutr* 45:693, 1987.

72. Heard GS and others: Distribution and bioavailability of biotin in human milk, *Fed Proc* 46:897, 1987.

73. Block G and others: Nutrient sources in the American diet: quantitative data from the NHANES II Survey. I. Vitamins and minerals, *Am J Epidemiol* 122:13, 1985.

74. Committee on Nutrition, American Academy of Pediatrics: Vitamin and mineral supplement needs in normal children in the United States, *Pediatrics* 66:1015, 1980.

75. Greer FR and others, Vitamin K status of lactating mothers, human milk, and breast-feeding infants, *Pediatrics* 88:751, 1991.

76. Cook, CC, Payne IR: Effect of supplements on the nutrient intake of children, *J Am Diet Assoc* 74:130, 1979.

77. Farris RP and others: Dietary studies of children from a biracial population: intakes of vitamins in 10- and 13- year-olds, *J. Am Coll Nutr* 4:539, 1985.

78. Breskin MW and others: Water-soluble vitamins: intakes and indices in children, *J Am Diet Assoc* 85:49, 1985.

CHAPTER

3

Collecting and Assessing Food Intake Information

Peggy L. Pipes
Judith Bumbalo
Robin Pritkin Glass

Objectives

✦✦

After studying this chapter, the student should:

✔ *Be cognizant of all of the information that needs to be collected for a comprehensive evaluation of infants' and children's food intake.*

✔ *Be able to select the appropriate dietary methodology for any particular case or setting.*

✔ *Recognize the advantages and limitations of the various approaches to evaluating dietary intake.*

✔ *Be able to appropriately screen children who need evaluation of motor and psychosocial parameters that affect food intake.*

✔ *Be aware of the advantages and limitations of computer programs designed to calculate nutrient intake.*

Nutrition screening, evaluation, counseling, and education have become integral parts of many health care, public health, and supplemental food programs that provide services to infants and children. In addition, children perceived as having feeding problems, those who must consume modified diets, and those whose parents are concerned about the adequacy of their food intakes are frequently referred to a program for a team management approach. Plans for modifying food intake in childhood should be based on information more comprehensive than that which identifies excesses or deficits in energy and nutrient intakes and cultural food practices. Health care professionals must work jointly to synthesize information and develop programs that can be carried out by children or their parents. Goals for change in food intake should be identified and periodically reassessed. Therefore, it is imperative that health care professionals recognize the necessity of accurate data collection in relation to the nutrient intake from the food consumed, the developmental level of feeding behavior (oral motor screening), psychosocial issues that affect behavior, and mother-child interactions that affect food and nutrient intake.

It is important to recognize that an assessment of food intake is not an **assessment** of nutritional status. The latter requires anthropometric data and biochemical and clinical evaluations as well as dietary intake data. Adequately collected food intake data can, however, provide information on which judgments of the adequacy of a child's current food intake can be made and plans for resolving concerns of food and nutrient intake can be designed and assessed. It is important for individuals who collect this information to be aware of the variety of methods of collecting food intake information and to develop skills for screening oral motor difficulties of feeding and psychosocial factors that may compromise a child's nutrient intake.

TOOLS FOR COLLECTING DIETARY INTAKE DATA

Health care professionals in clinical settings use a variety of tools for collecting dietary data, each tool having limitations and varying degrees of reliability. The choice of tool depends on the purpose of the interview, the time commitment of the professional, and the cooperation of the child or parents. Information sought will vary with the problem. For example, detailed documentation of an early feeding history may be important for counseling parents of young children with feeding problems, whereas this would be inappropriate if the patient were an obese adolescent. Only one tool is used in some instances, whereas a combination of tools is appropriate at other times. It is important to recognize that valid methods for assessing the dietary intake of groups differ from those designed to collect information on one child for whom plans for nutrition education and counseling are to be developed. The tools most often used in the clinical setting are the 24-hour recall, the dietary history, and the 3- and 7-day food records. Food frequencies may be applicable in some circumstances.

The interview is the most important aspect of any of the tools used, the validity of the information obtained being dependent on the client's understanding of the reasons for the interview and the information sought, the client's comfort with the interviewer, and the interviewer's skills at probing for and validating information. Whether the child or parents should be interviewed depends on several developmental and psychosocial factors. Beal found that with few exceptions, girls under 12 years of age and boys under 13 to 14 years of age were unlikely to give reliable nutrition histories.[1] However, if there is considerable conflict between a preadolescent and the parents about food intake, it may be important to interview the child both individually and with the parents so that an appropriate counseling relationship can be established.

It must be remembered that assessment data are only as valid as the child's or parent's willingness to share information with the interviewer. It is important that they feel comfortable with the interview and the individual conducting the assessment. The interviewer should give a friendly greeting, a clear definition of the purpose of the interview, and the reasons for the questions asked, which aid in establishing rapport with the client. Providing an adequate diet for children is an important aspect of parenting. Parents may feel threatened when questioned about a child's food intake. In addition, the interviewer must have reasonable expectations for the respondent. The parent of several children cannot be expected to give information as precisely for one child as does a parent who devotes his or her time to an only child. A number of meals or snacks may be consumed outside the home in a daycare center or at school, and parents may not know what children eat in these settings.

During the interview the interviewer must be careful to avoid suggesting time, meals, food, or amounts consumed. For example, the question "When does your child first have something to eat or to drink?" is appropriate, whereas the question "When does your child first eat breakfast?" is inappropriate. The tone of voice is also important. Neither approval nor disapproval should be expressed verbally or nonverbally by facial expression. Food preferences of the interviewer should never be indicated. Silences must be accepted with comfort, and parents should be permitted time to formulate answers to questions and to ask questions of their own.

24-Hour Recall

The most common method used for collecting dietary data to characterize the nutrient intake of populations is the 24-hour recall, often used in combination with 1-, 3-, or 7-day food records. The 24-hour recall has also been used successfully to screen children at nutritional risk and can give some indication as to compliance with a dietary regimen during clinical follow-up. It cannot be substituted for more intensive methods when judgments regarding the adequacy of an individual child's food intake are to be made.

The child or the parents are asked to relate every food in portion sizes that the child has consumed for the past 24 hours. Errors in the 24-hour recall have been reported to result from inability of the parents or children to remember exactly what was eaten, difficulties in estimating portion sizes, and lack of commitment of the individual who is being interviewed.[2] Often, parents are not aware of the foods consumed between meals. There is no assurance that the recall of the day selected is typical of other days. The accuracy with which portion sizes are reported can be increased by the use of food models and by skillful probing.

Klesges and others[3] found that parental reports of 24-hour intakes of 24- to 48-month-old children correlated highly with weighed food intake. However, Todd, Hudes, and Calloway[2] compared the 24-hour recall and 30-day recorded food intakes by graduate students and found that a single recall did not give an accurate assessment of the intake for that day or for the 30-day mean. There was, however, no consistent bias. Some subjects overestimated their intake, and others underestimated it.

Self-Administered Workbooks

In an effort to find a cost-effective approach to collecting nutrient intakes of groups of children, Farris and others[4] compared a self-administered workbook with the 24-hour recalls of 10- to 18-year-old children.

When the workbook was completed by the children after instruction on how to record food intake, it was found that the evening meal accounted for the greatest difference in recorded intake between the two methods. The workbook method yielded higher intakes of energy, protein, carbohydrates, and cholesterol than did the 24-hour recall. Omitted foods and inaccurate portion size were the reasons for differences. The workbook method is considered effective only when studies with a large sample size are made.[4]

3- and 7-Day Food Records

The 3- or 7-day food record or a written diary of all food and beverages consumed is a tool commonly used to characterize current intakes of individual children (see Food Diary for Children, page 63, and Food Diary for Infants, page 62). Parents are instructed to measure or weigh portions of food offered and amounts not eaten and record the amounts consumed. Parents report that measuring and weighing pose no problems but that they find the rigidity of recording each time the child eats difficult. Sometimes they forget foods that are added to other foods; for example, catsup, butter, or jelly may be unintentionally omitted from the record. Therefore careful instruction as to how to record food intake is important. Also, training with food models has been shown to be effective in improving the accuracy of the portions recorded for a week. The effect, however, did not persist for all portions studied for 4 weeks.[5] This emphasizes the need for continuing review if records are to be kept for long periods.

Debriefing, reviewing the records, and clarifying information on the records can increase the accuracy of information because portion sizes, brand names, and constituents of recipes can be clarified.[6]

Basiotis and others[7] found that the number of days required for valid estimates of an individual's intake varied with the nutrient to be investigated. Accurate estimates of energy intake required 30 days of food intake records,

❖

FOOD DIARY FOR INFANTS (BIRTH TO 1 YEAR)

- **Instructions**
1. Record *all* formula, milk, and food that the baby consumes immediately *after* each feeding.
2. If your baby is breast-fed, record the time of day the baby is fed and how long the baby feeds.
3. If your baby is formula-fed, record the time of day the baby eats, the kind of formula the baby is fed, and the amount actually consumed.
   Infant formula preparation:
   Is the formula iron fortified?
   ☐ Yes   ☐ No
   Formula (brand name): _____
   _____ oz liquid *or*
   _____ T powder
   Water
   _____ oz
   Other (describe): _____
   _____ oz
   _____ T
   Total prepared formula
   _____ oz
4. If the baby spits up or vomits, estimate the amount.
5. Measure the amounts of any other foods carefully in terms of ounces of liquid (e.g., 2 oz apple juice), level T (e.g., 2 T dry rice cereal), or portions of commercially prepared or home prepared foods (e.g., $\frac{1}{2}$ of a 4.7 oz jar or level T of strained peaches).
6. Does the baby take a vitamin supplement? ☐ Yes   ☐ No
   If yes, what kind? _____
- **Day 1**
Date _____ Day of week _____
Most recent weight _____ on (date) _____

Time	Food or Formula	Amount	Time	Food or Formula	Amount

Modified from Food diary for infants, Child Development and Mental Retardation Center, Seattle, 1975, University of Washington.

whereas accurate estimates on vitamin A intake required 433 days of food intake records.

Stuff and others[8] compared 1-, 3-, and 7-day records of food intake with food frequency records and found the 3-day records did not provide good individual estimates of nutrient intake compared with 7-day records, but did provide an estimate of the general quality of the diet.

A study comparing calculated nutrient intake of weighed and estimated portion size recorded in food diaries found intraindividual variations smaller for weighed food records than diary estimates. However, weighing food was reported

❖

FOOD DIARY FOR CHILDREN

• *Instructions*

1. Record all foods and beverages immediately after they are consumed.
2. Measure the amounts of each food carefully with standard measuring cups and spoons. Record meat portions in ounces or as fractions of pounds, e.g., 8 oz of milk; 1 medium egg; $\frac{1}{4}$ lb of hamburger; 1 slice of bread, white; $\frac{1}{2}$ of small banana.
3. Indicate method of preparation, e.g., medium egg, fried; $\frac{1}{2}$ c baked beans with a 2-inch slice of salt pork; 4 oz of steak, broiled.
4. Be sure to record any condiments, gravies, salad dressings, butter, margarine, whipped cream, relishes, e.g., $\frac{3}{4}$ c of mashed potatoes with 3 T of brown gravy, $\frac{1}{4}$ c of cottage cheese salad with 2 olives, $\frac{1}{2}$ c of cornflakes with 1 t of sugar and $\frac{1}{3}$ c of 2% milk.
5. Be sure to record all between-meal foods and drinks, e.g., coffee with 1 oz of cream, 12 oz of cola, 4 sugar cookies, 1 candy bar (indicate brand name).
6. If you eat away from home, please put an asterisk (*) in the food column beside the food listing.

• *Day 1*

Date _____ Day of week _____ Weight _____

Time	Food	Amount	How Prepared	

Modified from Record of food intake, Child Development and Mental Retardation Center, Seattle, 1975, University of Washington.

to be tedious for the client and expensive for the investigator, who provided scales.[2] The provision of cassette recorders, which made it possible for individuals to record their intake on tape, seems to have alleviated some of this difficulty in the study with graduate students.[2]

Dietary History

Another method to review dietary intake in retrospect is the research dietary history method developed by Burke[9] and modified and redescribed by Beale.[1] During an interview the investigator obtains an estimate of the fre-

quency and amounts of food and nutrient supplements consumed in a specified period, usually 1 to 6 months. Parents are questioned about the child's food likes and dislikes. If parent-child interaction or early feeding experiences are suspected to be factors in the nutrition concern, information is elicited on the early feeding history. The interview is often cross-checked with a 24-hour recall or 3-day record of food consumed and a food frequency questionnaire.

This method requires a skilled interviewer. The dietitian or nutritionist must gain the confidence of the parent or child, make good estimates, and judge if the answers are reliable. The process is time consuming and cannot be adequately completed in less than 1 hour. The finding that dietary histories administered to 5-, 9-, and 13-year-old children could not be replicated is not surprising in view of previous studies, and it emphasizes the need to include parents in obtaining food intake information for young children.[10]

Several researchers have cautioned against using this tool as the sole source of data. One study compared the research-type dietary history with 10- to 14-day weighed food records for a group of subjects 6 to 16 years of age and found that no history agreed within 20% for all constituents; the greatest deviations were for vitamins A and D, calories, riboflavin, and thiamin. Other investigators compared dietary histories with 7-day food records and 24-hour recalls and found that dietary histories gave distinctly higher values than 7-day food records and 24-hour recalls for groups.[11] Trulson[12] compared 7-day food records, an average of three or more 24-hour recalls, and dietary histories of clinic patients 7 to 12 years of age. She found no proof that one method was more reliable than another, but she preferred the interview method, since it might reveal long-range dietary practices. The 7-day food records and detailed dietary histories gave results showing closest similarity, but findings were not consistent.

Food Frequency Questionnaires

Several researchers have developed food frequency questionnaires. Clients are asked to estimate the portion size and frequency with which they currently consume specified foods and mixed dishes. Since the format is computer compatible, it can be keypunched and calculations are quickly returned. Advantages offered by the food frequency method include high response rates, minimal burden to the respondent, and the fact that they can be administered by nonprofessionals. They generally give higher estimates of intake than do food records.[13]

When collecting food intake information, the interviewer must keep in mind that dietary history and food frequency methods yield higher intakes than 3- or 7-day food intake records.[14]

Using both the dietary history and a record of food intake is likely to add credibility to the assessment. The interviewer must, however, recognize the life-style demands of the respondent and negotiate a reasonable approach for both the client and health care professional. If parents are literate, concerned, and motivated, they may agree to keep the food records. Daycare workers and preschool teachers are generally agreeable about keeping records. However, it may be necessary to accept a 3-day, rather than a 7-day, record from a working mother with a large family. If the parents clearly do not want to keep the diet diary, the interviewer must be satisfied with the dietary history but recognize its limitations.

ASSESSING DIETARY INTAKE INFORMATION

When the dietary intake information has been collected, the adequacy of nutrients in the foods consumed is assessed. The decisions of which method of evaluation should be used and which nutrients will be calculated are based on the precision and reliability of the information collected, the foods that appear in the dietary records, the interviewer's knowledge of foods as sources of nutrients, and the problem presented for evaluation.

In some instances intake data may be compared to food groups; other times, knowledge of foods that are present or absent in the dietary history as sources of nutrients may give sufficient indication of the presence or absence of problems of nutrient intake. If precise and complete information has been collected, hand or computer calculations of nutrients in the foods consumed may be compared with a standard.

When parents are unable or unwilling to give information that can be quantitated, such as when they report intake as bites of meat instead of one fourth of a 2 oz hamburger patty or when cross-checks reveal inconsistencies, the analysis of food groups or foods as sources of nutrients seems appropriate. However, if the child is underweight or overweight or if food sources of a particular nutrient appear on the record only occasionally, calculations of nutrient intake are important.

TABLE 3-1   *Nutritionist III Computer Report of One Day's Food Intake**

Quantity	Food	Gram	Energy (kcal)	Calcium (mg)	Total Protein (gm)	Vit C (mg)	Thiamin (mg)	Niacin (mg)	Riboflavin (mg)	Folate (µg)	Vit A RE	Vit D µg	Fe (mg)
1 large	Egg, whole, hardboiled	50.0	75	25	6.2	—	tr	tr	0.3	23	95.2	0.6	0.7
1 slice	White bread, enriched	25.0	67	31.5	2.0	—	—	0.9	tr	8.7	—	†	—
12 fl oz	Whole milk, fluid	366.0	225	—	—	—	—	—	—	18	138	3.8	—
0.25 c	Rice, white enriched	51.25	66	5.7	1.3	—	tr	0.7	—	1.7	†	—	0.6
57 gm (8/lb)	Frankfurter, Oscar Mayer, cooked	57.0	183	6	6.2	15	0.1	1.5	tr	2.0	†	0.5	0.6
1 c	Orange juice, fresh	248.0	112	21.9	—	96.5	—	0.5	tr	109	19.3	†	0.2
125 gm	Macaroni & cheese, Stouffer's	125.0	269	226	10.6	0.0	0.1	1.1	0.3	—	108	—	1.1
45 gm	Green beans, cut style, canned, solids drained	45.0	9	11.6	0.5	2.2	—	tr	tr	14.3	15.7	—	0.4
35 gm	Chicken drumstick, fried in veg. fat	35.0	85.8	4.2	9.4	—	tr	2.1	0.1	2.8	8.8	.19	—
1	Tortilla, wheat, baked/steamed	43.4	137	66.5	3.6	—	tr	1.4	—	†	.2	—	1.6
	TOTAL		1228	835	54	117	0.85	8.81	1.53	179	385	5.1	6.6

tr, Trace.

*Data are for a 2-year-old female child with a height of 82.4 cm and weight of 14.5 kg.

†Indicates there are no data on the item specified for that nutrient.

Computer Programs

Assessment of nutrient intake using a computer data base is in many ways an ideal task for computer technology because it is a frequently performed task. The technology to approach this task is rapidly changing and thus poses some problems for the practitioner while it solves others. There are well over 100 programs available to meet computational needs. The choice of the program that has a "best fit" is based on several important aspects of each program.

The best method of approach is to specifically identify the tasks appropriate to the setting. This is based on whether clients are outpatient or inpatient, whether analysis is for individual patient nutrient or screening intakes, and whether recipes and diaries are to be analyzed. The investigator should evaluate for the specific setting: (1) the most convenient hardware, e.g., personal or handheld computer; (2) the data entry format, e.g., code numbers or selection from food groups; and (3) the presentation of the output data, e.g., tabular or graphic printouts. The data base itself must be evaluated for the number of foods (data bases vary from 250 to 5000+ foods), the number of nutrients calculated for each food (varies from 3 to 90 nutrients), and the number of missing values for each nutrient. It is necessary to understand the source of the nutrient data for the data and the capacity and availability of updating it. Other considerations are features that may be desirable such as comparison of the calculated intake data to normative information, e.g., the RDA; emphasis on specific components, e.g., fats or amino acids; proposal of a menu based on specified restrictions; inclusion of food items especially used by infants and children such as formulas; and an activity analysis.

While these programs need care in selection, maintenance, and periodic evaluation, they provide a time-efficient way of making calculations once the evaluator learns to use the programs. A much larger number of nutrients can be calculated by computer than is possible by hand (Table 3-1).

Evaluating Intake Information

When calculations are complete, the data must be compared with a standard. All formulated standards are intended to be used to interpret data on groups of people and are not intended to be used for evaluating the adequacy of nutrient intakes of individuals.

Many of the computer programs compare nutrient intake to the RDA. These allowances for children are generally based on studies of adults from which extrapolations were made for children. A margin of safety above the average requirement is applied to each nutrient. This margin is not standard but varies for each nutrient.

When interpreting the data one must be keenly aware of the **bioavailability** of the nutrients. In addition, changes in nutrient concentration of foods during storage and preparation must be considered.

Some programs define children at nutritional risk as those who consume less then two thirds or three fourths of the recommended daily dietary allowances of any nutrient, and include these children and their families in intensive nutrition follow-up. It may also be important for these children to have a more intensive nutrition evaluation, including biochemical evaluation of their nutritional status.

Anthropometry (height, weight, and skinfold measurements) can give indications of the appropriateness of the child's energy intake. If rates of weight gain are excessive or inadequate, calculations of the child's energy intake provide important data on which plans for adjustments in energy intake can be made.

SCREENING CHILDREN AT NUTRITIONAL RISK

The objective of screening is to identify infants and children who appear to have nutritional problems that require further investigation. The interview is brief, and information sought is qualitative. It is often performed by **paraprofessionals** (e.g., community health workers or nutrition aides), nurses, or other professionals who assume the role of case manager. The 24-hour recall screening questionnaires or questionnaires filled out by parents may be used (see Screening Questionnaire for Infants, pages 67 to 68 and Screening Questionnaire for Young Children, pages 69 to 70).

SCREENING QUESTIONNAIRE FOR INFANTS (BIRTH TO 1 YEAR)

	Yes	No
1. Is the baby breast-fed?	☐	☐
If yes, does he/she also receive milk or formula?	☐	☐

If yes, what kind? _____

	Yes	No
2. Does the baby receive formula?	☐	☐

If yes ☐ Ready-to-feed
   ☐ Concentrated liquid
   ☐ Other: _____

How is formula prepared (especially dilution)?

_____

_____

	Yes	No
Is the formula iron fortified?	☐	☐
3. Does the baby drink milk?	☐	☐

If yes ☐ Whole milk
   ☐ 2% milk
   ☐ Skim milk
   ☐ Other: _____

4. How many times does the baby eat each day, including milk or formula? ____

	Yes	No
5. Does the baby usually take a bottle to bed?	☐	☐

If yes, what is usually in the bottle? _____

6. If the baby drinks milk or formula, what is the usual amount in a day?
   ☐ Less than 16 oz
   ☐ 16-32 oz
   ☐ More than 32 oz

7. Please indicate which (if any) of these foods the baby eats and how often:

	Never or Hardly Ever (Less Than Once a Week)	Sometimes (Not Daily But at Least Once a Week)	Every Day or Nearly Every Day
Eggs	☐	☐	☐
Dried beans or peas	☐	☐	☐
Meat, fish, poultry	☐	☐	☐
Bread, rice, pasta, grits, cereal, tortillas, potatoes	☐	☐	☐
Fruits or fruit juices	☐	☐	☐
Vegetables	☐	☐	☐

8. If the baby eats fruits or drinks fruit juices every day or nearly every day, which ones does he/she eat or drink most often (not more than three)? _____

_____

9. If the baby eats vegetables every day or nearly every day, which one does he/she eat most often (not more than three)? _____

_____

	Yes	No
10. Does the person who cares for the baby have use of a		
Stove?	☐	☐
Refrigerator?	☐	☐
Piped water?	☐	☐

From Fomon SJ: *Nutritional disorders of children: prevention, screening, and follow-up,* Pub No 76-5612, Rockville, Md, 1976, Department of Health, Education and Welfare.

Continued.

❖

SCREENING QUESTIONNAIRE FOR INFANTS (BIRTH TO 1 YEAR)—*cont'd*

	Yes	No
11. Does the baby take vitamin or iron drops?	☐	☐

11. Does the baby take vitamin or iron drops?
    If yes, how often? _____
    What kind? _____
12. Is the baby on a special diet now?
    If yes, what is the reason?
    Allergy—specify type of diet: _____
    Weight reduction—specify type of diet: _____
    Other—specify type of diet: _____
    Who recommended the diet? _____
13. Does the baby eat clay, paint chips, dirt, or anything else that is not usually considered food?
    If yes, what? _____
    How often? _____
14. Do you think the child has a feeding problem?
    If yes, describe: _____

Screening programs are designed to reach as many individuals as possible at a minimum cost. Adequately nourished individuals may be mistaken as at risk; however, this is acceptable, since many others who are not adequately nourished will be identified.

Anthropometric data plotted on growth charts are also used in screening. In general, when children's growth patterns plot at less than the 10th percentile, when they are underweight or overweight for their lengths (see Chapter 1), or when interviews show patterns of intake that indicate a nutrient consumed is in short supply, the children are referred for more intensive counseling.

From information on the screening questionnaire, parents of infants and children who need further evaluation or counseling can also be identified. A red flag could be raised when the infant screening questionnaire indicates that an infant was offered overdiluted or underdiluted formulas, if homogenized milk was offered to infants under 1 year of age, or if nonfat or 2% milk was offered anytime in the first year. Other infants who may be identified as at risk include those who receive semisolid foods before 4 months of age and those who are bottle-fed as they go to sleep.

As the child ages, the quantity of milk consumed and the frequency in which the listed food groups are eaten can identify older children at risk.

All infants or children who require a modified diet to control chronic disease or whose parents perceive them as having a feeding problem need further assessment.

DIETARY ASSESSMENT

Parents and children referred for intensive evaluation of nutrient and energy intake should anticipate a more extensive interview. Even so, the dietitian/nutritionist should carefully explain the purpose of the questions to be asked and reasons for continuing "how much" and "how often" questions. Decisions regarding which tool will be used may be made after the parents and children arrive and express their concern or lack of concern.

The dietary history, in combination with a 7-day food record, is the preferred tool currently available for dietary assessment in a clinical setting. These procedures require a skilled nutritionist and are costly in time, and not all parents and children can respond with validity even though they may wish to do so.

SCREENING QUESTIONNAIRE FOR YOUNG CHILDREN (PRESCHOOL CHILDREN AND YOUNG SCHOOL-AGE CHILDREN)

	Yes	No
1. Does the child drink milk?	☐	☐

    If yes ☐ Whole milk
          ☐ 2% milk
          ☐ Skim milk
          ☐ Other: _____

    If yes, how much?
    ☐ Less than 8 oz
    ☐ 8-32 oz
    ☐ More than 32 oz

2. Does the child drink anything from a bottle (for children less than 4 years of age)?   ☐ Yes ☐ No

    If yes ☐ Milk
          ☐ Other: _____

3. Does the child take a bottle to bed?   ☐ Yes ☐ No

    If yes, what is usually in the bottle? _____

4. How many times a day does the child usually eat (including snacks)? _____

5. Please indicate which (if any) of these foods the child eats and how often:

	Never or Hardly Ever (Less Than Once a Week)	Sometimes (Not Daily But at Least Once a Week)	Every Day or Nearly Every Day
Cheese, yogurt, ice cream	☐	☐	☐
Eggs	☐	☐	☐
Dried beans, peas, peanut butter	☐	☐	☐
Meat, fish, poultry	☐	☐	☐
Bread, rice, pasta, grits, cereal, tortillas, potatoes	☐	☐	☐
Fruits or fruit juices	☐	☐	☐
Vegetables	☐	☐	☐

6. If the child eats fruits or drinks fruit juices every day or nearly every day, which ones does he/she eat or drink most often (not more than three)? _____

_____

7. If the child eats vegetables every day or nearly every day, which ones does he/she eat most often (not more than three)? _____

8. Does the child usually eat between meals?   ☐ Yes ☐ No

    If yes, name the 2 or 3 snacks (including bedtime snacks) that the child has most often: _____

9. Does the person who cares for the child have use of a

	Yes	No
Stove?	☐	☐
Refrigerator?	☐	☐
Piped water?	☐	☐

From Fomon SJ: *Nutritional disorders of children: prevention, screening, and follow-up,* Pub No 76-5612, Rockville, Md, 1976, Department of Health, Education and Welfare.

Continued.

SCREENING QUESTIONNAIRE FOR YOUNG CHILDREN (PRESCHOOL CHILDREN AND YOUNG SCHOOL-AGE CHILDREN)—cont'd

	Yes	No
10. Does the child take vitamin or iron drops or tablets?	☐	☐

If yes, how often? _____

What kind? _____

	Yes	No
11. Is the child on a special diet now?	☐	☐

If yes, what is the reason? _____

☐ Allergy—specify type of diet: _____

☐ Weight reduction—specify type of diet: _____

☐ Other—specify reason for diet and type of diet: _____

Who recommended the diet? _____

	Yes	No
12. Does the child eat clay, paint chips, dirt, or anything else that is not usually considered food?	☐	☐

If yes, what? _____

How often? _____

13. How would you describe the child's appetite?

☐ Good

☐ Fair

☐ Poor

☐ Other: _____

Some programs use a food frequency questionnaire and 24-hour recall, a method that requires less time and is less taxing on the client but yields less valid and less useful information.

During this interview the nutritionist collects information about family interactions that affect a child's food intake (e.g., family members present at mealtimes, the use of food as rewards), the food budget and money spent for food, the frequency in which the family and children eat away from home, and the family's use of community resources that provide food or nutrition education (Figure 3-1).

The case of a 13-month-old girl referred for dietary assessment because of inadequate weight gain may clarify the process. The girl was the unplanned child of the second marriage of a couple who also had teenage children in their home. All medical reasons for failure to thrive had been ruled out. The interview with both father and mother proceeded as follows:

Interviewer: Let's begin with the early feeding history. Was the baby breast- or bottle-fed?

Mother: She was and still is breast-fed. I do not want her to drink formula or cow's milk. I have given her a little goat's milk from a cup.

Interviewer: Did she have any problems sucking at the breast?

Mother: None at all until she was 6 months. Then she wouldn't take much at a time but wanted to feed often. I want to breast-feed her as long as she wants to.

Interviewer: When was she introduced to foods other than milk?

Mother: I gave her cereal when the doctor told me to, about 5 months, then vegetables and fruits, and I think meat about 9 months. I made them for her from only fresh pure foods. I give her only "natural foods" now.

Interviewer: When did she begin finger-feeding?

Mother: About 6 months, I think. She feeds herself rice crackers.

Interviewer: When did she eat table foods that were not pureed?

Mother: I began mashing up vegetables and grinding meat when she was 8 months old.

Interviewer: Does she drink from a cup?

Mother: She has a little goat's milk from a cup, but I have to help her hold it.

FIG. 3-1 Nutritionist evaluates nutritional adequacy of preschooler's intake.

Interviewer: Does she try to feed herself?

Mother: She tries to get the spoon, but I can't stand the mess she makes so I feed her.

Interviewer: Now I would like for you to tell me how she lives her day with food. When does she first have something to eat or drink?

Mother: Well, she wakes about 3:00 or 4:00 in the morning and breast-feeds.

Interviewer: Then when does she have something to eat or drink again?

Mother: Well, she wakes again about 8:00, and I give her rice cereal from the health food store.

Interviewer: How much does she eat?

Mother: She's not too interested. Maybe $\frac{1}{4}$ cup.

Interviewer: Do you put anything on the cereal?

Mother: A little goat's milk.

Interviewer: How much?

Mother: An ounce or so.

Interviewer: Do you put anything else on the cereal?

Mother: Nothing else.

Interviewer: How often (out of 7 days) does she have rice cereal?

Mother: Oh, she has it 7 days at breakfast.

Interviewer: When does she have something else to eat or to drink?

Mother: She usually breast-feeds sometime in the morning.

Interviewer: How long does she stay at the breast?

Mother: About 10 minutes. She's learning to bite.

Interviewer: And when does she have something to eat again?

Mother: Between 11:00 and 12:00 I give her lunch.

She likes yogurt and sardines. Sometimes I give her a cracker with sunflower seed butter on it, or if I have leftovers from the night before, I may give them to her.

Interviewer: What's next?

Mother: She usually breast-feeds after lunch and again midafternoon, and she has a bottle of pear juice some time in the afternoon.

Interviewer: How much pear juice does she drink?

Mother: Six or seven ounces.

Interviewer: How often does she have the juice?

Mother: Three or four times a week. If she doesn't have juice, she gets half of a small banana.

Interviewer: When does she eat again?

Mother: She eats with us about 7:00.

Interviewer: What does she usually eat?

Mother: I offer her fish, or yogurt, or cottage cheese, but she won't eat much. If we have hamburger or a vegetable she'll eat, I'll give her that.

Interviewer: How much does she eat?

Mother: About a tablespoon of two or three foods.

Interviewer: What do you do when she does eat?

Mother: I offer her more.

Interviewer: What do you do when she refuses to eat?

Mother: I try to find something else for her to eat or try to get her to eat another bite.

It became apparent during the interview that the *mother was unable to give information that could be quantitated, so a 7-day record of the child's food intake was requested.* A sample of the

❖

FOOD INTAKE RECORD

4:30 AM	Breast-fed
8 AM	Rice bran, 2 t
	Rice puffs, 1 T
	Goat's milk, $\frac{1}{2}$ oz
9 AM	Breast-fed
10:15 AM	Banana, $\frac{3}{4}$ small
11:30 AM	Wheat grain crackers, $\frac{1}{3}$
	Goat's milk, 2 oz
	Raw sunflower butter, 1 t
	Alfalfa sprouts, 1 t
	Mozarella cheese, grated, 1 t
	Beets, 1 t
	Sardines, 3
	Goat's milk yogurt, 2 T
1 PM	Breast-fed
4:30 PM	Pear juice, 6 oz
5:30 PM	Sardines, 2
	Brown rice cracker, 1
	Sprouts, taste
7:50 PM	Goat's milk yogurt, 2 T
8 PM	Breast-fed

---

record received is shown in the box above. Quantitation of the 7-day food record showed an intake of 500 kcal/day or less in addition to the breast milk consumed. On this basis, inadequate energy and nutrient intake was diagnosed to be the cause of the infant's inadequate weight gain. *Therapy for this family involved much more than nutrition counseling. Psychosocial and parenting issues had to be dealt with as well.*

If children are overweight, activity patterns are explored. Discussions about the consumption of vending machine food and the effects of television on eating patterns may also provide important information.

It may be necessary to discontinue the detailed probing necessary for dietary history and use only a cross-check if parental tolerance for the continued questions is limited. It is also important to recognize that it may not be possible to obtain sufficient information during one interview; several follow-up clinic or home visits may be necessary to obtain a true picture of the child's feeding history and food intake.

Preschool teachers and public health nurses often provide information about a child's food intake at school and family food patterns.

When dietary data have been collected, an assessment is made of the following:

1. Parental knowledge of nutrition and appropriate foods for children
2. The adequacy of nutrients provided by the food offered to the child
3. The adequacy of the diet consumed by the child
4. Parental knowledge and use of community resources to improve the nutritional status of the child
5. Delays in feeding skills that affect food and nutrients consumed
6. Real or potential behavior patterns that can or do compromise a child's nutrient intake
7. The motivation of parents and the child to change the patterns of food intake

If this assessment indicates that adjustments need to be made only in the kinds of food or size of portions offered to and consumed by the child, or if a therapeutic diet is indicated, plans for modifying the child's food intake should be made with the child or parents. The counselor should be aware of community resources that help with the provision of food, such as the Supplemental Food Program for Women, Infants, and Children (WIC), the food stamp program, and school lunch programs. Clients may need help in contacting agencies that administer the programs. Plans for modifying food intake should be communicated to teachers, school lunch personnel, and others in the child's food environment.

If it appears that the child has delays in feeding skills or eating patterns or that parent-child interactions are also operative in problems presented, the investigator may need to screen for these specific problems so that appropriate referrals can be made.

EVALUATION OF ORAL MOTOR AND SWALLOWING FUNCTIONS

Children who are developmentally delayed or have abnormal muscle coordination may have difficulty with the various oral, swallowing, and fine motor skills needed for the process of eating. Failure to gain weight or eat appropriate foods for the child's age can be an early indication of a developmental or motor problem. Infants and children with these types of problems therefore may first be identified during a dietary intake interview and observation of feeding behavior. The nutritionist therefore needs a basic understanding of the development of normal oral skills so that early motor or oral motor difficulties can be perceived and appropriate referrals can be made. Ideally, a knowledgeable pediatric therapist should be involved in the evaluation and planning of treatment for any individual with motorically based feeding problems.

Evaluation of Motor and Oral Motor Skills

Incoordination of **oral motor skills** or basic motor skills may be identified by an interview with the parents and by observation of the child's eating and drinking skills. The examiner should observe not only the level of the child's eating and self-feeding skills, but also the level of assistance assumed by the parent. Not only will this provide the examiner with information regarding the child's skill level, but it may also provide information about the relationship between the parent and child while eating.

The Screening of Eating Abilities form (pages 74 to 78) can be used by the dietitian or nutritionist during the dietary assessment when the child has not yet been seen by a skilled therapist. This screening tool was developed at the Child Development and Mental Retardation Center (CDMRC) of the University of Washington to provide comprehensive assessment of feeding behavior. Once the screening tool is completed, the evaluator should be able to determine if the feeding difficulties are caused by abnormalities in overall motor and oral motor control or if they are caused by developmental delay.

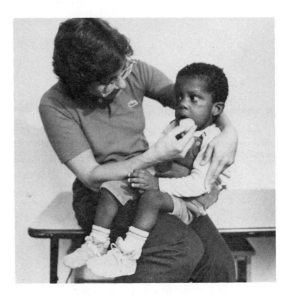

FIG. 3-2 Occupational therapist evaluates oral motor patterns of child with cerebral palsy.

It should be noted that where age guidelines are mentioned, they are intended to be lenient in recognition of the normal range in acquisition of feeding skills. For more comprehensive evaluation tools the reader is directed to Morris and Klein[15] and Jelm.[16] Morris and Klein[15] also provide a more detailed description of the normal oral motor sequence and many more examples of guiding questions that may be used during a parent interview.

During the nutritional and oral motor assessment, the evaluator should not only observe the types of foods the child currently eats, but if developmentally appropriate, should also offer food textures at the next higher level. In this way, it can be determined if the oral delays are caused by a lack of oral motor control or by lack of opportunity for more mature performance. For example, a child may demonstrate more mature lip, tongue, and jaw movements if foods are placed laterally between the gums or molars than if pureed foods are offered by spoon (Figure 3-2).

Difficulties in oral motor or swallowing con-

Text continued on p. 78.

❖

SCREENING OF EATING ABILITIES

Child's name: _____ ID#: _____ B.D.: _____
Medical diagnosis, if known: _____
Name of evaluator: _____
Name of parent or caregiver: _____ Phone: _____
Other agencies involved: _____

I. Questions to ask of parent or caregiver
   A. What are your greatest concerns in regard to feeding?
   B. What are the food likes and dislikes of your child in relation to texture, temperature, color, and flavor?
   C. Are some foods more difficult for your child to eat than others?
   D. Are there any foods that your child cannot eat?
   E. Does your child take any medication or food supplements?
   F. When does your child have meals and snacks?
   G. Does your child eat with the family?
   H. Who assists at mealtimes (home, school, other)?
   I. How much assistance is given?
   J. What textures are usually eaten (thin liquid, thick liquid, soft spoon food, soft chewy food, ground food, chopped food, crunchy food—see list below)?

II. Tactile sensitivity
   These stimuli are applied toward the beginning of the evaluation before offering food, but after the child has had some opportunity to adjust to you as a stranger. Tell the child what you are going to do before applying the stimuli. Be cautious in overinterpreting inappropriate responses that may be social or behavioral and not necessarily tactile.
   First, lightly stroke the front and back of each of the child's hands. Then stroke the front aspect of the skin on each arm. Finally, stroke the face, lips, and gums with firm pressure of your fingertips.

• *Appropriate*
Neutral or positive response to touch
  ☐ Hand, arm
  ☐ Face
  ☐ Gums, outside teeth, when stroked with
    a fingertip

• *Questionable appropriateness*
Muscle tension, moving away from stimulus
  or vocal protest
  ☐ Hand, arm
  ☐ Face
  ☐ Gums, outside teeth, when stroked with
    a fingertip

Questionable appropriate responses may be caused by situational variables, but if the caregiver reports consistent negative responses, a therapy referral is indicated.

III. Food offered
   These foods are listed in sequence according to difficulty and are grouped into three levels of corresponding normal developmental skills. Ask the caregiver to first offer foods commonly eaten at home, then try some of the other textures at more difficult levels.

Modified from Carman P: *Screening of eating abilities,* Occupational Therapy Department, Child Development and Mental Retardation Center, WJ-10, Seattle, 1980, University of Washington.

SCREENING OF EATING ABILITIES—*cont'd*

Watch carefully for amount of chewing, movement of food within the mouth, and tendency to choke. Small amounts of food are offered from each category appropriate to the child's developmental level so that satiation does not occur too quickly. Thin liquid is offered to every child, but soft spoon foods or soft chewy foods should be omitted when the child has demonstrated higher level skills. Thick liquid is offered only when thin liquids are difficult (evidenced by choking, liquid running out of mouth).

A. *Child less than 5 months of age developmentally* (needs head and trunk support while eating, e.g., needs to be held in adult's arms, infant seat, special support chairs).
   - ☐ Thick liquid (optional, offered when thin liquid is taken with difficulty): milkshake, thinned applesauce, thinned yogurt
   - ☐ Thin liquid: milk, water, fruit juice
   - ☐ Soft spoon food: applesauce, pudding, yogurt
   - ☐ Soft chewy food: cheese, tuna fish, vienna sausage

B. *Child 5 to 12 months of age developmentally* (good head control, needs some trunk support while eating, sits upright in chair).
   - ☐ Ground solid food: "junior foods," ground table foods (dry consistency)
   - ☐ Crunchy food that dissolves readily: cracker, potato stick
   - ☐ Oblong finger food (easier to grasp): potato stick, green bean
   - ☐ Small finger food (harder to grasp): Cheerio, puffed cereal
   - ☐ Hard crunchy food: melba toast, bread stick

C. *Child more than 12 months of age developmentally* (with good head and trunk control and tongue mobility, lateralization).
   - ☐ Chopped table foods
   - ☐ Bite-sized table foods: raisins
   - ☐ Multitexture foods (solid plus liquid): apple, celery, soup
   - ☐ Chewy food: chicken, hamburger, small pieces of well-cooked meat
   - ☐ Hard foods that break into diffuse pieces: carrots, nuts (if older than 2 years of age)

IV. Observations of child eating

   Caregiver is asked to feed the child in the usual way. Ask whether any particular equipment or furniture is used that may not be present for this observation.

   Mark NA (not applicable) if child is younger than stated age. Asterisks indicate posture or movement that is always abnormal; other activity of questionable appropriateness may be caused by neurological immaturity or other factors.

   A. *Positioning*

• *Appropriate*
   - ☐ Held by caregiver (if younger than 1 year of age) within 30° of upright
   - ☐ Within 30° of upright, propped, or special seat (hips flexed 90° in usual sitting angle)
   - ☐ High chair
   - ☐ Other: _____

• *Questionable appropriateness*
   - ☐ Held by caregiver (lying back, asymmetrical, or otherwise unusual)
   - ☐ Held by caregiver (older than 1 year of age)
   - ☐ Lying on flat surface
   - ☐ Other: _____

Continued.

❖

SCREENING OF EATING ABILITIES—*cont'd*

The health professional may wish to discuss alternative means of positioning if the usual method is questionably appropriate. If the child has abnormal muscle tone, appropriate positioning is much more difficult to achieve. Consultation with a physical therapist or occupational therapist should be obtained. Any of the following behaviors under the "questionable" column indicate need for a consultation or a therapy program.

B. *Posture and movement*

• *Appropriate*

- ☐ Head in alignment with body
- ☐ Head control stable (expected by 4 or 5 months of age)
- ☐ Arms forward, hands midline (frequent by 4 to 6 months of age)
- ☐ Hands, legs, and feet move freely, without stiffness
- ☐ Hips flex easily for sitting, knees spread apart spontaneously for wide sitting base
- ☐ Trunk straight when sitting (expected by 5 to 6 months of age)

• *Questionable appropriateness*

- ☐ Head frequently back or to one side, rotated to one side
- ☐ Lack of head stability, excess motions, floppy, pushes back, falls forward (older than 5 months of age)
- ☐ Arms frequently retracted at shoulders, hands do not come together (older than 4 to 5 months of age)
- ☐ Legs and feet seem stiff, seldom move, or move in stereotyped patterns
- ☐ Hips resist bending or intermittently extend; narrow sitting base, knees pull together
- ☐ Trunk tilted, slumped, rotated, or arched backwards (older than 5 months of age)

C. *Oral motor coordination*

• *Appropriate*
JAW

- ☐ Jaw opens and closes easily, controlled to receive food
- ☐ Jaw stabilized with little movement
- ☐ Jaw moves up and down with slight lateral movements when chewing ("rotary")

• *Questionable appropriateness*

- ☐ Jaw opens too wide or with tension
- ☐ Delayed jaw opening response to receive food
- ☐ Jaw moves up and down while drinking from a cup so liquid is lost (older than 12 months of age)
- ☐ Jaw clamps down intermittently (older than 2 years of age)
- ☐ Lack of up and down movement with solid food

• *Appropriate*
TONGUE

- ☐ Tongue stays within mouth while drinking
- ☐ Tongue stays within mouth with foods
- ☐ Tongue lateralized, food placed at side (6 months of age); food placed midline (9 months of age)

• *Questionable appropriateness*

- ☐ Tongue protrudes past border of lips while drinking
- ☐ Tongue protrudes with spoon foods
- ☐ Tongue moves forward and backward when solid foods are placed at side of mouth or presented midline, no lateral movement

SCREENING OF EATING ABILITIES—*cont'd*

• *Appropriate*

LIPS
- ☐ Lips seal on nipple or cup rim
- ☐ Lips close on and clean spoon
- ☐ Lips move actively while chewing

SWALLOW
- ☐ Swallows readily
- ☐ Swallows liquids, no choking
- ☐ Swallows solids, seldom chokes

GAG REFLEX
- ☐ Normal **gag reflex** (readiness to vomit when pressure applied to pharyngeal wall, soft palate, posterior tongue)

SALIVA CONTROL
- ☐ Swallows saliva (doesn't drool)

• *Questionable appropriateness*

- ☐ Liquids not retained well by lips with nipple, with cup (older than 24 months of age)
- ☐ Spoon foods not retained well by lips (older than 8 months of age)
- ☐ Passive lips while chewing

- ☐ Delayed swallow, slows eating
- ☐ Chokes two or more times when drinking liquid from a cup
- ☐ Chokes two or more times when drinking liquids other than from a cup (bottle, etc.)
- ☐ Chokes two or more times when solids are fed

- ☐ Gag reflex hyposensitive (slow or absent)
- ☐ Gag reflex hypersensitive (occurs to pressure on middle or front of tongue or at sight of certain food)

- ☐ Drools when not eating (older than 24 months of age) and when not teething

D. **Prehension**

Grasping of objects starts with a reflexive closing when the palmar surface of the hand is stimulated; the grasp becomes voluntary with maturity and is gradually refined to use of opposed fingertips. Any observations of questionable quality or prolonged primitive skill level should be cause for further evaluation.

• *Appropriate*
- ☐ Reflexive grasp (fading by 3 months of age)
- ☐ Raking grasp, whole hand (by 6 months of age)
- ☐ Thumb to side of fingers (8 months of age and older)
- ☐ Thumb to fingertips of index and/or middle fingers

• *Questionable appropriateness*
- ☐ Wrist flexed, hand often in awkward position
- ☐ Hand usually fisted (older than 3 months of age)
- ☐ Hand usually limp or grasp weak
- ☐ Grasps food too tightly
- ☐ Raking, use of whole hand (older than 12 months of age)
- ☐ Difficulty releasing grasp (older than 12 months of age)

Continued.

❖

SCREENING OF EATING ABILITIES—cont'd

E. *Hand and arm movement*

A child must have head and upper trunk control before the hand can be used for purposeful reaching. At first the hand and arm movements appear to be random. Purposeful movements are first seen as a child brings the hands to the mouth and the hands together at midline. Reaching for toys and bringing them to the mouth precedes finger-feeding. As control of the trunk improves, arm and hand use matures. A child will usually grasp the spoon and help bring it to the mouth long before he or she is able to control it independently. The effort of holding a cup is seen initially as the cup is pushed tightly against the mouth to stabilize it; it is difficult at this stage to stop drinking and put a partially full cup back to the table without spilling. Abnormal muscle tone or lack of head and trunk stability interferes with the quality and effectiveness of hand use.

* *Appropriate*
  - ☐ Hand to mouth
  - ☐ Hands to midline, hands together
  - ☐ Hand touches object purposefully
  - ☐ Toy to mouth
  - ☐ Holds bottle or drinks from cup (hands may be on cup, adult controls)
  - ☐ Self-feeds finger foods
  - ☐ Helps with spoon
  - ☐ Independent with spoon, spills
  - ☐ Independent with spoon, no spills
  - ☐ Holds cup with some assistance
  - ☐ Independent with cup

* *Questionable appropriateness*
  - ☐ Arms tight, limited movement
  - ☐ Hands usually fisted (older than 2 to 3 months of age)
  - ☐ Hand frequently misses object, overshoots (older than 6 months of age)
  - ☐ No attempt to reach for food or spoon, even when hungry and food is within reach (older than 6 months of age)
  - ☐ Uses spoon with much extraneous movement and spilling
  - ☐ Other: _____

F. *Cooperation*

* *Appropriate*
  - ☐ Motivated to eat
  - ☐ Accepts food passively
  - ☐ Participates to best of ability
  - ☐ Socially appropriate behavior

* *Questionable appropriateness*
  - ☐ Does not seem to care about eating
  - ☐ Actively resists eating (turns mouth away or slow to open mouth)
  - ☐ Physical skills not used to potential for self-assistance
  - ☐ Socially disruptive, attention seeking

Any observations of questionable cooperation tend to reduce the validity of other observations. A more thorough evaluation of parent-child interaction during mealtime may be indicated and may be the primary area requiring assistance.

---

trol may be observed as a child moves to the next higher level of food texture, particularly when making the initial transition to solid food. The child may continue to use primitive oral patterns that were appropriate for the lower texture food until oral skills and familiarity are developed at the next level. Loss of food from the mouth, mild coughing or sputtering, or rejection of food should not necessarily be considered problems during this transition stage. Should these behaviors persist, however, more careful evaluation of oral motor control and responses to varied sensory stimuli should occur.

If the oral motor screen identifies delays in feeding behavior that do not appear to be secondary to abnormalities in oral motor control, changes in the diet can be suggested to support developmental progress as outlined in Chapter 13. If abnormal oral and basic motor patterns are observed, however, referral to a specialized pediatric occupational, physical, or speech therapist is necessary. Resources for names of treatment centers or private therapists may be available from individual state therapy associations, the local school district, or the nearest regional children's hospital.

When specialized services are not immediately available, initial steps may be attempted to improve the quality of food intake by using the basic principles of positioning discussed in Chapter 13. The family's concerns, strengths, and resources are an important consideration in the development of any treatment program. The final feeding plan should be the distillation of the nutritionist's/therapist's goals and the family's goals. The rationale for suggested changes should be thoroughly explained and expectations for follow-through must be reasonable. It may take longer to feed a child in the desired position or when using therapeutic techniques, especially when they are first implemented. Implementing the new procedures at only a portion of the meal, or at the least stressful meal of the day, may ease the transition. Consideration of the client's and caregiver's comfort, feelings, and opinions is a key factor in developing an effective feeding program. Changes in motor or oral motor control may be slow to achieve. Changes in the feeding environment, however, may be easier to make and have significant impact on the long-term social, nutritional, and physical development of the individual.

Evaluation of Swallowing Function

Effective eating is not only the product of movements of the tongue, lips, jaw, and cheeks, but also includes an efficient and safe swallowing mechanism. Since swallowing dysfunction can lead to aspiration, difficulties in swallowing function not only may influence children's food intake and thus their nutrition, but also may have an impact on their overall health. Therefore some assessment of the swallowing function should occur during a screening of the motor skills necessary for eating.

Typically, the swallowing function is divided into three phases: the oral phase, the pharyngeal phase, and the esophageal phase. The child's oral motor control is a reflection of the

---

❖

INDICATIONS OF SWALLOWING DYSFUNCTION

1. History of frequent upper respiratory infections or pneumonias of unknown etiology
2. Consistent coughing or choking during swallowing
3. Noisy or "wet"-sounding upper airway sounds after individual swallows, or noisiness that increases over the course of the feeding
4. An inability to handle own oral secretions
5. More than one swallow needed to clear a single bolus

---

oral phase of swallowing. The oral phase sets the stage for the pharyngeal phase by forming the foodstuff into a cohesive bolus, moving it backwards in the mouth, and propelling it into the pharynx at the appropriate time when the pharyngeal swallow is initiated. Thus oral motor difficulties may not only affect the type of diet the child is able to eat, but also contribute to difficulties in swallowing.

The pharyngeal phase is what has typically been thought of as the swallow. During this phase the airway is closed and protected from aspirating food or liquid, and the bolus is propelled through the pharynx into the esophagus. Precise timing and closure of nasopharynx and larynx are needed to channel the bolus in the appropriate direction without aspiration. Although the clinician is able to make direct observations about the oral phase of swallowing, only inferences about the function of the pharyngeal phase can be made during clinical evaluation. The box above lists a number of clinical indications of swallowing dysfunction. If one or more of these indications are present, further detailed evaluation of swallowing is needed.

Detailed evaluation of the swallowing mechanism can be made only through a radiologic procedure. This test is known as the videofluoroscopic swallowing study (VFSS) or modified barium swallow. The procedure is structured to simulate the child's typical feeding regimen in

FIG. 3-3   A child positioned for videofluoroscopy. The x-ray table is tilted vertically. A small child sits in a "Tumbleform" feeder seat. Wheelchairs or other adapted chairs may be used for larger children.

From Wolf LS, Glass RP: Feeding and swallowing disorders: assessment and management, Tucson, Ariz, 1991, Therapy Skill Builders.

terms of seating, food types, and textures. Special devices may be needed to position the motor-impaired child for the procedure. Foods are mixed with barium, then feeding is viewed real-time with the fluoroscope and recorded on videotape for later review. The function and safety of the swallowing mechanism can be determined (Figure 3-3).

This procedure is generally available only at tertiary-level hospitals. The personnel completing the study typically include a speech or occupational therapist and radiologist or radiology technician. These individuals should have a solid background in pediatric feeding processes to make the most reliable interpretation of the test results. This is a highly specialized procedure and may not be available in all locations. If, however, the child has significant nutritional, oral motor, and health problems, and swallowing dysfunction is a contributing factor, efforts should be made to obtain this radiologic evaluation of the swallowing function.

CONSIDERATION OF PSYCHOSOCIAL FACTORS

Whenever and wherever the nutrition of a child is discussed, consideration must also be given to factors that have no direct relationship on the feeding process. Eating behavior serves as a sensitive barometer of the general adjustment of child, parent, and family. For this rea-son intrapersonal and interpersonal factors that influence food intake should also be taken into consideration when collecting and assessing information.

Since parents are primarily responsible for providing infants and children with both food and the environment in which it is consumed, attention should be given to the parents' psychosocial well-being, adaptation to the parenting role, and general level of parenting skills. Because patterns of food intake, even in young children, can be altered by emotional status, screening should also consider the socioemotional development of the child. When appropriate food is available and there is no evidence of biological or organic problems in the child, it is not unusual to find that the cause of a disturbance in food intake is within the psychosocial/emotional category. Such problems can manifest themselves in a variety of ways, for instance, parent or child dissatisfaction with the feeding or mealtime situation, parental neglect or overconcern with food or feeding, anorexia or vomiting, and food aversions or food gorging.

Stress Level and Family Coping

Infants and children are sensitive to the feelings and attitudes of parents, particularly at feeding time or bedtime. Research by Brandon[17] on the epidemiological factors of childhood eating disturbances found that the parents

---

❖

SCREENING QUESTIONNAIRE FOR FAMILY STRESS

	Yes	No
1. During the past year have any of the following occurred in your immediate family?		
Family moved?	☐	☐
Death, divorce, separation, loss of family member?	☐	☐
Marriage, reconciliation, pregnancy, new family member?	☐	☐
Serious injury or illness, problem with aging relative?	☐	☐
Loss of work, change of job, retirement?	☐	☐
Frequent or serious arguments or fights?	☐	☐
Money problems?	☐	☐
Drug or drinking problems?	☐	☐
Trouble with the law?	☐	☐
Some other serious problem?	☐	☐
If yes, what? _____		
2. During the past year:		
Has anyone in your family been seriously upset, depressed, or moody?	☐	☐
Have you been generally happy with your family's way of life?	☐	☐
Have you often felt lonely or cut off from other people?	☐	☐
Have you or your mate had serious differences that you feel may be related to differences in religion, race, nationality, or family background?	☐	☐
3. Have you and your children been separated for more than 1 day in the past year?	☐	☐
Do you have someone reliable to take care of your children when you need it?	☐	☐
Are your children cared for daily by someone outside the family?	☐	☐
If yes, has it been the same person for the past year?	☐	☐

Modified from Metz JR and others: *Pediatrics* 58:4, 1976.

of the maladjusted group, as compared with control groups, were younger, were more dependent on relatives, were regarded as unstable or suffering from mental problems, reported unhappy childhoods, experienced marital conflict, or were regarded as showing disturbed relationships with their children. It is reasonable to hypothesize that parents who are anxious or distressed somehow communicate these states to their babies and young children, which in turn affects feeding behavior. Older children are also quick to identify tension or conflict between adults at the dinner table and to respond accordingly. Reality stressors like a job or financial worries, recent change of domicile, and illness or injury of child or parent are additional factors that can disrupt routines and can be associated with temporary symptoms related to food or feeding behavior. Personal problems of adult family members, for instance, marital discord, unresolved grief, depression, drug use, or lack of self-esteem, may also influence the feeding situation involving children. When the feeding problem appears to be nonorganic, it is appropriate to ask parents a few simple questions to determine the emotional climate in the home. This can be done selectively in an interview or by using a questionnaire as a routine part of the assessment process (see Screening Questionnaire for Family Stress above).

Parental Feelings of Competence and Satisfaction

Clinical observations indicate that parental *feelings* of competence and satisfaction or dissatisfaction with the parental role are psychological factors that also have an influence on the food intakes and feeding behaviors of children. When an individual, for whatever reason, experiences minimal feelings of success in carrying out the activities associated with parenting, the opportunity for experiencing satisfaction decreases proportionately and the stage is set for problems in parent-child interaction. If the parent does not feel adequate in handling child-care activities outside of feeding, lack of confidence or feelings of incompetence can eventually be manifested in a dysfunctional feeding situation. The mother who reported the following impressions was trying to deal with a 3-year-old boy whose diet consisted only of olives, avocados, and salmon:

I'll never forget what I felt like when he was 2 weeks old and I had to care for him completely on my own. It wasn't at all what I expected. I was scared to death and sure that every time he cried I must have done something wrong. There were half-filled bottles all over the house because I worried that the milk might spoil if Gary didn't drink it in 10 or 15 minutes. My mother-in-law didn't help. She is still always giving me suggestions for a better way to do something.

In early infancy the close relationship to and dependence on the mother, in particular, often become linked with the feeding process. For this reason many individuals equate successful mothering with a well-nourished infant or child and a nonproblematic feeding situation. The comments of the mother of a developmentally delayed toddler with congenital heart disease (still on a diet of pureed foods) are illustrative:

I couldn't do anything about his heart, but I did pretty well at feeding him by that nasogastric tube. Nobody else could do it as well as I did. Now when he doesn't eat, I fix a special high kcalorie pudding for him so that he doesn't lose weight. He really gobbles it down!

Factors like past experience, age, knowledge of child growth and development, and the input of significant family members or professionals are important determinants of parental feelings of competence.[18] The standards of performance or values that parents hold for themselves, along with their more general feelings of self-esteem, are also related to perceptions of competence. But probably the most significant influence on parental feelings of success or satisfaction is the responsiveness of the child; that is, does the child show developmental and social evidence of a positive response to parenting? With these determinants in mind the following questions can serve as guidelines for eliciting data on the adjustment to parenting and its associated emotional responses:

1. As you were growing up, did you observe or assist with the upbringing of younger children such as brothers or sisters, relatives, friends, or neighbors?
2. How would you rate your maternal feelings on a scale of 1 to 5, with 1 being very maternal and 5 being nonmaternal?
3. What has been the biggest surprise or thing you least expected about being a parent?
4. How satisfied are you with your child's physical growth and development?
5. How satisfied are you with your child's social adjustment?
6. How much influence does your spouse have on your ideas about childrearing? Do you usually agree or disagree on child-rearing concerns?
7. Who or what has had the most influence on your ideas about child rearing? Books, magazines, or the media? Religion? Friends, neighbors, or relatives? Professionals? Formal education or parenting classes?
8. When you and your child are getting along as you usually do, how does your relationship with your child make you feel as a parent?
9. How competent do you feel about how you handle your life in general?
10. How competent do you feel as a parent?
11. How competent a parent do you think you are *from the viewpoint of others* who know you well?
12. Before you had your own family, how did you feel about children?

Parent-Child Interaction

An integral component of assessment and data collection related to food intake is consideration of the interaction between child and parent. To have an indication of the effects of food and the feeding situation on the parent-child dyad, such data should be based on observation of both mealtime and nonmealtime situations. It is important to determine if food-related parent-child problems are situation specific or part of a more basic discord. Ideally, the assessment should be done in the home setting during mealtime *and* free-play situations. If this is not possible, every attempt should be made to simulate natural conditions in the clinic, office, or hospital environment.

Several research methods and standardized tools have been developed to evaluate parent-child interaction, for instance, Verbal Interaction Record,[19] Mutual Problem Solving Task,[20] Nursing Child Assessment Feeding Scales,[21] and Nursing Child Assessment Teaching Scales.[22] Some practitioners may want to obtain training in the use of standardized assessment techniques, however less formalized methods can also be helpful in collecting data. Using the concepts of **affectional ties, propensity to interact, feedback,** and **reciprocity** as organizers, it is possible to identify the essential elements of most interaction between parents and children.

I. **Affectional ties** (refers to the emotional attachment and degree of psychological involvement between parent and child)
   A. Appropriate interview questions
      1. Do you believe in unconditional mother love? Would you ever use such a term to describe your feelings about ____?
      2. How old was ____ when you really felt that he/she was *your* child?
      3. How does ____ know that you love and care about him/her?
      4. How do you know that ____ loves you?
      5. To whom or what is ____ most attached?
      6. Have you ever regretted the decision to become a parent? Occasionally? Frequently?

   B. Direct observation
      1. Attentiveness of parent to child's distress; physical comforting
      2. Use of expressions of love or special designations to refer to child *or* use of negative terms to refer to child; no reference to child by name
      3. Evidence of parental pleasure when child is complimented or comments are made regarding parent-child physical resemblances
      4. Evidence of strong mutual need for togetherness and a maximum avoidance of separation *or* parent or child tendency/preference for isolated activity
      5. Willingness to relinquish child to care of a stranger

II. **Propensity to interact** (refers to the ability and desire of parent or child to give and receive communication)
   A. Appropriate interview questions
      1. When ____ is not around, do you ever find yourself thinking of something you want to do with him/her or something you want to tell him/her?
      2. Have you been (or are you ever) so preoccupied with adult worries or concerns that you don't have any energy left to interact with ____?
      3. Can you identify any person, thing, or situation that interferes with your relationship or communication with ____?
      4. How would you describe your relationship with ____?

   B. Direct observation
      1. Evidence of physical intactness (especially sensory and perceptual) of parent and child
      2. Evidence of emotional intactness of parent and child
      3. Presence or absence of reality stressors (as in Family Stress Questionnaire, page 81)

III. **Feedback** and **reciprocity** (refers to chains of response between parent and child; activity of one that occurs as a direct result of stimuli from the other)

A. Appropriate interview questions
 1. How does _____ let you know that he/she needs something or wants your attention? What is your usual response to this?
 2. Who or what usually initiates the interaction between you and your child?
 3. What do you do for _____? What does _____ do for you?
B. Direct observation
 1. Efforts on the part of either parent or child to remain in touch (physically or verbally) that are successful
 2. Conversation, singing, laughing, or smiling that maintains an extended interaction (one partner answers the other, the latter responds in turn, and so on)
 3. Presence or absence of eye contact between parent and child
 4. Presence or absence of caregiving activity on the part of the parent in response to behavior (e.g., cry, yawn, request)
 5. Manner in which infant or young child is held
 6. Attention of parent to cues in the feeding situation (e.g., satiation, hunger, pacing)

When data indicate that the cause of a child's feeding or food intake problem is most likely psychosocial, intervention must be planned accordingly. The primary focus of treatment most likely is on strategies to alleviate stress and to support family coping abilities, on increasing parental knowledge and skill regarding childrearing, or on facilitating the parent-child relationship. In some situations these goals may be accomplished within the context of the feeding situation; however, in the majority of instances more specific treatment is indicated. Reality-based family needs demand rapid provisions of concrete services to relieve situational demands. For this reason, referral to a public or private family service or social welfare agency may be appropriate. Those situations that require supportive counseling or education and anticipatory guidance may be handled in a variety of ways, for instance, with family therapy, enrollment in parenting classes, referral to a parent group, or one-on-one work with a qualified professional.

The variety of concerns presented about infants' and children's food intake clearly indicates that information sought must be based on problems presented and the health care professional's judgment. In some instances dietary intake data may provide sufficient information to design plans with parents and children to modify energy and nutrient intakes. In many cases, if plans are to be effective, the behavioral and psychosocial influences on a compromised food intake must be investigated. Parents of children with oral motor and self-feeding delays may need help in identifying specific foods to support developmental progress. Those with abnormal motor patterns need therapy.

Screening procedures may identify children with feeding problems of multiple etiological factors for whom an interdisciplinary assessment is appropriate. Factors that must be considered are adequacy of nutrient intake, structural abnormalities of the oral cavity, oral tissue health, medical status, speech development, living environment, social environment, and neurological integrity (including sensation). The collective data provide a base on which the cause of the problem may be determined, effective treatment plans may be designed, and progress may be assessed.

The team approach facilitates identification of priorities for treatment and use of logical step-by-step approach. Periodic reevaluations of identified concerns indicate the effectiveness of programs designed.

Summary

Several studies have attempted to assess dietary methods. Most of these studies have found that children who provide information are not as reliable as adults. Even so, all methods have inherent limitations that should be recognized. The results of diet histories have not agreed with those of weighed food records when applied to individual children. Most studies have indicated that diet histories and food frequency questionnaires of children overestimate intake by individuals compared with 3- and 7-day food records. Children who have delays in feeding skills should be screened to determine whether the delays are because of abnormal motor patterns or because of an overall delay, which should determine the need for an occupational or physical therapy evaluation. Because many feeding difficulties in childhood are caused by parent-child interactions, it may be necessary to evaluate the family level of stress and coping and the interaction between parent and child.

REVIEW QUESTIONS

1. When is it necessary to collect dietary intake information?
2. Describe the advantages and disadvantages of the 24-hour recall.
3. How many consecutive days of food intake data is required for an accurate estimate of an individual's energy intake?
4. How does one identify the most appropriate computer program to use?
5. How does screening differ from assessment?
6. Under what circumstances is it important to screen children for oral motor difficulties when assessing food intake?
7. Why is it important to understand psychosocial factors that influence a child's food intake?

SUGGESTED LEARNING ACTIVITIES

1. Interview parents of a preschool child to collect a diet history. Assess the validity of the information collected.
2. Measure (in standard household measures) portions appropriate for children for 1 day; compare these with adult size portions.
3. Keep a 7-day record of all food and beverages consumed. Assess the difficulty in keeping such a record.
4. Assess stress in the family of a preschool child whose parents consider the child to have a feeding problem.
5. Observe a comprehensive nutrition/feeding evaluation of a child who has oral motor feeding delays. Using appropriate tools, record dietary intake information, eating abilities, and level of family stress.

Terms and Concepts

Provided here for your review is a listing of terms and concepts within this chapter. The definitions for terms can be found in the glossary, which begins on page 413. To aid your understanding of the terms' and concepts' application within this text, the page number designating the first mention of each term or concept within the chapter is given.

affectional ties, 83
anthropometry, 66
assessment, 60
bioavailability, 66
feedback, 83
gag reflex, 77
oral motor skills, 73
paraprofessionals, 66
prehension, 77
propensity to interact, 83
reciprocity, 83

REFERENCES

1. Beal VA: The nutrition history in longitudinal research, *J Am Diet Assoc* 51:426, 1967.
2. Todd KS, Hudes M, Calloway H: Food intake measurements: problems and approaches, *Am J Clin Nutr* 37:139, 1983.
3. Klesges RC and others: Validation of the 24-hour dietary recall in preschool children, *J Am Diet Assoc* 86:1383, 1986.
4. Farris RP and others: A group method for obtaining dietary recalls of children, *J Am Diet Assoc* 85:1315, 1985.
5. Bolland JE, Ward JY, Bolland TW: Improved accuracy of estimating food quantities up to 4 weeks after training, *J Am Diet Assoc* 88:1250, 1988.
6. Garrahie EJ and others: The value of debriefing mothers of 3 to 7 year old children when analyzing children's diets, *J Am Diet Assoc* 91:710, 1991.
7. Basiotis PP and others: Number of days of food intake records required to estimate individual and group intake with defined confidence, *J Nutr* 117:1638, 1987.
8. Stuff JE and others: A comparison of dietary methods, *Am J Clin Nutr* 37:300, 1983.
9. Burke BS: The dietary history as a tool in research, *J Am Diet Assoc* 23:1031, 1947.

10. Rasanen L: Nutrition survey of Finnish rural children. VI. Methodological study comparing the 24 hour record and dietary history, *Am J Clin Nutr* 32:2560, 1979.

11. Medlin C, Skinner JD: Individual dietary intake methodology: a 50 year review of progress, *J Am Diet Assoc* 90:1402, 1990.

12. Trulson MF: Assessment of dietary study methods. I. Comparison of methods for obtaining data for clinical work, *J Am Diet Assoc* 30:991, 1954.

13. Bergman EA, Boyungs JC, Erickson ML: Comparison of a food frequency questionnaire and 3 day diet record, *J Am Diet Assoc* 90:1431, 1990.

14. Larkin FA and others: Comparison of estimate and nutrient intakes by food frequency and dietary records in adults, *J Am Diet Assoc* 89:215, 1989.

15. Morris SE, Klein MD: *Pre-feeding skills,* Tucson, Ariz, 1987, Therapy Skill Builders.

16. Jelm JM: *Oral-motor/feeding rating scale,* Tucson, Ariz, 1991, Therapy Skill Builders.

17. Brandon S: An epidemiological study of eating disturbances, *J Psychosom Res* 14:253, 1970.

18. Sutherland S: *An exploratory study of the factors which contribute to a material sense of competence among mothers of children in preschools, parenting classes and a day care center,* Unpublished master's thesis, Seattle, 1980, University of Washington.

19. Lambie DL, Bond JT, Weikart DP: Verbal interaction record, monograph 2, high scope monograph series, home teaching with mothers and infants. The Ypsilanti-Carnegie infant education project: an experiment, Ypsilanti, Mich, 1974, High Scope Press.

20. Epstein A, Weikart DP: Mutual problem solving task, monograph 6, high scope monograph series. The Ypsilanti-Carnegie infant education project: longitudinal follow-up, Ypsilanti, Mich, 1980, High Scope Press.

21. Nursing child assessment feeding scales. In Barnard KE, Eyres SJ editors: *Child health assessment, part 2: the first year of life,* Pub No HRA 79-25, Washington, DC, June 1979, US Department of Health, Education and Welfare.

22. Nursing child assessment teaching scales. In Barnard KE, Eyres SJ editors: *Child health assessment, part 2: the first year of life,* Pub No HRA 79-25, Washington, DC, June 1979, US Department of Health, Education and Welfare.

4 *Infant Feeding and Nutrition*

Peggy L. Pipes

Objectives

✱✱

After studying this chapter, the student should:

✔ *Recognize differences in human and other milks available for infants.*

✔ *Define the appropriate use of the various formulas and whole milk for infants.*

✔ *Recognize developmental landmarks during infancy that indicate a readiness for the infant to progress in feeding behaviors and a readiness for change in the varieties and textures of food that should be offered.*

✔ *Be aware of infant foods as sources of nutrients and appropriate use of foods to optimize the baby's nutritional status.*

✔ *Be aware of the variability among the personalities, growth patterns, and nutrient needs of infants at any age and the need to individualize what, when, how often, and how much each baby should be fed.*

At no time in the life cycle are as many changes in food and nutrient intake observed as they are during the first year of life. Influenced by a rapid but declining rate of physical growth, maturation of the oral, fine, and gross motor skills, and relationships established with their parents, infants who are prepared at birth to suck liquids from a nipple are at 1 year of age making attempts to feed themselves table food with culturally defined utensils. The need for nutrients and energy depends on the infant's requirement for maintenance, physical growth, and energy expenditure, while the foods offered to infants reflect culturally accepted practices. Infants' acceptance of food is influenced by both neuromotor maturation and their interactions with their parents. Because of the variability of the preceding parameters among infants, a variety of combinations of foods and milks are consumed by well-nourished children at any month during the first year.

MATURATION OF DIGESTION AND ABSORPTION

The newborn is a functionally immature organism. Although the normal neonate is well prepared to digest and absorb human milk, modified cow's milk formula, or soy formulas at birth, maturation of many of the enzyme systems occurs during and after the first year.

The stomach capacity of infants increases from 10 to 20 ml at birth to 200 ml by 12 months of age. The rate of stomach emptying depends on the size and the composition of the meal. During the first weeks after birth gastric acidity decreases, and for the first few months it remains lower than in the adult.

Protein

Proteolytic activity of duodenal juice is as great in infancy as in adulthood. However, the total quantity of protein that can be digested per hour is less during infancy and childhood and increases with age.[1]

Fat

A higher percentage of fat is absorbed in later life than in infancy. Adults absorb about 95% of ingested fats, whereas newborns absorb about 85% to 90% of ingested fats provided by human milk. Many infants absorb less than 70% of the fat in cow's milk.[2] Vegetable oils mixed with commercially prepared infant formulas are well absorbed, although the reason for the degree of absorption of those containing oleo oil remains unclear.[2] Absorption of fat begins to reach adult levels between 6 and 9 months of age.

Pancreatic lipase activity is low in the newborn, especially in the premature infant. The bile acid pool, although present, is reduced. When compared with an adult on the basis of body surface, the newborn, although able to synthesize bile, has a bile acid pool one-half that of the adult.[3]

During infancy the position of the saturated fatty acid on the glycerol molecule influences absorption. Stearic acid is poorly absorbed in any position. Free palmitic acid hydrolyzed from positions 1 and 3 is poorly absorbed, whereas palmitic acid, which occupies position 2 on the glycerol molecule, remains as a monoglyceride and appears to be well absorbed.[4]

Carbohydrates

Maltase, isomaltase, and sucrase activity reaches adult levels by 28 to 32 weeks' gestation. Lactase, present at low levels at 28 weeks' gestation, increases near term and reaches adult levels at birth.[5] Salivary and pancreatic **amylase** are low during the first months after birth. Concentrations of salivary amylase rise to adult levels between 6 months and 1 year of age. Concentrations of salivary amylase increase to two thirds of adult levels by 3 months of age, and reach full adult levels between 6 months and 1 year of age. Large variations in enzyme activity, however, have been noted among groups of infants. There appears to be no relationship between the activity of salivary amylase, the size of the infant, and intakes of starch-containing food before 3 months of age. Concentrations of pancreatic amylase increase from birth through the preschool years. Hadorn and others[6] found that output of amylase per kilogram in children less than 6 months of age was two to four times less than in children 1 year of age. There also appears to be an increase in output of amylase from the preschool to the school-age years.

Most health care professionals believe that the introduction of infant cereal before 3 to 4 months of age is inappropriate.

RENAL FUNCTION

The newborn has a functionally immature kidney. The glomerular surface area/tubular volume ratio in an infant's kidney is high compared with the kidney of an adult. The glomerular filtration rate is low. The concentrating capacity of some neonates has been reported to be as limited as 700 mOsm/L, and for others it is as great as that of older children and adults, 1200 to 1400 mOsm/L. Therefore infants are vulnerable to water imbalance.

MILK IN THE INFANT'S DIET

That human milk from adequately nourished lactating mothers offers nutritional, immunological, and psychosocial benefits to infants has never been questioned. However, the incidence of breast-feeding of the newborn infant fell to 18% in 1966. A renewed interest in promoting breast-feeding and supporting the lactating mother resulted in an increase of infants who were breast-feeding when they left the hospital to 56.9% in 1986. More recent surveys indicate a decline in both initiation and continuation of breast-feeding. Between 1984 and 1989 the initiation of breast-feeding declined to 52.2%.[7] An even greater reduction in the continuation of breast-feeding was noted. Only 18.1% of mothers were breast-feeding their 6-month-old infants in 1989 compared with 21.6% in 1984.

The incidence of breast-feeding is highest among mothers who are white, who have some college education, who have a normal birth weight infant, and who are of increased maternal age. It is greater in the Pacific and Mountain regions, and least in the East and South Atlantic areas. The decline in breast-feeding was greater in those who were less affluent and in those women who were younger and who had delivered their first child. Formula supplementation of breast-feeding has been consistently associated with a shortened breast feeding duration.[8]

Most normal full-term infants who are not breast-fed receive a cow's milk–base formula; very few receive fresh cow's milk. Milk-free formulas, including soy and hydrolyzed casein formulas, are fed to infants who do not tolerate milk.

Colostrum and Transitional Milk

For the first few days after birth, the breast-fed infant ingests a yellowish, transparent fluid called **colostrum.** Human colostrum contains more protein but less fat, carbohydrate, and energy than does mature human milk. Concentrations of sodium, potassium, and chloride are greater in colostrum than in later-produced milk. Between the third and sixth day colostrum changes to a milk that, compared with mature human milk, has a high protein content. This is referred to as transitional milk. By the tenth day the breast-fed infant receives mature human milk.

Comparison of Nutrient Compositions of Human Milk and Cow's Milk

Nutrients secreted in human milk vary and reflect individual biochemical variability among women, the diet consumed, the stage of lactation, and the length of time the mother has breast-fed.[9] When milk is analyzed for nutrient content, the time of day the milk was expressed and whether foremilk or hindmilk is analyzed influence the results. Wide ranges of many vitamins and minerals have been reported. Table 4-1 lists estimated concentrations of nutrients in human milk, and Table 4-2 lists minimum federal standards for homogenized milk.

Both human milk and cow's milk are complex liquids containing more than 200 components in the fat-soluble and water-soluble fractions. However considerable differences in the quantity and availability of the nutrients in the two milks are evident. Differences are thought to reflect species' specific nutrient needs to support individual maintenance and growth needs of the offspring. This hypothesis is further supported by the fact that changes occur in the nutrient composition of human milk during lactation. For example, the concentrations of iron, copper, and zinc decline between 2 weeks and 5 to 9 months of lactation.[10] Protein concentration decreases from the first week through 6 to 9 months of age and then rises slightly, reflecting the infant's declining needs during declining rates of growth.

Human milk provides similar amounts of water and approximately the same amount of energy as does cow's milk. The nutrient sources of the energy are, however, different. Protein supplies approximately 7% of the kcalories in human milk and 20% of the kcalories in cow's milk; the carbohydrate lactose supplies approximately 42% of the kcalories in human milk and 20% of the kcalories in cow's milk. The percentage of kcalories supplied by fat is similar in both milks.

The protein content of human milk is approximately 0.9 gm/100 ml compared with 3.5 gm/100 ml in cow's milk. Nonprotein nitrogen accounts for 25% of total nitrogen in human milk and 5% of total nitrogen in cow's milk.

TABLE 4-1   *Estimates of Concentrations of Nutrients in Mature Human Milk*

Nutrient (Per Liter)	Amount in Human Milk[a]	Nutrient (Per Liter)	Amount in Human Milk[a]
	gm/liter ± SD[b]		μg/liter ± SD
Lactose	72.0 ± 2.5	Vitamin A, RE[d]	670 ± 200
Protein	10.5 ± 2.0		(2,230 IU[e])
Fat	39.0 ± 4.0	Vitamin D	0.55 ± 0.10
	mg/liter ± SD	Vitamin K	2.1 ± 0.1
Calcium	280 ± 26	Folate	85 ± 37[f]
Phosphorus	140 ± 22	Vitamin B$_{12}$	0.97[g,h]
Magnesium	35 ± 2	Biotin	4 ± 1
Sodium	180 ± 40	Iodine	110 ± 40
Potassium	525 ± 35	Selenium	20 ± 5
Chloride	420 ± 60	Manganese	6 ± 2
Iron	0.3 ± 0.1	Fluoride	16 ± 5
Zinc	1.2 ± 0.2	Chromium	50 ± 5
Copper	0.25 ± 0.03	Molybdenum	NR[i]
Vitamin E	2.3 ± 1.0		
Vitamin C	40 ± 10		
Thiamin	0.210 ± 0.035		
Riboflavin	0.350 ± 0.025		
Niacin	1.500 ± 0.200		
Vitamin B$_6$	93 ± 8[c]		
Pantothenic acid	1.800 ± 0.200		

Adapted from the Committee on Nutrition, Institute of Medicine: *Nutrition during lactation*, National Academy of Sciences, Washington, DC, 1991, National Academy Press.
[a]Data taken from the Committee on Nutrition, 1985 unless otherwise indicated. The values are representative of amounts of nutrients present in human milk; some of them may differ slightly from those reported by investigators cited in the text.
[b]Standard deviation.
[c]From Styslinger L, Kirksey A: *Am J Clin Nutr* 41:21, 1985.
[d]RE, Retinol equivalents.
[e]IU, International units.
[f]From Brown CM, Smith AM, Piccino MF: *J Pediatr Gastroenterol Nutr* 5:278, 1986.
[g]From Sandberg DP, Begley JA, Hall CA: *Am J Clin Nutr* 34:1717, 1981.
[h]Standard deviation not reported; range 0.33 to 3.20.
[i]NR, Not reported.

During lactation protein levels decrease. Anderson, Atkinson, and Bryan[11] noted a linear decrease in protein nitrogen content of milk during the first 4 weeks of lactation. Chavalittamrong and others[12] found a decrease from 1.56 gm/100 ml at 1 to 7 days to 0.60 gm/100 ml at 180 to 270 days, then a gradual increase at 270 days in the mothers' milk.

Casein and **whey** constitute the protein in both human milk and cow's milk. Amounts of whey protein are similar in each. Cow's milk contains six to seven times as much casein as does human milk, and differences in the casein/whey ratios of the two milks are great. The casein/whey ratio of human milk is 40:60, whereas the casein/whey ratio of cow's milk is 82:18. β-Lactoglobulin, the dominant whey protein in cow's milk, is absent in human milk, in which α-Lactoalbumin and lactoferrin are the dominant whey proteins.

During digestion in the stomach, the protein in milk mixes with hydrochloric acid. The result

TABLE 4-2 **Estimates of Concentrations of Nutrients in Cow's Milk**

Nutrient (Per Liter)	Cow's Milk
Lactose (gm)	49
Protein (gm)	35
Fat (gm)	38
Calcium (mg)	1200
Phosphorus (mg)	940
Magnesium (mg)	120
Chloride (mg)	1060
Iron (mg)	0.5
Zinc (mg)	3-4
Copper (mg)	1100
Vitamin E (mg)	0.4
Vitamin C (mg)	17
Thiamin (mg)	3.7
Riboflavin (mg)	1.7
Niacin (mg)	0.9
Vitamin B_6 (mg)	42
Vitamin A (RE*) (μg)	295 (1025 IU†)
Vitamin D (μg)	10
Vitamin K (μg)	170
Folate (μg)	2.9-68
Vitamin B_{12} (μg)	4
Iodine (μg)	80
Selenium (μg)	30
Manganese (μg)	20-40
Fluoride (μg)	3
Chromium (μg)	20

From Blanc B: *World Rev Nutr Diet* 36:1, 1981.
*RE, Retinol equivalents.
†IU, International units.

of this process is the formation of curds from the casein and calcium and a liquid that contains whey. Because of its lower casein content, human milk forms a soft, flocculent, easy-to-digest curd in the infant's stomach. The increased casein content of fresh cow's milk causes it to form a tough, cheesy, hard-to-digest curd. Homogenization, boiling, and dilution of cow's milk modify the curd and prevent the formation of the hard curd in the stomach so that it is easily digested by the infant.

The amino acid composition of human milk meets the needs of the neonate with an immature enzyme system, whereas that of cow's milk may be inappropriate. The newborn has a limited ability to metabolize phenylalanine to tyrosine. Human milk has a low content of tyrosine and phenylalanine compared with cow's milk. The level of cystathionase, an enzyme that catalyzes the transulfuration of methionine to cystine, is low in the neonate. Taurine and cystine are present in much higher concentrations in human milk than in cow's milk.

The total fat content of human milk is similar to that of cow's milk. Saturated fatty acids predominate in cow's milk. The fatty acid pattern of human milk resembles that of the maternal diet. About 98% of the fat in human milk is triglycerides in which palmitic acid is in position 2, enhancing its absorbability. The average content of linoleic acid is 10% of fat, but ranges of 1% to 43% have been reported. Linoleic acid provides an average of 4% of the kcalories in human milk but only 1% of the kcalories in cow's milk. The cholesterol content of human milk averages 20 mg/100 ml, but there is considerable variability. Values up to 47 mg/100 ml have been reported. Cow's milk contains 7 to 25 mg/100 ml of cholesterol. Diurnal variations occur in human milk; the fat content is higher in early mornings, the short-chain fatty acid content is greater in cow's milk, and the fat content percentage of human hindmilk is higher than that of foremilk.

Both cow's milk and human milk contain lipoprotein lipase in the cream fraction that is stimulated by serum and inhibited by bile salts. Human milk contains an additional lipase that is stimulated by bile salts and contributes significantly to the hydrolysis of milk triglycerides. These enzymes contribute significantly to a higher percentage absorption of human milk fat as compared with butter fat.

The concentration of lactose is greater in human milk than in cow's milk. This nutrient is incorporated into galactolipids in the brain and spinal cord. Trace amounts of glucose, galactose, glucosamines, and other nitrogen-containing carbohydrates are also present in both milks. Human milk contains L-bifidus factor, a nitrogen-containing carbohydrate, in concentrations 40 times greater than that in cow's milk. This carbohydrate requires the *Lactobacillus* bacteria for growth.

Human milk from adequately nourished mothers is a reliable source of fat-soluble vitamins A and E and the water-soluble vitamins. The concentration of vitamin D in human milk has been shown to be influenced by maternal intake of vitamin D. The effect of sunlight on the infant is difficult to quantitate. However, vitamin D deficiency rickets continues to be identified in breast-fed infants, and has occurred most often in infants with dark skin and who have had little exposure to sunlight. Most breast-fed infants have exhibited normal growth and development without symptoms of vitamin D deficiency. A vitamin D supplement continues to be recommended for breast-fed infants, but evidence that supplements are necessary for infants with light skin is not convincing.[13]

Cow's milk is a reliable source of vitamin A and the B vitamins. It contains less vitamin E and more vitamin K than human milk. Most dairies fortify homogenized, 2%, and nonfat milk with vitamin D. Evaporated milk that is reconstituted with equal amounts of water is fortified with 400 IU/qt. Cow's milk is low in vitamin C.

Cow's milk contains four times as much vitamin K as human milk. In breast-fed infants the prothrombin level is 20% to 50% of that of the adult in the first few days. Hemorrhagic disease of the newborn may occur if vitamin K is not given. A prophylactic dose of 0.5 to 1 mg is usually given to breast-fed infants at birth.

Infants who are born at home and then breast feed are at risk of vitamin K deficiency if they do not receive the supplement at birth. O'Connor and others[14] describe two infants delivered at home who were not given vitamin K and required hospitalization at 4 to 5 weeks of age because of vitamin K deficiency. Women who plan to have home deliveries should be counseled before delivery about the infant's need for vitamin K.

Inadequate amounts of water-soluble nutrients in the maternal diet are reflected in milk produced for the infant. Infantile beriberi is well known in East Asians when maternal intakes of thiamin are inadequate. Vitamin B_{12} deficiency has been reported in a breast-fed infant whose mother had been a vegan for 8 years before her pregnancy, and in another infant whose mother had pernicious anemia.[15] Supplementation of a folate-deficient woman resulted in a prompt increase in her milk folate.[16]

Because vitamin B_6 is critical to the development of the central nervous system, researchers have investigated the need for maternal supplementation to support optimal levels in their milk. They have found that only when mothers are supplemented with 10 to 20 mg pyridoxine hydrochloride does their milk meet American Academy of Pediatrics standards.[17]

The mineral content of cow's milk is several times greater than that of human milk. Cow's milk contains more than three times as much calcium and six times as much phosphorus as does human milk. The high phosphate load and calcium/phosphate ratio have been implicated as causes of late hypocalcemic tetany of the neonate.

The iron content of human milk declines from 0.5 to 0.3 mg/100 ml between 2 weeks and 5 months of age; that of cow's milk remains at 0.5 mg/100 ml. It has been reported that 5- to 7-month-old infants absorbed 49% of the iron in human milk but only 10% of the iron in cow's milk.[18]

Studies of the iron status of solely breast-fed infants indicate that a substantial number will become iron deficient by 9 months of age as evidenced by low total body iron. Iron supplements are desirable for breast-fed infants.[13]

Human milk contains less zinc than does cow's milk. In cow's milk zinc binds strongly to casein, but very little is bound to whey. The zinc-binding capacity of human milk protein is assumed to be minimal. Because the stomach acid secretion is low in early infancy, ingested zinc may not be released from casein or its curd, making zinc from cow's milk inaccessible to infants. Studies suggest that the bioavailability of zinc in human milk is 59% and in cow's milk, 43% to 51%.[19]

Plasma fluoride is poorly transferred to breast milk; thus breast-fed infants receive almost no fluoride. They should receive supplements of fluoride.

The high protein and mineral content of cow's milk places a much greater osmolar load on the kidney of the infant and obligates a greater amount of water for excretion. The margin of safety is smaller. Cow's milk may not supply sufficient amounts of water when the environmental temperature is high. Neither milk may provide adequate amounts of water when requirements are increased by fever, vomiting, or diarrhea.

Antiinfective Characteristics of Human Milk

In addition to nutrients, human colostrum and human milk contain antibodies, enzymes, and other factors that are absent or present in only minute amounts in cow's milk; factors that provide infants with protection against enteric infections.[20] Table 4-3 lists important antiviral and antibacterial factors that are present in breast milk.

Lactobacillus microorganisms in the gastrointestinal tract, whose growth is dependent on L-bifidus factor, produce acetic and lactic acids. The resulting acidic environment interferes with the growth of certain pathogenic organ-

TABLE 4-3   *Antiviral and Antibacterial Factors in Human Milk*

Factor	Shown in Vitro to be Active Against
Secretory IgA	*Escherichia coli* (also pili and capsular antigens), *Clostridium tetani, Clostridium diphtheriae, Klebsiella pneumoniae, Salmonella* (6 groups), *Shigella* (2 groups), *Streptococcus, Streptococcus mutans, Streptococcus sanguis, Streptococcus mitis, Streptococcus salivarius, Streptococcus pneumoniae, Coxiella burnetii, Haemophilus influenzae*
	E. coli enterotoxin, *Vibrio cholerae* enterotoxin, *Clostridium difficile* toxins, *H. influenzae* capsule
IgM, IgG	*V. cholerae* lipopolysaccharide; *E. coli*
IgD	*E. coli*
Bifidobacterium bifidum growth z factor	Enterobacteriaceae, enteric pathogens
Factor binding proteins (zinc, vitamin B_{12}, folate)	Dependent *E. coli*
Lactoferrin	*E. coli*
Lactoperoxidase	*Streptococcus, Pseudomonas, E. coli, Salmonella typhimurium*
Lysozyme	*E. coli, Salmonella, M. lysodeikticus*
Carbohydrate	*E. coli* enterotoxin
Lipid	*Staphylococcus aureus*
Ganglioside (GMI-like)	*E. coli* enterotoxin, *V. cholerae* enterotoxin
Glycoproteins (receptor-like) + oligosaccharides	*V. cholerae*
Analogues of epithelial cell receptors (oligosaccharides)	*S. pneumoniae, H. influenzae*
Milk cells (macrophages, neutrophils B and T lymphocytes)	By phagocytosis and killing: *E. coli, S. aureus, Salmonella enteritidis* By sensitized lymphocytes: *E. coli* By phagocytosis: *Corpus albicans, E. coli* Lymphocyte stimulation: *E. coli*, K antigen, tuberculin PPD Monocyte chemotactic factor production: PPD

From May JT: *Microbiol Sci* 5:42, 1988.   *Continued.*

TABLE 4-3 *Antiviral and Antibacterial Factors in Human Milk—cont'd*

Factor	Shown in Vitro to be Active Against
Secretory IgA	Polio types 1, 2, 3, Coxsackie types A9, B3, B5, echo types 6, 9, Semliki Forest virus, Ross River virus, rotavirus, cytomegalovirus, reovirus type 3, rubella, herpes simplex virus, mumps virus, influenza, respiratory syncytial virus
IgM, IgG	Rubella, cytomegalovirus, respiratory syncytial virus
Lipid (unsaturated fatty acids and monoglycerides)	Herpes simplex; Semliki Forest virus, influenza, dengue, Ross River virus, Japanese B encephalitis virus, sindbis, West Nile
Nonimmunoglobulin macromolecules	Herpes simplex; vesicular stomatitis virus, Coxsackie B4, Semliki Forest virus, reovirus 3, poliotype 2, cytomegalovirus, respiratory syncytial virus, rotavirus
α_2-Macroglobulin (like)	Influenza hemagglutinin, parainfluenza hemagglutinin
Ribonuclease	Murine leukemia
Hemagglutinin inhibitors	Influenza, mumps
Milk cells	Induced interferon: virus or PHA
	Induced lymphokine (LDCF): phytohemagglutinin (PHA)
	Induced cytokine: by herpes simplex virus
	Lymphocyte stimulation: rubella, cytomegalovirus, herpes, measles, mumps, respiratory syncytial

isms such as *Escherichia coli* and *Shigella* organisms and provides a medium in which lysozymes are stable. Lysozymes exert their effect by destroying bacterial cell membranes after the organisms have been inactivated by peroxides and ascorbic acid also present in human colostrum and human milk.

Immunoglobulins (antibodies) to many different types of organisms, including pertussis, staphylococci, *E. coli*, and *Salmonella*, have been identified in colostrum and, in smaller amounts, in mature human milk. Since these immunoglobulins are not absorbed, they exert an effect only through the gastrointestinal tract. Infants who are breast-fed by mothers with high titers of antibodies to poliomyelitis are resistant to infection with orally administered polio vaccine. This effect is not believed to be operative after

the infant is 6 weeks of age. Lactoperoxidase, an enzyme present in human milk and saliva, aids in killing streptococci and may act on other organisms.

Large amounts of lactoferrin and small amounts of transferrin (iron-binding proteins) in human milk exert a bacterial effect. Lactoferrin is less than 50% saturated with iron. It is bacteriostatic because it deprives bacteria of the iron-containing environment necessary for their normal cell growth.

There is no question that breast-feeding reduces infant mortality and morbidity in developing countries. The presence of the antiinfective and antiviral factors in human milk, in addition to the potential for unsanitary bottle-feeding, makes breast-feeding important for 1 to 2 years.[21] Questions remain about the effect of antiinfective factors in human milk in populations in which environmental sanitation is not an issue. Some feel breast-feeding has no demonstrable effect on the incidence of infection; others believe it reduces the incidence of hospitalization after an infection.[22,23]

Antiallergenic Characteristics of Human Milk

The intestine of the newborn infant is permeable to macromolecules. Secretory IgA in human milk promotes closure of the gut and therefore decreases the permeability of **allergens.** Cow's milk protein β-lactoglobulin and serum bovine albumin are the most common allergens in infancy. Breast-feeding is the best prophylaxis for food allergy during infancy.

Modified Cow's Milk Formula for Infants

Modified, commercially manufactured formulas prepared from nonfat cow's milk are readily available and are generously used for feeding infants.

Cow's milk formulas are prepared by modifying whole cow's milk to reduce the solute load by reducing the protein and mineral content. The curd tension is reduced through homogenization and heat treatment to produce an easily digested protein.

Three manufacturers (Wyeth, Mead Johnson, and Carnation) combine demineralized whey with nonfat milk to produce a product with a whey/casein ratio similar to that of human milk. Minerals removed from the whey by electrodialysis are added in concentrations similar to that of human milk, resulting in simulated human milk. Two manufacturers (Ross Laboratory and Gerber) market a modified casein-predominant formula.

Combinations of vegetable oils, a high percentage of which are absorbed in infancy, are included, and carbohydrate is added to increase the kcaloric concentration to approximately that of human milk and cow's milk. Vitamins and minerals are added. Formulas are marketed

both with and without ferrous sulfate in amounts that provide 12 mg of iron/qt.

Infant Formulas

The Committee on Nutrition of the American Academy of Pediatrics, concerned about the composition of proprietary infant formulas, issued a policy statement on standards for these products.[24] These standards are based on the composition of milk from a healthy mother and are given in Table 4-4. The minimum amount for each nutrient is close to that of human milk and thus is the preferable quantity. The maximum amount is given for formulas intended for low birth weight or sick infants who take less formula and therefore need the higher nutrient content.

Nutrients provided by commonly used formula preparations are given in Table 4-5.

Hypoallergenic Formulas

The most commonly used products for infants who have conditions that contraindicate the use of cow's milk are the soy milks. The most frequently used formulas are constructed of protein isolated from soy meal fortified with methionine and corn syrup or sucrose, and soy or vegetable oils to which vitamins and minerals have been added. The trypsin inhibitor in raw soybean meal is inactivated during heat processing. The **goitrogenic effect** of soy is diminished by heating and by adding iodine.

The American Academy of Pediatrics has stated that the soy formulas are useful for potentially allergic infants but should not be used for infants with a documented allergy to cow's milk.[25] Soy formulas are commonly used for infants who are recovering from diarrhea, and for children with galactosemia and lactase deficiency because these formulas contain no lactose.

Other formulas are marketed for infants who do not tolerate either soy or cow's milk. Nutramigen is prepared from a casein hydrolysate and corn oil, Pregestimil contains a casein hydrolysate and medium-chain triglycerides, and Alimentum contains free amino acids, medium-chain triglycerides, safflower, and soy oils.

TABLE 4-4   *Recommended Ranges of Nutrient Levels in Infant Formulas[a]*

Nutrient (Per 100 kcal)	Adequate	Not to Exceed
Protein (gm)	1.8[b]	4.5
Fat (gm)	3.3 (30% of kcal)	6 (54% of kcal)
Including essential fatty acid (linoleate) (mg)	300 (2.7% of kcal)	
Vitamins		
A (IU)	250 (75 µg)[c]	750 (225 µg)[c]
D (µg) cholecalciferol[d]	1	2.5
K (µg)	4	—
E (tocopherol equivalents)[e]	0.5 (at least 0.5/gm linoleic acid)	
C (ascorbic acid) (mg)	8	—
B_1 (thiamin) (µg)	40	—
B_2 (riboflavin) (µg)	60	—
B_6 (pyridoxine) (µg)	20 µg/gm protein	—
B_{12} (µg)	0.15	
Niacin (µg)	250 (or 0.8 niacin equivalent)	—
Folic acid (µg)	4	—
Pantothenic acid (µg)	300	—
Biotin (µg)	1.5	—
Choline (mg)	7[f]	—
Inositol (mg)	4[f]	—
Minerals[g]		
Calcium (mg)	60[i]	—
Phosphorus (mg)	30[i]	—
Magnesium (mg)	6	—
Iron (mg)	0.15	2.5[i]
Iodine (µg)	5	25
Zinc (mg)	0.5	—
Copper (µg)	60	—
Manganese (µg)	5	100
Selenium (µg)	3	—
Sodium (mg)	20 (5.8 mEq/L)	60 (17.5 mEq/L)
Potassium (mg)	80 (13.7 mEq/L)	200 (34.3 mEq/L)
Chloride (mg)	55 (10.4 mEq/L)	150 (28.3 mEq/L)

[a]AAP Committee on Nutrition, 1976 Recommendations with 1982 Modifications.
[b]Nutritionally equivalent to casein. For use of other proteins refer to the Commentary on Breast Feeding and Infant Formulas, including Proposed Standards for Formulas. *Pediatrics* 57:278, 1976.
[c]Retinol equivalents.
[d]1 µg cholecalciferol = 40 IU vitamin D.
[e]1.49 IU = 1 mg *d*-α-tocopherol equivalent. The β and γ isomers have less activity.
[f]Average present in milk-based formulas; should be included in this amount in other formulas.
[g]Formula should be made with water low in fluoride and in all cases contain less than 45 µg/100 kcal. For explanation see Statement on Fluoride Supplementation: Revised Dosage Schedule. *Pediatrics* 63:150, 1979.
[h]Calcium to phosphorus ratio should not be less than 1.1 or more than 2.
[i]Prudence indicates there should be an upper limit for iron. If formula is labeled "infant formula with iron," it must not contain less than 1 mg/100 kcal.

TABLE 4-5 Nutrient Content of Commercially Available Cow's Milk–Base Formula

	Similac	Enfamil	SMA	Gerber	Good Start
Nutrient source					
Protein	Casein	Reduced mineral whey, casein	Demineralized whey, casein	Nonfat milk	Hydrolyzed, reduced-mineral whey
Fat	Soy oil, coconut oil, corn oil	Soy oil, coconut oil	Oleo; soybean, safflower, and coconut oils	Soy oil, coconut oil	Palm, safflower, and coconut oil
Carbohydrate	Lactose	Lactose	Lactose	Lactose	Lactose, corn syrup
Nutrients per 100 ml—normal dilution					
Energy (kcal)	68	67	67	67	67
Protein (gm)	1.5	1.5	1.5	1.5	1.6
Fat (gm)	3.6	3.8	3.6	3.6	3.4
Carbohydrate (gm)	7.2	6.9	7.2	7.1	7.4
Vitamin A (IU)	200	207	240	200	200
Vitamin D (IU)	40	42	42	40	40
Vitamin E (IU)	2	2	1	2	8
Vitamin C (mg)	5.5	5.5	5.8	6.0	5.3
Thiamin (µg)	65	53	71	67	40
Riboflavin (µg)	10	11	11	10	9
Niacin (mg) (equiv.)	0.7	0.8	1.0	0.7	0.5
Pyridoxine (µg)	40	42	40	40	40
Vitamin B_{12} (µg)	0.15	0.16	0.11	0.16	0.17
Folic acid (µg)	10	10.5	5.3	10	6
Calcium (mg)	51	46	44	50	42
Phosphorus (mg)	39	31.7	33	38	24
Magnesium (mg)	4	4	5	3.3	4.5
Iron (mg)	tr.	tr.	tr.	tr.	tr.
Zinc (mg)	0.5	0.5	0.37	0.5	0.5
Copper (µg)	60	63.4	48	60	53
Iodine (µg)	10	6.8	7	5.3	5.6

tr, Trace.

TABLE 4-6 *Nutrient Content of Soy Formulas and Other Milk Substitutes for Infants*

	Prosobee	Isomil	Nutramigen	Pregestimil	Alimentum
Nutrient source					
Protein	Soy protein	Soy protein	Casein hydrolysate	Casein hydrolysate	Casein hydrolysate, amino acids, medium-chain triglycerides,
Fat	Soy oil	Coconut oil, soy oil	Corn oil	Corn oil, medium chain triglycerides	fats, safflower, soy oils
Carbohydrate	Corn syrup solids	Sucrose, corn syrup solids	Modified tapioca, sucrose	Corn syrup solids, modified tapioca starch	Sucrose, modified tapioca starch
Nutrients per 100 ml—normal dilution					
Energy (kcal)	67	68	67	68	68
Protein (gm)	2.0	2.0	1.9	1.9	1.9
Fat (gm)	3.1	3.6	2.7	2.8	3.7
Carbohydrate (gm)	7.1	6.8	9.4	9.4	6.9
Vitamin A (IU)	210	203	210	250	203
Vitamin D (IU)	42.0	41.0	42.0	51.0	41.0
Vitamin E (IU)	2.2	2.0	2.1	2.5	2.1
Vitamin C (mg)	6.0	5.5	5.5	7.9	6.0
Thiamin (μg)	52.0	41.0	52.0	52.0	41.0
Riboflavin (μg)	63.0	61.0	63.0	63.0	61.0
Niacin (mg) (equiv.)	0.8	0.9	0.8	0.8	0.9
Pyridoxine (μg)	42.0	41.0	42.0	42.0	41.0
Vitamin B_{12} (μg)	0.2	0.3	0.2	0.2	0.3
Folic acid (μg)	11.0	10.0	10.6	10.6	10.0
Calcium (mg)	63.0	71.0	63.0	63.0	71.0
Phosphorus (mg)	50.0	51.0	42.0	42.0	51.0
Magnesium (mg)	7.4	5.1	7.4	7.4	5.1
Iron (mg)	1.3	1.2	1.3	1.3	1.2
Zinc (mg)	0.5	0.5	0.5	0.5	0.5
Copper (μg)	63.0	51.0	63.0	63.0	63.0
Iodine (μg)	7.0	10.0	4.8	4.8	4.8

These formulas have an unpleasant odor and taste and are rarely accepted by infants if not introduced before 8 or 9 months of age. The composition of non–cow's milk–base formulas is given in Table 4-6.

Goat's milk should be used with care during infancy. It is low in iron, folate, and vitamins C and D. It has a high solute load relative to cow's milk and may cause metabolic **acidosis** if fed in the first month of life.[26] If goat's milk is used before 6 months of age, it should be diluted with water and carbohydrate should be added.

Feeding infants formulas made from recipes that have not been proved to support adequate nutrition should be strongly discouraged. Malnutrition has been observed in infants fed a barley water, corn syrup, and whole milk formula.[27] Kwashiorkor has been reported in infants fed a nondairy creamer as a substitute for milk.[28] Beriberi has been diagnosed in a 6-week-old infant whose intake was limited to a nondairy creamer.[29]

Formula Preparation

Manufacturers market formulas as liquid concentrates to be prepared for feeding by mixing equal amounts of the liquid and water. Ready-to-feed formulas that require no preparation are available in an assortment of sizes (4-, 6-, 8-, and 32-oz bottles and cans). Powdered formula that is prepared by mixing 1 level tbsp of powder in 2 oz of water is also available. All of the formulas, when properly prepared and adequately supplemented, provide the nutrients important for the infant in an appropriate kcaloric concentration and present a solute load reasonable for the normal full-term infant. Errors in dilution caused by misunderstanding the proper method of preparation, improper measurements, or the belief of the parents that their child should have greater amounts of nutritious food can lead to problems.

Result of Errors in Formula Preparation

Failure to appropriately gain in height and weight has been observed as a result of dilution of ready-to-feed formulas in the manner concentrates are prepared. Mothers have been known to add extra water to formula in the belief that a more dilute formula might reduce spitting up by their infants.

Feeding undiluted concentrated formula increases kcalories, protein, and solutes presented to the kidneys for excretion and may predispose the young infant to **hypernatremia,** tetany, and obesity. Problems of improper formula preparation have most frequently been reported with the use of powdered formula and occur most often when an increased need for water caused by fever or infection is superimposed on consumption of an already high solute formula. Infants fed concentrated formula during such illnesses may become thirsty, demand more to drink, or refuse to consume more liquid because of anorexia secondary to illness. When the body is presented with more milk concentrated in the protein and solutes, the osmolality of the blood increases and hypernatremic dehydration may result. Cases of cerebral damage and gangrene of the extremities have been reported to be the result of hypernatremic dehydration and metabolic acidosis.[30,31] Feeding undiluted evaporated milk for 5 days after an illness during infancy has been reported to be the cause of gangrene resulting in the loss of limbs in a 61-week-old infant.[32] Infants who have been fed improperly prepared concentrated and ready-to-feed formulas with less dramatic long-term effects have been noted by many who counsel parents of very young infants.

Overdiluting formula or offering water as a substitute for milk or as a pacifier can lead to serious consequences. Water intoxication resulting in hyponatremia, irritability, and coma has been reported in several infants fed 8 oz of water after each feeding or fed water as a substitute for milk because of financial inability of parents to buy more formula.[32]

Anticipatory guidance of parents of young infants should include information on the variety of formulas available to feed their infants, differences in methods of preparation of each product, and the dangers of overdiluted formula and excessive water intake.

PREPARATION OF FORMULAS

Terminal sterilization of formulas is no longer practiced in North America. Most parents prepare formulas by the clean technique, one bottle at a time. It is important that the hands of the person preparing the formula be first carefully washed. All equipment to be used during preparation, including the cans that contain the milk, the bottles, and the nipples, must be thoroughly washed and rinsed. Once opened, cans of formula must be covered and refrigerated. The formula is prepared immediately before each feeding. After the formula has been heated and the infant has been fed, any remaining milk should be discarded. Warm milk is an excellent medium for bacterial growth.

FORMULA AND MILK FOR OLDER INFANTS

One manufacturer markets a cow's milk–base formula for older babies. It is designed to accompany the feeding of semisolid foods and is higher in protein and lower in fat than formula for the younger infant. However, examination of the nutrient intakes of infants from 6 months to 1 year reveals intakes of nutrients completely adequate without the additional protein. Pediatricians believe there is no advantage to the use of this milk; in fact, they believe there is no reason for its existence. Formulas prepared for younger infants are perfectly adequate for the first year.[33,34]

The use of whole milk is strongly discouraged in the first year. It has been noted to contribute to the incidence of anemia. Not only is there no iron in this milk, but it may cause a tiny blood loss from the intestinal tract. If a test of the baby's feces is done with paper impregnated with guiac solution or a fecal hemoglobin test is performed, small amounts of blood may be found. Over time this may lead to anemia.[35]

Nonfat and 2% milk are not recommended in the first 2 years. Infants fed nonfat milk increase their intake and continue to gain weight but at a slower rate. They lose body fat, as evidenced by decreases in skinfold thickness, and lose energy reserves. Because milk solids are often added to 2% milk, it may increase the renal

solute load. Even though one researcher suggested that infants over 6 months of age can achieve adequate growth and nurture consuming this milk in combination with infant food, it is not recommended.

Substitute or imitation milks should not be offered to infants. These milks, defined by the Food and Drug Administration as nutritionally equivalent to whole milk or skim milk based on the content of only 14 or 15 nutrients, omit many nutrients recommended as components for infant formulas and are not appropriate for infants.

ECONOMICS OF INFANT FEEDING

Several attempts have been made to compare the economic impact of the provision of energy and nutrients to support human lactation with the use of prepared infant formula. Investigators have reported disadvantages both to breast-feeding and to formula-feeding.

It must be remembered that the numbers of foods that supply important nutrients for lactation are large. Therefore the economic impact can range from a minimal increase to a sizeable increase over basic food costs.

The cost of commercially prepared formula varies with packaging. Concentrated formulas are the least expensive; ready-to-feed formulas are the most costly. The nutrient support for breast-feeding costs about 50% to 60% as much as the ready-to-feed formula.

Feeding the infant human milk can be less expensive or more expensive than commercially prepared formula depending on the parents' food purchasing practices and selection of foods. The many advantages of human milk far exceed any small monetary advantage for prepared formula. Parents may need help in the selection of appropriate low-cost foods, but breast-feeding should never be discouraged on an economic basis.

Bonding

Klaus and Kennell[36] have shown that the first few minutes and hours of life are important to maternal-infant **bonding.** This leads to attachment, the unique relationship between two people that is special and lasts forever. Mothers who have immediate skin contact with their infants shortly after birth have significantly more attachment behaviors. Breast-feeding facilitates this attachment.

FOODS IN THE INFANT'S DIET

Although no nutritional advantage can be expected from the early introduction of semisolid foods, many families feed them to their infants in the first month of life. Semisolid foods are introduced by parents on the advice of physicians, neighbors, and friends and because parents think that it is time for their infants to eat foods other than milk. Some parents add semisolid foods in the hope that they will encourage their infants to sleep through the night, a commonly held belief that has been proved untrue.[37] Other parents feed semisolid foods because they think that their infants are hungry, or because they consider the acceptance of these foods a developmental landmark.

Many infants receive table food by the time they can sustain a sitting posture. As infants begin to finger feed, increasing amounts of table food are included in their diets.

Semisolid Foods

The age of introduction of semisolid foods to infants in the United States declined from 1920, when these foods were seldom offered before 1 year of age, to 1960 to 1970, when they were frequently offered in the first weeks and months of life. Concern that this early introduction of semisolid foods predisposed infants to obesity and allergic reactions caused many health care professionals in the pediatric community to reexamine the appropriate age for the introduction of these foods. It is currently recommended that the feeding of semisolid foods be delayed until the infant's consumption of food is no longer a reflexive process, and the infant has the fine, gross, and oral motor skills to appropriately consume them (e.g., at approximately 4 to 6 months of age). Even so, many parents are reported to offer semisolid foods in the first month of life. Table

TABLE 4-7   *Suggested Ages for the Introduction of Semisolid Foods and Table Foods*

Food	Age (Months)		
	4-6	6-8	9-12
Iron-fortified cereals for infants	Add		
Vegetables		Add strained	Gradually delete strained foods, introduce table foods
Fruits		Add strained	Gradually delete strained foods, introduce chopped well-cooked or canned foods
Meats		Add strained or finely chopped table meats	Decrease the use of strained meats, increase the varieties of table meats
Finger foods such as arrowroot biscuits, oven-dried toast		Add those that can be secured with a palmar grasp	Increase the use of small-sized finger foods as the pincer grasp develops
Well-cooked mashed or chopped table foods, prepared without added salt or sugar			Add
Juice by cup			Add

4-7 gives suggested guidelines for the introduction of semisolid foods to normal infants.

A vast number of commercially prepared canned and frozen foods are marketed for feeding the infant. The new mother may select organically grown products or products prepared from farms and vineyards that probably use fertilizers and insecticides. She will find single foods and juices, vegetables with meat dinners, and mixed juices in $2\frac{1}{2}$-oz, 4-oz, or 6-oz jars (first foods, second foods, and third foods). Juices are marketed in 4-oz, 8-oz, and 25.3-oz bottles; some juices are prepared from fresh fruit, others from concentrates. Some children may find toddler meals interesting. Frozen meals of two or three foods in varying textures are available for babies.

Ready-to-serve single-grain dry cereals, such as rice cereal, are commonly the first food offered to infants because rice is considered the least allergenic of the cereal grains and because most cereals are fortified with electrolytic iron.

It appears to make little difference whether fruits or vegetables are introduced next. New foods should be added singly at intervals of no more than every 3 days. The introduction of nitrate-containing vegetables (e.g., carrots, beets, and spinach) is usually delayed until the infant is at least 4 months of age because the nitrate can be converted to nitrite in the stomach of the young infant. This can result in **methemoglobinemia.**

Infant's acceptance of semisolid foods. Parents report both immediate acceptance and rejection of semisolid foods, a fact that may relate to the mother's skill in feeding and her attitudes and feelings about these foods. Some parents who believe that the use of semisolid foods is important add them to the formula, cut a larger hole in the nipple, and feed the infant semisolid foods in this manner. One manufacturer markets a syringe with a plunger and a nipple with which mothers can force feed their babies by pushing the strained food through the nipple. These practices increase the energy and nutrient composition of the formula and may deprive the infant of experiences that are important in the development of feeding behavior.

Parents are reported to mix milk with cereal until it is almost liquid and can easily be fed by spoon. Fruits are commonly reported as favorites. Vegetables appear to be accepted without problems. Yellow vegetables, green beans, and peas have been reported to be preferred vegetables; spinach and beets are often reported to be rejected. Strained meats, especially liver, are frequently rejected by infants. Parents state that the infants reject the sticky, granular texture rather than the taste of meats. Older infants are, as a result, often fed strained and junior vegetable and meat mixtures and high-meat dinners.

Food additives and fortification in semisolid foods. Concern that intakes of sodium in the first year might predispose infants to later **hypertension** has resulted in the deletion of salt from commercially prepared infant foods. Sugar is added only to desserts. All cereals are fortified with niacin, thiamin, riboflavin, calcium, and phosphorus. All dry infant cereals are fortified with electrolytically reduced iron.

Strained, jarred cereals with fruit are fortified with ferrous sulfate. High-meat and mixed dinners are prepared with rice or wheat flour or tapioca to increase shelf life. Modified corn starch or tapioca starch is included in some desserts. Fruits and fruit juices are enriched with vitamin C.

Home preparation of semisolid foods. It is both possible and economical for parents to prepare semisolid foods for their infants with a food grinder, blender, or strainer. The foods should be carefully selected from high-quality fresh, frozen, or canned fruits, vegetables, and meats and should be prepared so that nutrients are retained. The area in which the foods are prepared and the utensils used in preparation should be meticulously cleaned. Salt and sugar should be used sparingly, if at all. When the food has been cooked, pureed, and strained, it should be packaged in individual portions and refrigerated or frozen so that a single portion can be heated and fed without compromising the quality and bacterial content of the entire batch. Directions for preparation of infant foods are given in the box on page 103. Home-prepared infant foods have a greater energy content than commercially prepared foods, and many have a higher salt content. Mothers who feed higher sodium intakes to infants are re-

---

✤

DIRECTIONS FOR HOME PREPARATION OF INFANT FOODS

1. Select fresh, high-quality fruits, vegetables, or meats.
2. Be sure all utensils, including cutting boards, grinders, and knives, are thoroughly clean.
3. Wash your hands before preparing the food.
4. Clean, wash, and trim the foods in as little water as possible.
5. Cook the foods until tender in as little water as possible. Avoid overcooking, which may destroy heat-sensitive nutrients.
6. Do not add salt. Add sugar sparingly. Do not add honey to foods for infants less than 1 year of age.*
7. Add enough water so that the food has a consistency that is easily pureed.
8. Strain or puree the food using an electric blender, a food mill, a baby food grinder, or a kitchen strainer.
9. Pour puree into ice cube tray and freeze.
10. When food is frozen hard, remove the cubes and store in freezer bags.
11. Unfreeze and heat in serving container the amount of food that will be consumed at a single feeding (in water bath or microwave oven).

From Pipes PL: *Nutrition in infancy.* In Krause MV, Mahan LK: *Food, nutrition, and diet therapy,* ed 8, Philadelphia, 1992, WB Saunders.
*Botulism spores have been reported in honey, and young infants do not have the immune capacity to resist this infection.

ported to add salt to their food more vigorously and have less education than mothers who offer lower sodium intakes.[38]

Fruit juice. When a high percentage of infants were fed evaporated milk formulas, fruit juices containing vitamin C were commonly introduced in the first month of life; the widespread use of vitamin-fortified formula and vitamin supplements made this practice unnecessary. Because a sucrose-containing liquid consumed as infants go to sleep sometimes results in extensive dental caries (see pages 114 and 115), it is generally recommended that the introduction of fruit juice be delayed until it can be consumed from a cup.

Nutrients in semisolid foods. Ranges of nutrients found in any group of foods for infants are sizeable (Table 4-8).

Jarred cereals are fortified with ferrous sulfate, and dry infant cereals are fortified with electrolytically reduced iron. Absorption of electrolytically reduced iron is approximately 5% of that of ferrous sulfate.

Strained and junior fruits contribute one third more kcalories, only a fraction of vitamin A, but twice as much vitamin C, as do vegetables when fed in equal amounts. Vegetables contribute small but important amounts of iron. Fruit juice is fortified with abundant amounts of vitamin C.

Strained and junior meats contribute significant amounts of protein and iron. High-meat dinners contribute less than half as much protein as pure meat; vegetables and meat contribute less than one fifth as much protein as pure meat. Strained and junior meats and high-meat dinners contribute similar amounts of iron; strained vegetables and meat contribute much less iron. Strained vegetables and meat provide slightly less than half as many kcalories as meat; high-meat dinners provide 75% as many kcalories as pure meat. Strained egg yolks have the highest kcalorie concentration of the prepared infant foods.

Strained and junior desserts are rich in carbohydrates and kcalories. A few are fortified with vitamin C. All have a sweet taste, and indiscriminate use of these items should be discouraged.

Infants receive table food soon after the in-

TABLE 4-8   *Ranges of Selected Nutrients Per Ounce in Commercially Prepared Infant Foods*

Food	Energy (kcal)	Protein (gm)	Iron (mg)	Vitamin A (IU)	Vitamin C (mg)
Dry cereal	102-114	2.0-10.2	17.0-21.0	0-20	0-1.4
Strained and junior fruits	11-23	0.0-0.2	0.0-0.2	3-206	0.2-35.3
Strained and junior vegetables	7-18	0.2-1.0	0.1-0.4	9-3348	0.6-3.6
Strained and junior meats	27-42	3.6-4.4	0.3-1.5	8-10811	0.3-0.7
Strained egg yolks	58	2.8	0.8	355	0.4
Strained and junior meats and vegetable dinners	20-33	1.6-2.6	0.0-0.3	22-237	0.1-0.5
Strained and junior vegetables and meat dinners	9-70	0.1-1.5	0.1-0.3	4-1114	0.2-1.2
Strained and junior desserts	17-25	0.0-0.8	0.0-0.1	4-71	0.2-8.9

From Gebhardt SE, Cutrufelli R, Matthews RH: Composition of foods, baby foods, raw, processed, prepared, *Agriculture Handbook No 8-3,* Washington, DC, 1978, US Department of Agriculture.

troduction of supplemental foods. Most often the foods offered to infants are the same foods prepared for the remainder of the family. Data from the HANES II study indicate that at 7 to 12 months of age the energy intake from table food increases dramatically and that from commercially prepared foods declines. At 1 year of age over 50% of the energy intake of infants is provided by table food.[39] Little guidance has been provided for parents to determine appropriate table foods to feed their infants, and cases of choking and aspiration have occurred. Hot dogs, nuts, grapes, carrots, and round candies should be avoided. Appropriate table foods for infants are shown in the box at right.

Honey, sometimes used as a sweetener for home-prepared infant foods and formulas and recommended for use on pacifiers to promote sucking in hypotonic infants, has been implicated as the only food source of spores of *Clostridium botulinum* during infancy. These spores are extremely resistant to heat and are not destroyed by present methods of processing

APPROPRIATE INTRODUCTORY TABLE FOOD FOR INFANTS

Mashed potatoes
Well-cooked mashed vegetables (carrots, stringless green beans)
Soft, mashed fruits (bananas, peaches, pears)
Peeled, mashed vienna sausage
Well-cooked, *finely ground,* ground meats
Yogurt
Canned, drained tuna or salmon (no bones)
Egg yolk, mashed with milk or water
Mashed or refried beans

honey. **Botulism** in infancy is caused by ingestion of the spores, which germinate into the toxin in the lumen of the bowel. Honey should not be fed to infants less than 1 year of age.[40]

Stages of development of feeding behavior indicate readiness to progress in textures of

TABLE 4-9 *Nutrient Content of Selected Table Foods Commonly Fed to Infants*

Food	Portion Size	Energy (kcal)	Protein (gm)	Iron (mg)	Vitamin A (IU)	Vitamin C (mg)
Cooked cereal (farina)	$\frac{1}{4}$ c	26	0.8	Dependent on level of fortification		
Mashed potato	$\frac{1}{4}$ c	34	1.1	0.2	10	5
French fried potato	3, 1″ to 2″	29	0.4	0.2		
Spaghetti	2 T	19	0.6	0.2		
Macaroni and cheese	2 T	54	2.1	0.2	107	
Liverwurst	$\frac{1}{2}$ oz	45	2.1	0.8	925	
Hamburger	$\frac{1}{2}$ oz	41	3.4	0.5	5	
Eggs	1 medium	72	5.7	1.0	520	
Cottage cheese	1 T	5	1.9		23.7	
Green beans	1 T	3	0.15	0.2	43	1
Cooked carrots	1 T	2.81			952	
Banana	$\frac{1}{2}$ small	40	0.5	0.35	90	5
Pudding	$\frac{1}{4}$ c	70	2.2	Trace	102	
Lollipop	1 oz hard candy	109				
Saltine crackers	1	12	0.2			
Vanilla wafer	$\frac{1}{4}$″ thick, $1\frac{3}{4}$″ diameter	18	0.2			
Cheese strips	$\frac{1}{4}$ oz	28	1.78		92	

From Adams CF: Nutritive value of American foods in common units, *Agriculture Handbook No 456*, Washington, DC, 1975, US Department of Agriculture.

food and are discussed in the section on development of feeding behavior. The energy and nutrient composition of foods offered must also be considered. Examples of table foods often offered and their contribution to an infant's dietary intake are given in Table 4-9.

INTAKES OF INFANTS

Volume of intake and energy consumption is influenced not only by the infant's requirements for maintenance, growth, and activity but also by the parents' sensitivity to and willingness to accept cues of hunger and satiety, parental eagerness for the infant to feed, and the parents' skill at feeding. The kcaloric concentration of the formula is also a determinant of the volume of intake, kcalorie intake, and growth in early infancy.[41]

Infants feed differently and mothers vary in their sensitivity to their child's cues. Thoman[42] found that primiparous mothers spent more time stimulating their infants during feeding than did multiparous mothers, yet their infants spent less time sucking during breast-feeding and consumed less from bottles at feeding than did infants of multiparous mothers in the newborn period. Primiparous mothers stimulated their infants during pauses between sucking. The stimulation prolonged the pause and reduced the total consumption of food.

Growth Response to Feeding

Normal breast-fed infants regulate their milk intake to meet their needs for normal growth and development. Formula-fed infants have been reported to regain their birth weights more rapidly than breast-fed infants.

Exclusively breast-fed infants grow in length more slowly than formula-fed infants. Rates of weight gain and energy deposition are greater in bottle-fed babies than those who are breast-fed.[43]

Energy intakes. Per unit of size, infants consume the greatest number of kcalories between 14 and 28 days of age, a time known to many pediatricians as the hungry period. Mothers who are breast-feeding may find talking to a lactation counselor helpful when demands for milk suddenly increase. After this time, although total quantity and energy intakes increase, intakes per unit of size decrease. Infants consume greater amounts of food and nutrients at a decreasing amount per unit of body size as they grow older.

Wide ranges of volume of intake and energy consumption throughout the first year of life have been noted in both breast- and formula-fed infants by several researchers.[44,45]

Breast-fed infants consume less milk than bottle-fed infants. When semisolid foods are added to the infant's diet, they replace. rather than supplement, milk.[46] This decrease in milk intake appears to be progressive as the intake of semisolid foods increases.

Table 4-10 shows ranges of intakes of breast-fed and bottle-fed babies in an Australian study.[47]

Studies by Fomon and others[41] have shown

TABLE 4-10 *Consumption in kcal/kg Body Weight (Mean and Range of Breast Milk Substitutes [BMS] and Breast Milk [BM] by 150 Infants Aged 1-3 Months and Fed Ad Libitum)*

Age (Months)	BMS (kcal/kg)	BM (kcal/kg)
1	120	112
	(78-201)	(74-146)
2	107	108
	(75-168)	(74-145)
3	101	96
	(76-130)	(70-120)

From Hofvander Y and others: *Acta Paediatr Scand* 71:953, 1982.

that the kcaloric concentration of the formula influences kcalorie intake during the first 41 days of life. Female infants who were fed formulas kcalorically concentrated to 100 kcal/100 ml (30 kcal/oz) reduced their volume of intake but consumed greater numbers of kcalories, whereas those who were fed formulas kcalorically diluted to 54 kcal/100 ml (16.5 kcal/oz) increased their volume of intake but consumed fewer kcalories, as compared with infants who were fed formulas of normal kcaloric concentration. After this period, adjustments in volume of intake were sufficient so that kcalorie intakes were similar for the entire 111-day study period. Infants who were fed the kcalorically concentrated formula were, however, heavier for their lengths at 111 days of age than were infants who had been fed the kcalorically dilute formulas.[41] Male infants who were fed formulas concentrated to 133 kcal/100 ml (40 kcal/oz) reduced their volume of intake but consumed greater numbers of kcalories during the first 84 days of life. They experienced supernormal rates of growth in both length and weight during the first 42 days of life compared with infants who were fed formulas providing 67 kcal/100 ml (20 kcal/oz).[41]

FEEDING BEHAVIORS

Defining developmental readiness for changes in textures of food and the acquisition of self-feeding skills is important in establishing realistic goals for normal and handicapped infants and children. Illingworth and Lister[48] have defined a critical or sensitive period of development in relation to eating, a time at which a specific stimulus, solid food, must be applied for the organism to learn a particular action, that of accepting and eating table food, which is more difficult to masticate. They point out that an infant learns to chew at about 6 or 7 months of age; thus he or she is, at this point, developmentally ready to consume food. If solid foods are withheld until a later age, the child will have considerably more difficulty in accepting them.

In 1937 Gesell and Ilg[49] published observations of their extensive studies of the feeding behavior of infants. Their observations are as valid today as they were then. **Cineradiographic** techniques developed since then have permitted more detailed descriptions of sucking, suckling, and swallowing.[50,51] More recently physiologic studies have refined and clarified the original observation.[52]

Development of feeding behavior depends on the maturation of the central nervous system, which controls the acquisition of fine, gross, and oral motor skills, each of which influences the child's ability to consume food and the manner in which he or she suckles, sucks, chews, and swallows. Normal development proceeds in an orderly and predictable **cephalocaudal** sequence. Likewise, the sequence of acquisition of feeding skills occurs in a predictable order influenced by the acquisition of function and behavior.

It is important to recognize that, even though the normal neonate is well prepared to suck and swallow at birth, the physical and neuromotor maturation during the first year alters both the form of the oral structure and the methods by which the infant extracts liquids from a nipple. Each of the parameters of change influences the infant's eating skills. At birth the tongue is disproportionately large in comparison with the lower jaw and essentially fills the oral cavity. The mandible is retruded relative to the maxilla, which protrudes over the mandible by approximately 2 mm. When the mouth is closed, the jaws do not rest on top of each other, but the tip of the tongue lies between the upper and lower jaws. There is a fat pad in each of the cheeks. It is thought that these pads serve as a prop for the buccinator muscle, maintaining rigidity of the cheeks during suckling. The lips of the neonate are also instrumental in sucking and suckling and have characteristics appropriate for their function at this age. A mucosal fold on the free edge of the gums in the region of the eyetooth buds of both jaws is instrumental in sealing off the oral cavity as the lips close around a nipple. The mucosal fold disappears by the third or fourth month when the lips have developed muscular control to seal the oral cavity.

The sucking, swallowing, and respiratory centers are located in close proximity within the brain stem. The rhythmic functions must be co-ordinated to allow for the crossing of the alimentary and respiratory pathways in the **pharynx.** Normal full-term newborn infants coordinate sucking, breathing, and swallowing. Newborn infants suck reflexively; they can breathe and suck simultaneously.

SUCKING

Cineradiographic studies by Ardran, Kemp, and Lind[50,51] led investigators to believe that processes of breast- and bottle-sucking were similar. More recent physiological studies have shown differences in the sucking pattern of breast- and bottle-fed infants.[52] In the initial phase of sucking the facial muscles constrict to form a seal around the nipple. The nipple is compressed against the palate by the tongue.

During breast-feeding the human nipple elongates to approximately twice its length; rhythmic movements of the tongue and lower lip during suck result in lowering of the mandible and protrusion of the tongue. Both positive and negative pressure create a suction. The bottle-fed infant creates a suction by pistonlike movements of the tongue, allowing for extraction of the milk.

At the beginning of a feed infants suck vigorously and continuously. This initial sucking is followed by a period when bursts alternate with periods of no sucking, or a pause. Sucking frequencies are relatively constant during bottle-feeding, but pressures vary markedly. There is considerable variability in milk flow within and among the types of nipples on the market, the most important determinant being the size of the nipple hole. Several factors influence the sucking pattern. Sweet solutions increase the continuity and speed of sucks. The infant's state of wakefulness influences the pressure and time between sucks. Near the end of a feeding there is a decrease in sucking pressure and an increase in the time between sucking clusters.

During swallowing the food lies in a swallow preparatory position on the groove of the tongue. The distal portion of the soft palate is raised toward the adenoidal pad in the roof of the epipharynx. The tongue is pressed upward against the nipple so that the bolus of milk follows gravity down the sloping tongue reaching the pharynx. As the bolus moves downward, the posterior wall of the pharynx comes forward to displace the soft palate toward the dorsal surface of the tongue, and the larynx is elevated and arched backward. The bolus is expressed from the pharynx by peristaltic movements of the pharyngeal wall toward the back of the tongue and the larynx. The bolus spills over the pharyngoepiglottic folds into the lateral food channels and then into the esophagus.[51]

The tonsils and lymphoid tissue play an important role as infants swallow; they assist in keeping the airway open and in keeping food away from the posterior pharyngeal wall as the infant is fed in a reclining position, thus delaying nasopharyngeal closure until food has reached the lower pharynx.

As the infant grows older, the oral cavity enlarges so that the tongue no longer fills the mouth. The tongue grows differentially at the tip and attains motility in the larger oral cavity. The elongated tongue can be protruded to receive and pass solids between the gum pads and

TABLE 4-11   Sequence of Development of Feeding Behavior

Age	Reflexes	Oral, Fine, Gross Motor Development
1-3 months	Rooting, suck, and swallow reflexes are present at birth Tonic neck reflex present	Head control is poor Secures milk with a suckling pattern, the tongue projecting during a swallow By the end of the third month, head control is developed
4-6 months	Rooting and bite reflexes fade Tonic neck reflex fades by 16 weeks	Changes from a sucking pattern to a mature suck with liquids Sucking strength increases Munching pattern begins Grasps with a palmar grasp Grasps, brings objects to mouth, and bites them
7-9 months	Gag reflex is less strong as chewing of solids begins and normal gag is developing Choking reflex can be inhibited	Munching movements begin when solid foods are eaten Rotary chewing begins Sits alone Has power of voluntary release and resecural Holds bottle alone Develops an inferior pincer grasp
10-12 months		Reaches for a spoon Bites nipples, spoons, and crunchy foods Grasps bottle and foods and brings them to the mouth Can drink from a cup that is held Tongue is used to lick food morsels off the lower lip Finger feeds with a refined pincer grasp

Modified from Gesell A, Ilg FL: *Feeding behavior of infants,* Philadelphia, 1937, JB Lippincott.

erupting teeth for mastication. Mature feeding is characterized by separate movements of the lip, tongue, and gum pads or teeth.

Sequence of Development of Feeding Behavior

The sequence of development of feeding behavior is given in Table 4-11 and Figure 4-1.

Newborn infants can neither focus their eyes nor direct their hands, yet they find nourishment. The **rooting** reflex, caused by stroking of the perioral skin including the cheeks and lips, causes an infant to turn toward the stimulus so that the mouth comes in contact with it. Stimulus placed on the lips causes involuntary movements toward it, closure, and pouting in

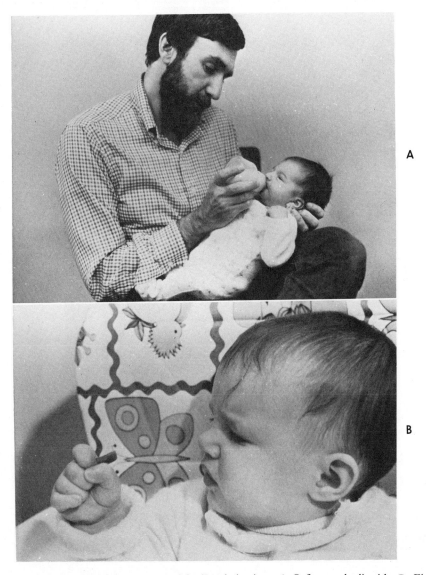

FIG. 4-1 Sequence of development of feeding behaviors. **A,** Infant sucks liquids. **B,** Five-month-old infant begins to finger feed.

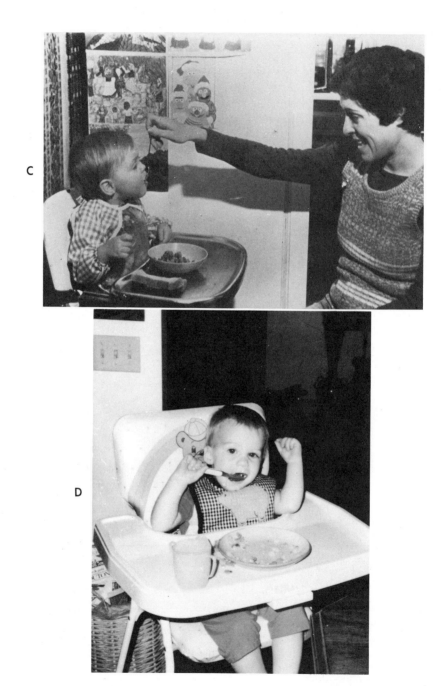

FIG. 4-1, *cont'd*.   Sequence of development of feeding behaviors. **C,** Eight-month-old infant is fed table food. **D,** Eleven-month-old infant begins to feed himself.

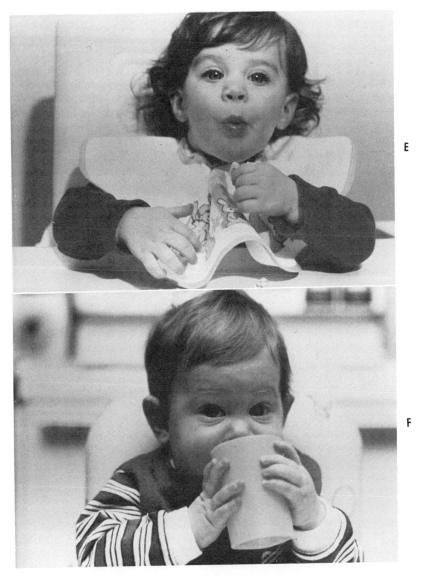

FIG. 4-1, cont'd Sequence of development of feeding behaviors. **E,** Ten-month-old infant purses her lips. **F,** Twelve-month-old infant drinks from cup.

preparation for sucking. These reflexes thus enable the infant to suck and receive nourishment. Both rooting and suckling can be elicited when the infant is hungry but are absent when the infant is satiated. During feeding the neonate assumes a **tonic** neck position; the head is rotated to one side and the arm on that same side is extended while the other is fisted. The infant seeks the nipple by touch and obtains milk from the nipple with a rhythmic suckle. Semisolid foods, introduced at an early age into diets of many infants and fed by spoon, are secured in the same manner as is the milk, by stroking movements of the tongue with the tongue projecting as the spoon is withdrawn. Frequently, food is expelled from the mouth.

By 5 weeks of age the infant can focus the eyes on faces, and by 12 weeks of age the gaze can be shifted. At 10 weeks of age the infant is able to recognize the breast or bottle as the source of food.

4 to 6 months. By 16 weeks of age a more mature sucking pattern has become evident, with the tongue moving back and forth as opposed to the earlier up-and-down motions. Spoon-feeding is easier because the infant can draw in the lower lip as the spoon is removed. The tonic neck position has faded, and the infant assumes a more symmetrical position with the head at midline. The hands close on the bottle. By 20 weeks of age the infant can grasp on **tactile** contact with a palmar squeeze. By 24 weeks of age the infant can reach for and grasp an object on sight. In almost every instance the object goes into the mouth.

7 to 9 months. Between 24 and 28 weeks of age the beginning of chewing movements, an up-and-down movement of the jaws, occurs. This, combined with the ability to grasp, the hand-to-mouth route of grasped objects, and sitting posture, indicates a readiness of the infant to finger feed. Infants at this age grasp with a **palmar grasp.** Therefore the shape of the food presented for the child to finger feed is important. Cookies, melba toast, crackers, and teething biscuits are frequently introduced at this stage.

Between 28 and 32 weeks of age the infant gains control of the trunk and can sit alone without support. The sitting infant has greater mobility of the shoulders and arms and is freer to reach and grasp. The grasp is more digital than the earlier palmar grasp. The infant is able to transfer items from one hand to another and learns to voluntarily release and resecure objects. The beginning of chewing patterns (up-and-down movements of the jaws) is demonstrated. The tongue shows more maturity in regard to spoon-feeding than to drinking. Food is received from the spoon by pressing the lips against the spoon, drawing the head away, and drawing in the lower lip. The infant is aware of a cup and can suck from it. Milk frequently leaks from the corners of the mouth as the tongue is projected before swallowing.

Critical stage of development. The introduction of soft, mashed (but not strained) foods is appropriate at this stage of development. In fact, it is at this stage of development that Illingworth and Lister believe it is critical to introduce the infant to harder-to-masticate foods.[48]

Between 6 and 12 months of age the infant gradually receives greater amounts of food from the family menu and less and less of the pureed and strained items. Foods should be carefully selected and modified so that they are presented in a form that can be manipulated in the mouth without the potential of choking and **aspiration,** as may occur with small grains of rice or corn. Many parents mash well-cooked vegetables and canned fruits and successfully offer them to their infants. Well-cooked ground meat dishes, such as ground meat in gravies or sauces, appear to be easily accepted, as are liverwurst, minced chicken livers, and drained tuna fish. Custards, puddings, and ice cream soon become favorites.

Self-feeding. By 28 weeks of age infants are able to help themselves to their bottle in sitting postures, although they will not be able to tip the bottle adaptively as it empties until about 32 weeks of age. By the end of the first year they can completely manage bottle-feeding alone.

By 32 weeks of age infants bring their heads forward to receive the spoon as it is presented to them. The tongue shows increased motility and allows for considerably increased manipulation of food in the mouth before swallowing.

At the end of the first year, infants are able to manipulate food in the mouth with definite chewing movements.

9 to 12 months. During the fourth quarter of the first year, the child develops an increasingly precise **pincer grasp.** The bottle can be managed alone and can be resecured if it is lost. Infants at this age are increasingly conscious of what others do and often imitate the models set for them. By 1 year of age the patterns of eating have changed from sucking to beginning rotary chewing movements. Children understand the concept of the container and the contained, have voluntary hand-to-mouth movements and a precise pincer grasp, and can voluntarily release and resecure objects. They are thus prepared to learn to feed themselves, a behavior they learn and refine in the second year.

Infant feeding. Presented with the breast of an adequately fed, lactating mother or the nipple on a bottle of properly prepared formula, the hungry infant receives both biochemical and psychosocial nurturance. Most mothers warm the milk to body temperature. The infant held in a semireclining position who is offered the nipple sucks and receives the major portion of nourishment in 20 minutes. Most physicians recommend a flexible self-demand schedule. Newborn infants initially feed six to eight times a day at intervals of 2 to 4 hours and will consume 2 to 3 oz at a feeding (Figure 4-2).

Parents should recognize that infants are quite variable in their eating patterns. Not uncommonly they may want to eat at an interval

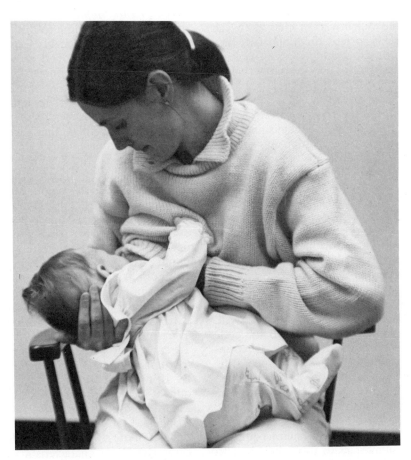

FIG. 4-2   Mother breast feeds her 4-month-old infant.

of 2 hours, then wait 5 hours for the next feeding.

By 2 weeks of age most infants have increased the amount of milk consumed at a feeding and reduced the number of feedings to six. By 2 months of age, most infants are fed five times a day and sleep through the night. By 6 months of age, most consume three meals and four milk feedings a day.

Infants swallow air as well as formula during feeding. Holding the child in an upright position and gently patting the back encourages expulsion of swallowed air and prevents distention and discomfort.

Difficulties in infant feeding. During feeding both the parents and the infant receive satisfaction and pleasure. The infant is pleased because hunger is satiated; the parents are pleased because they have fulfilled the needs of their newborn infant. Infants learn that they can trust their parents to feed them and that they please their parents by eating. Successful feeding provides the basis for the warm, trusting relationship that develops between infants and their parents.

Difficulties in feeding resulting from a weak suck, maternal difficulty in establishing adequate lactation, improper equipment such as firm nipples with small holes, or other causes are frustrating to both infants and their mothers. Hungry infants cry more frequently, demand to be fed more often, and may create anxiety in conscientious and concerned mothers.

Since infants have not yet learned to separate themselves from others in the environment, they perceive the feelings of others as their own immediate feelings in any particular situation. Thus they are easily susceptible to parental anxieties and may reflect these by crying and not eating well. When the infant does not eat well, parental anxieties may increase. Thus the cycle can begin. It is possible that such bottle-fed infants will feed more easily when presented the bottle by a less intense person. However, when the infant is successfully fed by another, the parents' feelings of inadequacy and anxiety may be increased.

To achieve successful parent-child feeding experiences, it is important to work directly with the parents. It may be necessary for the professional to determine any problems with equipment used and positioning, then to model a calm, relaxed feeding situation for the parents. Care should be taken not to usurp the parents' role, thus increasing their feelings of inadequacy. An approach that seems to be beneficial to all concerned is to (1) model a feeding, (2) sit beside the parents and talk them through a feeding while showing them how to use a relaxed position, (3) reinforce parenting behaviors, and (4) help them to become aware of cues from the infant that he or she is relaxed.

This method may need to be used for several feedings until the parent and infant can achieve a successful, relaxed experience. Even then, parents may need further support in their continuing efforts to create a relaxed and warm relationship with their infants during feeding.

Inadequate human milk. Several cases of malnutrition and failure to thrive have been reported in breast-fed infants secondary to an inadequate milk intake, and thus an inadequate energy and nutrient intake.[53] Most of the mothers were primiparous women who seemed intelligent and mature. They appeared to be unaware that their babies were not gaining or were losing weight or that their milk production was inadequate.

Feeding the baby at both breasts more frequently may help to increase the mother's milk supply. However, if weight gain continues to be less than adequate, the temporary use of supplemental feedings is appropriate.

It is important for parents to recognize that newborn infants demonstrate a pattern of crying in early life and that a crying infant is not a symptom of inadequate mothering. The amount of time an infant cries increases from 2 weeks of age to approximately 6 weeks of age, when it peaks. After this time crying decreases. The major concentration period is from 6 PM to 11 PM. Other periods of crying occur in the morning from 4 AM to 7 AM and 9 AM to 11 AM. By 10 weeks of age most infants become more quiet.[54] Seldom is this crying a symptom of an allergy, and it is no indication for formula change.

Baby Bottle Tooth Decay. **Baby bottle decay (BBTD),** a characteristic pattern of tooth decay of all the upper and sometimes the lower posterior teeth, is often observed in children who are given sweetened liquids by bottle at naptime and nighttime as they go to sleep. As the children suck, the tongue protrudes slightly from the mouth, covering the lower front teeth. Liquids then spread over the upper and lower posterior teeth. Sucking stimulates the flow of saliva, which washes the debris from the teeth and promotes the secretion of compounds that buffer the acids in plaque. When babies are awake, they swallow the liquid quickly. However, if they fall asleep, sucking stops and the salivary flow and buffering are reduced. The sweetened liquid pools around the teeth unprotected by the extended tongue, and bacterial plaque has contact with the carbohydrate during the hours of sleep.[55]

Infant formulas, fruit juice, human milk, and cow's milk consumed when infants are falling asleep may cause decay. To prevent this dental destruction it has been suggested that infants be held when fed, burped, and put to bed without a bottle.

Colic. Parents of colicky babies—those who are otherwise healthy and well fed but who have an inconsolable agonizing cry for several hours each day, draw their legs onto the abdomens, and pass large amounts of gas—often request changes in the infants' formula. A number of psychosocial and dietary causes have been suggested as the cause of colic. Food allergy or intolerance is one of the causes in 12% to 15% of colicky infants. A 2- to 3-month trial of hypoallergenic formula such as Nutramigen may be warranted, but parents should not be led to believe that their colicky baby will have a lifetime of food allergy problems. Food intolerances or allergies in infants may be short lived.[57,58] The response to the formula change may be to mechanisms other than allergy. It has been suggested that colic in some breast-fed infants be resolved by eliminating milk from the mothers' diets.[59]

Spitting. Both spitting and regurgitation can occur in infants and usually cause concern for parents. During the early months of life some otherwise healthy infants spit a small amount of any milk or food ingested at each feeding. Although the infants do not fail to thrive, parents may seek help in resolving this situation. There is no therapy. The problem usually resolves itself by the time the infants can sustain sitting.

Regurgitation, the effortless expulsion of gastric contents, is a symptom that demands medical evaluation. The most common cause of persistent regurgitation is gastroesophageal reflux, the result of decreased pressure in the lower esophageal sphincter. A prone position in contrast to a seated position increases sleep time and reduces crying time in these infants. There seems to be no difference between the prone or seated position regarding awake crying time.[60] Surgery may be indicated.

Distractions. Some infants are easily distracted by noise or by other influences in the environment. Such infants feed more easily at the night feeding. Presentation of the bottle in a quiet, partially darkened room by a rested parent may promote successful feeding for both the parent and the infant.

Parental perception of feeding problems. Many parents perceive their infants as having feeding problems. Problems include refusal of a particular food because of taste or texture, dissatisfaction with amount consumed, spitting up, developmentally related problems such as refusing the bottle or refusing to be fed, and only finger-feeding. Such difficulties are usually of short duration and rarely compromise an infant's nutrient intake or physical growth. Parents, however, may need reassurance that their infant's development is normal and that their food-related behaviors are not of nutritional concern.

Recognizing Satiation Cues and Readiness to Progress

Successful infant feeding is generally regarded in our society as a measure of competent parenthood. As such, it is a reinforcing experience to parents. They must learn to recognize and to accept their infant's cues, since the infant uses a variety of cries and vocalizations to express needs. Parents, for one reason or another, cannot always discriminate their infant's cries. Consequently, they give food to satisfy all types of infant discomforts. The infant, in turn, may not learn to discriminate hunger from other discomforts and may learn to rely on eating to satisfy a wide variety of needs. Parents must learn to recognize satiation of hunger in infants and be willing to accept their infant's expressions of satisfaction, to set limits on

TABLE 4-12   *Satiety Behaviors in Infants*

Age	Behavior
4-12 weeks	Draws head away from nipple
	Falls asleep
	When nipple is reinserted, closes lips tightly
	Bites nipple, purses lips, or smiles and lets go
16-24 weeks	Releases nipple and withdraws head
	Fusses or cries
	Obstructs mouth with hands
	Increases attention to surroundings
	Bites nipple
28-36 weeks	Changes posture
	Keeps mouth tightly closed
	Shakes head as if to say "no"
	Plays with utensils
	Hands become more active
	Throws utensils
40-52 weeks	Behaviors of above period typical
	Sputters with tongue and lips
	Hands bottle or cup to parent

From Pipes PL: *Health care professionals.* In Garwood G, Fewell R: *Educating handicapped infants,* Rockville, Md, 1982, Aspen Systems. With permission by Aspen Systems; modified from Gesell A, Ilg FL: *Feeding behavior of infants,* Philadelphia, 1937, JB Lippincott.

amounts of food offered to eager eaters, and to decline the natural inclination to overfeed infants who please others by accepting more food. Satiety behaviors of infants are given in Table 4-12.

Parents who are eager for their infant to empty the bottle encourage excessive intakes of food and can reinforce eating to the extent that obesity may result. Infants may be offered food and formula by many people: parents, baby sitters, aunts, siblings, and others.

Parents who are dissatisfied with their infant's food intake may find that the infant has reduced the intake to compensate for food offered by others. Additional cues that parents must recognize are those that indicate the infant's readiness for increasingly independent feeding experiences. The infant's ability to put objects in his or her mouth and to chew on them indicates a readiness to use increasingly solid foods and to begin finger-feeding. Anticipatory guidance to parents during this period about developmental changes is an important factor in their acceptance of and adaptation to their infant's behavior.

Recognizing Nutrients and Energy Needs in the Infant's Diet

Most infants consume foods that provide nutrients in excess of recommended amounts, with the exception of iron. Human milk and formula provide the major source of protein and calcium and important sources of vitamin A and the B vitamins in early life. Breast-fed infants should receive supplements of iron, vitamin D, and fluoride. Iron-fortified formulas contribute appreciable amounts of iron in early infancy.

Most lactating mothers need to be away occasionally when it is time to feed their infant. It is therefore advantageous for the infant to have an occasional bottle with a rubber nipple after lactation is well established. Ready-to-feed formulas can be used, but many mothers prefer to express their own milk for such occasions. Manual expression is the choice of most mothers. However, manual and electric pumps are on the market and may be preferred by mothers who work and express for a day or more.

Once expressed, the milk must be stored so that it will be microbiologically safe with a minimal loss of nutrients. Freezing protects it from contamination with minimal change in milk composition. Immunoglobulin levels and nutritional properties are essentially unchanged. Milk should be refrigerated or frozen at once. It can be safely held in a refrigerator for 24 hours and in a freezer for up to 3 months.

Often breast-fed infants refuse a rubber nipple from their mother. They usually accept such a feeding from their father, a friend, or a babysitter.

Because of the great variability in kcalories and nutrients provided by foods offered to infants, selection of foods and the amounts offered should be based on the infant's rate of gain in height and weight as well as on nutrient needs. The introduction and acceptance of heme iron–containing foods before the time homogenized milk replaces iron-fortified formula or before iron supplements are discontinued is important because the infant must continue to consume foods that provide this nutrient as it is deleted from milk or supplements. Fruit juice offers sources of vitamin C when vitamin-containing formulas are no longer consumed. It seems reasonable to encourage parents of infants whose gains in weight are more rapid than gains in length to feed the infants lower-kcalorie infant foods such as vegetables and dinners. Parents of infants whose increments of weight gains are small should be encouraged to feed greater amounts of the higher-kcalorie strained meats and fruits. Amounts of semisolid foods offered to infants should be adjusted to their appetites and rates of weight gain. Experiences with a variety of flavors and textures are thought to be conducive to acceptance of a variety of foods in later life.

Programs to Help Parents Optimize the Nutritional Status of Infants

Various federal and state programs include a component to improve the nutritional status of infants. State and local health departments have always considered nutrition services during pregnancy, lactation, and infancy an essential component of preventive health care. Nutritionists in these programs provide information about nutrition in infancy by preparing materials for public distribution, serving as a resource for other health workers, and participating in mother-infant and other classes.

Nutritionists provide nutrition education and individual counseling to parents in a number of federally funded programs designed to meet the needs of children at risk. These services may be found in local health departments and Migrant Health, Appalachian Health, and Indian Health programs. Diagnostic clinics for infants and children also provide nutrition services, including nutrition screening, counseling, education, referral, and follow-up. Such clinics are included in programs funded to serve children, youth, and the developmentally delayed.

One program, the Special Supplemental Food Program for Women, Infants, and Children (WIC), provides specific food supplements to pregnant and lactating women and to infants and children up to 5 years of age who are at nutritional risk because of nutritional needs and inadequate income. The program provides only formula for the first 3 months, then the following food for formula-fed infants 4 to 12 months of age:

Iron-fortified infant formula

Infant cereal containing 45 mg iron/100 gm

Single-strength canned, frozen concentrated, or infant juices that contain a minimum of 30 mg vitamin C/dl

Mothers of breast-fed infants may be certified to receive the supplemental food themselves. Some breast-fed infants may be certified to receive partial food packages that include iron-fortified cereal and fruit juice.

It is important to recognize that the specific formulas, quantities of food provided, and the methods of implementation vary from state to state. Many states provide vouchers that can be redeemed at grocery stores for the specific foods; a few give the foods directly to the parents. Breast-feeding promotion and nutrition education are required components of this program.

Summary

Various combinations of milks, supplements, and semisolid foods can provide an adequately nourishing diet for infants. Maturation of the oral and fine motor skills indicate appropriate stages for the introduction of semisolid and solid foods. Current recommendations include breast-feeding by an adequately nourished mother, the introduction of semisolid foods at 4 to 6 months of age, and the introduction of finger foods when infants reach out, grasp, and bring items to their mouths.

If the mother is unable or unwilling to breast feed, many properly constructed infant formulas are marketed that have been proved to support normal growth and development in infants. It is to the formula-fed baby's advantage to receive a formula with iron.

Infants should be permitted to establish their own feeding schedule and to be fed to satiety. When they develop a voluntary mature sucking pattern, the introduction of semisolid food is appropriate. When munching and rotary chewing begin, the introduction of soft-cooked table food is appropriate. Infants can begin to drink from a cup with help between 9 and 12 months of age.

Difficulties in infant feedings that indicate a need for intervention include inadequate milk production by the mother, poor suck, improper formula preparation, and parental anxiety about feeding their infants.

REVIEW QUESTIONS

1. Why are infants vulnerable to water imbalance?
2. List nutritional and other advantages of human milk.
3. Which formulas are suitable for infants allergic to cow's and soy milk formula?
4. Describe oral differences in the manner babies consume milk from the breast and from the bottle.
5. List developmental landmarks that indicate readiness for nonliquid milk foods.
6. How does a mother know if an infant has had enough to eat?

SUGGESTED LEARNING ACTIVITIES

1. Investigate the incidence of breast-feeding in the maternity unit of a local hospital.
2. Investigate local agencies in the community that provide support for the lactating mother.
3. Describe formula products available for feeding infants in the community.
4. Compare the cost of homemade and commercially available foods for infants.
5. Describe how useful mothers find the nutrition information found on commercially prepared baby food container labels.
6. Observe infants feeding at 2, 4, 7, and 9 months of age, and describe changes in the way babies secure their food.
7. Describe appropriate therapy for breast-fed babies who are thought to be gaining weight too fast.

Terms and Concepts

Provided here for your review is a listing of terms and concepts within this chapter. The definitions for terms can be found in the glossary, which begins on page 413. To aid your understanding of the terms' and concepts' application within this text, the page number designating the first mention of each term or concept within the chapter is given.

acidosis, 99

allergens, 95

amylase, 88

aspiration, 104

baby bottle tooth decay, 114

bonding, 100

botulism, 104

casein, 90

cephalocaudal, 107

cineradiographic, 107

colostrum, 89

goitrogenic effect, 95

hypernatremia, 99

hypertension, 102

methemoglobinemia, 102

palmar grasp, 112

pharynx, 107

pincer grasp, 113

rooting, 109

tactile, 112

tonic, 112

whey, 90

REFERENCES

1. Lindberg T: Proteolytic activity in duodenal juice in infants, children, and adults, *Acta Paediatr Scand* 63:805, 1974.
2. Fomon SJ: *Infant nutrition,* ed 2, Philadelphia, 1974, WB Saunders.
3. Watkins JB: Bile acid metabolism and fat absorption in newborn infants, *Pediatr Clin North Am* 2:501, 1974.
4. Filer LJ, Mattson FH, Fomon SJ: Triglyceride configuration and fat absorption by the human infant, *J Nutr* 99:293, 1969.

5. Bayless TM, Christopher NL: Disaccharidase deficiency, *Am J Clin Nutr* 22:181, 1969.

6. Hadorn B and others: Quantitative assessment of exocrine pancreatic function in infants and children, *J Pediatr* 73:39, 1968.

7. Ryan AS and others: Recent declines in breast-feeding in the United States, 1984 through 1989, *Pediatrics* 88:719, 1991.

8. Kurinij N, Shiono PH: Early formula supplementation of breast-feeding, *Pediatrics* 88:745, 1991.

9. Subcommittee on nutrition and lactation, Committee on Nutritional Status during Pregnancy and Lactation, Food and Nutrition Board, Institute of Medicine, National Academy of Sciences: *Nutrition during lactation,* Washington, DC, 1991, National Academy of Sciences.

10. Siimes MA, Vuori E, Kuitunen P: Breast milk iron—a declining concentration during the course of lactation, *Acta Paediatr Scand* 68:29, 1979.

11. Anderson GN, Atkinson SA, Bryan MH: Energy and macronutrient content of human milk during early lactation from mothers giving birth prematurely and at term, *Am J Clin Nutr* 34:258, 1981.

12. Chavalittamrong B and others: Protein and amino acids of breast milk from Thai mothers, *Am J Clin Nutr* 24:1126, 1981.

13. Fomon SJ: Reflections on infant feeding in the 1970s and 1980s, *Am J Clin Nutr* 46:71, 1971.

14. O'Connor ME and others: Vitamin K deficiency and breast feeding, *Am J Dis Child* 137:601, 1983.

15. Higginbottom L, Sweetman L, Nylan WL: A syndrome of methylmalonic aciduria, homocystinuria, megaloblastic anemia, and neurological abnormalities of a B_{12} deficiency in an infant strictly breast-fed by a mother with latent pernicious anemia, *J Pediatr* 100:917, 1982.

16. Cooperman JM and others: The folate in human milk, *Am J Clin Nutr* 36:576, 1982.

17. Borschel MW, Kirksey A, Hannemann RE: Effects of vitamin B_6 intake on nutriture and growth of young infants, *Am J Clin Nutr* 43:7, 1986.

18. Saarinen UM, Siimes MA, Dallman PR: Iron absorption in infants: high bioavailability of breast milk iron as indicated by the extrinsic tag method of iron absorption and by the concentration of serum ferritin, *J Pediatr* 91:36, 1977.

19. Johnson PE, Evans GW: Relative zinc availability in human breast milk, infant formulas, and cow's milk, *Am J Clin Nutr* 31:416, 1978.

20. May JT: Microbial contaminants and antimicrobial properties of human milk, *Microbiol Sci* 5:42, 1988.

21. Cunningham AS, Jeliffe DB, Jeliffe EFP: Breast-feeding and health in the 1980s: a global epidemiologic review, *J Pediatr* 118:659, 1991.

22. Rubin AH and others: Relationship between infant feeding and infectious illness: a prospective study of infants during the first year of life, *Pediatrics* 85:464, 1990.

23. Leventhal JM and others: Does breast-feeding protect against infections in infants less than 3 months of age? *Pediatrics* 78:896, 1988.

24. Committee on Nutrition, American Academy of Pediatrics: Commentary on breast-feeding and infant formulas, including proposed standards for formulas, *Pediatrics* 57:279, 1976.

25. Committee on Nutrition, American Academy of Pediatrics: Soy-protein formulas: recommendations for use in infant feeding, *Pediatrics* 72:359, 1983.

26. Harrison HL and others: Goat milk acidosis, *J Pediatr* 94:927, 1979.

27. Fabius RJ and others: Malnutrition associated with a formula of barley water, corn syrup, and whole milk, *Am J Dis Child* 135:615, 1981.

28. Sinatra FR, Merritt RJ: Iatrogenic kwashiorkor in infants, *Am J Dis Child* 135:21, 1981.

29. Wyatt DT, Noetzel MJ, Hillman RE: Infantile beriberi presenting as subacute necrotizing encephalomyelopathy, *J Pediatr* 110:888, 1987.

30. Comay SC, Karabus CD: Peripheral gangrene in hypernatremic dehydration of infancy, *Arch Dis Child* 50:616, 1975.

31. Abrams CAL and others: Hazards of overconcentrated milk formula, *JAMA* 232:1136, 1975.

32. Partridge JC and others: Water intoxication secondary to feeding mismanagement, *Am J Dis Child* 135:38, 1981.

33. Fomon SJ, Sanders KD, Ziegler EE: Formulas for older infants, *J Pediatr* 116:690, 1990.

34. Committee on Nutrition, American Academy of Pediatrics: Follow-up or weaning formulas, *Pediatrics* 83:1067, 1989.

35. Ziegler EE and others: Cow's milk feeding in infancy: gastrointestinal blood loss and iron nutritional status, *J Pediatr* 98:540, 1991.

36. Klaus MH, Kennell JH: *Maternal-infant bonding: the impact of early separation or loss on family development,* St Louis, 1976, Mosby–Year Book.

37. Macknin ML, Medendorp SV, Maier WC: Infant sleep and bedtime cereal, *Am J Dis Child* 143:1066, 1989.

38. Schaefer LJ, Kumanyika K: Maternal variables related to potentially high-sodium infant-feeding practices, *J Am Diet Assoc* 85:434, 1985.

39. Montalto MS, Benson JD, Martinez RA: Nutrient intake of formula fed infants, and infants fed cow's milk, *Pediatrics* 75:343, 1985.

40. Arnon SS and others: Honey and other environmental risk factors for infant botulism, *Pediatrics* 94:331, 1979.

41. Fomon SJ and others: Influence of formula concentration on calorie intake and growth of normal infants, *Acta Paediatr Scand* 64:172, 1975.

42. Thoman EB: Development of synchrony in mother infant interaction in feeding and other situations, *Fed Proc* 34:1587, 1975.

43. Salmenpera L, Perheentupa J, Siimes MA: Exclusively breast-fed healthy infants grow slower than reference infants, *Acta Paediatr Scand* 19:307, 1985.

44. Butte NF, Smith EO, Garza G: Energy utilization of breast-fed and formula-fed infants, *Am J Clin Nutr* 51:350, 1990.

45. Ernst JA, Brady MS, Rickard KA: Food and nutrient intake of 5 to 12 month old infants fed formula or cow milk: a summary of four national surveys, *J Pediatr* 117(suppl):586, 1990.

46. Stuff JE, Nichols BL: Nutrient intake and growth performance of older infants fed human milk, *J Pediatr* 115:959, 1989.

47. Hofvander Y and others: The amount of milk consumed by 1-3 months old breast or bottle fed infants, *Acta Paediatr Scand* 71:953, 1982.

48. Illingworth RS, Lister J: The critical or sensitive period with special reference to certain feeding problems in infants and children, *J Pediatr* 65:839, 1964.

49. Gesell A, Ilg FL: *Feeding behavior of infants,* Philadelphia, 1937, JB Lippincott.

50. Ardran GM, Kemp FH, Lind J: A cineradiographic study of breast feeding, *Br J Radiol* 31:156, 1958.

51. Ardran GM, Kemp FH, Lind J: A cineradiographic study of bottle feeding, *Br J Radiol* 31:11, 1958.

52. Mathew OP: Science of bottle feeding, *J Pediatr* 119:511, 1991.

53. Roddey OF, Martin ES, Swetenburg RL: Critical weight loss and malnutrition in breast-fed infants, *Am J Dis Child* 135:597, 1981.

54. Brazelton TB: Crying in infancy, *Pediatrics* 29:579, 1962.

55. Johnson, S, Nowjack-Raymer, R: Baby bottle tooth decay (BBTD): issues, assessment and an opportunity for the nutritionist, *J Am Diet Assoc* 89:112, 1989.

56. Forsyth BWC: Colic and the effect of changing formulas: a double-blind multiple-crossover study, *J Pediatr* 115:521, 1989.

57. Sampson HA: Infantile colic and food allergy: fact or fiction? *J Pediatr* 115:583, 1989.

58. Clyne PS, Kulczycki A: Human breast milk contains bovine IgG: relationship to infantile colic? *Pediatrics* 87:439, 1991.

59. Orenstein SR: Effects on behavior state of prone versus seated positioning for infants with gastroesophageal reflux, *Pediatrics* 85:765, 1990.

5

The Preschool-Age Child

Peggy L. Pipes
Cristine M. Trahms

Objectives

+++

After studying this chapter, the student should:

✔ *Be aware of nutrition concerns of preschool-age children.*

✔ *Understand that both physical and psychosocial development affects food choices in young children.*

✔ *Recognize that changes in growth rates, e.g., slowed and erratic, during the preschool-age period are reflected in food intake.*

✔ *Recognize cultural and community factors that affect food availability and choices for young children.*

✔ *Recognize factors that influence parents' provision of food for young children.*

✔ *Recognize factors that must be considered to prevent choking in children.*

✔ *Be aware of the value of snacks to a young child's daily total nutrient intake.*

✔ *Be aware of common concerns about food intake encountered by parents of preschool-age children.*

✔ *Have knowledge of feeding programs designed to improve the nutritional status of young children.*

The preschool-age period is considered to be 1 to 6 years of age. During this period, changes occur in children's rates of growth and continuing maturation of fine and gross motor skills. Personality development influences not only the amounts of food young children consume but also the foods that are acceptable to them. Food habits, likes, and dislikes begin to be established, some of which are transient and many of which form the base for a lifetime of food and nutrient intake. Environmental influences and parental behavior reinforce or extinguish food-related behavior.

There are common patterns of food and nutrient intake among preschool-age children. Feeding programs at day care and preschool contribute significantly to young children's total nutrient intake. Although evidence of malnutrition has been reduced in the past 10 years, populations of children who exhibit significant biochemical evidence of inadequate nutrient intake continue to be found in the United States.

NUTRITION OF PRESCHOOL-AGE CHILDREN

Although overt clinical signs of **malnutrition** are rarely found in children in North America, evidence proves that children do receive diets that are inadequate in quantity or quality. Iron and zinc are the nutrients most frequently of concern.[1,2] The Nationwide Food Consumption Survey also identified calcium and vitamins A and C as nutrients that are frequently consumed in less-than-recommended amounts.[1,3]

If concerns over the intake of preschool children can be generalized, iron and zinc appear to be the main nutrients at risk for a lower-than-acceptable intake. Many surveys, comprehensive cross-sectional populations studies, and evaluations of small groups have been collected since 1936 to evaluate intake and, less frequently, biochemical status of young children.

Regardless of population group, geographical location, or ethnic origin, some sociocultural factors appear to affect the nutrient intake of young children. A discussion of some of this information with a 15- to 20-year perspective will aid in the understanding of factors that have changed the pattern of nutrient intake of young children. Supplemental food programs, for example, have had a positive impact on iron intake of low-income children.

The data presented may appear to be contradictory, e.g., preschool children are poorly nourished and poorly grown,[4] children have achieved acceptable height and weight attainment, and being overweight is more of a concern than being underweight.[5] These apparent contradictions are due to circumstances affecting family economics, cultural influences, and

food availability. They reflect the differences in subgroups of young children and point to areas of nutritional concern. Most of the reports of the intakes of preschool children appropriately focus on those children believed to be at highest risk for deficient intakes—poor children. Younger children are more likely to be poor than older children or adults; one in four children under 6 years of age lives below the official **poverty line** (annual income of $10,419 for a family of three in 1990).[6]

Not all of the reports evaluated all nutritional components; for example, zinc, copper, and manganese have only recently emerged as nutrients of high concern. Many surveys provide information on nutrient intake or food groups consumption with a focus on specific nutrients or food groups. Few studies report biochemical parameters.

Nutrient intakes of young children tended to be higher in families with incomes above poverty level. Recent intake data suggest that family income affects the energy intake of young children. Children whose families have incomes less than 131% of the poverty guidelines had energy intakes of 1427 kcal/day, and those children in families with incomes greater than 300% of the poverty guidelines had energy intakes of 1478 kcal/day.[3] Groups of young children appear to be at risk for a diminished intake of specific nutrients because of family circumstances, especially poverty.

A lower calcium density was noted in the diets of Hispanic and black children than in other populations. The vitamin A density was lowest for the Hispanic children compared with other groups. The place of residence also influenced the nutrient density of the diets consumed. Intakes of niacin and vitamins B_6 and C per 1000 kcal were lower in nonmetropolitan areas than in the central city and suburban areas studied.[7]

Race is often described as a factor negatively affecting nutrient intake. In a recent comparison, race did not discriminate adequacy of intake among three groups of young children (African-American, Mexican-American, and Caucasian) observed at day care centers.[8]

The National Nutrition Status Study of preschool children conducted by Owen and others[9] found that black children consumed iron at an average of 1 mg/day more than white pre-

TABLE 5-1 *Mean Intakes of Preschool Children as a Percent of Standard (RDA, 1968)*

Nutrient (Unit)	Range of Intakes
Kcalories (kcal)	110-130
Protein (gm)	215-240
Calcium (mg)	170-230
Vitamin A (IU)	80-190
Vitamin C (mg)	195-220
Thiamin (mg)	160-170
Riboflavin (mg)	210-215
Iron (mg)	
2-3 yr/o	48-55
4-5 yr/o	83-94

From *Caloric and selected nutrient values for persons 1 to 74 years of age:* First Health and Nutrition Examination Survey, United States, 1971-1974, DHEW Pub No (PHS) 79-1657, 1979.

schoolers at all ages. Cereal grains were the major contributors of iron. Vitamin C intakes were unrelated to energy intakes, and children of parents who had more money to spend for food consumed greater amounts of ascorbic acid.

Data collected in the late 1970s from a larger sample of children indicated a wide range of intakes when expressed as a percent of the RDA (Table 5-1).[10] Preschool-age children as a group (2 to 5 years of age), regardless of income (above or below poverty level), race (black or white), or gender received intakes in excess of the standard (RDA, 1968) for energy, protein, calcium, vitamins A and C, thiamin, and riboflavin. Intakes of iron varied with age. Iron is the nutrient of most significant concern.

A comparison of data from Food Consumption Surveys from 1977, 1985, and 1986 is shown in Table 5-2. Iron, calcium, zinc, and vitamin B6 emerge as nutrients of concern across the time span.

TABLE 5-2 *Selected Food Consumption Survey Data for Children, 1 to 5 Years of Age*

Nutrients	1977	1985	1986
Mean intake			
Food energy	1335 kcal (<RDA)	1446 kcal (97% RDA)	1447 kcal
Food energy as			
Fat		34%	35%
Carbohydrate		52%	51%
Mean intake			
Calcium	<RDA	96% RDA	
Iron	74% RDA	84% RDA	86% RDA
Zinc		76% RDA	82% RDA
Copper			
1 to 3 years		0.8 mg	
4 to 6 years		0.9 mg	
Cholesterol		254 mg	
Children consuming vitamin/mineral supplements	47%	60%	59%

Comparisons compiled from Food consumption survey examines eating habits, *Nutrition Week,* CNI Newsletter, Jan 16, 1986 and Nationwide food consumption survey: continuing survey of food intakes by individuals. *Nutr Today,* Nov/Dec:31, 1986 and *Nutr Today,* Sept/Oct:36, 1987.
RDA comparison = 1980 RDA.

TABLE 5-3   *Fat and Carbohydrate Intakes of Preschool Children (NHANES II)*

Component	Reported Intake— All Children	Recommended Dietary Guidelines
Total fat	33%-36% of kcal	30% of kcal
Carbohydrate	49%-51% of kcal	55% of kcal
Protein	15%-16% of kcal	15% of kcal
Saturated fat	13% of kcal	10% of kcal
Polyunsaturated/ saturated fat intake ratio	0:4	1:1

Modified from Kimm SYS and others: *Prev Med*, 19:432, 1990.

The children enrolled in the Bogalusa Heart Study reported higher fat and carbohydrate intakes and lower protein intakes than the children surveyed for NHANES II.[11] The intake data of children enrolled in NHANES II are reported in Table 5-3. These children as a group had fat intakes that were higher than those recommended for fat and cholesterol intakes in Healthy People 2000: Nutrition Objectives[12] and Dietary Guidelines for Americans.[13] Black children generally had higher total fat and cholesterol intakes, and white children had higher kcaloric intakes as complex carbohydrates. The reported protein intakes were similar for both racial groups.[14]

A high percentage of children in all studies have been found to be receiving multiple vitamin and mineral supplements. Table 5-1 shows the Food Consumption Survey data on the intake of vitamin and mineral supplements for young children. In general, supplements are more often used by children from families with a head who is white and better educated. Fewer children have been noted to take iron supplements than vitamin supplements. Supplemental iron is consumed most often as part of a multiple vitamin supplement.[15]

Nutrition Concerns of Children

Ethnic and geographical variations in nutrient deficiency concerns have been found in var-

ious populations. For example, Navajo children were found to have low dietary intakes of calcium and vitamins A and C. Biochemical evidence of inadequate intakes of iron, vitamin A, and riboflavin was also noted.[16] White Mountain Apache children in Arizona were noted to have biochemical evidence of inadequate intakes of vitamins A and C.[17]

A nutritional status study of low-income preschool children indicated that, although improvement in the nutritional status of the children had been effected in 10 years, 9% to 18% of the children studied had low or deficient serum levels of vitamins A and C, thiamin, riboflavin, or hemoglobin. Also, income level had dropped further and a greater number of the children were categorized as thin than 10 years previously.[18]

Biochemical evidence of vitamin B_6 deficiency has been reported in 9% of children studied in Virginia.[19]

Unfortunately, homelessness is a way of life for many young children. When homeless children were compared with children living in homes, but of similar ages and income levels, homeless children showed a growth pattern compatible with moderate, chronic nutritional deprivation, e.g., stunting without wasting. It was believed that the diets of these young children, 2 to 6 years of age, were not deficient in total energy but rather were inadequate in content of some nutrients and contained excessive amounts of cheaper, carbohydrate-rich foods.[20] Calculated intakes of nutrients indicated iron intakes at 40% of the RDA, and folic acid at 30% of the RDA. All other nutrients were ingested at amounts greater than or equal to 60% of the RDA. However, the overall dietary adequacy score was low at 9.8 (NORM = 16).[21]

The numbers of young children in foster care are also increasing. Although little is known of the nutritional intake of this group, these children are vulnerable to nutritional deficiency and negative eating behavior because of the crises in their lives and the high incidence of health problems.[22]

Availability of specific nutrients has a positive impact on the diets of young children. Children of ages 1 to 5 years from low-income households were more likely to have low intakes of energy, vitamin C, and iron than children from high-income households. Children participating in the Supplemental Nutrition Program for Women, Infants, and Children (WIC) were less likely to have low-iron intakes than low-income children who were not enrolled in WIC. Vitamin A and calcium intake did not vary with WIC participation or by household income level.[23] Another WIC program documented intakes that did not meet the RDA for vitamins A and C, calcium, iron, protein, and folacin.[24]

Iron. In some poverty-level populations, groups of children have been identified that show both clinical and biochemical evidence of malnutrition. All preschool children are at risk for iron-deficiency anemia, which appears to be a greater problem in children of low-income families than in children of other groups.

Iron-deficiency anemia causes long-term developmental effects. Costa Rican children whose iron status was documented in infancy were evaluated again at 5 years of age. All of the children had appropriate growth and iron status at age 5. However, those children who had moderately severe iron-deficiency anemia in infancy (hemoglobin levels less than 100 g/L) had lower scores of mental and motor functioning at entrance into school.[25] In the United States the WIC program has demonstrated its effectiveness in improving the iron status of young children when the iron was measured as increased hemoglobin measurements before and after the provision of supplemental food containing iron.[24]

Iron intake appears to be a problem even for those children whose families have an annual income of more than $35,000 and provide day-care for the children. Since 93% had height and weight measures within normal achievement, the apparently low energy intakes (mean = 70% of the RDA) were adequate to support growth. All nutrients met 75% of the RDA (1989) except for iron and folic acid (50% of the RDA). These children also had low biochemical indexes for iron status.[26]

Healthy People 2000: Nutrition Objectives[12] proposes to reduce iron deficiency to <3% among children 1- to 4 years-old from a baseline of 9% for children ages 1 to 2 years and 4% for children ages 3- to 4 years. For children of low-income families the target is 10% of children 1 to 2 years

old and 5% for children 3 to 4 years old. Achievement of this target would reduce iron deficiency from baselines of 21% and 10%, respectively, for children of low-income families.

Other Concerns

Lead. Lead poisoning in young children can cause permanent stunting of growth, cognitive deficits, and other neurological problems. Children under 6 years old are at significant risk for lead toxicity because of their higher rate of lead absorption in the intestines, rapidly developing nervous system, and frequent exposure to lead (e.g., mouthing objects). Poor dietary intakes of energy, calcium, phosphorus, iron, and zinc increase susceptibility to lead effects (e.g., increased absorption and toxicity).[27] Improving intake and nutritional status of vulnerable groups offers some protection against toxicity.

Moderate concentrations of lead in children's blood (0.14 to 1.92 µmol/L) are associated with growth retardation (e.g., short stature).[28] Improving the nutritional status of children at risk increases the effectiveness of removal of lead from the environment. Low calcium and low iron status in young children increases the absorption of lead. The FDA goal is to reach lead intakes of less than 100 µg/day from all food sources for children 1 to 5 years of age.[29]

A statement by the Centers for Disease Control offers these guidelines[30]: (1) offer regular meals to children, since more lead is absorbed on an empty stomach; and (2) include plenty of iron and calcium in the child's diet.

Dental caries. Dental caries, as a result of excessive intakes of sweet foods, poor dental hygiene, and lack of dental care, is common among all groups of children.

Foods as Nutrient Sources

Food Consumption Survey data (Table 5-4) indicate reported food intakes for young children. Most young children consume milk and meat, poultry, or fish as sources of protein. The percentage of young children consuming milk remains constant over the years while the proportion consuming low-fat or nonfat milk increases. About one third of the vegetables reported to be consumed are white potatoes and over two thirds of the fruits consumed are non-citrus fruits. Young Mexican-American children

TABLE 5-4   *Selected Food Consumption Survey Data for Children, 1 to 5 Years of Age*

Intake of Foods	1977	1985	1986
Total meat, poultry, fish consumed		104 gm	105 gm
Meat mixtures consumed	45 gm	45 gm	
(Stews, casseroles, sandwiches, hamburgers, frozen dinners)			
Total using meat, poultry, fish		86%	89%
Using beef		18%	25%
Consuming milk	88%	89%	89%
Whole milk	65%	54%	49%
Lowfat or nonfat milk	26%	38%	43%
Milk consumed	357 gm	381 gm	341 gm
Grain consumed		202 gm	
Grain mixtures consumed	50 gm	69 gm	
(Macaroni and cheese, spaghetti with tomato sauce, pizza)			
Vegetables consumed, total		91 gm	
White potatoes		35 gm	
Fruits consumed, total		162 gm	
Noncitrus fruits		109 gm	
Beverages, total		204 gm	
Soft drinks	77 gm	70 gm	80 gm

Comparisons compiled from Food consumption survey examines eating habits, *Nutrition Week,* CNI Newsletter, Jan 16, 1986 and Nationwide food consumption survey: continuing survey of food intakes by individuals, *Nutr Today,* Nov/Dec:31, 1986, and *Nutr Today,* Sept/Oct:36, 1987.

are reported to consume vegetables less often than other groups of children; for example, 25% of the Mexican-American children did not consume vegetables daily.[31]

FAMILY RESPONSIBILITY AND CHILDREN'S FOOD INTAKES

Preschool-age children depend on their parents or other care providers for the selection of food they consume (Figure 5-1). Since the preschool period is important in the formation of attitudes toward food, it is essential that foods that supply a variety of nutrients be available to young children. Parents also need to understand and support children in their food-related behaviors so that food habits are formed that are conducive to an adequate nutrient intake. Young children need some experience selecting food, yet parents and care providers need to set

limits so that children eat foods that provide adequate amounts of nutrients.

The research knowledge base for nutrition knowledge of parents and child care providers is limited. The data available have focused on nutrition knowledge and practices of mothers classified by income level rather than family constellation, e.g., single-parent households and blended families. Recently, the role of day-care providers in the nutritional well-being of young children has been appreciated and evaluated.

The educational level and nutrition knowledge of the mother influence the nutritional quality of the diet. It has been noted that as the nutrition knowledge of the mother increased, preschool children's intakes of calcium, iron, riboflavin, and ascorbic acid increased. Nutrition knowledge was significantly related to positive attitudes toward meal planning and food preparation.[32,33] Also, the more positive mothers

FIG. 5-1   Children consume food successfully in a comfortable setting free from stress.

felt about meal planning, the importance of good nutrition for their children, and their roles as homemakers, the more likely were the children to receive good-quality meals; the more discontent, nervous, and unhappy the mothers were with their roles as homemakers, the lower was the dietary quality of the children's food intakes.[34]

More recently it has been documented that although preschool children whose mothers were employed outside the home ate more meals at day-care centers, maternal employment did not negatively affect the dietary quality of these children.[35] This may also be related to other factors such as higher household incomes and fewer siblings in homes in which the mother was employed part time or full time outside the home.

Parents often need both help in interpreting the nutrition information to which they have been exposed and direction to valid sources of information. Sources of nutrition information vary among groups of parents. Low-income families reportedly receive their nutrition information from relatives and friends. Other families rely heavily on lay sources such as magazines, newspapers, books, radio, and television.

Some of the information presented in these sources lacks validity, and conflicting information is often presented in any two sources. In addition, advertising and merchandising play on parents' emotional responses to suggestion and imply a false need for certain foods or supplements.

Preschool children often accompany their mothers to the grocery store and request specific foods. In this situation, 68% of mothers have reported that they sometimes buy foods that are requested and 18% stated that they always purchase the items. Sugar-coated cereal is the food most frequently requested.[36]

Young children have a significant impact on how families spend their food dollars. Child-prompted purchases comprised about 14% of the family food budget. The range was wide, as expected, varying from 1% to 44%. It is noteworthy that over half of the child-prompted food items were calorie dense.[37] Mothers also reported a sense of guilt because they realized that their families, including young children, ate foods they preferred rather than foods the mothers felt to be nutritious.[38]

The ordinal position of the preschool child

affected food choices and availability of foods, especially presweetened cereal. Preschool-aged children who were the oldest or the only child in their family received more foods that they specifically requested.[39]

Convenience is another factor many mothers consider when they select food for their families. Working mothers may rely heavily on convenience food and fast-food establishments. They have been known to leave the decision to the child as to what he or she would like to eat. Parents may need help selecting convenience foods and combinations of other foods that, when served together, provide a balanced nutrient intake. Parents may also need to learn how to plan other meals so that the daily intake is adequate when fast foods are consumed frequently.

Table 5-5 indicates trends in food consumption patterns of young children. Nearly half of young children receive foods away from home, and these meals comprise about 20% of their daily total energy intake. Snacks comprise about the same percentage of the total energy intake as meals consumed away from home.

Low-income families have less money for food than more affluent families. If the purchasing power is reduced significantly, foods that provide essential nutrients may be partially or completely eliminated from the diet. However, not all children from low-income families are at risk for undernutrition. Undernourished, low-income children had parents who prepared fewer regular meals, and these children were less likely to eat vegetables and milk than adequately nourished children from homes with similar incomes. More convenience foods and fewer foods requiring preparation were available to undernourished children than to well-nourished children.[40]

Day Care

By 1995, it is estimated that mothers of 15 million preschool children will be working outside the home: Of these 15 million children, 26% will be enrolled in child-care centers (facility of 12 or more children); 22% will be enrolled in family day-care (6-12 children in the caregiver's home); and 52% will receive alternate care (with a relative).[41] Many children are in care centers or homes 8 to 10 hours/day, which means child care centers are responsible for two thirds of the child's total nutritional intake.

It is clear that out-of-home child care has a remarkable impact on the foods and nutrients provided to young children. Although nutrition standards for day-care programs have been enacted[42-46], the question still remains of whether day-care programs provide adequate nourishment for young children.

Menus at child-care centers are primarily planned by either the center director or the cook. Both reported having received some

TABLE 5-5   Selected Food Consumption Survey Data for Children, 1 to 5 Years of Age

Food Patterns	1977	1985	1986
Frequency of eating/day	3 times	4 times	
Snacks (1 or more/day)		83%	76%
Snacks, total nutrient intake	6%-16%	9%-22%	9%-18%
Snacks, total energy intake		19%	16%
Food away from home	30%	43%	45%
1-3 years			39%
4-5 years			53%
Total energy intake		10%-14%	14%-20%

Comparisons compiled Food consumption survey examines eating habits, *Nutrition Week*, CNI Newsletter, Jan 16, 1986 and from Nationwide food consumption survey: continuing survey of food intakes by individuals. *Nutr Today*, Nov/Dec:31, 1986, and *Nutr Today*, Sept/Oct:36, 1987.

training and viewed foods served at the center as an important part of the growth and health of the young child.[47] There is concern that foods provided at child-care centers are those usually accepted by young children (hamburgers, fried potatoes, applesauce, cookies, milk) but not in large enough quantities to meet energy and iron needs of these children.[48] Poor selection and combinations of foods provided less than 67% of the 1989 RDA for energy, iron, thiamin, and niacin even when foods were served at the recommended portion sizes.[49] The menus at family day-care homes had similar shortcomings.[50]

The intakes of Canadian preschool-aged boys (also in day-care) were appraised for nutrient adequacy. These boys as a group had intakes within recommended ranges.[51]

The goal of Healthy People 2000 is to increase to 50% the number of child care food services that provide foods consistent with the Dietary Guidelines for Americans.[12]

Table 5-5 indicates trends in food consumption patterns of young children. Nearly half of young children receive foods away from home, and these meals comprise about 20% of their daily total energy intake. Snacks comprise about the same percentage of calories as foods eaten away from home.

As family life-styles have grown increasingly

TABLE 5-6   Microwaveable Foods for Children: Supermarket Survey and Comments

Manufacturer: Brand Name	Food Name	Cost Per Serving	Weight Per Serving (oz)	Protein (g)	Fat (g)	Kcalories	Sodium (mg)
Con Agra: Kid Cuisine	Macaroni and cheese with mini-franks, green beans, applesauce, brownie	$1.99	9	9	13	360	790
Comment	Entree was too salty and applesauce got too hot						
	Beef patty sandwich with cheese, potato, sliced apples, cookie	1.99	6.25	13	22	430	550
Comment	Sandwich was OK, potato was mushy not crisp						
	Chicken nuggets, pasta with tomato sauce, sliced apples, brownie	1.99	6.8	11	17	360	660
Comment Tyson: Looney Tunes	Nuggets were mushy, pasta was too salty	2.29	7.25	12	11	270	630
	Fish sticks, green beans, mashed potato						
Comment	Fish sticks were mushy, not crisp, and too salty	2.29	7	17	11	290	440
	Chicken chunks, applesauce, carrots*						
Comment	Chicken chunks were too mushy, applesauce got too hot.						

Compiled by Anna Trahms-Neudorfer.
*Healthy Food Report Card = no artificial colors or flavorings, low fat, and low sodium as defined by manufacturer.
Comments: A representative adult dinner has 9 oz of food, 500 kcal, 960 mg sodium, and costs $2.25. These foods seem to be relatively more expensive than 'adult' microwaveable dinners because of the smaller portion per package for a similar amount of money (e.g., $.29–$.32/oz for children's dinners compared with $.25/oz for adult's dinners).

complex, children at younger ages are increasingly independent in acquisition and preparation of food for themselves. Survey results show that children ages 5 to 8 years are frequently allowed to operate a microwave oven without supervision.[52] So it is no surprise that marketing for microwaveable frozen dinners is aimed at young children. A supermarket survey (Table 5-6) indicates some of the items available and their relative acceptance. Young children are a target market for, and are influenced by, advertising on television. Younger children are not able to differentiate commercial content from program content.[53] The advertising aimed at shaping the food choices of young children is for foods high in sodium, fat, and sugar.[54]

FACTORS AFFECTING FOOD INTAKE

Provision of appropriate amounts and kinds of food does not ensure that preschool-age children will consume foods that support an appropriate nutrient intake. Children imitate the models of food acceptance set for them. They learn to control concerned parents by the food they accept or reject.

Emotional factors influence food acceptance and intake. Parents and siblings provide a model of food acceptance and feeding behaviors that children imitate (Figure 5-2).

Attitudes of parents toward child rearing influence food intake. Permissiveness of parents in relation to eating was found to be negatively

FIG. 5-2   Parents provide role models for food choices and eating styles.

related to the nutritive value of food consumed by the children, adversely affecting all dietary components except fat. Less permissive mothers regulated the child's food intake to some degree, and as a result children consumed greater amounts of protein, vitamins, and minerals.[55] Children of more affluent, nonauthoritarian mothers had higher intakes of calcium and ascorbic acid, whereas children of parents with authoritarian attitudes toward child rearing had higher intakes of kcalories, carbohydrates, iron, and thiamin.[56] Parental monitoring (or threat of parental monitoring) decreased the number of nonnutritious foods chosen and thus the total energy content of a meal.[57]

The emotional environment at mealtime may influence food and nutrient intake. The dinner table is not the place for family battles or punitive action toward children. For eating to be successful, it should occur at a time and in a setting that is comfortable and free from stress and unreasonable demands.

THE PRESCHOOL CHILD'S DEVELOPMENTAL PROGRESS

During the preschool years rates of growth decrease, and as a result appetites decrease. Children learn to understand language and how to talk and ask for food. Development of gross motor skills permits them to learn to walk and seek food for themselves. Development of fine motor skills allows them to learn to feed themselves and to prepare simple foods such as cereal with milk and sandwiches. They learn about food and the way it feels, tastes, and smells. Preschool children learn to eat a wider variety of textures and kinds of food, give up the bottle, and drink from a cup. They demand independence and refuse help in many tasks in which they are not skillful, such as self-feeding. As they grow older, they become less interested in food and more interested in their environment. They test and learn limits of behavior that are acceptable.

Self-feeding

Children learn to feed themselves independently during the second year of life. Spilling and messiness are marked during the first half of the year, but by their second birthday most children spill very little (Figure 5-3). Handedness is established after 1 year of age. The 15-month-old child will have difficulty scooping food into the spoon and bringing food to the mouth without turning the spoon upside down and spilling its contents because of lack of wrist control. By 16 to 17 months of age a well-defined ulnar deviation of the wrist occurs and the contents of a spoon may be transferred more steadily to the mouth. By 18 months of age the child lifts the elbow as the spoon is raised and flexes the wrist as the spoon reaches the mouth so that only moderate spilling occurs, in contrast to earlier stages of self-feeding. By 2 years of age spilling seldom occurs.

Younger preschool children are interested in how food feels and often prefer finger-feeding and feeding themselves. Foods that provide opportunities for finger-feeding should be provided at every meal. Children frequently will place food in the spoon with their fingers and may finger-feed foods commonly spoon-fed, such as vegetables and pudding (Figure 5-4).

By 15 months of age children can manage the cup, although not expertly. They have difficulty in lifting and tilting a cup and in lowering it to a tray after drinking. The cup is tilted, using the palm, and often is tilted too rapidly. By 18 to 24 months of age the cup is tilted by manipulation of the fingers.

Rotary chewing movements are refined in the second year and are well established by 2 years of age.

As the young child matures, self-help skills become more sophisticated. In general, a 2-year-old child uses arm muscles for tasks, a 3-year-old child uses hand muscles, and a 4-year-old child uses finger muscles.[58] This maturation enables the child to wipe, scrub, pour, mix, and peel foods for consumption.

Risk of Choking

Young children, especially preschoolers, are at risk of choking on food. Death from **food asphyxiation** has been described mostly in younger preschool children less than 2 years of age. Foods

FIG. 5-3   Preschool children refine their self-feeding skills as they grow older.

FIG. 5-4   Preschool children enjoy learning to feed themselves.

❖

GUIDELINES FOR FEEDING SAFETY— PRESCHOOL CHILDREN

Insist that children eat sitting down. It lets them concentrate on chewing and swallowing.

An adult should supervise children while they eat.

Food on which preschoolers often choke, such as hot dogs, peanut butter, hard pieces of fruit, and vegetables, should be avoided for children under 3 years of age.

Well-cooked foods, modified so that the child can chew and swallow without difficulty, should be offered.

Eating in the car should be avoided. If the child starts choking it is hard to get to the side of the road safely.

Rub-on teething medications can cause problems with chewing and swallowing because the muscles in the throat may also become numb. Children who receive such medications should be carefully observed during feeding.

---

most often responsible for the deaths include hot dogs, candy, nuts, and grapes.[59]

Actually children can choke on almost any food but are most likely to have trouble with foods that are hard, slippery, or just the right size to plug up the throat (e.g., hard candy, popcorn). If the food becomes stuck, the plug prevents the child from coughing and bringing it back up. Other foods that may cause problems are thick, sticky foods such as peanut butter. These foods can line the back of the throat and build up so the children cannot clear their throats.

Prevention is the most reasonable approach to childhood choking. Educating parents about developmentally appropriate foods is important. Guidelines for preventing choking are given in the box above.

Patterns of Food Intake

Few children pass through the preschool years without creating concern about their food intakes (Figure 5-5). Between 9 and 18 months of age a disinterest in food becomes apparent; this lasts from a few months to a few years.[60] Idiosyncratic food choices are common. Likes and dislikes may change from day to day and week to week. For example, a child may demand only a specific kind of cereal for snacks for a week and completely reject it for the next 6 months. Rituals become a part of food preparation and service. Some children, for example,

accept sandwiches only when they are cut in half, and when parents quarter the sandwiches the children may throw tantrums. Others demand that foods have a particular arrangement on the plate or that their dishes be placed only in certain locations on the table.

Appetites are usually erratic and unpredictable during this period. The child may eat hungrily at one meal and completely refuse the next. The evening meal is generally the least well received and is of the most concern to the majority of parents. It is possible that a child who has consumed two meals and several snacks has met the energy and nutrient needs before dinnertime; in this instance consumption of limited amounts of food may be appropriate. It is also important to recognize that much social interaction occurs during the evening meal. This may be overwhelming for the preschooler who is learning not only to eat and interact at the same time but also to master the use of utensils and to eat harder-to-masticate foods.

A high percentage of parental dissatisfaction with children's appetites and interest in food between 2 and 4 years of age has been reported.[55,60] Concerns most frequently expressed are selection of a limited variety of foods, dawdling, limited consumption of fruits and vegetables, and consumption of too many sweets and too little meat.

More recently, mothers have described feed-

FIG. 5-5   Children want to eat the same food as their siblings, even if it means regressing to baby food.

ing problems among 2- to 7-year-old children that are very similar (see the box at right).[61] It is apparent that such problems are those of the parents' lack of insight into normal child development and, if properly managed, need not compromise a child's nutrient intake. Anticipatory guidance about children's food behavior is important for all parents, and intervention is imperative when battles are waged between parents and children about what is to be eaten.

Ellyn Satter[62] has summarized the research on early childhood feeding into a useful manual.

Frequency of eating. It has been noted that we are raising a generation of nibblers. Nearly 60% of 3- to 5-year-old children eat more than 3 times a day. Young children consume food an average of 5 to 7 times a day, although ranges of 3 to 14 times a day have been noted.[63] The frequency of food intakes was unrelated to nutrient intakes except when children consumed food less than 4 or more than 6 times a day.[64]

> ## *FOOD BEHAVIORS OF CHILDREN 2 TO 7 YEARS OF AGE VIEWED AS PROBLEMS BY MOTHER (IN ORDER OF FREQUENCY CITED)*
>
> Child consumes a restricted range of foods.
> Child's eating habits are poor.
> Child eats insufficient quantity of food.
> Child is not interested in eating.
> Child dislikes new foods.
> Child likes "junk foods."

From Pelchat ML, Pliner D: *J Nutr Ed* 18:23, 1986.

Children who consumed food less than 4 times a day consumed fewer kcalories and less calcium, protein, ascorbic acid, and iron than average intakes of other children their age. Those who consumed food more than 6 times a day consumed more energy, calcium, and ascorbic acid than average intakes of children their age. Snacks have been noted to provide one fourth to one third of the total kcalories, over one third of the total sucrose, one fifth of the total calcium and ascorbic acid, and one fifth of the protein ingested by children.[65] Recent food consumption data indicate that nearly all children have snacks and these snacks provide about one fifth of the total daily energy intake (see Table 5-5).

Food preferences. Parents report that preschool children enjoy meat, cereal grains, baked products, fruits, and sweets. They frequently ask for dairy products, cereals, and snack items such as cookies, crackers, fruit juice, and dry beverage mixes. Preschoolers seem to prefer the carbohydrate-rich foods that are easier to masticate. Cereals, breads, and crackers are often selected in preference to meat and other protein-rich foods. Dry fortified cereals are used as a primary source of many nutrients. Yogurt and cheese are popular among young children and provide calcium and protein.

Concerns of Parents

A concern of parents of many children between 1 and 3 years of age is that their children do not like meat and will not eat it. In the description of their dissatisfaction, it may become apparent that the children do eat and enjoy chicken and hamburger but refuse the more fibrous and harder-to-chew steaks and roasts. Foods have not yet been classified in relation to the pressure that must be applied to chew them well. Empirical observations, however, indicate that fibrous meats require the greatest pressure of any food consumed and may be difficult for the preschooler to eat. It may be important to focus parents' attention on the many softer, easier-to-chew meats and protein-rich foods that their children are consuming.

Food dislikes in childhood consistently include cooked vegetables and mixed dishes. Children accept raw vegetables more readily than they do cooked ones but often accept only a limited number. Acceptance of new foods appears to be age related. Only 6% of the youngest preschoolers but 18% of the oldest in their study would flatly refuse a new food.[8] Since fa-miliarity with food is believed to influence its acceptance, new foods should be offered frequently, even though they have been previously refused.

Milk intakes are erratic and change with age. A reduction in milk intake begins at approximately 6 months of age.[60] Milk may be completely refused at times. Intakes of milk between ages 1 and 4 years approximate 1 to $2\frac{1}{2}$ cups/day. After this age, the total volume of milk consumed increases.

Nutrient Intake Patterns

Both longitudinal and cross-sectional studies of nutrient and energy intakes of children have shown large differences in intakes between individual children of the same age and gender; some children consume two to three times as much energy as others.[36,66] Children are capable of regulating energy intake over a complete day, even though meal by meal, intake appears to be sporadic.[67] After a rapid rise in intake of all nutrients during the first 9 months of life, reductions can be expected in the intakes of some nutrients as increases occur in intakes of others.

Gender differences in intakes of energy and nutrients have been noted by several researchers. In all studies males consumed greater quantities of food and thus greater amounts of nutrients and energy.

During the preschool years a decrease occurs in intakes of calcium, phosphorus, riboflavin, iron, and vitamin A because of the omission of iron-fortified infant cereals in the diets of children, the reduction in milk intake, and the disinterest in vegetables. During this period children increase their intakes of carbohydrates and fats. Protein intakes may plateau or increase only slightly.[66] Between 3 and 8 years of age a slow, steady, and relatively consistent increase occurs in intake of all nutrients. Since intakes of vitamins A and C are unrelated to energy intakes, greater ranges of intakes of these nutrients have been noted. Black preschoolers in California have been noted to have higher intakes of sodium because of their frequent use of undiluted commercially prepared soups.[36] Young Hispanic children were reported to have high intakes of sodium[68] as were young children in Nebraska of whom 89% reported intakes of greater than the estimated safe and adequate range.[69]

Selection of a Nutritionally Appropriate Diet

Some clinicians mistakenly believe that if children are given a wide variety of food choices, they will instinctively select an adequate diet. These opinions are the results of studies designed to prove that infants and young children could tolerate and should receive a variety of foods in the first years of life. The studies, conducted in the 1920s and early 1930s, involved 6-month-old to $4\frac{1}{2}$ -year-old foundlings in a Chicago hospital.[70] The children under investigation were presented with 10 different fresh, unprocessed foods. They could eat as much or as many of the foods presented as they wished. At the completion of this study, the children were described as in good health, judged by physical growth, appearance, and vigor. It is important to note that the foods offered included only nutrient-dense, unsweetened items. There were no environmental factors that influenced food selection during the studies.

These studies indicate the kinds of food from which young children can select nutritionally adequate diets. They show that when natural, unmixed, unprocessed foods are presented in a neutral environment, children are likely to consume quantities to support normal growth and development. They do not prove that children in the free-living population and exposed to the number of combined and convenience foods available today will innately consume an appropriate nutrient and energy intake.[67,71]

Feeding Preschool Children

In spite of the reduction in appetite and erratic consumption of food, preschool children do enjoy food and gradually increase their average daily energy intakes. If simply prepared foods that provide a balance of nutrients are presented in a relaxed setting, children will consume an appropriate nutrient intake. Understanding and supportive help from parents and others who offer food to children lay the groundwork for the development of nutritionally sound and satisfying eating practices. Meals and snacks should be timed to foster appetite. Intervals necessary between meals and snacks may vary from one child to another; rarely can the clock be depended on to let one know appropriate intervals and times when it may be important for a child to eat.

Appetites may be satiated when energy needs are met regardless of a child's need for nutrients; thus a variety of food should be provided to ensure adequate nutrients and kcalories. The food should be presented without comment and the child permitted to consume amounts desired without any conversation focused on what or how much is being eaten. Portions served should be scaled to the child's appetite. When the meal is over, food should be removed and the child should be permitted to leave the table.

Intervention for nutrition and feeding difficulties. Occasionally, anxious or concerned parents need help replacing food sources of nutrients usually supplied by food refused, or in establishing limits to preschoolers' food intakes and feeding behavior. Of the commonly expressed concerns, limited intakes of milk, refusal of vegetables and meat, consumption of too many sweets, and limited intakes of food appear to cause the most problems. It is important to recognize that 1 oz of milk supplies 36 gm of calcium, and many children receive 6 to 8 oz of milk on dry cereal daily. Although they consume only 1 to 2 oz at a time, their calcium intakes may be acceptable when they consume milk with meals and snacks. When abundant amounts of fruit juice or sweetened beverages are available, children may simply prefer to drink them rather than milk. Other dairy products can be offered when milk is rejected. Cheese and yogurt are usually accepted. Powdered milk can be used in recipes for soups, vegetables, and mixed dishes.

Parents' perceptions of children's dislike of meat may need to be clarified. If preschoolers do consistently refuse all food sources of heme iron, their dietary intakes of iron should be carefully monitored. Parents concerned about children's excessive intakes of sweets may need help in setting limits on amounts of sweet foods they make available to their children. It may also be important to help parents convey their concern and the need to set limits on the availability of these foods to other family members, day-care providers, and preschool teachers.

When vegetables are consistently refused, wars between parents and children should not be permitted to erupt. Small portions (1 to 2 teaspoons) should continue to be served without comment and should be discarded if the child does not consume them. Preschool behavior modification programs that included token rewards when children consumed vegetables and another that provided education about specific vegetables served at mealtime have been found to increase children's acceptance and intake of them.[72]

If children's food intakes are so limited that their intakes of energy and nutrients are compromised, parents may need help in establishing guidelines so that the children develop appetites. They should offer food sufficiently often that children do not get so hungry that they lose their appetite, yet not so often they are always satiated. Intervals of 3 to 4 hours are often successful. Very small portions of food should be offered, and second portions should be permitted when children consume the foods already served. Attention should always be focused on children when they eat and never when food is refused.

Group Feeding

As increasing numbers of children eat some of their meals outside the home, the role of child-care providers and preschools becomes more important in providing food, nourishment, and education in eating well. Day-care facilities and preschools offer snacks and meals, and food experiences are often included as part of the learning exercises provided for children.

Day-care centers are licensed by state agencies that mandate the meal pattern and types of snacks to be provided for the children and the percentage of the RDAs that must be included in the menus. Licensed centers may receive financial assistance by entering into an agreement with the Food and Nutrition Service of the Department of Agriculture. Rates of reimbursement are variable based on family size, income, and number of children in the program. Meal requirements for children 1 to 6 years of age are based on USDA guidelines (see Tables 6-1 and 6-2).[73]

The Head Start guidelines indicate that part-day programs should receive one third of their daily nutritional needs. Those children in full-day programs should receive one half to two thirds of their daily needs depending on the length of the program day.[44]

In day-care centers or schools, breakfast needs to be provided for children who receive none at home. Snacks should be planned to complement the daily food intakes. Small portions of food should be served, and children should be permitted second servings of those foods they enjoy. Disliked or unfamiliar foods may be offered by the teaspoon, and the child's acceptance or rejection should be accepted without comment. Children who eat slowly need to be served first and should be permitted to complete their meals without being rushed to other activities. Teachers should eat with the children without imposing their attitudes about food on them.

A new setting provides an opportunity for children to have exposure to many new foods. Day-care centers, kindergartens, and preschools can provide an important educational setting for both children and their parents. Children learn how to prepare food, how food grows, how foods smell, and what nutrients foods contain. Parents learn through participation, observation, and conversations with the staff. An organized approach to feeding children must include parents, teachers, and others who offer food to young children. Teachers and day-care workers can provide parents with important information about how children successfully consume food, the nutrients children need, and the foods that provide these nutrients. Parents offer important information to the centers about their children's food acceptance and needs. Parents and professionals need to positively reinforce each other to successfully provide food for children.

A study of 48 day-care and Head Start programs found that all participating children consumed appropriate intakes of nutrients. Total

---

RESOURCE MATERIALS FOR CHILD-CARE PROVIDERS AND PRESCHOOL PROGRAMS

A planning guide for food service in child care centers, USDA, Food and Nutrition Service, Jan, 1985.
> Meal patterns, menus, food preparation, sanitation and nutrition education guidelines for young children in child care centers

Head start program performance standards, US Department of Health and Human Services, Office of Human Development Services, Administration for Children, Youth, and Families, Head Start Bureau, 1984.
> Performance standards for menus, nutritional requirements and meal service that support developmental milestones for young children

Caring for our children—national health and safety performance standards: guidelines for out-of-home child care programs: Joint Project of American Public Health Association and American Academy of Pediatrics, 1992.

Nutrition and your health: dietary guidelines for Americans, ed 3, Home and Garden Bulletin No 232, USDA, US Department of Health and Human Services, US Government Printing Office, Washington, DC 1990.
> Provides guidelines for appropriate intakes of foods to support good health

Nutrition standards in day-care programs for children: technical support paper, J Am Diet Assoc 87:504, 1987.
> Provides support for appropriate nutrient intake, emotional climate of food service, and nutrition education for young children

Meal pattern requirements and offer versus serve manual, USDA, Food and Nutrition Service, FNS-265, Aug, 1990.
> Provides USDA guidelines for foods to be served to young children at breakfast, lunch, or supper and snacks

Healthy People 2000: Nutrition Objectives, *J Am Diet Assoc* 91:1515, 1991.
> Based on dietary guidelines for Americans, proposes achievable goals for improved nutritional status

---

daily energy intakes were similar for all children regardless of whether one meal and one snack or two meals and two snacks were provided. In fact when children consumed one meal and one snack in this setting, 82% of their energy intake was provided, but when they consumed two meals and two snacks, 84% of their energy intake was provided.[73]

The box above provides a listing of guidelines and recommendations that affect provision of nourishment to young children.

Summary

Children between 1 and 6 years of age develop at a steady rate. They acquire many new skills, learn much about the environment in which they live, and test the limits of behavior that the environment will accept. All of these factors influence their food and therefore nutrient intake. Parents need to provide appropriate foods and supportive guidance so that food patterns that support an appropriate nutrient intake are developed. Nutrition knowledge of the parents positively influences children's nutrient intake. Advertising and television programs also affect children's requests for and acceptance of food.

Although most young children are well nourished, groups exist within our population with both clinical and biochemical evidence of malnutrition. Nutrients most often consumed in inappropriately limited amounts are iron, calcium, and vitamins B_6 and C.

REVIEW QUESTIONS

1. Which nutrients are most likely to be consumed at low levels in the preschool-age period?
2. What influence does rate of growth have on energy intake?
3. Which physical and developmental factors most influence the foods that young children are willing and capable of consuming?
4. How do family food habits most significantly effect the foods that are consumed of young children?
5. In what ways do cultural and community factors effect the foods that are available to young children?
6. What are the most common concerns of parents about the food intake of young childen?

SUGGESTED LEARNING ACTIVITIES

1. Assess the nutrient intake of a preschool child.
2. Observe a preschool feeding program and describe the feeding environment.
3. Describe factors that influence food acceptability in the preschool child.
4. Describe appropriate snacks for preschool-age children.
5. Describe factors that influence foods acceptable to preschool-age children.
6. Plan a nutrition lesson for a Head Start Program class.
7. Plan brown bag lunches for a preschool-age child for one week that provide variety and are nutritionally appropriate.

Terms and Concepts

Provided here for your review is a listing of terms and concepts within this chapter. The definitions for terms can be found in the glossary, which begins on page 413. To aid your understanding of the terms' and concepts' application within this text, the page number designating the first mention of each term or concept within the chapter is given.

malnutrition, 122
food asphyxiation, 131
Healthy People 2000: Nutrition Objectives, 125
poverty line, 122

REFERENCES

1. Nationwide food consumption survey—continuing survey of food intake by individuals—1985: Nutrition Monitoring Division, Human Nutrition Information Service, *Nutr Today* Nov/Dec:31, 1986.
2. Food consumption survey examines eating habits: *Nutr Week,* Community Nutrition Institute, Washington, DC, Jan 16, 1986.
3. Nationwide food consumption survey: CSFII—continuing survey of food intake by individuals—1986: Nutrition Monitoring Division, Human Nutrition Information Service, *Nutr Today* Sept/Oct:36, 1987.
4. Jones DY, Nesheim MD, Habicht JP: Influences in child growth associated with poverty in the 1970's: an examination of HANES I and HANES II, cross-sectional US national surveys, *Am J Clin Nutr* 42:714, 1985.
5. Kumanyika SK and others: Stature and weight status of children in an urban kindergarten population, *Pediatrics* 85:783, 1990.
6. Leave no child behind: an opinion maker's guide, *Nutr Week* XXI:4, Community Nutrition Institute, Washington, DC, Dec 6, 1991.
7. Windham CT and others: Nutrient density of diets in the USDA Nationwide Food Consumption Survey, 1977-1978. I. Impact of socioeconomic status on dietary density, *J Am Diet Assoc* 82:26, 1983.
8. Friedman BJ: Differences in dietary intake of young Caucasian, Mexican-American, and African-American children, *J Am Diet Assoc* 91:A-77, 1991.
9. Owen GM and others: A study of nutritional status of preschool children in the United States, 1968-1970, *Pediatrics* 53:597, 1974.
10. Caloric and selected nutrient values for persons 1-74 years of age: First Health and Nutrition Examination Survey, US, 1971-1974. US Department of Health, Education and Welfare, Public Health Service, Office of Health Research, Statistics, and Technology, National Center for Health Statistics, DHEW Pub No (PHS) 79-1657, 1979.
11. Nicklas TA and others: Cardiovascular risk factors from birth to 7 years of age: the Bogalusa Heart Study—dietary intake, *Pediatrics* 80(suppl 5):797, 1987.
12. Healthy People 2000: Nutrition objectives, *J Am Diet Assoc* 91:1515, 1991.
13. *Nutrition and your health: dietary guidelines for Americans,* ed 3, Home and Garden Bulletin No 232, USDA, US Department of Health and Human Services, Washington, DC, 1990, US Government Printing Office.

14. Kimm SYS and others: Dietary patterns of US children: implications for disease prevention, *Prev Med* 19:432, 1990.
15. Terry RD, Oakland MJ: Parents' reasons for giving vitamin and mineral supplements to their preschoolers, *Top Clin Nutr* 5:67, 1990.
16. Van Duzen J, Carter JP, Vander Zwaag R: Protein and calorie malnutrition among preschool Navajo Indian children, *Am J Clin Nutr* 29:657, 1976.
17. Owen GM and others: Nutrition survey of White Mountain Apache preschool children in nutrition, growth, and development of North American Indian children, Pub No (NIH) 72-76, Washington, DC, 1972, Department of Health, Education and Welfare.
18. Zee P and others: Nutritional improvement of poor urban preschool children: a 1983-1977 comparison, *JAMA* 253:3269, 1985.
19. Fries ME, Crisley BM, Driskell JA: Vitamin B_6 status of a group of preschool children, *Am J Clin Nutr* 34:2706, 1981.
20. Fierman AH and others: Growth delay in homeless children, *Pediatrics* 88:918, 1991.
21. Drake MA: Dietary adequacy of children residing in temporary shelters, *J Am Diet Assoc* 91:A-77, 1991.
22. DuRousseau PC and others: Children in foster care: are they at nutritional risk? *J Am Diet Assoc* 91:83, 1991.
23. Brown E, Tieman P: Effect of income and WIC on the dietary intake of preschoolers: results of a preliminary study, *J Am Diet Assoc* 86:1189, 1986.
24. Smith AL and others: Effectiveness of a nutrition program for mothers and their anemic children under 5 years of age, *J Am Diet Assoc* 86:1039, 1986.
25. Lozoff B and others: Long-term developmental outcome of infants with iron deficiency, *N Engl J Med* 325:687, 1991.
26. Drake MA: Anthropometry, biochemical iron indexes, and energy and nutrient intake of preschool children: comparison of intake at day care center and at home, *J Am Diet Assoc* 91:1587, 1991.
27. Mahaffey KR: Environmental lead toxicity: nutrition as a component of intervention, *Environ Health Perspect* 89:75, 1990.
28. Frisancho AR, Ryan AS: Decreased stature associated with moderate blood lead concentrations in Mexican-American children, *Am J Clin Nutr* 54:516, 1991.
29. Mushak P, Crocetti AF: Methods for reducing lead exposure in young children and other risk groups: an integrated summary of a report to the US Congress on childhood lead poisoning, *Environ Health Perspect* 89:125, 1990.
30. Preventing lead poisoning in young children: a statement by the Centers for Disease Control, US Department of Health and Human Services, Public Health Service, Centers for Disease Control, Oct, 1991.
31. Murphy SP and others: An evaluation of food group intakes by Mexican-American children, *J Am Diet Assoc* 90:388, 1990.
32. Eppright ES and others: Nutrition of infants and preschool children in the North Central region of the United States of America, *World Rev Nutr Diet* 14:269, 1972.
33. Eppright ES and others: The North Central Regional study of diets of preschool children. II. Nutrition knowledge and attitudes of mothers, *J Home Econ* 62:327, 1970.
34. Caliendo MA and others: Nutritional status of preschool children, *J Am Diet Assoc* 71:20, 1977.
35. Johnson RK and others: Effect of maternal employment on the quality of young children's diets—NFCS 1987-1988, *J Am Diet Assoc* 91:A-67, 1991.
36. Crawford PB, Hankin JH, Huenemann RL: Environmental factors associated with preschool obesity, *J Am Diet Assoc* 72:589, 1978.
37. DeWalt KM: The use of itemized register tapes for analysis of household food acquisition patterns prompted by children, *J Am Diet Assoc* 90:559, 1990.
38. Kirk MC, Gillespie AH: Factors affecting food choices of working mothers with young families, *J Nutr Educ* 22:161, 1990.
39. Phillips DE and others: Use of food and nutrition knowledge by mothers of preschool children, *J Nutr Educ* 10:73, 1978.
40. Karp R and others: Parental behavior and the availability of foods among undernourished inner-city children, *J Fam Pract* 18:731, 1984.
41. *Dietitians teach value of good nutrition in foodservice for young children,* ADA Courier 31:1, 1992.
42. Nutrition standards in day-care programs for children: technical support paper, *J Am Diet Assoc* 87:504, 1987.
43. *A planning guide for food service in child care centers,* Food and Nutrition Services, USDA, Washington, DC, 1985.
44. Head Start Program Performance Standards, US Department of Health and Human Services, Office of Human Development Services, Administration for Children, Youth, and Families, Head Start Bureau, 1984.

45. Caring for our children: national health and safety performance standards: guidelines for out-of-home child care programs: joint project of American Public Health Association and American Academy of Pediatrics, 1992.

46. Position paper on nutrition in child care settings, *J Nutr Educ* 23:49, 1991.

47. Briley ME and others: Who plans the menu at the child care center? *J Am Diet Assoc* 91:A-75, 1991.

48. Briley ME and others: What is on the menu at the child care center? *J Am Diet Assoc* 89:771, 1989.

49. Briley ME: Nutrition of young children in child care programs, *Food and Nutr News* 62(4):21, 1990.

50. Briley ME and others: Nutrition knowledge and attitudes and menu planning skills of family day-home providers, *J Am Diet Assoc* 89:694, 1989.

51. McNichol J and others: Nutrient intakes of preschool-aged boys, *J Can Diet Assoc* 50:31, 1989.

52. Microwave meals attract children, *J Am Diet Assoc* 91:720, 1991.

53. Kunkel D: Children and host-selling television commercials, *Comm Res* 15:17, 1988.

54. Windhauser MM and others: A nutritional evaluation of food and beverage products as advertised to children on Saturday morning television, *J Am Diet Assoc* 91:A-83, 1991.

55. Eppright ES and others: Eating behavior of preschool children, *J Nutr Educ* 1:16, 1969.

56. Sims LS, Morris PM: Nutritional status of preschoolers, *J Am Diet Assoc* 64:492, 1974.

57. Klesges RC and others: Parental influence on food selection in young children and its relationship to childhood obesity, *Am J Clin Nutr* 53:859, 1991.

58. Hertzler AA: Preschoolers' food handling skills—motor development, *J Nutr Educ* 21:100B, 1989.

59. Harris CS and others: Childhood asphyxiation by food: a national analysis and overlook, *JAMA* 251:2231, 1984.

60. Beal VA: On the acceptance of solid foods and other food patterns of infants and children, *Pediatrics* 20:448, 1957.

61. Pelchat ML, Pliner P: Antecedents and correlates of feeding problems in young children, *J Nutr Educ* 18:23, 1986.

62. Satter E: *How to get your kid to eat . . . but not too much,* Palo Alto, Calif, 1987, Bull Publishing.

63. Huenemann RL: Environmental factors associated with preschool obesity. II. Obesity and food practices of children at successive age levels, *J Am Diet Assoc* 64:489, 1974.

64. Eppright ES and others: The North Central Regional study of diets of preschool children. III. Frequency of eating, *J Home Econ* 62:407, 1970.

65. Frank, GC and others: Dietary studies of rural school children in a cardiovascular study, *J Am Diet Assoc* 71:31, 1977.

66. Beal VA: Dietary intake of individuals followed through infancy and childhood, *Am J Public Health* 51:1107, 1961.

67. Birch LL and others: The variability of young children's energy intake, *N Engl J Med* 324(4):232, 1991.

68. Sanjur D and others: Dietary patterns and nutrient intakes of toddlers from low-income families in Denver, Colorado, *J Am Diet Assoc* 90:823, 1990.

69. Stanek K and others: Diet quality and the eating environment of preschool children, *J Am Diet Assoc* 90:582, 1990.

70. Davis CM: The self-selection of diet experiment: its significance for feeding in the home, *Ohio State Med J* 34:862, 1938.

71. Story M, Brown JE: Do young children instinctively know what to eat? The studies of Clara Davis revisited, *N Engl J Med* 316:103, 1987.

72. Ireton CL, Guthrie HA: Modification of vegetable-eating behavior in preschool children, *J Nutr Educ* 4:100, 1972.

73. *Meal pattern requirements and offer versus serve manual,* USDA, Food and Nutrition Service, FNS-265, Aug, 1990.

74. Williams S, Henneman A, Fox H: Contribution of food service programs in preschool centers to children's nutritional needs, *J Am Diet Assoc* 71:610, 1977.

6

Nutrition and the School-Age Child

Betty Lucas

Objectives

✦✦

After studying this chapter, the student should:

✔ *Be aware of nutrition concerns of school-age children.*

✔ *Recognize factors that influence food choices and attitudes of children and their families.*

✔ *Be aware of the value of snacks to a child's daily total nutrient intake.*

✔ *Have knowledge of feeding and educational programs designed to improve the nutritional status of children.*

✔ *Understand nutrition and food intake approaches to the control of dental caries.*

✔ *Understand the primary nutritional considerations for children participating in sports.*

✔ *Recognize the effects of diet on learning and school performance.*

✔ *Be familiar with the various dietary treatments for hyperactivity and the studies of their effectiveness.*

✔ *Understand the natural course and dietary management of lactose intolerance.*

The school-age years, generally considered to be 6 to 12 years of age, are marked by more quiet, stable changes compared to the extremes of growth and development seen in infancy and adolescence. Children in this age group show a consistent but slow rate of physical growth, continuing maturation of fine and gross motor skills, and gains in cognitive and social-emotional growth. By the end of this period, girls are typically well into puberty, and boys will soon follow.

There are common patterns of food and nutrient intake among school-age children. Food habits, likes, and dislikes are established, many of which form the base for a lifetime of food and nutrition intake. Food choices are influenced more by factors from outside and less by parents and family. Feeding programs at day-care and school continue to contribute significantly to children's total nutrient intake.

NUTRITIONAL STATUS OF SCHOOL-AGE CHILDREN

Although clinical signs of malnutrition are rarely found in children in North America, there are children who receive diets inadequate in quantity or quality (e.g., low income, Native Americans, homeless). Nutrients most likely to be low or deficient are calcium, iron, vitamins B_6 and A, and ascorbic acid.[1,2] The more limited the diet is in energy, the more likelihood for low or deficient nutrient intakes.[3]

Vitamin and Mineral Supplements

The use of multiple vitamin and mineral supplements decreases after infancy to about 23% of school-age children.[4] Supplements are generally used by families who are better educated and in less need of them. Most children take iron supplements as part of a multiple vitamin supplement.

Except for fluoride supplementation in unfluoridated areas, the American Academy of Pediatrics does not support routine supplementation for healthy children. Four groups of children at nutritional risk, however, are identified as potentially benefitting from supplements. These include: (1) children from deprived families, especially those abused or neglected; (2) children with anorexia, poor appetites, and poor eating habits; (3) children consuming vegetarian diets without dairy products; and (4) pregnant adolescents.[5]

Children needing supplements can be determined by a nutritional assessment, and in addition to the above, might include those with food allergies, limited food acceptances, or frequent or chronic illness. There is no risk if parents wish to give their children a standard pediatric multivitamin but **megadose** levels should be discouraged.

FACTORS AFFECTING FOOD INTAKE

There are several influences that determine the food habits and intake of children. Major factors include family, peers, and the media.

Family

Eating habits and food likes or dislikes are formed in the early years and continue into adulthood. Parents and siblings provide a model of food acceptance and feeding behavior that children imitate. In a study of parents and 6- to 19-year-old children, there was a positive correlation between parent and child intakes of kcalories, carbohydrates, saturated fats, and polyunsaturated fats.[6] The correlation was greater for black children than for white children.

The emotional environment at mealtime may influence food and nutrient intake. The dinner table is not the place for family battles or punitive action toward children. For eating to be successful, it should occur at a time and in a setting that is comfortable and free from stress and unreasonable demands.

With more women employed outside the home, there may be less time available for food preparation and more use of fast food, eating out, and prepared foods from restaurants or grocery delicatessens. Although convenience may be a major factor, parents often need help selecting these foods and others so that a balanced nutrient intake is provided.

Low-income families have less money for food than more affluent families. The large percentage of single-parent families headed by women often means a reduced purchasing power. Foods that provide essential nutrients may be partially or completely eliminated from the diet. However, not all children from low-income families are at risk for undernutrition. One study found that undernourished children from low-income families had parents who prepared fewer regular meals and who were less likely to eat vegetables and milk than parents of adequately nourished children from homes with similar incomes. More **convenience foods** and fewer foods requiring preparation were available to undernourished children than to the well-nourished children.[7]

An emerging trend in the United States is the increased responsibility for family shopping and cooking by children not yet in their teenage years. Some of these children frequently prepare their own breakfasts, lunches, snacks, and even evening meals.[8] They also shop for food on a regular basis and have a significant influence on family food purchases. Factors contributing to this trend include working parents, increased use of microwave ovens, more money available to spend on convenience and prepared foods, and less emphasis on family meals. Along with this trend there is increasingly sophisticated advertising aimed at these children.[8] Although children need experience selecting food, parents need to provide guidance so that children select foods that provide adequate amounts of nutrients.

Peers

As children move into the wide world, their food choices are influenced by those outside the immediate family. Day-care, the homes of friends, and school provide broad food experiences, with both positive and negative impacts on nutritional status. The credibility of parents is often questioned in the face of advice from teachers, peers, or peers' parents. The school-age child has more access to money, to grocery stores, and therefore to foods with questionable nutrient value.

Participation in the school lunch program may be determined as much by friends as by the menu. Being part of the group can be a problem for a child who has a chronic illness or disorder that requires diet modification such as diabetes, food allergies, or phenylketonuria (PKU). These children need education regarding diet rationale appropriate to their developmental level and methods of problem-solving food choices when in a group of peers.

Media

Television is the primary media influence on children of all ages. The typical school-age child watches about 26 hours of television per week.[9] Nearly half of all commercials advertise food with a higher percentage of food commercials aired during children's programs.[9] Foods most frequently advertised are those high in fat, sugar, and salt (e.g., sweetened cereals, fast foods, snack foods, and candy). The message from these food commercials has a primary emotional and psychological appeal, with little basis on sound nutrition. Although school-age children are better at cognitive discrimination between the program and commercial messages than younger children, they are still very responsive to these commercials.

FEEDING THE SCHOOL-AGE CHILD

The school-age period is one of relatively steady growth and few apparent feeding problems. School schedules provide a more ordered routine. Children attempt to master physical skills, and they expend energy in organized sports and games. A natural increase in appetite is responsible for normal increases in food intake. Differences in intake between males and females increase gradually up to 12 years of age and then become marked. Boys consume greater quantities of energy and nutrients than do girls.

School-age children are not without food and nutrition concerns. Unresolved conflicts from the preschool years may persist. Children in their early school years often continue to refuse a food that touches another on the plate or to demand a special arrangement of dishes and utensils on the table. Likes and dislikes, although established, are not necessarily permanent, but they may become so if parents do not offer the food or if the food dislike is such a frequent focus that children become fully patterned into their **food idiosyncrasies.**

Undernutrition may have serious consequences for the school-age child; for example, the child may become easily fatigued, unable to sustain prolonged physical effort, or unable to participate fully in learning experiences. Because the risk of infection is greater in undernourished children, a child with limited nutrient reserves may have frequent absences from school.

Food Intake Patterns

School-age children eat less frequently than younger children, about four to five times per day on school days. They almost always want snacks after school, which they often prepare themselves. It has been reported that their snacks contribute about one third of their total energy intake.[10] Although some children increase the variety of foods they accept, many continue to reject vegetables, mixed dishes, and some meats, or to accept a limited range of foods.

Breakfast is an important meal. Children have to rise early to eat an unhurried and balanced meal and may have to prepare it themselves. Most children consume breakfasts that contribute at least one fourth of the RDA.[11] A larger percentage of children in the lower grades eat breakfast than of those in the middle and upper grades. One study found that children who consumed ready-to-eat cereals three or four times a week skipped breakfast less frequently than children who ate cooked cereal.[11]

Regular family meals may be less frequent as participation in organized sports, music lessons, and other activities increases. Even when eating at the same time, some family meals have been moved from the dining room to trays in front of the television. In addition to limiting the social interaction of family meals, it has been observed that some children become so engrossed in the shows that they lose interest in their food.

Snacking between meals and while watching television is an important factor in the school-age child's nutrient intake and food habits. Not only does television viewing encourage snacking, but it is a **sedentary** activity and has been linked to the development of obesity in childhood.[12] Parents can help by planning regular snack times and providing appropriate foods (see Chapter 12 for a thorough discussion of obesity and its management).

SCHOOL MEALS

Feeding and nutrition education programs in schools, when adequately implemented, provide not only important nutrients for children, but also an opportunity for them to learn to make responsible choices regarding dietary intake. Since its inception in 1946, the **National School Lunch Program (NSLP)** has been ad-

ministered by the US Department of Agriculture (USDA), which provides cash reimbursement and supplemental foods to feeding programs that comply with federal regulations. These regulations require that school meals be sold at reduced prices or be given free to children whose families cannot afford to buy them.

Begun as a pilot project in 1966, the **School Breakfast Program (SBP)** is also administered by USDA. Supported by consumer groups and low-income advocates, the program has slowly expanded in the past 25 years. Some states have passed legislation requiring breakfast programs in schools where there is a high percentage of children receiving free or reduced price lunches. In 1991, breakfasts were provided in more than one half of the schools participating in the lunch program.[13]

Menus must be planned to meet the guidelines established for the NSLP. Lunch provides about one third of the RDA for the particular age group. Tables 6-1 and 6-2 show minimum quantities of food required for the lunch and breakfast patterns for the various age groups.

Unfortunately not all schools have provided well-prepared food or an optimum environment to encourage acceptance of the NSLP. Problems with the program have included **plate waste**, poor menu acceptance by students, competition from vending machines, and concerns regarding excessive amounts of fat, sugar, and salt.

Factors believed to be responsible for food waste include unpalatability of the food, limited menu choice, off-site food preparation, children's low preference for vegetables, and the availability of sweets and sodas in vending machines. **Family style service** has been shown to result in less waste than cafeteria style service.[14] Other factors believed to compromise children's food intakes include short lunch periods, long cafeteria lines, and a hurried, unsupervised atmosphere.

Efforts have addressed these problems by including students in menu planning, improving the eating environment, program promotion, and related activities. Programs have offered popular foods that comply with the NSLP (e.g., pizza, hamburger, tacos, salad bars, and fruits). To provide variety and to increase par-

TABLE 6-1   *School Lunch Pattern—National School Lunch Program*

Components	Minimum Quantities				Recommended Quantities*
	Group I: Age 1-2; Preschool	Group II: Age 3-4; Preschool	Group III: Age 5-8; Gr. K-3	Group IV: Age 9 and Older; Gr. 4-12	Group V: Age 12 and Older; Gr. 7-12
Milk Whole and unflavored lowfat milk must be offered†	$\frac{3}{4}$ c (6 fl oz)	$\frac{3}{4}$ c (6 fl oz)	$\frac{1}{2}$ pt (8 fl oz)	$\frac{1}{2}$ pt (8 fl oz)	$\frac{1}{2}$ pt (8 fl oz)
Meat or meat alternate (quantity of the edible portion as served)					
Lean meat, poultry, or fish	1 oz	$1\frac{1}{2}$ oz	$1\frac{1}{2}$ oz	2 oz	3 oz
Cheese	1 oz	$1\frac{1}{2}$ oz	$1\frac{1}{2}$ oz	2 oz	3 oz
Large egg	$\frac{1}{2}$	$\frac{3}{4}$	$\frac{3}{4}$	1	$1\frac{1}{2}$
Cooked dry beans or peas	$\frac{1}{4}$ c	$\frac{3}{8}$ c	$\frac{3}{8}$ c	$\frac{1}{2}$ c	$\frac{3}{4}$ c
Peanut butter or an equivalent quantity of any combination of above	2 T	3 T	3 T	4 T	6 T
Vegetable or fruit 2 or more servings of vegetable or fruit or both to total	$\frac{1}{2}$ c	$\frac{1}{2}$ c	$\frac{1}{2}$ c	$\frac{3}{4}$ c	$\frac{3}{4}$ c
Bread or bread alternate (servings per week) Must be enriched or whole-grain—at least $\frac{1}{2}$ serving‡ for group I or one serving‡ for groups II-V must be served daily	5	8	8	8	10

From Food and Nutrition Service, US Department of Agriculture: *Meal pattern requirements and offer versus serve manual*, FNS-265, 1990.

*The minimum portion sizes for these children are the portion sizes for group IV.

†This requirement does not prohibit offering other milk, such as flavored milk or skim milk, along with the above.

‡Serving, 1 slice of bread; or $\frac{1}{2}$ cup of cooked rice, macaroni, noodles, other pasta products, other cereal products such as bulgur and corn grits; or 1 biscuit, roll, muffin, and similar products; or any combination of these.

TABLE 6-2   *School Breakfast Pattern—School Breakfast Program*

Food Components		Minimum Quantities		
		Age 1-2	Age 3-5	Age 6 and Older
Milk	Beverage, on cereal, or both	$\frac{1}{2}$ c (4 fl oz)	$\frac{3}{4}$ c (6 fl oz)	$\frac{1}{2}$ pt (8 fl oz)
Fruit/vegetable/juice*	Fruit or vegetable or both or full-strength fruit or vegetable juice	$\frac{1}{4}$ c	$\frac{1}{2}$ c	$\frac{1}{2}$ c
Select *one* serving from each of the following components or *two* servings from one component.				
Bread or bread alternate	Whole-grain or enriched bread	$\frac{1}{2}$ slice	$\frac{1}{2}$ slice	1 slice
	Whole-grain or enriched biscuit, roll, muffin	$\frac{1}{2}$ serving	$\frac{1}{2}$ serving	1 serving
	Whole-grain, enriched, or fortified cereal	$\frac{1}{4}$ c or $\frac{1}{3}$ oz	$\frac{1}{3}$ c or $\frac{1}{2}$ oz	$\frac{3}{4}$ c or 1 oz
Meat or meat alternate	Lean meat, poultry, or fish	$\frac{1}{2}$ oz	$\frac{1}{2}$ oz	1 oz
	Cheese	$\frac{1}{2}$ oz	$\frac{1}{2}$ oz	1 oz
	Large egg	$\frac{1}{2}$	$\frac{1}{2}$	$\frac{1}{2}$
	Peanut butter	1 T	1 T	2 T
	Cooked dry beans or peas	2 T	2 T	4 T
	Nuts or seeds or both	$\frac{1}{2}$ oz	$\frac{1}{2}$ oz	1 oz

From Food and Nutrition Service, USDA: *Meal pattern requirements and offer versus serve manual*, FNS-265, 1990.
*A citrus fruit or juice or a vegetable that is a good source of vitamin C is recommended daily.

ticipation and consumption, schools are encouraged to provide a selection of foods. Students may be permitted to decline one or two items, depending on age and local discretion.

School meals do not always accommodate the needs of a child on a weight management program, and more recent concerns about preventing cardiovascular disease have focused on the levels of fat, sugar, and salt in the menus. Using a visual plate waste study, Ho and others[15] reported that the school lunch as consumed provided 39% of the kcalories as fat and 14% of the kcalories as saturated fat. Current guidance from USDA has encouraged the development of menus that will strive to meet the U.S. Dietary Guidelines, including reducing the fat content of recipes, offering fewer baked desserts and more fresh fruits and vegetables, and incorporating more whole-grain products.

Vending machines and school stores used as fundraisers for school activities have been a concern to many interested in dental health, prevention of obesity, and the development of sound food habits for all children. Although common items offered are candy, soda pop, and chips, some school districts have made efforts to provide more fruit, juice, milk, nuts, and seeds. These more healthy options have met with partial success, since they may not sell as well and the profit margin is slimmer than with the candy and soda.

Federal legislation stipulates that foods sold in competition with school lunch in snack bars or vending machines must provide at least 5%

of the RDA for one or more of the following nutrients: protein, vitamin A, ascorbic acid, niacin, riboflavin, thiamin, calcium, and iron. The original legislation was amended to restrict this competition to the food service area during the lunch period. Other items not meeting this criteria (e.g., soda pop, chewing gum, some candies) can be sold anytime outside the restricted area. Thus, these competitive foods continue to be daily choices for schoolchildren.

Children who do not participate in the school lunch program generally bring a packed lunch from home. Studies have indicated that, compared with the school lunch, sack lunches provide significantly fewer nutrients, but are also lower in saturated fats.[15] Little variety is seen in the packed lunches because favorite foods tend to be consistently packed and lack of refrigeration limits the food choices.

Although elementary school children are making more decisions regarding food selection, some supervision and supportive guidance may be necessary at lunchtime. Children may give priority to activities other than eating, often rushing through their meals. They may prefer to do without meals rather than reveal the fact that they must receive reduced price or free lunches. Some may refuse to eat many foods on the menu. In addition, disposable trays and plastic utensils are not always easy for children to use.

Some children and their families may need assistance in making school meals meet the child's needs. Overweight and obese children will need more fresh fruit desserts and fewer sauces and gravies as well as a low-fat milk. An undernourished or homeless child may need to be offered whole milk even if the usual offering is low-fat milk. As children with special health care needs enter mainstream education, careful planning with parents will be necessary to ensure that mealtimes at school provide appropriate foods and nutrients for these children.

NUTRITION EDUCATION

As children grow older, have money to spend, attend school, and interact with larger numbers of individuals, their selection of food increasingly becomes their own. Nutrition education during the school years is an important method of developing a nutritionally informed population. This occurs formally in school classrooms and clubs such as 4-H, but also informally from the media, advertising, written materials, family, and peers.

Unfortunately nutrition is frequently a low priority in the curriculum and few teachers have had basic nutrition information during their teacher training. Many have considered it a boring subject and difficult to integrate into an already crowded curriculum. Other reasons cited for ineffective nutrition education programs include lack of adequate research, resource materials, and specific curriculum guidelines that would be interdisciplinary and sequential.[16] Nutrition education activities have been a part of some private sector programs, primarily the Dairy Council, and of some governmental agencies.

Children's developmental level should be taken into consideration when teaching nutrition concepts. **Piaget's theory of learning** through the growing years is the basis of many educational programs.[17] Table 6-3 correlates Piaget's learning theory with progress in feeding and nutrition. School-age children will do best with a hands-on food experience that relates to them personally, not written or verbal nutrition concepts. They frequently respond well to computer-assisted programs that use their individual dietary profiles or teach nutrition concepts through a game format.

Nutrition Education Training Program

Because of concern that lack of adequate nutrition information was contributing to unwise food choices and to food waste in the school lunch programs, Congress enacted the **Nutrition Education Training Program (NETP)** in 1977. Administered by the USDA, the program offered states grants to develop and implement a state nutrition education plan. Congress identified the following needs for this program in the NETP legislation[18]:

1. The proper nutrition of the nation's children is a matter of highest priority.

TABLE 6-3   Piaget's Theory of Cognitive Development in Relation to Feeding and Nutrition

Developmental Period	Cognitive Characteristics	Relationships to Feeding and Nutrition
Sensorimotor (Birth-2 years)	Progression from newborn with automatic reflexes to intentional interaction with the environment and the beginning use of symbols	Progression is made from sucking and rooting reflexes to the acquisition of self-feeding skills Food is used primarily to satisfy hunger, as a medium to explore the environment, and to practice fine motor skills
Preoperations (2-7 years)	Thought processes become internalized; they are unsystematic and intuitive Use of symbols increases Reasoning is based on appearances and happenstance Approach to classification is functional and unsystematic Child's world is viewed egocentrically	Eating becomes less the center of attention than social, language, and cognitive growth Food is described by color, shape, and quantity but there is limited ability to classify food into "groups" Foods tend to be classed as "like" and "don't like" Foods can be identified as "good for you" but reasons are unknown or mistaken
Concrete operations (7-11 years)	Child can focus on several aspects of a situation simultaneously Cause/effect reasoning becomes more rational and systematic Ability to classify, reclassify, and generalize emerges Decrease in egocentricism permits child to take another's view	Beginning of realization that nutritious food has a positive effect on growth and health, but limited understanding of how or why this occurs Mealtimes take on a social significance The expanding environment increases the opportunities for, and influences on, food selection (peer influence rises)
Formal operations (11 years and older)	Hypothetical and abstract thought expand Understanding of scientific and theoretical processes deepens	The concept of nutrients from food functioning at physiological and biochemical levels can be understood Conflicts in making food choices may be realized (knowledge of nutritious food vs. preferences and nonnutritive influences)

From Mahan LK, Arlin MT: *Krause's food, nutrition, and diet therapy,* ed 8, Philadelphia, 1992, WB Saunders.

2. The lack of understanding of the principles of good nutrition and their relationship to health can contribute to a child's rejection of highly nutritious foods and consequent food waste in school food service operations.

3. Many school food service personnel have not had adequate training in food service management skills and principles, and many teachers and school food service operators have not had adequate training in the fundamentals of nutrition or in how to convey this information to motivate children to practice sound eating habits.

4. Parents exert a significant influence on children in the development of nutritional habits, and lack of nutrition knowledge on the part of parents can have detrimental effects on children's nutritional development.
5. There is a need to create opportunities for children to learn about the importance of the principles of good nutrition in their daily lives and how these principles are applied in the school cafeteria.

During the program's most active phase, states provided nutrition education for school lunch employees and teachers. Curriculum guidelines and materials for children in schools and child-care settings were also developed. Classroom activities that involved the cafeteria were initiated in some schools.

When the effect of these programs was evaluated, they were found to have a strong positive impact on nutrition-related knowledge. There was an increase in the number of children willing to select and taste new foods and in reported food preferences and food-related attitudes. However, the behavioral and attitudinal effects were neither as strong nor as consistent across grade levels as were the effects on knowledge. In grades one to three a positive impact was noted in self-reported measures of food preference and willingness of children to select unfamiliar fruits and vegetables when offered a choice during the school lunch.[19] In grades four to six, children who participated in the programs were more willing to taste previously unfamiliar foods than were children who had not participated in the program. Although nutrition education has been noted to decrease food waste, ongoing education efforts are needed to maintain the positive changes in food consumption.[20]

During the 1980s, the NETP budget was drastically reduced with little program impact noted at the local level. Recent years have seen a modest increase in funding, to a level of $15 million nationally for 1992. Current efforts are directed toward school food service employee training, coordination of curriculum and food service activities, and integration of nutrition into health education and other curriculums.

As children prepare to enter adolescence, attitudes toward food will be well established. The nutrition knowledge and attitudes acquired during this period become a basis for the future when decisions of food selection become their own. It is important that we learn new methods of nutrition education that may have a greater impact on behavioral change in school-age children.

SPORTS AND FITNESS

Interest in sports and physical fitness has increased dramatically among children and adolescents. No longer are athletic competition and training restricted to boys in varsity team sports. Much enthusiasm has developed among girls, and individual sports have gained in popularity among girls and boys of all ages.

On the other hand, overweight and obesity has increased substantially in the school-age and adolescent population compared with children of the same age groups in the 1970s.[21] It has been reported that American youth are becoming less fit. A decline in physical activity throughout childhood is observed and accepted, although results of national fitness tests are not necessarily linked to health outcomes.[22]

Some factors believed to be at blame for a sedentary life-style include an increase in time spent watching television and playing computer and video games and less physical education in the school curriculum. With two working parents there is less free or spontaneous play and more organized sports, dance classes, swimming lessons, and gymnastics classes. Budget cuts can eliminate extramural school sports or recreational activities in community centers. In addition, safety issues, especially in urban areas, frequently mean that children are restricted to their homes.

Interest in athletic performance is beneficial to the health of our youth, provided that the intensity of involvement is not excessive. Activities that focus on winning rather than skill development and pleasure can have negative physical and emotional consequences. Positive goals for children in sports are listed in the box on page 151. Sensible health practices for growing

❖
THE YOUNG ATHLETES' BILL OF RIGHTS

1. The right to have the opportunity to participate in sports regardless of one's ability level.
2. The right to participate at a level commensurate with the child's developmental level.
3. The right to have qualified adult leadership.
4. The right to participate in a safe and healthy environment.
5. The right of each child to share leadership and decision-making.
6. The right to play as a child and not as an adult.
7. The right to proper preparation for participation in sports.
8. The right to equal opportunity to strive for success.
9. The right to be treated with dignity by all involved.
10. The right to have fun through sports.

From Strong WB: *Am J Dis Child* 142:143, 1988.

TABLE 6-4   *Activities of Different Energy Expenditures**

Energy Output	Activities
Low (<4 kcal/min; up to 240 kcal/hr)	Baseball, cycling (up to 9 mi/hr), walking, gymnastics, table tennis, moderate football
Moderate (4-7 kcal/min; 240-420 kcal/hr)	Basketball, cycling (10-13 mi/hr), roller skating, ice skating (9 mi/hr), running (more than 12 min/mi), touch football, hiking with a pack (3 mi/hr)
High (>7 kcal/min; ≥420 kcal/hr)	Cycling (more than 14 mi/hr), running (more than 6 mi/hr), judo, karate, vigorous calisthenics (e.g., some aerobic dance)

Modified from Peterson M, Peterson K: *Eat to compete,* St Louis, 1988, Mosby–Year Book.
*Based on a reference child weighing 100 lbs.

athletes are multifaceted, including attention to appropriate diet, fluid, sleep, and training and an accepting, supportive home environment.

Few studies have been done on the nutritional needs of growing athletes. Most published research has been taken from adolescents who agreed to be studied while training for specific sports.

Adequate energy and water are the key nutrients to be considered in the typical school-age athlete. Besides being needed for basal metabolism and physical activity, energy is required to support normal growth. Growing athletes therefore demand more kcalories per kilogram of body weight than adults performing the same activity. During adolescence when the growth rate is extremely rapid (especially for boys), the kcaloric needs may be great.

The amount of energy needed will depend on the intensity, duration, and frequency of the activity (Table 6-4 gives examples of activities with different levels of energy expenditure). The average 10-year-old boy may expend between 2000 and 2800 kcal/day, but those who are running long distances or exerting themselves in other physical activities may need an additional 300 to 700 kcal/day. The kcaloric needs of preadolescent girls are similar to those of boys for moderate and heavy exercise, but may be greater at ages 11 to 12 as they go into puberty.

Fluids are especially critical in hot, humid weather or when participating in endurance activities. Dehydration not only decreases performance but also can result in serious health consequences such as increased body temperature, muscle cramps, and heatstroke. Children are more at risk for these disorders than adults, so diligent attention to fluids is needed during children's physical activities.[23] Although thirst is a normal cue to drink, children frequently do not instinctively drink enough fluid to replenish losses during prolonged exercise. They should be encouraged to drink plenty of fluids before, during, and after exercise. A rule of thumb is to drink every 15 minutes during practice. Electrolytes lost from sweat can be replenished easily by eating food after the physical exertion, and the use of special supplements will not be necessary.

A group particularly at health risk are competitive wrestlers who may restrict food and fluids in order to "make weight" in their weight class. Studies of college wrestlers have shown that they are unable to fully rehydrate themselves by competition time, and may enter a match in a state of dehydration with compromised performance as a result.[24] The American Medical Association's guidelines for weight management in young wrestlers should be used as the foundation for practice by coaches and trainers in this sport (see box at right).

Diet and sports is unfortunately filled with superstition and myth about "optimum practices." Special diets or foods are sometimes promoted, and supplements are frequently recommended. These diets and supplements often have no scientific proof to support their use; however, the enthusiasm of the coach or trainer may influence the child to follow these practices. Carbohydrate-loading is inappropriate for children, extra protein will not increase performance, and various supplements will not energize the body.[25]

Common sense is much needed in assessing the nutritional needs of the growing athlete. Sufficient kcalories must be consumed to support growth and activity. For the young athlete with a busy schedule, frequent, portable snacks are essential in addition to regular meals. Fluid and electrolytes lost during practice or competition must be replaced to avoid the consequences of dehydration and electrolyte imbalance. Weight management efforts should be approached sensibly without trying to achieve minimal weight through promotion of fluid loss. Eating before competition should be scheduled to allow enough time to avoid retention of undigested food material in the gut at

AMERICAN MEDICAL ASSOCIATION'S GUIDELINES FOR WEIGHT MANAGEMENT IN YOUNG WRESTLERS

1. The amount of body fat desirable for the wrestler is 7% to 10%.
2. The wrestler should participate in a 6-week intensive training and conditioning program with no regard for his weight.
3. Weight at the end of this period is to be his minimum effective weight for competition and certification.
4. Any effort to maintain a weight below this would be a hardship to the body.

the time of the event. Foods that are easy to digest should be selected, avoiding unnecessary fat, fiber, and gas-forming fruits and vegetables. No special diets or supplements are recognized to be the answer to greater performance or success. However, if eating a particular food provides a psychological edge, choosing it might be considered potentially advantageous.

Many children do not participate in organized sports because of lack of interest, finances, or family support. However, all children should be encouraged and supported in physical fitness through individual activities of their interest, unorganized group play, or other recreational activities (e.g., camping, hiking, nature exploration). The optimal physical activities or sports are those that the child can continue to perform into and throughout adulthood (Figure 6-1). Parents and other family members are significant models and should provide opportunities for family activities such as biking, walking the dog, or exploring a local park or beach. Families may also consider limiting the time children spend watching television or playing computer games. Beyond the family, the fitness of youngsters will be boosted by local support for community recreational programs and the availability of physical education in the school curriculum.

FIG. 6-1 Biking is a physical activity that can be enjoyed throughout life.

HEALTH PROMOTION

Increased interest in health and concern about heart disease, cancer, and obesity have caused Americans to change their eating habits in recent years. Various recommendations from the government and nonprofit organizations, such as the Dietary Guidelines, are promoting healthy eating to the public.

The **National Cholesterol Education Program (NCEP)** recommends that everyone over 2 years of age consume a diet of no more than 30% of kcalories from fat (10% or less from saturated fat, up to 10% from unsaturated fat, 10% to 15% from monounsaturated fat) and no more than 300 mg cholesterol per day.[26] Cholesterol screening is also recommended for children at risk for cardiovascular disease. Secular trends over the past 15 years have been reported by the Bogalusa Heart Study, including significant decreases in total fat intake, saturated fat intake, and percent of kcalories from fat (from 38% in 1973 to 1974 to 36% in 1987 to 1988).[27] These dietary trends, however, did not alter serum lipid and lipoprotein levels and

do not meet the NCEP guidelines. Although there remains controversy about the appropriateness of the dietary and screening recommendations for children, school-age children and adolescents apparently are able to consume low-fat diets (less than 30% of kcalories from fat and less than 300 mg cholesterol) without negatively influencing the level of micronutrients.[28]

Prevention of **osteoporosis** in later years is critically dependent on calcium retention during adolescence and young adulthood. Calcium needs in childhood are usually met by the inclusion of typical amounts of dairy products in the diet. By ages 10 to 12 years in females, however, the needs increase significantly to match pubertal growth. Balance studies suggest that adolescent girls less than 16 years of age may need to consume more than the RDA level of 1200 mg/day in order to achieve maximum calcium intake and balance.[29] Therefore the preteen years are critical for establishment of dietary habits that include optimal calcium sources to carry them through the next decades.

Common sense and moderation are probably the best policy in promoting a healthy diet in school-age children. Beneficial food habits consolidated in these years will likely be maintained into adulthood. The use of low-fat dairy products, lean animal protein, and fewer high-fat foods is appropriate for healthy, growing children. Restricting the intake of fermentable carbohydrate in the diet will improve dental health and nutrient density. Increasing children's intake of fruits, vegetables, whole grains, and legumes above usual reported levels has several benefits including (1) increasing the fiber content, (2) reducing the percentage of dietary fat, (3) increasing the amount of beta-carotene and other dietary factors that may help in cancer prevention, and (4) providing a diet that is more nutrient dense.

NUTRITION CONCERNS
Diet and Behavior

Does sugar make a child "hyper"? Does skipping breakfast really make any difference in school performance? Are food additives or allergies a cause of behavioral problems in children? These and similar questions are often asked by parents, teachers, and health care workers. A good deal of information on diet and behavior is available, but some of it is myth, some of it is controversial, and some of it is based on sound scientific research.

Nutrition and learning. Dozens of studies over the last few decades have documented the negative effect of malnourishment on children's intellectual development (see Chapter 1 for a thorough discussion). A more gray area of any diet-cognitive connection is whether "marginal" malnutrition or skipping meals affects behavior or school performance. In the past, nutrition and school performance studies suggested that children who go to school without breakfast are likely to be more inattentive, lethargic, and irritable, but there was no strong documentation to support this association.[30]

Studies of healthy school-age children in a laboratory setting have measured cognitive abilities, such as problem solving, memory, and attentiveness, after the children had eaten or not eaten breakfast. The children who had fasted generally made more errors in their performance.[31] Another report using similar methodology compared healthy children with those stunted, those experiencing severe malnutrition in early life, and those currently wasted (low weight for height). Although variation occurred among the groups in their response to the cognitive tests, all of the malnourished and undernourished children were adversely affected in their performance when they missed breakfast.[32]

In a recent community-based study, the academic performance of children in six schools in a low-income area was compared before and after the schools began the SBP. The children participating in the breakfast program showed improved performance as measured by standardized achievement tests compared with children qualifying for the breakfast program but not participating.[33] These results support the expansion of nutrition education and feeding programs so that children at risk might be successful in school.

Iron deficiency, a common nutrient deficiency in children, has long been implicated in negative changes in behavior and performance. Iron is involved in the functioning of many molecules in the brain and nervous system, and these systems are sensitive to lowered iron levels long before overt anemia is diagnosed. Compared with control subjects, iron-deficient infants and preschool children (with and without anemia) tend to score lower on standard scales of mental development and are less likely to pay attention to relevant cues in problem-solving situations.[34,35] A recent report suggests that iron deficiency's negative impact on cognitive performance can have long-term consequences on children into the school years.[36] This information has clinical implications in terms of assessing the overall nutrient quality of the diet of a "behavior problem" child, as well as implications for public policy in addressing the nutrition needs of low-income, high-risk children.

A relatively new research focus has been on the relationships between nutrition and behavior and the brain. Studies have addressed the influence of dietary components on the synthesis of brain neurotransmitters which affect behaviors such as appetite, mood, and depression. Tryptophan and choline intake can stimulate the increased release of the neurotransmitters serotonin and acetylcholine.[37] Studies in adults suggest that mental alertness is lower and lethargy and drowsiness are greater after a high-carbohydrate rather than a high-protein meal.[37] One study of newborns showed that those fed a tryptophan-carbohydrate formula entered active and quiet sleep sooner than infants fed a valine–low-carbohydrate formula.[38] Although there seems to be a general relationship between diet, brain chemistry, and behavior, further research will be needed to reveal the significance of individual variability and to discern clinical implications for children.

Attention deficit hyperactivity disorder. Frequently referred to as hyperactivity, **attention deficit hyperactivity disorder (ADHD)** is most commonly seen among school-age children in the United States. ADHD is a clinical diagnosis requiring the following specific criteria: inattention, impulsivity, and hyperactivity; onset before 7 years of age and duration of at least 6 months; and absence of schizophrenia, affective disorder, or mental retardation.[39]

An estimated 3% to 5% of schoolchildren are believed to be affected by ADHD with boys affected six to nine times more often than girls.[39] Although a true diagnosis is a result of assessment by medical or educational specialists, many children are labeled hyperactive by less formal measures of behavior in the school or home. Regardless of the looseness of the diagnosis, the main focus of those involved with the child becomes treatment and management.

Various causes of ADHD have been proposed over the years, yet the etiology remains relatively unknown. Perinatal complications such as anoxia, toxemia, prematurity, and infection have long been suggested as causes, as have insults during the early years including head injuries, seizures, toxic agents, or infections. Greater incidence of a family history of hyperactivity and learning disabilities in the identified children suggests a genetic component. Some studies have suggested a biochemical basis for ADHD, and environmental factors such as exposure to fluorescent lights and heavy metals (e.g., lead) have also been suggested. Dietary factors, including food additives, sugar, and allergies, have also been implicated as causes of hyperactivity.

Stimulant medication. The most widely used and accepted forms of treatment for ADHD are stimulant medications, behavioral management, and special education. Methylphenidate (Ritalin) is the most common medication, with dextroamphetamine (Dexedrine) and pemoline (Cylert) used less frequently. Although the exact mechanism of these medications is not fully understood, children with ADHD respond to them with reduction in such undesirable behaviors as motor restlessness, short attention span, and irritability. Many people assume that when the child is calmed down and paying more attention, academic performance improves. Some evidence, however, suggests that stimulant medications do not necessarily improve school learning and that long-term outcomes are no different from those of children who have no medication.[40]

One of the appeals of stimulant medication is its immediate results with few toxic side effects. Anorexia is frequently noted and can eventually result in growth suppression.[41] There appears to be a direct relationship between the dosage and the degree of suppressed appetite.[42] Although more tolerance to the medication's negative effect on growth is expected over time, the response is very individual. Children discontinuing the medication during vacations and summers usually have a growth rebound, but this is unlikely to compensate completely for the growth suppression incurred during the school year.[43] Other evidence suggests that adult height of boys treated with Ritalin for up to 5 years was no different from control boys, suggesting a compensatory growth rebound after discontinuation of the medication.[44]

Although the mechanisms by which stimulant medication inhibits growth is unclear, decreased energy intake is a factor. Children receiving stimulant medication present a variety of feeding problems including being picky about foods eaten, dawdling at mealtime, refusing school lunches or returning sack lunches home, and being disinterested in food. Some children have been observed to consume large amounts of concentrated carbohydrates and other low-nutrient foods because parents are concerned that the child will refuse to eat something. Because of poor appetites and slow growth, families frequently resort to bribery, indulgence, and threats to induce their children to eat. It is easy to understand how a preoccupation with food and eating can lead to frustration for parents and children, resulting in inappropriate behaviors and interactions at mealtimes. When the children discontinue medication during vacations, their parents often note dramatic increases in appetite and food consumption.

Since stimulant medications can result in growth suppression, frequent measurement of weight and height is essential to monitor longitudinal changes in growth. The efficacy of the medication should be assessed periodically using standard double-blind procedures. For practical dietary management, it is important to know the type, dosage, and administration time of the medication. Since it takes about 30 minutes for the medication's effect to be clinically manifested, the medication should be given before or with meals to take advantage of optimal appetite. The medication's effect is usually minimal or absent after 4 to 6 hours, and foods of high energy and nutrient density should be offered then. Each child should be evaluated with regard to medication administration, meal and snack routine, and appetite response. Some families may benefit from counseling regarding specific feeding problems.

Food additives. Of the various proposed dietary causes of ADHD, artificial colorings and flavorings in food is one of the most common. This theory, supposedly supported by parallel increases of food additives in the food supply and the prevalence of ADHD, was proposed by Feingold and became popular in the 1970s.[45] Although most concerns regarding additives center on safety issues and potential carcinogenicity, adverse physical reactions are reported with monosodium glutamate, which precipitates the Chinese restaurant syndrome, and tartrazine, which causes an allergic response in persons who are also sensitive to aspirin.[37]

Treatment by the Feingold diet consisted of removing these additives, natural salicylates

(found mostly in fruits), and some preservatives (BHA, BHT) from the child's diet. Initial reports, mostly open trial and subjective, were positive and caused the diet to become popular with the public at a time when medication use and overuse were being questioned. Subsequent challenge and diet replacement studies using controlled double-blind procedures have not supported the Feingold diet as an effective therapy for ADHD.[46,37] It is accepted, however, that as many as 5% to 10% of children may benefit from a trial of the diet, and preschool children appear to be more sensitive to these substances than older children.[37] One diet replacement study in preschool hyperactive boys used the Feingold diet plus elimination of any other foods to which the child seemed to react (e.g., chocolate, sugar, or caffeine). Using accepted rating scales, results showed some behavioral improvement in almost one half of the boys.[47]

For families using the Feingold diet, nutritional evaluation of the modified version (including the natural fruits and vegetables) has shown that it compares favorably with the RDA and thus poses little nutritional risk for the child.[48] It is certainly understandable that a family with a child with ADHD might expect a positive outcome from a diet that is relatively simple and without side effects. In addition to the possibility of a placebo effect the diet may create a positive focus for the family rather than the negative attention to problem behaviors. Children using the diet should receive nutritional assessment, and families should be counseled not to disregard the potential help provided by special education, behavioral management, and other therapies that can combine appropriately with the diet.

Sugar. Sugar (sucrose) has been implicated, mainly in popular books and anecdotal reports, as a causative factor in a multitude of diseases and disorders. Some of these include diabetes, obesity, heart disease, and hypoglycemia, as well as mental and behavioral disorders such as ADHD, depression, and psychoses. Some practitioners believe that sugar is the most common food substance causing adverse behavior reactions in children. In addition, parents, teachers, and school nurses report dramatic negative changes in some children after receiving a load of sugar. Anecdotal stories describe children "climbing the walls" the day after Halloween. All of these reports, however, are subjective and are not based on controlled studies.

An initial report by Prinz, Roberts, and Hantman[49] suggested that there was a positive correlation between sugar consumption and destructive-aggressive behavior in 4- to 7-year-old hyperactive children. Correlation, however, does not imply a cause-effect role for sugar in behavior problems of children. Other factors such as a permissive home environment or a child who demands foods high in sucrose may be involved.

Sucrose double-blind challenge studies have failed to detect significant negative behavioral effects of sucrose. Behar and others[50] studied sugar and behavior in 21 boys who, according to their parents, respond adversely to sugar. Behavior ratings, motor activity, memory, and blood levels were monitored for 5 hours after a double-blind challenge of glucose, sucrose, or saccharin. These researchers found no significant effect of sugar on any of the behavioral measures in these children. Contrary to popular belief, the children who consumed sugar were less active and quieter than those given the placebo. These results may support the theory that a high carbohydrate intake facilitates production of serotonin, or the results may derive from other unknown factors.

In another study, hyperactive boys were challenged with a sucrose or aspartame drink and then evaluated by measures of behavior, motor activity, and cognitive performance.[51] No significant differences were found between the sucrose and aspartame challenges for any of the tests. Similar studies, including those with preschool children, have reached the same conclusions.[37] There are some limitations to the design of the challenge studies that may affect results, e.g., the load of the sucrose challenge, the need to have a placebo substance that is sweet (usually artificial sweeteners), and the possibility that any behavioral response is within a narrow window of time.

At this time the only direct cause-effect rela-tionship between sugar and disease is the role of sugar in dental caries, but this does not preclude the possibility that an individual child might be responsive to a large sucrose load. More, well-designed investigations of the relationship between sugar intake and behavior may help clarify the issue.

Americans consume approximately 125 pounds of sweeteners per year, of which sucrose represents about 65 pounds.[37] Many foodstuffs that are high in sugar are low in nutrients, and thus they dilute the nutrient quality of the diet. Reducing or eliminating sugar in the diet serves to improve the overall nutritional and dental health of both child and family. These positive changes in families' diets have been observed in personal clinical experience. The professional can reinforce the dietary changes while stressing the lack of data supporting a sugar-behavior association.

Megavitamin therapy. The use of large doses of certain vitamins to treat ADHD frequently originates from lay groups, the popular press, and some professionals. The basis of megavitamin therapy is that children with ADHD or learning problems have biochemical imbalances and that these disturbances can be eliminated by this therapy.

Megavitamin therapy, using nicotinic acid, was first used to treat schizophrenia. Suspecting vitamin deficiency as a cause of mental and behavioral problems is a result of existing nutritional knowledge on deficiency states. Classic examples are the neurological and mental changes noted in persons with niacin deficiency (pellagra) and thiamin deficiency (beriberi).

Most commonly, megavitamin therapy includes niacin, ascorbic acid, pyridoxine, and calcium pantothenate. On the other hand, personal clinical experience has indicated that children receiving megavitamin therapy may be taking a wide assortment of vitamin or mineral supplements with or without professional guidance.

A few studies have tested megavitamin therapy using double-blind controlled studies. Arnold and others[52] reported on 31 children with minimal brain dysfunction who received either placebos or megavitamins during a 2-week trial. The megavitamin regimen was advocated by Cott—1 gm niacin, 1 gm ascorbic acid, 100 mg pyridoxine, 200 mg pantothenate calcium, and 500 mg glutamic acid, all twice daily. Parent and teacher behavior ratings taken before and after the trial showed no significant difference in the two groups. Only two children responded so well that stimulant medication was not considered necessary; they were both in the placebo group.

Other studies have had similar results. In one, children with learning disabilities were put on a low-carbohydrate, high-protein diet and then given either megavitamins or placebos for 6 months.[53] Evaluations before and after this period with a combination of intellectual, school achievement, perceptual, and behavioral measures showed no difference between the two groups. In another report, behavioral and classroom performance of children with ADHD actually worsened following megavitamin therapy, while the behavior of those receiving a placebo improved.[54]

Studies have been unable to support the theories advocated by proponents of megavitamin therapy, and established medical professionals have not supported the treatment. In addition, potential dangers exist from consuming large doses of vitamins. Toxicity can result from excessive intake of fat-soluble vitamins A and D. These vitamins are not included in the standard megavitamin treatment, yet clinical experience reveals that some practitioners commonly recommend vitamins A and D, or that families on their own initiative may include them in their regimen. Other complications that have been reported from megadoses of water-soluble vitamins are **hyperbilirubinemia** and liver damage from large doses of nicotinic acid, and sensory neuropathy from large doses of vitamin B_6.[37] Megavitamin therapy as an unfounded treatment for mental retardation is discussed in Chapter 14.

It is easy to understand why a family would respond to the appeal of megavitamin therapy, but too often it plays on the false hopes and guilt of the parents or provides a focus for blame. Some families can spend considerable money on vitamins and yet not deal with the basic problem related to the child's behavior. Although there are no sound data to support the use of megavitamins with hyperactive children, it is possible that some individuals may have increased needs for certain nutrients. The nutritional status of each child should be assessed and appropriate dietary intervention should be planned. In working with parents who choose to use megavitamins for their child, one needs to help them recognize the practice as helpful, neutral, or harmful and to provide accurate information. At times counseling may be indicated to help families recognize and consider other treatment options.

Dental Health

Dental caries, one of the most common nutritional diseases, affects children at all ages and income levels. Despite great strides in the dental field in the past few decades, U.S. schoolchildren in 1987 averaged 3.07 decayed, missing, or filled permanent tooth surfaces (DMFS). The rate increased with age to an average of 8.04 DMFS by age 17.[55]

Once the tooth has erupted, the composition of the diet, the presence of acid-producing bacteria, and the buffering capacity of the saliva interact and result in the control or development of dental caries. Some children appear to be more susceptible to dental caries than others, suggesting a hereditary influence. Calcified dental tissues, unlike the long bones, which are subject to constant remodeling and repair, do not have the ability to repair themselves. Tooth destruction by decay is permanent.

The development of dental caries requires fermentable carbohydrate, bacteria, and a susceptible tooth. The decay process starts with the interaction of bacteria *(Streptococcus mutans)* and a carbohydrate on the surface of the tooth. The bacteria, within the sticky, gelatinous dental plaque, metabolize the carbohydrate, producing organic acids. When the pH is decreased to 5.5 or less, degradation and demineralization of the tooth enamel begin.[56] The saliva, with a pH of 6.5 to 7.0, acts as a buffer and provides mechanical cleansing of the teeth. Although any fermentable sugar is cariogenic, sucrose is considered the most cariogenic because it is the most common in the diet. The three major food sources of sucrose in the diets of children and adolescents are beverages, candies, and desserts. Starch is considered to be less cariogenic than sugars, but it is readily broken down to fermentable carbohydrate by salivary amylase. In addition, many high-starch foods also contain sucrose, which could make them more cariogenic than sugar alone because starch is retained longer in the mouth.[56]

The presence of sugar, or even the total amount of carbohydrates in the diet, may not be the determining factor in the incidence of dental caries. Other important factors are the frequency of eating and the retentiveness of the food to the teeth. These elements as a whole influence the length of time that the teeth are exposed to an acidic environment, which leads to tooth decay.

Protein foods such as hard cheeses, nuts, eggs, and meats do not reduce plaque pH and thus are believed to be protective against caries.[57] The exact mechanism involved is unknown, but these foods have a relatively high protein content with basic amino acids, a moderate fat content, a strong buffering capacity, a high mineral content including calcium and phosphorus, and a pH greater than 6.0. They also stimulate saliva flow.

❖ NUTRITIONAL SNACKS FOR DENTAL HEALTH

- *Protein foods**
  Natural cheese (cheddar, jack, string)
  Milk
  Cooked turkey, chicken, beef, ham
  Plain yogurt
  Peanut butter
  Cottage cheese
  Unsalted nuts and seeds
  Tuna
  Hard-cooked egg
- *Breads and cereals†*
  Whole-grain breads
  Whole-grain cereals
  Whole-grain, low-fat crackers
  Tortillas
  English muffins
  Rice crackers
  Pita bread
  Popcorn
  Bagels

- *Fruits†*
  Apples
  Bananas
  Pears
  Berries
  Oranges, other citrus fruits
  Melon
  Grapes
  Unsweetened canned fruit
  Unsweetened fruit juices
- *Vegetables*
  Carrots
  Celery
  Green pepper
  Radishes
  Cucumbers
  Cabbage
  Cauliflower
  Broccoli
  Tomatoes
  Jicama
  Vegetable juices

Examples: Apple wedges with peanut butter; egg salad sandwich; raw vegetables with yogurt or cottage cheese dip; plain yogurt with unsweetened applesauce and cinnamon; tortilla with melted cheese; pita bread with tuna; popcorn with parmesan cheese; frozen banana rolled in plain yogurt and chopped nuts; rice cracker with peanut butter or cheese.

---

*These foods may be protective against lowering plaque pH when eaten with foods that contain fermentable carbohydrate.
†Fruits, juices, and most cereal/bread products contain fermentable carbohydrate; limit to 1 serving in a snack.

Prevention and control of caries. Fluoride is the single most effective factor in caries prevention. It reduces the incidence of dental caries by suppressing sugar metabolism by bacteria, making enamel more resistant to acid, and stimulating remineralization of the teeth. A fluoridated water supply is a critical part of prevention. In areas without fluoridation, a supplement is recommended through the growing years.

Dietary management continues to be a most important and effective approach to the control of dental caries. Three factors are interdependent in determining the cariogenicity of a particular food: (1) sucrose content; (2) physical properties; and (3) consumption patterns. For example, sweets and desserts eaten with meals will be less cariogenic than when eaten alone; dried fruits are less retentive when in cereal, baked goods, or salads; and sweetened beverages may be less damaging than starchy foods containing sugar.[56]

Snacks for children should emphasize foods that are low in sucrose, are not retentive, and stimulate saliva flow (the box on page 159 lists some examples). Eating cheese, nuts, and meats at the same time as higher sugar foods will help prevent a decrease in plaque pH. Chewing sugarless gum after eating fermentable carbohydrate may also be beneficial in controlling acidity, but this remains controversial.[58]

Good dental health will be most likely when families purchase few cariogenic foods, provide routine eating schedules, encourage daily oral hygiene, and schedule routine dental examinations. In addition, group feeding at schools, day care facilities, camps, and other programs should practice positive dental nutrition, and dental health education should be a part of the school health curriculum.

Lactose Intolerance

Many adults throughout the world experience lactose malabsorption or intolerance. The exceptions include Northern Europeans, the Fulani and Tussi tribes of Africa, the Punjali of India, Finns, Hungarians, and probably Mongols. An estimated 70% of black American adults and 100% of homogenous Native Americans have limited ability to hydrolyze lactose.[59]

The onset of reduced lactase levels occurs in childhood and adolescence, but rarely before 3 years of age. In some countries (e.g., Greece and Israel) there is a linear progression in the prevalence of lactose malabsorption throughout the school-age years, but in other countries (e.g., China, Jamaica, Peru, and Bangladesh) this transition occurs more quickly between 3 and 5 years of age.[60] In the United States, clinical symptoms are usually not manifested until after 5 to 7 years of age.

Unaffected individuals hydrolyze and absorb ingested lactose in the small intestine. If lactase activity is low, only a portion of the sugar will be hydrolyzed to glucose and galactose. Undigested lactose remains in the lumen of the intestine and has a hyperosmolar effect, drawing large amounts of fluid into the gut. As the sugar is transported to the ileocecal region and the first part of the colon, it is fermented by bacterial flora. This causes production of carbon dioxide, hydrogen, and low molecular weight acids that interfere with the reabsorption of fluids and electrolytes. The increased fluid load and products of bacterial fermentation cause the symptoms of bloating, flatulence, abdominal cramping, and diarrhea.

The response of individuals with lactase deficiency to the ingestion of milk varies. Some manifest no symptoms, and others experience symptoms shortly after milk is ingested. The amount of milk that must be consumed at one time to produce symptoms ranges from less than 240 ml to 1000 ml. Many persons with lactase deficiency are not intolerant to lactose or to milk. Adults and older children with low lactase levels have usually consumed milk in infancy and early childhood without symptoms.

There are two common tests for lactose intolerance.[59] A lactose tolerance test measures change in blood glucose for 2 to 3 hours after a load of lactose is given. A flat glucose curve suggests lactose intolerance, but is not diagnostic for lactose malabsorption. The lactose breath-hydrogen test, which more directly indicates lactose maldigestion, measures expired breath hydrogen.

Milk is an important source of protein, calcium, riboflavin, and vitamins D and A. Children in racial groups known to have a high incidence of lactose intolerance should not be limited in their milk intake unless they manifest symptoms. Those with symptoms should be encouraged to consume dairy products in which lactose has been fermented (e.g., yogurt, buttermilk, and aged cheese). Heating or pasteurizing yogurt loses its effectiveness because the bacteria are killed; thus products with active cultures are most beneficial.[61] Ice-cold milk and milk consumed alone seem to cause greater discomfort than milk consumed with food or at room temperature. Many children can tolerate up to one cup of milk at a time when consumed with meals.

Lactose-free milks or milk treated with lactase are commercially available for children whose symptoms are severe. These products provide a 70% to 100% reduction of the lactose.[61] Commercial preparations are also available either as drops to add to milks or formulas, or as tablets to take orally at the same time as a lactose-containing meal. Since lactose is added to many prepared foods, parents of children with lactose intolerance should read labels carefully so that additional loads of lactose can be avoided. Lactose is found in whey powder, casein, casein hydrolysate, sodium caseinate, and lactalbumin.[61]

Diets of all children who limit their intakes of milk should be carefully monitored for vitamin D and calcium levels. Supplements should be prescribed when appropriate. In healthy subjects the percentage of calcium absorbed from carbonate, acetate, gluconate, and citrate salts is similar to the percentage absorbed from whole milk.[62]

The previous discussion applies to primary lactase deficiency acquired after the weaning years. Primary lactase deficiency can occur in infancy as a result of a congenital condition or inborn error of metabolism, but this is rare.[61] Secondary lactase deficiency may result from infectious diarrhea, medications that alter the intestinal mucosa, and gastrointestinal diseases. These periods are usually temporary, and normal levels of lactase activity usually return when the disease is controlled. Despite long-standing therapy to omit the offending sugars in these cases, current practice suggests continuing to offer the dairy products after an initial 24-hour glucose-electrolyte solution.[61]

Summary

School-age children grow at a steady rate and acquire many physical and cognitive skills. Their food and nutrient intake is influenced by many factors, including family, peers, and media. As children prepare to enter adolescence, their attitudes toward food will be well established. Parents need to provide appropriate foods and supportive guidance so that positive food patterns are developed. School feeding programs and educational curricula provide an opportunity for nutrition education that can improve nutrition knowledge and behavior.

Although most school-age children clinically appear to be well nourished, some groups are at risk for malnutrition because of socioeconomic factors, limited food resources, lack of education, or health conditions. Others are at risk for obesity and poor physical condition as a result of poor food selection and poor life-style habits.

REVIEW QUESTIONS

1. Discuss the major problems and criticisms of the NSLP. What factors are responsible for these problems?
2. List the NCEP dietary guidelines for children.
3. Discuss the various dietary treatments for ADHD and critique the rationale for each.
4. List three practical, but reasonable, dietary recommendations that would decrease the risk of dental caries in children.
5. Describe major societal trends in the United States over the last two decades that have influenced the dietary intake and health status of school-age children.
6. List the four groups of at-risk children who might benefit from routine vitamin-mineral supplements.

SUGGESTED LEARNING ACTIVITIES

1. Assess the nutrient intake of a school-age child.
2. Review a daily activity log of an elementary school child and categorize according to levels of energy expenditure.
3. Describe factors that influence food choices in the school-age child.

4. Assess the nutritional status of a child who has been on long-term stimulant medication. What is the growth pattern? The appetite?
5. Eat a school lunch with children and assess the menu, palatability, cafeteria atmosphere, amount of time to eat, and children's interaction.
6. Plan a nutrition lesson emphasizing dental nutrition for an elementary school class.
7. Plan brown bag lunches for a school-age child for one week that provide variety and are nutritionally appropriate.

Terms and Concepts

Provided here for your review is a listing of terms and concepts within this chapter. The definitions for terms can be found in the glossary, which begins on page 413. To aid your understanding of the terms' and concepts' application within this text, the page number designating the first mention of each term or concept within the chapter is given.

REFERENCES

1. Dietary Intake Source Data: United States, 1976-1980. Data from the National Health Survey, Vital and Health Statistics Series 11, No 231, DHHS Publication No (PHS) 83-1681, 1983.
2. Science and Education Administration: Nationwide Food Consumption Survey, 1977-1978, Preliminary Rep. No 2, Food and nutrient intakes of individuals in 1 day in the U.S., Spring, 1977, Hyattsville, Md, 1980, US Department of Agriculture.
3. Windham CT and others: Nutrient density of diets in the USDA Nationwide Food Consumption Survey, 1977-1978. I. Impact of socioeconomic status on dietary density, *J Am Diet Assoc* 82:26, 1983.
4. Bowering J, Clancy KL: Nutritional status of children and teenagers in relation to vitamin and mineral use, *J Am Diet Assoc* 86:1033, 1986.
5. Committee on Nutrition, American Academy of Pediatrics: Vitamin and mineral supplementation needs in normal children in the United States, *Pediatrics* 66:1015, 1980.
6. Laskarzewski P and others: Parent-child nutrient intake interrelationships in school children ages 6 to 19: the Princeton School District Study, *Am J Clin Nutr* 33:2350, 1980.
7. Karp R and others: Parental behavior and the availability of foods among undernourished inner-city children, *J Fam Pract* 18:731, 1984.
8. Guber S: Marketing to kids: it's elementary, *Prepared Foods* 158:48, 1989.
9. Cotugna N: TV ads on Saturday morning children's programming—what's new? *J Nutr Educ* 20:125, 1988.
10. Nicklas TA and others: Nutritional studies in children and implications for change: the Bogalusa Heart Study, *J Adv Med* 2:451, 1989.
11. Morgan KJ, Zabik MZ, Leville GA: The role of nutrient intake of 5- to 12-year-old children, *Am J Clin Nutr* 34:1418, 1981.
12. Dietz WA, Gortmaker SL: Do we fatten our children at the television set? Obesity and television viewing in children and adolescents, *Pediatrics* 75:807, 1985.
13. Community Nutrition Institute, vol 22, no 1, Jan 3, 1992.
14. Lind BA and others: Effect of family versus cafeteria style service on students' attitudes, food intake, and food waste, *Sch Food Serv Res Rev* 10:18, 1986.
15. Ho CS and others: Evaluation of the nutrient content of school, sack and vending lunch of junior high students, *Sch Food Serv Res Rev* 15:85, 1991.
16. O'Donnell NL, Alles WF: School nurse demonstrates that mini-grant funding can improve elementary nutrition education, *J Sch Health* 5:316, 1983.

17. Brainerd CJ: *Piaget's theory of intelligence,* Englewood Cliffs, NJ, 1978, Prentice-Hall.

18. GAO/CED: What can be done to improve nutrition education? Gaithersburg, Md, 1982, US Government Accounting Office, Document Handling and Information Services Facility.

19. St. Pierre RG, Rezmovic V: An overview of the national nutrition education and training program evaluation, *J Nutr Educ* 14:61, 1982.

20. Green NR, Munroe SG: Evaluating nutrient-based nutrition education by nutrition knowledge and school lunch plate waste, *Sch Food Serv Res Rev* 11:112, 1987.

21. Gortmaker SL and others: Increasing pediatric obesity in the United States, *Am J Dis Child* 141:535, 1987.

22. Rowland TW: *Exercise and children's health,* Champaign, Ill, 1990, Human Kinetics Books.

23. American Academy of Pediatrics: Clinical heat stress and the exercising child, *Phys Sports Med* 11:155, 1983.

24. Vaccaro P, Zauner CW, Cade JR: Changes in body weight, hematocrit and plasma protein concentration due to dehydration and rehydration in wrestlers, *J Sports Med Phys Fitness* 16:45, 1976.

25. Berning JR, Steen SN, editors: *Sports nutrition for the 90's: the health professional's handbook,* Gaithersburg, Md, 1991, Aspen Publishers.

26. National Cholesterol Education Program: *Report of the expert panel on blood cholesterol levels in children and adolescents,* NIH Pub No 91-2732, National Heart, Lung, and Blood Institute, NIH, Public Health Service, Bethesda, Md, 1991, US Department of Health and Human Services.

27. Nicklas TA and others: Secular trends in dietary intakes and cardiovascular risk factors of 10-year-old children: the Bogalusa Heart Study (1973-1988), *Am J Clin Nutr* in press.

28. McPerson RS and others: Intake and food sources of dietary fat among schoolchildren in The Woodlands, Tex, *Pediatrics* 86:520, 1990.

29. Matkovic V and others: Factors that influence peak bone mass formation: a study of calcium balance and the inheritance of bone mass in adolescent females, *Am J Clin Nutr* 52:878, 1990.

30. Pollitt E, Gersovitz M, Gargiulo M: Educational benefits of the United States school feeding program: a critical review of the literature, *Am J Public Health* 68:477, 1978.

31. Pollitt E, Leibel RL, Greenfield D: Brief fasting, stress, and cognition in children, *Am J Clin Nutr* 34:1526, 1981.

32. Simeon DT, Grantham-McGregor S: Effects of missing breakfast on the cognitive functions of school children of differing nutritional status, *Am J Clin Nutr* 49:646, 1989.

33. Meyers AF and others: School breakfast program and school performance, *Am J Dis Child* 143:1234, 1989.

34. Pollitt E and others: Iron deficiency and behavioral development in infants and preschool children, *Am J Clin Nutr* 43:555, 1986.

35. Walter T and others: Iron deficiency anemia: adverse effects on infant psychomotor development, *Pediatrics* 84:7, 1989.

36. Lozoff B, Jimenez E, Wolf AU: Long-term development outcome of infants with iron deficiency, *N Engl J Med* 325:687, 1991.

37. Kanarek RB, Marks-Kaufman R: *Nutrition and behavior: new perspectives,* New York, 1991, Van Nostrand Reinhold.

38. Yogman MW, Zeisel S: Diet and sleep patterns in newborn infants, *N Engl J Med* 309:1147, 1983.

39. American Psychiatric Association: *Diagnostic and statistical manual of mental disorders,* ed 3 (rev), Washington, DC, 1987, The Association.

40. Varley CK: Attention deficit disorder (the hyperactivity syndrome): a review of selected issues, *Dev Behav Pediatr* 5:254, 1984.

41. Mattes JA, Gittelman R: Growth of hyperactive children on maintenance regimen of methylphenidate, *Arch Gen Psychiatry* 40:317, 1983.

42. Lucas B, Sells CJ: Nutrient intake and stimulant drugs in hyperactive children, *J Am Diet Assoc* 70:373, 1977.

43. Safer DJ, Allen RP, Barr E: Growth rebound after termination of stimulant drugs, *J Pediatr* 86:113, 1975.

44. Klein RG and others: Hyperactive boys almost grown up. III. Methylphenidate effect on ultimate height, *Arch Gen Psychiatry* 45:1131, 1988.

45. Feingold BF: *Why your child is hyperactive,* New York, 1974, Random House.

46. Lipton MA, Mayo JP: Diet and hyperkinesis—an update, *J Am Diet Assoc* 83:132, 1983.

47. Kaplan BJ and others: Dietary replacement in preschool-aged hyperactive boys, *Pediatrics* 83:7, 1989.

48. Harper PH, Goyette CH, Conners CK: Nutrient intakes of children on the hyperkinesis diet, *J Am Diet Assoc* 73:515, 1978.

49. Prinz RJ, Roberts WA, Hantman E: Dietary correlates of hyperactive behavior in children, *J Consult Clin Psychol* 48:760, 1980.

50. Behar D and others: Sugar challenge testing with children considered behaviorally "sugar reactive," *Nutr Behav* 1:277, 1984.

51. Wolraich M and others: Effects of sucrose ingestion on the behavior of hyperactive boys, *J Pediatr* 106:675, 1985.

52. Arnold LE and others: Megavitamins for minimal brain dysfunction: a placebo-controlled study, *JAMA* 240:2642, 1978.

53. Kershner J, Hawke W: Megavitamins and learning disorders: a controlled double-blind experiment, *J Nutr* 109:819, 1979.

54. Haslam RHA, Dalby JT, Rademaker AW: Effects of megavitamin therapy on children with attention deficit disorders, *Pediatrics* 74:103, 1984.

55. US Department of Health and Human Services: *Oral health of United States children: the national survey of dental caries in US school children* (1986-1987), NIH Pub No 89-2247, Bethesda, Md, 1989.

56. White-Graves MV, Schiller MR: History of foods in the caries process, *J Am Diet Assoc* 86:241, 1986.

57. The role of diet and nutrition in oral health, *Dairy Council Digest* 57, May-June, 1986.

58. Jensen ME: Responses of interproximal plaque pH to snack foods and effect of chewing sorbitol-containing gum, *J Am Dent Assoc* 113:262, 1986.

59. Committee on Nutrition, American Academy of Pediatrics: The practical significance of lactose intolerance in children, *Pediatrics* 86(suppl):643, 1990.

60. Ladas SD, Katsiyiannaki-Latoufi E, Raptis SA: Lactose maldigestion and milk intolerance in healthy Greek schoolchildren, *Am J Clin Nutr* 53:676, 1991.

61. Sinden AA, Sutphen JL: Dietary treatment of lactose intolerance in infants and children, *J Am Diet Assoc* 91:1567, 1991.

62. Sheikh MS, and others: Gastrointestinal absorption of calcium from milk and calcium salts, *N Engl J Med* 317:532, 1987.

7

Development of Food Patterns in Young Children

Miriam E. Lowenberg

Objectives

✢✢

After studying this chapter, the student should:

✔ *Recognize differences between hunger and appetite.*

✔ *Be aware of appropriate furniture and utensils for use when feeding young children.*

✔ *Be aware of the factors to consider when writing menus for young children.*

✔ *Have knowledge of appropriate foods and methods of preparation for young children.*

✔ *Know common difficulties encountered by concerned parents when feeding young children.*

✣ Introduction

Investigations of child feeding began in the early 1900s and have continued throughout this century. Among those who will long be remembered for their contribution to our understanding of children's food behavior and child feeding are Arnold Gesell, Lydia Roberts, Icie Macy Hoobler, Virginia Beal, and Miriam E. Lowenberg, the author of this chapter. Dr. Lowenberg's studies have provided the information on which the philosophy of preschool feeding that has persisted throughout the last half of this century was developed. Because of her interest in cultural food habits, Dr. Lowen-berg later developed a course and co-authored a book emphasizing cultural influences on food patterns.[1]

Dr. Lowenberg at 95 years of age remains vitally interested in nutrition and feeding of children. This chapter presents her philosophy and approaches to feeding young children. It is a classic that anyone interested in food for young children must read, assimilate, and apply.

FOOD PATTERNS

Food patterns in the United States show distinct cultural characteristics that change as life-styles change. Hurried small breakfasts, mid-morning coffee breaks, and light lunches followed by heavy evening dinners show modern adjustments to change. In the home, snacking is known to have increased as television has become an integral part of the day and night activities of the American family.

There are many different meal patterns in modern America. There are inner-city patterns of poor or rich families, suburban patterns, and rural patterns of nonfarm and farm families. The rich and the poor have throughout the ages had different food patterns. In fact, careful professional observers of young children eating in a group can often predict the home environment of an individual child.

The current enthusiasm for behavioral control of food intake points to a need to examine the day's program to learn when unneeded kcalories in food are consumed. Researchers now believe that what happens during the first year of life, as well as during the preschool years, is of paramount importance. During the first five or six years of life it is undoubtedly easier to learn to like all foods than it will be later.

At present the young child is introduced early to hamburgers and french fries when families eat out; attesting to this is one fast-food company's yearly sales—the highest in the restaurant industry. Eating out becomes a helpful respite for the young homemaker or working mother, and a pattern is established for the young child. When parents hope to establish a basic food pattern of meals enjoyed at home, they must deal with the child's desire to eat out, even if the child only knows about it because other children talk about eating out.

Goals for the development of food patterns are the following:
1. Children should be able to eat in a matter-of-fact way sufficient quantities of the foods that are given to them, just as they take care of other daily needs. Preschool children who truly enjoy most foods but are able to eat without fuss those they do not especially like will be fortunate later.
2. Children should be able to manage the feeding process independently and with dispatch, without either unnecessary dawdling or hurried eating.
3. Children should be willing to try new foods in small portions the first time they are served to them and to try them again and again until they like or at least willingly accept them.

Professionals interested in guiding parents or prospective parents must know which patterns produce healthy children and adults. We must also believe that it is possible to set up a home environment to foster the development of desirable food patterns in young children. Often an impersonal professionally trained outsider can point out to parents how they can set up such an environment. It must be understood that food patterns begin to be formed from the day of an infant's birth. This reminds me of a healthy, happy young mother who telephoned from her hospital room to report the birth of a daughter 4 hours before. She said with joy that her baby had already tried to nurse; this mother, although still tired from the birth process, had already enjoyed the process of even feeble breast-feeding.

Those who are concerned about obesity as our chief problem of malnutrition wisely point out that prevention, the preferred cure, should begin early in infancy. Parents who give their newborns the privilege of deciding that they have had enough food are well on the way to solving this problem. It is believed that when an individual forms a pattern of quitting to eat at the first indication of satiety, the food intake regulatory mechanism is encouraged to continue to function. Of course, food that produces the growth of good body tissues must be provided so that more than kcalorie satiety is provided. This is an important part of early food patterning of a child.

The food patterns established in a home are reinforced by love of mother and father and therefore have far-reaching effects on lifetime patterns. No one has ever phrased the functions of parents more aptly than did Aldrich and Aldrich[2] 40 years ago when they said:

According to nature's plan then parents are meant to enter the feeding situation for three reasons:
First, to provide the food,
Second, to support a child's progress from simple to mature methods of eating, and
Third, to make it easy for him to establish his own satisfying feeding habits.

Long ago I observed another principle that we need to emphasize with parents: it really is easier and quicker to change the food than it is to change the child. For instance, young children often have trouble swallowing dry food, and when extra milk is added to thin their mashed potatoes they seem thankful. Such methods are explained in detail later in this chapter.

To know what foods children like requires careful observations of young children while they are eating. Table 7-1 on pages 168-169 gives approximate amounts of foods that one can expect the average child to eat.* *In no way are these amounts to be used to force a certain amount of food on any specific child.* If any child, however, habitually eats less than the amount in the chart, the reasons should be determined. As always, a particular child's food dislikes, health condition, or spe-

---

*For 12 years I observed daily 20 nursery school children eating their noon meals. Later, for 2 years, the ideas generated by this observation were used in the daily feeding of 1000 children, mostly 18 months to 6 years of age, in two shipyard World War II nursery schools. My commission as chief nutritionist was to be in charge of feeding and nutritional development. Feeding for the 9 hours at nursery school was carefully planned, and mothers and fathers were also advised and helped to feed their children at home.

The knowledge gained while studying the eating patterns and food preferences of the nursery school children for 12 years was used to teach college students about feeding young children. All food was measured onto the child's plate before it left the kitchen serving area; second helpings and leftover foods were measured and recorded. For one school year, the adult who ate at a table with two or three children was asked to record each child's reaction to each food and to the menu as a whole. They were to record: was a food too dry? too tough? too acid to be easily eaten? Were there other characteristics that made the food unsuitable? Were the combinations of foods acceptable and liked by the children? As these criticisms came in daily, corrections were made in the menus and recipes for the foods. During the following year the corrected menus and specific foods were again studied, and further corrections were made. During this study, each day a chart was made of the amounts of each food to be served to each child. The head teacher confirmed that when the children's appetites were closely studied a child's specific food intake could be accurately judged. Most thoughtful mothers can do this.

The advice in this chapter is based on the ideas gained from this meticulous study as well as on extensive tests of these ideas.

cific family circumstances need to be considered.

CULTURAL PATTERNS

Many ethnic groups make up the population of the United States. Each ethnic food pattern, based on foods available and preferred, comes from the home country and is based firmly on tradition and often on long usage. Specific ways of cooking foods are always dependent on such factors as the fuel available, the time and the energy available for food preparation, and the interests and patience of the cook. For example, the generous use of rye breads and fish in the Scandinavian countries is a result of the cool and short growing season, the long coastlines, and the Scandinavian people's knowledge of successful fishing. Even after such countries are able to import other foods, the preferred foods are still used as tradition dictates. The cause for the abundant use by Polynesian peoples of the coconut, tropical fruits and vegetables, and fish that are abundant in tropical waters is obvious.

The history of a people is written in their preferred foods. This explains why schoolchildren in North Dakota and in Georgia react in radically different ways to rice used as a vegetable. For instance, rice, which grew well in the American south from early colonial times, has become a preferred food in that part of the country, yet when first used in lunches in some schools in North Dakota, rice was rejected as an unfamiliar food. Another vegetable of historic importance to the southern United States is okra. This vegetable is said to have been brought by slaves from Africa, and its popularity has even withstood the memory of those sad journeys to which those slaves were subjected. Blends in Creole dishes could only occur where Spanish, French, black African, and American Indian influences came together. During the latter part of the twentieth century most Americans have come to prize their cultural backgrounds, cultural foods, and cultural differences in food patterns.

In summary, two points should be emphasized. First, every ethnic diet must be based on **nutritional adequacy,** at least to some degree, for the group using it to survive. For example,

TABLE 7-1 *Food Pattern for Preschool Children**

Food	Portion Size	Number of Portions Advised	
		Ages 2 to 4 Years	Ages 4 to 6 Years
Milk and dairy products			
Milk†	4 oz	3 to 6	3 to 4
Cheese	$\frac{1}{2}$ to $\frac{3}{4}$ oz	May be substituted for one portion of liquid milk	
Yogurt	$\frac{1}{4}$ to $\frac{1}{2}$ c	May be substituted for one portion of liquid milk	
Powdered skim milk	2 T	May be substituted for one portion of liquid milk	
Meat and meat equivalents			
Meat‡, fish§, poultry	1 to 2 oz	2	2
Egg	1	1	1
Peanut butter	1 to 2 T		
Legumes—dried peas and beans	$\frac{1}{4}$ to $\frac{1}{3}$ c cooked		
Vegetables and fruits			
Vegetables		4 to 5 to include 1 green leafy or yellow‖	4 to 5 to include 1 green leafy or yellow
Cooked	2 to 4 T		
Raw	Few pieces		
Fruit		1 citrus fruit or other vegetable or fruit rich in vitamin C	1 citrus fruit or other vegetable or fruit rich in vitamin C
Canned	4 to 8 T		
Raw	$\frac{1}{2}$ to 1 small		
Fruit juice	3 to 4 oz		

the very poor and food-deficient Irish people of the nineteenth century, who had an extremely limited diet, could scarcely have chosen any two foods as nutritionally adequate as buttermilk and potatoes. The nutritional adequacy for a desirable state of health may point, in some ethnic patterns, to a need for supplementation with some other foods. Adding needed foods to this basic diet is often much easier than changing the **staple food** of a group. This, however, means that it is desirable to maintain the basic pattern with only the needed supplementation. American Indian children who have been taught to like the wild greens that their families eat, for instance, should be encouraged to follow these food patterns. Second, children who learn the cues of ethnic food patterns at an early age should be allowed to make these patterns as permanent as possible in a new environment. Respect for differences in food patterns influences the way individuals view themselves and their worth.

TABLE 7-1 *Food Pattern for Preschool Children—cont'd*

Food	Portion Size	Number of Portions Advised	
		Ages 2 to 4 Years	Ages 4 to 6 Years
Bread and cereal grains			
Whole grain or enriched white bread	$\frac{1}{2}$ to 1 slice	3	3
Cooked cereal	$\frac{1}{4}$ to $\frac{1}{2}$ c	May be substituted for one serving of bread	
Ready-to-serve dry cereals	$\frac{1}{2}$ to 1 c		
Spaghetti, macaroni, noodles, rice	$\frac{1}{4}$ to $\frac{1}{2}$ c		
Crackers	2 to 3		
Fat			
Bacon	1 slice	Not to be substituted for meat	
Butter or vitamin A-fortified margarine	1 t	3	3 to 4
Desserts	$\frac{1}{4}$ to $\frac{1}{2}$ c	As demanded by kcalorie needs	
Sugars	$\frac{1}{2}$ to 1 t	2	2

*Diets should be monitored for adequacy of iron and vitamin D intake.

†Approximately $\frac{2}{3}$ c can easily be incorporated in a child's food during cooking.

‡Liver once a week can be used as liver sausage or cooked liver.

§Should be served once or twice per week to substitute for meat.

‖If child's preferences are limited, use double portions of preferred vegetables until appetite for other vegetables develops.

POSITIVE REINFORCEMENT

Experience with helping young children form desirable feeding patterns shows that positive reinforcement of desirable behavior is sound. (For further discussion of behavior modification, see Chapter 15.) Some 40 years ago it was found that children developed desirable feeding patterns when they felt successful and when negative behavior was ignored. It is wise to find out why a child does not like or does not readily eat a certain food or combination of foods. Often it is easy to change the food or menu.

There are many ways to help children eat successfully. Portion size is of paramount impor-tance. When children are presented with less food than they normally eat, they can accomplish the goal that the adult has set; they can then ask for second helpings. This allows them to receive adult approbation, which is a reward to them. If for some reason children cannot eat all the food that has been given to them, allowing them to set their own limit shows respect for them and lets them feel successful. However, when children restrict their food intake to much less than expected over a number of days, parents should investigate. Improving an environmental situation often corrects this low intake of food (see pages 172-173 for specific suggestions).

HUNGER AND APPETITE

Food is taken into the body to satisfy the primal urge of **hunger.** According to physiologist Dr. Anton J. Carlson,[3] two unpleasant sensations are involved in what we call hunger. The first is a generalized weakness and restlessness all over the body, which is probably caused by a need for more sugar in the blood. The second is a definite localized sensation of pains of tension in the upper part of the stomach. These pangs of hunger are comparatively brief and are followed by periods when hunger pain is not felt. The infant and the young child are thought to have frequent and severe hunger pains. These sometimes are severe enough to cause an outcry as they awaken the infant from sleep. Infants' stomachs have been observed to show feeble hunger contractions 1 hour after nursing and strong hunger contractions 2½ to 3 hours after a feeding. The length of time the stomach shows in this way that it is ready for food varies with the individual infant. In the young child of 2 to 5 years of age these hunger pains are somewhat less frequent or pronounced than in the young infant, but they are still quite definite. Normally, food taken into the body gives immediate pleasure to a child when it eases the pain of hunger. If nothing else interferes, food is associated with the easing of pain, and pleasure results from eating.

Hunger is quite different from **appetite.** Most authorities agree that although hunger is an unpleasant sensation, appetite is a pleasurable experience. Appetite is usually defined as the pleasant association of a food with past experiences with that food. Appetite, associated with the sight and odor of food, stimulates the flow of digestive juices and is therefore a vital part of good digestion, as has often been demonstrated in the clinic and laboratory.

Many people have searched diligently and long for foods that taste like those mother used to cook when they were children. No doubt her foods were good, but they were probably not incomparable. The remembered foods were eaten at times when the child was thoroughly happy, and as a result, a strong appetite for them was created. As an individual grows older, the zest for the same food may be lessened. There is only the memory of or the appetite for the former food. Thus appetites for certain foods are undoubtedly built up in children not only from the flavor, color, and texture of the food itself, but also from the many associations with the food.

It is normal for a young child to be hungry. To be persistently nonhungry is decidedly abnormal. The child who is not hungry should be taken to a physician who will carefully assess his or her physical well-being (looking possibly for a chronic infection) and his or her daily habits. This child may not get enough brisk exercise in the open air or may need more sleep, a more regular diet pattern, sleep and rest, or a less stimulating environment.

If a child is in good health and is hungry, with a stomach calling urgently for food, food will be eaten to satisfy that urge rather than to satisfy whims. As has been so aptly said, hunger should control the child rather than the child control hunger. This fact may be taken advantage of in many ways. New foods in very small portions may be served at the time of the day when the child is hungriest. It should be remembered that for a young child a new food is a step in the dark; children are generally not as adventuresome as adults. If a child eats the new food when hungry, it will probably leave a pleasant sensation, and the next time this food is served it will be recognized as a friend. Children learn to like a food by tasting it time after time, even though the first tastes are but a few tiny bites.

SETTING UP A FOOD ENVIRONMENT

In helping parents to understand why children eat as they do, it is important to direct their attention to the fact that *behavior is caused.* When causes of behavior are understood, a food problem is on the way to being cured. Parents who understand why children eat as they do can usually set up an environment that promotes a healthy appetite. Often an outside professional person can help a parent to discover these causes and to restructure the environment. Preparental education in which specific appetite problems are discussed can help prevent them. Part of this education must emphasize the requirements of a good food environment.

How does a parent help a child develop desirable food patterns? The following are suggestions:

1. The parents, as "gatekeepers," must recognize that the kinds of food available to the preschool child in the home are what they buy and provide. Many parents need to be shown that, in this, they are *really in command*. In a well-child clinic, a mother complained that her 3-year-old child was eating too many potato chips, yet she admitted that she was the one who bought them. Of course, other family members must also cooperate in not having foods of this kind available.

2. Often parents must decide which of their own food patterns they want to pass on to their children. Some parents need to be assured that they can change their own food patterns; they may even need to be helped to do this.

3. Feeding programs for groups of preschool children have proven again and again that the eating habits of young children can be repatterned under skilled guidance. This should give parents added confidence.

DEVELOPMENTAL PATTERNS

Children develop for the most part in an orderly pattern—physically, emotionally, and psychologically.

Eating is always dependent on the abilities of the eater. For instance, when normal infants are born, they are able to root for a nipple and to suck vigorously to ingest milk. When infants are given a chance to satisfy their hunger in this manner, they attain their first success in eating. As parents discover the child's hunger patterns and provide foods to satisfy hunger, they set up the condition for successful eating.

DIFFICULTIES IN THE FORMATION OF GOOD FOOD HABITS AND WAYS TO AVOID THEM

When most infants are fed the first semisolid food, they often spit it out rather violently— not because they do not want the food but because they know only the sucking motion they have used thus far to ingest food (see Chapter 4). Now they try this motion again, and the semiliquid cereal or food spatters everywhere. They must learn an entirely new feeding technique. If they fail in the first efforts, a parent may be spattered and naturally quite upset. The infants have met their first feeding disaster. To laugh at these efforts is unwise because the infant learns to do this to make parents laugh. Parents should prepare themselves in advance so that they can remain undisturbed by the incident.

Another difficulty enters into this situation— all the previous food has been liquid. Now, suddenly, here is a food with a new texture, as well as a new flavor that is different from the usual, mildly sweet milk. Difficulties may be avoided by giving the infant minute amounts of the new food, well moistened and thinned by the familiar milk, until the new food is easily accepted. **Weaning** begins at this time. The infant is being weaned away gradually from an exclusively fluid diet.

In this discussion weaning is used to mean a general process involving, as far as food is concerned, any change in food flavor, texture, consistency, temperature, or method of feeding. Many feeding difficulties arise because the changes are expected to take place too abruptly or because adults fail to realize how difficult some of these tasks are for the infant and the young child. A child can and will learn these new things, but neither the parent nor child should become upset over failures at first. Nor must the child learn to get attention by spitting food out or by refusing it. The problem can be avoided by demonstrating the technique for spoon feeding.

At approximately 6 months of age, even before the first tooth appears, most infants make chewing movements with their gums. At this time infants should be given foods such as small strips of oven-dried toast, which offer a chance for chewing at the same time as they soften to allow easy swallowing. It has been observed that when an infant is not given a chance to chew at this time, trouble in mastering this skill may occur later.

When the infant begins to gain the muscular ability to pick up small particles using the thumb and forefingers, particles of soft green beans or peas can be fed (see Chapter 4 for a more detailed discussion of this). These efforts, along with reaching for the bottle and later holding it, are the infant's first efforts to learn to feed independently.

The stage of developing independence at 9 to 18 months of age can be either exciting or distressing for parents. If parents understand that exploring everything new is very important to an infant, they can encourage this exploration by providing new textures and flavors in foods; this allows an infant to discover what a food such as oatmeal feels like. At this stage many infants have learned to crawl out from their former sitting position or to walk. It is no longer satisfying to them to just look at something; they now want to examine it. Wise parents take advantage of this new learning by providing a wide variety of food. They should not be discouraged at first if the child only feels a food before chewing it.

During the first year an infant has tremendous adjustments to make, only one of which is learning new foods and new methods of eating. In helping this infant to form good patterns, we will be most successful if we provide thoughtful and understanding guidance in the following ways:

1. Introducing new textures and flavors gradually
2. Enlarging the child's experience with as many individual foods in as many different forms as possible
3. Feeding individual foods and not mixtures so that the infant may learn to appreciate foods for their own flavors and textures
4. Observing at what time of day the infant takes the new food most easily and giving it then
5. Being patient with the first efforts and allowing the infant to learn to feed himself or herself; offering help when the infant becomes too tired to finish the process easily
6. Being understanding of the infant's efforts in each new feeding process
7. Above all, securing the entire family's cooperation

The high level of nutritive need of the first year of life is superseded by a slower metabolic rate and a slower rate of growth; therefore the child does not need as much food per unit of body weight as before. What is eaten and how it is eaten are now more important than how much is eaten. To watch a young child grow increasingly independent in feeding himself or herself can be as thrilling for a parent as watching the taking of the first steps from chair to chair. Perhaps in no other area of development in young children is progress more individual. Each child should be allowed to try new skills over and over with no record of failures unless development is obviously too slow to show any progress.

When parents understand what children are telling them in the way they eat, rebellion against food can be lessened and future food refusals can be reduced. For instance, the realization that the 2-year-old child may have a sporadic appetite, which should not be the cause for undue alarm, may prevent the long-lasting influence of battles over food.

SPECIFIC SUGGESTIONS FOR SETTING UP A FOOD ENVIRONMENT

Perhaps no arrangements for eating are more important than those that afford physical comfort to a child. Children should always feel secure on a sturdy, well-balanced chair with their feet well supported on the floor or other structure. They should be able to reach their food easily without straining their muscles. This also provides a better opportunity to eat without spills, although wise parents also prepare table surfaces and floors for children's spills. Dishes and utensils as well as table arrangements can foster success in eating. It is desirable to give the child sturdy and as nearly unbreakable utensils as possible so that spills and breaking utensils will not give a sense of failure. Also it is important not to laugh at the child, because if parents laugh at a child's mistakes, the child may gain an undue feeling of being the center of attention.

When children's chairs are being purchased, these should be "tried on" as clothing is. Some chairs, for instance, are designed to fit a child's torso and are much more comfortable than are perfectly straight chairs.

Sometimes children, who for some months have eaten at the family table, may suddenly be happier eating at their own small table with a parent nearby. Some mothers even find it possible to eat a quiet noon meal with the child at a small table.

Colorful table arrangements intrigue young children and are worth the trouble to provide. When children have developed some skill in eating, they will appreciate eating from the family's best china. Parents who show confidence in a child's accomplishment are usually rewarded by the child's care in handling prized possessions. These children who have had help in gaining skill in successful eating are easy to recognize as one observes families eating together in restaurants.

Forks and spoons should be chosen for their suitability for young hands. The spoon, which is the first eating implement a child uses, should have a round shallow bowl and a blunt tip that allows the child to shove food from the plate into the mouth. A handle that is blunt, short, and easily held in the child's palm is desirable; at this age a child uses the hand as a mass of muscles. Only after 5 or 6 years of age is control of the finer muscles of the fingers accomplished. Forks with short, blunt tines are best adapted to the child's palm. Although some parents report that their children enjoy sharper tines with which they can spear food, sharp tines can be dangerous.

Glasses that sit firmly on the table and are small enough for children's hands to encircle are best for 2- to 4-year-old children. Small delicate handles on cups are difficult for small hands to maneuver.

The shape and weight of the dishes are also important. The young child delights in pouring his or her own milk. Interesting, squat pitchers with broad handles from which the child can easily pour milk are recommended. Parents can be encouraged to experiment with dishes and utensils for their children and to look for those that satisfy children's needs.

FOOD LIKES

Patient observation and long experience in feeding young children, as well as in counseling parents, have given me an insight into what children want in their food. When this knowledge of children's preferences is combined with the knowledge of nutrients, children can be adequately and happily fed. The results of these observations are discussed on the following pages.

Menus

Simplicity in menus is important. At the same time there must be variety to allow young children to learn to know many foods, since variety in foods is a good foundation for an adequate diet.

The following outline gives a general meal pattern that should satisfy nutrient needs in a hungry preschool child.

A. Breakfast
1. One high-protein food
   a. 1 egg *or*
   b. 2 oz muscle meat *or*
   c. $\frac{3}{4}$ c cereal, cooked, *or*
   d. 1 c dry cereal with 4 to 6 oz milk
2. Bread with butter or margarine (1 slice whole grain or white enriched bread, plus 1 t butter)
3. 6 to 8 oz milk
4. Fruit—preferably one serving of citrus
   a. 4 oz orange juice *or*
   b. $\frac{1}{3}$ to $\frac{1}{2}$ medium-sized grapefruit *or*
   c. 1 medium-sized orange
B. Noon meal
1. One high-protein food (see breakfast for list of high-protein foods)
   a. 1 serving thick soup or stew *or*
   b. 1 serving casserole dish of a protein food in a starchy base
2. Vegetables
   a. 1 cooked (see Table 6-1 for amounts)
   b. 1 raw (see Table 6-1 for amounts)
3. Bread (1 slice whole grain *or* enriched white bread with 1 t butter)
4. 6 to 8 oz milk
5. Dessert
   a. Simple dessert based on a combination of milk, eggs, and fruit *or*
   b. Serving of fruit
C. Evening meal
1. One high-protein food
   a. 2 oz meat *or*
   b. 1 oz cheese *or*
   c. 1 egg *or*

d. Combinations of these and vegetables
2. Vegetables
   a. 1 or 2 cooked *or*
   b. 1 raw
3. Bread and butter (1 slice whole grain or enriched white bread with 1 t butter)
4. 6 to 8 oz milk
5. Dessert (see noon meal, dessert)
D. Snacks (between meals or at bedtime). These should provide some of the needed nutrients and be low in sugar and fat so that they do not interfere with the appetite for the following meal; use, for example, any of the following:
   1. Fruit juices with a cracker or a piece of bread *or*
   2. Small pieces of fruit *or*
   3. Small pieces of raw vegetables *or*
   4. Small pieces of cheese with a small piece of bread or cracker

Combinations of Food

Most children eat most easily those foods with which they are familiar. It is advisable that a very small portion of a new food be introduced with a familiar and popular food. If the child only looks at the new food or just feels or smells it at first, this is a part of learning to accept it.

Dry foods are especially hard for children to eat, as is discussed later in this chapter. In planning a menu, dry foods should always be carefully balanced with one or two moist foods. For instance, it is wise to put a slice of meat loaf (relatively dry) with mashed potatoes and peas in a little cream sauce.

Combinations of sharp, rather acid-flavored foods with mild-flavored foods are popular with young children.

Ease of Manipulation

The ease of eating food with the unskilled and seemingly clumsy hands of a young child is important. Many small pieces of foods such as cooked green peas or beans are difficult for a child to spoon up. These can be mixed with mashed potatoes for easier eating.

When a 2-year-old child eats a bowl of thin soup, many trials are made before it is finished. Although it is advisable to serve young children soups occasionally, one must realize that the process of spooning it is tiring. Two things may be done to make soup easier for a child to eat. It may be drunk from a cup, or the soup may be made slightly thicker so that it does not spill from the spoon easily. I suggested a two-way soup to a prominent soup company. The company promoted a canned soup that was to be thinned, preferably with milk, and then strained so that a child could spoon up the solid portion and drink the liquid. Soup for young children should be either spoonable or drinkable. Later, the child may have soup to be eaten with a spoon when he or she is able to manage a spoon without spilling its contents.

Many foods can be prepared so that a child can eat them with the fingers (Figure 7-1). Hard-cooked eggs may be served in quarters, cooked meat can be cut in small strips, and cooked green beans can be served as finger foods. Children have been observed to like oranges that have been cut in wedges (skin and all) much better than peeled and diced oranges. Young schoolchildren prefer simple pieces of raw vegetables with no salad dressing to mixed-up salads, which are much more difficult to eat. It is best to serve cottage cheese or similar foods separate from the lettuce leaf on a child's plate. Creamed foods served on tough toast are difficult for children to manage.

The size of pieces of food for children must be given serious consideration. Handling silverware and conveying food to the mouth at this early age is a greater task than many adults realize. Pieces of carrots that slide across the plate and are too small to remain on the fork or cubes of beets so large that they must be cut into bite-size pieces exhaust the patience of a 2- or 3-year-old child. Most foods served to young children should be cut into bite-size pieces. When the child is 4 years of age and older, the skills to cut up some foods may have been developed. If, however, much difficulty in managing is noticed, small pieces should usually be served, accompanied by occasional encouragement to cut up some foods. Canned pears and other soft fruits are usually easily cut into bite-size pieces.

Stringy spinach or tomatoes are a trial for anyone to eat. Much can be done with a handy pair of food shears in the kitchen to make these foods easier to eat. Finger foods, such as pieces of lettuce or toast, should be used in meals in which some of the foods are difficult to handle. Small sandwiches—that is, a large one cut into four squares—are popular with young children.

Texture

I have found it wise to serve one soft food (for easy eating), one crisp food (to allow easy chewing and enjoyment of the sounds in the mouth), and one chewy food (to use emerging chewing skills without having too much to chew) in each meal for young children.

Some children can fall into the habit of rejecting all foods of a certain texture; this limits the kinds of foods the child tries to eat (see pages 177-178 for suggestions on how to handle this problem).

Pieces of meat are hard for young children to eat because the teeth of 2- or 3-year-old children do not grind meat as easily as adult teeth do. This explains why children often prefer hamburgers or frankfurters and why thrice-ground meat is often popular with nursery school children. Most children's meat can be served as ground meat. When parents want a steak, a roast, or a pot roast, the mother can cook a small portion of ground meat from the freezer for the young child. Ground meat should be cooked only long enough for the color to change to brown. It should not be allowed to become dry with a hard crust, which is hard for a child to eat. Some children may prefer moderately rare meat, which is even more moist.

Flavor

In general, young children reject strong flavors. Many children, however, do seem to like pickles, some spicy sauces, and beer, preferences that may seem to contradict this. In general, it has been found that children like food that is mildly salted, with about half as much salt as is used in adult recipes. Because some authorities now believe that all of us would profit by taking less salt, this may be a good health habit to foster (Chapter 12). In general, sharp spices such as pepper and acids such as vinegar should also be used sparingly on children's food.

Strong-flavored vegetables such as cabbage and onions are more popular with young children when served raw. If these vegetables are cooked, it is recommended that they be prepared in excessive amounts of water so that some of the strong flavor can be thrown away. Of course, water-soluble nutrients are lost if the water is discarded, but teaching children to eat these foods is most important at this time in their lives. A mild-flavored cream sauce also helps to make these vegetables more palatable. This was shown in a nursery school when some children asked for very mild-flavored creamed onions after they had eaten dessert.

Because young children often reject sharply tart fruits, such fruits should be diluted with those of mild flavor. Tart oranges were found to be popular when mixed with cooked peaches or bananas. The rule of one tart, one mild, and one crisp is good to follow. The crisp fruit may be small unpeeled pieces of apples.

In general, when helping children develop desirable food patterns, keep the natural flavor of the food so that only small amounts of sugar are needed. The use of a little honey is also recommended because it is sweeter than an equal amount of granulated sugar and less can be used.

Color

Children have a natural interest in color in their foods, and teaching them to appreciate the lovely fresh color of foods is a worthy aim. Young children are delighted when they may choose one of several different colored desserts. Green, orange, yellow, and pink are popular colors in food. Children in nursery schools rarely failed to comment on the food to which a tiny sprig of parsley had been added or to notice bits of hidden color such as tomato, carrot, or parsley in sandwiches.

Cakes, cookies, and candies containing molasses, dried fruits, and nuts provide other nutrients in addition to kcalories. Natural fruit juices have more of the needed nutrients than sweetened, colored, and artificially flavored drinks. Because the water that fruit juices contain is also desirable for children, strong-fla-

FIG. 7-1   Eighteen-month-old twins enjoy finger-feeding one another.

vored juices should be diluted, giving additional water to the child.

SPECIFIC FOOD PREPARATION

Children should be considered when the family plans meals. Many parents do, of necessity, vary their life-styles when they are raising their families, so the importance of food-patterning during this period is emphasized. Young children can be taught that just as adults wear different clothes from children, so there are adult-type foods and drinks. Children often prefer an orange or a serving of another fruit to the cherry pie that is being served to adults.

Foods can be made soft enough in texture for young children by adding extra milk to a dry, starchy food.

If the parents prefer strong-flavored vegetables, a small portion for the young child can be rinsed under the hot water faucet before it is served.

A young child may prefer food served at room temperature. In fact, preschool children often appear frightened by hot food. They also often stir hard ice cream until it is soupy and less sharply cold.

While the father serves dinner at the table, the mother may prefer to dish the preschool child's food in the kitchen. This can serve two purposes: (1) young children's hunger makes them impatient participants at a meal, so rapid service of food is desirable, and (2) the mother can easily regulate the amount of food served or can make any sudden changes. Fathers sometimes have more difficulty serving small enough portions to a child than mothers do.

Table 7-1 has been devised from my many years of careful observations of how much the average child can eat easily. Some pediatricians who believe that children should not be forced to eat a specific amount of any food object to setting up such expectations in a chart. Yet mothers often need some help in the amount of food the *average* child can eat easily to get the needed nutrients. Such goals may also prevent mothers from expecting their children to eat more than their children want. These average portion sizes may be too large for a new food, for a disliked food, or for a nonhungry child. Of course, the hungry child can have extra servings.

FOOD DISLIKES

It is safe to allow every person to have at least one or two food dislikes. Unless a child is on a medically prescribed diet, no one food has to be eaten assuming that a family can afford a varied diet.

Some food dislikes, as has been previously discussed, have unusual causes. One woman reports that sugared oranges always have a flavor of castor oil to her, though she enjoys oranges without sugar. When she was young she was given doses of the then strong-flavored castor oil with sugared oranges to cover its flavor. Though she knows that she only imagines the castor oil flavor in the oranges, she says that even now she thinks, "What has been on my spoon, castor oil?" The association of sugared oranges and castor oil has survived with her over many years.

Substitutions for liquid milk, which children sometimes dislike, can temporarily be made. Powdered milk (4 T substituted for 8 oz of fluid milk) can be added to foods, and cottage or cheddar cheese can be used.

When children are in control of their appetite and hunger, they sometimes refuse all foods. This can be handled by structuring the environment in which they eat. One cold, winter day in a nursery school when we were weary of preparing food for nonhungry children, we decided to give the children a shock. On the usual array of dishes, we placed only 1 T of vegetable meat stew in the soup bowl. No other food was in evidence in the entire dining room, no baskets of sandwiches, no pitchers of milk, no trays of dishes of desserts. When the children took one look, they at once exclaimed, "Where's our dinner? Is this all of our dinner?" Rather slowly, second servings were brought in from the kitchen. The food records showed that more food was eaten that day than any day for several weeks before.

Telling a child that we know he or she doesn't like boiled potatoes and can have more green beans often encourages a good appetite. However, when a child rejects many foods, for example, all vegetables or all meat, the parents should try to find out the reasons. Adequate substitutions may need to be made. For instance, in hot summer weather, fruits can replace cooked vegetables in a child's diet if the family budget can tolerate the extra cost. This serving of fruit sometimes stimulates failing appetites.

At times parents may need to seek professional help from someone who understands children both from closer observation of many children eating and from knowing the findings of research in the area. My observation and research have shown me the importance of the following:

1. Belief that changes can occur in a child's eating patterns is of primary importance. Eating is one of the pleasures of life. The individual who likes the foods he or she needs to eat for the adequate nutrition of the body is fortunate.

2. The goals set by someone counseling parents about children's eating should be easy to accomplish. Success in following the advice of professional people promotes confidence and positively reinforces the child who succeeds in eating what is presented. When a food dislike is firmly established before the parent seeks help, it will probably not disappear suddenly; only gradual correction can be expected. Progress may not be consistent, and temporary failures to reach the goal must be expected. Often the best methods of correction are progressive. For instance, to help a child learn to eat food with texture, a mother can gradually add coarser textured food to those that are usually eaten.

3. Parents should accept a child's strong dislike for a particular food and should substitute another food that provides the same nutrients. Often a temporary release of pressure concerning eating a specific food causes the child to try it later. A mother who was looking at her 3-year-old son's noon meal food consumption record

in a nursery school said, "But he never eats eggs at home and this noon he had seconds!" That is exactly the reason that a parent enrolling a child is not asked about the child's food dislikes, but only about the foods that make the child ill. Another mother said to her son as she looked at the school records, "But you don't like turnips!" Whereupon her son answered, "Yours are black. They are white at nursery school. I like them white!"

4. Children are good judges of well-prepared food. Sometimes classes in food preparation for parents or prospective parents would be the best approach to handling children's food dislikes.

5. Sometimes the war over children's eating becomes so sharp that withdrawing one of the combatants is the only solution. Someone other than the parent feeding the child temporarily may be a solution to the problem.

6. Because children are usually rhythmic in all they do, the satisfaction of their hunger should also be kept rhythmic. This means that meals served at the same time each day generally promote a good appetite. Fatigue, the most defeating factor in children's appetites, is thus avoided. I have found again and again that starving a child to get the child to eat does not promote good eating.

COMMON PROBLEMS

Healthy, hungry children will eat if they are given a calm atmosphere in which to eat. This is the first and most important consideration.

One of the most common problems, that of fatigue, has just been discussed. Sympathy should be extended to the child who, eating at a tearoom in a large store after a morning of shopping, just looks at the food and cries when urged to eat. The child probably needs to rest more than he or she needs to eat.

When a child is regularly more hungry at a certain time of day than at other times, this should be accepted. Perhaps the greater hunger at the evening meal is caused by having rested while watching a favorite television program

before dinner. Sometimes healthy outdoor running followed by a quiet rest restores a lagging noontime appetite. It was found that nursery school food costs increased when the children played outdoors in a warm Iowa March after a cold and confining February.

Some of the earliest eating skills learned by a young child are those of chewing and swallowing. Each of these is accomplished to a great extent by trial and error. Some impatient parents worry over this slow progress.

Swallowing seems to be difficult for some children. They tend to swallow only after the food is thoroughly chewed and finely ground. In fact, some children hold food in the cheeks like chipmunks, and some children eat their dessert and still have the vegetable in their cheeks. The fact that some children apparently gain more enjoyment from filling their mouths full of food than from taking small mouthfuls makes learning to chew and swallow a bit complicated for them. These children may almost appear helpless as they sit with packed mouths. Encouraging them to take small bites and to chew and swallow each mouthful has been successful in some cases.

No discussion of children's food problems would be complete without a discussion of the so-called vegetable war. Sometimes this may be created at first by a generally disgruntled parent who really wants to have the child reinforce his or her own belief that all vegetables are horrible. Perhaps a father associates cooked vegetables with his mother with whom there was always a clash. Histories of American colonial times tell of husbands who refused their wives the money to buy seeds for green leafy vegetables because they considered these foods fodder. This was, of course, in the "previtamin days." This idea of fodder appears too often in the history of food patterns. Yet we also find in these histories stories of gathering wild greens for use during the so-called hunger weeks of spring when the food preserved for winter was either all gone or too spoiled to be used. It is also interesting to observe in tropical countries of Asia and Africa the vast array of what are to us strange-looking green leafy vegetables that are bought eagerly from native markets.

The rejection of some kinds of foods can easily be passed down from parents to their children. Sometimes a dislike for the usually popular milk can be directly accounted for in this way. The labeling of salads as "women's food" may also have caused some boys to reject them.

All of these influences, although subtle, are definitely effective in the development of food prejudices. Being branded as someone who does not like carrots often prevents a child who would later like to try them from doing so. When we begin to understand the basis of a food prejudice, we are on the way to counteracting it.

However, many children do like vegetables. Some raw vegetables are preferred, but well-cooked vegetables are accepted also. Of course, I am assuming here that strong acrid odors and unpleasant flavors are not present in these cooked vegetables. When a person, coming in from outdoors and the fresh air, smells unpleasant cooking odors in a poorly ventilated kitchen, a prejudice may precede the actual meal. Sometimes better selection at the market of tender young root vegetables is necessary to prevent the unpleasant "woodiness" in root vegetables.

Another specific food problem concerns the child who is exceptionally fond of sweet foods; often parents who are very fond of such foods have patterned the child to be overfond of them. Sweet foods used as rewards or as special treats also reinforce the child's desire for sweets. The use of cake for a birthday celebration is too well grounded in American tradition to be uprooted, but we should recognize that a wonderful birthday cake reinforces the value of a sweet food. One child asked whether fruit cake (always served in his home at Christmas time) was Christ's birthday cake.

Summary

In no other area are family influences stronger than in food preferences. The association of mother's food and her love lasts over years and may supersede all outside influences. Studies have shown that of all meal patterns, Sunday dinner meal patterns change most slowly when a family moves to a new country. A father's influence on a child's food preferences was shown in one study in which children were found to dislike the foods that the father disliked.[4] The principal reason was that since mothers did not serve the food fathers disliked, these foods were unfamiliar to the children and they refused them when they were served later.

Modern parents, buffeted by their children's faith in television advertisements for food as well as by the sweets offered in vending machines at school, sometimes lose faith in their role as the "home gatekeeper." They may need professional bolstering to reinforce their faith in themselves so that they actually do control the food in their homes and in their children's lives.

To assist children to develop desirable food patterns, I recommend the following:

1. All foods should be well prepared and attractive in color, flavor, and texture, so that the child will approach the meal and eat it happily. Children appreciate and enjoy an attractive plate and often comment on foods being "pretty"; they eat with greatest enthusiasm when there is a variety of flavors and textures in the meal.
2. The environment for eating should be suited to the abilities and comfort of the young eater. This includes appropriate tables and chairs as well as suitable dishes and implements.
3. A child should be expected to have a good appetite and to be hungry when in good physical and emotional health.
4. Appetite will be fostered if the child is hungry and happily excited over the fact that it is mealtime.
5. Pleasant associations with the food are fostered if the meal can be eaten successfully with reasonable effort. Fatigue often defeats children's desire for food. They should come to the meal rested, and the eating process should not be tiring.

REVIEW QUESTIONS

1. What is the difference between hunger and appetite?
2. How does one help an infant to accept new foods?
3. Describe dishes and utensils appropriate for preschool-age children.
4. How can foods be prepared so that they are easy for the child to eat?

5. How can tastes and textures of food be combined to make a meal pleasing for the young child?

SUGGESTED LEARNING ACTIVITIES

1. During observation of a preschool feeding program, identify food preferences of the children.
2. Describe factors in the environment that, at mealtimes, influence children's food acceptance.
3. Discuss appropriate portions for 2- and 5-year-old children.
4. How can parents facilitate a child's acceptance of new textures?
5. Describe appropriate tables, chairs, and utensils for feeding young children.

Terms and Concepts

Provided here for your review is a listing of terms and concepts within this chapter. The definitions for terms can be found in the glossary, which begins on page 413. To aid your understanding of the terms' and concepts' application within this text, the page number designating the first mention of each term or concept within the chapter is given.

appetite, 170
hunger, 170
nutritional adequacy, 167
staple food, 168
weaning, 171

REFERENCES

1. Lowenberg ME and others: *Food and people,* New York, 1979, John Wiley & Sons.
2. Aldrich CA, Aldrich MM: *Feeding our old-fashioned children,* New York, 1946, Macmillan Publishing.
3. Carlson AJ: *The control of hunger in health and disease,* Chicago, 1916, University of Chicago Press.
4. Bryan MS, Lowenberg ME: The father's influence on young children's food preference, *J Am Diet Assoc* 34:30, 1958.

8

Factors That Shape Food Patterns in Young Children

Cristine M. Trahms

Objectives

✦✦

After studying this chapter, the student should:

✔ *Understand the development of taste preferences of infants and young children.*

✔ *Understand the role of adult and peer influences on children's food acceptance.*

✔ *Recognize social and cultural influences on food patterns of children.*

✔ *Understand the effect of television on food preferences and intake of children.*

✔ *Understand the role of learning in the development of food preferences, regulation of food intake, and ability to distinguish between food and inedible substances.*

We all have developed our own unique set of food habits without necessarily understanding the factors that have shaped our individual patterns and choices. As nutrition professionals and educators, we have long been curious about the forces that shape food habits and consequently health status. It has been generally accepted that patterns of food choices are developed early in life and that parents are influential in shaping food-related behaviors. The traditional manner of counseling parents has been to provide nutrition information and to hope for a concomitant increase in knowledge and change

in attitudes and behaviors related to nutrition and food choices. Guidance on shaping food-related behaviors has been primarily based on observation and common sense principles.

This chapter is a sequel to Dr. Lowenberg's discussion of earlier research and the practical aspects of the development of the food habits of young children. It describes some of the research that has helped us begin to understand the interactions of genetics and environment that shape food-related behaviors. It is difficult to define in a measurable manner those terms related to food behavior, such as food choices, food preferences, dawdling, and coaxing. It is then equally difficult to measure the intervening and confounding variables that may affect food behavior. Parents clearly no longer, if they ever did, have the single significant impact on the food choices of their young children.

Currently the interaction of factors that shape food choices is being evaluated using appropriate theoretical constructs. These factors include nutrition attitudes and knowledge of parents and child-care providers, economic and social status of the family, ordinal position of the preschool child, siblings and peers, and media advertising.

It is difficult but necessary to begin to incorporate both an assessment of individual nutritional adequacy and an evaluation of food patterns and choices in an effort to assess the effect of food preferences on long-term health status.

Factors that have recently been evaluated for the young child are texture, taste, familiarity of food, preferences of the child compared with those of parents and other significant adults, and interaction patterns of parents and children around food. The limitations of these reports are the usual qualifications encountered when dealing with a complex set of interacting factors. However, these reports do indicate a direction for clinical practice and suggest important considerations in developing multidimensional research models that build a solid base for that practice.

PHYSIOLOGICAL BASIS OF TASTE

Brillat-Savarin noted in his 1825 book *The Physiology of Taste,* "It is not easy matter to determine the precise nature of the organ of taste. It is more complicated than it would appear at first sight."[1] The nature of taste is still largely unknown. It is an essential part of our lives, influencing our food choices and our willingness to consume enough of specific foods to provide adequate nourishment. Some aspects of taste are believed to be innate to the human organism, whereas others are dictated by genetics, and still others are believed to be developed by physical maturation and experience. Willingness

to ingest food is affected by a series of factors that include the sensory attributes of food, as well as immediate hunger, nutritional status, prior experience with the food, and beliefs and feelings about food. Recent work with infants and young children has endeavored to measure these almost immeasurable aspects of taste.

It is believed that preference for sweet tastes is innate to the infant.[2] However, this preference may be modified in early life. Sugar water must be offered to the infant to maintain the newborn level of preference for sweetness. Without this exposure in the early newborn period, the relative acceptance of this beverage diminishes.[3]

Aversion to bitter tastes appears at an early age (Figure 8-1). Reactions to salty tastes are initially neutral.[2] This indifference for the taste of salt shifts to relative preference for salt at about 4 months of age when this taste interacts with other tastes in foods. Younger children and infants prefer a saltwater solution. However, preschoolers reject this solution, favoring instead relatively high levels of salt in foods that are usually associated with a mildly salty taste. For example, preschoolers prefer a much higher level of salt in soup than do most adults.[4]

The genetic makeup of an individual affects basic taste responses, which in turn affect food acceptance. The classic genetic difference is capability to be a "taster" for 6-N-propylthiouracil (PROP) or a "nontaster" for the compound. Tasters to PROP are more sensitive to bitter taste. However, only recently has the link between genetics of taste and food preference been explored for young children. The young children who were nontasters preferred cheese and milk more than the tasters.[5] The implication for selecting foods as sources of nutrients based on the genetic status of taste is noteworthy and warrants further evaluation.

DEVELOPMENT OF FOOD PREFERENCES

Innate tastes are only one aspect of food preference. Factors that influence the food habits of young children are listed in the box on page 183. Infants and young children often favor

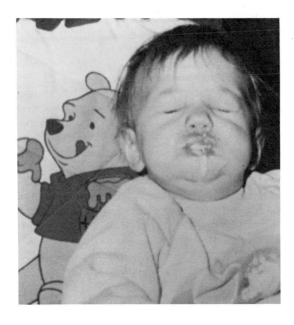

FIG. 8-1   Infants recognize sour and bitter tastes and make their dislikes known.

FACTORS THAT SHAPE FOOD CHOICES

- ***Characteristics of parents and child care providers***
Nutrition knowledge
Nutrition attitudes
Personal food choices
Personal eating style (e.g., pace and frequency of eating)
Nonnourishment uses of food
- ***Characteristics of family***
Family composition
Economic status
Social status
Educational level of adults
Occupation of adults
Ordinal position of child
Number and age of children in home
- ***Characteristics of peers and siblings***
Food preferences
Nonnourishment uses of foods
Nutrition attitudes

- ***Characteristics of child***
Age
Genetics of taste
Conditioned responses
- ***Interactions with adults around food***
Satiety cues respected
Pace and frequency of eating that adults expect from the child
Social interaction and communication patterns around food
Type of food offered
Benefit versus threat contingencies
- ***Characteristics of foods***
Texture
Taste
Familiarity of food
Sweetness
Appearance of food
- ***Media***
Foods advertised
Promotion of foods for nonnourishment capabilities
Promotion of desired body shape

foods because they are offered or because their parents and peers enjoy them. For preschool children, sweetness and familiarity are primary enhancers of choice; familiarity becomes less important with older children.[6] Preference rankings made by preschool children are highly correlated with consumption,[7] and the preferences of children can be strongly influenced by their peers. Fear of a new food can be diminished by increasing exposure to the food.

It would also seem that the food preferences of young children would be significantly influenced by the adults who provide their care and thus their food. Child-parent preference associations would be expected to be strong because of intimate social contact inside the family. However, the evidence is contradictory. One study suggests that both the mother and the father influence a child's food preferences equally, possibly because of the high priority given to the father's preferences in the family menu.[8] Another study shows that unrelated adults of the same subcultural group, such as day-care teachers, exert an influence equal to that of parents in development of food preferences.[9] In a comprehensive evaluation of family resemblance in food patterns, mother-child choices were similar, whereas father-child choices had no relationship. Parent–older child similarities in food choices were stronger than parent–younger child similarities. The food preferences of young children were more similar to those of their siblings than to those of their parents,[10] perhaps because children in a given family generally accept a narrower range of foods than the adults accept (Figure 8-2).

Even though the family constellation has changed with increasing numbers of single-parent and blended families, the relationship between gender and food roles appears not to have changed much.[11] Women are still the primary "purchasers and preparers" of foods brought into the home. The change has been in the frequency of meals eaten away from home

FIG. 8-2   Siblings exert influence on food preferences.

by children—at day-care, preschool, school breakfast or lunch, or fast-food restuarants.

While it would appear that roles in the home have not changed much, many women are preparing food less often for their young children. However, the report of the Continuing Survey of Food Intakes of Individuals (CSFII) indicates that these changes in maternal employment appear to have no detrimental effect on the nutritional adequacy of the diets of young children. In fact, reported intakes of total fat, saturated fat, cholesterol, and sodium did not increase with maternal employment.[12] The impact of these changes on nutrition and long-term health is not understood.

LEARNED RESPONSES THAT AFFECT FOOD INTAKE

The role of learning in the process of regulation of intake, food preferences, and differentiating food from nonfood substances is important. Young children must learn to differentiate food from nonfood substances. It has been demonstrated that the young child learns by experience to place "items" into edible foods and inedible categories, such as disgust (feces), danger (poisons), inappropriate (grass, sticks), and unacceptable combinations (catsup on cookies). The youngest children had a high to moderate level of acceptance of all categories of food and nonfood items offered. Fortunately, the acceptance of dangerous and disgusting substances decreased with age. However, almost all of the children accepted combinations that were unacceptable to adults (e.g., a hot dog with chocolate sauce).[13]

Young children must also learn to differentiate hunger from other cues, since the failure to learn to discriminate among various cues can lead to inappropriate eating and perhaps intake regulation disorders. Birch and Deysher[14] found that young children show clearer evidence for kcaloric compensation than adults. Nearly all of the children studied (95%) ate less at lunch following a high-kcaloric density preload than a low-kcaloric density preload. Only 60% of the adults had this same pattern.

A significant learned food behavior is the response to the parent's admonition to eat specific foods "or else!" (Figure 8-3). A preschool child usually knows that foods presented as the

FIG. 8-3 Young children have their own ideas about when and how to eat.

means in the contingency are the ones that are usually disliked (e.g., "Eat your spinach before you can have more french fries"). When a food is placed as the means component of a contingency to increase the consumption of a particular food, the consumption of that food increases while the contingency is in effect. However, the consumption of the food is actually reduced after the contingency is removed.[15]

Young children responded in a more positive manner to nutrition guidance that was presented in a benefit appeal rather than a threat appeal format. The benefit appeal stresses the positive aspects of changing practices and the threat appeal presents the consequences of not changing practices.[16] Accenting the positive aspects of healthy food choices appealed to young children. This learning style needs to be more fully evaluated for long-term effect.

Nutrition awareness is a component of development of long-term food habits. How parents communicate with children about foods sets a baseline for development in this area. The nutrition messages from parents to children could be categorized as general nutrition, specific nutrition, encouragement, passive and nonverbal, example, authoritarian, bribe and rewards, and positive or negative messages in each category. The children responded to positive messages that were general but frequent (this food will make you strong) and to specific nutrition messages (milk gives you strong bones) from parents.[17]

EXTERNAL CONTROLS OF FOOD PREFERENCES

"Attempts to externally control the child's intake reflect an implicit assumption that children are incapable of self-regulation and the attempts at control often have effects counter to those intended."[14] External control strategies may lead the young child to see that external cues, such as the amount of food remaining on the plate, rather than the internal cues of hunger and satiety are important to the regulation of food intake.

Satiety is specific to particular foods and in-

fluences both the choice of a food and the amount of a food that is eaten; this specificity can lead to a greater intake when a variety of foods is available. Food intake in humans increases as the variety of foods offered at a meal increases.[18] Children who are not exposed to coercive parenting strategies (e.g., have a safe, comfortable eating environment), are able to modify their intake based on the energy content of their diets. Children were offered a fixed volume as a first course of either high or low energy content and then allowed to choose foods as desired. These children chose less after the high energy content fixed volume and more after the low energy content fixed volume of food.[14]

Davis,[19] supported by recent work of Story and Brown[20] and Birch and others,[21] documents the differing roles of parents and children in facilitating and making appropriate food choices and eating on the development of food patterns. Primary guidelines to the role differentiation are (1) to offer foods of highest nutritional value; and (2) to recognize the appetites of young children are a *reliable* guide to the amount of food that needs to be consumed. To offer nonnutritional foods and to override the individual's ability to respond to hunger and satiety cues is to do a grievous disservice to our children.

SOCIAL INFLUENCES ON DEVELOPMENT OF FOOD HABITS

Social influence is one of the most important aspects of food acceptance and rejection. An estimated 50% of all people have conditioned taste aversions. The relationships between food rejection and other personality variables such as anxiety, instability, and poor self-concept have been questioned. Mothers of 2- to 7-year-old children were asked, "Is there anything about your child's current eating behavior that bothers you?" The most frequent response was finicky behaviors; the most common food listed was vegetables. Mothers were also concerned about eating habits, especially dawdling and messiness. Even with cautious interpretation there was a relationship between the feeding problems score and psychological-behavioral problems. For example, greater acting-out, toileting problems, and fearfulness were reported for children who had higher feeding problems scores.[22]

Evidence suggests that the adolescent preoccupation with dieting and body shape may actually begin in elementary school. By age 7 years, children appear to have adopted the adult cultural values of attractiveness. In a survey children always ranked the drawings of obese children the lowest.[23] Of children in grades three to six, nearly half wanted to be thinner, and most of these children had already tried to lose weight. The boys and girls were nearly equally preoccupied with body shape.[24] This indicates the need to better understand the development of eating behavior and attitudes of children.

CATEGORIZATION OF FOODS

How children categorize foods is a facet of food choice that has been only recently evaluated. Children 5 to 11 years of age were asked to separate food into groups by whatever criteria they chose to use.[25] The children, regardless of age, used some common characteristics to divide foods into categories, such as sweet versus nonsweet foods, meal entrees versus drinks or breakfast foods. None of the children used nutrient terminology to classify foods into groups (e.g., protein foods), nor was dislike of a particular food used as a basis for classification. The cognitive stage of the children indicated the ability of the child to sort foods into groups and to follow guidelines established by Piaget.[26]

The younger children who are classified as preoperational in Piaget's terminology used concrete features to classify foods (e.g., sweet versus bitter taste or liquid versus solid). They also used the occasion of eating as a basis for classification (e.g., meal entrees versus breakfast foods). As cognitive development increased, so did the basis for food classification. Those children in Piaget's concrete operational category were able to classify foods in more than one category and by more than one characteristic (e.g., both amount of processing and plant or animal origin). All of the children formed a sweets group, 50% a fruits group, 50% a vegetable group, about 50% a drinks group, about 25% a dairy group, and 20% a breads and cereals group.[25] It may be reasonable to use these spontaneous notions about food groups as the basis for nutrition education even when the goal is to foster a more sophisticated understanding of nutrition.

NUTRITION KNOWLEDGE OF CAREGIVER

Nutrition knowledge of parents and other caregivers is an important factor to consider in the shaping of the food preferences of children. The degree to which knowledge of nutrition is incorporated into family meal planning appears to be related to positive attitude toward self, problem-solving skills, and family organization in spite of a professed concern by all mothers interviewed about the total diet offered to young children and importance of mealtime with children.[27] The ordinal position of the preschool child in the family appears to influence choices of specific foods regardless of equivalent knowledge of nutrition of mothers.[28] When preschool children were the youngest children in a family, mothers were found to be less susceptible to children's requests for new products. They were willing, however, to accommodate that preference when the preschool-age child was the oldest child in a family.

Day-care teachers would presumably also have an impact on the development of food preference in young children. In a survey day-care teachers reported that they knew little about nutrition, but they thought it was important.[29] Since young children are responsive to early influences, the role of the day-care teacher in shaping positive food-related attitudes needs to be strongly supported by the nutrition community. Day-care providers readily acknowledged that they need more information and guidance on developing good food habits and planning meals for preschool children.[30]

INFLUENCE OF FAMILY

Hertzler[31] has encouraged the development of a broader conceptual framework for studying children's food behavior and urged that the family unit be included in the research model. The influence of the family unit on changing food-choice patterns to manage obesity has been reviewed.[32] Families can provide the appropriate role models and reinforcements that are most likely to bring about appropriate food habit changes. Mealtime companionship is important to young children. The food intake and consequently nutrient intake were determined to be more adequate for those children who had positive adult companionship at meals.[33]

The child-parent interactions have an important influence on food consumption. There appeared to be differences between the interactions of thinner children and their mothers and fatter children and their mothers in both food and nonfood situations.[34] The thinner children and their mothers talked more with each other, ate less food, ate more slowly, and in general had a more positive, supportive relationship than the fatter children and their mothers. This type of study begins to look at the broader construct of family units as related to food and eating and needs to be further researched.

Mothers of obese 3- to 4-year-old children reported that they exercised less control over the foods the child ate and were less satisfied with the child's food choices than the reports from the parents of normal weight children.[35] These parents of obese children were also dissatisfied with the amount of food the child consumed between meals. These parents controlled time, frequency, and type of food eaten by their children, but not the amount of food eaten. The location and activity at meals were reported as managed by the parent. However, this same management did not extend to snacks while watching television. All parents reported that children's food preferences were considered when making food purchases. Sweets were offered frequently after children had eaten a "good meal." Normal weight children were offered sweets only after a good meal was eaten more often than obese children. Parents of obese children felt that their children ate too much food between meals. Many of these parents felt that their own food behavior influenced the children's food behavior. Time of eating, types of foods liked or disliked, location of eating, and watching television were the parental habits that by their report influenced the children's behavior. The parents did not feel that the amount of food they ate influenced the amount of food their children ate. However, these parents felt that the influence their personal food habits had on the children's food behavior decreased as the amount of time the parent spent working outside the home increased.

Obviously children respond to the social environment when they make food choices for themselves. It has been demonstrated that preferences for foods were enhanced when foods were offered as a reward or with brief positive social interactions with adults.[36] Parenting behaviors that have been recognized as related to increased nutritional adequacy of the intakes of young children are (1) allowing the child enough time to eat; (2) asking the child to help prepare food or set the table; (3) allowing the child to make decisions about the type of food eaten; and (4) giving small portions when introducing a new food.[33]

When parents overtly monitored or only said they would monitor the food choices of children, the children adjusted the foods they selected. In general, they chose foods lower in sugar than when supervised.[37]

Hertzler[38] discussed the negative influences of development of inappropriate choices, which are primarily too much stimulation and attention at meals and negative or inappropriate parenting. When surveyed, more than half of the parents interviewed promised foods as a reward and also withheld foods as a punishment.[33]

NUTRITION EDUCATION

The overt shaping of food choices and food behaviors by educational strategies happens less specifically than we would like for optimal nourishment. Results suggest that healthy snack choices increased in school in the training setting. However, without a strategy for promoting generalization of healthy snack choices such as cueing, little generalization across settings

FIG. 8-4   Food patterns are influenced by nutrition education activities such as making bread.

occurred even at school. Furthermore, generalization to healthy snack choices at home was achieved only when individualized procedures to program at home choices were organized and implemented. Unfortunately, even with cueing, the change was not permanent. After withdrawal of the reinforcement procedures snack choices eventually returned to baseline levels.[39] It is obvious that knowledge of healthy eating alone is not sufficient to change the children's eating behavior. Parental involvement in the nutrition education programs has been more successful in changing food choices and eating behaviors. Kirks and Hughes[40] have demonstrated that the diets of young children whose parents concomitantly received nutrition education were better than those of children whose parents were not directly involved (Figure 8-4).

Efforts have been made to teach young children to consume diets lower in total fat. When children were asked, "What does it mean to be healthy?" 82% responded, "Eat the right foods." All of the children thought it was important to be healthy. The right kinds of foods were described as foods from the fruit and vegetable group. Unhealthy foods were listed as foods high in sugar. Most children defined health in a positive fashion.[41]

Parents of fourth graders felt that the schools should have a significant role in nutrition education, but were not overly eager to participate themselves. The goals the parents wanted achieved were to learn about nutrition and to learn label reading. Parents felt that barriers to good nutrition in the home were (1) differing likes and dislikes of family members; (2) children's desire for foods that are advertised; (3) the difficulty of "breaking" faulty habits; and (4) lack of time to prepare nutritious meals.[42] In contrast, it has been documented that changes in behavior and knowledge of nutrition implemented at school do not necessarily carry over at home. Nutrition edu-

FIG. 8-5 Play activities help young children explore and develop food preparation skills.

cation with parents as part of the program is more effective than without parents' participation.

Recent work with innovative techniques (e.g., open ended questions and concept maps), to assess nutrition knowledge and beliefs of young children indicate that young children are intellectually ready to learn more about food, nutrition, and positive health habits than previously believed (Figure 8-5).[43] These types of innovative techniques warrant more exploration.

INFLUENCE OF MEDIA ON THE FOOD BEHAVIORS OF YOUNG CHILDREN

In addition to the many familial, cultural, and psychosocial influences on children's food habits, mass media have an impact on children's requests for and attitudes toward food. Of the forms of mass media, television has the greatest impact on children because it reaches many children before they are capable of verbal communication. Children spend more time watching television than they spend at school and more than they spend in any activity other than sleeping. Children from low-income families watch more television than do children from moderate- to high-income families.[44] It has been estimated that, as a group, children watch television for 26 hours per week from preschool to junior high school.[45] This means that the average child watches 3 hours of television advertising per week and 19,000 to 22,000 commercials per year.

Children often are unable to separate commercials from the program and frequently explain them as part of the program especially if a host-selling format is used. Slightly older children (7 to 8 years of age) were more favorably influenced by the host-selling format than younger children.[46] School-age children (11 to 12 years of age) are conscious of the concept of commercials, the purpose of selling, and the concept of sponsorship and are less likely to accept advertisers' claims without question. They perceive that television commercials are designed to sell products rather than entertain or educate.

It has been pointed out that certain attributes of food are promoted as superior to others. The main characteristics presented positively are sweetness, chocolateyness, and richness.[47] Many food manufacturers, in other words, de-emphasize the physiological need for nutrients and encourage selection on the basis of sweet flavor. Exposure to such messages may distort a child's natural curiosity toward other characteristics of food, such as the fresh crispness of celery or apples.

In the past 10 years little has changed in terms of the kinds of foods advertised with programs targeted at young children, e.g., Saturday morning cartoons. In a recent survey 71% of the commercials were for food products and 80% of those were for foods of low nutritional value.[48] The foods most frequently advertised contained amounts of energy, fat, and sodium high enough to be noteworthy.[49]

There has been ongoing concern about the influence of television on the growth and health of young children. It has been demonstrated that television influences the eating habits and thus the nutritional status of children in three significant ways: (1) television advertising influences family food purchases and the snacking patterns of young children; (2) the use of food as depicted by television programs shows food being used for many activities other than the satisfaction of hunger; and (3) the few overweight children used on television programs suggests that inappropriate use of foods has no impact on health or nutritional status.[50] Dietz and Gortmaker[45] outline other aspects of television watching and television advertising that are of concern: (1) the relationship between increased television watching and increased snacking; (2) the relationship between consumption of foods advertised on television and viewing time; and (3) the relationship between

increased viewing time and the number of attempts by the young child to influence the food purchases of the parent. The foods advertised on weekend children's programming are usually high–kcaloric density foods that if purchased and consumed without an increase in activity, can lead to inappropriate weight gain and poor eating habits. The larger intake of highly concentrated sweet and fat foods plus the decrease in activity that is associated with excess television watching has led to an increase of obesity among children in the United States.

Parents must set limits on their children's requests for advertised food and may need support in their efforts to do so. They may need guidance in principles of behavior modification (see Chapter 15) and reassurance that it is to the child's advantage to learn that not all advertised products are a part of every child's meal pattern.

Other advertising also influences children's food requests. Prize offers lead to increased demand for and consumption of certain foods. Door-to-door sales of candy and cookies for charitable causes may adversely influence the distribution of the food dollar and encourage consumption of foods that provide sugar but few nutrients.

The influence of media, especially television, cannot be overemphasized. Children are susceptible, vulnerable, and responsive to its carefully crafted messages of consumption.

Summary

The feeding relationship between the child and the parent or caregiver is an important one. The tempo of parent-child interaction gives the child cues on how much and how fast to eat. The shaping of this tempo and pattern ultimately affects nutritional status and overall well-being. Young children are shaping patterns for a lifetime. They are developing a sense of food as nourishment, as well as an appropriate sense of food's uses in comfort, sociability, and satisfaction.

The child has innate taste. Adults are responsible for enhancing the sense of taste or defeating it by setting the tone of the interaction around food. Clearly adults must be mindful of the nutrient needs of children. Satter[51] states that the parent or caregiver is responsible for

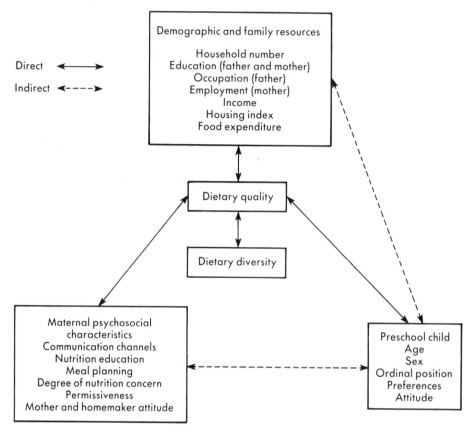

Direct ◄────►

Indirect ◄----►

Demographic and family resources

Household number
Education (father and mother)
Occupation (father)
Employment (mother)
Income
Housing index
Food expenditure

Dietary quality

Dietary diversity

Maternal psychosocial
characteristics
Communication channels
Nutrition education
Meal planning
Degree of nutrition concern
Permissiveness
Mother and homemaker attitude

Preschool child
Age
Sex
Ordinal position
Preferences
Attitude

FIG. 8-6   Factors related to child's dietary status.
(From Caliendo MA, Sanjur D: *J Nutr Educ* 10:69, 1978.)

what is offered; the child is responsible for how much to eat. Although there are still many unanswered questions about the formation of food preferences, it is clear that preferences are a major determinant of food selection. If allowed free choice, children select sweet foods over nonsweet, more nutritious foods. Giving children free access to highly preferred but nutritionally weak foods encourages the development of nutritional problems during childhood and beyond.

To exert a maximum influence on the health and well-being of young children, nutrition educators must attend to the influences that shape the food preferences and eating patterns of

young children. These influences are dynamic and multidirectional. Figure 8-6 indicates one approach to describing these influences. Young children are shaped by their particular family unit in several ways. Effective nutrition work with young children and their families requires nutrition educators to forge strong ties with the social scientists.

REVIEW QUESTIONS

1. Which factors are most important in determining food preferences for young children?
2. How do developmental stage and age of the young child affect food preferences?

3. What is the role of the media, especially television, in the food preferences of young children?
4. What role do parents and other caregivers play in the development of food habits?
5. How does social interaction shape food choices for young children?

SUGGESTED LEARNING ACTIVITIES

1. Ask a group of 3-year-old children and a group of 4-year-old children to separate a group of edible and nonedible items from two containers. Describe the differences of food choices by age groups.
2. Describe the effectiveness of food contingencies in getting a child to accept a specific food.
3. Plan and implement a 30-minute nutrition education program for children 5 to 6 years old.
4. Watch children's television for 1 hour and describe the food commercials presented during that hour.
5. If you were asked to provide a diet of 1000 kcal/day for a very overweight 2-year-old boy (weight: 40 pounds, greater than 95th percentile; height: 90th percentile, NCHS), what factors would you need to consider in relation to the family unit and eating environment?
6. If you were a nutrition consultant to a preschool that provides morning and afternoon snacks for the children and provides milk at lunch although children bring their own lunches: a. What easy, nourishing snacks that can be linked to activities for the children would you recommend? b. What basic concepts do you consider important in developing guidelines or inservice education for parents who prepare their children's lunches?

REFERENCES

1. Brillat-Savarin A: *The physiology of taste,* New Haven, Conn, Leete's Island Books.
2. Lawless H: Sensory development in children: research in taste and olfaction, *J Am Diet Assoc* 85:577, 1985.
3. Beauchamp GK, Cowart BJ: Congenital and experimental factors in the development of human flavor preferences, *Appetite* 6:357, 1985.
4. Cowart BJ, Beauchamp GK: The importance of sensory context in young children's acceptance of salty tastes, *Child Dev* 57:1034, 1986.
5. Anliker JA and others: Children's food preferences and genetic sensitivity to the bitter taste of 6-n-propylthiouracil (PROP), *Am J Clin Nutr* 54:16, 1991.
6. Birch LL: Dimensions of preschool children's food preferences, *J Nutr Educ* 11:77, 1979.
7. Birch LL: Preschool children's food preferences and consumption patterns, *J Nutr Educ* 11:189, 1979.
8. Burt JV, Hertzler AA: Parental influence on the child's food preference, *J Nutr Educ* 10:127, 1978.
9. Birch LL: The relationship between children's food preferences and those of their parents, *J Nutr Educ* 12:14, 1980.
10. Pliner P, Pelchant ML: Similarities in food preferences between children and their siblings and parents, *Appetite* 7:333, 1986.
11. Schafer RB, Schafer E: Relationship between gender and food roles in the family, *J Nutr Educ* 21:119, 1989.
12. Johnson RK and others: Effect of maternal employment on the quality of young children's diets: the CSFII experience, *J Am Diet Assoc* 92:213, 1992.
13. Rozin P and others: The child's conception of food: differentiation of categories of rejected substances in the 16 months to 5 year age range, *Appetite* 7:141, 1986.
14. Birch LL, Deysher M: Conditional and unconditional caloric compensation: evidence for self-regulation of food intake in young children, *Learning and Motivation* 16:341, 1985.
15. Birch LL, Marlin DW, Rotter J: Eating as the "means" activity in a contingency: effects on young children's food preferences, *Child Dev* 55:431, 1984.
16. Lawatsch DE: A comparison of two teaching strategies on nutrition knowledge, attitudes and food behavior of preschool children, *J Nutr Educ* 22:117, 1990.
17. Anliker JA and others: Parental messages and the nutrition awareness of preschool children, *J Nutr Educ* 22:24, 1990.
18. Rolls BJ: Experimental analysis of the effects of variety in a meal on human feeding, *Am J Clin Nutr* 42:932, 1985.
19. Davis CM: Self selection of diet by newly weaned infants: an experimental study, *Am J Dis Child* 36:651, 1929.
20. Story M, Brown JE: Do young children instinctively know what to eat? The studies of Clara Davis revisited, *N Engl J Med* 316:103, 1987.
21. Birch LL and others: The variability of young children's energy intake, *N Engl J Med* 324:232, 1991.
22. Pelchant ML, Pliner P: Antecedents and correlates of feeding problems in young children, *J Nutr Educ* 18:23, 1986.

23. Feldman W and others: Culture versus biology: children's attitudes toward thinness and fatness, *Pediatrics* 81:190, 1988.
24. Maloney MJ and others: Dietary behavior and eating attitudes in children, *Pediatrics* 84:484, 1989.
25. Michela JL, Contento IR: Spontaneous classification of foods by elementary school–aged children, *Health Educ Q* 11:57, 1984.
26. Bybee RW, Sund RB: *Piaget for educators,* ed 2, Columbus, Ohio, 1982, Charles E Merrill Publishing.
27. Swanson-Rudd J and others: Nutrition orientations of working mothers in the North Central region, *J Nutr Educ* 14:132, 1982.
28. Phillips DE, Bass MA, Yetley E: Use of food and nutrition knowledge by mothers of preschool children, *J Nutr Educ* 10:73, 1978.
29. Gillis DEG, Sabry JH: Daycare teachers: nutrition knowledge, opinions, and use of food, *J Nutr Educ* 12:200, 1980.
30. Dirige OV and others: An assessment of the nutrition education needs of day-care providers, *J Am Diet Assoc* 91:714, 1991.
31. Hertzler AA: Children's food patterns—a review. I. Food preferences and feeding problems. II. Family and group behavior, *J Am Diet Assoc* 83:551, 1983.
32. Hertzler AA: Obesity—impact on the family, *J Am Diet Assoc* 79:525, 1981.
33. Stanek K and others: Diet quality and the eating environment of preschool children, *J Am Diet Assoc* 90:1582, 1990.
34. Birch LL and others: Mother-child interaction patterns and the degree of fatness in children, *J Nutr Educ* 12:17, 1981.
35. Seagren JS, Terry, RD: WIC female parents' behavior and attitudes toward their children's food intake—relationship to children's relative weight, *J Nutr Educ* 23:223, 1991.
36. Birch LL, Zimmerman SI, Hind H: The influence of social-affective context on the formation of children's food preferences, *J Nutr Educ* 13:115, 1981.
37. Klesges RC and others: Parental influence on food selection in young children and its relationship to childhood obesity, *Am J Clin Nutr* 53:859, 1991.
38. Hertzler AA: Review of nutrition education programs for preschoolers, *Top Clin Nutr* 5:35, 1990.
39. Stark LJ and others: Using reinforcement and cueing to increase healthy snack food choices in preschoolers, *J Appl Behav Anal* 19:367, 1986.
40. Kirks BA, Hughes C: Long-term behavioral effects of parent involvement in nutrition education, *J Nutr Educ* 18:203, 1986.
41. Perry CL and others: Modifying the eating behavior of young children, *J Sch Health* 55:399, 1985.
42. Crockett SJ and others: Nutrition intervention strategies preferred by parents: results of a marketing survey, *J Nutr Educ* 21:90, 1989.
43. Singleton JC and others: Role of food and nutrition in the health perceptions of young children, *J Am Diet Assoc* 92:67, 1992.
44. Reid LN, Bearden WO, Teel JE: Family income, TV viewing, and children's cereal ratings, *Journalism Q* 57:327, 1980.
45. Dietz WH, Gortmaker SL: Do we fatten our children at the television set? Obesity and television viewing in children and adolescents, *Pediatrics* 75:807, 1985.
46. Kunkel D: Children and host-selling commercials, *Comm Res* 15:17, 1988.
47. Gussow J: Counternutritional messages of TV ads aimed at children, *J Nutr Educ* 4:48, 1972.
48. Cotuga N: TV ads on Saturday morning children's programming—what's new? *J Nutr Educ* 20:125, 1988.
49. Windhauser MM and others: A nutritional evaluation of food and beverage products as advertised to children on Saturday morning television, *J Am Diet Assoc* 91:A-83, 1991.
50. Palumbo FM, Dietz WH: Children's television: its effect on nutrition and cognitive development, *Pediatr Ann* 14:793, 1985.
51. Satter EM: The feeding relationship, *J Am Diet Assoc* 86:352, 1986.

9

Normal Adolescent Nutrition

Jane Mitchell Rees

Objectives

✦✦

After studying this chapter, the student should:

✔ *Be able to define and contrast the terms* adolescence *and* puberty.

✔ *Know the milestones of adolescent physical development.*

✔ *Be able to describe the emotional and intellectual components of adolescent psychological development.*

✔ *Be able to list influences on adolescent eating habits.*

✔ *Know the elements of nutritional assessment of males and females during puberty.*

Adolescence is a dynamic phase of life. The normal human develops a mature body in the 5 to 7 years during puberty. The mind also develops, advancing to adult thought patterns and emotions. To understand nutritional issues of this stage of the life cycle, students need to learn about growth and development processes. These processes determine what teenagers need nutritionally and how they eat. Learning about adolescence is an exciting challenge and a valuable lesson because it gives the student a basis for understanding much about human life and the principles of nutrition that support it.

ADOLESCENT GROWTH AND DEVELOPMENT

Physiological Growth

Puberty. During late childhood slow growth begins to accelerate with the initiation of **pu-**berty until linear growth (in centimeters per year) during the teen years compares with that of the second year of life (Figure 9-1). About 20% of adult height and 50% of adult weight are acquired during pubertal growth.[1] Most body organs double in size. The body develops sexual organs, larger hips and thighs, and breasts (in females) called the **secondary sexual characteristics.**

Initiation of puberty. The exact factor, or combination of factors, that triggers the upsurge in hormonal activity to initiate puberty is still unknown.[1] Recently a sequence of hormonal changes culminating in feedback mechanisms that allow increased production of estrogen, testosterone, and progesterone with the onset of puberty has been described.[2] Others have observed an association between **menarche** and the attainment of a critical body weight in North American and most European females. They theorize that the achievement of the criti-

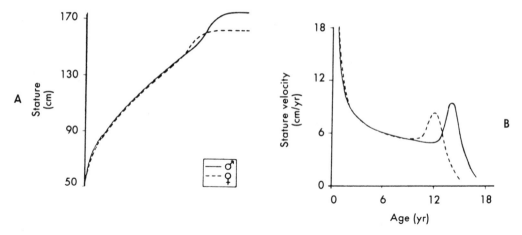

FIG. 9-1 **A,** Growth in stature of typical boy *(solid line)* and girl *(interrupted line).* **B,** Growth velocities at different ages of typical boy *(solid line)* and girl *(interrupted line).* (From Marshall WA: *Clin Endocrinol Metab* 4:4, 1975.)

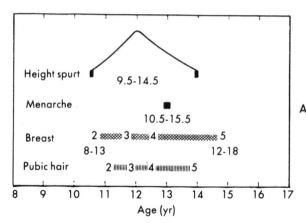

FIG. 9-2 Diagram of sequence of events at puberty in, **A,** girls and, **B,** boys.

(From Marshall WA, Tanner JM: *Arch Dis Child* 45:13, 1970.)

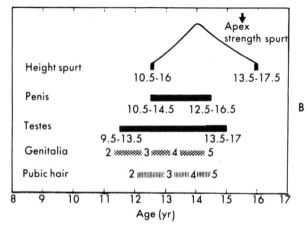

TABLE 9-1   *Stages of Sexual Maturation (Sexual Maturity Ratings)*

Boys	Pubic Hair	Genitalia
Stage 1	None	No change from childhood
Stage 2	Small amount at outer edges of pubis; slight darkening	Beginning penile enlargement; testes enlarged to 5 ml volume; scrotum reddened and changed in texture
Stage 3	Covers pubis	Longer penis; testes 8-10 ml; scrotum further enlarged
Stage 4	Adult type; does not extend to thighs	Larger, wider, and longer penis; testes 12 ml; scrotal skin darker
Stage 5	Adult type; now spread to thighs	Adult penis; testes 15 ml

Girls	Pubic Hair	Breasts
Stage 1	None	No change from childhood
Stage 2	Small amount; downy on labia majora	Breast bud
Stage 3	Increased; darker and curly	Larger; no separation of nipple and areola
Stage 4	More abundant; coarse texture	Increased size; areola and nipple form secondary mound
Stage 5	Adult type; now spread to thighs	Adult distribution of breast tissue; continuous outline

Modified from Tanner JM: *Growth at adolescence,* ed 2, Oxford, 1962, Blackwell Scientific Publications. In Mahan LK, Rees JM: Seattle, Wash, 1989. Originally published in Mahan LK, Rees JM: *Nutrition in adolescence,* St Louis, 1984, Mosby–Year Book.

cal body weight of 47.8 kg (105 lb) or body fatness of 17% causes a change in metabolic rate, which triggers menarche. Most researchers acknowledge an association between change in body composition and the onset of menarche, but they do not view it as triggering puberty.[3]

Physical Growth and Development

Stage. Each characteristic of sexual maturity and growth occurs gradually but at any one time can be described as being at a certain stage (or phase). The stages of sexual development are listed in Table 9-1.

Sequence. Maturation takes place in a predictable sequence. For example, genital development always occurs before the period of most rapid growth in height. The sequence of sexual maturity and growth in height is shown in Figure 9-2.

Timing. The "tempo" (or timing) of initiation and moving from one stage to another during physical maturation is different from one individual to another (see Figure 9-2).[4] The years of age at which sexual maturation may begin or end are shown with each characteristic listed. The menarche typically occurs between 10.5 and 15.5 years of age, for example. Males of the same chronological age may be very different in size as shown in Figure 9-3 because they are at different stages of development.

Sexual development. Sexual maturity begins with enlargement of genitalia in males and breast development in females (Figures 9-4 and 9-5). Pubic hair distribution is first sparse and becomes thicker and covers a large area. Completion of genital growth in males corresponds with stage 5, or adult status of sexual maturity.

FIG. 9-3   Two boys of same chronological age in different stages of adolescent development.

(Copyright Mahan LK, Rees JM: Seattle, Wash, 1989. Originally published in Mahan LK, Rees JM: *Nutrition in adolescence,* St Louis, 1984, Mosby–Year Book.)

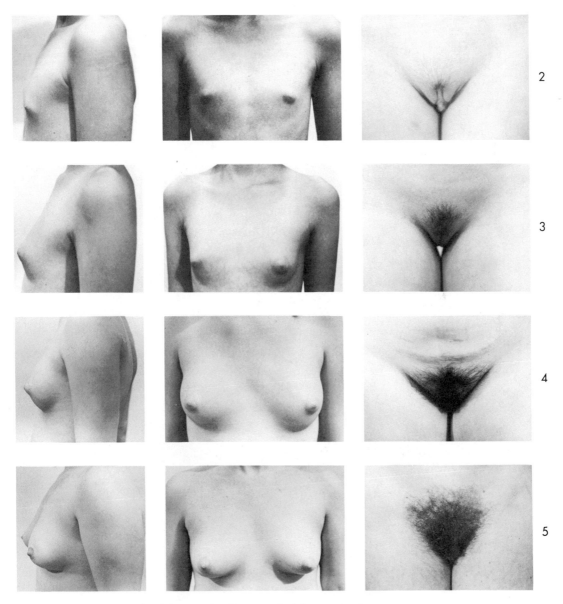

FIG. 9-4 Female adolescents in all stages of adolescent development.

(Copyright Mahan LK, Rees JM: Seattle, Wash, 1989. Originally published in Mahan LK, Rees JM: *Nutrition in adolescence,* St Louis, 1984, Mosby–Year Book.)

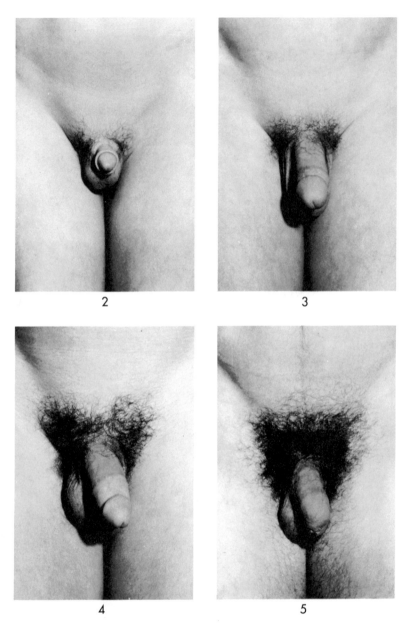

FIG. 9-5 Male adolescents in all stages of adolescent development.
(From Farrow JA: *Semin Fam Med* 2[3]:146-153, 1981. By permission of Grune & Stratton, Inc.)

In females menstrual cycles begin when breasts are nearly mature and height growth is nearly complete.

Existing data indicate that during the past century young women have gradually come to experience the menarche at a younger age. The so-called **secular trend** is probably due to improved nutrition, sanitation, and health care, allowing modern children to mature more rapidly. The current mean age of menarche is 12 years and 4 months compared with approximately 16 years in 1890. This theory is generally accepted, although records of menstrual age are scarce enough that it has been criticized. Total maturation probably occurs earlier for males as well. The mean age of onset of sperm emission (**spermarche**) currently is 13.4 years.

Height and weight. Throughout the approximately 5 to 7 years of pubertal development, rapid growth continues although a great percentage of height will be gained during the "growth spurt." Like the initiation of puberty, the 18 to 24-month period of the peak growth velocity will occur at different ages for different individuals, fitting into the sequence of overall sexual development. Peak growth velocity occurs earlier for girls than for boys. Following the achievement of sexual maturity, linear growth and weight acquisition continue at a much lower rate and then cease, as shown by the downward slope of the height spurt curve (see Figure 9-2). For rare females it will continue into the late teens and for males into the twenties. Most females will gain no more than 2 to 3 inches (5.1 to 7.6 cm) after the onset of menses (Table 9-2) Approximate weight gain following the menarche is shown in Table 9-3.

Body composition. Body composition changes during maturation. The proportion of fat and muscle in prepubertal males and females tends to be similar, with body fat about 15% and 19%, respectively, and lean body mass is about equal for both sexes. During puberty females gain proportionately more fat. By age 18 body fat is normally about 27% in females and 16% in males.[5] Males, meanwhile, gain twice as much muscle as females do (Figure 9-6). This striking difference in adolescent growth between males and females influences nutritional needs. Since adolescent males experience greater gain in bone and lean tissue than females, they require more protein, iron, zinc, and calcium for development of these tissues. The male's larger requirements for these nutrients is also related to his greater *rate* of growth.

Monitoring growth. Knowing the relationship between the milestones of sexual development and physical growth will enable the clinician to assess growth in an adolescent at a particular time and indicate the extent of future growth. Thus pubertal development can be monitored clinically by using weight and height tables and sexual maturity ratings. Excessive or less-than-normal growth can be detected by

TABLE 9-2   *Postmenarcheal Growth in Stature (N=408)*

Growth (in)	Percent of Sample
<1.00	6.0
1.00-1.99	21.0
2.00-2.99	34.0
3.00-3.99	22.0
4.00-4.99	9.0
5.00-5.99	4.0
6.00-6.99	1.5
7.00-7.99	1.5

Data from Fried RI, Smith E: *J Pediatr* 61:562, 1962.

TABLE 9-3   *Approximate Increments in Weight of Postmenarcheal Women*

Postmenarcheal Year	lbs	kg
1	10.12	4.6
2	6.16	2.8
3	2.42	1.1
4 and 5	1.76	0.8

Data from Frisch RE: *Hum Biol* 48:353, 1976. Copyright Mahan LK, Rees JM: Seattle, Wash, 1989. Originally published in Mahan LK, Rees JM: *Nutrition in adolescence,* St Louis, 1984, Mosby–Year Book.

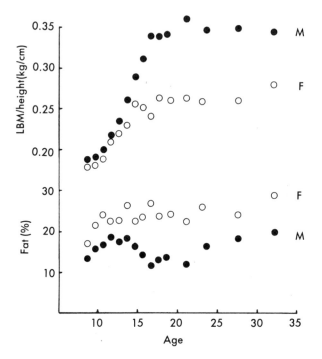

FIG. 9-6 Mean lean body mass/height ratio and percent body fat. *LBM*, Lean body mass. (From Forbes GB: *Nutritional requirements in adolescence*. In Suskind RM, editor: *Textbook of pediatric nutrition*, New York, 1981, Raven Press.)

plotting height changes on standard growth charts (see Appendix). Height and weight changes should be plotted on gender-specific charts. The major cause of short stature during adolescence is genetically late initiation of puberty, although such conditions as chronic disease and skeletal or chromosomal abnormalities also account for certain children being shorter than normal. Hormonal imbalances leading to abnormal growth are rare. Malnutrition is also rarely a primary cause of short stature in the United States.

Weight can be plotted on a grid similar to the one for height to determine if an individual is either keeping pace with or exceeding the weight of peers at a particular year of age. Because of the wide variation in weights seen in sample individuals in the adolescent period, some of whom were obese, the frequency distribution represented by the grids cannot be used

for evaluation of weight-for-height proportion as it is used for younger children. Evaluation of weight-for-height proportion in adolescents is described in the assessment section of this chapter.

Psychosocial Development

Tasks of adolescence. The term "adolescence" refers to the period when both mind and body are maturing and therefore applies to humans before and after, as well as during puberty. Emotional, social, and intellectual development are rapid during adolescence.[6] Milestones in psychological development of humans are shown in Table 9-4. The ability to use abstract thinking that adolescents develop, as opposed to the concrete thought patterns of childhood, enables the individual to accomplish these tasks. Planning ahead and connecting facts into integrated ideas become possible.

TABLE 9-4   *Erikson's and Piaget's Models for Emotional and Cognitive Development*

Age (Years)	Erikson (Emotional)	Piaget (Cognitive)
0-2		
	Phase I Basic trust versus mistrust	**Sensorimotor period** Learning through senses and manipulation
2-4		
	Phase II Autonomy versus shame and doubt	**Preconceptual period** Classification by a single feature (e.g., size); no concern for contradictions
4-8		
	Phase III Initiative versus guilt	**Initiative thought period** Intuitive classification (e.g., awareness of con- servation of mass concept)
8-12		
	Phase IV Industry versus inferiority	**Concrete operations period** Logical thought development; learning to organize
12-20		
	Phase V Ego identity versus role confusion	**Formal operations period** Comprehension of abstract concepts; forma- tion of "ideals"
20 and older		
	Phase VI Intimacy versus isolation	—
Middle adulthood		
	Phase VII Generativity versus stagnation	—
Late adulthood		
	Phase VIII Integrity versus despair	—

Developed by LL Eggert, University of Washington. Copyright Mahan LK, Rees JM: Seattle, Wash, 1989. Originally published in Mahan LK, Rees JM: *Nutrition in adolescence,* St Louis, 1984, Mosby–Year Book.

With the accomplishment of the developmental **tasks of adolescence** as shown in Figure 9-7, the person is prepared for a role in adult society. An adolescent can plan to get the food he or she needs throughout the day, for example, while a younger child will need to have food provided by others.

Successfully accomplishing the tasks of adolescence contributes to the nutritional health of the individual. For example, emotional maturity allows teenagers to develop their own value system. As a result they can choose foods that will enhance their health rather than responding to less healthful characteristics of foods as they may have done in childhood. They may go through a time of experimentation while they are learning to make choices.

Body image. Developing an image of the physical self that includes an adult body is an intellectual and emotional task intertwined with nutritional issues. Adolescents often feel uncomfortable with their rapidly changing bodies. At the same time, being much affected by influences outside themselves, they want to be like their most perfect peers and the idols of their culture. Stereotypes in the mass media reinforce

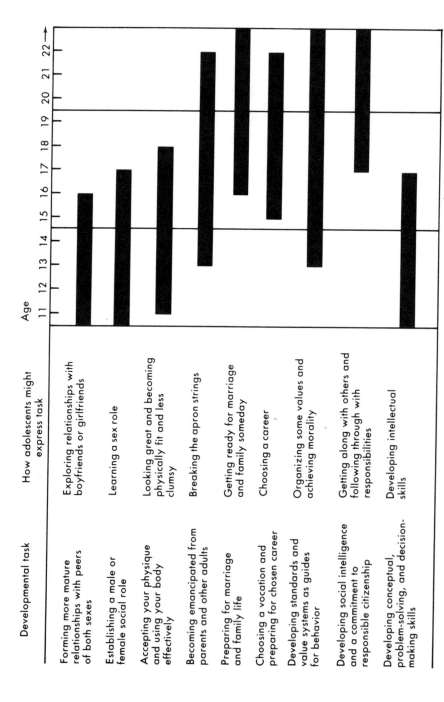

FIG. 9-7 Developmental tasks in adolescence.

(Developed by LL Eggert, University of Washington. Modified from Thornburg H: *Contemporary adolescence: readings*, ed 2, Monterey, Calif, 1975, Brooks/Cole Publishing. Copyright Mahan LK, Rees JM: Seattle, Wash, 1989. Originally published in Mahan LK, Rees JM: *Nutrition in adolescence*, St Louis, 1984, Mosby–Year Book.

such images. Teenagers may wish that certain body parts were larger and that other parts were smaller. They may want to grow faster or slower. Moore[7,8] found in recent studies that 67% of females and 42% of males were dissatisfied with their body weight. These feelings can lead them to try to change their bodies by manipulating their diets.

Young women who have not developed a mature **body image** may restrict food to reduce the size of hips and thighs they have developed during puberty. Young men are tempted to use nutritional supplements, steroids, or growth hormones to speed up their muscular development.[9,10]

REQUIREMENTS FOR NOURISHMENT
Nutritional Requirements Related to Growth

Limitations of the Recommended Dietary Allowance. Studies of the nutritional requirements of adolescents take not only age, but stage, of physical maturity into account.[11] The research base on which recommendations are made is limited because appropriate studies are not generally available. The Recommended Dietary Allowance (RDA)[12] for three adolescent age groups is stated, not related to stages of maturity. The highest levels of nutrients are recommended for the group assumed to be growing at the most rapid rate. Adolescents at the peak of their growth velocity have been shown to incorporate twice the amount of calcium, iron, zinc, magnesium, and nitrogen into their bodies during the years of the growth spurt as compared with that of other years (Table 9-5).

Calculation of individual needs. Dividing the RDA total of a nutrient by the reference individual's height in centimeters provides a quantity of the nutrient in units per centimeter that can be applied to any size teenager.[13] For example, the RDA for protein for the male 11 to 14 years old is 45 g/day. The reference height is 157 cm. Thus 0.29 g/cm would be recommended. Then the total protein need would be 39 g for the 135-cm male and 54 g for the 185-cm male. This example of variation in size during the teenage years is quite realistic,

TABLE 9-5   *Daily Increments in Body Content Due to Growth*

	Average for Period 10-20 yr (mg)	At Peak of Growth Spurt (mg)
Calcium		
Male	210	400
Female	110	240
Iron		
Male	0.57	1.1
Female	0.23	0.9
Nitrogen*		
Male	320	610 (3.8 g protein)
Female	160	360 (2.2 g protein)
Zinc		
Male	0.27	0.50
Female	0.18	0.31
Magnesium		
Male	4.4	8.4
Female	2.3	5.0

From Forbes GB: *Nutritional requirements in adolescence.* In Suskind RM, editor: *Textbook of pediatric nutrition,* New York, 1981, Raven Press.
*Maintenance needs (2 mg/basal calorie) at age 18 are 3500 mg and 2700 mg for males and females, respectively.

since persons experience the growth spurt at different ages. Nutrient recommendations will come closest to meeting needs when the largest quantity of nutrient per centimeter is suggested for those experiencing the most rapid growth, even if the age does not coincide with the age at which the highest RDA is made.

Recommendations for Specific Nutrients

Energy. The recommended energy intake in the RDA for adolescents as shown in Table 9-6 reflects average needs of teenagers. To determine the needs of the individual, level of exercise and growth rate will need to be considered.[14]

Protein. Less is known about the protein requirements of adolescents than of other age groups. The recommendation is that the energy value of the protein intake should make up 7%

to 8% of the total energy consumed. Sex, age, nutritional status, and quality of the protein must be considered in estimating the amount an individual will need. The range of total protein need will be about 39 to 56 gm, usually obtained in the normal diet. Protein consumption should not be overly emphasized. Protein stores of adolescents should be carefully monitored and supported in situations in which nu-

tritional depletion may occur so that physical development will not be impaired.

Calcium. The calcium requirement is based on the amount needed for skeletal growth.[15] Of the total bone growth, 45% occurs during this period. The total recommendations are the same for both sexes, although males will accumulate more than females as they develop larger frames.

Iron. Males and females have high requirements for iron during adolescence as shown in Table 9-7. Males require more iron because the buildup of muscle mass is accompanied by greater blood volume. Adolescent females require more than children because they lose iron monthly during menstruation.

Zinc. Zinc is known to be essential for growth and sexual maturation and is therefore of great importance in adolescence. The retention of zinc increases, especially during the growth spurt, leading to more efficient use of dietary sources of the nutrient.[16]

Other minerals. The roles of other minerals in the nutrition of adolescents have not been extensively studied. Magnesium, iodine, and phosphorus as well as copper, chromium, cobalt, and fluoride, however, are known to be important. The possibility that these nutrients interact cannot be overlooked. The recommendations for safe levels should be followed so that imbalances will not develop.

Vitamins. Adolescents require large amounts

TABLE 9-6 *Recommended Dietary Allowances for Energy for Adolescents (Kcalories Per Day)*

Age (Years)	Allowance	Reference Height (cm)	Energy (kcal) Per cm Height
Children			
7-10	2000	132	15.2
Males			
11-14	2500	157	15.9
15-18	3000	176	17.0
Females			
11-14	2200	157	14.0
15-18	2200	163	13.5

Data from Food and Nutrition Board, National Research Council: *Recommended Dietary Allowances,* ed 10, Washington, DC, 1989, National Academy of Sciences.

TABLE 9-7 *Calculated Iron Requirements for Males and Females at the 3rd, 25th, 75th, and 97th Percentile for Body Weight (From 10 to 16 Years of Age)*

	Calculated Iron Requirements (mg)					
	Daily Dietary Need*		Peak Daily Dietary Need*		Cumulative Need†	
Percentile Rating	Male	Female	Male	Female	Male	Female
3rd	6.6	5.1	13.2	10.3	966	751
25th	9.3	5.2	18.6	10.4	1360	772
75th	11.0	5.5	21.9	11.0	1610	794
97th	12.9	5.7	25.8	11.9	1885	836

From McKigney JI, Munro HN, editors: Nutrient requirements in adolescence, Cambridge, Mass, 1978, The MIT Press.
*Period of adolescent growth spurt.
†Total body iron increment represented by muscle tissue increase during 10 to 16 year interval.

of thiamin, riboflavin, and niacin because of their high energy requirements. Vitamin D is especially needed for rapid skeletal growth. Recommended amounts of vitamins A, E, C, and B$_6$ and folic acid are the same as those for adults. Often the quantity of vitamins recommended for adolescents has been interpolated from studies in adults and children.[13,14]

PHYSICAL FITNESS

All teenagers should be encouraged to fit exercise into their lives as part of balanced nourishment. Adolescents who participate in sports should adopt personal fitness programs between seasons.

Lack of Fitness

As the energy requirements of modern life are decreasing, adolescents are less fit than in earlier decades.[17] Only about 50% of young people today are regularly involved in vigorous exercise. When tested, 30% of males and more than 50% of females ages 6 to 17 years could not do one pull-up.[18]

Benefits of Physical Fitness

Physical activity can benefit individuals because it[19]:
1. Helps maintain optimal body composition
2. Facilitates weight loss (when necessary)
3. Increases the efficiency of energy use by muscle fibers
4. Increases the efficacy of hormones (insulin, lipoprotein lipase, epinephrine) in the regulation of energy metabolism
5. Decreases the production of lactic acid, which interferes with energy production
6. Strengthens the heart, lungs, and circulatory system
7. Increases levels of HDL over LDL and decreases some triglycerides
8. Raises rates of basal metabolism
9. Helps control appetite

Elements of Fitness

Each teenager should participate in activities that maintain the elements of fitness, which are (1) cardiorespiratory function, (2) body composition, and (3) Muscular strength, endurance, and flexibility.[20]

Maintaining Fitness

The principles of maintaining fitness are incorporated into the testing and improvement protocol (page 208). Raising the heart rate to at least 50% but not more than 75% of the maximum heart rate for 15 minutes with 5 minutes warm-up and cool-down at least 3 days a week will maintain cardiorespiratory fitness. The maximum heart rate of adolescents is about 200. This number can be used until age 20, when the usual calculation for adults, subtracting the age from 220 to determine the maximum heart rate, can begin. Stressful exercise is ineffective, but continuous gradual improvement and maintenance is effective. A few well-chosen calisthenics will maintain muscular strength, flexibility, and endurance.

EATING HABITS
Nutrient Consumption

Surveys of nutrient intake have shown adolescents likely to be obtaining less vitamin A, thiamin, iron, and calcium than recommended.[21-23] They also ingest more fat, sugar, protein, and sodium than is thought to be optimal.[24,25]

Snacks

Concern is often expressed about the habit of eating between meals. Although many choose fatty, sugary foods without fiber, other teenagers obtain substantial nourishment from foods eaten outside traditional meals.[26,27] The choice of foods they make is of greater importance than the time or place adolescents eat.[28] Emphasis should be placed on fresh vegetables, fruits, and whole-grain products to complement the foods high in energy value and protein that they commonly choose.

Meals

The number of meals teenagers miss and eat away from home increases from early adolescence to late adolescence, reflecting the growing need for independence and time away from home. The evening meal appears to be the most regularly eaten meal of the day. Females have been found to skip meals more often than males.[29]

FITNESS: TESTING AND PLANNING IMPROVEMENT PROGRAMS

1. a. Have client sit quietly and relax for 3 to 5 minutes.
   b. Take pulse for 10 seconds.*
   c. Record resting heart rate (RHR):_____.
2. a. Find intensity of exercise required to reach training heart rate (THR)†immediately after exercise (THR for teens: 20 to 22 beats/10 seconds).
      Stop with the exercise that achieves 20 to 22 beats/10 seconds. This is the exercise to us initially in the improvement program.

	Run for 5 minutes
↑	Jog for 5 minutes
Intensity increases	Jog for 2 minutes—walk for 2 minutes—jog for 2 minutes
	Walk uphill or upstairs for 2 to 3 minutes
	Walk for 5 minutes at a more rapid pace
START	Walk for 5 minutes at a moderate pace

   b. Monitor pulse return toward RHR after each exercise level—it should be below 16 beats/10 seconds

Immediate →	1 minute →	2 minutes →	3 minutes →	5 minutes →

3. Improvement program: To maintain THR for 15 minutes 4 to 5 days/week:
   a. Work with client to design an individualized program that is comfortable for him/her.
   b. Plan 5-minute warmup—move at level below the level that maintains THR.
   c. Exercise at intensity that maintains THR.
   d. 5-Minute cool down—back to warmup speed—client should not sit or lie down immediately.
   e. Use a combination of exercise levels and types, if necessary.
   f. If the client is ill, he/she should begin after illness at lower intensity and return slowly to intensity achieved before illness.
4. a. Retest every 3 to 4 weeks.
   b. Increase intensity of exercise to maintain THR.
   c. Client can increase time spent doing the exercise by 5-minute increments, up to 30 minutes.
   d. When client has reached jogging level and maintained it for 6 to 8 weeks, increase THR to 22 to 25 beats/10 seconds.
   e. Client can use any aerobic activities (e.g., jogging, bicycling, skating, or dancing) or combinations that the client prefers.

Developed by Scott B, Rees J: Adolescent Program, University of Washington, Seattle.
*10-Second time segment is easiest to measure and use.
†*Maximum heart rate* (MHR): ≈ 200 beats/minute for persons under 20 years of age (Cumming GR, Everatt D, Hastman L: Bruce treadmill test in children: normal values in a clinic population, *Am J Cardiol* 41:69, 1978). THR is 60% of MHR for persons with poor initial fitness, 75% of MHR for persons who are fit (e.g., 60% of 200 = 120 beats/minute = 20 beats/10 seconds [20 to 22 beats/10 seconds for normal variation]).
Note: Contraindications for testing and initiating fitness program are revealed by routine medical history and physical examination.

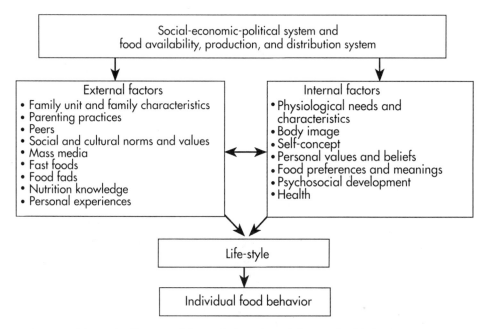

FIG. 9-8   Schematic diagram of factors influencing adolescent food behavior.
(Developed by M Story, University of Minnesota. Copyright Mahan LK, Rees JM: Seattle, Wash, 1989. Originally published in Mahan LK, Rees JM: *Nutrition in adolescence*, St Louis, 1984, Mosby–Year Book.)

Breakfast is frequently neglected and is omitted more often by teenagers and young adults under 25 years of age than by any other age group.[30] A likely explanation for why females are more likely to miss breakfast than are males is the pursuit of thinness and frequent attempts at restricting food intake. Many teenage girls believe that they can control their weight by omitting breakfast or lunch. Young women who are attempting to manage their weight should be counseled that this approach is likely to accomplish just the opposite. By midmorning or lunchtime they may be so hungry that they eat more than if they had eaten at least simple foods in the early morning.

Influences on Eating Habits

By the time a person reaches adolescence, the influences on eating habits are numerous. Formation of those habits is extremely complex (Figure 9-8). Adolescents' growing independence, increased participation in social life, and generally busy schedule of activities have a decided impact on what they eat. They are beginning to buy and prepare more food for themselves, and they often eat rapidly and away from home.[29]

Advertising

While families provide the basic foundation for eating habits, many influences on eating behavior originate outside the home. Teenagers are vulnerable to the kind of advertising messages seen in Figure 9-9. Television food commercials and the eating habits portrayed in program content have influenced people for more than a decade by the time they become adolescents.[31] The average teenager will have watched over a million food commercials, the majority of which are for products with a high concentration of sugar and fat.

FIG. 9-9   Examples of enticements and advertisements for weight-loss products featured in popular magazines.

(Developed by M Story, University of Minnesota. Copyright Mahan LK, Rees JM: Seattle, Wash, 1989. Originally published in Mahan LK, Rees JM: *Nutrition in adolescence,* St Louis, 1984, Mosby–Year Book.)

Ready-to-Eat Foods

The ease of obtaining food that is ready to eat also influences the eating habits of teenagers. In vending machines and at movies, sporting events, fast-food outlets, and convenience groceries, food is available at numerous times throughout the day. During the time of their peak growth velocity, adolescents may need to eat often and in large amounts and are able to use foods with a high concentration of energy. However, they will usually need to eat more carefully when growth has slowed.

Nutritional Limitations of Fast Food

The following factors appear to be the major nutritional limitations of **fast-food** meals[32]:

1. **Calcium, riboflavin, and vitamin A.** These essential nutrients are low unless milk or a milkshake is ordered. In addition, extensive consumption of soft drinks contributes to low intakes of magnesium and vitamin C.[33]
2. **Folic acid and fiber.** There are few fast-food sources of these key factors.
3. **Fat.** The percentage of energy from fat is high in many meal combinations.
4. **Sodium.** The sodium content of fast-food meals is high.
5. **Energy.** Common meal combinations contain excessive energy when compared with the amounts of other nutrients provided.

Although fast foods can contribute nutrients to the diet, they cannot completely meet the nutritional needs of teenagers. Both adolescents and health professionals should be aware that fast foods are acceptable nutritionally when they are consumed judiciously and as *part* of a well-balanced diet.[26] When they become the mainstay of the diet, there is cause for concern.[34] A nutrient imbalance may not *appear* to be a problem until a number of years has gone by, or unless some specific problem such as a chronic disease exists. However, evidence is accumulating to show that food intake patterns of teenagers affect their health in later life.[14]

SUBSTANCE USE AND ABUSE

Adolescent Experience

Substance use and abuse among adolescents are of major concern.[35] Tobacco, smokeless tobacco, alcohol, marijuana, and cocaine are the substances most widely abused. Over 90% of high school seniors have consumed alcohol, and in one study one in seven seniors admitted they had been inebriated once a week. The use of marijuana has been declining in recent years while there was a steady increase in cocaine use throughout the 1980s. Although rates of tobacco use have remained stable since the early 1980s, the rate among females has increased and the age of beginning use has declined for all teenagers. Smokeless tobacco is typically used by 7% to 25% of male adolescents in rural areas and young white male athletes in populations studied. It is responsible for significant oral damage, including cancer.

Overall, about 10% to 15% of teenagers have had no experience with drugs and alcohol, 70% to 80% have experimented, 10% to 15% have definable problems, and less than 1% are chemically dependent. Cognitive, emotional, and social development is likely to be retarded in the last group.[35]

Impact on Nutritional Status

In studies of nutritional status of drug and alcohol abusing teenagers, one study of a racially mixed and the other of a Native American population, deficient nutrient levels were not found in blood samples from either group (Table 9-8).[36,37] Neither reported consuming less of the nutrients studied than they needed or than nonusing peers. However, abusers acquired nutrients from a different group of foods than nonabusers. They consumed more snack foods and meat products while fruits, vegetables, and milk were left out of their dietary patterns.[36] The long-term effects of alcohol abuse coupled with an imbalance of nutrients probably account for development of nutritional disorders as they reach adulthood. Overall, the effect of substance abuse on nutritional status of any individual depends on the substance, the amount, duration and frequency of use, prior health and nutritional status, stage of physical growth, and nutritional adequacy of the diet consumed.

TABLE 9-8 *Energy Intake (From Alcohol) and Tissue Nutrients (N = 49)*

| | Abuse Group | | | |
	Alcohol and Marijuana	Marijuana	Nonusers	P Value
Alcohol energy value (kcal/d)	1894	147	22	.001
Thiamin (0.93-1.30 AC)*	1.10	1.10	1.04	NS (.10)
Pyridoxine (1.4-2.0 AC)*	1.31	1.43	1.33	NS (.70)
Riboflavin (0.90-1.30 AC)*	1.15	1.14	1.18	NS (.64)
Plasma ascorbic acid (0.36-1.48 µg/dL)	.52	.63	.91	NS (.08)
Plasma copper (73-127 µg/dl)	111.20	106.00	115.00	NS (.80)
Plasma zinc (71-126 µg/dl)	96.60	85.50	113.00	NS (.20)
Plasma magnesium (1.5-2.0 mEq/L)	1.75	1.71	1.74	NS (.94)
Blood protopophyrin/heme ratio (<80)	15.60	14.40	18.30	NS (.60)

From Farrow JA, Rees JM, W-Roberts, BS: *Pediatrics* 79:220, 1987.
*Enzyme activation test method. AC, activity coefficient.

Identification and Rehabilitation

All health professionals need to be aware of the indicators of drug use listed in the box at the right so that they can refer adolescents with a definable problem for treatment before they reach a more advanced stage of chemical dependency.[35] Nutritional assessment, intervention, and support are included in rehabilitative programs for adolescent substance abusers.

Role of Parents in Supporting Healthful Habits

To encourage adolescents to form reasonably healthy eating habits, parents should give their children increased responsibility and choice of nourishing foods as they are growing up. By the time they are teenagers, they will need some freedom to use the kitchen; this is true for young men as well as for young women.

NUTRITIONAL ENVIRONMENT

Because adolescent life is increasingly complex, the health professional will need to know a great deal about a teenager to assess his or her nutritional status.[13] Intelligence, emotional status, social functioning, and physical status are relevant factors. General medical history, socio-

---

❖ *DRUG USE INDICATIONS*

Rash	Dyspnea on exertion
Muscle weakness	Faintness
Vomiting	Hangover
Diarrhea	Blackouts
Stomach pain	Nervousness
Nausea	Depression
Indigestion	Tiredness
Bleeding gums	Insomnia
Sore tongue	Somnolence
Taste loss	Headache
Appetite loss	Seizures
Memory loss	

---

economic status, medications, alcohol or tobacco use, family attitudes, and peer group food practices are part of the nutritional environment of an adolescent and influence food choices. Table 9-9 summarizes the significance of each of these influences. A probing interview by a nutritionist who has had experience communicating with adolescents about these topics will reveal how an individual teenager feels about and manages food.

TABLE 9-9 **Nutrition Environment Evaluation Guide**

Influences	Key Issues	Significance
Likes and dislikes	Does patient dislike any particular food that is a major source of a specific nutrient (for example, milk is a major source of calcium; citrus fruits of vitamin C; meat of high-quality protein)?	Points out need to explore alternative ways to supply nutrients (for example, substitute cheese and yogurt for milk; broccoli and green peppers for citrus fruit; proper combinations of plant foods for meat)
Environment and attitudes		
Individual	Does patient express interest in his or her diet?	Gives clues to attitude toward role of nutrition in health care
	Are there any behavioral problems that influence patient's food choices?	May indicate need to work with other health team members to resolve problem that temporarily precludes nutrition intervention
	Has patient ever followed a special diet? If so, who prescribed it, what type of diet was it, and when was it prescribed? What instructions did patient receive?	Self-prescribed diet may signal inappropriate or unreliable approach toward control of health by diet; points out medical and educational considerations needed in design of care plan
	Does patient think he or she has been following the diet? Is there evidence to substantiate this?	If discrepancy exists, indicates lack of understanding of diet by patient or unwillingness or inability of patient to make dietary changes
	What difficulties if any does patient see in making dietary changes?	Focuses on issues that need consideration in design of individualized care plan
Family	Who purchases and prepares food in home (that is, partially controls patient's food supply)?	Sets scene for type of action plan suitable to patient and family
	Does patient have adequate cooking facilities and equipment or access to other resources?	May indicate need to provide basic nutrition guidelines, including personalized menu plan
	Are there any cultural, regional, or religious factors that affect patient's food choices?	Requires consideration to tailor care plan to individual needs
Peers	How often does patient eat away from home? Where and with whom does patient eat? Are there specific food intake patterns related to peer influences?	Indicates potential influences of peers on food choices; points out potential efficacy of patient- versus family-oriented care plan

Continued.

TABLE 9-9 *Nutrition Environment Evaluation Guide—cont'd*

Influences	Key Issues	Significance
Environment and attitudes—cont'd Schools	Does patient eat at school? Does patient participate in school feeding programs?	School feeding programs with their standardized composition assure minimal nutrient availability and provide reference for accuracy of reported information
	Is there anything about school schedule or cafeteria environment that may discourage appropriate nutrient intake?	"Too little time for lunch" or "no one to eat with" may necessitate consultation with other team members or school to resolve lifestyle problems
	Is patient in appropriate grade in school? Has patient received food and nutrition information in school courses?	Gives clues to current knowledge of nutrition and level of intellectual functioning; allows practical planning for educational aspects of care plan
Limited food funds	Is patient or family eligible for food stamps; Women, Infants, and Children program (WIC), reduced-price, or free school lunch? Do they participate in programs? Does patient or family receive other social assistance?	Indicates family has limited income and may need assistance with food buying and preparation to assure nutritionally adequate diet; points out need to consider referral to appropriate food program or nutrition education resource
Health-related concerns	Does patient have any food allergies or intolerances (as distinguished from dislikes)?	Excludes foods from diet; indicates need to plan and assure adequacy with alternative food choices
	Are there any physical conditions affecting ability to consume adequate nutrients (for example, mouth sores, swallowing problems, taste abnormalities)?	Indicates need to consider flavor, consistency, and temperature of food in care plan
	Are there any problems in digestion, absorption, or metabolism that will interfere with nutrient utilization? Will any other therapy (drugs, exercise, radiation) affect nutrient needs?	Indicates need to address these problems in diet preparation

Developed by R Rosebrough, University of Maryland. Copyright Mahan LK, Rees JM: Seattle, Wash, 1989. Originally published in Mahan LK, Rees JM: *Nutrition in adolescence*, St Louis, 1984, Mosby–Year Book.

TABLE 9-10 **Weight in Kilograms of Girls Aged 17 Years at Last Birthday, United States, 1966 to 1970**

Height (cm)	Percentile						
	5th	10th	25th	50th	75th	90th	95th
145-149.9	38.6	38.8	40.1	45.1	45.7	51.1	51.2
150-154.9	41.6	42.3	44.6	48.9	53.5	59.2	64.1
155-159.9	44.4	45.5	48.7	53.2	57.7	61.6	76.2
160-164.9	46.8	48.0	50.2	55.4	61.5	72.3	82.3
165-169.9	47.9	50.3	55.1	59.3	65.1	69.4	71.6
170-174.9	50.6	52.9	55.5	60.2	65.7	76.1	82.7
175-179.9	54.9	56.7	60.1	61.7	75.2	75.9	83.0

Modified from National Center for Health Statistics: *Height and weight of youths 12-17 years, United States.* In Vital and health statistics, series 11, no 124, Health Services and Mental Health Administration, Washington, DC, 1973, US Government Printing Office. Data from the national health survey, 1973, US Department of Health, Education and Welfare.

Evaluating Nutritional Status

To fully assess the nutritional status of adolescents, the health professional will evaluate the progress of physical development (see list), the usual laboratory tests, and the measures of dietary intake.

Weight/age/sex
Height/age/sex*
Weight/height/age/sex
Mid (upper) arm circumference/age/sex*
Triceps skinfold/age/sex*
Subscapular/skinfold/age/sex*
Arm fat area/age/sex*
Arm muscle circumference/age/sex*
Arm muscle area/age/sex*
Percentage body fat/age/sex
Sexual maturity rating of males and females
Females
    Age (or absence) of menarche
    Timing of menses

Anthropometrics

Weight, height, weight-for-height proportion, skinfold measurement, and muscle mass are evaluated by comparing the measurements of an individual with measurements of subjects

---

*Measurements for African-American adolescents available.[5]

of the same age and sex in large studies.[5,38] Measurements are also available for African-American adolescents as indicated previously. It is not possible to use the growth charts to determine ideal body weight of adolescents as is the practice for younger children because weight-for-height charts were not constructed for adolescents.

The detailed tables of the National Health and Nutrition Examination Survey (NHANES) compiled by the National Center for Health Statistics can be used to evaluate the relationship between the weight and height of an individual adolescent (Table 9-10).[38] For each 2 cm increment in height at a particular year of age, a range of weights is given. Weight and height values for age and sex between the 25th and the 75th percentiles allow for differences in body build of individuals and can be considered to be in the normal range.

In addition, a skinfold evaluation will yield a more precise assessment of the proportion of fat to muscle and therefore weight to height. For example, a low value for triceps skinfold measurement in an individual above the 75th percentile for weight and height indicates that the adolescent is overweight but not overfat. An assessment of midarm circumference and arm muscle area will confirm the muscular body

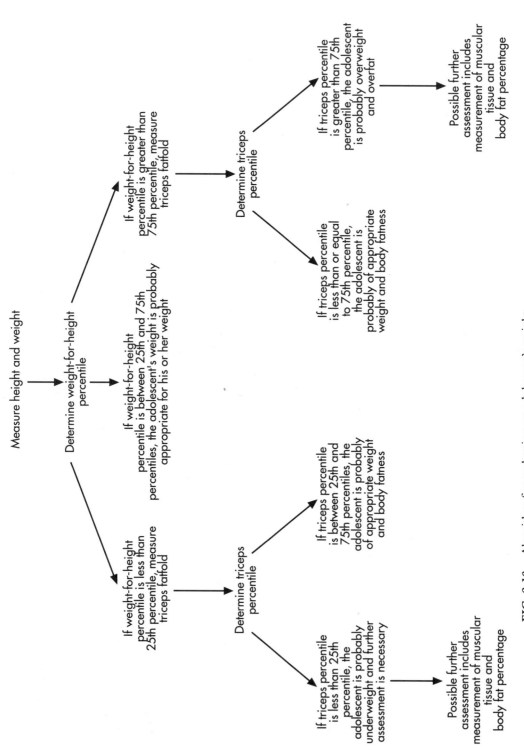

FIG. 9-10 Algorithm for evaluating an adolescent's weight.

(Developed by LK Mahan, University of Washington. Copyright Mahan LK, Rees JM: Seattle, Wash, 1989. Originally published in Mahan LK, Rees JM: *Nutrition in adolescence,* St Louis, 1984, Mosby—Year Book.)

composition. This type of evaluation is diagrammed in Figure 9-10.

Sexual Maturity Rating

The evaluation of **sexual maturity** is an essential factor in making a valid nutrition assessment of an adolescent in a normal clinical setting. By knowing the stage of sexual maturity of the adolescent (see Figure 9-2) it is possible to determine if the full height has been reached or if growth can still occur. Also it is possible to determine whether the proportion of fat to lean body mass measured in a person at a given time is likely to change because maturation is incomplete. Thus if a young woman at stage 1 of sexual maturity is at the 90th percentile of weight-for-height, she will continue to grow in height and has a greater potential to achieve more normal body composition by maintaining a stable weight as she grows than has a female of the same age, the same weight-for-height, but who has experienced menarche and is at stage 4 of sexual maturity. The young woman described last would not grow taller and would have to lose weight to improve the proportion of weight-to-height.

Prevention of Hyperlipidemia and Hypertension

All adolescents should be cautioned against a high intake of sodium, fat, and total energy because of the suspected link with cardiovascular disease.[39,40] In the case of hyperlipidemia, fat and total energy intake should be controlled as described in the Chapter 10. The risks of particular levels of blood lipids for ages 2 to 19 years are listed in Figure 9-11. If an adolescent is hypertensive or has a strong family history of hypertension, a diet controlled in sodium and total energy is part of long-term nutritional care.

Dental Caries and Periodontal Disease

The cause of dental caries is a complex process involving the interaction of several factors. The minerals of the tooth enamel are in constant equilibrium with the oral environment. It is necessary therefore to consider not only the presence of fermentable carbohydrate but also such factors as food solubility, mineral composition, and the buffering capacity of the oral en-

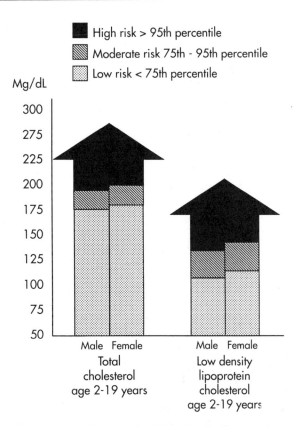

FIG. 9-11   Cholesterol and low density lipoprotein cholesterol (LDL-C) reference ranges for risk assessment.

(Developed by MS Jacobson, Director, Center for Atherosclerosis Prevention, Schneider Children's Hospital, New Hyde Park, NY.)

vironment. Adolescents' propensity to snack on refined carbohydrates is conducive to tooth decay. Since 80% of the average person's total incidence of dental lesions occurs in the teenage years, this is the time to encourage habits built on choosing alternatives to sugar-containing foods.

Gingivitis increases in prevalence during the teenage years, and periodontal disease often follows. Little is known about nutrition's role in periodontal disease, although deficiency in ascorbic acid has received a great deal of attention as an important cause. Vitamin A deficiency has also been implicated because it is common in underdeveloped countries with high incidences of periodontal disease. Inadequate intake of these nutrients in the teen years can have an adverse effect on the health of the gums in later life.

Acne

About 85% of all adolescents have acne caused by action of high levels of hormones on the sebaceous glands. Severity in individual teenagers varies. Stress and phase of the menstrual cycle are two of the factors that determine severity. Traditionally, dietary factors have been blamed for the appearance of acne, but studies have shown no correlation between ingestion of foods and the appearance or degree of this condition.

Education about the cause of acne helps teenagers learn to control it. Antibiotics given orally and benzoyl peroxide and tretinoin to apply on skin surfaces are usually effective, as are special cleansing agents.

Medicinal levels of vitamin A derivatives are useful in treating acne. They should not be used by young women who may become pregnant because they are linked to deformities in fetal development. In general, while no research is available to confirm the effect, it would seem that the optimally nourished body will be best able to cope with the development of acne as with many conditions.

NUTRITION EDUCATION
Potential Application

Well-developed nutrition education has components devoted to (1) communicating facts, (2) influencing attitudes, and (3) changing behavior.[41] Print media are usually the most successful in communicating information, while audio, visual, combined audio-visual, and hands-on experience communication techniques effectively influence attitudes and model healthful behavior.

Because teens normally begin to look outside the family for information, it is logical to expect that they can be educated about nutrition by institutions with which they interact in the community at large. Coordinated efforts could edu-cate them in schools, malls, libraries, grocery stores and convenience stores, fast-food outlets, detention facilities, and mass media (magazines, television, radio, newspapers, and books).

Current Status

At present, nutrition education of adolescents is not well designed or financed so they are generally influenced more by advertising, sensationalized material in magazine and newspaper stories, and peer-generated information than by health educators. Health education is usually confined to primitive print techniques, brief units in the health curriculum, and occasional encounters with health professionals. As a result typical teenagers know something about healthy use of foods but do not put most of that knowledge into practice.[42,43] It is obviously a challenge, but health educators and health policymakers will have to build coalitions to develop strategies for funding and carrying out programs for teenagers to improve the health of the adults of the future.[44]

Summary

Physical and psychosocial developments are rapid and all encompassing in the adolescent period of human life. The nature of physical growth is the basis for determining nutritional needs. Eating behavior is influenced to a great extent at this time by the developing body image and, as a result of breaking ties with the family, by the total culture. Emphasis must be placed on physical fitness to help all adolescents balance energy intake and output. The multitude of factors influencing teenagers at a time of so much change makes it an ideal time to provide nutrition education. Messages relayed in a style that they find appealing can help them sort out the conflicting information they get from family, peers, mentors, and media.

REVIEW QUESTIONS

1. What are the main characteristics of adolescent eating behavior patterns?
2. Why might two 16-year-old males be of different heights?
3. Discuss the current age of menarche as compared with 1900 and the reasons for the difference.
4. What is the relationship between puberty and adolescence?

5. What elements of a nutritional assessment are unique to adolescents?
6. How do the thinking patterns of older teenagers compare with those of younger children?
7. Describe the sequence of events in adolescent maturity for males? For females?

SUGGESTED LEARNING ACTIVITIES

1. Seek out a fast food restaurant that provides information to customers about nutrient content of its foods. Pick out a menu that contains the major nutrients and appropriate energy for an adolescent female whose statural growth is complete.
2. Assess 3-day food records kept by an adolescent male and an adolescent female who are still growing. How do their intakes and eating patterns compare with published reports?
3. Assess the material in a magazine popular among teenagers. Are the weight management methods safe? Is the nutrition information sound? Do the human images portray healthy weights and varied body types?
4. Interview an adolescent to obtain the types of information needed to assess that person's nutritional environment.
5. Prepare a talk describing physical growth and development during puberty and the interaction with nutrition for a Girl Scout group.

Terms and Concepts

Provided here for your review is a listing of terms and concepts within this chapter. The definitions for terms can be found in the glossary, which begins on page 413. To aid your understanding of the terms' and concepts' application within this text, the page number designating the first mention of each term or concept within the chapter is given.

REFERENCES

1. Tanner JM: *Fetus into man: physical growth from conception to maturity,* Cambridge, Mass, 1978, Harvard University Press.
2. Neinstein LS: *Adolescent health care: a practical guide,* ed 2, Baltimore, 1991, Urban & Schwarzenberg.
3. Trussel J, Frisch RE: Menarche and fatness: re-examination of the critical body composition hypothesis, *Science* 200:1506, 1978.
4. Tanner JM: Issues and advances in adolescent growth and development, *J Adolesc Health Care,* 8:470, 1987.
5. Frisancho AR: *Anthropometric standards for the assessment of growth and nutritional status,* Ann Arbor, Mich, 1990, University of Michigan Press.
6. Newman B, Newman P: *Adolescent development,* Columbus, Ohio, 1986, Merrill Publishing.
7. Moore DC: Body image and eating behavior in adolescent girls, *Am J Dis Child* 142:1114, 1988.
8. Moore DC: Body image and eating behavior in adolescent boys, *Am J Dis Child* 144:475, 1990.
9. Johnson MD and others: Anabolic steroid use by male adolescents, *Pediatrics* 83:921, 1989.
10. Rickert VI and others: Human growth hormone: a new abused substance among adolescents? (Abstract), *J Adolesc Health Care* 13:47, 1992.
11. McKigney JI, Munro HN, editors: *Nutrient requirements in adolescence,* Cambridge, Mass, 1976, MIT Press.
12. Food and Nutrition Board, National Research Council: *Recommended Dietary Allowances,* ed 10, Washington, DC, 1989, National Academy of Sciences.
13. Mahan LK, Rosebrough RH: *Nutrition requirements and nutritional status assessment in adolescence.* In Mahan LK, Rees JM: *Nutrition in adolescence,* St Louis, 1984, Mosby–Year Book.
14. Gong E, Heald FT: *Diet, nutrition and adolescence.* In Shils M, Young VR, editors: *Modern nutrition in health and disease,* ed 7, Philadelphia, 1988, Lea & Febiger.
15. Peacock M: Calcium absorption efficiency and calcium requirements in children and adolescents, *Am J Clin Nutr* 34:261s, 1991.
16. Thompson P and others: Zinc status and sexual development in adolescent girls, *J Am Diet Assoc* 86:892, 1986.
17. Raunikar RA, Strong WB: The status of adolescent physical fitness, *Adolesc Med: State of Art Rev* 2:65, 1991.

18. American Medical Association and American Dietetic Association: *Targets for adolescent health: adolescent nutrition and physical fitness,* Chicago, 1991, American Medical Association.

19. McArdle WD, Katch FI, Katch VL: *Exercise physiology: energy, nutrition and human performance,* ed 2, Philadelphia, 1986, Lea & Febiger.

20. Mahan LK: *Physical fitness, athletics, and the adolescent.* In Mahan LK, Rees JM: *Nutrition in adolescence,* St Louis, 1984, Mosby–Year Book.

21. Farthing MC: Current eating patterns of adolescents in the United States, *Nutr Today* 26:35, 1991.

22. Pennington JAT and others: Mineral content of foods and total diets: the selected minerals in foods survey, 1982 to 1984, *J Am Diet Assoc* 86:876, 1986.

23. Chan G: Dietary calcium and bone mineral status of children and adolescents, *Am J Dis Child* 145:631, 1991.

24. Witschi JC, Capper AL, Ellison RC: Sources of fat, fatty acids and cholesterol in the diets of adolescents, *J Am Diet Assoc* 90:1429, 1990.

25. Read MH, Harveywebster M, Usinger-Lesquereaus J: Adolescent compliance with dietary guidelines: health and education implications, *Adolescence* 23:567, 1988.

26. Bigler-Doughten S, Jenkins MR: Adolescent snacks: nutrient density and nutritional contribution to total intake, *J Am Diet Assoc* 87:1678, 1987.

27. McCoy H and others: Snacking patterns and nutrient density of snacks consumed by southern girls, *J Nutr Educ* 18:61, 1986.

28. Leverton RM: The paradox of teenage nutrition, *J Am Diet Assoc* 53:13, 1968.

29. Story M: *Adolescent lifestyle and eating behavior.* In Mahan LK, Rees JM: *Nutrition in adolescence,* St Louis, 1984, Mosby–Year Book.

30. Morgan KJ, Zabik ME, Stampley GL: Breakfast consumption patterns of U.S. children and adolescents, *Nutr Research* 6:635, 1986.

31. Morton HN: A survey of the television viewing habits, food behaviors and perception of food advertisements among South Australian year 8 high school students, *J Home Econ Assoc Aust* 22:34, 1990.

32. Franz MJ: Fast food facts: *Nutritive and exchange values for fast-food restaurants,* Wayzata, Minn, 1990, Diabetes Center Inc.

33. Guenther PM: Beverages in the diets of American teenagers, *J Am Diet Assoc* 86:493, 1986.

34. Portnoy B, Christenson GM: Cancer knowledge and related practices: results from the National Adolescent Student Health Survey, *J Sch Health* 59:218, 1989.

35. Farrow JA: Adolescent chemical dependency. In Farrow JA editor: Adolescent medicine, *Med Clin North Am* 74:1265, 1990.

36. Farrow JA, Rees JM, Worthington-Roberts BS: Health, development and nutritional status of adolescent alcohol abusers, *Pediatrics* 79:218, 1987.

37. Story M, Van Zyl York P: Nutritional status of Native American adolescent substance users, *J Am Diet Assoc* 87:1680, 1987.

38. National Center for Health Statistics: Height and weight of youths 12-17 years, United States. Vital and Health Statistics, Series 11, No 124, DHEW, Washington, DC, 1979, US Government Printing Office.

39. Heald FP: Atherosclerosis during adolescence. In Farrow JA, editor: Adolescent medicine, *Med Clin North Am* 74:1321, 1990.

40. Jacobson MS, editor: *Atherosclerosis prevention: identification and treatment of the child with high cholesterol,* Philadelphia, 1991, Harwood Academic Publishers.

41. Rees JM, Dixon-Docter A, Worthington-Roberts BS: *Nutrition education: a support for reproduction.* In Worthington-Roberts B, Williams SR: *Nutrition in pregnancy and lactation,* ed 5, St Louis, 1983, Mosby–Year Book.

42. Story M, Resnick, MD: Adolescents' views on food and nutrition, *J Nutr Educ* 18:188, 1986.

43. Resnicow K, Reinhardt J: What do children know about fat, fiber, and cholesterol? a survey of 5,116 primary and secondary school students, *J Nutr Educ* 23:65, 1991.

44. Panzarine S, editor: *Promoting the health of adolescents: proceedings from the 1990 state adolescent health coordinators conference,* Washington, DC, 1991, National Center for Education in Maternal and Child Health.

10

Nutrition in Special Situations During Adolescence

Jane Mitchell Rees

Objectives

✤✤

After studying this chapter, the student should:

✔ *Be able to describe the major eating disorders.*

✔ *Know the psychological and physiological factors fostering obesity.*

✔ *Be able to describe dietary issues for adolescents who are athletes.*

✔ *Understand how the growth of the fetus influences the growth of the adolescent during pregnancy.*

✔ *Be aware of the main principles of counseling adolescents.*

Nutritional support for growth and development in such diverse circumstances as eating disorders, competitive sports, and pregnancy follows specific principles. Modifications may be required to ensure that physical development is normal and continuous in the face of wide swings in nutritional requirements based on the characteristics of an adolescent's life. The nature of psychological development requires that the most sophisticated counseling techniques available to the social sciences today be applied in helping teenagers change long-standing food-related behaviors that are impairing their nutritional health.

✤Eating Disorders in Adolescence

Although recent precise figures are not available, as many as 30% of American teenagers are said to be obese. The number with diagnosed **anorexia nervosa** or **bulimia nervosa** is growing, and many adolescents with **eating disorders** remain undiagnosed and untreated. Because these disorders are so common among adolescents, health professionals interested in adolescent nutrition must understand them. Eating disorders provide effective models for study of other adolescent nutrition problems and their treatment. Therefore this chapter will explore these disorders in depth.

✤Eating Disorder Spectrum

Characteristics

The physical symptoms of eating disorders can be viewed as a spectrum, with **developmental obesity** at one end and anorexia nervosa at the other (Figure 10-1). In the middle of this spectrum are persons at normal and abnormal

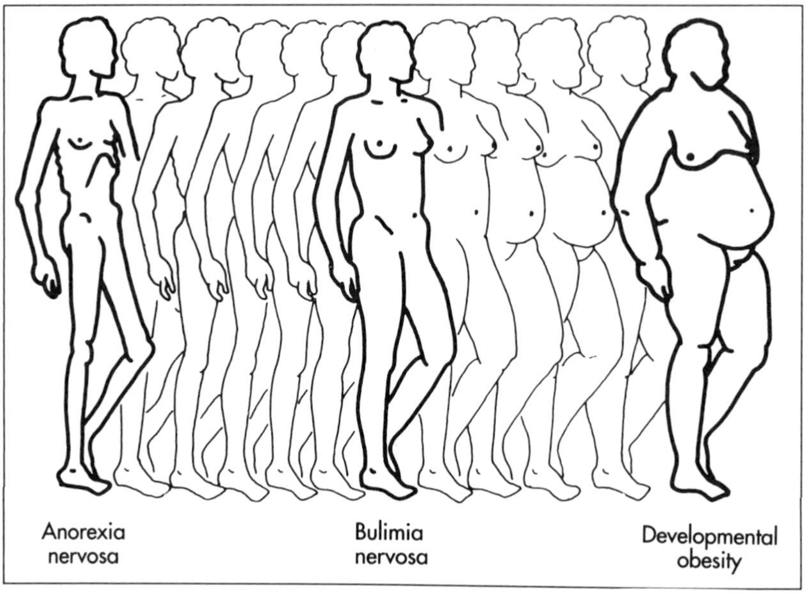

FIG. 10-1   Spectrum of eating disorders. Although physical conditions vary, underlying psychological characteristics are held in common across the spectrum.
(From Rees JM: *Eating disorders.* Copyright Mahan LK, Rees JM: Seattle, Wash, 1989. Originally published in Mahan LK, Rees JM: *Nutrition in adolescence,* St Louis, 1984, Mosby–Year Book.)

weights. Along the spectrum these persons have in common basic underlying psychological problems that interfere to varying degrees with normal functioning. In developing responses to life, affected persons often use food inappropriately. Food-related behaviors and the resulting deviation in weight, the two most obvious aspects of these disorders, are usually the main focus of attention of the person affected, the public, and often the health professional. The underlying neurophysical and psychodevelopmental mechanisms, however, are the essential features of knowledge needed by nutritionists.

Adolescent Growth and Body Image Development

Because of rapid physical growth and body image development in adolescence, eating disorders are of special concern at this stage of life. These changes intensify associated **self-esteem** problems. Anorexia nervosa, for example, is a disorder so tied to **body image distortion** that it is most commonly seen in adolescence, the period when a person is struggling with self-identity and is most vulnerable to body image problems. Progress in adopting a normal adult body image will be interrupted for the teenager with an eating disorder. Bruch[1] has provided classic descriptions of distorted body images in both anorexic and obese adolescents.

Psychosocial Developmental Tasks

Teenagers with severe eating disorders fail in varying degrees to accomplish the developmental tasks of adolescence. The developmental problems of these persons are summarized in the box on page 223. The most striking of their problems is failure to develop autonomy.

FAMILY INTERACTION

In recent years studies of factors contributing to the origin of these problems have turned to the structure and interaction of the adolescent's

DEVELOPMENTAL PROBLEMS
ASSOCIATED WITH EATING
DISORDERS IN ADOLESCENCE

Inability to develop and use formal
operational thought processes, especially in
reference to themselves
Inability to experience bodily sensations
originating within themselves as "normal"
and "valid"
Unrealistic perceptions of body size
Preoccupation with weight and food,
reflecting dependence on social opinion and
judgment
Failure to normalize eating and exercise
patterns
Unrealistic expectations for themselves
Failure to develop autonomy
Difficulty in accomplishing the normal tasks
of adolescence

From Rees JM: *Eating disorders*. Copyright Mahan LK,
Rees JM: Seattle, Wash, 1989. Originally published in Mahan LK, Rees JM: *Nutrition in adolescence*, St Louis, 1984,
Mosby–Year Book.

family. Although obese teenagers are a much less homogeneous group than anorectic persons, the family patterns have much in common. Minuchin and others[2] have described families of persons with anorexia as being psychosomatic. They are enmeshed, rigid, and overprotective and have a low tolerance for conflict.

Biopsychosocial Etiology

Eating disorders are very complex and may have developed throughout life or appear in adolescence. Individual and familial, biological, and psychological characteristics influenced by the modern social milieu contribute to their origin.

ANOREXIA NERVOSA
Symptoms

The term *anorexia nervosa* is actually a misnomer.[1] The implication that affected persons have a lack of appetite has been shown to be invalid. Superficially, the motivation to be thin keeps the person with anorexia nervosa from eating. In over 100 years of description in the literature, however, a combination of symptoms has come to be recognized as characteristic of the disorder. Although certain of these symptoms may be seen in other disorders, the combination is unique in anorexia nervosa. This unique combination of symptoms has been defined by the American Psychiatric Association[3] and are as follows:

Refusal to maintain body weight over minimal normal weight for age and height

Loss or failure to gain weight with maintenance weight 15% below expected

Fear of gaining weight or becoming fat, although underweight

Disturbance in body weight, size, or shape perception

Person feels fat or that body parts are fat, although underweight

Absence of three consecutive menstrual cycles

The above criteria focus more on physical symptoms at the crisis stage than on the underlying psychological symptoms. Recognition of the psychological symptoms, however, is of equal importance. The principal psychological features of anorexia nervosa are "a relentless pursuit of thinness" and "a misuse of the eating function in efforts to solve or camouflage problems that otherwise would appear insolvable," that is, problems resulting from arrested normal development.[1]

Incidence

The majority of persons with anorexia nervosa are adolescents, although it has been seen in other age groups. About 1% of young women are thought to be affected. The disorder has not been commonly seen in males, but 5% to 10% of anorectic teenagers are male. Males who develop the disorder appear to experience anorexia nervosa in essentially the same form as females.[4] Because of the predominance of females in the population seen with anorexia nervosa, the feminine pronoun will be used in this discussion.

Anorexia nervosa occurs predominantly in affluent classes and nations and is supported by a

cultural paradox in which food is abundant and used lavishly for purposes other than survival on the one hand, and slimness is highly valued on the other. These cultural values are strong internal messages that have great impact on a young adolescent who has not developed autonomy. The lack of a similar value on slimness in males probably accounts for the small number of males seen with the disorder, although the influence of rock stars and other celebrities with excessively thin bodies is beginning to have an impact on the ideals of young males.

Etiology

Theories about the etiology of anorexia nervosa have evolved from the initial psychoanalytic idea that the disease stemmed from an inability to deal with innate sexual drives, through periods when it was ascribed to endocrine deficits, and then disturbed patterns of family interaction, to the present when a combination of these biological, psychological, and social factors is thought to contribute to the development of the disorders.

Mother-daughter relationship. Bruch's work[1] was the first to incorporate a broader focus than simply the patient and her symptoms. An interaction pattern prevails in which the mother misperceives the needs of her child from infancy on or the child fails to express her needs clearly. In any case the child acquiesces to the mother's misguided ministrations. During the period of infancy and childhood, the daughter is so controlled by her mother that she does not develop a true sense of self as distinguished from mother.

Effect of adolescence. As adolescence approaches, the body develops and life requires decisions and performance in many areas. The teenager panics at her lack of ability to cope independently. She develops rituals related to eating in an effort to be thin and "good." To gain her "independence," the teenager regresses to the period when independence ordinarily begins. In this early stage the principal manner to demonstrate growing independence open to the child is eating behavior.

Family system. Minuchin and others'[2] more recent approach describes how not only relationships with the mother, but also interrelationships within the family system, foster anorexia nervosa. If family members are enmeshed in a system that does not allow development of appropriate roles, the system can produce a variety of psychosomatic problems. The particular direction toward anorexia nervosa may be determined when the main themes of family interaction are related to food, fitness, and appearance.

Biochemical processes. The possibility that a biochemical process may be responsible for development of anorexia nervosa continues to be investigated. Although various mechanisms have been proposed, so far none have been shown to be primary or causative. These mechanisms appear to result from psychological stress, malnutrition, and starvation. The fact that patients and their families fit such characteristic and complex patterns would raise doubt that a single primary physiological cause exists in most cases. However, it may be found that biochemical factors contribute to the development of the disorder.

Psychological State

The physical manifestations of anorexia nervosa may be sudden, although unrecognized underlying characteristics may have been previously present. Intervention strategies must address both the psychological and physiological states of the patient.

Progressive development. From the family's point of view, the anorectic teenager is usually a "model child" until she begins to develop a compulsive attitude about her weight. She has fit into the family unit and met their high expectations. She has worked extremely hard at school, being satisfied with nothing less than excellent grades.

Suddenly the whole family erupts in conflict over her eating behavior. The teenager herself has become troubled about her role in life. She is unable to sustain peer friendships and she is very anxious about relationships with males. She is confused by the need to establish more adult behavior patterns and clings to the rigid standards of childhood. She isolates herself. Life appears to be out of her control. She has conflicting feelings about living as her parents direct her to live, and she is hurt by their critical comments and begins to realize that she must assert herself. She takes a stand and will not compromise on her eating and exercise habits. She feels that she is too fat and must be slim to prove that she is a worthy person. She is increasingly preoccupied with her rituals and is angry when her family interferes. She denies her illness.

Distorted perceptions. A wide range of distorted perceptions has been noted, related specifically to body size, sex, hunger, rest, satiety, body temperature, pleasure, control, and "feeling states" in general. The anorectic teenager has often been described as wishing to stave off adulthood. But the question remains as to whether she wishes to avoid maturation or whether maturation eludes her.

Family problems. Although most families with anorectic teenagers would describe themselves as normal and without problems until the manifestations of anorexia nervosa arise, these families often have a multitude of problems. The parents may have been dominating and intrusive. They may have overlooked the *actual* (including nutritional) needs and emotions of their children, even in times when the children have been ill. By adopting a "helpless" stance, the affected children may be thoroughly manipulative and involved in their parents' conflicts. Both parents and children become locked into a system in which problems go unresolved and responses are stereotyped.[2]

Physiological State

In the initial stage of anorexia nervosa, physical symptoms are related to weight, diet, exercise, menses, and nutritional status.

Weight. In some cases the anorectic teenager is overweight when the disorder begins. The anorectic young woman is typically hypersensitive to developing breasts and hips. These young patients often recall a chance statement about their needing to lose weight by a relative or close friend, or a weight reduction plan suggested by a health professional, as the trigger for their initial weight loss behavior.

Diet. The anorectic adolescent usually develops a personal philosophy about her diet, limiting herself by eating food only from certain categories and in certain ways. She may manipulate the fluid or sodium content of her intake. In addition, she may force herself to vomit and misuse laxatives or diuretics to rid herself of food energy and weight. Vomiting may follow episodes of gorging.

Exercise. The practice of exercise rituals is equally varied. Anorectic teenagers include excessive calisthenics and other strenuous activities in their schedules. They may limit rest and use stimulants. They are so frequently involved in junior and senior high school athletics and dancing that coaches and teachers should be educated about the disorder. Good coaches should recognize which of their students may be exercising to their detriment by compulsively training beyond reasonable endurance while losing weight at a rapid rate.

Menses. Although a young woman in a state of starvation would be expected to become **amenorrheic,** indications are that cessation of menses occurs in most patients with anorexia nervosa before they have lost sufficient weight and body fat to cause an interruption of the cycle and lasts beyond the time they have regained weight and body fat.[5,6] Psychological factors probably contribute to the problem as well as true hormonal disturbance since stressful states are known to interfere with the endocrine system regulating the menstrual cycle.

Nutritional status. During the initial phase of an anorectic teenager's energy restriction, the body does not exhibit the effects of malnutrition to a measurable degree other than a decrease in weight. Infections are not generally seen. Deficiencies in specific nutrients have not been reported, but they may exist subclinically depending on the food habits of the individual. If weight loss continues unchecked, however, the symptoms of severe starvation may become apparent and additional nutritional problems such as those listed on page 227 begin to undermine basic health. This state indicates the onset of a crisis.

Intervention Strategies

Early recognition of symptoms. A recognition of the developing symptoms is the most important early intervention strategy. A protocol for assessing anorexia nervosa and bulimia nervosa is provided in the box on page 226.

❖

ISSUES TO ADDRESS IN A CLINICAL ASSESSMENT OF EATING DISORDERS

• **Motivation**
Appropriateness of weight goals
Desire to change unhealthful habits
Insight into problem
• **Emotional/psychological status**
Depression
Locus of control
Body image
Self-esteem
Oral expression
Coping skills
Compulsivity
Perfectionism
Independence
• **Mental function**
Intellectual ability
School performance
Attitude toward school
Ability to articulate
• **Family characteristics**
Eating disorders
Other diseases
Natural or other parent
Intrusiveness
Enmeshment
Rigidity
Conflict resolution
Role of food
Exercise patterns
Perceptions of problem
Attempts to intervene
Willingness to participate in therapy

• **Social relationships**
Friends
Social habits
Social skills
Attitude of peers
• **Eating behavior**
Knowledge/acknowledgment of nutritional
   needs
Meal pattern
Bizarre eating habits
Personal philosophy toward eating
Nutritional adequacy
Control over food supply
• **Physical status**
Signs of bulimia
Signs of starvation
Terminal signs of starvation
Thyroid status (obesity)
Resting heart rate
Exercise to reach 60% maximum heart rate
• **Growth and adiposity**
Weight/height/age percentile
Triceps skinfold/age percentile
Arm muscle area/age percentile
Weight/height history
Growth velocity
Maturational stage
Age
• **Physical activity**
Exercise patterns
Hobbies/interests
Personal feelings about exercise

From Rees JM: *Eating disorders.* Copyright Mahan LK, Rees JM: Seattle, Wash, 1989. Originally published in Mahan LK, Rees JM: *Nutrition in adolescence,* St Louis, 1984, Mosby–Year Book.

Friends, school personnel, family, and health professionals are among those who observe the growing problems and can take steps to initiate treatment.

Psychotherapy. Individual and family psychotherapy by experienced therapists will enable both the affected adolescent and her family to adopt more appropriate roles. It will also help the anorectic teenager to complete the psychological developmental processes that have been arrested.[1]

Nutritional therapy. Other than general monitoring of height and weight, it may not be necessary to treat the patient physically at this stage. Refocusing her attention on the primary emotional and interactional problems rather than the power struggle over food and exercise patterns will often enable the patient to abandon her compulsive striving for thinness. The patient should have access to a professional who can answer her questions about nutrition and make sure that she has the information she needs to begin to regulate her eating patterns to meet her physical needs. Information should be given in the context of the adolescent's desire to change rather than imposed as a rigid system of dietary planning by a professional. The overall disorder should not be defined as solely a nutritional problem, although nutrition counseling is an important component of therapy.

Crisis Stage: Psychological State

Overall, a lack of progress toward positive family interaction patterns during the initial therapy or continuing avoidance of intervention will often lead to physical and mental deterioration. When the crisis stage of anorexia nervosa develops, severe psychological and physiological symptoms appear and intervention must be directed toward the deteriorating condition.

Psychological effects of starvation. The anorectic teenager in crisis can cause panic among family, friends, and professionals. The family generally sees the adolescent's bizarre eating behavior as the problem and fails to understand the extent of developmental and interactional patterns. As a result, they often seek treatment that does not demand their involvement with the patient in therapy. As she becomes truly **cachectic,** the psychological changes inherent in starvation described by Keys and others[5] in his classic studies become evident:

1. Cognitive processes center around food. Thoughts of food intrude constantly; the major part of the waking hours are spent in contemplating it.
2. Behavior around food includes toying with it and hoarding, especially during **renourishment.**
3. Coherent creative thinking is impaired.
4. Mental function is characterized by apathy, dullness, exhaustion, and depression.
5. Interest in sexual function is lacking.

These effects of starvation are superimposed on the anorectic teenager's already disturbed psychological state. The behavior pattern, distorted perceptions, and weight phobia become more pronounced.

Behavior pattern. Many patients resist what they see as intrusions by professionals. They are secretive and hide the fact that they are carrying out their rituals. Their behavior may otherwise reflect the apathy typically seen in starving people. In obsessional preoccupation, they plan menus, read recipes, cook and serve food to others, cut or manipulate food before eating it, and record all that they eat. They usually have a detailed knowledge of "calorie content," but not of the energy value of foods. They may pretend to eat and then hide and dispose of the food. The disturbed adolescent's fear of gaining weight becomes increasingly evident as her weight phobia intensifies.

Crisis Stage: Physiological State

In the crisis stage of anorexia nervosa, the physiological state deteriorates with physical signs of starvation, endocrine abnormalities, and undeniable signs of approaching terminal starvation.[7]

Physical signs of starvation. As the crisis stage develops, the individual is unable to take care of herself. The physical state of starvation is now superimposed on the other problems inherent in the disorder. These physical signs of starvation include:

Fat store depletion
Muscle wasting
Amenorrhea
Cheilosis
Desquamation
Dry skin
Hirsutism
Thin, dry, brittle hair
Alopecia
Degradation of fingernails
Acrocyanosis
Postural hypotension
Inability to regulate body temperature

Additional nutritional problems. In addition to the clinical signs, recent research has focused on zinc nutriture, bone demineralization, growth failure, and structural changes in the brain, which result from severe long-term malnutrition in anorectic patients.[8,9] The possibility that bone demineralization, growth retardation, and brain structural abnormalities may prove irreversible to some degree is especially troublesome and warrants further examination.[10-12] The relationship of depressive symptoms, sex role, and body image distortion to lowered body weight, and suggestion that fewer than the expected number of children are born to patients formerly diagnosed with anorexia nervosa are equally disturbing long-term effects of chronic malnutrition with implications for dancers, gymnasts, and other athletes who keep themselves in a state of starvation as well as to anorectics.[13-15]

Endocrine abnormalities. The endocrine abnormalities in women with anorexia nervosa are such that the body essentially reverts to a prepubertal hormonal state. As a result of hypothalamic change, the anorectic adolescent is amenorrheic, is unable to adapt to heat and cold, suffers sleep disturbances, and is unable to conserve body water. There is no interest in sex.

Terminal starvation signs. During the crisis, professionals must monitor the physical state of the patient and take remedial action when signs of starvation approach a terminal state. The most outstanding of these signs include:

Fluid and electrolyte imbalance indicating inability of the body to maintain homeostasis (dehydration and edema)

Severe cardiac abnormalities in the absence of electrolyte imbalances, indicating a wasted myocardium

Absence of ketone bodies in the urine, indicating a lack of fat stores for metabolic fuel

Concurrent infection, indicating increasing nutritional needs

Crisis Intervention Strategies

When the anorectic adolescent's condition reaches the crisis stage, hospitalization is necessary to provide comprehensive care involving nutritional therapy.

Hospitalization. For some clinicians, the decision to hospitalize an anorectic patient depends on her reaching a life-threatening physical state. However, if the goal is to renourish the individual so that she will be able to benefit from psychotherapy without semistarvation

neurosis, as many authoritative therapists recommend, the anorectic patient must be hospitalized before a critical stage has been reached. The patient can be released from the hospital when she has been nutritionally rehabilitated, usually confirmed by reaching a particular weight-for-height goal.

Comprehensive treatment. Nutritional components of therapeutic regimens for anorexia nervosa patients in the crisis stage are intertwined with the psychological aspects of the treatment. Team care is essential. Certain principles can be observed that will apply regardless of the treatment modality. Renourishment obviously will begin with a gradual increase in energy intake.

Diet therapy. In some programs the patient will be allowed to choose anything available on the hospital menu. Other programs impose rules, make additions to what is ordered, or serve a set menu. If a diet is prescribed following the principles established for renourishing malnourished individuals, it should have adequate protein to meet basic needs with additional energy made up of complex carbohydrates and a small amount of fat.

Nutritional supplements. If a patient refuses food, a nutritional supplement, which is prescribed and dispensed as a medicine, may be used. If a life-threatening state is reached at any time with the patient refusing oral feeding, nourishment by nasogastric tube or parenteral methods may be necessary. These methods will be presented as life-saving procedures and not as punishment for refusing to eat. Nourishment by mouth is the preferred route and is possible in most cases.

Renourishment edema and body image. Edema generally appears with renourishment and can be a problem because of the anorectic patient's phobia of weight gain. The edema is seen by her as proof that she will "expand" as she feared. Some anticipatory guidance can help her accept such a development. Assurance that professionals will aid her in gaining appropriate weight, which will be strengthening for her but will not form excess fat, can help desensitize the issue.

Role of the clinical nutritionist. The clinical nutritionist/dietitian on the therapeutic team provides nutritional care while maintaining the psychotherapeutic goal of redirecting the focus of the patient's concern. The nutritionist's knowledge of energy balance as it applies to the individual is needed in determining appropriate weight goals throughout therapy, especially as related to the patient's release from the hospital.

Long-Term Therapy

Psychological state. The anorectic teenager who has recovered from a starvation crisis by gaining a certain amount of weight to improve her physical state will still have to deal with the developmental arrest that brought her to the crisis, a process that usually requires several years. There will continue to be problems concerning vocational choices and preparation, economic stability, relationships with peers and especially with the opposite sex, weight management, and body image.

Physiological state. The anorectic young woman will often experience wide swings in weight from extreme thinness to obesity before she will be able to bring her anorexia into control. She may see herself as somewhat detached from her body and experiment with various food habits before putting food into a more normal perspective. She may keep herself sufficiently thin that she may not resume her menses. She may feel bloated and have bouts of edema, physical responses to starvation and refeeding, and **carotenemia,** a symptom of anorexia.

Intervention strategies. In the recovery period the psychotherapeutic goal will be to facilitate normal development in the anorectic teenager, to prepare her for a full adult role in society, and to enable her to function without depending on bizarre eating and exercise habits. She will need information and retraining about food and the physical aspects of life. Many of the techniques described in the section on obesity will be useful. Issues such as the state of nourishment necessary to maintain the menstrual cycle will resurface from time to time as development proceeds. Returning to such issues will enable her to deal more capably with them as time goes on. Guided food experiences in cafeterias, grocery stores, cooking, and entertaining help ready the person for managing food in her environment. The objective is to help the individual put food into a reasonable perspective and give up overfocusing on food out of ignorance. A team consisting of medical, psychological, and nutrition specialists may provide care, or the care may be left to a single therapist who will be responsible for all aspects of therapy with consultation from others.

Outcome. Common features of anorexia nervosa are the strong resistance to treatment and the high incidence of relapse and partial recovery. Some patients will manifest varying degrees of the anorectic symptoms in adulthood. Although outcome criteria have been inconsistently used by researchers, results reported to date indicate that although weight-for-height proportion improved in about 75% of the patients, menstrual cycles were often unsatisfactorily maintained, ideas about food and weight were disturbed, and psychosocial maladjustment was common.

BULIMIA NERVOSA

First called bulimarexia, *bulimia nervosa* is the most recently recognized eating disorder and is characterized by gorging followed by self-induced vomiting or diarrhea. Although these symptoms may be a part of anorexia nervosa, they also constitute a separate syndrome.

Symptoms

The person suffering from bulimia nervosa generally maintains close-to-normal weight (Figure 10-1) while gorging, binging, eating abnormally large amounts of food, and vomiting or purging (forcing bowels to empty) on a regular basis. The bulimic teenager may have somewhat less severe distortions in body image and less restrictive weight goals than the adolescent with anorexia nervosa. She is often older at age of onset.

American Psychiatric Association criteria. The diagnostic criteria established by the American Psychiatric Association (APA) includes the following behaviors[3]:

Recurrent episodes of binge eating, rapid consumption of large amounts of food in a discrete period

Lack of control over binges

Regular self-induced vomiting, use of laxatives or diuretics, strict dieting or fasting, or vigorous exercise

Average of two binge-eating episodes a week for at least 3 months

Overconcern with body shape and weight

Incidence

The syndrome of bulimia nervosa should be differentiated from the recent behavior of many normal adolescent females who occasionally use self-induced vomiting as a means of controlling weight.[16] As many as 20% of college age females may engage in bulimic behaviors with an estimated 2% to 4% meeting the criteria for diagnosis of bulimia nervosa.

A serious condition will be uncontrollable, and the psychological features of the disorder will impair normal functioning. Bulimia nervosa sometimes develops after a serious bout with anorexia nervosa or obesity. The bulimic person is more likely to be fertile than the individual with anorexia nervosa. Therefore, certain young women will be bulimic during pregnancy.

Psychological State

Separation anxiety is one of the important issues for the bulimic teenager. Her self-esteem is extremely low and is tied to her feelings about her body. She demonstrates excessive need for control and approval. She thinks of herself as physically unattractive, although she is well groomed and has a normally attractive physique. She develops guilt over her habits and her secret feelings of inadequacy. Superficially, she may be responsible and keep a heavy social schedule. In reality she has few close friends and feels that no one really knows her. In contrast to the more rigid anorectic adolescent, the young woman with bulimia nervosa often demonstrates poor impulse control, abuses substances, and becomes easily enraged. By all accounts, the gorging, vomiting, and purging serve to release tension for the sufferers. However, the residual guilt feelings bring renewed tension that perpetuates an uncontrolled cycle. Social isolation is also perpetuated because of the fear that the secret will be found out. If pregnant, the bulimic teenager may be committed to protecting the fetus but retain ideas that

inhibit normal nourishment of herself, her fetus, and the child after birth.

Food behavior. The bulimic teenager periodically eats large amounts of food and then voluntarily vomits or purges. Each person with bulimia nervosa defines what a binge is for herself. Because of distortions in thinking about food, as little as one doughnut may be thought of as a binge by one person while as much as an entire package of doughnuts may constitute a binge for another. As the duration of the habits extends, it becomes easier for her to vomit. Eventually, the vomiting is a nearly automatic response. In addition, she may take laxatives to purge herself of the energy she has ingested or use diuretics to remove body fluid.

Physiological Symptoms

As a result of these behaviors, physiological symptoms of the bulimic adolescent will include:

Tooth damage

Throat irritation

Esophageal inflammation (all of the above symptoms are caused by exposure of unprotected tissues to acidic vomitus)

Swollen salivary glands (caused by acidic reflux or constant stimulation)

Broken blood vessels in face (from force of vomiting)

Cracked, damaged lips

Rectal bleeding (caused by overuse of laxatives)

Life-threatening situations are rarer in bulimics than in anorectics. They are:

Dehydration and electrolyte imbalance

Fistulas or ruptures in the upper gastrointestinal tract

Kidney damage

Concerns during pregnancy are the adverse biochemical environment for the mother and fetus, the mother's abnormal weight gain pattern (weight loss, lack of weight gain, inordinate gain), and the mother's unrealistic ideas about infant feeding.

Intervention Strategies

The techniques most frequently reported in treating bulimia nervosa patients are similar to those used during the long-term recovery period of anorexia nervosa patients. Psychotherapy, nutritional therapy, and care of any pregnancy that may occur must be included.

Psychotherapy. The emphasis of therapy is on freeing the person from guilt, facilitating gains in self-esteem, and helping her deal with anxiety as well as challenging distorted goal setting based on perfection. Ideally, the young woman's family or partner will be included in the therapy.

Nutritional therapy. While she deals with the psychological problem, the bulimic individual will still have an eating disorder and will need reeducation to nourish herself properly. Physical and nutritional education can fill gaps in knowledge these teenagers have about their body functions. Over time, myths about weight management can be dispelled and more normal eating habits developed. Because of distorted feelings about food, the bulimic person may feel guilty every time she eats, despite the fact that food is necessary for life. The family often reinforces the guilt by a misguided overfocus on food, thinness, and the physical aspects of life. The bulimic teenager usually restricts her food intake to match the ideal plan she conceives for herself. Binges may thus arise from the natural need for adequate food and the desire for additional gratification.[17]

Role of the clinical nutritionist. The clinical nutritionist on the professional team will help the young person with bulimia nervosa to see food in a more appropriate context and accept more realistic weight goals using the techniques described in the following section. Helping her understand the physiological processes of energy balance and nutrient functions as well as the effects of binging, vomiting, and purging as they affect her personally is especially useful. This education, however, must be done gradually in a counseling mode, allowing time for alteration of her rigid system of beliefs. Family and individual psychotherapy will continue concurrently. It is necessary to deal with the underlying causes of the obsessional food behavior. Group therapy has also been used.

Pregnancy care. The bulimic teenager who is pregnant can be helped to accept the idea that the baby she wants must be nourished. She can then be supported in learning to retain those foods that the fetus needs even if she cannot give up binging and vomiting totally. She should also be helped in learning to recognize natural hunger signals from her baby after it is born.

OBESITY

At the other end of the physical spectrum of eating disorders is obesity. Unlike anorectic adolescents, persons who are abnormally heavy do not fit into a homogeneous group and may be carrying excessive weight for a variety of reasons. Factors leading to obesity can be broadly divided into those that are psychological and those that are physiological. In any individual a combination of these factors may operate in the development and maintenance of obesity. Because of the cultural response to obesity, the adolescent whose obesity may be physiologically based will generally be subject to many of the same problems as those whose obesity is more psychologically based.

Psychological Factors

Various psychological factors are associated with adolescent obesity, whether it develops during earlier childhood or is related to more severe psychiatric disorders.

Developmental obesity. Bruch[1] described a form of obesity that primarily results from psychological factors within the family. Thus it is termed *developmental obesity*. It is an eating disorder comparable to anorexia nervosa in that it originates in the early life of the child. The families of developmentally obese teenagers fit descriptions of the psychosomatic family. The family's attitudes and behavior thus stunt the child's psychological development and serve as primary causes of the obesity. The obesity itself further inhibits normal development, and this in turn leads to maintenance or increase of body weight. The affected children are made to feel pressure, inappropriate responsibility, and specialness to an abnormal degree in family interactions. They become rigid, isolated, and enmeshed. They develop misperceptions about their basic physical needs and rely on coping skills based on the abuse of food. As obese teenagers, these persons may not develop their full potential as competent, well-functioning adults, but they are less likely to experience the complete developmental arrest that the anorectic teenager does.

Body image. The teenager who is overweight is vulnerable to body image disturbances. The type and extent of the disturbance depend on the length of time the person has been heavy, the amount of excessive weight carried, the person's sex, and the life situation surrounding the individual's unique development. For example, teenagers who have been heavy from childhood may react differently from those who have gained weight only during later adolescence. Like anorectic teenagers, many tie thoughts of success or failure to their weight status.

Associated psychological disorders. In some teenagers, obesity may be associated with severe psychiatric disorders. In others, the overeating behavior may act as an emotionally stabilizing influence helping to maintain the person at a functioning level. Interference in such a situation without substantial support provided can cause the disintegration of the person's affect into an anxious or depressed state.

Cultural and Family Influences

The abundance of food and lack of necessity to expend energy in American society make it easy for children to gain unwanted weight. In families where food intake and exercise patterns are not appropriate for dealing with this situation, an overweight state can result without other specific psychological or physiological origins.

Behavior Patterns in Obese Teenagers

The usual overweight or obese teenager is passive in interactions with others and with the environment. This response further reinforces the weight problem and leads to social isolation, lack of exercise, and disturbed patterns of eating and family interaction.

Social isolation. The **passive response pattern** of the obese adolescent in contact with others creates social isolation and an increased dependence on the family for relationships, even though the family interaction patterns may be unpleasant and the parents may constantly exhibit intrusive

and negative attitudes. Adolescents often react to the stigma of obesity by adopting a stereotyped life-style with a narrow range of activities.

Sedentary life-style. The eating and exercise functions in the lives of obese teenagers generally become distorted. They may never feel comfortable eating in social situations. Their isolation leads them to opt out of many activities that would expend energy. They fear being seen wearing gym clothes or swimsuits or doing physical activities because they feel they are the object of attention and even ridicule. Instead they spend an inordinate amount of time in passive pursuits such as watching television or reading. Both of these activities may be paired with eating. Commercial television, especially, fosters this behavior with frequent food-related cues.

Eating patterns. Although many studies of teenagers after they have become obese have shown that on the average they eat no more, and sometimes less, than their normal weight peers, they often have disturbed, unstructured patterns of eating. They may eat only in the latter part of the day, feeling nausea when eating earlier, and eat rapidly and indiscriminately.

Family patterns. Parents in some families may be locked into power struggles with their children, attempting in vain to control what they eat. Overanxiety regarding even slight overweight may actually contribute to growing obesity. In other families overeating may be the main theme, with most interactions revolving around food.

Physiological Factors

In certain individuals physiological factors are principally responsible for their obesity. These factors are summarized in Table 10-1. Two of these underlying factors deserve note here.

Set-point theory. One theory that cannot be overlooked is that certain individuals may be subject to a body weight "set-point." A certain body weight may be physiologically normal for each person, and body characteristics may be tuned to keep the body at that weight.

Lower basal energy needs. A decreased requirement of the amount of energy used in biochemical reactions may increase the amount of

TABLE 10-1   *Processes Leading to and Sustaining Obesity: Therapeutic Implications*

Process	Therapeutic Implications
Genetic predisposition Certain inherited biochemical, morphological, and histological features foster excess storage of energy as fat.	Teach to control energy intake and output to exert any possible control and need to be vigilant even if unable to avoid being greater than normal size.
Sodium pump activity Less activity in cells of obese decreases energy usage, making more available for storage.	No direct intervention; not known if process is reversible.
Body temperature differences Defect in regulation with failure to maintain normal core temperature by obese increases energy available for storage.	As above
Adipose tissue lipoprotein lipase activity Rate limiting enzyme in triglyceride storage is more active in the obese, enhancing adipose tissue synthesis.	As above
Brown adipose tissue activity Responsible for increased facultative thermoclines in animals; also being investigated in humans to no avail so far.	As above
Insulin resistance Obese bodies are less sensitive to insulin. Resulting hyperinsulinemia tends to maintain obese state.	Exercise improves sensitivity to insulin even without weight loss; also reversible with weight loss.
Thermogenesis Less energy is spent in obligatory (food processing) or facultative (response to sympathetic nervous system) thermogenesis in obese.	Complex carbohydrates increase obligatory thermogenesis in some individuals; timing exercise before or after meals increases facultative thermogenesis in some.
Adipocyte hypertrophy When energy is available for storage fat cells enlarge.	Decrease energy available by changing intake/output; cell size is reduced with energy deficit.

Modified from Rees JM: *Eating disorders.* Copyright Mahan LK, Rees JM: Seattle, Wash, 1989. Originally published in Mahan LK, Rees JM: *Nutrition in adolescence*, St Louis, 1984, Mosby–Year Book.

Continued.

TABLE 10-1 *Processes Leading to and Sustaining Obesity: Therapeutic Implications—cont'd*

Process	Therapeutic Implications
Adipocyte hyperplasia When fat cells are filled, new cells will be formed if energy continues to be available for storage.	Already obese can decrease energy available to prevent formation of even more cells; cell number does not decrease even with energy deficit.
Regional distribution of adipose tissue Typically, males have more central (abdominal) adipose tissue with higher waist/hip ratios than females who have more peripheral (femoral and gluteal) fat with lower waist/hip ratios. Male distribution associated with diabetes, hypertension, and cardiovascular disease; female distribution more difficult to change. Difference in cell size and lipoprotein lipase activity in various sites may be important.	Assessing waist/hip ratio helps determine difficulty of achieving weight loss and harm in adults remaining obese. Not yet explored in adolescents.
Set-point weight Bodies of certain individuals defend high body weights. Others defend low weights or no particular weight.	Decrease excess energy through exercise and substituting complex carbohydrates for fat, so as to reverse any processes that are reversible. If obese adolescents have control of energy intake and output, psychological support for physiologically sustainable weight is reasonable.

❖

COMPONENTS OF A COMPREHENSIVE WEIGHT MANAGEMENT PROGRAM WITH APPLICABLE TREATMENT MODALITIES

* *Food management*
Food use retraining
Nutrition education
Behavior modification
Diet prescription

* *Energy time management*
Fitness testing and improvement programs
Relaxation training
Movement and dance therapy
Expanded interest stimulation

* *Psychosocial adjustment*
Supportive counseling
Family counseling
Social skills training
Assertion training
Psychotherapy
Group support

From Rees JM: *Eating disorders.* Copyright Mahan LK, Rees JM: Seattle, Wash, 1989. Originally published in Mahan LK, Rees JM: *Nutrition in adolescence,* St Louis, 1984, Mosby–Year Book.

energy available in the systems of some people for storage as fat. Based on present theory, the longer the teenager has been obese and the greater the extent of the obesity, the greater the effect these factors will have. The adolescent whose obesity was originally caused by other factors such as social, psychological, or family influences will, as time passes, have added problems of physiological obesity. This pattern increases the complexity of the obese state.[18]

Intervention Strategies

An effective program in working with obese teenagers and their families will provide personalized care, giving attention to identifying individual needs and attitudes, setting realistic goals, developing related strategies within a comprehensive approach (see box, page 234), and evaluating outcome.

Assessment

The combination of psychological and physiological circumstances by which an individual teenager has become obese must be identified so that intervention can be directed toward specific aspects of the problem. The degree of overweightness must be considered. The material in the assessment section, especially Figure 9-10 on page 216, may be used to evaluate the size of heavy adolescents. Generally they will be (1) *overweight,* only moderately above weight-height midranges for health; (2) *obese,* about 20% or more above normal weight-height ranges with a higher degree of fatness; or (3) *morbidly obese,* much higher weight for height ranges and greater amount of fat tissue, associated with multiple health problems. Among all of these persons some will suffer from hidden eating disorders such as bulimia nervosa or anorexia nervosa (recovery stage). The information needed to assess adolescent obesity (Figure 10-2) may best be gathered by a team of professionals. Many of these aspects will need to be explored over time. The basic initial steps to assess physical status and personal attitude include:

1. Physical status. A physical examination will disclose the stage of puberty and rule out any endocrine abnormalities or com-

plications of the obese state. Endocrine disorders are rarely found. Most physiological abnormalities associated with obesity indicated by clinical laboratory measures will respond to weight reduction.

2. Personal attitude. The most important aspect of initial evaluation is whether the individual is committed to making changes. The teenager's feelings must be assessed initially and at each visit. It is of no value for other persons to have goals related to weight management if the teenager is not ready to change the status quo. The question needs to be, "Are you ready to make changes?" rather than, "Do you want to lose weight?" Many teenagers will answer "yes" to the second question but remain totally passive, the implication being that the process of weight management for them is a passive one in which the professional administers treatment.

Reasons for Not Starting a Weight Loss Program

A weight loss program should not be instituted if (1) the adolescent has not reached full height; (2) there is a lack of commitment; (3) it is likely to be another in a series of failures harmful to the individual's self-esteem; or (4) the individual is obviously predisposed to obesity by overwhelming physiological factors. If obese teenagers keep fit, maintain energy equilibrium, and are emotionally healthy, they will be candidates for weight loss only if they understand the physiological aspects of obesity and are determined to test these aspects in a healthful manner. Those adolescents who are still growing in height should not be encouraged to lose weight because the level of energy restriction required to do so is inadequate to support growth.

Goals

Realistic planning of goals includes a series of short-term steps to achieve the long-term goal:

1. Short-term goals. These continuing short-term goals need to be based not on changes in weight but on positive changes in food intake and exercise-related atti-

Rate on a scale of 0 to 5 the contribution to weight management
0 = Minimum; 5 = Maximum

	0	1	2	3	4	5
NOURISHMENT						
Knowledge of:						
Meaning of "kcalories"						
Role of food in life						
Relationship of energy intake/output						
Major nutrients—physiological role						
energy value						
amount needed						
food sources						
amount of food needed						
Choosing food in a variety of situations						
Behavior modification techniques						
Appropriate wt/ht/age/genetic heritage						
Attitude						
Acceptance of responsibility for nourishing self						
Commitment to health-promoting habits						
Obtaining appropriate foods						
Nutrition education						
Eating behavior						
Control of food supply						
Fat content						
Types of food						
Amounts of food						
Meal pattern						
Between meal eating						
Binges/night eating/other aberrations						
Uses behavior modification techniques						
Eats in social situations—						
with family						
with peers						
Family						
Eating meals together						
Place						
Distractions (TV)						
Serving methods						
Support for weight control via use of:						
Food						
Knowledge						
Autonomy allowed to choose food						

FIG. 10-2 Format for weight management assessment of adolescents. The initial rating in each category can be used to set short-term goals and subsequently can be used to monitor improvement between assessments.

ENERGY TIME MANAGEMENT	0	1	2	3	4	5
Knowledge of:						
Exercise in energy balance						
Fitness—cardiorespiratory						
muscular.						
Exercise—aerobic						
anaerobic						
Monitoring pulse						
Attitude						
Committment to exercising regularly						
Without others, equipment, or money						
if necessary						
Interest in fitness education						
Pleasure in moving						
Behavior						
Fitness tested						
Program planned						
Program maintained						
Level of fitness						
Relaxation						
Rest/sleep						
Activities shared—with friends						
with family						
Consciously plans exercise/relaxation/rest						
Family						
Support of activities						
Family activities						
Understanding of exercise in weight						
management						
PSYCHOSOCIAL HEALTH						
Knowledge of:						
Emotional factors in weight management						
Cues to eat—internal						
external						
Impact on emotional health of:						
physical activity						
nourishment						
Responsibility for weight management						
Need to seek guidance for insoluble problems . . .						
Attitude						
Commitment to mental health						
Learning about weight control						
Solving problems						

Continued.

FIG. 10-2, cont'd.   For legend see opposite page.

PSYCHOSOCIAL HEALTH—cont'd	0	1	2	3	4	5
Behavior						
Pleasurable experiences						
Relationships—peers						
family						
teachers						
counselors						
School activities						
Social skills						
Intellect—insight						
communication						
problem solving						
school performance						
Goal setting—short term						
long term						
Self-rewards						
Emotional status						
Body image						
Self-efficacy						
Locus of control						
Depression vs. nondepression						
Sense of humor						
Oral gratification						
Coping skills						
Compulsivity						
Perfectionism						
Independence						
Parental support						
Perception of weight problem						
Support vs. intrusion—emotional						
financial						
Rigidity						
Conflict resolution						
Commitment to treatment						

FIG. 10-2, cont'd. For legend see page 236.

OBJECTIVE

Age _____ yr

Length of obesity	Infancy	Toddlerhood	Early childhood	Elementary school	Jr. high	Sr. high
Reduction attempts	Yo-yo	Severe	Diets	Exercise	None	Reasonable
	Anorexia nervosa	Bulimia nervosa				
Parents	Natural	Adoptive				
	Anorexia nervosa	Bulimia nervosa	Obesity	Overweight		
Grandparents	Natural	Adoptive				
	Anorexia nervosa	Bulimia nervosa	Obesity	Overweight		
Maturation stage	0	1	2	3	4	5
Menarche	0	+1 yr	+2 yr	+3 yr	+4 yr	+5 yr

Thyroid screen

Cholesterol (mg/dL) _____   HDL (mg/dL) _____   LDL (mg/dL) _____

Wt percentile*	>95	95	95-75	75	75-50	50
Ht percentile*	95	90	75	50	25	10
Wt/Ht percentile*	(100-50 lb) >95	(50-25 lb) >95	>95	95	95-75	75
BMI†						
TSF percentile‡	>95	95	95-75	75	75-50	50
SSF percentile (male)‡	>95	95	95-75	75	75-50	50
MAC percentile‡	>95	95	95-75	75	75-50	50
AMC percentile‡	>95	95	95-75	75	75-50	50

Waist circumference _____ in
Hips circumference _____ in
Waist/hip ratio _____

---

*National Center for Health Statistics: *Height and weight of youths 12-17 years*, United States. In Vital and health statistics, series 11, no 124, Health Services and Mental Health Administration, Washington, DC, 1973, US Government Printing Office. Above 75th percentile wt/ht/age/sex considered obese if TSF also greater than 75th percentile. Normal range includes 25th-75th percentile wt/ht/age/sex. From Mahan LK, Rees JM: *Nutrition in adolescence,* St Louis, 1984, Mosby – Year Book.
†Body Mass Index (kg/m^2). Standards in Hammer LD and others: Standardized percentile curves of body-mass index for children and adolescents, *Am J Dis Child* 145:259, 1991.
‡TSF triceps skinfold; SSF, subscapular skinfold; MAC, midarm circumference; AMA, arm muscle area. Standards in Frisancho AR: *Anthropometric standard for the assessment of growth and nutritional status,* Ann Arbor, 1990, University of Michigan Press.   *Continued.*

EXERCISE

HR to reach 120 beats/min	Slow walk	Moderate walk	Fast walk	Walk up hill	Walk/jog	Jog
Entry		+3 mo	+6 mo	+12 mo	+18 mo	+24 mo
Date ____		____	____	____	____	____

Weight ___ lb
- +10 _____
- + 5 _____
- − 2.5 _____
- − 5 _____
- −10 _____
- −15 _____

%BF§ ____
- + 3 _____
- + 2 _____
- − 2 _____
- − 5 _____

RHR‖ ____ beats/min
- + 5 _____
- + 3 _____
- − 3 _____
- − 5 _____

Height ____ in
- + 3 _____
- + 2 _____
- + 1 _____

AMA‡ ____ mm²
- +500 _____
- +200 _____
- +100 _____
- −100 _____
- −200 _____

From Rees JM: Management of obesity in adolescents. In Farrow JA, editor: Adolescent medicine, *Med Clin North Am* 74:1275, 1990.

‡TSF triceps skinfold; SSF, subscapular skinfold; MAC, midarm circumference; AMA, arm muscle area. Standards in Frisancho AR: *Anthropometric standard for the assessment of growth and nutritional status,* Ann Arbor, 1990, University of Michigan Press.

§Percent body fat

‖Resting heart rate

FIG. 10-2, cont'd.   For legend see page 236.

tudes and behaviors with appropriate rewards built in. It is especially necessary to build a program around short-term manageable goals related to behavioral change, since physiological factors may make actual weight loss a difficult, long-term achievement. The teenager should be made aware that over the long term, deficit will eventually lead to weight loss, however slowly. Working toward improved knowledge, attitudes, or behav-

[receipt obscures text]

```
HEALTH SCIENCES STORE    310/825-7721
WESTWOOD PLAZA LOS ANGELES, CA 90024

ALE              857211 02005 39575
        0200 09/15/93  04:04 PM

74319220305 4X4 QUAD
  1 @ 1/1.10                      1.10
800801665679
  NUTRITION IN IN
    1 @ 1/28.25                  28.25
           SUB TOTAL             29.35
           8.25% TAX              2.42
           TOTAL               $31.77
           CHECK                31.77
ACCT# / ID# / FORM#
  3255618
AUTH    9999

        IPV LN  31760  17806063

ASUCLA: STUDENTS HELPING STUDENTS
```

Factors

Strategies planned to deal with the physiological factors of obesity must be based on the laws of energy exchange and balance, address positive changes in personal food behaviors, avoid the dangers of "crash diets and life-threatening situations, and increase physical activity and fitness.[18]

Basic individual energy balance. Whatever the reasons are for a teenager's being overweight, the method for intervention remains the same: decreasing the body's energy intake and increasing the energy output until the appropriate deficit state is established. There is no way of knowing the exact use of energy by a particular body except by testing it over time. To lose weight an energy deficit must be achieved at the cellular level. Because this state is not measurable under normal clinical circumstances, there is no set formula that ensures weight loss. It is an error to count kcalories of food energy being eaten and assume that this amount of energy will be available within the biochemical system. Thus a deficit of 3500 kcalories calculated at the point of intake does not necessarily lead to a loss of 1 lb of body weight. This does not imply that the second law of thermodynamics is inoperative, but simply that energy from food may be used in a variety of ways once it is in the body, as indicated previously (Table 10-1). Thus both the physiological and the psychological aspects of weight management are unique to the individual.

Eating habits. Each individual teenager must be guided in learning the level of energy intake and output that produces weight gain, loss, and maintenance for that individual if the treatment is to be effective. An understanding of physiological factors must be incorporated. The teenager must be made aware that however bleak the physiological situation appears, the possibility of weight management has not been tested until the individual has control over energy intake and output. There is usually some potential for improvement in the diet that will help even those persons who are physiologically prone to obesity to become more fit and healthy and to stabilize and perhaps to reduce their weight in small amounts.

Dietary change. Strategies for dietary change must address the issues of (1) energy and nutrient content of the food intake; (2) circumstances of eating related to timing, place, accompanying social factors, and emotions; and (3) principles of nutrition regarding weight management.

Food use retraining. Specific diets have rarely achieved long-term changes in eating behavior. This result is especially true for teenagers, who tend to rebel against authoritarian techniques and hold a number of negative views about diets. Food use retraining, a series of habit changes planned jointly by the teenager and the therapist and instituted in succession over time, will be more acceptable to most adolescents and is a more realistic way to approach a complex problem.

Time factor. Because eating habits have been developed over a number of years, the teenager will need considerable time to make changes. A person cannot suddenly pick up a musical instrument and play it well but will need education, practice, and support to become proficient. Even so, most teenagers will not be able to learn a new food pattern or "diet" and perfect it immediately. Usually, intensive treatment will need to be continued for a year or more to accomplish major dietary changes. Breaking down the problem of food misuse into small components makes change more probable. What habit will be the initial focus, how change will be accomplished, what foods will be eaten, and what motivations and rewards will be effective are topics to be developed and clarified in counseling sessions between the therapist and the teenager.

Therapy objective. The nutritional therapist's objective is eventually to focus on each time of day and point of environment where teenagers meet with food and to help them to *retrain themselves* in the use of food. Most teenagers will have some reasonable habits that can be supported and used as a foundation for the emerging positive patterns.

Self-responsibility. Teenagers will need help at every stage to take responsibility for their actions. Coupled with psychological support, the process can lead to effective change. Even those who are unsuccessful in retraining themselves during the adolescent period will have a model for the future, when they may be able to take greater control. Education regarding the physiological factors of obesity will help teenagers avoid the harmful quick-loss plans to which they are so vulnerable.

Dangers of "crash" diets. An important component of programs in weight management education involves helping the teenager understand that rapid weight loss by either starvation or too low an energy intake is ineffective. Since the loss is in lean body mass and fluids, inevitably weight will be regained when usual eating is resumed and muscle (and the ability to use energy), not fat, will have been lost.[19] The deprivation in such a regimen often leads to even greater overeating. Thus the final result of a "crash" diet is often a net gain.[20] It is not difficult to convince those who have had the experience a few times that such practices are ineffective, but it is important to support their impressions by teaching them the physiological reasons. Teenagers who will not be convinced that such methods and "diet aids" are unhealthy will be deterred from using them by the knowledge that they will not lose fat.

Morbid obesity. There are certain life-threatening situations for very obese persons when drastic intervention will be necessary. The physical condition should be monitored to detect any rapid deterioration. The following conditions warrant hospitalization:

Sudden changes in cardiac or respiratory function

Inability to move, maintain balance, or travel

Rapid weight increase because of the above factors

Inability to fit into furniture and having to rest on the floor

Ulcerations at pressure points and friction areas

As with the anorectic teenager, a period of separation from the family may break up a pernicious cycle leading to physical deterioration.[21] Comprehensive treatment using a **modified fast** as the dietary component is at present the most practical therapy. Although it is still controversial whether lean body mass can be spared, such dietary methods appear less objectionable than other radical procedures.

Physical activity and fitness. One of the most important concepts of weight management is that energy output must be increased. Individualized exercise programs need to be developed with the obese teenager to achieve a gradual increase in physical activity. The fitness test shown in Chapter 9 is designed to be a conservative tool that can safely be used with even an extremely obese person. It can be used with or without professional help. Increasing activity can be rewarding in itself, whereas denying oneself an accustomed food may seem more like punishment. Besides fitness testing and improvement, various strategies can be directed toward increasing energy output by increasing physical activity. Activities should be (1) built into everyday life; (2) something the person enjoys or finds useful; (3) independent of help from others or complex equipment; and (4) nonstressful by not causing embarrassing exposure of the body or awkwardness.

Intervention Strategies: Psychological Factors

Weight management for teenagers should be a total rehabilitation program. It demands a significant length of time and must be individualized. Like the physiological component, the psychological component of any weight management problem cannot be overlooked. Activities planned to meet these needs include motivational support, psychotherapy, and counseling.[22-24]

Motivation. In a short-term situation where the teenager has only a few pounds to lose, the problem is one of motivation. This support can be provided in school settings and in many other community settings.

Psychotherapy. With extreme developmental obesity, changes usually require extensive psychotherapeutic intervention. This includes the family when the teenager is living at home.[25]

Counseling. For teenagers falling between these two extremes, a variable degree of supportive counseling will be needed to increase self-acceptance, to decrease stress, to facilitate development, and to enable adolescents to carry out weight management strategies. Teenagers need help in learning to experience the body's signals related to hunger and satiety and to adopt nondestructive coping mechanisms to replace the misuse of food.

Comprehensive Approach

To provide a comprehensive approach to a weight management program for teenagers, attention must be given to additional resources available. These resources include group activi-

BE SIZEWISE
Don't Lose Your Balance.

Nourishment	Activities	Feelings
Be good to your body—give it what it needs	Do interesting things—quiet as well as energetic	Learn to know and like yourself
Don't starve or stuff yourself	Take time to relax every day	Have realistic goals for yourself
Know what's in the food you eat	Don't let eating be your only recreation	Don't substitute food for love and companionship
	Do some strenuous activity every day	Build satisfying relationships with your family and friends
	Share active and quiet time with friends	Get help for problems you can't cope with alone

FIG. 10-3 Be sizewise—materials for clinicians, educators, and teenagers.
(From Rees JM and others: *Be size wise,* Seattle, 1979, American Heart Association of Washington.)

ties applied with professional guidance, parent education and counseling, and school and community support.

Group activities. Strategies such as camp settings, support groups, peer counseling, social skills and assertiveness training, body awareness experience, physical fitness training, and behavior modification can be used successfully with some individuals. Groups and preplanned programs will help those adolescents with mild, relatively simple problems. *Camps and other groups that provide for only short-term weight loss are detrimental and should be avoided.*

Professional guidance. No group setting provides a solution for all aspects of obesity. To be effective, weight management techniques must be applied within the context of ongoing supportive counseling by professionals who assess the specific problems of the individual over time and choose appropriate treatment methods. A team of professionals will be best able to carry out a comprehensive program as described here.

Parent education and counseling. Counseling will enable parents to support their teenagers in learning to manage weight. Education about the physiological factors involved and rational approaches to management will help dispel parents' myths. Helping them develop a nonintrusive attitude toward their teenagers is extremely important. The counselor can demonstrate this by stressing the need for the teenager, not the counselor or the parent, to establish his or her own goals.

School and community support. Although they are rarely in the position to carry out therapy because of the complexity of the problem, teachers, school counselors, nurses, coaches, and other community leaders have many opportunities to educate and support overweight teenagers. Curriculum materials such as those represented in Figure 10-3 have been designed to help adolescents understand the complexity of weight management.

Outcome

Reviews of the outcome of weight management therapies for teenagers are uniformly gloomy. In general, such programs are designed as studies of *weight loss* when informed workers in the field of adolescent health have stressed the importance of focusing on the other benefits of *weight management* programs such as increased self-esteem. Added knowledge, increased readiness to work for change, and improved practices are important outcomes of weight management programs for adolescents.

SUMMARY: EATING DISORDERS

The spectrum of eating disorders affects adolescents physically, psychologically, personally, and socially. Intervention strategies must be directed toward both the nutritional and the developmental aspects of these disorders for them to be effective. Goals must be established in relation to all aspects of eating disorders. Helping teenagers put food into reasonable perspective in their lives will be a principal goal of nutritional therapy. A recognition of the amount of time required for effective intervention is essential for a basic understanding of eating disorders.

✣ Athletics
NUTRITIONAL SUPPORT FOR ADOLESCENT ATHLETES

Adolescent athletes require nutritional support to maintain normal growth and physiological maturation in spite of physical stress. Energy is the basic factor here. The additional energy needed depends on the intensity, duration, and type of exercise and the size and state of development of the adolescent.

Source of Energy

Energy is best utilized if it is supplied as carbohydrates. The need for carbohydrate as fuel instead of protein to build muscle even for a teenager who is still growing is one of the most misunderstood principles among adolescent athletes.

Protein requirement. An additional intake of 6 to 7 gm of protein/day is sufficient in a muscle-building phase (during initial training). Thereafter, intakes of 2 to 3 gm of protein/day above the recommended daily allowance

(RDA) will support body maintenance in most athletes. Abnormally high levels of protein or amino acid supplements are counterproductive, leading to dehydration as the body rids itself of nitrogenous waste products.

Weight Management

Weight should be gained or lost following safe effective methods. To support normal growth successfully, weight should be maintained at an optimal level over the long term rather than be subjected to seasonal, or especially weekly, manipulation as is often urged by wrestling and crew coaches during competition. The development pattern of skeletal growth and weight gain must be considered. Two problems in this area are common among teenage athletes who become too thin in trying to reduce the percentage of body fat: (1) women interrupt their menses, and (2) men stunt their linear growth. **Anabolic steroids** taken by men to increase weight cause stunting of growth and disturbed development of secondary sex characteristics. Both males and females may increase the tendency to gain weight as fat if they repeatedly gain and lose weight rapidly through drastic dietary and related manipulation.[26,27]

Supplements

The increased dietary intake should provide sufficient amounts of vitamins and minerals, including the B vitamins essential in energy production.[28] Supplementation of nutrients in amounts above those recommended has not resulted in benefits during competition.

Iron Nutriture

Of the non-energy-producing nutrients, iron is particularly important to young athletes because "sports anemia" is associated with reduced oxygenation. There is some evidence that adolescents involved in athletics are more likely to become iron deficient than adolescents who are not athletes. The increased needs of both males and females during physical growth and development may impair their ability to maintain body stores when they engage in strenuous activity. Teenage athletes should be tested for iron deficiency before and during each season

and treated for any problem found. Other than consuming foods with enough iron to meet the RDA and taking supplements at that level if dietary sources are inadequate, teenagers are not advised to use additional iron on a routine basis.[17,29]

Anabolic Steroids

An estimated 5% to 10% of adolescents are using anabolic steroids. Use is greater among male athletes who say they use them to increase muscle, size, strength and speed and to improve personal appearance and athletic performance. Young people are using these substances without appropriate knowledge of the profound effects they have been found to have throughout the bodies of adults. Studies of the effects on adolescents are not available.

Dietary Issues for Adolescents in Competition

The science of managing food and drink to keep athletes healthy and in condition for competing is constantly advancing.[30,31] All teenagers who are participating in athletics, as well as their coaches and parents, need to know the latest principles of dietary intake with the following issues in mind as they apply to younger athletes.

Adequate fluids and electrolytes. Younger people are at greater risk for dehydration and heat illness than adults. They have a lower output of water from the sweat glands and lower cardiac output, resulting in less blood being carried to the skin to lower the core body temperature. Adolescents are especially at risk when they start strenuous workouts at the beginning of a season in an unconditioned state and when humidity as well as temperature is high.[32]

Appropriate balance between complex and simple carbohydrates during competition and training. Because adolescents are vulnerable to advertising and mythology repeated by others, they may follow unsound practices instead of using glucose and starches effectively. Teenagers may not take the time or realize the need to appropriately nourish their bodies for grueling, long-term sporting events.

Teenagers also do not clearly understand the need for sufficient but not excess fuel for short-term sporting events. The subtleties of balancing the various sources of simple and complex carbohydrates are especially important during these often anaerobic events because sufficient oxygen cannot be provided by the cardiorespiratory system without adequate fuel.

Because young teenagers may lack experience in choosing foods, they may not choose a meal of reasonable composition before competition and thus may impair their performance. Foods that should be eliminated are those with excess roughage or fats and gas-forming foods.

Long-term adequacy. Food intake must be balanced with energy output, but also with sufficient energy and nutrients to support growth and development. Total energy and calcium are especially important for normal skeletal development and maintenance.[33]

Support from Adults

Maintaining appropriate weight for height as the adolescent grows is a good general guide to dietary adequacy as long as the foods eaten to attain that weight are nutrient rich. Obtaining sufficient food may prove difficult for teenage athletes whose days are filled from early morning to late evening with practices as well as normal activities including classes and study assignments. Parents, coaches and school officials need to support teenagers by helping them plan specifically to obtain adequate acceptable foods at times when rigorous schedules allow them to eat.

✤Adolescent Pregnancy
DEVELOPMENTAL ISSUES

Teenage pregnancy must be studied in light of the highly dynamic nature of adolescence. Both the psychological and the physical status of the adolescent have implications for the course of any pregnancy. The many interactions of factors in adolescent development and reproduction have great clinical significance for all aspects of the pregnancy including nutrition.[34]

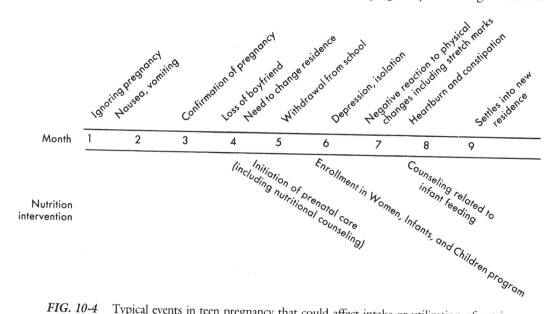

FIG. 10-4 Typical events in teen pregnancy that could affect intake or utilization of nutrients.

(From Rees JM, Worthington-Roberts BS: *Adolescence, nutrition and pregnancy: interrelationships.* Copyright Mahan LK, Rees JM: Seattle, Wash, 1989. Originally published in Mahan LK, Rees JM: *Nutrition in adolescence,* St Louis, 1984, Mosby–Year Book.)

Indeed, adolescents are changing so profoundly that pregnancy for the younger, less mature teenager will be different than for the older, more mature adolescent.

Less mature teenagers will be more dependent on others and less able to act and make decisions on their own. They will be more **narcissistic** and less able to comprehend the needs of others. These young women will be less realistic, engage in more fantasy and wishful thinking, and have less insight into their own behaviors and motives. In general, younger teenagers will have fewer intellectual and physical skills to be able to cope with any situation, especially a complex reproductive experience. Many of the difficulties related to pregnancy in adolescence stem from this immaturity. As development advances, a person is able to carry out reproduction and child-rearing in a more normal, less problem-fraught way. As shown in Figure 10-4, the timeline of events in teenage pregnancy has great potential for affecting the nutritional well-being of the adolescent.

✥Reproduction During Adolescence

The pregnant adolescent's nutritional needs are influenced by many factors. Primary influences are her growth and nutrient stores, her gynecological age, and her nutritional status at conception.

ADOLESCENT GROWTH AND NUTRIENT STORES

The assumption that pregnant adolescents need an additional supply of nutrients to support their own growth plus that of the growing fetus has been questioned. Because hormone levels are high in pregnancy, even the slower statural growth that usually follows menarche may not occur. According to recent studies, growth does continue to some degree during adolescent pregnancy.[35,36] Whether or not actual growth continues for an adolescent who becomes pregnant, she will have experienced rapid growth more recently than her adult counterparts. There will have been less opportunity for storage of nutrients. Thus there may be greater physiological risk to young women who conceive in the early years after the onset of menses.

GYNECOLOGICAL AGE

The number of years between the onset of menses and conception is calculated to determine gynecological age. Those adolescents who are more sexually mature, that is, of greater gynecological age, share a vulnerability to physiological stresses but appear to have no more physically based complications during pregnancy than adult women. It is the young women of lower gynecological age who carry more risk and need more nutritional support. The number of adolescents who become pregnant in the first 2 years following menarche will be relatively small because most of them will not be ovulating during that time, although they are menstruating. Those who do become pregnant, however, are of great concern to clinicians and researchers.

NUTRITIONAL STATUS AT CONCEPTION

Pregnant adolescents who are of young gynecological age and are malnourished at the time of conception are at double risk. They appear to have the greatest need for nutrients to support a pregnancy and maintain optimal health themselves.[36]

HAZARDS TO THE MOTHER

Given the complexity of pregnancy in the adolescent period, it is logical to question how these young women fare during pregnancy. They have more complications, a higher risk of maternal mortality, and more problems in personal psychological development and education that carry long-term implications for economic well-being.

Complications

The variety of complications often described for the teenage mother during gestation includes:

First and third trimester bleeding
Anemia
Difficult labor and delivery
Cephalopelvic disproportion
Pregnancy-induced hypertensive disorders including preeclampsia and eclampsia
Infections

Of these complications, the most common physical problem is infection, while the most serious problem nature is preeclampsia, which usually manifests itself in the third trimester by increased weight gain, fluid retention, high blood pressure, and proteinuria and does not appear to run a different course in pregnant teenagers than in older women. Some researchers point out that it is a disease of first pregnancies. In addition, the harmful effects of preeclampsia, or the more serious state of eclampsia, may be greater in teenagers. Damage to the cardiovascular and renal systems initiated with a first pregnancy early in life and intensified by insults such as other pregnancies can increase the risk of developing renal and cardiovascular problems with increasing age.

Maternal Mortality

The serious risk of maternal mortality is also a problem. The rate is $2\frac{1}{2}$ times greater for mothers under 15 years of age than for those 20 to 24 years of age.

Effect on Normal Developmental Steps

Apart from the physical sequelae, pregnancy often affects teenagers' psychological development, education, and ability to gain economic independence. Clearly these developmental steps are difficult to achieve in any case, and for many adolescents pregnancy is not a cause of failure but a coinciding event. The situations responsible for early pregnancy often remain unresolved, and many teenage mothers have additional pregnancies before the adolescent years are over.

HAZARDS TO THE INFANT

Infants born to teenage mothers suffer a higher incidence of morbidity and mortality in the perinatal period than do infants of older mothers. Problems seen more frequently include[37]:

Prematurity
Stillbirth
Low birth weight (LBW), the major hazard in adolescent pregnancy
Perinatal and infant deaths
Physical deformities

It is difficult to compare the likelihood of these problems occurring in infants born to teenage versus older mothers, or to younger versus older teenage mothers, but it is generally agreed that the problems do occur in a considerable number of teenage pregnancies. For example, the incidence of LBW is far greater when the mothers are adolescents.

WEIGHT GAIN
Specific Requirements

There is evidence that adolescents need to gain substantial weight during gestation to deliver optimal weight infants. Their infants will be somewhat smaller than the infants born to adults with the same gestational weight gain.[38,39] For example, when adolescents gain 26-35 lbs, the incidence of LBW (under 2500 gm) is 6.3%, equivalent to the incidence for adult women who have gained 21 to 25 pounds.[40] The incidences of fetal mortality and morbidity are thus linked to weight gain because they are linked to LBW.

TABLE 10-2   *Approximate 9-Month Increments in Weight of Postmenarcheal Women*

Postmenarcheal Year	Pounds	Kilograms
1	8	3.45
2	5	2.0
3	2	.90
4 and 5	1.32	.60

Modified from Frisch RE: *Hum Biol* 48:353, 1976.
In Rees JM, Worthington-Roberts BS: *Adolescence, nutrition and pregnancy: interrelationships.* Copyright in Mahan LK, Rees JM: Seattle, Wash, 1989. Originally published in Mahan LK, Rees JM: *Nutrition in adolescence,* St Louis, 1984, Mosby–Year Book.

The continuing growth and development of the adolescent may account for the extra weight that is needed. Table 10-2 shows the amount of weight a young woman could be expected to gain in the 9-month period corresponding to her gynecological age if she were not pregnant. That amount plus the amount she would have to gain to be normal weight for her height and age if she is underweight probably constitute the extra amount she will gain in pregnancy.[41] Some authors refute this idea, theorizing (1) that teenagers may retain extra weight following delivery if they gain more than adults, and (2) that the teenagers' infants may be small in a natural adaptation to the less mature maternal biological state of the adolescent, and therefore not at risk simply because their birth weights are lower.[42,43] Many questions about the gestational weight gain of adolescents remain to be answered by future research. For example:

Is delivery of an infant weighing 3000 to 4000 gm between 39 and 41 weeks' gestation an optimal outcome for adolescents as well as adults?

Is weight gain controlled by the biological makeup in adolescence so it is not possible for a young woman to gain more weight even if it is well known that achieving a certain range of weight gain would allow her to deliver an optimal weight infant?

If adolescent mothers retain larger amounts of body fat as a result of gaining at a higher rate than adult women, is the adverse effect to the mother of potentially retaining 5 extra pounds (for example) more serious than the actual risk to an infant born at a lower than optimal birth weight after a pregnancy during which the adolescent mother gained less than optimal weight?

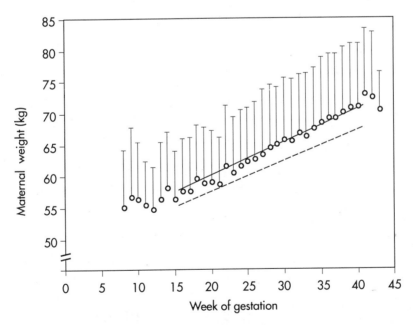

FIG. 10-5 Rate of weight gain of adolescent mothers of 3000-4000 gm (———) and <3000 gm (– – – –) infants described by regression statistics from 15 to 40 weeks' gestation (n of week 8 to 15 and after 40 too small to include in analysis). Means of weekly weight measures are shown for the total study population (o) and standard deviation (T). Symbols represent 6 to 313 measures at a given week.

(From Rees JM and others: *Am J Clin Nutr*, in press, 1992.)

Rate of Gain

Provisional recommendations in the 1990 Institute of Medicine Report are that women gain at the following rates in the last two trimesters of pregnancy, depending on their prepregnant weight status[44]:

.361 to .529 (.440 average) kg/wk if normal weight

.386 to .588 (.490 average) kg/wk if underweight

.218 to .386 (.300 average) kg/wk if overweight

Further, it was suggested that adolescents gain at the upper portion of these ranges. The report stated, however, that there was insufficient evidence to make separate recommendations for teenage mothers.

In the meantime, data are accumulating to show that the rate of gain by adolescents in the final trimesters of pregnancy is, on average, above .500 kg/wk. In one study a multiethnic group of adolescents who delivered term infants with a mean birth weight of 3258 gm (calculated from data given) gained at the rate of .505 to .531 kg/wk (50th percentile) during the last 18 weeks.[45] Weight gain at the rate of .692 to .893 kg/wk represents the 75th percentile. Of term infants delivered following relatively uncomplicated pregnancies, 5% weighed under 2500 gm, putting them in the category of high risk. To decrease the number of infants weighing less than optimal, the average rate would have to be greater.

In another study the mean rate of gain during the second and third trimesters of mothers delivering normal weight (3000 to 4000 gm), term infants was .588 kg/wk, while mothers of less than 3000 gm infants gained at the rate of .510 kg/wk in the same period (Figure 10-5).[46] The mean rate of gain for adolescents to bear infants weighing close to 3500 gm would appear to be about .588 kg/wk.

In summary, the evidence does not suggest restricting the natural gain of adolescents to levels recommended for adults. The upper and lower limits of optimal weight gain still need to be established to guide young women who find it difficult to gain at a reasonable rate.

MONITORING WEIGHT IN PRENATAL CARE

In both studies described above, the rates of gain were observed during prenatal care, rather than from the mother's report of what she weighed when she conceived. Keeping track of weekly weight gains is an effective way to evaluate the progress of adolescents during pregnancy.

In addition, measuring triceps skinfolds indicates adequacy of initial stored energy while changes have been related in later pregnancy to infant birth weight (Figure 10-6).[47]

ASSESSMENT AND MANAGEMENT OF NUTRITION

Risk Factors

So that nutrition services can be provided efficiently and effectively, pregnant teenage clients should be screened for those risk factors most closely linked to poor outcomes. Significant factors include:

Low gynecological age

Low prepregnancy weight for height or other significant evidence of malnutrition

Low pregnancy weight gain

Infections during pregnancy

Excessive pregnancy weight gain

Excessive weight for height at conception

Anemia

Other risk factors gathered from history include:

Unhealthy life-style (including use of tobacco, drugs, and alcohol)

Unfavorable reproductive history

Chronic diseases or eating disorders

Overall assessment of nutritional status of the pregnant teenager follows more or less the general pattern for nutritional assessment of all pregnant women.

Nutrient Needs

A summary of recommended amounts of nutrients is provided in Table 10-3. It combines the allowance for pregnancy in adult women with the amounts recommended for nonpregnant adolescents. A clinically practical way of ensuring nutrient adequacy is to encourage the

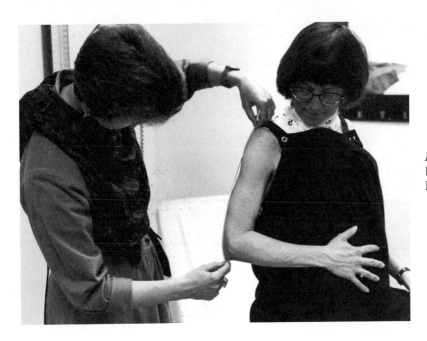

FIG. 10-6 Monitoring body composition of adolescent during prenatal care.

TABLE 10-3   *Recommended Dietary Allowances for Pregnant Adolescent Females*

Nutrient	Age (Reference Height)			
	11-14 Years (157 cm)		15-18 Years (163 cm)	
	Total RDA	RDA/cm	Total RDA	RDA/cm
Energy (kcal)*	2500	15.9	2500	15.3
Protein (gm)	56	0.38	54	0.36
Calcium (mg)	1200	7.6	1200	7.4
Phosphorus (mg)	1200	7.6	1200	7.4
Iron (mg)	30	0.19	30	0.18
Magnesium (mg)	300	2.0	320	2.1
Iodine (μg)	175	1.1	175	1.1
Zinc (mg)	15	0.09	15	0.09
Vitamin A (μg RE)	800	5.1	800	4.9
Vitamin D (μg)	10	0.06	10	0.06
Vitamin E (mg α-TE)	10	0.06	10	0.06
Ascorbic acid (mg)	60	0.38	70	0.43
Niacin (mg NE)	17	0.11	17	0.10
Riboflavin (mg)	1.6	0.01	1.6	0.01
Thiamin (mg)	1.5	0.01	1.5	0.01
Folate (μg)	400	2.3	400	2.5
Vitamin B_6 (mg)	2.0	0.01	2.1	0.01
Vitamin B_{12} (μg)	2.2	0.01	2.2	0.01

Data modified from Food and Nutrition Board, National Research Council: Recommended dietary allowances, ed. 10, Washington, DC, 1989, National Academy of Sciences.
Modified from Rees JM, Worthington-Roberts BS: *Adolescence, nutrition and pregnancy: interrelationships.* Copyright Mahan LK, Rees JM: Seattle, Wash, 1989. Originally published in Mahan LK, Rees JM: *Nutrition in adolescence,* St Louis, 1984, Mosby–Year Book.
*Second and third trimester.

pregnant adolescent to gain the recommended amount of weight by consuming nutrient-rich foods. Sources of protein, calcium, iron, micronutrients, and dietary fiber are also important. The box on page 252 shows warning signs that a pregnant adolescent may demonstrate when having nutritional problems.

Contact with health professionals during prenatal care provides many important opportunities to teach adolescents about feeding themselves and their families. A clinical protocol for nutritional management of adolescent pregnancy is provided here (see box on page 253).

Economic and Psychosocial Needs

The economic instability of pregnant adolescents makes it impossible to assume that they will have an adequate food supply. The impact of life-style, economics, and other stressful issues on the nutritional well-being of young pregnant women is great and must be acknowledged in any program to improve their nutritional status.[48,49] A summary of these issues is provided here (see box on page 254). Above all, the stage of social and emotional development will determine the mother's ability to cope with all aspects of reproduction.

WARNING SIGNS OF NUTRITION PROBLEMS IN PREGNANT ADOLESCENTS

* ***Medical/obstetrical factors***
Adolescent with a gynecological age (chronological age minus age at menarche) of <3
A previous pregnancy
History of poor obstetrical or fetal performance
Chronic systemic disease
Past or present eating disorder: anorexia nervosa or bulimia nervosa
Underweight or overweight before pregnancy
Inadequate weight gain during pregnancy
Excessive weight gain during pregnancy
Persistent nausea or vomiting during pregnancy
Iron deficiency anemia or other nutritional deficiencies
Infections during pregnancy
Heavy smoker
Alcohol or drug use

* ***Nutrition/dietary factors***
Inadequate refrigeration or cooking facilities
Lack of transportation or accessibility to grocery store
Cultural or religious dietary restrictions
Frequent eating away from home
Frequent snacking
Poor appetite
Limited, monotonous, or highly processed diet
Irregular meal patterns (skipping meals)
History of frequent dieting
Exclusion of a major food group(s)
Binge eating episodes
Eating of nonfood substances (pica)
Nontraditional dietary pattern (e.g., vegetarianism)
Overuse of nutritional supplements
Heavy caffeine intake

* ***Psychosocial factors***
Inadequate income
Living alone or in an unstable family or other environment
Little family or peer support
Denial or failure to accept the pregnancy
Significant emotional stress or depression

From Story M: *Nutrition assessment of pregnant adolescents.* In Story M, editor: *Nutrition management of the pregnant adolescent: a practical reference guide.* Arlington, Va, 1990, National Center for Education in Maternal Child Health US Department of Health and Human Services.

PROTOCOL FOR ASSESSMENT AND MANAGEMENT OF NORMAL TEENAGE PREGNANCY

• *Initial evaluation (if possible)*

Review intake material, social and life-style history

Review clinical data
    Height and weight
    Gynecological age
    Physical signs of health
    Expected delivery date

Review laboratory data
    Hematocrit or hemoglobin
    Urinalysis

Begin to build relationship with the client (and partner if available)

Assess clients' perspective of nutrition issues

Assess attitude about, and acceptance of, prepregnancy with and feelings about weight gain during pregnancy

Assess intake patterns using dietary methodology best suited to client and professional

Make preliminary assessment of food resources and refer to supportive agencies if necessary

Check for nausea and vomiting and suggest possible remedy

Discuss supplemental vitamins and minerals

Make initial plan that sets priorities for issues

Come to agreement with patient about any initial changes and steps to take; have client state plan as she perceives it

Determine client understanding of relation between nutrition and health

Do initial anthropometrics, calculate reasonable weight gain

• *Second visit*

Check on referrals to other agencies

Discuss results of initial evaluation and suggest any changes necessary in dietary patterns (use printed materials as appropriate)

Do any further investigations when necessary

Perform laboratory studies
    Specific diagnosis of anemia
    Protoporphyrin heme or serum ferritin
    Serum or red cell folate

Serum vitamin B_{12}

Further probing of dietary habits if necessary

Monitor weight gain; discuss projected weight gain for following visit and total for gestation

Assess and address issues affecting nutritional status in order of priority for the individual
    Activity level
    Appetite changes
    Pica, food cravings, and aversions
    Allergies/food intolerances
    Supplementation practices (prescribed and self-selected)

• *Subsequent visits*

Monitor and support appropriate weight gain: include discussion of fitness and encourage habitual safe exercise

Support upgrade in nutritional pattern in support of the woman and the developing infant; augment knowledge of principles of nutrition; continue to address issues affecting nutritional status

Check for heartburn, small food intake capacity, and elimination problems; suggest dietary interventions

Begin preliminary discussion and comparison of advantages/disadvantages of breast feeding and formula feeding

• *Final prenatal visit(s)*

Discuss infant feeding if client will keep infant

If breast-feeding is chosen, provide preliminary guidance about breast-feeding practices

If formula-feeding is chosen, discuss product selection and preparation; define important details about feeding techniques

• *Postpartum visits*

Help client understand safe methods of managing weight following delivery

Review infant feeding practices and infant growth; provide assistance when problems are identified

Modified from Rees JM, Worthington-Roberts BS: *Adolescence, nutrition and pregnancy: interrelationships.* Copyright Mahan LK, Rees JM: Seattle, Wash, 1989. Originally published in Mahan LK, Rees JM: *Nutrition in adolescence,* St Louis, 1984, Mosby–Year Book.

ISSUES IN ADOLESCENT PREGNANCY THAT INFLUENCE NUTRITIONAL WELL-BEING

• *Acceptance of the pregnancy*
Desire to carry out successful pregnancy
Acceptance of responsibility (even if child is to be relinquished)
Clarification of identity as mother separate from her own mother
Realistic acceptance versus fantasy and idealization
• *Food resources*
Family meals (timing, quantity, quality, responsibility)
Self-reliance
School lunch
Fast-food outlets
Socially related eating
Food assistance (WIC program and others)
Mobilization of all resources
• *Body image*
Degree of acceptance of an adult body
Maturity in facing bodily changes throughout pregnancy
• *Living situation*
Acceptance by living partners and extended family
Role expectations of living partners
Financial support
Facilities and resources
Ethnic group (religious, cultural, and social patterns)
Emancipation vs. dependency
Support system vs. isolation
• *Relationship with the child's father*
Presence or absence of father
Quality of relationship
Influence on decision making
Contribution to resources
Influence on mother's nutritional habits and general life-style
Understanding of physiological processes
Tolerance of physical changes in pregnancy and physical needs of mother and child
Influence on child feeding

• *Peer relationships*
Support from friends
Influence on nutritional knowledge and attitudes
Influence on general life-style
• *Nutritional state*
Weight-for-height proportion
Maturational state
Tissue stores of nutrients
Reproductive and contraceptive history
Physical health
History of dietary patterns and nutritional status, including weight-losing schemes
Present eating habits
Complications of pregnancy (nausea and vomiting)
Substance use
Activity patterns
Need for intensive remediation
• *Prenatal care*
Initiation of and compliance with prenatal care
Dependability of supporting resources
Identification of risk factors
• *Nutritional attitude and knowledge*
Prior attitude toward nutrition
Understanding of role of nutrition in pregnancy
Knowledge of foods as sources of nutrients and of nutrients needed by the body
Desire to obtain adequate nutrition
Ability to obtain adequate nutrition and to control food supply
• *Preparation for child feeding*
Knowledge of child-feeding practices
Attitude and decisions about child feeding
Responsibility for feeding
Understanding the importance of the bonding process
Support from family and friends

From Rees JM, Worthington-Roberts BS: *Adolescence, nutrition and pregnancy: interrelationships.* Copyright Mahan LK, Rees JM: Seattle, Wash, 1989. Originally published in Mahan LK, Rees JM: *Nutrition in adolescence,* St Louis, 1984, Mosby–Year Book.

Involving the Baby's Father

When the partner of the young pregnant woman is available, he should be included in counseling sessions to build mutual nutritional support for the pregnancy. Specific outreach to the father of the baby can be beneficial.[50] If he is employed or in school, an effort should be made by the counselor to see him at least occasionally. This effort will be especially important if for some reason he is interfering with the young woman's ability to nourish herself. Sharing what is known about the father's contribution to the outcome of pregnancy helps some adolescent males become more interested in maintaining healthy living habits.

Individualized Counseling

To be effective, the clinician must work within the context of an individualized counseling relationship with the young pregnant adolescent and her partner.[51] The counselor will not "prescribe," but will make practical suggestions and give support to help the teenager change her habits, usually in small increments throughout the pregnancy.

Benefits of Nutrition Counseling

The benefits of nutrition counseling will be seen more in the long term than in a particular pregnancy. Prenatal care is one of the best opportunities to teach a vulnerable group of teenagers sound nutritional information. Even if they seek care later in pregnancy and miss appointments, for most of them these contacts constitute the greatest input of health care during their adolescence.

Effective Counseling Strategies

Helping pregnant adolescents follow the suggested rate of gain can ensure sufficient energy intake to support the pregnancy and the mother's own developmental needs. Following the guidelines demonstrates dramatically in a few months the possibility of exerting personal control over eating, as well as the effect on both weight and nutritional status, in a way the teenager can understand. There is great appeal in discussing with adolescents the effects of various events on their bodies and on the growing fetus. Learning about the physiological needs of both her own body and her developing infant can be the teenager's impetus for upgrading the quality of her diet to keep pace with the increase in energy intake needed to support adequate weight gain. Repeated counseling sessions to review those needs may motivate the young mother to try new foods to obtain additional sources of nutrients. Attention to nutritional health in the prenatal period can become a model for taking responsibility for feeding a family. The young woman can gain experience in the use of community resources to obtain food for herself and her family.

In summary, nutrition counseling in prenatal care for teenagers can accomplish the following goals:

1. Serve as a model for exerting control over what a person eats with visible results in terms of the optimal weight gain pattern and the quality of foods contributing to it.
2. Be an impetus for trying new foods.
3. Serve as a model for taking responsibility and using community resources to feed a family.

The nutrition counselor will be most effective when working within a clinical program designed especially for adolescents. Such programs have been shown to improve overall outcome in adolescent pregnancy.[37]

✤ Nutritional Counseling for Adolescents
FACILITATING CHANGE

Attempts to help adolescents improve their nutritional status must be approached with skill, especially because of their growing independence. Nutrition counselors must know adolescents' physical and psychological development, life-styles, and habits as well as appropriate methods of communicating with the adolescents.[51]

Strategies for Change

Sophisticated strategies to add knowledge, alter attitudes, and change behavior must be used in any setting if the objective is to influence an adolescent's eating habits.[52] Providing knowledge or teaching can be done in a variety of settings from the classroom to the hospital bedside. Altering attitudes is much more difficult and usually demands an individualized experience. Facilitating the adoption of new behavior is even more difficult and requires a lengthy period of time. The adolescent will have to feel positive about any plan before it can succeed. In fact, much effort must be directed toward encouraging the person to want to change before introducing steps to bring about the change.

Personalized counseling. Besides changes in attitude, the counselor must impart knowledge in an especially meaningful and individualized manner. Finally, behavior change can be approached in increments that are sufficiently realistic to ensure personal success.[53]

Nutritional counseling, unlike nutrition education activities or specific dietary teaching techniques, is based on a continuing interactive relationship between counselor and client. The mutual goal for the relationship is improvement of the adolescent's nutritional well-being. This relationship has been characterized as one of mutual participation, as opposed to the activity-passivity relationship seen in acute care or guidance-cooperation model, which usually is used with younger children.[54] The way in which a message is presented is as important as the message itself.

Nature of counseling process. The counseling process is a specialized conversation that has a specific purpose and takes place within a relationship.[55] The professional will be primarily responsible for guiding the process so that the mutual goals are met. It can never be a unilateral responsibility, however, but must be shared by the adolescent client. In fact, the professional will need to help clients feel a responsibility for contributing if they do not do so spontaneously. In these conversations the purposes will be to obtain information about the client, to provide information to the client, and to stimulate the client to take action.

Content vs. process. The exchanges in counseling can be divided into the content (the information exchanged) and the process (the way the exchange takes place).[56,57] The content that is brought forth for discussion by adolescents consists of what they want to talk about, what they are concerned about, and in some situations, irrelevant material used to avoid focusing on problems. It ultimately will be the responsibility of the counselor to guide them in presenting material that contributes to the overall goals of counseling. The counselor will also be responsible for bringing in content that is suited to the client's needs in terms of quantity, type, and level of understanding.

The process on the adolescents' part is made up of their attitude toward the discussion, the way they express themselves, and their emotional response to the counseling session. The counselor's expression (beginning from the first meeting with the client in the waiting room or at the bedside), verbal and nonverbal reinforcement of the client's responses, and overall guidance of the session constitute the counselor's contributions to the process. Examples of the content of a nutritional counseling session would include information from the client about his or her eating habits and recommendations from the counselor about changes that need to be made. The process would include the way the client described his or her eating patterns and the kind of approach the counselor took in securing the information and in suggesting changes following an evaluation.

Both the content and process of counseling exchanges contribute to the results of a therapeutic relationship. When the approach of the clinician is overly authoritarian, a working relationship becomes impossible. The other extreme is the relationship that builds rapport on irrelevancies but fails to deal with difficult issues.

Obtaining and providing information are relatively common processes, and it is easy to conceive of how this is done in counseling. Stimulating a client to take action by means of a conversation, however, is a much more complex process to visualize and to accomplish than that of obtaining information. The following are descriptions of accomplishments in counseling that lead to change on the part of the client:

> ❖
> ## STRATEGIES FOR FOSTERING CLIENT DIGNITY
>
> Address the client's presenting agenda.
> Provide information so that a structure can be developed that will encourage and support an honest, mutual interaction.
> Assess and respect the client's coping style (e.g., What is her behavior telling you? Is she withdrawn? Talkative? A caretaker? Childlike? Mature beyond her years?).
> Allow the client choices whenever possible so that she can feel she is making her own decisions.
> Normalize variations in feeling and mood so that the client does not fear or harshly judge the changes in her emotions since pregnancy.
> Provide words for feelings.
> Provide education about physical and emotional aspects of pregnancy so that the client has a simple base of knowledge from which to participate in her pregnancy.
> Reinforce adult (not childlike) behaviors.
> Focus on her positive attributes to foster self-esteem and positive coping.
> Draw out positive coping by recognizing and complimenting coping behaviors that are obviously functional and healthy.
> Focus away from pathology and avoid unhelpful commiseration so that you will represent a person who can remain a neutral mirror for her.
> Proceed at a pace that is comfortable for the client.

From Reynolds S, Faulkner P: *Interviewing and counseling skills.* In Story M, editor: *Nutrition management of the pregnant adolescent: a practical reference guide,* Washington, DC, 1990, National Center Education Maternal Child Health.

Increasing self-awareness
Realizing existence of alternatives
Problem solving
Experiencing positive communication style
Experiencing control over one's life
Building self-esteem

Building self-esteem. Adolescents must believe that they are worthy individuals so that they may find the energy to make changes in their lives. The box above describes some of the specific methods nutritionists use to foster self-esteem in encounters they have with adolescents.

Role of parents. Parents must be appropriately involved in the counseling process. They need help in being supportive, as opposed to being intrusive, as the adolescent makes changes. Both adolescents and their parents must be helped to see the importance of focusing on the process of making change rather than solely on the desired goal of self-care. An understanding of both the physical and social

sciences, along with a liberal injection of art, is needed in nutrition counseling for adolescents and their parents. It is indeed a challenging field.

Common problems in counseling. Health care professionals must often overcome a lack of training in counseling techniques. Some of the common pitfalls that indicate a need for improved skills are listed below:

Setting inappropriate goals
Communicating in overly authoritarian style
Losing the adolescent's attention
Being deterred by the adolescent's defenses
Losing control and therefore losing credibility
Being confused over the direction counseling should take
Failing to treat the adolescent as an individual

Preparation for counseling. By constantly improving skills, a counselor will be more effective in a greater variety of settings. Resourc-

❖

ADAPTATIONS TO COUNSELING IN UNDESIRABLE SETTINGS

Verbally acknowledge and apologize for the inconvenience, reassuring the adolescent of your concern for her.

Reschedule the appointment if conditions might be better another day.

Acknowledge your own feeling of anger, frustration, anxiety, or tension elicited by the situation, and be aware that the adolescent may feel similarly.

Consider going for a walk or sitting outside to conduct the counseling session.

When time is inadequate, prepare in advance and prioritize needs:

Review the chart and previous "progress notes" (if available) before the meeting.

Have available at the meeting any materials that might be useful.

If there are no immediate or obvious needs, allow her to use the time as she wants (e.g., ask if she has any particular questions or concerns that she'd like to discuss).

If permissible, display in the lobby or examination room posters that might be appealing and informative to pregnant adolescents.

From Reynolds S, Faulkner P: *Interviewing and counseling skills.* In Story M, editor: *Nutrition management of the pregnant adolescent: a practical reference guide,* Washington, DC, 1990, National Center Education Maternal Child Health.

es for improving counseling skills are listed below:

Classes
Workshops
Experience
Observation of others
Working with other disciplines
Reading
Self-monitoring
    Video or audio
    Client surveys
Feedback from colleagues
Assessing clinical outcome
Self-assessment

Counseling environment. Adolescents will often need to be counseled in their own environment, whether that be in a school, a mall, or a community-based clinic.

The box above provides suggestions for making adolescents feel comfortable in any setting.[52] Taking a walk with a teenager or inviting the teenager to share some other activity often puts him or her more at ease than sitting face to face with a counselor (Figure 10-7). An adolescent who has had little experience conversing with adults will often be more verbal when he or she can move freely.

FIG. 10-7   Nutritional counseling in out-of-doors environment can be effective.

(From Rees JM: *Nutritional counseling in adolescence.* Copyright Mahan LK, Rees JM: Seattle, Wash, 1989. Originally published in Mahan LK, Rees JM: *Nutrition in adolescence,* St Louis, 1984, Mosby–Year Book.)

TABLE 10-4 *Suggested Members of Health Care Team to Guide Adolescents in Issues Arising in Pregnancy*

Issues	Obstetrician	Adolescent Medical Specialist	Nurse	Nutritionist	Social Worker	Psychologist
General health and planning of continuous care		X	X	X	X	
Complications of pregnancy	X	X	X	X		
Labor and delivery preparation	X	X	X			
School program					X	X
Economic resources			X		X	
Substance abuse (cessation and education)		X	X	X	X	X
Psychological adjustment and stress	X	X	X	X	X	X
Developmental delay			X		X	X
Infant-care education		X	X	X		
Relinquishment counseling			X		X	X
Nutritional care		X	X	X		
Education		X	X	X		
Resource coordination			X	X	X	
Family or marital conflict					X	X

From Rees JM: *Nutritional counseling in adolescence.* In Mahan LK, Rees JM: *Nutrition in adolescence,* St Louis, 1984, Mosby–Year Book.

✥The Health Care Team

Adolescent health care is one of the most demanding of clinical problems. As such, it is best handled as a team effort. Any one professional will generally not possess the skills to meet all the client's needs. Table 10-4 lists some of the types of issues that will arise throughout the course of teenage pregnancies with a suggested list of professionals to guide clients in managing these issues. This does not mean that certain problems are the responsibility of any one profession to the exclusion of others. Each professional team member can support the messages and guidance provided by other team members. Team conferences aid in coordination of care and team efficiency in meeting identified needs and noting the client's progress in solving various problems. Nutritionists and other professionals who are in positions to influence program planning can help develop clinical teams for care of adolescents.

Working with a team requires specialized skill. Team members bring their backgrounds, both professional and personal, with them. These characteristics determine how that professional will carry out a role on a team. The structure of the team, which may be any one of

Structure	Communication pathways	Best serves
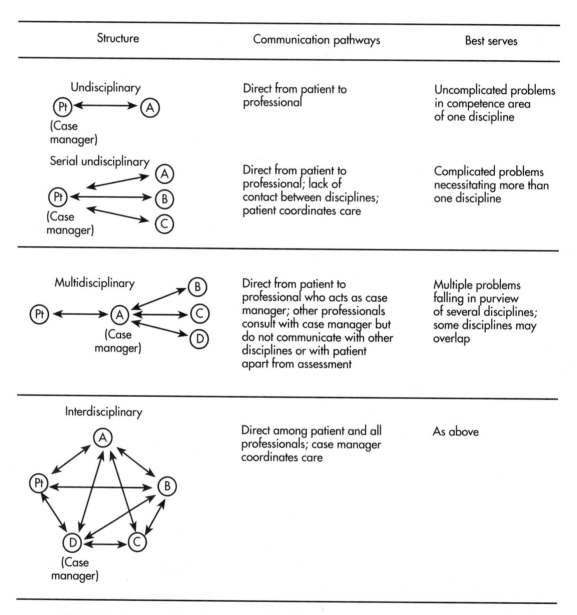	Direct from patient to professional	Uncomplicated problems in competence area of one discipline
	Direct from patient to professional; lack of contact between disciplines; patient coordinates care	Complicated problems necessitating more than one discipline
	Direct from patient to professional who acts as case manager; other professionals consult with case manager but do not communicate with other disciplines or with patient apart from assessment	Multiple problems falling in purview of several disciplines; some disciplines may overlap
	Direct among patient and all professionals; case manager coordinates care	As above

FIG. 10-8 Structure of health care teams. *Pt,* Patient; *A, B, C, D,* health care specialists of various disciplines.

(From Rees JM: *Nutritional counseling in adolescence.* In Mahan LK, Rees JM: *Nutrition in adolescence,* St Louis, 1984, Mosby–Year Book.)

those in Figure 10-8, will affect their work in a basic fashion. Structure determines communication patterns between professionals and between professionals and clients. Interrelationships between team members are complex and must be carefully developed by clinicians who are highly motivated to work together. The reward will be seen in improved comprehensive care for adolescents with complex problems.

Summary

In the context of rapid physical and psychological growth during adolescence, appropriate nourishment cannot be taken for granted. Extrapolations cannot always be made from the known requirements of adults or children. There will be specific nutritional objectives in each of the special circumstances of adolescent life.

In dealing with a client with an eating disorder, the overall objective is to help the individual put the eating function into proper perspective. The athlete must obtain sufficient nourishment to support a growing body that is subjected to stress. If a pregnancy should occur, the adolescent will need support in nourishing herself and her developing infant during a chaotic time. While a great deal is still unknown about nutritional needs of adolescents, the growing interest in this age group should stimulate the research necessary to close gaps in our knowledge.

REVIEW QUESTIONS

1. Discuss the commonalities and differences of specifically recognized syndromes across the spectrum of eating disorders.
2. Describe how a comprehensive weight management program would be set up for teenagers in a community where none had previously existed.
3. It has been proposed that adolescents need to gain more weight during pregnancy than adult women. What aspects of adolescent growth and development lead to the idea that these larger gains are beneficial?
4. What are the most important dietary issues for adolescent athletes?
5. What are the characteristics of effective counseling for adolescents?

SUGGESTED LEARNING ACTIVITIES

1. Prepare a discussion about the specific dietary issues important to adolescent athletes for a high school track team.
2. Develop an explanation you can give to a 15-year-old pregnant teenager as to why she will be counseled to gain more weight than her mother did when she was pregnant with her daughter.
3. Explain to an obese teenage boy who has not experienced a growth spurt why he should not try to lose weight rapidly. Test his fitness (as described in Chapter 9) and help him develop an improvement plan.
4. Speak with a teenager about lowering the fat content of his or her diet.
5. Develop a graph depicting all the factors that contribute to the development of eating disorders in adolescents.

Terms and Concepts

Provided here for your review is a listing of terms and concepts within this chapter. The definitions for terms can be found in the glossary, which begins on page 413. To aid your understanding of the terms' and concepts' application within this text, the page number designating the first mention of each term or concept within the chapter is given.

acrocyanosis, 227
alopecia, 227
amenorrhea, 225
anabolic steroids, 245
anorexia nervosa, 221
body image distortion, 222
bulimia nervosa, 221
cachexia, 227
carotenemia, 229
cheilosis, 227
cultural paradox, 224
desquamation, 227
developmental obesity, 231
eating disorder, 221
hirsutism, 227
modified fast, 242
morbidly obese, 235
narcissism, 247

REFERENCES

1. Bruch H: Developmental considerations of anorexia nervosa and obesity, *Can J Psychiatry* 26:212, 1981.
2. Minuchin S and others: *Psychosomatic families: anorexia nervosa in context,* Cambridge, Mass, 1978, Harvard University Press.
3. *Diagnostic and statistical manual of mental disorders,* ed 3 (revised), Washington, DC, 1987, American Psychiatric Association.
4. Farrow JA: The adolescent male with an eating disorder, *Pediatr Ann* (in press), 1992.
5. Keys A and others: *The biology of human starvation,* vols I and II, Minneapolis, 1950, University of Minnesota Press.
6. Meyer AE and others: Psychoendocrinology of remenorrhea in the late outcome of anorexia nervosa, *Psychother Psychosom* 45:174, 1986.
7. Commerci G: Medical complications of anorexia nervosa and bulimia nervosa. In Farrow JA, editor: Adolescent medicine, *Med Clin North Am* 74:1293, 1990.
8. Bachrach LK and others: Decreased bone density in adolescent girls with anorexia nervosa, *Pediatrics* 86:440, 1990.
9. Nussbaum M and others: Cerebral atrophy in anorexia nervosa, *J Pediatr* 96:867, 1980.
10. Rigotti NA and others: The clinical course of osteoporosis in anorexia nervosa: a longitudinal study of cortical bone mass, *JAMA* 265:1133, 1991.
11. Nussbaum MP and others: Blunted growth hormone responses to clonidine in adolescent girls with early anorexia nervosa: evidence for an early hypothalmic defect, *J Adol Med* 18:145, 1990.
12. Dolan RJ and others: Structural brain changes in patients with anorexia nervosa, *Psychol Med* 18:349, 1988.
13. Laessle RG and others: Depression as a correlate of starvation in patients with eating disorders, *Biol Psychiatry* 23:719, 1988.
14. Steiger H and others: Relationship of body-image distortion to sex-role identification, irrational cognitions, and body weight in eating-disoriented females, *J Clin Psychol* 45:61, 1989.
15. Brinch M and others: Anorexia nervosa and motherhood: reproduction pattern and mothering behavior of 50 women, *Acta Psychiatr Scand* 77:611, 1988.
16. Polivy J, Herman CP: Diagnosis and treatment of normal eating, *J Consult Clin Psychol* 55:635, 1987.
17. Rowland TW and others: The effect of iron therapy on the exercise capacity of nonanemic iron-deficient adolescent runners, *Am J Dis Child,* 142:165, 1988.
18. Rees JM: Management of obesity in adolescents. In Farrow JA, editor: Adolescent medicine, *Med Clin North Am* 74:1275, 1990.
19. Pencharz PB and others: The effect of a weight-reducing diet on the nitrogen metabolism of obese adolescents, *Can J Physiol Pharmacol* 66:1469, 1988.
20. Bennett W: Dietary treatments of obesity, *Ann NY Acad Sci* 499:250, 1987.
21. Boxer GH, Miller BD: Treatment of a 7-year-old boy with obesity hypoventilation (Pickwickian syndrome) on a psychosomatic inpatient unit, *J Am Acad Child Adolesc Psychiatry* 26:798, 1987.
22. Hoerr SLM, Nelson RA, Essex-Sorlie D: Treatment and follow-up of obesity in adolescent girls, *J Adolesc Health Care* 9:28, 1988.
23. Ikeda JP and others: Two approaches to adolescent weight reduction, *J Nutr Educ* 14:90, 1982.
24. Mellon LM, Slinkard LA, Irwin CE: Adolescent obesity intervention: validation of the SHAPE-DOWN program, *J Am Diet Assoc* 87:333, 1987.
25. Kinston W and others: Interaction in families with obese children, *J Psychosom Res* 32:513, 1988.
26. Steen SN, Oppliger RA, Brownell KD: Metabolic effects of repeated weight loss and regain in adolescent wrestlers, *JAMA* 260:47, 1988.
27. Woods ER, Wilson CD, Masland RP: Weight control methods in high school wrestlers, *J Adolesc Health Care* 9:394, 1988.
28. Buzina K and others: Vitamin C status and physical working capacity in adolescents, *Int J Vitam Nutr Res* 54:55, 1984.
29. Nickerson HJ and others: Causes of iron deficiency in adolescent athletes, *J Pediatr* 114:657, 1989.

30. Mahan LK, Arlin M: *Krause's food, nutrition and diet therapy,* ed 8, Philadelphia, 1992, WB Saunders.

31. McArdle WD and others: *Exercise physiology: energy, nutrition, and human performance,* ed 2, Philadelphia, 1986, Lea & Febiger.

32. Squire DI: "Heat illness: fluid and electrolyte issues for pediatric and adolescent athletes," *Pediatr Clin North Am* 37:1085; 1990.

33. Drinkwater BL and others: Bone mineral density after resumption of menses in amenorrheic athletes, *JAMA* 256:380, 1986.

34. Story M, editor: *Nutrition management of the pregnant adolescent: a practical reference guide,* Washington, DC, 1990, MCH National Clearinghouse.

35. Scholl TO and others: Maternal growth during pregnancy and decreased infant birth weight, *Am J Clin Nutr* 51:790, 1990.

36. Harrison KA and others: Growth during pregnancy in Nigerian teenage primigravidae. In Harrison KA, editor: Child-bearing, health and social priorities: a survey of 22,774 consecutive hospital births in Zario, Northern Nigeria, *Br J Obstet Gynaecol* 55:32, 1985.

37. Rees JM and others: Position of the American Dietetic Association: nutrition management of adolescent pregnancy, and technical support paper, *J Am Diet Assoc* 89:900, 1989.

38. Haiek L, Lederman SA: The relationship between maternal weight for height and term birth weight in teens and adult women, *J Adolesc Health Care* 10:16, 1988.

39. Frisancho AR and others: Developmental and nutritional determinants of pregnancy outcome among teenagers, *Am J Phys Anthropol* 66:247, 1985.

40. Taffel S: *National Center for Health Statistics: maternal weight gain and the outcome of pregnancy,* United States, 1980, Vital and Health Statistics, Series 21, No 44, DHHS Pub No (PHS) 86-1922, Washington, DC, June 1986, US Government Printing Office.

41. Rosso P, Lederman SA: *Nutrition in the pregnant adolescent.* In Winick M, editor: *Adolescent nutrition,* New York, 1982, John Wiley & Sons.

42. Garn SM, Petzold AS: Characteristics of the mother and child in teenage pregnancy, *Am J Dis Child* 137:365, 1983.

43. Stevens-Simon C, McAnarney ER: Adolescent maternal weight gain and low birth weight: a multifactorial model, *Am J Clin Nutr* 47:948, 1988.

44. Institute of Medicine, National Academy of Sciences: *Nutrition during pregnancy,* Washington, DC, 1990, National Academy Press.

45. Hediger ML and others: Rate and amount of weight gain during adolescent pregnancy: associations with maternal weight-for-height and birth weight, *Am J Clin Nutr* 52:793, 1990.

46. Rees JM and others: Weight gain in adolescents during pregnancy: rate related to birthweight outcome, *Am J Clin Nutr,* In press 1992.

47. Maso MJ and others: Anthropometric predictors of low birth weight outcome in teenage pregnancy, *J Adolesc Health Care* 9:188, 1988.

48. Farrow JA: *Homeless pregnant and parenting adolescents: service delivery strategies,* Maternal and Child Health Technical Information Bulletin, Public Health Service, USDHHS, Nov, 1991.

49. Ketterlinus RD, Henderson SH, Lamb, ME: Maternal age, sociodemographics, prenatal health and behavior: influences on neonatal risk status, *J Adolesc Health Care* 11:423, 1990.

50. Hardy J, Duggan AK: Teenage fathers and the fathers of infants of urban, teenage mothers, *Am J Public Health* 78:919, 1988.

51. Rees JM: *Nutritional counseling in adolescence.* In Mahan LK, Rees JM: *Nutrition in adolescence,* St Louis, 1984, Mosby–Year Book.

52. Reynolds S, Faulkner P: *Interviewing and counseling skills.* In Story M, editor: *Nutrition management of the pregnant adolescent: a practical reference guide,* Washington, DC, 1990, National Center Education Maternal Child Health.

53. Faulkner PL: *Strategies for dietary change.* In Story M, editor: *Nutrition management of the pregnant adolescent: a practical reference guide,* Washington, DC, 1990, National Center Education Maternal Child Health.

54. Silber TJ: Physician-adolescent patient relationship, *Clin Pediatr* 19:50, 1980.

55. Rogers CR: A counseling approach to human problems, *Am J Nurs* 56:994, 1956.

56. Hackney H, Cormier LS: *Counseling strategies and objectives,* Englewood Cliffs, NJ, 1979, Prentice-Hall.

57. Brill NI: *Teamwork: working together in the human services,* Philadelphia, 1976, JB Lippincott.

FURTHER READINGS

1. Carruth BR, Skinner JD: Pregnant adolescents report infrequent use of sugar substitutes, *J Am Diet Assoc* 91:608, 1991.

2. Jacobson MS, editor: *Atherosclerosis prevention: identification and treatment of the child with high cholesterol,* Philadelphia, 1991, Harwood Academic Publishers.
3. Killen JD and others: Is puberty a risk factor for eating disorders? *Am J Dis Child* 146:323, 1992.
4. Paperny DM, Starn JR: Adolescent pregnancy prevention by health education computer games: computer-assisted instruction of knowledge and attitudes, *Pediatrics* 83:742, 1989.
5. Scholl TO and others: Maternal weight gain, diet and infant birth weight: correlations during adolescent pregnancy, *J Clin Epidemiol* 44:423, 1991.
6. Skinner JD, Carruth BR: Dietary quality of pregnant and nonpregnant adolescents, *J Am Diet Assoc* 91:718, 1991.
7. Wells RD, McDiarmid J, Bayatpour M: Perinatal health belief scales: a cost-effective technique for predicting prenatal appointment keeping rates among pregnant teenagers, *J Adolesc Health Care* 11:119, 1990.

11

Vegetarian Diets for Children

Cristine M. Trahms

Objectives

✦✦

After studying this chapter, the student should:

✔ *Be aware of the effect of vegetarian and vegan food patterns on the nutritional status and growth of infants and children.*

✔ *Understand nutritional and growth parameters that should be monitored for children who follow vegetarian food patterns.*

✔ *Understand which combinations of foods provide adequate energy, protein, and all other nutrients for children who follow vegetarian food patterns.*

✔ *Be able to provide guidance for texture modification of foods for young children on vegetarian food patterns.*

✔ *Understand appropriate ways to counsel children and families who follow vegetarian food patterns.*

Using plant foods as the primary source of nutrients in the food pattern, for example, a vegetarian diet, is both a traditional and a recent dietary pattern. Many religious groups have traditionally advocated a meat-free food pattern, and this practice continues today. The people of many countries have also historically been vegetarian or near vegetarian, not necessarily by choice, but because of limited food availability.

Currently, many people are choosing a non-meat food pattern for a variety of religious and health reasons. Thus the pattern may be prescribed by the group or based on the personal choices of the individual. The generally accepted definitions of nonmeat food patterns are shown in the box on page 266. Many people who describe themselves as **vegetarians** may eat meat as often as once a week or twice a month, while other vegetarians may choose rigid food patterns that forbid them even yeast and honey. For example, in Boston young adult vegetarians come from relatively affluent and educated families. More than half of those interviewed were **lacto-ovo vegetarians,** and less than 10% adhered to a **vegan** food pattern.[1] Few of those interviewed had parents who were also vegetarian, but most expected their own children to continue the vegetarian food pattern. About one fourth of these vegetarians were affiliated

❖
> ## DESCRIPTION OF FOOD CHOICE PATTERNS
>
> Vegetarian: consumes no poultry, meat, or fish
> Lacto-ovovegetarian: uses eggs and dairy products
> Lacto-vegetarian: uses dairy products
> Vegan: a strict, pure, or total vegetarian who avoids consumption of all animal products
> Macrobiotic vegetarian: restricts additional foods or beverages in addition to those derived from animals; may use supplements and advocate fasting

with traditional religious groups. Since individuals seldom make their personal food choices based on these descriptive categories, it is reasonable to evaluate foods as sources of nutrients rather than to impose labels on individual food patterns. This method of evaluation also provides an appropriate basis for nutrition education.

The practice of eating meat does not inherently ensure good health, just as the practice of omitting meat does not ensure poor health. The interrelationships of nutritional needs, food choices, health practices, religious convictions, and social mores are complex. The exclusion of one food or group of foods does not necessarily swing the pendulum of health or nutritional adequacy in either the positive or the negative direction. Dissimilar food and health practices among groups often make it difficult to interpret reported data. Therefore when discussing vegetarianism—the concept of not eating meat—one must carefully consider all other factors.

HEALTH ADVANTAGES AND DISADVANTAGES

It is important to understand that there are adequate and inadequate vegetarian and vegan diets. Among the health advantages of a non-meat food pattern for adults are decreases in cholesterol, triglycerides, and other blood lipid

constituents.[2] Although there is disagreement on the specific dietary factors that support these changes, the vegetarian food pattern, both in long-term and short-term evaluations, appears to exert a positive effect on blood lipids. A vegetarian food pattern also seems to reduce the incidence of obesity,[3,4] hypertension,[5] coronary artery disease,[6] diabetes,[7] and gallstones[8] and maximize endurance performance.[9] These reports are evaluations of adults in industrialized countries who have made other life-style changes in addition to omitting meat from their food patterns. Life-style factors, such as abstinence from smoking and alcohol use, a high level of exercise, or seclusion from the rest of society, must be considered potential intervening or modifying variables in the impact of the vegetarian diet on long-term health.

Many of the reports that indicate nutritional disadvantages to a vegetarian food pattern have been conducted in developing countries where the total amount of food and food choices available are limited. In these situations, lack of food to provide adequate energy and nutrient intakes determines nutritional status rather than a conviction to be vegetarian. A negative impact of a vegetarian food pattern for adults has also been reported in the United States. Young adults have become overzealous in following specific teachings or omitting specific foodstuffs from their food patterns. One example is the Zen **macrobiotic** followers who felt that tea and brown rice were the way to purity. Even the leaders of the group warned against this extreme practice and encouraged a more moderate food intake pattern that included grains, legumes, fruits, and vegetables.

In general, the more restricted the pattern of food choices, the more likely the individual is to be at high nutritional risk. (The same can be said for popular weight-reduction formats.) Young children and pregnant women, who are generally considered to be at high nutritional risk, are thought to be particularly vulnerable to food intake patterns that limit both the quantity and the kinds of food consumed.

Growth of Children

Birth weight. There appear to be no detrimental effects to the offspring of the vegetarian or vegan mother if she chooses a food pattern

TABLE 11-1 *Selected Reported Weight and Height of Vegetarian and Vegan Children*

Report, Year	No. of Subjects	Mean Age	Food Pattern	Growth Reference	Size of Children
Brown, Bergan 1975[27]	10	1-6 yr	Zen macrobiotic (vegan)	—	Mean weight and height = 40%
Fulton and others, 1980[33]	48	3.8 yr	Vegan "The Farm"	HANES	Mean height and weight less than mean of HANES; height more affected; 83% had height < 50th percentile
Shull and others, 1977[10]	72	< 5 yr	Vegetarian	Harvard	Greater than 2 years of age, subjects are the same as control for weight and height; less than 2 years of age, subjects are shorter, lighter than control
			Macrobiotic (vegan)		Slightly lower size attainment than vegan (not significant)
Dwyer and others, 1982[32]	39	4 yr	Vegetarian	NCHS	Height, weight within normal limits
Dwyer and others, 1978[16]	119	2.33 yr	Vegetarian extensive vs. limited food group avoidances	Harvard	Adjusted for mid-parent height, 61% < 10th percentile, the difference is more pronounced with increased avoidances
van Staveren and others, 1985[19]	92	1-3 yr	Vegetarian macrobiotic (vegan)	Dutch	Height and weight for age shorter and lighter; weight for length OK
Sanders, 1988[34]	37	1-6 yr	Vegan	British	Girls <50% for weight Boys <50% for height and weight

Continued.

TABLE 11-1 *Selected Reported Weight and Height of Vegetarian and Vegan Children—cont'd*

Report, Year,	No. of Subjects	Mean Age	Food Pattern	Growth Reference	Size of Children
van Staveren, 1988[14]	300	0-8 yr	Macrobiotic	Dutch	Growth delay after 5 months, Height and weight for age are shorter and lighter but within reference limits
O'Connell and others, 1989[11]	404	4 mo-10 yr	Vegan "The Farm"	NCHS	1-3 year olds were shorter, by age 10 height for age, weight for age, and weight for height were in the 25th to 75th percentiles
Rona and others, 1987[21]	7103	Primary schoolage	Vegetarian	British	Weight for height, TSF is similar to nonvegetarian
Tayter, Stanek, 1989[29]	17 + controls	10-12 yr	Lacto-ovovegetarian	NCHS	Boys height >50th percentile, weight >30th percentile Girls height is in the 45th percentile, weight is in the 50th percentile

that provides the required nutrients in appropriate quantities to support the pregnancy. No differences in birth weights between the vegetarian infants (both extensive and limited food group avoidances) and the control infants were noted.[10] Infants born to vegan mothers on "The Farm" (a collective community in Tennessee) had weights comparable to the U. S. average.[11] Birth weight was 180 gm lower for macrobiotic than for control group women; however, increasing birth weight was associated with increasing maternal weight gain and frequency of consumption of dairy products and

fish by macrobiotic women.[12] Birth weight appears to be affected by maternal serum zinc status. Women with low serum zinc levels were more likely to have infants of low birth weight regardless of vegetarian status.[13]

Infants

Growth success and growth failure have been reported for children on vegetarian and vegan food patterns as shown in Table 11-1. Similar patterns of growth for infants have been described for the Dutch and Boston children, for whom weight and length were within the nor-

TABLE 11-1 *Selected Reported Weight and Height of Vegetarian and Vegan Children—cont'd*

Report, Year,	No. of Subjects	Mean Age	Food Pattern	Growth Reference	Size of Children
Dagnelie and others, 1988[12]	243	0-8 yr	Macrobiotic	Dutch	0-8 months = normal growth; 8-18 months = growth lag; 2-4 years = catch-up for weight and skinfolds, not height
Dagnelie and others, 1989[30]	53 + controls	4-18 mo	Macrobiotic	Dutch	Weight gain less for macrobiotic infants, after 14 months growth stabilized at 10th percentile
Sabate and others, 1990[20] Sabate and others, 1991[28]	2272 + controls	6-18 yr	Lacto-ovovegetarian (SDA)	NCHS	Average height and weight > 50th percentile: boys taller than controls, girls no different; both boys and girls leaner than controls
Dwyer and others, 1983[15]	142 + controls	0-6 yr	Macrobiotic vegetarian	NCHS	Length more affected than weight; macrobiotic children are shorter than vegetarian; females shorter for age than males

mal limits for the first 6 to 8 months of life.[14,15] In general, infants who receive an appropriate quantity and quality of breast milk or formula grow well. Vegetarian and vegan women tend to breast-feed their infants until the end of the first year, which supports growth in early infancy.

Growth rate declined fairly rapidly in late infancy and then reached its nadir by 18 months of age.[12,14] Weaning is a time of nutritional vulnerability for all children. This vulnerability is demonstrated by changing growth patterns. Weaning from breast milk to foods of a lesser energy density and biological value of protein can negatively affect the growth of young children, regardless of whether they are vegan or vegetarian. Weaning poses a problem to vegetarian and vegan infants if the biological value of protein and energy density of foods are reduced when breast milk is discontinued and dairy foods are omitted when solids are added. Growth for all of the children was improved if they consumed some dairy products.

Preschool Children

Deficits in height and weight occurred among young children on vegan diets.[14-17] Young vegan children were significantly shorter and lighter than were age- and gender-matched vegetarian children and control children.[18] Some catch-up growth has been demonstrated between 2 and 4 years of age.[11,12,17]

When the data are adjusted for midparental height, 61% of 119 preschool vegetarian children were in less than the 20th percentile for height. Nearly half of the children had parents who consumed macrobiotic food patterns; the remaining children were almost equally members of yoga groups, Seventh-Day Adventists, or without group affiliation. Almost all (96%) of the children had been breast-fed. The vegetarian children younger than 2 years of age showed mean weight and length velocities that were lower than the reference charts, whereas those of the older vegetarian children were comparable with reference charts.[10] This pattern of growth was also reported for Dutch children.[19]

School-Age Children

When growth patterns of vegetarian and nonvegetarian schoolchildren were compared, the two groups of children demonstrated growth patterns that were compromised[15] or

TABLE 11-2   Selected Reported Mean Nutrient Intakes of Vegetarian and Vegan Children

Report, Year,	No. of Subjects	Mean Age (yr)	Food Pattern	Energy (kcal)	Protein (gm)
Brown, Bergan 1975[27]	10	1-6	Zen macrobiotic (vegan)	1002-1267	34.4-41
Fulton and others, 1980[33]	48	3-8	"The Farm" vegan, boys	1580-2141	52-62
			"The Farm" vegan, girls	1509-2249	49-65
Dwyer and others, 1982[32]	39	4	Vegetarian	103/kg	3.3/kg
van Staveren and others, 1985[19]	92	1-3	Vegetarian	1020 (84-98/kg)	36 (2.8-3.5/kg)
			Macrobiotic (vegan)	1010 (85-92/kg)	31 (2.2-3.3/kg)
Sanders, 1988[34]	37	1-6	Vegan (British)	30% kcal from fat	10% kcal
Dagnelie and others, 1988[12]	50 + controls	10-20 mo	Macrobiotic (Dutch)	—	—
Taytor, Stanek, 1989[29]	17 + controls	10-12	Lacto-ovovegetarian (SDA)	Boys = 2315 Girls = 1650 (28%-31% kcal from fat)	67 56.5 (↓ than controls)
Dagnelie and others, 1989[30]	53 + controls	4-18 mo	Macrobiotic	(↓ than controls)	80% of rec (↓ than controls)
RDA, 1989*		1-3 4-6		1300 1700	16 24

*Recommended Dietary Allowances, 1989.

similar.[20,21] It appeared that the more limiting the food choices were, the more growth was affected. In general, length was more affected than weight, although measurements were generally within normal limits. Evaluation of food intakes suggested that protein intakes for these children were adequate, and energy intakes were less than the accepted recommendations.

The availability of adequate nutrients to the individual child was a more significant factor than the beliefs of the parents and the concomitant prescribed food pattern. The more restrictive the food choices and quantities of food available, the greater the negative effect on growth. However, the lower relative weight of the well-nourished vegetarian school children may provide health advantages in adulthood.

Nourishment

Nutrients of concern. Young children consuming food patterns consisting only of plant foods seem to be at greater risk for nutritional inadequacies. The most commonly reported low dietary intakes are in protein, calcium, total energy, essential fatty acids, riboflavin, iron, zinc, folate, and vitamins B_{12} and D. A summary of reported nutrient intakes of vegan and vegetarian children is shown in Table 11-2. Table 11-3 indicates that nutrient intakes may be compromised or enhanced by food choices.

Factors Influencing the Intakes of Children

The young child depends on caregivers to provide adequate foods as sources of nutrients. The young infant being exclusively breast-fed

Calcium (mg)	Iron (mg)	Vit D (µg)	Vit B_{12} (µg)	Fiber (gm)
359-402	0.1-11.9	—	—	—
323-426	18-25	—	10.8-19.2	—
296-340	14-16	—	10.9-15.8	—
685	12-16	1.3-9.9 (51-395 IU)	0.6-4.4	—
783	7.1	0.5	—	16
345	10.8	0.3	—	24.9
52% of rec	142% of rec	Sunlight	280% of rec	—
	15% iron deficiency	—	Significantly less than controls	—
1400	17	—	—	5
1040 (↑ than controls)	10.7 (↑ than controls)	—	—	4.5 (similar to controls)
280 (↓ than controls)	5.1 (↑ than controls)	↓ than controls	0.3 (↓ than controls)	—
800	10	10 (400 IU)	0.7	—
800	10	10	1.0	—

by a mother who has a marginal or definite vitamin B_{12} intake may have an increased risk of deficiency. Older children who consume diets restricted in animal foods may also be at risk for vitamin B_{12} deficiency if the choices of foods available to them are severely restricted and exclude all animal foods. The adequacy of nutrient intake may also be affected by food preferences, which are demonstrated early in life. The older infant and toddler with rigid food preferences may be at risk for deficits of protein, energy, calcium, iron, zinc, and vitamins D and B_{12} despite adequate food availability.

Infants who are breast-fed but whose food patterns are not supplemented with additional foods may suffer adverse nutritional and growth effects after 4 to 6 months of age, especially if they are weaned to a cereal gruel or other form of predominantly vegan food pattern.[17,22]

Limitations in nutrient availability may be in part related to family food choice patterns and to the individual preferences of the child, who may not eat the foods that are offered. An example of nutritional risk caused by limited food choices is the young child who was offered a grain beverage consisting of rice, sesame seeds, and oats in a reasonable protein complement. However, the quantities that the child was willing to consume did not provide adequate nutrients to support normal growth.

The young child on a food intake pattern composed totally or primarily of plant proteins may have problems obtaining an adequate intake of energy if the volume of food required to meet energy needs is large. Often a fortified soy formula will provide an easily ingested volume of protein, energy, and other nutrients for the infant and young child.

In addition to volume, texture may influence the adequacy of the intake of the young child. Many foods that contain adequate quantities of protein and are rich sources of nutrients must be texture modified for the young child; for instance, beans must be well cooked and mashed or pureed. Even rice must be mixed with liquid and mashed for the infant. The young child may not chew whole grain breads well, and consequently the nutrients may not be well absorbed. The same is true for nuts, seeds, dried fruits, and some vegetables.

Cases of kwashiorkor (protein and energy deficiency) among infants whose parents were vegetarian[23,24] and poor weight gain in children fed cereal-base formulas[25-27] have been described. The infants were fed restricted quantities of kokoh (a grain milk) and other foods. The children were rehabilitated on appropriate vegetarian or near vegetarian food patterns within a few months. In all of these reports the number of children evaluated was small, and long-term observations on growth, cognitive development, or nutrient intake were not available. More recent reports do not support this degree of neglect or lack of knowledge about provision of adequate nutrients and energy to young children.

The school-age, Seventh-Day Adventist vegetarian children ingested less junk food and dairy products, but more starchy foods, protein products, fruits, and vegetables than nonvegetarian peers.[20,28] Girls had lower intakes of energy, protein, and fat, and boys had greater carbohydrate and iron and less protein intakes than nonvegetarian peers.[29] For school-age children, the more restrictive the food pattern, the shorter the child and the more compromised the intakes of energy, protein, vitamin D, and iron.[21]

Nutrient Intakes

There are adequate and inadequate vegan, vegetarian, and meat-containing food patterns. Children are at greater risk than adults for manifestation of nutrient deficiencies. Macrobiotic infants were breast-fed until about 13 months of age, and then solids consisting of porridge, vegetables, sesame seeds, and legumes were introduced. No fruits or animal products were offered. The food patterns for these infants were calculated to contain less energy, protein, fat, cholesterol, calcium, riboflavin, and vitamin B_{12} and greater amounts of fiber, iron, and thiamin than for control infants.[30]

Calculation of nutrient intakes of preschool children has shown that children whose food patterns excluded all animal foods consumed significantly less total protein, fat, calcium, and riboflavin than did vegetarian children and control children.[31] Intakes of iron and calcium were also calculated at lower than acceptable levels. Recently the intakes of a small number of children (mean age of 4 years) consuming different types of vegetarian food patterns were evaluated. The findings suggested that these food patterns met the dietary goals for the United States for carbohydrate, fat, protein, sodium, and cholesterol. Some children had intakes limited in iron and in vitamins D and B$_{12}$.[32,33] Young children who received some appropriate nutrients, for example, 142% of the British recommendations for iron from whole meal bread, 280% of the recommendations for vitamin B$_{12}$ because of supplementation, and 10% of kcalories from protein, but only 52% of calcium all from nuts and legumes, were shorter and lighter than their peers.[34]

Vitamin D. Vitamin D deficiency rickets has been reported in breast-fed infants of vegan and vegetarian mothers. All of the infants had hypocalcemia, and three fourths had **tetany** or convulsions.[35] Rickets has been identified in infants who do not receive a vitamin D supplement, whether breast- or formula-fed[36] or whether vegetarian or not.[37]

Clinical identification of rickets has recently been reported in older infants who demonstrated the classic symptoms: growth failure, listlessness, delayed motor development, and abnormal gait.[38] Bone deformity was evident on further investigation. The children received little or no cow's milk or formula and no vitamin D supplements. Not all of the children were vegetarian or vegan, again demonstrating the need to evaluate food patterns for specific nutrients.

However, healing occurred with dietary changes in all cases. Of 52 children on macrobiotic food patterns, 88% had vitamin D intakes of less than 100 IU/day compared with vegetarian children, of whom only 18% had vitamin D intakes this low.[39] Although five children had pathological findings related to bone mineralization, roentgenograms did not indicate rickets. Clinically, only three children demonstrated signs (bowed legs) that could possibly be attributed to vitamin D deficiency. The serum calcium and serum phosphorus levels of the children on both macrobiotic and vegetarian food patterns were within normal limits. Eight of the children on macrobiotic food patterns and two of the vegetarian children had elevated serum alkaline phosphatase levels.

Calcium. Calcium deficiency and osteomalacia in the presence of an adequate intake of protein and energy further emphasize the need to evaluate all of the nutrient components of a food pattern.[40] In the presence of vitamin D, calcium is absorbed at about 30% to 35%; without vitamin D, this rate decreases to about 10%.

Vitamin B$_{12}$. Vegan women who do not take vitamin B$_{12}$ supplements may have low vitamin B$_{12}$ levels in their milk, and their infants may demonstrate compromised metabolic status.[41] Case reports cite growth failure and other clinical signs of vitamin B$_{12}$ deficiency in infants who were breast-fed by vegan women.[42] Apparently these infants required more vitamin B$_{12}$ than could be supplied by breast milk of women with marginal vitamin B$_{12}$ stores. The more restricted the food pattern, the greater the risk for deficiency for vitamin B$_{12}$.[43,44]

Zinc. The status of zinc nutriture for vegan and vegetarian children has not been fully evaluated. It would seem that zinc intake may be limited in some restricted food patterns. A combination of increased fiber intake, calcium, and phytic acid plus low bioavailable zinc led to decreased serum zinc levels in adults.[45]

Iron. Vegan and vegetarian food patterns rely on nonheme iron from plant sources to meet iron needs for growth and development. The absorption of nonheme iron is increased when ingested in the presence of ascorbic acid. There is also an important dose-effect relationship between iron absorption and the phytate content of the food pattern. Fermentation (e.g., bread with yeast) breaks down the phytate components and increases the availability of the iron in whole grains.

Fiber. Absorption of nutrients may be a problem if the fiber content of the infant's or young child's food pattern is high. High fiber intakes render intakes less kcalorically dense and are believed to decrease intestinal transit time, lead to high fecal energy loss, and bind iron, calcium, zinc, and other trace metals.

Energy. The volume of food required to meet the energy needs of young children may interfere with adequate intakes. This is especially true for children who are offered bulky foods without texture modification. A model proposed by Payne[46] suggests that an adequate, safe protein/energy ratio in young children is close to 5% of total kcalories from protein. Since most cereal grains seem to provide protein levels close to this, energy deficit rather than protein deficit may be the cause of protein/energy malnutrition in children. Energy intake should be adequate to promote acceptable growth.

Protein. Protein utilization is affected by a variety of factors, including quality and quantity of ingested protein, percent of kcalories as fat, total energy intake, biological variation of the individual, and growth and maintenance needs (e.g., age and nutritional state). Protein utilization among young children has been evaluated in terms of the ability of vegetable protein to maintain growth and nitrogen balance for young children. Commercially formulated legume products and combinations of grains, legumes, and milk solids promote rehabilitation from malnutrition.[47-49] In the United States few if any children must exist on a single food that in turn must supply all or the majority of nutrients. The young breast- or formula-fed infant is the exception. Infant food must be chosen carefully to meet the rigorous nutrient requirements for supporting normal growth and development.

Fat. Fat absorption in young children depends on levels of dietary protein intake.[50] Low protein intakes, even with adequate energy intakes, are detrimental to maximum fat absorption and may ultimately increase total energy requirements. Children on diets containing 5% or more of total kcalories as protein (FAO/WHO recommendation) showed improvement of apparent fat absorption as protein intakes increased.

Choosing Foods for Young Children

Protein. It is important that the protein sources offered to children be appropriately combined so that the pattern of amino acid intake will be adequate to support normal growth. Careful attention to combining plant proteins in the best proportion for optimal utilization is a must, especially for the child of a vegan family. Appetites of young children fluctuate widely on a day-to-day basis, making it important that all foods eaten provide nutrients rather than only energy.

In combining plant proteins, not only must foods that supplement the most limiting amino acids be combined, but they should be combined in proportion for the most efficient utilization of protein. This ratio becomes of little concern when adequate quantities of protein and energy are available to the young child. Protein complementation is also a useful and practical way to enhance the value of foods readily accepted by young children. One can accomplish this by adding a small amount of soy grits while oatmeal is being cooked or by adding wheat germ, soy flour, or dry milk to muffins, pancakes, cookies, and breads. Some combinations that are practical and acceptable to young children are shown in Table 11-4.

Preschool-age children are in the process of developing individual food patterns and are not amenable to eating foods because they are good sources of protein. It is often difficult to persuade children to eat foods in a proportional relationship or to eat a sufficient volume of legumes, grains, seeds, and nuts in a form they can easily digest. Therefore it is difficult to provide sufficient quality and quantity of proteins and an adequate amount of kcalories to support normal growth for young children without a concentrated source of high–biological value protein such as dairy foods or eggs in their food pattern.

Meeting the Nutrient Needs of Vegetarian Children

Examples of recorded food intakes of vegan, vegetarian, and nonvegetarian children that show the variety of foods and general quantities needed to provide reasonable intakes of nutrients are given in Table 11-5. Calculated nutrient intakes from these food records are shown in Table 11-3. Special attention needs to be paid to providing adequate sources of vitamins, minerals, and trace metals in a form that is bioavailable in the food patterns of young children. Factors that interfere with absorption of nutrients and ways to enhance absorption are shown in Table 11-6. Commercially prepared and fortified soy formulas are appropriate sources of all of the critical nutrients for young children. Other sources of nutrients that are of concern for young children are shown in Table 11-7. Nutrient values of foods common to nonmeat

TABLE 11-3   *Calculated Nutrients in Recorded Intakes of Young Children*

Nutrient	Child 1 Inadequate Vegan	Child 2 Better Vegan	Child 3 Vegetarian	Child 4 Non-vegetarian	RDA* 1-3 Years
Protein (gm)	11.3	36.4	67.3	56.5	16
Energy (kcal)	547	1105	1323	1961	1300
Dietary fiber (gm)	9.4	25.7	13	1.8	—
Vitamin A (RE)	383	599	667	746	400
Vitamin D (μg)	0	0	10	11	10
Vitamin C (mg)	27	31	45	26	40
Vitamin B_{12} (μg)	0	0	3.3	5.2	0.7
Zinc (mg)	2.3	8.3	8.5	7.4	10
Calcium (mg)	80	490	1422	1335	800
Iron (mg)	4	12.9	9.9	3.9	10
Fat (gm)	5	24.5	61.7	33.6	—
%kcal as fat	8	20	42	31	30

*Recommended Dietary Allowances, 1989.

TABLE 11-4   *Combinations of Food to Improve Protein Quality*

Food	Ingredients
Oatmeal, cooked	$\frac{3}{4}$ c cooked oatmeal with 2 t soy grits, $\frac{1}{3}$ c milk
Scalloped potatoes	$\frac{1}{2}$ c potatoes, $\frac{1}{2}$ c milk
Macaroni and cheese	$\frac{1}{2}$ c cooked macaroni, 3 T grated cheese
Rice pudding	$\frac{1}{2}$ c dry rice, 1 c milk or $\frac{1}{4}$ c milk powder
Peanut butter sandwich on whole wheat bread	$\frac{1}{2}$ T peanut butter, 1 slice bread
Tortillas with beans	2 tortillas, $\frac{1}{4}$ c cooked mashed beans
Whole wheat and soy muffin	2 T whole wheat flour, 1 t soy flour, 1 T milk
Sesame and oatmeal cookies	1 T oatmeal, 1 T whole wheat flour, 1 $\frac{1}{2}$ t sesame, $\frac{1}{2}$ T milk
Rice and beans	1 c dry rice, $\frac{1}{4}$ c dry red beans
Cornell Triple Rich Flour	1 T soy flour, 1 T milk powder, 1 t wheat germ plus whole wheat flour to fill the cup

food patterns and generally accepted by young children are shown in Table 11-8.[12]

Zinc. Although the information on zinc intakes of children is limited, it is known that zinc intakes are likely to be at risk for inadequacy in a vegan food pattern. Phytate and fiber in cereal are known to bind zinc and decrease its avail-ability. It has been suggested that foods highest in zinc and lowest in fiber, such as tofu (soy cheese) and hard cheeses, be emphasized in the vegetarian food pattern to maintain an adequate intake of this nutrient.[51] Miso, wheat germ, legumes, nuts, and sprouts are also reasonable food sources of zinc.[52]

TABLE 11-5 Recorded 1-Day Intakes of Young Children

Food	Portion Size	Food	Portion Size
Child 1 (age 12 months)—inadequate vegan intake		**Child 3 (age 13 months)—vegetarian intake**	
Oatmeal, cooked	$\frac{1}{2}$ c	Milk, whole	9 oz
Raisins	1 t	Cereal mixture	
Yellow squash, cooked	$\frac{1}{2}$ c	Cornmeal, dry	$\frac{1}{4}$ c
Apple	1 medium	Wheat germ	3 T
Oatmeal, cooked	1 c	Milk, whole	$\frac{1}{4}$ c
Yams, cooked	$\frac{1}{2}$ c	Apple	1 T
Pudding		Soybeans, cooked	1 c
Apple cider	1 c	Apricot, dried	2 halves
Arrowroot flour	1 t	Apple	$\frac{1}{2}$ medium
No supplements		Potato, baked	$\frac{1}{2}$ small
		Tomato	1 small
Child 2 (age 14 months)—better vegan intake		Cheddar cheese, grated	$\frac{1}{4}$ c
Kokoh (cereal mixture)	$1\frac{1}{4}$ c	Soy oil	2 t
Rice	$\frac{1}{2}$ c	Milk, whole	9 oz
Sweet rice	$\frac{1}{4}$ c	Milk, whole	9 oz
Whole oats	$\frac{1}{8}$ c	No supplements	
Sesame seeds	$\frac{1}{8}$ c		
Wakame (sea weed)	$\frac{1}{2}$ t	**Child 4 (age 12 months)—nonvegetarian intake**	
Squash, baked	$\frac{1}{3}$ c	Peach, canned	$\frac{1}{2}$
Whole wheat noodles	$\frac{1}{2}$ c	Link sausage	2
Miso soup		Toast, white	$\frac{1}{2}$ slice
Miso (fermented soy)	1 t	Margarine	$\frac{1}{2}$ t
Scallions	1 t	Egg yolk	1
Onion	1 t	2% Milk	8 oz
Kokoh	$1\frac{1}{4}$ c	2% Milk	8 oz
Nori (sea weed)	1 piece	Veal	50 gm
Cauliflower	$\frac{1}{4}$ c	Cracker	1
Adzuki beans, cooked	$\frac{1}{3}$ c	Rice, cooked	$\frac{1}{2}$ c
Watercress	1 sprig	Tomato	$\frac{1}{4}$ medium
Brown rice pudding	$1\frac{1}{4}$ c	2% Milk	8 oz
Squash, cooked	$\frac{1}{4}$ c	2% Milk	8 oz
Apple, baked	2 T	Supplement: Poly-vi-sol	6 ml/day
Raisins	1 t		
No supplements			

Vitamin B$_{12}$. Since animal foods are the primary sources of vitamin B$_{12}$, care must be taken to avoid vitamin B$_{12}$ deficiency for the infant and young child by ensuring adequate maternal stores during lactation and by providing overt sources for the young child. These sources may be supplemented brewer's yeast, vitamin B$_{12}$ tablets, dairy foods, or eggs. Recent data suggest that vitamin B$_{12}$ from algae and other plant foods is not bioavailable.[53,54]

Vitamin D. Vitamin D needs may be met via exposure to sunlight, fortified milk or soy formula, vitamin D supplements, or cod liver oil. No one is sure how much sunlight a person needs to make vitamin D because it depends on exposure, time, and the angle of the sun. However, children who are exposed to sunlight on a regular basis do not demonstrate vitamin D deficiency.

Calcium. Calcium is readily available from cow's milk or a commercially prepared and fortified soy formula. Dark, green leafy vegetables and legumes are also reasonable sources as is firm tofu that has been precipitated with calcium sulfate instead of magnesium (e.g., 115 mg vs. 13 mg calcium/100 gm tofu).[55] A calcium supplement may be needed if adequate food sources are not ingested.

Iron. Iron deficiency anemia is a common occurrence in childhood regardless of food choice patterns. The most bioavailable sources of iron are muscle meats. The bioavailability of plant sources of iron is variable and less than that of heme sources.[56] However, nonheme iron

TABLE 11-6 Factors that Influence Utilization of Nutrients

Factor Limiting Utilization	To Enhance Absorption
Phytate (binds zinc)	Use cooked or leavened grain products, include dairy foods
Fiber (binds iron, zinc, calcium)	Cook legumes well
Nonheme iron	Consume with ascorbic acid–rich foods
Bulk	Modify texture and offer concentrated sources of energy (e.g., nut butters, dried fruit spreads, avocado)
Oxalate (binds calcium)	Offer milk

TABLE 11-7 Sources of Nutrients of Concern for Young Children Consuming Vegetarian Diets

Nutrient of Concern	Sources
Iron: plant foods do not contain heme iron	Legumes, green leafy vegetables, whole grains, fortified cereals, dried fruits, blackstrap molasses
Vitamin B$_{12}$: plant foods do not contain vitamin B$_{12}$	Eggs, dairy foods, vitamin B$_{12}$–fortified foods such as nutritional yeast, breakfast cereals, soymilks, meat analogues, and supplements (not miso, tempeh, sea vegetables)
Vitamin D: limited sunlight exposure	Regular exposure to sunlight, or source of vitamin D from fortified milk, supplement, or cod liver oil (infants should receive supplement)
Calcium: without dairy foods, bioavailable calcium intake may be limited	Dairy foods, fortified soy formulas, legumes, tofu processed with calcium sulfate, almonds, sesame seeds, low-oxalate green leafy vegetables
Zinc: without meat and dairy foods, zinc may be limited	Legumes, hard cheeses, whole grain breads and cereals, wheat germ, fortified cereals, tofu, miso, nuts

TABLE 11-8   Nutrient Values of Selected Foods Providing Nutrients of Concern for Vegetarian Children

Food	Amount	Protein (gm)	Energy (kcal)	Ca (mg)	Fe (mg)	Zn (mg)	B_{12} (μg)
Baby cereal, dry	4T						
Mixed		1.2	36	68	7.2	.44	
Oatmeal		1.2	40	72	7.2	3.6	
Rice		.8	36	80	7.2	2.0	
Baby vegetables, strained	1 jar, 128 gm						
Green beans		1.7	32	49	.96	.26	0
Carrots		1.1	34	29	.47	.2	0
Peas		2.8	68	16	.72	.5	0
Squash		1.1	30	30	.38	.18	0
Meat analogues: (Loma Linda)							
Chicken, frozen	2 sl, 57 gm	10	160	25	1.1	.63	2.0
Ocean fillet, frozen	1, 47 gm	11	130	45	.9	.66	2.0
Vege-burger, canned	$\frac{1}{2}$ c, 108 gm	22	110	32	2.7	1.1	2.0
Sizzle franks, canned	2, 70 gm	10	170	49	1.6	.78	2.0
Sandwich spread, canned	3 T, 48 gm	4.0	70	21	.7	.62	2.0
Vege-scallops	6 pc, 78 gm	14	70	17	1.1	1.1	2.0
Stew pac, canned (Millstone)	2 oz, 57 gm	10	70	17	.73	.62	1.0
Meatless loaf	1 oz	9.9	90	67	2.2	.46	
Vege-burger (Worthington	$\frac{1}{2}$ c, 108 gm	20	110	12	1.1	2.7	
Choplets	2, 92 gm	19.1	105	11	1.9		
Cereals, cooked							
Cream of Rice	$\frac{3}{4}$ c	1.6	95	6	.3	.29	
Cream of Wheat	$\frac{3}{4}$ c	2.9	100	38	7.7	.24	
Farina, enriched	$\frac{3}{4}$ c	2.5	87	3	.88	.12	
Oatmeal	$\frac{3}{4}$ c	4.5	108	15	1.2	.86	
Cereals, ready-to-eat, fortified							
Cheerios	$\frac{1}{2}$ c	2.1	55	24	2.2	.29	.75
Corn Chex	$\frac{1}{2}$ c	1	55	1	.9	.06	.75
Crispy Rice	$\frac{1}{2}$ c	.9	56	2.5	.35	.23	.4
Kix	$\frac{3}{4}$ c	1.2	55	17.5	4	.14	.75
Wheat Chex	$\frac{1}{3}$ c	1.4	50	5.5	2.2	.37	.75
Cheese							
Cheddar	1 oz	7.1	114	204	.19	.88	.23
Cottage	1 T	3.5	29	17	.7	.2	.18
Cream cheese	2 T	2.1	99	23	.34	.15	.12
Mozzarella, part skim	1 oz	7.8	79	207	.7	.89	.26
Parmesan, grated	1 T	2.1	23	69	.5	.16	
Ricotta, part skim	$\frac{1}{4}$ c	7.2	85	168	.27	.83	.18
Swiss	1 oz	8.1	107	272	.5	1.11	.48

TABLE 11-8 *Values of Selected Foods Providing Nutrients of Concern for Vegetarian Child—cont'd*

Food	Amount	Protein (gm)	Energy (kcal)	Ca (mg)	Fe (mg)	Zn (mg)	B$_{12}$ (µg)
Egg, large	1, 50 gm	6.1	79	28	1.04	.72	.66
Dairy products							
Milk, whole	8 oz	8	150	288	—	1.0	1.34
Lowfat, 2%	8 oz	8.1	121	297	.12	.95	.89
Yogurt, whole	8 oz	7.9	139	274	.11	1.34	.84
Infant formulas							
Mead Johnson							
Enfamil	8 oz	3.2	160	112	3.04	1.28	4
Prosobee	8 oz	4.8	160	152	3.04	1.28	4.8
Ross Labs							
Similac	8 oz	3.2	160	120	2.88	1.2	4
Isomil	8 oz	4.0	160	168	2.88	1.2	7.2
Soy products							
Soy milk	1 c	6.6	79	10	1.38	.54	0
Soy meal, defatted	$\frac{1}{4}$ c	15	103	74	4.2	1.5	0
Miso	$\frac{1}{4}$ c	4.1	71	23	.9	1.1	—
Tempeh	$\frac{1}{4}$ c	3.9	41	19	.5	.4	—
Tofu, raw, firm	$\frac{1}{4}$ c	4.9	46	65	3.3	.5	0
Grains							
Mesa harina de maiz	$\frac{1}{3}$ c	3.5	137	77	2.93	1	0
Whole wheat flour	$\frac{1}{4}$ c	4	100	12.2	1	—	0
Wheat germ, toasted	1 T	2.1	27	3.2	.6	1.2	0
Tortilla, corn	1, 30 gm	2.1	67	42	.57	.43	0
Brown rice, cooked	1 c	4.9	232	23	1	—	0
Nut butters							
Almond butter	1 T	2.4	101	43	.59	.49	0
Cashew butter	1 T	2.5	83	6	.72	.73	0
Peanut butter, creamy	1 T	4.6	95	5	.29	.47	0
Sesame butter, tahini	1 T	2.6	89	64	1.34	.69	0
Legumes, cooked							
Adzuki beans	$\frac{1}{4}$ c	4.3	73	16	1.2	1	0
Black beans	$\frac{1}{4}$ c	3.8	57	12	.9	.5	0
Garbanzo beans	$\frac{1}{4}$ c	3.6	67	20	1.2	.6	0
Black eye peas	$\frac{1}{4}$ c	3.3	49	11	1.1	.5	0
Kidney beans	$\frac{1}{4}$ c	4	55	29	1.3	.4	0
Split peas	$\frac{1}{4}$ c	4.1	58	6.5	.6	.5	0
Pinto beans	$\frac{1}{4}$ c	3.5	59	21	1.1	.5	0
Miscellaneous							
Molasses, blackstrap	1 T	0	43	137	3.2	—	—
Brewer's yeast	1 oz	11	80	60	4.9	—	—
Torula yeast, dried	1 oz	13.5	99	100	6.4	3.6	.17

Continued.

TABLE 11-8 **Values of Selected Foods Providing Nutrients of Concern for Vegetarian Child—cont'd**

Food	Amount	Protein (gm)	Energy (kcal)	Ca (mg)	Fe (mg)	Zn (mg)	B$_{12}$ (μg)
Fruits and vegetables							
Orange juice, frozen	8 oz	1.7	112	22	.24	.13	0
Apple juice	8 oz	0.2	116	16	.92	0.7	0
Tomato juice	6 oz	1.4	32	16	1.06	.26	0
Avocado	$\frac{1}{2}$ med	1.8	153	9.5	1	.36	0
Beet greens, cooked	$\frac{1}{2}$ c	1.9	20	82	1.37	.36	0
*Broccoli, cooked	$\frac{1}{2}$ c	2.3	23	89	.89	.12	0
*Collards, cooked	$\frac{1}{2}$ c	1.5	18	74	.39	.61	0
Spinach, cooked	$\frac{1}{2}$ c	2.7	21	122	3.21	.69	0
Chard, cooked	$\frac{1}{2}$ c	1.7	18	10	.18	—	0
*Kale, cooked	$\frac{1}{2}$ c	1.2	21	47	.59	.15	0
*Mustard greens, cooked	$\frac{1}{2}$ c	1.6	11	52	.49	—	0
*Turnip greens, cooked	$\frac{1}{2}$ c	0.8	15	99	.57	.1	0
Bamboo shoots, cooked	$\frac{1}{4}$ c	.47	4	6	1.2	—	0
Dried fruit							
Apricots	5 halves	.7	46	8	.8	.13	0
Currants, zante	$\frac{1}{4}$ c	1.8	102	31	1.17	.23	0
Dates	5	.8	114	13	.48	.12	0
Figs	1	.57	57	27	.44	.11	0
Raisins, seedless	$\frac{1}{3}$ c	1.6	150	48	5	.15	0
Prunes	2	.44	40	15	.41	.09	0
Sprouts							
Alfalfa, raw	10 gm	.1	1	1	.03	.03	0
Lentils, cooked	10 gm	.9	10	1.4	.3	.15	0
Mung beans, cooked	$\frac{1}{4}$ c	.7	7	3.54	.2	.14	0
Soy, cooked	$\frac{1}{4}$ c	2	19	14	.3	.25	0

Data from Pennington JAT: Bowes and Church's Food, Food Values of Portions Commonly Used, ed 15, Philadelphia, 1989, JB Lippincott.
*Low-oxalate green leafy vegetables.

iron bioavailability is improved if ascorbic acid–rich foods are consumed at the same meal.

Counseling the Vegetarian Family

The word *vegetarian* has a specific nuance or value system attached to it for all persons who have chosen to apply that label to themselves. Health care professionals in the counseling role should carefully examine their own biases and, whether they are negative or positive, try to approach the family or household as open mindedly as possible.

It seems reasonable that one should first ask the family to describe the foods regularly included and excluded in the family's food pattern and the individual's food pattern (see Chapter 2). A survey of women in Seattle indicated the importance of this approach.[57] Less than 50%

FIG. 11-1 A young child who enjoys a variety of foods and is healthy and well-nourished on a nonmeat food pattern.

of the persons who described themselves as vegetarians never ate meat, 30% ate meat once or twice per month, and nearly 10% ate meat as often as once per week.

Every food pattern that a person chooses has some positive aspects that should be defined and reinforced (Figure 11-1). Clinical experience indicates that a counseling and supportive role is much more effective than a directive or argumentative approach. People can, in fact, adequately meet their nutrient needs in a variety of ways, and the individual variability of nutritional needs is wide.

SPECIAL CONCERNS FOR INFANTS AND CHILDREN

For the infant and young child, linear growth and rate of weight gain can be used as indices of appropriate energy intake. The mother of an exclusively breast-fed infant should be asked to describe her own intake and should be advised of all the usual guidelines regarding adequate

fluid, protein, calcium, and energy to maintain health and support lactation.

Some provisions should be made to ensure that the breast-fed infant receives adequate supplies of iron and vitamins B_{12} and D. Evidence indicates that iron in breast milk is well absorbed by the infant.[58] Well-nourished lactating women who are following a vegetarian food pattern have adequate supplies of nutrients in their breast milk.[59,60] However, vitamin B_{12} may be a concern, especially if the mother's levels are low or if she has chosen a vegan food pattern. A supplement or additional food choices may be necessary to provide adequate quantities of this nutrient. Usually, if the need for the particular nutrient can be clearly documented, the parents are willing to reexamine their philosophical basis for making food choices, and a reasonable decision or compromise can be reached for the ultimate nutritional welfare of the child.

When breast-feeding is not feasible, the infant needs to receive adequate quantities of a properly prepared infant formula. This can be a soy or a cow's milk infant formula, but it must provide adequate quantities of critical nutrients such as protein, calcium, iron, energy, and vitamins B_{12}, A, and D. It has been demonstrated that fortified soy infant formulas can promote normal growth and development in infants.

Home-prepared infant formulas made with cow's milk, goat's milk, or soy base and supplemented with calcium, yeast, lactose, and other vitamin and mineral preparations are not advised. These types of formula are susceptible to errors in measurement and dilution; thus they put the infant at risk of excess or deficiency of specific nutrients and potential renal solute problems.

SPECIAL CONCERNS FOR ADOLESCENTS

Many adolescents and young adults who choose vegetarian or semivegetarian food pat-terns are concerned with their own health and the nutrition that is basic to it. Often their food choices are based, at least in part, on political and philosophical convictions. These young people need information and supportive counseling to make sound health decisions while they continue to make the political or philosophical statement of their choice.

Young adolescents who are not yet emancipated from the nuclear family may use food selection as a means of establishing independence. In this situation parents must remain flexible, tolerant, and interested in the adolescent's convictions regarding food choices. When there is little understanding, the food pattern can quickly become another point of intense family conflict. It must be remembered that an unusual food pattern is not necessarily a harmful food pattern. The parents and the adolescent need guidance to discern the difference. Any direct criticism of food choices may be considered personal criticism, so counseling must be sup-

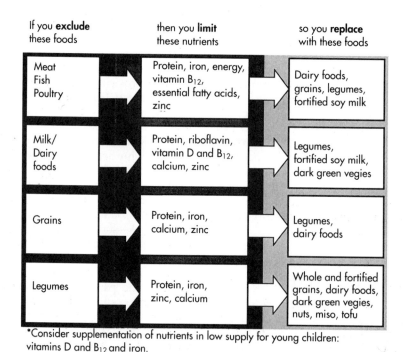

*Consider supplementation of nutrients in low supply for young children: vitamins D and B_{12} and iron.

FIG. 11-2 Thoughtful food choices provide all *key nutrients* for a nonmeat food pattern. (From Trahms CM: *Body Basics* 4(5), 1991, University of Washington.)

portive. It should reinforce the positive aspects of the chosen food pattern and consider the energy and nutrient needs required for growth, development, and physical activity. Nonjudgmental discussion of alternatives and a mutual decision-making process among the health care professional, the adolescent, and the parent can guide adolescents in making healthful and responsible food choices.

Many nutrient needs can be met by careful planning and by including foods that are equivalent sources of specific nutrients. Figure 11-2 defines foods as sources of nutrients and the foods that can be exchanged to provide the equivalent nutrients. This scheme may be used not only by vegetarians but also by those who have specific food likes and dislikes or by those who for some other reason feel the need to restrict the variety of choices in their food intake patterns.

Guidance for Families

In addition to the food guide (Table 11-9), the following point should be kept in mind when counseling a family that has chosen to become vegetarian: the goal of the health care professional is the same as when counseling a nonvegetarian family, that is, to promote good health through reasonable food choices. Responsibilities include the following:

1. To support the individual and the family in every positive aspect of the chosen food pattern
   a. By being nonjudgmental about the stated reasons for specific food choices
   b. By recognizing the wide variety of food choices that are appropriate to maintain good health
   c. By understanding the food taboos and food preferences and the reasons for them

TABLE 11-9 Vegetarian Food Guide

Food Group	Portion Size	Number of Daily Portions		
		Pregnant	2 to 3 Years	4 to 6 Years
Breads, cereals, pasta	1 slice bread $\frac{1}{3}$ c granola $\frac{3}{4}$ c cooked cereal 1 biscuit, muffin 1 T wheat germ $\frac{3}{4}$ c cooked rice	6	3	3
Protein foods				
Legumes, meat analogues	1 c cooked beans $\frac{1}{4}$ c peanut butter 6 oz tofu	$\frac{3}{4}$	$\frac{1}{8}$	$\frac{1}{4}$
Nuts and seeds	3 T	1	$\frac{1}{8}$	$\frac{1}{4}$
Dairy products				
Milk	1 c milk, yogurt 1 oz cheese 4 T cottage cheese	4	2-3	2-3
Eggs		$1\frac{1}{2}$	1	1
Fruits and vegetables	1 c, raw $\frac{1}{2}$ c, cooked $\frac{1}{2}$ c juice	5-6	2	3
Extra foods	No requirement (recommendation)			

Modified from Smith EB: *J Nutr Educ* 7:109, 1975.

2. To evaluate the food intake of a specific family member, identifying possible nutrients at risk for a deficient intake because of food choices or food preparation methods
   a. By helping the family recognize the differing needs of infants, young children, adolescents, adults, pregnant women, and sedentary individuals
   b. By working with the individuals to identify food as sources of nutrients
3. To encourage the family members to purchase foods that provide the most nutrients for the money
   a. By encouraging the evaluation of foods for their nutrient content, packaging, and processing
   b. By encouraging the use of simple foods, whole grains, fresh fruits, and vegetables
   c. By encouraging the use of cooking methods that conserve nutrients

Summary

The more restrictive food choices become, the more difficult it is to plan a nutritionally adequate food pattern. Dietary inadequacy is more likely to occur in children than in adults. Vegetarian food patterns that include prudently chosen plant foods and a reasonable amount of dairy foods are adequate to support normal growth and development for people of all ages, including young children and pregnant and lactating women. These recommendations are supported by a position paper from the American Dietetic Association,[61] as well as others.[62-64] General recommendations to support an adequate nutritional intake for young children who are vegetarians and vegans include the following:

1. Use of a variety of fruits and vegetables
2. Use of whole grain breads and cereals
3. Provision of nutrient-dense foods to meet energy and nutrient needs and limitation of foods that are high in energy and low in nutrient density
4. Provisions of adequate bioavailable quantities of the limiting nutrients iron, calcium, folate, zinc, and vitamin B_{12} by either appropriate food choices or fortified food supplements

5. Use of an appropriately supplemented cow's milk formula or soy formula for infants who are not breast-fed
6. Use of a suitable supplement or daily exposure to sunlight to provide adequate amounts of vitamin D
7. Modification of texture of foods to be in concert with the developmental skills of the child
8. Judicious use of dairy foods to promote appropriate growth achievement for older infants and children

The "New" Laurel's Kitchen [65] and Jane Brody's Good Food Book [66] are helpful manuals that include nutrition information as well as recipes for those who choose nonmeat food patterns.

It should be noted that these recommendations for an appropriate vegetarian food pattern are in accord with the Healthy People 2000 Objectives[67] for lower fat, higher complex carbohydrate food choices for all people.

REVIEW QUESTIONS

1. Why are infants of vegan mothers susceptible to vitamin B_{12} deficiency?
2. What is the most critical time of growth for all infants, but especially for vegan infants?
3. List the nutrients most likely to be present in marginal or deficient amounts on (a) vegetarian and (b) vegan diets for children.
4. Describe an adequate food intake pattern for a vegetarian child.
5. What are the most likely nutritional problems for a vegan child?
6. What bioavailable sources of protein, energy, zinc, and vitamins B_{12} and D would be most reasonably suggested for a vegan child?

SUGGESTED LEARNING ACTIVITIES

1. Plan a menu for a 2-year-old vegetarian boy who weighs 10 kg. He is unwilling to consume beans of any kind. His mother is unwilling to offer more than 1 cup of milk or yogurt per day because "it causes phlegm."
2. Outline teaching objectives and a food pattern for a young woman with a 6-month-old infant who is at the 25th percentile for length and weight. The mother prefers to avoid all animal products. The infant is totally breast-fed. The mother plans to continue breast-feeding until the infant is 1 year of age.

3. Judy is a 4-year-old girl enrolled in the Head Start Program. She has been labeled "anemic" on the entrance physical examination. Her weight/stature is at the 10th percentile. Her mother is strongly opposed to all supplements. The family is vegan. Outline a plan for the family and for the classroom.

4. A mother of two young children (5 and 6 years of age) has recently become vegetarian and is adjusting her cooking habits and the family food pattern. Her children are picky eaters in both the variety and quantity of food they are willing to consume. She feels that they may have lost weight on the vegetarian food pattern. Suggest how she can provide appropriate intakes for her children.

Terms and Concepts

Provided here for your review is a listing of terms and concepts within this chapter. The definitions for terms can be found in the glossary, which begins on page 413. To aid your understanding of the terms' and concepts' application within this text, the page number designating the first mention of each term or concept within the chapter is given.

lacto-ovovegetarian, 265

lacto-vegetarian, 266

macrobiotic vegetarian, 266

tetany, 273

vegan, 265

vegetarian, 265

REFERENCES

1. Freeland-Graves JH and others: A demographic and social profile of age- and sex-matched vegetarians and nonvegetarians, *J Am Diet Assoc* 86:907, 1986.
2. Masarei JRL and others: Vegetarian food patterns, lipids and cardiovascular risk, *Aust NZ J Med* 14:400, 1984.
3. Slattery ML and others: Meat consumption and its associations with other diet and health factors in young adults: the CARDIA study, *Am J Clin Nutr* 54:930, 1991.
4. Mäenpää P and others: Effects of low-fat lactovegetarian diet on health parameters of adult subjects, *Ecol Food & Nutr* 25:255, 1991.
5. Sacks FM, Kass EH: Low blood pressure in vegetarians: effects of specific foods and nutrients, *Am J Clin Nutr* 48:795, 1988.
6. Resnicow K and others: Diet and serum lipids in vegan vegetarians: a model for risk reduction, *J Am Diet Assoc* 91:447, 1991.
7. Snowdon DA: Animal product consumption and mortality because of all causes combined, coronary heart disease, stroke, diabetes, and cancer in Seventh-Day Adventists, *Am J Clin Nutr* 48:739, 1988.
8. Dwyer JT: Health aspects of vegetarian diets, *Am J Clin Nutr* 48:712, 1988.
9. Nieman DC: Vegetarian dietary practices and endurance performance, *Am J Clin Nutr* 48:754, 1988.
10. Shull MW and others: Velocities of growth in vegetarian preschool children, *Pediatrics* 60:410, 1977.
11. O'Connell JM and others: Growth of vegetarian children: The Farm study, *Pediatrics* 84:475, 1989.
12. Dagnelie PC and others: Do children on macrobiotic diets show catch-up growth? *Eur J Clin Nutr* 42:1007, 1988.
13. Neggers YH and others: A positive association between maternal serum zinc concentration and birth weight, *Am J Clin Nutr* 51:678, 1990.
14. van Staveren WA and others: Food consumption, growth, and development of Dutch children fed alternative diets, *Am J Clin Nutr* 48:819, 1988.
15. Dwyer JT and others: Growth in "new" vegetarian preschool children using the Jenss-Bayley curve fitting technique, *Am J Clin Nutr* 37:815, 1983.
16. Dwyer JT and others: Preschoolers on alternate lifestyle diets, *J Am Diet Assoc* 72:264-1978.
17. Dwyer JT and others: Size, obesity and leanness in vegetarian preschool children, *J Am Diet Assoc* 77:434, 1980.
18. Trahms CM and others: Restriction of growth and elevated protoporphyrin in children deprived of animal protein, *Clin Res* 25:179, 1977.
19. van Staveren WA and others: Food consumption and height/weight status of Dutch preschool children on alternative food patterns, *J Am Diet Assoc* 85:1579, 1985.
20. Sabate J and others: Anthropometric parameters of schoolchildren with different life-styles, *Am J Dis Child* 144:1159, 1990.
21. Rona RJ and others: Vegetarianism and growth in Urdu, Gujarati, and Punjabi children in Britain, *J Epidemiol Community Health* 41:233, 1987.
22. Poskitt EME for Nutrition Standing Committee of the British Paediatric Association: Vegetarian weaning, *Arch Dis Child* 63:1286, 1988.

23. Chase HP and others: Kwashiorkor in the United States, *Pediatrics* 66:972, 1980.

24. Shinwell ED, Gorodisches R: Totally vegetarian diets and infant nutrition, *Pediatrics* 70:582, 1982.

25. Robson JRK and others: Zen macrobiotic dietary problems in infancy, *Pediatrics* 53:326, 1974.

26. Roberts LF and others: Malnutrition in infants receiving cult diets: a form of child abuse, *Br Med J* 1:296, 1979.

27. Brown PT, Bergan JG: The dietary status of "new" vegetarians, *J Am Diet Assoc* 67:455, 1975.

28. Sabate J and others: Attained height of lacto-ovovegetarian children and adolescents, *Eur J Clin Nutr* 45:51, 1991.

29. Tayter M, Stanek K: Anthropometric and dietary assessment of omnivore and lacto-ovovegetarian children, *J Am Diet Assoc* 89:1661, 1989.

30. Dagnelie PC and others: Nutritional status of infants aged 4 to 18 months on macrobiotic diets and matched omnivorous control infants: a population-based mixed-longitudinal study. II. Growth and psychomotor development, *Eur J Clin Nutr* 43:325, 1989.

31. Trahms CM, Feeney MC: Evaluation of diet and growth of vegans, vegetarian, and nonvegetarian preschool children, *Fed Proc* 34:675, 1975.

32. Dwyer JT and others: Nutritional status of vegetarian children, *Am J Clin Nutr* 35:204, 1982.

33. Fulton JR and others: Preschool vegetarian children: dietary and anthropometric data, *J Am Diet Assoc* 76:360, 1980.

34. Sanders TAB: Growth and development of British vegan children, *Am J Clin Nutr* 48:822, 1988.

35. Hellebostad M and others: Vitamin D deficiency rickets and vitamin B_{12} deficiency in vegetarian children, *Acta Paediatr Scand* 74:191, 1985.

36. Dagnelie PC and others: High prevalence of rickets in infants on macrobiotic diets, *Am J Clin Nutr* 51:202, 1990.

37. Inner-city babies susceptible to rickets, *Northwest Med* 7:28, 1991.

38. Rudolf M and others: Unsuspected nutritional rickets, *Pediatrics* 66:72, 1980.

39. Dwyer JT and others: Risk of nutritional rickets among vegetarian children, *Am J Dis Child* 133:134, 1979.

40. Marie PJ and others: Histological osteomalacia due to dietary calcium deficiency in children, *N Engl J Med* 307:584, 1982.

41. Specker BL and others: Vitamin B_{12}: low milk concentrations are related to low serum concentrations in vegetarian women and to methylmalonic aciduria in their infants, *Am J Clin Nutr* 52:1073, 1990.

42. Higginbottom MC and others: A syndrome of methylmalonic aciduria, homocystinuria, megaloblastic anemia and neurologic abnormalities in a vitamin B_{12} deficient breast fed infant of a strict vegetarian, *N Engl J Med* 299:317, 1978.

43. Dagnelie PC and others: Increased risk of vitamin B_{12} and iron deficiency in infants on macrobiotic diets, *Am J Clin Nutr* 50:818, 1989.

44. Miller DR and others: Vitamin B_{12} status in a macrobiotic community, *Am J Clin Nutr* 53:524, 1991.

45. Bindra GS and others: [Phytate] [Calcium]/[Zinc] ratios in Asian immigrant lacto-ovovegetarian diets and their relationship to zinc nutriture, *Nutr Res* 6:475, 1986.

46. Payne PR: Safe protein-calorie ratios in food patterns: the relative importance of protein and energy intake as causal factors in malnutrition, *Am J Clin Nutr* 28:281, 1975.

47. Graham GG and others: Dietary protein quality in infants and children. IX. Instant sweetened corn-soy-milk blend, *Am J Clin Nutr* 26:491, 1973.

48. Bressani R and others: Protein quality of a soybean protein textured food in experimental animals and children, *J Nutr* 93:349, 1967.

49. Knapp J and others: Growth and nitrogen balance in infants fed cereal proteins, *Am J Clin Nutr* 26:586, 1973.

50. MacLean WC and others: Effect of the level of dietary protein intake on fat absorption in children, *Pediatr Res* 11:774, 1977.

51. Freeland-Graves JH and others: Zinc and copper content of foods used in vegetarian food patterns, *J Am Diet Assoc* 77:648, 1980.

52. Truesdell DD and others: Nutrients in vegetarian foods, *J Am Diet Assoc* 84:28, 1984.

53. Dagnelie PC and others: Vitamin B_{12} from algae appears not to be bioavailable, *Am J Clin Nutr* 53:695, 1991.

54. Herbert V: Vitamin B_{12}: plant sources, requirements and assay, *Am J Clin Nutr* 48:852, 1988.

55. Poneros AG, Erdman JW: Bioavailability of calcium in tofu, tortillas, nonfat dry milk and mozzarella cheese in rats: effect of supplemental ascorbic acid, *J Food Sci* 53:208, 1988.

56. Lynch SR and others: Iron absorption from legumes in humans, *Am J Clin Nutr* 40:42, 1984.

57. Johnston PK: *Infant feeding among Seventh-Day Adventists,* master's thesis, Seattle, 1979, University of Washington.

58. Saarinen UM, Siimes MA: Iron absorption from breast milk, cow's milk, and iron supplemented formula, *Pediatr Res* 13:143, 1979.

59. Finley DA and others: Inorganic constituents of breast milk from vegetarian and nonvegetarian women: relationships with each other and with organic constituents, *J Nutr* 115:772, 1985.

60. Finley DA and others: Breast milk composition: fat content and fatty acid composition in vegetarians and nonvegetarians, *Am J Clin Nutr* 41:787, 1985.

61. American Dietetic Association: Position paper on vegetarian approach to eating, *J Am Diet Assoc* 88:351, 1988.

62. Truesdell DD, Acosta PB: Feeding the vegan infant and child, *J Am Diet Assoc* 85:837, 1985.

63. Jacobs C, Dwyer JT: Vegetarian children: appropriate and inappropriate diets, *Am J Clin Nutr* 48:811, 1988.

64. Dwyer JT: Nutritional consequences of vegetarianism, *Annu Rev Nutr* 11:61, 1991.

65. Robertson L, Flinders C, Ruppenthal B: *The new Laurel's kitchen*, Berkeley, Calif, 1986, Ten Speed Press.

66. Brody J: *Jane Brody's good food book*, New York, 1985, WW Norton.

67. Healthy People 2000: nutrition objectives, *J Am Diet Assoc* 91:1515, 1991.

12

Prevention of Chronic Disease with Dietary Intervention in Childhood

Peggy L. Pipes

Objectives

✤✤

After studying this chapter, the student should:

✔ *Be aware of nutritional approaches to the prevention of chronic disease by changes in current dietary intake during childhood.*

✔ *Recognize factors that must be considered in controlling children's weight.*

✔ *Recognize the diversity of opinions regarding the screening of children for cardiovascular heart disease.*

✔ *Be aware of the studies about the effect of salt on the development of hypertension.*

✔ *Be aware of acceptable blood pressure levels during childhood.*

A significant number of longitudinal and other studies have indicated that the prevention of chronic disease should begin in childhood. As a result researchers and experts recommend dietary changes in the current diet consumed in childhood and adolescence, and they believe that such changes could extend the years of a healthy life for many. They recommend that obesity in childhood be prevented or corrected, that the current diet children consume be modified to decrease intakes of total fat, saturated fats, and salt, and to increase intakes of fiber. They also recommend the identification of and tracking and intervention for children at high risk for chronic disease.

OBESITY

Obesity is a frequent concern in clinics that serve adolescents. The lack of success in achieving sustained weight reduction of obese adolescents has focused on identifying children at risk and motivating families to alter life-styles, environmental factors, and psychosocial factors that contribute to the development of this condition.

Obesity is a major health hazard predisposing affected adults to a greater risk of hypertension, cardiovascular disease, diabetes, gallbladder disease, and degenerative joint disorders than persons of normal weight. Even in children as young as 5 to 6 years of age a relationship has been found between fitness, fatness, and blood pressure.[1] In addition to these health risks, obese individuals are often subjected to sociocultural prejudices. For example, obese adolescents face discrimination at college entrance, and obese adults are discriminated against in job placement and advancement. Obese adolescents often exhibit psychosocial difficulties. They frequently have distorted body images and low **self-esteem** and may become socially isolated. They have been described as leading a "Cinderella-like" existence.

Incidence

Obesity in childhood is a growing problem. Data from the NHANES I study conducted between 1972 and 1974 and the NHANES II study conducted between 1976 and 1980 indicate that the prevalences of obesity and **superobesity** are increasing.[2] Defining obesity as triceps skinfold measures greater than or equal to the 85th percentile and superobesity as triceps skinfold measures greater than or equal to the 95th percentile, an increase of 54% in obesity and 98% in superobesity in 6- to 11-year-old children and of 39% in obesity and 64% in superobesity among 12- to 17-year-old children was noted in the years between the two studies. A prevalence of 27% obesity and 11.7% superobesity was noted among 6- to 11-year-old children, and a prevalence of 21.9% obesity and 9% superobesity was noted among 12- to 17-year-old children in the NHANES II study. Limited data exist on obesity in preschoolers. One study in Manhattan suggested an incidence of greater than 13%.[3]

Prognosis of Obesity

Many obese children become obese adolescents and adults. It has been estimated that 40% of obese children at 7 years of age and 70% of obese adolescents are obese as adults.[4] Retrospective investigations have shown that approximately 30% of the obese adults had a history of juvenile obesity.[5] Data from the U.S. Health Examination Study showed that three fourths of those classified as obese between 6 and 11 years of age were classified as obese 3 to 4 years later.[6] Early-onset obesity is more severe and resistant to treatment than is obesity acquired later in life.

Definition

Obesity is defined as an excessive deposition of adipose tissue. It differs from **overweight,** which implies only weight in excess of the average for height. Overweight can result from increased lean body mass, adipose tissue, or both. Forbes[7] has suggested that there may be two types of obesity in childhood and adolescence: one type characterized by increased lean body mass in addition to fat, a tendency for tallness, advanced bone age, and a history of overweight since infancy; and another type with no increase in lean body mass, normal bone age and height, and weight gain in the midchildhood or late childhood years.

Weight greater than 20% of normal for height is one criterion that has been used to define obesity. Such standards, although they show trends for populations, are not applicable to individual children. The use of weight standards tends to underestimate fatness in children less than 6 or 7 years of age and frequently overestimates adiposity in adolescents. Diagnosis of grossly obese children is easily made by visual inspection. Differentiating between less severely obese children and those who are overweight because of increased muscle mass requires measurements that give indications of body composition. Identification of children who are overfat and are settled into patterns of growth indicative of future obesity also requires that measurements of body composition be included in health examinations, just as other measurements of growth are obtained. As described in Chapter 1, standards for triceps fatfold measures with calipers have been published for all age groups. Use of these measurements to define greater than normal increases in adipose tissue of infants and children as they grow older helps identify children for whom preventive measures should be applied.

Etiological Factors

Studies of rats and other animals have definitively shown that, in animals, genes carrying obese traits are transmitted to offspring.

Definition of human genetic obesities has been more difficult because of the mixed racial heritage of most individuals and the many environmental factors known to contribute to obesity that cannot be controlled in studies. The high incidence of obesity among parents of obese children and the fact that early onset obesity appears to be almost intractable lead one to believe that hereditary factors are important. Studies have shown that 60% to 70% of obese adolescents have one or both obese parents, and 40% of obese adolescents have obese siblings.[8] Other studies have found that less than 10% of children of average weight parents are obese.[9] A study of Danish adoptees found that an individual's relative weight strongly correlated with the body masses of his or her biological parents. There was no relation between the body masses of the individuals studied and their adoptive parents.[10]

Another study investigated whether parental obesity influenced **resting metabolic rate (RMR)** in children 3 to 5 years of age and 12 years later. These researchers found that parental obesity predicted a more rapid growth and an earlier decline in resting metabolic rate in males but did not predict adiposity. Also, childhood energy intake per kilogram of body weight in earlier years was not predictive of obesity in adolescent males. Among females they noted the opposite. Energy intake per kilogram of bodyweight in the early years was predictive of obesity 12 years later, even more than parental obesity. The RMRs of daughters of obese parents did not differ significantly from that of their peers who had higher energy intakes in childhood. The researchers felt that the differences between the sexes resulted from differences in the rates of maturation. They propose that children who are preobese have a faster rate of growth and decline of RMRs per kilogram, leading to earlier adolescence. They predict that children of obese parents will become obese themselves. They also think that sons who become obese as adults will have metabolic rates per kilogram similar to those of their nonobese peers.[11]

Seltzer and Mayer[12] studied weight patterns of different body types. Using Sheldon's somatotypes they described obese adolescent females as more endomorphic and less ectomorphic than nonobese adolescent females. Inherited body type may predispose children to obesity.

Inactivity is another cause of obesity. Obese adolescents and school-age children are less active than are those of normal weight. Most become obese despite ingesting kcalorie intakes equivalent to or less than their peers. Activity patterns are acquired in childhood. Children learn to enjoy those activities in which their families and peers engage. Parents who enjoy hiking, swimming, and sports often teach their children to engage in and enjoy these physical activities. Parents who spend their hours at home urging their children to be still so that they can watch television or read reinforce inactivity and sedentary living.

Television viewing also contributes to obesity. Dietz and Gortmaker[13] found a dose-response effect: the more television viewed, the greater the risk of obesity. In addition to the inactivity while watching television, children are reported to eat more of the foods advertised on television as well as larger quantities of food during the programs than children not watching television.

Several researchers have reported increased birth weights of obese children compared with children of normal weight.[14,15] Others have found no differences in birth weights of the two groups of children. Fisch, Bilek, and Ulstrom[16] found that infants who were extremely obese at birth tended toward normal weight at 4 and 7 years of age, but an unusually high percentage retained their stocky physiques (Figure 12-1). The children who were obese at 4 and 7 years of age tended to have stocky physiques at birth. By 7 years of age, however, they were joined in their obese and overweight statuses by children who had normal physiques at birth.

There has been speculation in the past that formula-feeding and the early introduction of semisolid foods might be one cause of excessive intakes of energy and obesity in infancy, and that obese infants often become obese adults. However, a number of studies have shown that breast-feeding, bottle-feeding, and the age of introduction of semisolid foods do not cause obesity in infancy or later childhood.[17,18] Obe-

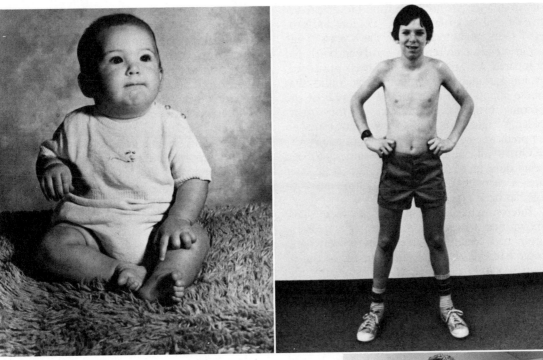

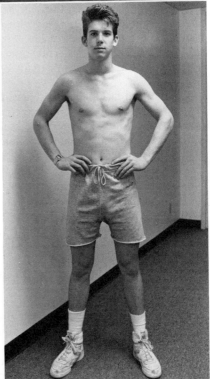

FIG. 12-1   Overweight infant became a lean, well-proportioned 12-year-old and a muscular 16-year-old boy.

sity in infancy has not been found to be predictive of obesity in later life.[19] Fomon and others[18] found measures of fatness at 8 years of age no greater in children who had been bottle-fed compared with those who had been breast-fed. A longitudinal study of children found that obese infants at 6 months and one year of age become progressively thinner as they grow older. Weight gain in infancy was not found to be predictive of obesity at 9 years of age.[19]

Obesity during the preschool- and school-age years does increase the risk of obesity in later life. A channeling tendency that increases with age has been noted.[20]

Interestingly, retrospective studies have shown that a large percentage of obese adolescents had feeding problems in infancy, and some had even been hospitalized for failure to gain weight. In a study by Hammer and others,[21] 7 out of 10 mothers of obese adolescents reported seeking advice at least six times about feeding their children during infancy. Of the obese adolescents, seven of the ten had allergic reactions to food in late infancy and early childhood. Massengale[22] found that 28% to 30% of 92 obese adolescents had histories of feeding problems in the first year of life. Two children had had pyloric stenosis, and eight had been hospitalized for poor weight gain or dehydration.

Psychosocial factors and parent-child interactions are important factors that contribute to obesity in childhood. The obese child is often an only child or the youngest child and frequently the result of an unwanted pregnancy. These children are often given food and material objects instead of love and the opportunity to have experiences that lead to the development of coping skills.[23] Anxious and insecure parents frequently overfeed children as expressions of their concern and love. They usually measure their success as parents by the amount of food their children eat and by how much weight the child gains.

Psychological trauma has been observed to be another factor associated with the onset of obesity. Bruch[24] noted that fear of hospitalization was associated with the onset of obesity in some children. Kahn[25] found a history of separation of the children from their mothers in 32% of 72 obese children under 12 years of age. Fourteen children had experienced rapid weight gains that began shortly after the separations. It has been noted in clinical practice that other psychological trauma found with some superobese children include sexual or physical abuse and other conflicts between their parents.

Differences have been noted in the incidence of obesity among children from the lower and higher socioeconomic groups. Garn, Clark, and Guire[26] reported, from analysis of data compiled during the Ten-State Nutrition Survey of 1968-1970 and the Preschool Nutrition Survey conducted by Owens and associates, that after the first few years of life and into adolescence the children of the poorest groups were leaner and the children of the affluent groups were fatter. The higher the socioeconomic status, the greater the amount of adipose tissue. Females were fatter than males at all ages at comparable income levels. White children had more adiposity than blacks. In adults the relationship between fatness and income continued in males, but it was reversed for females. Low-income female adults were fatter than those who had greater economic resources.

Garn, Hopkins, and Ryan[27] reevaluated the socioeconomic influences on adiposity with data from the Tecumseh, Michigan, Community Health Survey. Again they found low-income preadolescent males and females to be leaner than their higher income peers during the first examination. When the same individuals were reevaluated 18 years later, the low-income children had become fatter than their high-income peers.

Prevention

Regardless of its cause, obesity results when energy intakes exceed energy needs for growth, maintenance, and activity. Its manifestation is usually the result of small excesses of calorie intakes over expenditure for a period of weeks, months, or years. Monitoring rates of growth and deposition of adipose tissue helps to identify children who are accumulating more fat than would be anticipated, and measures to increase activity or decrease caloric intakes can be effected.

Adolescents often make their own decisions

FIG. 12-2   Previously obese child and her mother exercise as part of a program to control the child's weight.

about what and when they eat. Counseling must be directed to the teenagers themselves. Parents control the food available to younger children, create the environment that influences their acceptance of food, and can influence energy expenditure by the opportunities they create for physical activity for their children. It may be important to explore first with parents their reason for encouraging children to consume amounts of food that result in rapid weight gain. Some parents may not recognize that their expectations for the quantity of food they encourage their children to consume are excessive and that the chubby child is not necessarily the healthy child.

Parents may need help in developing appropriate parenting skills. They may need to learn how to respond to hunger and other needs of their infants or how to interact with their children. They may need help identifying ways to help their children develop initiative and cultivate friends and outlets in the community.[23]

The activity pattern of both the child and the family should be explored; it may be important to help parents find ways of increasing their child's level of activity (Figure 12-2). Parents who live in apartments often reinforce sedentary activities to reduce the noise level and complaints from neighbors. Those who live in one-family dwellings may have limited space for activities for children. City park departments, preschools, and schools frequently have programs that offer opportunities to increase children's activities.

The range of appropriate energy intakes at any given age is large. Overweight children and children with familial trends to obesity may need fewer kcalories than their peers. Griffith and Payne[28] found that normal weight 4- to 5-year-old children of obese parents expended 1174 kcal/day as compared with 1508 kcal/day expended by children of the same size and age of normal weight parents. Children of normal weight parents expended twice as much energy in physical activity as did those of obese parents. Families of children with a familial tendency to obesity may need help in identifying the kinds and amount of food that provide en-

TABLE 12-1   Approximate Energy Value of Common Snack Foods Offered Young Children

Food	Portion Size	kcal	Food	Portion Size	kcal
Cheese cubes	$\frac{1}{4}$ oz	25	Homogenized milk	3 oz	60
Hard-boiled egg	$\frac{1}{2}$ medium	36	Chocolate milk	3 oz	80
Frankfurter, 5" by $\frac{3}{4}$"	1	133	Cauliflower buds	2 small	2
Pretzel, 3" by $\frac{1}{2}$"	1	20	Green pepper strips	2	2
Potato chips	10	114	Cucumber slices	3 large	2
Popcorn with oil and salt	1 c	41	Cherry tomato	1	3
Bread stick, 4 $\frac{1}{2}$"	1	38	Raw turnip slices	2	5
Saltines	1	12	Dill pickle, large	$\frac{1}{3}$	5
Graham cracker	2 squares	55	Apple wedges	$\frac{1}{4}$ medium apple	20
Animal cracker	1	11	Banana	$\frac{1}{2}$ small	40
Brownie, 3" by 1" by $\frac{7}{8}$"	1	97	Orange wedges	$\frac{1}{4}$ medium orange	18
Chocolate cupcake	1	51	Orange juice	3 oz	35
Vanilla wafer	1	18	Grape juice	3 oz	60
Yogurt, plain	$\frac{1}{4}$ c	40	Lemonade	3 oz	40

From Adams CF: *Nutritive value of American foods in common units,* Agriculture Handbook No 456, Washington, DC, 1975, US Department of Agriculture.

ergy intakes that support normal growth and weight gain.

Nutrition counseling should be family oriented and based on normal nutrition, emphasizing foods that provide a balance of nutrients and appropriate kcalorie intakes. Families need to realize that efforts are directed at reduction in rates of weight gain and are not intended to effect weight loss. They must recognize that the food available and the models set for their child determine the child's response to efforts to control weight gain. Family meals may need to be modified to include fewer fried foods, less gravy, and fewer rich desserts. Parents and siblings may have to modify their own eating practices to set appropriate examples. Teachers, baby sitters and day-care workers should be alerted to and included in programs designed to control weight. Food experiences at school may need to be modified to exclude corn dripping with butter and chocolate cupcakes that are so frequently provided for special occasions. Low-kcalorie snacks such as raw fruits and vegetables can be provided instead of cookies, candy, and hot dogs. The use of food as reinforcers can be modified. Comparative energy values of snack foods are shown in Table 12-1.

Parents and children will need help in planning for parties and special occasions. Some children delete 50 kcal/day from their planned diet and have a kcalorie savings account that permits them to participate in the refreshments. Some prefer to have very special food. For example, one child has a "very special glass of water and a gingersnap" for his preschool snack.

Care should be taken in approaches to prevention of obesity because the preventive methods can have harmful results. For example, Pugliese and others[29] describe 14 normal children with growth failure and delayed maturation because of an inadequate intake because of fear of obesity.

If the child is grossly obese, a very slow rate of weight reduction may be attempted, however, linear growth should be frequently monitored. Epstein and others[30] found that behaviorally family-based treatment procedures did not compromise the linear growth of obese children when height was adjusted for parental height. My clinical experience has indicated that in grossly obese preschool- and school-age handicapped children, a weight reduction of 2 lbs/mo did not affect linear growth. Others, however, have reported that restricted kcalorie intakes did modify linear growth. Wolff and Lloyd[31] noted that children who had lost 2% or more of their weight per month grew in length at a less than expected rate. Children who (1) lost less than 2% of their body weight, (2) did not lose any weight, or (3) gained weight all grew at a rate faster than expected when energy intakes were increased to match energy expenditure. Knittle and others[3] reported that children on a protein-sparing, modified-fat diet may experience a transient slowed rate of growth, but 6 months after weight reduction, height-for-age is not affected.

The many factors in the etiology of childhood obesity indicate that a multidisciplinary approach may be necessary. The team might consist of a psychologist or behaviorist, a physician, and a dietitian-nutritionist.

Case Study

At the request of her local pediatrician, the $2\frac{1}{2}$-year-old daughter of a single parent was seen at the Child Development and Mental Retardation Center at the University of Washington. She needed evaluation and therapy from several professionals. The child was visibly obese. Her weight plotted above the 95th percentile, her length was between the 25th and 50th percentiles, and her weight-for-height, was over the 95th percentile.

During the nutrition interview it was reported that she was obviously overfat at 4 months of age. By 14 months of age her mother and grandmother became concerned. When she was 2 years of age she was often upset because she was "fat." Her mother tried offering her low-kcalorie foods. She, however, often gorged and sneaked food. The child, according to her diet history, was consuming 1500 to 1700 kcal/day, 75 to 85 kcal/kg, 16 to 18 kcal/cm of height. A diet supplying 850 kcal (9 cal/cm) was prescribed.

The mother and child lived with the mother's male friend and his father. The child was often cared for by her grandmother, and there was no coordination of efforts to control her food or energy intake.

The mother's friend, a rehabilitated drug addict, frequently told the child she was a "fatty" and ugly and then gave her food to keep her quiet. The child's mother did not want to move to her parents'

home and doubted that she could "make it" on her own.

In the following 3 months the child lost 2 kg. Her linear growth proceeded in channel. Often when she came to the clinic she was very reluctant to be weighed, stating "I not a fatty; I not ugly." Play therapy for the child and therapy sessions for the mother as well as nutrition counseling were incorporated into the monthly visits.

The child's mother applied for and received a scholarship to a junior college, which carried a monthly stipend, and she was able to move to her own apartment and enroll the child in a preschool program that included a variety of daily physical activities. When she had lost 3 kg her weight-for-height plotted below the 95th percentile, and her suggested energy intake was increased to 10.5 kcal/cm/day (950 to 1000 kcal/day) with a goal of weight maintenance. However, she began to gain weight.

It soon became apparent that each episode of weight gain was associated with psychosocial problems of the mother and that only the continuing counseling and play therapy made implementation of the plan for maintaining a normal weight possible. Even today, as a school-age child, her diet and weight gains must be carefully monitored. She is, however, no longer classified as obese. Continuing support has been necessary to maintain the gains toward prevention of future obesity (Figure 12-3).

Parents and their children need continuing support as they implement programs to prevent obesity and face unwitting responses from other members of society. Well-meaning merchants and bankers who provide sweets for children should be encouraged to provide nonfood items as alternatives. Neighbors, relatives, and other children's parents should support weight control programs.

As children grow older, they must learn to exercise willpower in refusing amounts of food that result in a positive energy balance. The children should receive positive reinforcement for control of weight gain. They need continuing support, education, and understanding as they get older. An 8-year-old boy who has been on a weight control program for 6 years, since obesity was reversed at 27 months of age, expressed the difficulties encountered on such a program. He stated during a recent clinic visit, "It's really hard to control my weight. I'm often hungry. I can't eat as much as the other boys, and my food is different from that of the other

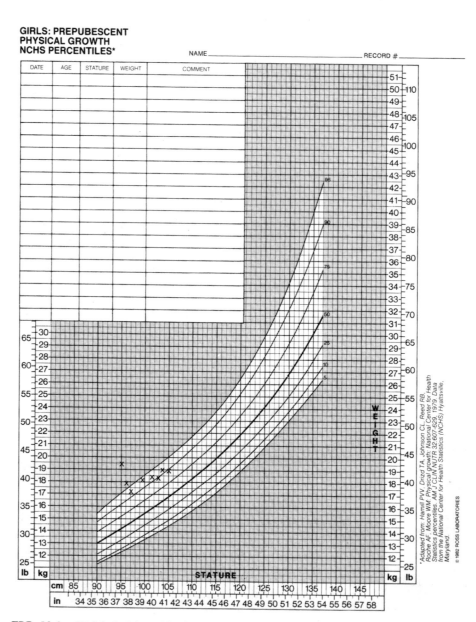

FIG. 12-3 Weight/height grid of obese preschooler during and after nutrition counseling and psychosocial intervention.

children in my class. I don't want to get fat, but I don't like being different." He, however, understands his program and knows he will receive the guidance and support he desires from his family as he assumes control of his own food selection and management of weight control.

DIETARY FATS

It is generally believed that intakes of cholesterol and saturated fatty acids and food habits established in childhood are important factors in the development of coronary artery disease in later life. Recommendations by the American Heart Association,[32] the American Health Foundation,[33] and the Expert Panel on Blood Cholesterol Levels in Children and Adolescents sponsored by the National Institutes of Health[34] include a reduction in dietary fat to 30% of total energy intake, 10% or less from saturated fat, 10% from monounsaturated fat, and less than 10% from polyunsaturated fat for all individuals over 2 years of age. They also recommended reducing cholesterol intakes to 250 to 300 mg/day or less.

The Expert Panel on Cholesterol Levels in Children and Adolescents recommends two approaches to the reduction of cardiovascular disease: (1) a population approach focusing on changes in the current diet of all children and adolescents over two years of age as described above, and (2) an individualized screening (determining cholesterol levels, and low-density lipoprotein cholesterol if indicated) for children and adolescents who are "at risk" (those with a family history of hyperlipidemia or early cardiovascular events). Even though population screening identifies a number of false positives (children with elevated lipoprotein levels that will not remain elevated in adulthood), some researchers feel that screening of only "high-risk" individuals will miss 50% of children with elevated lipid levels, and that all children should be screened.[34]

Hyperlipidemia

Both cholesterol and triglycerides in the plasma are derived from two sources, dietary intake and endogenous synthesis in the liver and intestines. Dietary cholesterol is absorbed in proportion to the amount consumed. Increases in intakes reduce endogenous synthesis only partially. Endogenous triglycerides are synthesized from carbohydrate, fatty acids, and a variety of two-carbon fragments.

All plasma lipids, cholesterol, triglycerides, and phospholipids are transported in the blood bound to protein, which solubilizes them. Four macromolecule families of plasma lipoproteins are found in the blood. **Chylomicrons** transport the major portion of dietary triglyceride. **Very low-density lipoproteins** (pre-beta-lipoproteins) transport endogenous triglyceride. **Low-density lipoproteins** (beta-lipoproteins) transport one half to two thirds of the total plasma cholesterol. **High-density lipoproteins** transport cholesterol and phospholipids. Low-density lipoprotein cholesterol is transported primarily to peripheral tissue and the smooth muscle of the arterial intima. High-density lipoprotein cholesterol travels through the capillary bed of peripheral tissue and acquires redundant-free cholesterol. It is ultimately carried to the liver where it is released and excreted. Low-density lipoproteins appear to damage the arteries, whereas high-density lipoproteins are beneficial. The ratio of low-density lipoprotein cholesterol to high-density lipoprotein cholesterol has been found to be a good predictor for coronary heart disease.

Cholesterol concentrations are lower in cord blood than in maternal blood and rise after newborns are fed. At 6 months of age infants fed human milk or cow's milk have higher serum cholesterol concentrations than those fed formulas containing soy or corn oil. These differences are modified when other foods are added to the diet. At 1 year of age differences in serum cholesterol levels between infants fed cow's milk or formula with unsaturated fatty acids and a variety of other food disappear. Total protein, total fat, and cholesterol intakes correlate with total serum lipoprotein cholesterol and serum low-density lipoprotein cholesterol at 1 year of age.[35] After weaning, serum cholesterol concentrations are unaffected by the method of feeding in early infancy.

Serum cholesterol levels vary at different age groups and into adulthood (Table 12-2). There are significant changes between birth and 2 years of age and during sexual maturation. Re-

TABLE 12-2   *Serum Lipids and Lipoprotein Levels for Infants, Children, and Young Adults (Bogalusa Heart Study)*

Age (Years)	Total Cholesterol		Triglycerides (mg/dl)	
	Median	(90th P)	Median	(90th P)
Birth	68	94	34	67
6 months	132	173	81	141
1-2	147	179	64	120
3-4	157	191	56	95
5-6	158	194	51	88
7-8	163	196	53	92
9-10	165	203	57	106
11-12	161	200	61	115
13-14	155	192	61	109
15-16	151	189	61	109
17-18	155	200	63	106
19-20	160	210	76	136
21-22	165	215	78	156
23-24	170	219	81	164
25-26	177	221	85	186

	Cholesterol Fractions (mg/dl)					
	HDL-C		LDL-C		VLDL-C	
Age (Years)	(10th P)	Median	Median	(90th P)	Median	(90th P)
Birth	18	35	29	43	2	9
6 months	27	51	73	99	9	22
1-2	33	55	85	113	6	16
3-4	36	59	92	122	4	13
5-6	43	67	86	117	4	13
7-8	43	66	91	123	4	14
9-10	40	67	91	127	5	17
11-12	38	62	90	123	7	19
13-14	37	61	84	117	7	19
15-16	35	58	82	118	8	19
17-18	35	57	89	128	8	19
19-20	24	51	101	143	9	22
21-22	23	50	102	155	10	27
23-24	23	52	106	155	10	29
25-26	23	52	116	156	12	34

From Berensen GS and others: Prevention of adult heart disease beginning in the pediatric age. In Frohoick ED (editor): *Preventive aspects of coronary disease,* and Brest AN: Cardiovascular Clinics, Philadelphia, 1990, FA Davis.

searchers in Louisiana noted dramatic rises in the first 2 years of life. Low-density lipoproteins account for the major increase during the first year. However, a slow but progressive rise in high-density lipoproteins occurs.[36]

No dramatic changes occur in lipid or lipoprotein levels in school-age children. During adolescence, race- and sex-specific changes in cholesterol levels occur. There is a decrease in high-density lipoprotein serum cholesterol levels accompanied by an increase in low-density lipoprotein serum cholesterol levels in white males between 10 and 16 years of age. High-density lipoprotein cholesterol levels decline in black males of the same age, although not as dramatically. Black males also experience a slight drop in low-density lipoprotein cholesterol levels. Declines occur in high-density lipoprotein cholesterol levels with almost no change in low-density lipoprotein cholesterol levels in both black and white females between 9 and 14 years of age. The ratio of mean serum levels of low-density lipoprotein cholesterol to levels of high-density lipoprotein cholesterol rises dramatically in white boys beginning at 11 years of age, but it remains unchanged in black adolescent males and black and white adolescent females.[36] After 24 years of age, a progressive rise in total cholesterol for the next 30 years occurs.

The Louisiana study found that cholesterol levels in the first year were the most predictive factors studied of subsequent cholesterol levels. Of the children at the 90th and 10th percentiles in the first year, 45% persisted at their respective levels in the second year. Children of parents with high serum cholesterol levels are 2.57 times more likely to have serum cholesterol levels greater than the 95th percentile.[37] Another longitudinal study in Iowa found that of those children with cholesterol levels above the 75th percentile 75% of boys and 56% of girls would not qualify for intervention as adults. Of the children with cholesterol levels above the 95th percentile, 57% of girls and 37% of boys would not qualify for intervention as adults.[38]

Studies have suggested that 5% of the children in the United States have serum cholesterol levels greater than 200 to 220 mg/100 ml. It appears that these individuals will maintain their elevated levels throughout childhood and into adulthood; they are considered at risk of developing coronary artery disease.[37] As they grow older, they will be joined by others who enter the ranks of the "at risk" population.

Etiological Factors in Atherosclerosis

Cardiovascular disease, considered epidemic in the western world, is responsible for more deaths in the United States than all other causes. **Atherosclerosis** is responsible for more than 50% of the deaths resulting from cardiovascular disease.

Atherosclerosis is a major specific type of **arteriosclerosis,** and involving primarily the large elastic and medium-sized arteries. Lipids similar to those circulating in the blood accumulate on the intima of the arteries, to which an accumulation of connective tissue and various blood products are added, and plaques result. Several complications such as hemorrhage, thrombosis, or ulceration can occur in the atherosclerotic lesion and can transform plaques into rough, complicated lesions. The plaques narrow the lumen of the arteries and may produce a deficiency of blood flow to some degree. They set the stage for complete occlusion.

Fatty flecks and streaks are present by 3 to 5 months of age in the aortas of all children of all populations. As children age, the number and size of the streaks increase. Studies of animals have suggested that dietary intakes of cholesterol and fatty acids determine whether the fatty deposits are reabsorbed, remain, or develop into atherosclerotic plaques.[39,40]

The average extent of intimal involvement is small in the first 10 years of life. After the first decade the extent of the intimal surface involved by fatty streaks increases rapidly. The lipid in the juvenile fatty streak is predominantly intracellular with minimal connective tissue. Black children have more extensive fatty streaks than do children of other ethnic groups. Females have more extensive streaking than do males. This is true in all populations studied, regardless of the incidence of atherosclerosis. After 25 to 29 years of age, differences appear. Fatty streaks progress through continued lipid accumulation and lead to plaque formation. These fatty streaks contain much of their lipid in the form of extracellular accumulations in areas where intact cells are scanty. An increase in extracellular components of connective tissue also becomes apparent. Fibrous plaques then appear in a significant number of cases.

Autopsies of male soldiers in their early twenties who died in the wars in Korea and Vietnam revealed a striking incidence of atherosclerotic plaques. Of the males killed in Korea, 77% were found to have evidence of atherosclerosis, ranging from minimal thickening to complete occlusion of one or more of the main artery branches.[41] Autopsies of soldiers killed in Vietnam revealed a lesser but significant incidence of atherosclerosis. Of the casualties on whom autopsies were performed during this war, 45% were found to have atherosclerosis, but only 5% had gross evidence of coronary artery involvement.[42]

Autopsy studies of children from the Bogalusa Heart Study found an adverse effect of elevated risk factor levels including serum cholesterol and lipoprotein levels in accelerating the development of fatty streaks and fibrous plaques in adolescence.[43]

Risk Factors Associated with Atherosclerosis

Two hundred and forty-six risk factors have been identified for cardiovascular disease. However, the major risk factors include elevated serum levels of low-density lipoprotein cholesterol, cigarette smoking, hypertension, obesity, sedentary life-style, and a family history of heart disease. There is also some evidence that there is a relationship between watching television and cholesterol levels. Children who watched the most television had the highest cholesterol levels, probably because they had less exercise. All risk factors have been found to be independent and continuous variables.[44] No arbitrary serum cholesterol level exists at which the risk of developing cardiovascular heart disease is increased. As the serum cholesterol level increases, the risk for atherosclerosis increases. Also, the risk of developing atherosclerosis increases as the number of risk factors increases. Two or three risk factors increase the risk for atherosclerosis in an exponential manner. For example, the obese individual with a moderately elevated serum cholesterol level who has

hypertension and smokes cigarettes has a higher risk of developing atherosclerosis than the person who has a more elevated serum cholesterol level but is lean, active, and does not smoke.

Elevated serum low-density lipoprotein cholesterol and low serum high-density lipoprotein cholesterol concentrations are clearly risk factors in the etiology of coronary artery disease. Populations that consume diets rich in cholesterol and saturated fats have higher serum cholesterol concentrations and higher incidences of and mortality rates from premature coronary heart disease than populations that consume diets low in cholesterol and saturated fats. The risk of developing premature atherosclerotic heart disease increases in any population group as the serum cholesterol concentration rises. The Framingham study showed that the risk of myocardial infarction for men 30 to 49 years of age increased five times if cholesterol levels were greater than 260 mg/100 ml as compared with less than 220 mg/100 ml.[45]

Effect of Dietary Intervention

It has been proved that dietary alterations can reduce serum lipids. Reduction in intakes of dietary cholesterol reduces serum lipids by 5% to 8%. Reductions in intakes of saturated fats accompanied by increases in intakes of polyunsaturated fats and reductions in cholesterol can reduce the serum cholesterol by 24%.[46] It has not been possible, however, to establish relationships in individuals between serum cholesterol levels and dietary consumption of fat and cholesterol. Morrison and others[46a] found few significant correlations between dietary lipid and lipoprotein levels in 10-year-old children. However, children in the top quartiles for serum cholesterol ingested more total fat, more saturated fat, and less polyunsaturated fat than those in the lowest quartile.

McGandy[47] reduced kcalories from fat from 39% to 34%, reduced cholesterol consumption from 720 to 380 mg/day, and increased the dietary P/S ratio from 0.2 to 1.2 in children 12 to 18 years of age. Boys whose initial serum cholesterol was 200 mg/100 ml experienced a reduction of 15%. However, those whose initial serum cholesterol was 199 mg/100 ml or less experienced a reduction of only 8.3%.

Dietary factors other than fats have been shown to influence cholesterol levels. For example, fiber, especially pectin, has a **hypocholesterolemic** effect.

Recommendations

An effort to prevent cardiovascular heart disease has been recommended and is currently being implemented in most areas of the United States. Two efforts are directed toward children and adolescents; a change in the diet for all children limiting intakes of total fat, saturated fatty acids, and cholesterol, and the identification of the child "at high risk" because of a family history of cardiovascular heart disease. In addition, efforts need to be made to reduce the other risk factors such as smoking, stress, and obesity.

Dietary Changes

The Expert Panel from the National Institutes of Health (NIH) recommends a pattern of food intake for children over 2 years of age that includes foods low in saturated fatty acids, total fat, and cholesterol and that provides sufficient energy to support normal growth and development.[34] Specifically, they recommend a diet that includes (1) less than 10% of kcalories as saturated fatty acids, (2) no more than 30% of kcalories from total fat, and (3) less than 300 mg cholesterol per day.

It is probable that a reduction in total fat intake will aid in the prevention of obesity, since fat is a more concentrated source of energy than other nutrients. However, it is important that energy intake be maintained to support normal growth. This means that intakes of carbohydrate will be increased. The panel recommends an intake of 55% of energy using mostly complex carbohydrates. They recommend increasing intakes of pastas, breads and cereals, legumes, and fruits and vegetables. Most of these foods will also provide fiber.

The recommendation that children consume no more than 300 mg cholesterol per day will not be hard to achieve. Most children do not now consume more than this: average intakes for children 1 to 5 years are 193 mg/day; for children 6 to 11 years, 255 mg/day; and for children 12 to 19 years of age, 297 mg/day. It

has been suggested that a cholesterol intake based on energy intake might be more appropriate.[37]

Lowering total fat in the current diet will mean that children will need to consume more low-fat dairy products, more low-fat cuts of meat, and few baked products made with fat. It will be important that the diets of children continue to be monitored for adequate energy intakes as children and adolescents implement the suggested changes. A diet that reduces total fat to the suggested level may include a number of high-fiber foods. The young child with a finicky appetite may soon be satiated. Careful planning will be necessary to ensure an adequate energy intake.

Since most children consume a considerable percentage of food away from home, implementation of the recommendations will involve not only nutrition education for the children and their parents but changes in the menu patterns of many day-care and school feeding programs. The contents of school vending machines, snack bars, and student stores will need to include "heart healthy" foods. The food industry also has an important role to play in the implementation of the suggested changes by providing appropriate low-fat foods for children and labeling foods so that parents and children can identify the saturated fatty acids in the products in the grocery store.

Dietary changes should be implemented by all of the health and educational professionals who interact with the child and family. Nutrition education at school can focus on teaching young children to make appropriate food choices at snack time and during meals; adolescents can assume responsibility for developing a "heart healthy" diet and life-style. Physicians, dietitians, and nurses should include an assessment of the child's fat intake in their health surveillance programs and help the children and their parents implement a diet that provides no more than 30% of the kcalories as fat, no more than 10% of the kcalories as saturated fat, and no more than 300 mg cholesterol per day.

Selective Screening

The second approach recommended by the NIH panel is selective screening; that is, identi-

TABLE 12-3   *Classification of Total and LDL-Cholesterol Levels in Children and Adolescents From Families with Hypercholesterolemia or Premature Cardiovascular Disease*

Category	Total Cholesterol (mg/dL)*	LDL Cholesterol (mg/dL)*
Acceptable	<170	<110
Borderline	170-199	110-129
High	≥200	≥130

From Expert Panel on Blood Cholesterol Levels in Children and Adolescents: *Report of the health panel on blood cholesterol levels in children and adolescents,* Public Health Service, National Institutes of Health, Pub No 91-2732, Washington, DC, 1991, US Department of Health and Human Services.
*To convert cholesterol values in mg/dL to millimoles per liter (mmol/L), multiply by 0.02586.

fication by physician and nurse practitioners of children "at high risk" for developing cardiovascular heart disease during health surveillance. Those at risk include children with a family history of **hypercholesterolemia** or cardiovascular disease, children who smoke, have high blood pressure, or whose diets include excessive amounts of cholesterol and saturated fatty acids. The screening protocol will vary with the reason for the high-risk designation. If one parent has high cholesterol levels, a determination of total cholesterol will be made. If the cholesterol level is borderline (Table 12-3), a second measurement will be made.[34] If the total cholesterol is high, a lipoprotein analysis will be obtained. If the child is being tested because of a family history of premature cardiovascular disease, a lipoprotein analysis will be the first test performed. Acceptable ranges are shown in Table 12-3.[3]

If children have borderline or high low-density lipoprotein cholesterol levels, implementation of the diet previously described for the entire population is recommended. If the low-density lipoprotein cholesterol level is high and the diet does not sufficiently lower the lipid levels, a diet providing less than 200 mg cholesterol and 7% of total kcalories as saturated fatty acids is recommended. If diet fails to lower the lipid levels sufficiently, the use of cholesterol-lowering drugs should be considered.[34]

The recommendation for selective screening is based on the fact that population screening is costly and identifies a significant number of children with high cholesterol levels who will not be hypercholesterolemic as adults.[38] However, researchers are concerned that selective screening will miss a significant number of children with hypercholesterolemia. Steiner, Neinstein, and Pennbridge[48] found that one third to one half of teenagers with hypercholesterolemia will have been missed with selective screening. It is likely that one will find individual and mass screening in health care agencies and among individual practitioners.

SALT INTAKE

Essential hypertension, another risk factor in cardiovascular heart disease, as well as stroke and renal disease, is also a major health problem affecting 20% of adults over 40 years of age. Epidemiological studies have suggested that as with hyperlipidemia, genetic and environmental factors interact to determine an individual's susceptibility to hypertension. Salt has been implicated as one factor that may cause this disorder.

Success in reducing blood pressure in hypertensive patients with the low-sodium rice diet designed by Kempner caused some researchers to hypothesize that excessive salt intakes could cause hypertension. Dahl[49] became so convinced that salt intakes were important in the development of hypertension that he devoted his life to this research. He studied the effect of salt intakes on thousands of rats, the effect of reduced sodium intake on hypertensive patients, and the relationship of sodium intakes to the incidence of hypertension in populations.

Evidence from Animal Studies

Meneely and others[50] induced hypertension in rats by mixing salt with their food and allowing them to consume as much water and food as they wished. They studied six groups of rats, each of which was fed an increasing amount of salt, and found that as sodium chloride intakes increased, elevations in blood pressures increased. Hypertension developed early in those animals who consumed the highest salt intakes. Although increases in blood pressure of groups of animals were related to the level of salt intakes, individual variations within groups were noted. They later fed diets that included extra amounts of salt to three groups of older animals who had been maintained on the basic food throughout their lives. Elevations in blood pressure did occur, but increases were always less than those of the young animals who ate the same rations.[51]

Dahl and others[52] found that in unselected rats, blood pressure increases in response to high salt intakes ranged from none to gradually increasing blood pressures, including the malignant phase. Some rats died from hypertension within a few months. One fourth of the animals showed no increase in blood pressure. The other animals developed increases in blood pressure that were associated with increasing morbidity and mortality.

In successive generations, rats were inbred and a strain of rats genetically susceptible to salt was developed. It was found that increased salt intakes of these animals during the first 12 to 13 months after weaning produced hypertension that was sustained regardless of later reductions in sodium intakes. Control rats fed low-sodium mixtures developed no hypertension.[53] Dahl, Heine, and Tassinari[54] concluded that salt intakes in infancy and early childhood may be more critical than those in later life to persons genetically determined to be responsive to salt intakes. In 1963 they fed commercially prepared salted infant foods to those rats bred to be genetically sensitive to salt. Five of seven rats developed hypertension, whereas none of the seven control rats who were fed low-sodium diets developed the disorder. At that time they suggested that there may be groups of human infants with similar genetic potentials who are at risk of induced hypertension from salt intakes in early life. They advocated reductions in salt intakes in infancy.

Srinivasan and others[55] found that systolic and diastolic blood pressure levels increased in spider monkeys that were fed salt and salt-sucrose diets as compared with the levels of monkeys fed a control diet. A greater rise was noted in blood pressure of those fed the salt-sucrose diet. They suggested a potentiating effect of sucrose on sodium-induced hypertension.

Studies of Populations

Dahl[49] studied five population groups whose lifetime salt intakes varied from 4 to 26 gm/day and found that as average salt intakes increased, the incidence of hypertension increased.

Gleibermann[56] reviewed studies of 27 populations. Sodium intakes had been estimated by urinary excretion of sodium for 24 hours in some and by estimated salt intakes in others. Her statistical analysis of these studies suggested a direct relationship between salt intakes and blood pressure across population lines.

The Intersalt Cooperative Research Group[57] studied the relationship between 24-hour urinary electrolytes and blood pressure in 10,079 men and women, 20 to 59 years of age, in 52 centers around the world. It was only centers in which very low sodium excretion was found that a population was identified with low blood pressure and in which there was little or no increase in blood pressure with age. In the other centers sodium excretion was related to the slope of blood pressure with age but not to the prevalence of hypertension nor median blood pressure of the subjects. Within centers sodium excretion was related to blood pressure in individuals. The sodium to potassium excretion ratio and blood pressure in individuals had a pattern similar to sodium alone but was stronger and more consistent. Body mass index and alcohol consumption were positively associated with blood pressure in individuals.

The relationship of salt intakes of individuals to blood pressure has not been established.

Data from the HANES I study and from a large population in Connecticut found no relationship between blood pressure and dietary sodium or salt intake.[58]

Studies in children have not conclusively established a relationship between salt intakes and blood pressure. Whitten and Stewart[59] studied two groups of black males starting at 3 months of age: one fed a low level of salt; the other fed a high level of salt. They found no difference in blood pressure levels of the two groups at 8 months or 8 years of age.

Siervogelm and others[60] found a strong relationship between urinary sodium and systolic blood pressure in 8- to 18-year-old white children. However, the relationship was not significant when body size, obesity, and age were considered.

Falkner, Oresti, and Angelakos[61] found that adolescents with normal blood pressure from families with a history of hypertension who were fed a high-salt diet for 2 weeks and then stressed with difficult mathematical problems had a greater heart rate and blood pressure than did a control group. No differences were noted in children fed the high-salt diet and then stressed if their families had no history of hypertension.

It has been estimated that 18% of the population is hypertensive and that about one third to one half of those individuals are salt sensitive. A practical method for identifying salt-sensitive individuals is not available.[62]

BLOOD PRESSURE DURING CHILDHOOD

Blood pressure in adults is correlated with childhood blood pressure and body size.[63] Some individuals who are likely to be hypertensive adults can be identified in childhood and preventive intervention can be suggested. Goals during childhood are (1) surveillance, (2) possible prevention, and (3) identification and treatment of children who are already hypertensive. However, no mass screening is recommended.[62] Ideally, blood pressure measurements are included during well child and subsequent medical visits and "at risk" children can be iden-

tified over time. Blood pressure readings increase from 3 months of age through adolescence. The definition of hypertension during childhood is age specific (Table 12-4).

SODIUM INTAKES

Sodium intake of infants is relatively low when human milk and commercially prepared infant foods are consumed and relatively high when cow's milk and table foods are eaten. As the transition is made to table foods, salt intakes will reflect family food habits and cultural patterns.

The use of convenience foods and the popularity of fast-food establishments for feeding children past infancy have given the food industry a major role in determining salt intakes of children.[64]

Commercially prepared infant foods have no salt added during preparation. Many parents prefer to make their own infant foods from a variety of foods prepared and seasoned for the family. Those who serve the highest sodium intakes to their infants have less education, feed salty snacks, and heavily salt their own food.[66] Salt intakes in the United States average 7 to 10 gm/day; intakes of 10 to 20 gm/day are common.

Need for Sodium

Sodium is an essential nutrient. It functions in the maintenance of water and acid-base balance and the regulation of blood volume. It regulates cell membrane and capillary permeability and is a constituent of tissues. It is estimated that total body sodium increases from 240 mEq in the 3.3-kg newborn to 3100 mEq in a 70-kg adult. Requirements are determined by the individual's needs for growth and by losses from the skin and in the urine and stools.[67] Needs for growth are estimated to be 0.5 mEq/kg/day during the first 3 months, 0.2 mEq/kg/day from 3 to 6 months, 0.1 mEq/kg/day from 6 to 12 months, and less than 0.1 mEq/kg/day after the first year. Skin losses depend on the ambient temperature. Sodium losses from stools are independent of intake, averaging 5% to 10% in the first year. Because of

TABLE 12-4   Classification of Hypertension by Age Group

Age Group	Significant Hypertension (mm Hg)	Severe Hypertension (mm Hg)
Newborn		
7 d	Systolic BP ≥96	Systolic BP ≥106
8-30 d	Systolic BP ≥104	Systolic BP ≥110
Infant (<2 yr)	Systolic BP ≥112	Systolic BP ≥118
	Diastolic BP ≥74	Diastolic BP ≥82
Children (3-5 yr)	Systolic BP ≥116	Systolic BP ≥124
	Diastolic BP ≥76	Diastolic BP ≥84
Children (6-9 yr)	Systolic BP ≥122	Systolic BP ≥130
	Diastolic BP ≥78	Diastolic BP ≥86
Children (10-12 yr)	Systolic BP ≥126	Systolic BP ≥134
	Diastolic BP ≥82	Diastolic BP ≥90
Adolescents (13-15 yr)	Systolic BP ≥136	Systolic BP ≥144
	Diastolic BP ≥86	Diastolic BP ≥92
Adolescents (16-18 yr)	Systolic BP ≥142	Systolic BP ≥150
	Diastolic BP ≥92	Diastolic BP ≥98

From Task Force on Blood Pressure Control in Children, American Academy of Pediatrics: *Pediatrics* 79:1, 1987.

the variability of losses, Fomon[68] suggests an advisable intake of 8 mEq/day from birth to 4 months of age, 6 mEq/day from 4 to 24 months of age, and 8 mEq/day from 24 to 36 months of age. Humans adapt to a wide range of sodium intake by varying excretion in relation to intake and nonrenal losses. Safe limits for normal children appear to be between 8 and 100 mEq/day.

The Task Force on Blood Pressure Control in Children[64] recommends limiting sodium intake to 5 to 6 gm (85 to 100 mEq)/day if a child is hypertensive. It is also important to increase potassium-rich foods in the diet when intakes of salt are limited.

It is important to remember that iodized salt is a major source of iodine in the United States. Intakes by children who consume low-sodium diets should be carefully monitored for iodine. A palpable goiter has been noted in two adolescent females whose family had adopted a low-sodium dietary intake because of diagnosed hypertension in the father.

Summary

Obesity, hypertension, and hyperlipoproteinemia are all risk factors for adult cardiovascular disease and other disorders. A number of studies have indicated that the atherosclerotic process begins in childhood and that total cholesterol, low-density lipoprotein cholesterol, very low-density lipoprotein cholesterol levels, and high-density lipoprotein levels are correlated with the extent of the atherosclerotic lesions in adolescents and young adults.

It has been demonstrated that the lipid levels in the blood can be reduced by altering the present diet. Efforts have been directed to reduce intakes of fats and saturated fatty acids in the current diet of children and adolescents in hopes that reducing the risk factors of individuals will reduce the incidence of and the morbidity and mortality from cardiovascular heart disease. Recommendations have also been made to prevent obesity and moderate salt intakes.

REVIEW QUESTIONS

1. Define obesity and superobesity in childhood.
2. When should a weight reduction diet be planned for an obese child?
3. Why are there differences of opinion regarding individual and population screening for hyperlipidemia?
4. What dietary changes are recommended for children in the United States to reduce the incidence of cardiovascular heart disease?
5. What level of sodium restriction is recommended for children who are hypertensive?

SUGGESTED LEARNING ACTIVITIES

1. Plan a week's menu for a 5-year-old girl who weighs 21 kg and is 109 cm tall. The diet should maintain her weight.
2. Investigate and report on physical activities that are developmentally appropriate to increase energy expenditure for 2- and 8-year-old girls.
3. Describe how you would counsel the parents of an obese 8-month-old boy.
4. Describe children at risk of hyperlipoproteinemia. How would one counsel parents of these children?
5. Investigate the salt content of fast-food menu items.

Terms and Concepts

Provided here for your review is a listing of terms and concepts within this chapter. The definitions for terms can be found in the glossary, which begins on page 413. To aid your understanding of the terms' and concepts' application within this text, the page number designating the first mention of each term or concept within the chapter is given.

arteriosclerosis, 299
atherosclerosis, 299
chylomicrons, 297
high-density lipoproteins, 297
hypercholesterolemia, 302
hypocholesterolemia, 302
low-density lipoproteins, 297
obesity, 288
overweight, 289
resting metabolic rate (RMR), 290
self-esteem, 289
superobesity, 289
very low-density lipoproteins, 297

REFERENCES

1. Gutin B and others: Blood pressure, fitness, and fatness in 5- and 6-year-old children, *JAMA* 264:1123, 1990.
2. Gortmaker SL and others: Increasing pediatric obesity in the United States, *Am J Dis Child* 141:535, 1987.
3. Knittle JL and others: *Childhood obesity.* In Suskin RM: *Textbook of pediatric nutrition,* New York, 1981, Raven Press.
4. Kalata G: Obese children: a growing problem, *Science* 232:20, 1986.
5. Mullins AG: The prognosis in juvenile obesity, *Arch Dis Child* 33:307, 1958.
6. Zack PM and others: A longitudinal study of body fatness in childhood and adolescence, *J Pediatr* 95:126, 1979.
7. Forbes GB: Lean body mass and fat in obese children, *Pediatrics* 34:308, 1964.
8. Angel JL: Constitution in female obesity, *Am J Phys Anthropol* 7:433, 1949.
9. Gurney R: The hereditary factor in obesity, *Arch Intern Med* 57:557, 1936.
10. Stunkard AJ and others: An adoption study of human obesity, *N Engl J Med* 314:193, 1986.
11. Griffiths M and others: Metabolic rate and physical development in children at risk of obesity, *Lancet* 336:76, 1990.
12. Seltzer CC, Mayer J: Body build and obesity—who are the obese? *JAMA* 189:677, 1964.
13. Dietz WH, Gortmaker SL: Do we fatten our children at the television set? Obesity and television viewing in children and adolescents, *Pediatrics* 75:807, 1985.
14. Shukla A and others: Infantile overnutrition in the first year of life: a field study of Dudley, Worcestershire, *Br Med J* 4:507, 1972.
15. Sveger T and others: Nutrition, overnutrition, and obesity in the first year of life in Malmo, Sweden, *Acta Paediatr Scand* 64:635, 1975.
16. Fisch RO, Bilek MK, Ulstrom R: Obesity and leanness at birth and their relationship to body habits in later childhood, *Pediatrics* 56:521, 1975.
17. Yeung DL and others: Infant fatness and feeding practices: a longitudinal assessment, *J Am Diet Assoc* 79:531, 1981.
18. Fomon SJ and others: Indices of fatness and serum cholesterol at age eight years in relation to feeding and growth during early infancy, *Pediatr Res* 18:1233, 1984.
19. Shapiro LR and others: Obesity prognosis: a longitudinal study of children from the age of 6 months to 9 years, *Am J Public Health* 74:968, 1984.

20. Committee on Nutrition, American Academy of Pediatrics: Nutritional aspects of obesity in infancy and childhood, *Pediatrics* 68:880, 1981.

21. Hammer SL and others: An interdisciplinary study of adolescent obesity, *J Pediatr* 80:373, 1972.

22. Massengale ON: The obese adolescent observations on etiology management prevention, *Clin Pediatr* 4:649, 1965.

23. Hertzler AA: Obesity-impact of the family, *J Am Diet Assoc* 79:525, 1981.

24. Bruch H: Obesity in childhood. III. Physiologic and psychologic aspects of food intake of obese children, *Am J Dis Child* 59:739, 1940.

25. Kahn EJ: Obesity in children: identification of a group at risk in a New York ghetto, *J Pediatr* 77:771, 1970.

26. Garn SM, Clark DC, Guire KE: *Growth, body composition and development of obese and lean children.* In Winick M, editor: *Childhood obesity,* New York, 1975, John Wiley & Sons.

27. Garn SM, Hopkins PJ, Ryan AS: Differential fatness of low income boys and girls, *Am J Clin Nutr* 34:1465, 1981.

28. Griffith M, Payne PR: Energy expenditure in small children of obese and nonobese parents, *Nature* 260:698, 1976.

29. Pugliese MT and others: Fear of obesity: a cause of short stature and delayed puberty, *N Engl J Med* 301:513, 1983.

30. Epstein L and others: Growth in obese children treated for obesity, *Am J Dis Child* 144:1360, 1990.

31. Wolff OH, Lloyd JK: Obesity in childhood, *Proc Nutr Soc* 32:195, 1973.

32. Weidman K and others: Diet in the healthy child, *Circulation* 67:1411, 1983.

33. Wynder EL and others: Summary and recommendations of the conference on blood lipids in children: optimal levels for early prevention of coronary artery disease, *Prev Med* 12:728, 1983.

34. Expert Panel on Blood Cholesterol Levels in Children and Adolescents: *Report of the expert panel on blood cholesterol levels in children and adolescents,* Public Health Service, National Institutes of Health, Pub No (NIH) 91-2732, Washington, DC, 1991, US Department of Health and Human Services.

35. Farris RP and others: Influence of milk source on serum lipids and lipoproteins during the first year of life, *Am J Clin Nutr* 38:42, 1982.

36. Berenson GS and others: *Prevention of adult heart disease beginning in the pediatric age.* In Frohoick ED, editor: *Preventive aspect of coronary disease,* and Brest AN: *Cardiovascular clinics,* Philadelphia, 1990, FA Davis.

37. Berenson GS and others: Serum high-density lipoprotein and its relationship to cardiovascular disease risk factor variables in children—the Bogalusa Heart Study, *Lipids* 14:91, 1979.

38. Lauer RM, Clarke WR: Use of cholesterol measurements in childhood for the prediction of adult hypercholesterolemia: the Muscatine study, *JAMA* 264:3034, 1990.

39. Armstrong ML, Warner ED, Connor WE: Regression of coronary atheromatosis in rhesus monkeys, *Circ Res* 27:59, 1970.

40. Wissler RW and others: Atherogenesis in the cebus monkey, *Arch Pathol* 74:312, 1962.

41. Enos WF, Holmes RH, Beyer JC: Coronary disease among United States soldiers killed in action in Korea, *JAMA* 152:1090, 1952.

42. McNamara JJ and others: Coronary artery disease in combat casualties in Vietnam, *JAMA* 216:1185, 1971.

43. Cresanta JL and others: Prevention of atherosclerosis in childhood, *Pediatr Clin North Am* 33:835, 1986.

44. Goldsmith MF: Youngsters dialing up cholesterol levels? *JAMA* 264:2976, 1990.

45. Dawber T and others: The epidemiology of coronary heart disease, *Proc R Soc Med* 55:265, 1962.

46. North AF: Should pediatricians be concerned about children's cholesterol levels? *Clin Pediatr* 14:439, 1975.

46a. Morrison JA and others: Parent-child association at upper and lower ranges of plasma cholesterol and triglyceride levels, *Pediatrics* 62:468, 1978.

47. McGandy RB: Adolescence and the onset of atherosclerosis, *Bull NY Acad Med* 47:590, 1971.

48. Steiner NJ, Neinstein LS, Pennbridge J: Hypercholesterolemia in adolescents: effectiveness of screening strategies based on selected risk factors, *Pediatrics* 88:269, 1991.

49. Dahl LK: Salt and hypertension, *Am J Clin Nutr* 25:231, 1972.

50. Meneely GR and others: Chronic sodium chloride toxicity in the albino rat. II. Occurrence of hypertension and a syndrome of edema and renal failure, *J Exp Med* 98:71, 1953.

51. Meneely GR, Ball COT: Experimental epidemiology of chronic sodium chloride toxicity and the protective effect of potassium chloride, *Am J Med* 25:713, 1958.

52. Dahl LK and others: Effects of chronic excess salt ingestion: modifications of experimental hypertension in the rat by variations in the diet, *Circ Res* 22:11, 1968.

53. Dahl LK: Effect of chronic excess salt feeding induction of self-sustaining hypertension in rats, *J Exp Med* 114:231, 1961.

54. Dahl LK, Heine M, Tassinari L: High salt content of Western infants' diet: possible relationship to hypertension in the adult, *Nature* 198:1204, 1963.

55. Srinivasan SR and others: Effects of dietary sodium and sucrose on the induction of hypertension in spider monkeys, *Am J Clin Nutr* 33:561, 1980.

56. Gleibermann L: Blood pressure and dietary salt in human populations, *Ecol Food Nutr* 2:143, 1973.

57. Intersalt Cooperative Research Group: Intersalt: an international study of electrolyte excretion and blood pressure: results for 24 hour urinary sodium and potassium excretion, *Br Med J* 297:319, 1988.

58. Harlan WR and others: *Dietary intake and cardiovascular risk factors. I. Blood pressure correlates: United States 1971-75,* Vital and Health Statistics, Series 11, No 226, DHHS, Pub No PHS 831676, Public Health Services, Washington, DC, Feb 1983, US Government Printing Office.

59. Whitten CF, Stewart RA: The effect of dietary sodium in infancy on blood pressure and related factors, *Acta Paediatr Scand Suppl* 279, 1980.

60. Siervogelm RM and others: Blood pressure, electrolytes, and body size: their relationships in young relatives of men with essential hypertension, *Hypertension* 2(part II):183, 1980.

61. Falkner B, Oresti G, Angelakos D: Effect of salt loading on the cardiovascular response to stress in adolescents, *Hypertension* 3(part III):195, 1981.

62. Task Force on Blood Pressure Control in Children, American Academy of Pediatrics: Report of the second task force on blood pressure control in children—1987, *Pediatrics* 79:1, 1987.

63. Lauer RM, Clarke WR: Childhood risk factors for high adult blood pressure: the Muscatine study, *Pediatrics* 84:633, 1989.

64. Committee on Nutrition, American Academy of Pediatrics: Sodium intake of infants in the United States, *Pediatrics* 68:444, 1981.

65. Select Committee on GRAS Substances: *Evaluation of the health aspects of sodium chloride and potassium chloride as food ingredients,* SCOGS 12, Bethesda, Md, 1979, Federation of American Societies for Experimental Biology, Life Science Research Office.

66. Schaefer LJ, Kumanyika SK: Maternal variables related to potentially high infant-feeding practices, *J Am Diet Assoc* 85:433, 1985.

67. Sperotto G: *Sodium chloride in pediatrics.* In Moses C, editor: *Sodium in medicine and health,* Baltimore, Md, 1980, Reese Press.

68. Fomon SJ: *Infant nutrition,* Philadelphia, 1974, WB Saunders.

13

Nourishing the Preterm and Low Birth Weight Infant

Mary J. O'Leary
Joan Zerzan

Objectives

****

After studying this chapter, the student should:

✔ *Be aware of the reasons why the premature infant is at greater risk for nutritional problems than the full-term infant*

✔ *Be aware of the vulnerability of the premature infant to a variety of medical problems that may limit nurtrient and energy intake and complicate methods of feeding.*

✔ *Be aware of factors that determine whether the premature infant will receive parenteral or enteral feeds.*

✔ *Recognize that human milk from the infant's mother is an appropriate milk for the low birth weight baby.*

✔ *Know differences between formulas designed for the low birth weight baby and those designed for the full-term infant.*

Many advances have been made in neonatal intensive care in recent years. New technologies, better understanding of pathophysiology, and cooperative interactions to regionalize the delivery of perinatal care have contributed to the increased survival of newborns requiring intensive care. As the prognosis for survival of preterm and low birth weight (LBW) neonates improves, attention is being focused on the nutritional support of these infants. Adequacy of postnatal nutrition affects the clinical course of critically ill babies and may influence their long-term developmental outcome. This chapter describes current recommendations for nutrient intake, methods of nutritional support, and guidelines for nutritional assessment and management of preterm and LBW infants requiring intensive care.

Some of the material in this chapter has been adapted from O'Leary MJ: *Nutritional care of the low birth weight infant.* In Mahan LK, Arlin M: *Krause's food, nutrition, and diet therapy,* ed 8, Philadelphia, 1992, WB Saunders.

NUTRITIONAL SERVICES IN NEONATAL CARE

Delivery of Neonatal Care

Practical considerations of limited economic, technical, and human resources prohibit the availability of intensive care facilities in all hospitals. A regionalized system of perinatal services has evolved over the past 20 years to insure that all infants have equal access to the highest quality of care. The regional perinatal network encompasses three levels of neonatal care. The system of classifying nurseries as level I, II, or III, based on the type of care they are capable of providing, has been described in several publications.[1-3]

Level I nurseries provide uncomplicated neonatal care for healthy infants who are products of normal, full-term pregnancies. The personnel in these nurseries are trained in early detection of potential complications and use coordinated mechanisms for referral and transport of high-risk infants to level II or level III units. When problems arise, care provided in level I nurseries usually consists of stabilization until the infant can be safely transferred.

The personnel in level II nurseries provide a full range of services for healthy newborns. They also provide expertise in screening and referral of high-risk infants and are prepared to care for moderately ill neonates or convalescing babies whose immaturity or medical risks preclude discharge.

Level III nurseries are specifically staffed and equipped to cope with the most serious types of neonatal illnesses and abnormalities. A level III neonatal intensive care unit often assumes a leadership role within its region by setting standards of clinical care, developing educational materials, and providing consultative services to other nurseries. The nutrition specialist of such a unit may also have a similar opportunity and responsibility to serve as a regional resource for improvement in nutritional care of high-risk newborns.

Role of the Nutritionist

The National Research Council Committee on Nutrition of the Mother and Preschool Child has identified specific skills required to provide clinical services at each of the **three levels of neonatal care.**[4] These skills should enable the nutrition consultant to screen for various nutrition problems, monitor and assess nutritional progress, and develop and implement management plans.

Providing adequate nutrition to intensive care neonates is a challenge that requires the skillful input of several disciplines, including physicians, nurses, pharmacists, and occupational therapists. The nutritionist functions as a member of the health care team to facilitate nutritional support of individual infants and to develop guidelines for safe and effective nutritional management of critically ill neonates.[5]

CHARACTERISTICS OF PRETERM AND LOW BIRTH WEIGHT INFANTS REQUIRING INTENSIVE CARE

Definition and Classification

Infants cared for in level III intensive care units typically include infants at high medical risk and critically ill babies with serious medical or surgical problems. Increasing numbers of preterm and LBW infants are being admitted to level III intensive care units (see box on page 311, top). Although the medical status of larger babies may warrant intensive care, this chapter will focus on nutritional management of preterm and LBW infants who require intensive care (Figure 13-1).

Accurate assessment of **gestational age** is important in classifying an individual infant. An infant may be classified as large for gestational age (LGA), appropriate for gestational age (AGA), or small for gestational age (SGA) as shown in the bottom box on page 311. Classification of an infant as LGA, AGA, or SGA may have implications for early glucose tolerance, nutritional needs, and growth potential. This information may be useful in establishing nutritional goals for individual infants and anticipating potential difficulties in meeting those goals.

Metabolic Reserve

Preterm and LBW infants have smaller metabolic reserves and are physiologically less well prepared to maintain homeostasis immediately

❖
DEFINITION OF PRETERM OR LBW INFANTS

Preterm	<37 weeks' gestation
Low birth weight (LBW)	<2500 gm or <$5\frac{1}{2}$ lb
Very low birth weight (VLBW)	<1500 gm or <$3\frac{1}{3}$ lb
Extremely low birth weight (ELBW)	<1000 gm or <$2\frac{1}{4}$ lb

❖
CLASSIFICATION OF INFANTS AS LGA, AGA, OR SGA

Large for gestational age (LGA)	Birth weight > 90th percentile for gestational age
Appropriate for gestational age (AGA)	Birth weight between the 10th and 90th percentile for gestational age
Small for gestational age (SGA)	Birth weight < 10th percentile for gestational age

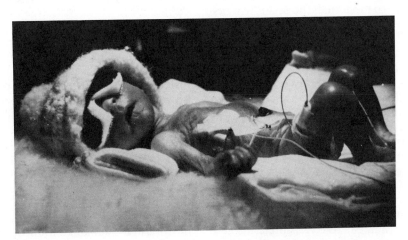

FIG. 13-1 Little girl born at 26 weeks' gestation weighing 650 gm. Her eyes are covered for protection from photography lights.

after birth than larger, full-term infants. Fat stores are limited because most fetal fat is deposited during the last 6 weeks of gestation. Fat contributes only 1% of the total body weight of the infant weighing 1000 gm. In contrast, 16% of the total body weight of a full-term infant (3500 gm) is fat.[6] Glycogen reserves of preterm infants are particularly small and are rapidly de-pleted. Babies who weigh 1000 gm have a glycogen and fat reserve of approximately 110 kcal/kg.[6,7] Because basal metabolic needs are about 50 kcal/kg/day, these babies will rapidly run out of fat and carbohydrate fuel unless adequate nutritional support is established. Depletion time will vary between 2 and 4 days depending on the volume and concentration of

TABLE 13-1 *Duration of Survival Expected in Starvation (H_2O Only) and Semistarvation ($D_{10}W$)*

Birth Weight (gm)	Estimated Survival Time (Days)	
	H_2O Only	$D_{10}W$
1000	4	11
2000	12	30
3500	32	80

From Heird WC and others: *J Pediatr* 80:351, 1972.

TABLE 13-2 *Examples of Problems Common to Preterm or LBW Infants*

System	Problem
Respiratory	Hyaline membrane disease, chronic lung disease (bronchopulmonary dysplasia)
Cardiovascular	Patent ductus arteriosus
Renal	Fluid and electrolyte imbalance
Neurological	Intracranial hemorrhage
Metabolic	Hypoglycemia, hyperglycemia, hypocalcemia, metabolic acidosis
Gastrointestinal	Hyperbilirubinemia, feeding intolerance, necrotizing enterocolitis
Hematological	Anemia
Immunological	Sepsis, pneumonia, meningitis
Other	ABCs (apnea, bradycardia, cyanosis)

IV dextrose that can be tolerated. Depletion time is even shorter for preterm or LBW infants who weigh less than 1000 gm.

It is often difficult to provide adequate nutrient intake during the first several days of life because of immaturity of organ systems and severe medical problems. When adequate dietary intake cannot be achieved and fat and glycogen reserves have been exhausted, the infant will begin to catabolize vital body protein tissue for energy. Heird and others[7] have theoretically estimated survival time of starved and semistarved infants assuming depletion of all glycogen and fat and about one third of body protein tissue at a rate of 50 kcal/kg/day with and without exogenous kcalories as intravenous dextrose (Table 13-1). The projected survival times are alarmingly short and occur at the expense of significant protein tissue catabolism. These numbers are estimates and lack empirical precision, but they do serve to demonstrate the disadvantage of the small infant when faced with inadequate nutritional support.

Because of limited reserves, preterm and LBW infants are particularly vulnerable to the potential consequences of **protein-energy malnutrition.**[8] Protein and energy malnutrition may have an impact on every organ system and may have long-term developmental consequences as noted. In adult and animal studies, undernutrition is associated with diaphragmatic muscle atrophy, decreased respiratory muscle force, alteration in ventilatory drive, and increased need for ventilatory support.[12] Although data are not available in infants, these studies suggest that undernutrition may further compromise the respiratory status of preterm infants with pulmonary disease. Animal and human studies also suggest that protein-energy malnutrition at critical periods of rapid brain growth may result in irreversible impairment of brain growth and function (see Chapter 1).[9-14]

Medical Complications

Preterm and LBW infants may have a variety of clinical problems in the early postnatal period. These problems vary in type and severity depending on such factors as the intrauterine health of the fetus, the degree of prematurity, birth-related trauma, and functioning of immature or stressed organ systems. Although a wide range of medical problems may complicate the neonatal course of preterm and LBW infants, certain problems occur with such frequency that they can be considered typical problems of prematurity. Small, immature infants are at risk for development of the problems listed in Table 13-2. Medical and nutritional management of these high-risk neonates therefore must anticipate the possibility that these problems may occur so that preventive measures or effective treatment modalities can be employed.

Immaturity. Problems of metabolic and physiological immaturity may also complicate medical management and nutritional support. Although the fetal gut resembles that of a newborn by 20 weeks' gestation, functional development is limited before 34 weeks' gestation. Key developmental factors and their implications for nutritional support are listed in Table 13-3.[15,16]

NUTRIENT REQUIREMENTS OF PRETERM INFANTS

The nutrient requirements of preterm infants are generally higher than those of full-term infants because of limited body stores, metabolic and physiological immaturity, and increased growth rates. The exact quantities of nutrients required by preterm infants are still being defined. These estimates were established on predominantly larger and more mature preterm infants and have been applied to ELBW infants in a clinical setting. This method has succeeded in extending the survival of small infants and producing growth without overt evidence of deficiencies. Whether this provides optimal nutritional support for a group of vulnerable infants will need further research and experience.

Route of delivery also affects nutrient needs[17]; parenterally administered nutrients are delivered directly into the vascular system, thus bypassing the gastrointestinal tract, and are not subject to digestive and absorptive losses. However, parenterally administered nutrients may be lost through nutrient-nutrient interactions in solution, adsorption to delivery sets, **photodegradation,** and increased renal losses.

ENERGY REQUIREMENTS

Parenteral energy requirements differ from enteral requirements (Table 13-4). **Basal energy needs** may be met with 50 to 75 kcal/kg/day. Increased energy is needed for growth. Preterm and LBW infants who are enterally fed require about 120 to 130 kcal/kg/day to grow while 70 to 90 kcal/kg/day supports growth in parenterally fed infants. A number of factors may alter the energy needs of preterm infants regardless of the method of nutritional support. These fac-

TABLE 13-3 *Developmental Maturity and Nutritional Implications in Preterm Infants*

Functional Development	Nutritional Implication
Immature suck-swallow-breathe coordination appears between 33-36 weeks' gestation	Impaired nippling ability and increased risk of aspiration
Lower levels of lactase in infants < 34 weeks' gestation	Potential for some lactose malabsorption
Lower lipase levels and bile acid pool	Potential for fat malabsorption (long chain fats)
Reduced gastric volume	Volume intolerance
Immature peristaltic and gastrointestinal motility patterns	Delays in gastric emptying, increased transit time, apparent feeding intolerance (e.g., residuals, regurgitation, abdominal distention), and constipation.
Alterations in renal and cardiac function	Fluid and electrolyte imbalance, alteration in protein tolerance (acidosis, azotemia, and hyperammonemia)

Adapted from Grant A, DeHoog S: *Nutritional assessment and support,* ed 4, 1991, Seattle.

tors are summarized in Table 13-5. The energy intakes of individual infants may need to be adjusted for appropriate growth to occur.

Parenteral

Studies of LBW infants generally show values for resting kcaloric expenditure to be about 50 to 60 kcal/kg/day, provided that measurements are made under thermoneutral conditions and that the infants are relatively inactive. Provisions for 60 kcal/kg/day and adequate amounts of protein meet resting metabolic energy needs and allow nitrogen retention to occur.[18,19] **Parenteral** protein intakes of 70 to 90

TABLE 13-4   *Energy Needs for Infants Receiving Parenteral vs. Enteral Support*

Type of Nutritional Support	Energy Needed For	
	Maintenance	Growth
Parenteral	50-60 kcal/kg/day	70-90 kcal/kg/day
Enteral	75 kcal/kg/day	120-130 kcal/kg/day

TABLE 13-5   *Factors to Consider in Estimating the Energy Requirements of LBW Infants*

Factor	Comment	Factor	Comment
Weight	Small babies may have: High heat losses secondary to a lack of subcutaneous fat insulation and a large body surface area High absorptive losses	Environmental stress	Energy needs may be increased by: Temperature instability Fluid losses (e.g., radiant warmers)
Classification	SGA infants often have: High basal metabolic rate Rapid growth rate	Feeding	Enterally fed infants require more kcalories for growth Inappropriate selection of a formula can increase absorptive losses In certain circumstances, continuous vs. bolus feeding may alter energy utilization. Nipple-feeding may increase energy expenditure in some infants
Postnatal age	Energy requirements may diminish with increasing postnatal age		
Physiological stress	Energy needs may be increased by: High absorptive losses Hypermetabolic states (e.g., fever, sepsis) Malabsorptive problems (e.g., short bowel syndrome) Respiratory distress and chronic lung disease	Growth	Energy needs are increased when catch-up growth occurs

TABLE 13-6   *Energy Requirements of LBW Infants*

Energy Used for (kcal/kg/day)		Energy Needed
Basal metabolic rate	50	
Activity	15	
Cold stress	10	
TOTAL MAINTENANCE		75
Specific dynamic action	8	
Fecal loss	12	
Growth	25	
TOTAL ADDITIONAL RE-QUIREMENTS		45
TOTAL ENERGY NEEDS FOR GROWTH		120

Adapted from Sinclair J and others: *Pediatr Clin North Am* 17:863, 1970.

kcal/kg/day and 2.5 to 3.0 gm/kg/day allow for greater tissue protein synthesis and weight gain approximating intrauterine rates.[20,21]

Enteral

Sinclair and others[22] have estimated energy needs for maintenance and growth in enterally fed LBW infants as shown in Table 13-6. Recent energy balance studies confirm total energy expenditure to be in the range of 44 to 88 kcal/kg/day with additional energy needed for growth and tissue deposition.[21] Most **enterally** fed preterm infants show appropriate growth on 120 to 130 kcal/kg/day. However, 130 to 150 kcal/kg/day may be required for adequate growth in some infants, particularly during periods of catch-up growth.

PROTEIN REQUIREMENTS

Protein needs of individual infants are influenced by the adequacy of energy intake and the quantity and quality of protein intake. Feeding studies corroborate the biochemical findings that preterm infants can digest and absorb an adequate quantity of protein for intrauterine rates of nitrogen accretion. Preterm infants have gastric, pancreatic, and intestinal enzymes

necessary for protein hydrolysis, and there is active transport of amino acids in fetal life.[23,24] However, preterm infants have limited activity of some enzymes involved in amino acid metabolism, particularly cystathionase, tyrosine transaminase, and arginosuccinate synthetase.

These immaturities influence the specific amino acid requirements and the metabolic response of preterm infants given various types of protein. Preterm infants are susceptible to **hyperammonemia, metabolic acidosis,** and abnormal **plasma amino acid levels** when given proteins that differ in quality or quantity. **Plasma amino acid patterns** reflect protein quality as well as quantity in both parenterally and enterally fed preterm infants.[21,24]

Parenteral

A provision of 2 to 2.5 gm/kg/day of crystalline amino acids and adequate energy to meet basal metabolic needs, for example, 60 kcal/kg/day, promotes positive nitrogen balance in parenterally fed preterm infants. A provision of protein in excess of an individual infant's needs or metabolic capability may result in metabolic acidosis, azotemia, and hyperammonemia and offers no apparent advantage. LBW infants are usually given a small amount of amino acids (0.5 to 1 gm/kg/day within the first 2 to 5 days of life) and the amount is gradually increased to 2 to 2.5 gm/kg/day as tolerated.[25]

Controversy surrounds the issue of the ideal amino acid mixture for LBW infants.[26,27] Three solutions have been designed for use in pediatrics: Trophamine (Kendell McGaw Laboratories), Aminosyn PF (Abbott Laboratories), and Neopham (KabiVitrum). Compared with other solutions used for adults, the use of these pediatric solutions results in plasma amino acid profiles more like those of healthy infants fed with breast milk. Amino acid solutions such as Aminosyn (Abbott Laboratories), Freamine (McGaw Laboratories), and Travasol (Travenal Laboratories) were not designed to meet the particular needs of immature infants and may provoke imbalances in plasma amino acid levels. For example, cysteine, tyrosine, and taurine in these solutions are low relative to the needs of the LBW infant, but the methionine and glycine levels are relatively high. However, many

LBW infants have received long-term parenteral nutrition with these amino acid mixtures without showing evidence of nutrient deficiency or excess. More research is needed to clarify which amino acid solutions are preferred for LBW infants.

Enteral

One approach to estimating the protein needs of enterally fed preterm infants considers the goal to be intrauterine rates of protein accumulation (factorial approach).[7] A reference fetus model is used to determine the amount of protein that would need to be ingested to match the quantity of protein that is deposited into newly formed fetal tissue.[28,29] To achieve these fetal accretion rates, additional protein must be supplied to compensate for intestinal losses and obligatory losses in urine and skin. Based on this approach, the American Academy of Pediatrics recommends 3.5 to 4.0 gm/kg/day of enteral protein.[30] Protein quality influences protein requirements, and whey-predominant proteins of high biological value, for example, human milk proteins, support growth in preterm infants at quantities less than 3.5 to 4.0 gm/kg/day. Preterm infants who ingest adequate kcalories and whey-predominant protein at 2.25 gm/kg/day show steady gains in weight and length although their rate of growth may be less than intrauterine rates of growth. Provisions of 2.9 gm/kg/day protein and 120 kcal/kg/day from human milk have been shown to support weight gain and nitrogen retention at intrauterine rates.[31-33]

The distribution of protein to nonprotein kcalories must also be considered. It is desirable that protein make up 7% to 16% of total kcalories. Feedings with less than 7% protein may limit growth; those with more than 16% may cause azotemia and acidosis.[34]

LIPID

The growing LBW infant needs an adequate intake of well-absorbed dietary fat to help meet the high energy needs of growth, to provide essential fatty acids, and to assist absorption of other important nutrients such as the fat-soluble vitamins and calcium. However, neonates in general, and premature and SGA infants in particular, are relatively inefficient in digestion and absorption of lipids.

The percentage of total kcalories as fat relative to carbohydrate and protein is another important consideration. Fat should constitute 30% to 55% of total kcalories; fat intake greater than 60% of kcalories may lead to ketosis. Furthermore, a diet that is high in fat and low in protein may yield more fat deposition than is desirable for the growing LBW infant. Linoleic acid must compose at least 3% of the total kcalories to meet essential fatty acid needs.[30]

VITAMINS AND MINERALS

Preterm infants are at risk for a number of nutrient deficiencies. Because fetal fat and minerals are deposited largely in the last trimester, the preterm infant is born with limited stores of many vitamins and minerals. Overt deficiencies have been documented in both parenterally and enterally fed preterm infants. For example, **osteopenia,** secondary to inadequate calcium and phosphorus intake, hemolytic anemia associated with vitamin E deficiency, and iron deficiency anemia have been extensively reported in this population.[34]

Parenteral

In 1986, a subcommittee of the Committee on Clinical Practice Issues of the American Society for Clinical Nutrition[35] was formed to review the existing data on vitamin and mineral needs of pediatric patients receiving parenteral nutrition. Guidelines for meeting nutrient needs of parenterally and enterally fed preterm infants are shown in Table 13-7.

The only IV multivitamin preparation currently approved for use in infants and children in the United States is MVI Pediatric (Armour Pharmaceutical Company). This product meets the 1979 recommendations of the Nutrition Advisory Group of the American Medical Association.[36] However, recent evidence suggests that LBW infants receiving this preparation often have low plasma vitamin A levels. Increasing the dose to provide higher intakes of vitamin A would result in excess intakes of water-soluble vitamins and vitamin E.[35] It has been recommended that the IV multivitamin prepa-

TABLE 13-7 *Parenteral and Enteral Vitamin and Mineral Requirements of Preterm Infants*

	Requirements	
	Parenteral	**Enteral**
Fat-soluble vitamins		
A	280 μg/kg/day	Same as term
D	4 μg/kg/day	500 IU
E	2.8 mg/kg/day	5-25 IU
K	—	Same as term
Water-soluble vitamins		
Vitamin C	25 mg/kg/day	35 mg/day
Thiamin	.48 mg/kg/day	Same as term
Riboflavin	.56 mg/kg/day	Same as term
Niacin	6.8 mg/kg/day	Same as term
Pantothenate	2.0 mg/kg/day	Same as term
Biotin	8.0 μg/kg/day	Same as term
B_6	.4 mg/kg/day	Same as term
Folic acid	56 μg/kg/day	50 μg/day
B_{12}	.4 μg/kg/day	Same as term
Minerals		
Calcium	500-600 mg/L	185-210 mg/kg/day
Phosphorus	400-450 mg/L	123-140 mg/kg/day
Magnesium	50-60 mg/L	8.5-10 mg/kg/day
Iron	—	2-3 mg/kg/day by 2 months of age
Zinc	400 μg/kg/day	0.5 mg/100 kcal
Manganese	1 μg/kg/day	5 μg/100 kcal
Copper	20 μg/kg/day	90 μg/100 kcal
Iodine	1 μg/kg/day	5 μg/100 kcal
Sodium		2.5-3.5 mEq/kg/day
		VLBW infants may require 4-8 mEq/kg/day to prevent hyponatremia
Potassium		2-3 mEq/kg/day
		2.5-3.1 mEq/kg/day
Other trace minerals		
Cobalt		
Molybdenum	.25 μg/kg/day	Insufficient data for recommendations
Selenium	2 μg/kg/day	
Chromium	.2 μg/kg/day	

Adapted from American Academy of Pediatrics, Committee on Nutrition: *Pediatrics* 75:976, 1985, and Greene HL and others: *Am J Clin Nutr* 48:1324, 1988.

ration should be reformulated to meet the more recent guidelines established by the Committee on Clinical Practice Issues (1988).[35]

Minerals are added to parenteral solutions. Preterm infants have a higher requirement for calcium and phosphorus than full-term infants.[37] Because of insolubility, it is difficult to add enough calcium and phosphorus to parenteral solutions to meet these requirements. To prevent precipitation, calcium, phosphorus, and magnesium intakes are described per liter and assume an average fluid intake of 120 to 150 ml/kg/day. Greene and others[35] suggest that these levels be used through a central venous line and not a peripheral line.

Trace elements are also added to parenteral solutions on an individualized basis. Whereas zinc may be given to all LBW infants receiving parenteral nutrition, other trace elements must be provided according to expected duration of TPN, renal and hepatic function, and availability of trace element preparations.[35] Manganese and copper should be omitted when obstructive jaundice occurs. Selenium, chromium, and molybdenum should be omitted for infants with renal dysfunction. Iron is not generally added to TPN solutions because of concerns about possible adverse effects, as well as lack of an acceptable intravenous preparation and insufficient data on compatibility and pediatric usage.[35]

Enteral

The Committee on Nutrition of the American Academy of Pediatrics[30] has established guidelines for meeting the nutrient requirements of enterally fed preterm infants (see Table 13-7). Preterm infants have increased needs for a number of nutrients including vitamins E and C, folic acid, calcium, phosphorus, and iron. The rationale for the current guidelines and current research issues have been reviewed.[28,30,37]

NUTRITIONAL SUPPORT

Medical and metabolic instability in the immediate postnatal period may interfere with providing optimal nutritional support. The

TABLE 13-8 *Goals of Nutritional Support for Preterm Infants*

Phase	Goal
One: stabilization	Support fluid and electrolyte balance and glucose homeostasis
Two: maintenance	Prevent tissue catabolism and promote positive nitrogen balance
Three: transition	Promote tolerance to increase in nutritional support
Four: growth	Provide sufficient protein, energy, and other nutrients to support optimal growth

goals for nutritional support in this population may be divided into four phases (Table 13-8). Transition from one phase to another depends on the individual infant's medical and metabolic status.

STABILIZATION

Immature preterm and LBW infants have an immediate need for fluid to replace ongoing water losses and rapidly become dependent on an exogenous source of glucose because of limited glycogen stores and decreased capacity for **gluconeogenesis.** To prevent hypoglycemia and to spare protein tissue, an IV solution containing dextrose is infused as soon as primary postnatal demands for resuscitation and stabilization have been met. In addition to fluid and glucose administration, most preterm newborns require sodium, chloride, and potassium to replace daily losses.

Fluid

Fluid management of preterm infants should allow normal transition of body fluids from fetal to neonatal status. Preterm infants have rela-

TABLE 13-9   Estimates of Water Losses and Requirements in LBW Infants

Source of Loss	Water Requirements
Evaporation	10-60 ml/kg/day
Fecal	10-15 ml/kg/day
Renal	2-5 ml/kg/hr
Growth	0-0.5 ml/kg/hr

tively more total body water than do full-term infants. Preterm infants may lose up to 15% of their birth weight in the early neonatal period.

Estimates for fluid requirements include the sum of the predicted losses and the requirements for growth. Fluid losses include evaporative losses through skin and respiratory tract, fecal losses, and renal losses. Evaporative losses are the most variable and can be substantial in the smallest, most immature infants secondary to increased skin permeability, larger body surface area relative to body mass, and greater skin blood flow relative to metabolic rate.[38-43] Estimates of fluid losses and requirements for growth are shown in Table 13-9.

Several factors can either increase or decrease the fluid requirements of LBW infants by altering fluid losses. For example, radiant warmers and phototherapy lights markedly increase water requirements by increasing insensible fluid losses.[44,45] On the other hand, heat shields and thermal blankets help to decrease the evaporative water losses of LBW infants.[39,46] To determine total water requirements, the various factors that alter fluid losses should be taken into account and the appropriate additions or subtractions should be made according to individual circumstances.

Because of the many variables affecting fluid needs, it is difficult to establish routine guidelines for fluid management of LBW infants. After initial fluid administration of 40 to 80 ml/kg/day, subsequent needs are determined by clinical examination of the infants. Evaluation of weight changes, urine output, specific gravity, serum electrolytes, blood urea nitrogen, blood pressure, peripheral circulatory status, mucous membrane moisture, and skin turgor aid in individualized fluid management.

Lack of diuresis in the early neonatal period may complicate the course of respiratory disease in the preterm infant. Excess fluid may contribute to heart failure, edema, and persistence of an open patent ductus arteriosus. Excess fluid administration in the early postnatal period has also been associated with intraventricular hemorrhage. Inadequate fluid intake in LBW infants may result in dehydration, electrolyte imbalance, and hypotension.[47-52]

Glucose

Preterm infants are metabolically dependent on glucose in the immediate postnatal period and are susceptible to glucose intolerance secondary to immaturity and metabolic instability. These infants are at risk for both hypoglycemia and hyperglycemia. Glycogen stores and pathways for gluconeogenesis may not be completely developed. In addition, insulin production and function may be impaired.

Preterm infants initially receive glucose intravenously as dextrose (D glucose). In the early postnatal period, fluid volume and dextrose concentration is adjusted to avoid hyperglycemia and hypoglycemia. Hyperglycemia may lead to **glucosuria** and an **osmotic diuresis.** If these conditions are uncorrected, dehydration will occur. To prevent hyperglycemia and the consequences of dehydration, LBW infants should be started on amounts of glucose that do not exceed what the infant is able to metabolize. The amount of glucose administered is determined by its concentration and the rate of administration (glucose load). Calculation of glucose load and suggested guidelines for increasing glucose load are shown in Table 13-10.

Electrolytes

Sodium, potassium, and chloride are added to intravenous solutions in the first few days of life unless daily monitoring of serum electrolytes indicates an imbalance. Electrolyte requirements for intravenous solutions are shown in Table 13-11. Actual electrolyte requirements

TABLE 13-10   Guidelines for Glucose Load in LBW Infants

Birth Weight (gm)	Initial Glucose Load* (mg/kg/min)	Daily Incremental Increase (mg/kg/min)
<1000	4-6	1.5-2.0
1001-1500	6-8	1.5-2.0
1501-2000	8	As tolerated

Modified from O'Leary MJ: *Nutritional care of the low-birth-weight infant.* In Mahan LK, Arlin M: *Krause's food, nutrition and diet therapy,* Philadelphia, 1992, WB Saunders.

$$\text{*Glucose load} = \frac{\dfrac{\text{gm glucose}}{100 \text{ ml}} \times \underline{\hspace{1cm}} \text{ ml/kg/day} \times \dfrac{1000 \text{ mg}}{\text{gm}}}{1440 \text{ min/day}} = \frac{\text{\%dextrose} \times \underline{\hspace{1cm}} \text{ ml/kg/day}}{144} = \text{ ml/kg/min}$$

TABLE 13-11   Recommended Daily Intakes of Electrolytes from Parenteral Nutrition Solutions

Electrolytes	mEq/kg/day
Sodium	2-4
Potassium	2-3
Chloride	2-3

From Poole RL: *Electrolyte and mineral requirements.* In Kerner JA, editor: *Manual of pediatric parenteral nutrition,* New York, 1983, John Wiley & Sons.

for preterm infants may vary depending on factors such as clinical status, renal function, and state of hydration. VLBW infants may require more sodium to prevent hyponatremia secondary to immature renal function and increased urinary losses. Medications such as diuretics may further alter electrolyte needs for individual infants.[37]

PARENTERAL NUTRITION

Parenteral nutrition (the intravenous administration of a hypertonic solution of amino acids, carbohydrate, fat, electrolytes, vitamins, and minerals) can provide all essential nutrients as the sole source of nutritional support. In this case the term **"total parenteral nutrition"** or **TPN** is used. Partial parenteral nutrition is used to supplement enteral feedings and is advantageous to preterm infants who are unable to tolerate full enteral feedings or who are being weaned from TPN to a program of complete enteral nutrition.

Indications

Parenteral nutrition is indicated in these infants when the projected time to establish adequate enteral support exceeds the infant's metabolic reserves. Because malnutrition complicates the clinical course of these tiny infants, TPN may be indicated in preterm or LBW infants who are unable to receive enteral feedings in the first 2 to 3 days of life or who receive some enteral feedings in the first week of life, but in amounts insufficient to meet basal needs and promote positive nitrogen balance.[53]

Route of Administration

It is possible to support growth and positive nitrogen balance with parenteral nutrition by either **central** or **peripheral vascular routes.**[54,55] Selecting the peripheral versus the central route of administration involves several considerations that should be individualized according to the unique circumstances of each infant. The principal factors to be considered in choosing one technique over another are the kcaloric needs of the infant and the projected duration

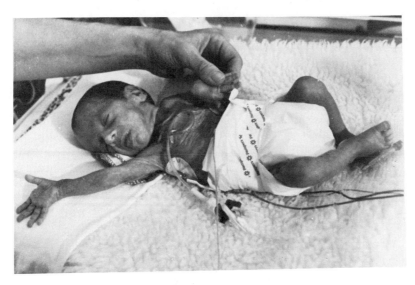

FIG. 13-2   A central venous catheter has been surgically implanted in the superior vena cava. This type of catheter permits delivery of hyperalimentation by a central venous route.

of need for parenteral support.[55,56] Peripheral parenteral solutions are usually not as kcalorically dense as central vein solutions. Peripheral veins are limited to dextrose concentrations of less than 10% to 15%. Blood flow through central vessels such as the superior vena cava is very rapid, and hyperosmotic fluids are quickly diluted. Central veins therefore may tolerate dextrose concentrations of 20% to 25%. This means that infants who receive parenteral nutrition through central veins can potentially receive more energy to promote positive nitrogen balance and growth. In the critically ill infant for whom prolonged parenteral therapy is projected, central vein nutrition is usually the treatment of choice (Figure 13-2).[57] If minimal stress is present, if vessel access is good, and if the anticipated duration of parenteral support is less than 2 to 3 weeks, then the peripheral route of administration is often preferred.

Consideration of the advantages and disadvantages of either route of administration also plays a role in selecting the method of delivery in individual infants. In general, there are more serious technical and infectious complications encountered in central delivery compared with peripheral delivery, but both routes have characteristic problems related to the method of administration. Although strict adherence to aseptic techniques and to established guidelines for catheter care and maintenance markedly decrease the incidence of these complications, neither method of delivery is benign.

Complications

Complications associated with parenteral nutrition may be **infectious, technical,** or **metabolic.** Table 13-12 lists the complications associated with parenteral support. The technical and infectious complications associated with parenteral support can be reduced by careful attention to aseptic conditions and judicious placement and maintenance of the catheters. Metabolic complications can be reduced by attention to solution composition, nutrient needs of individual infants, and monitoring nutritional tolerance. Development of new solutions to meet our growing knowledge of parenteral nutrition may further reduce the complications associated with parenteral support.[20,28,57]

TABLE 13-12 *Complications Associated with Parenteral Nutrition*

Infectious	Sepsis
Technical	Cardiac or vascular thrombosis
	Pneumothorax
	Emboli
	Cardiac/thoracic/ peritoneal effusion
	Clotting of catheter line
	Tissue necrosis
	Alterations in vascular perfusion
Metabolic	
Carbohydrate-related	Hyperglycemia/ hypoglycemia
	Fatty liver
Lipid-related	Hyperlipidemia
Protein-related	Metabolic acidosis
	Hyperammonemia
	Azotemia
	Abnormal plasma amino acid levels
	Hyperammonemia
	Fluid and electrolyte imbalance
Vitamin-related	Hypervitaminosis or hypovitaminosis
Mineral-related	Osteopenial rickets
	Hyperphosphatemia or hypophosphatemia
	Hypercalcemia or hypocalcemia
Other	Cholestatic jaundice
	Hepatic dysfunction

Solution Composition

Parenteral nutrition solutions can provide all essential nutrients to promote positive nitrogen balance and growth, but they must be tailored in their composition to meet the unique needs of each preterm and LBW infant. The theoretical and practical considerations involved in the management of pediatric parenteral nutrition have been summarized by Lebenthal.[57]

Carbohydrate. LBW infants are dependent on the availability of glucose. Glucose is provided as dextrose and is advanced as tolerated. Glucose tolerance is monitored by serum glucose levels and evidence of glucosuria.

In some preterm infants, particularly those who are extremely immature, stressed, or septic, glucose intolerance may persist despite administration of conservative glucose loads. Persistent hyperglycemia may severely limit the provision of adequate kcalories. Increased energy intake has been reported with persistent hyperglycemia by continuous insulin infusion.[58,59] Because of the difficulty in titrating insulin during infusion, there is concern that this therapy may result in extreme and precipitous fluctuations in serum glucose levels. Efficacy and long-term consequences of insulin infusion will require further investigation.

Protein. The first protein solutions available for IV use were hydrolysates of fibrin and casein, which have now largely been replaced by crystalline amino acid solutions. These solutions mimic the amino acid composition of naturally occurring proteins with high biological values, such as casein or egg albumin. Crystalline amino acid solutions show more efficient nitrogen utilization compared with protein hydrolysates.

Although current amino acid solutions were designed for adults, they support growth and positive nitrogen balance in LBW infants. In general, these solutions contain low or absent amounts of glutamate, aspartate, tyrosine, cysteine, and taurine and potentially excess amounts of methionine, glycine, and alanine. The plasma amino acid pattern of infants receiving parenteral nutrition reflect the amino acid composition of the solution.[60]

The impact of abnormal plasma amino acid levels on the premature infant is not clearly known. Glycine is a potent neurotransmitter inhibitor, and **hyperglycinemia** may have adverse effects on the developing central nervous system of premature infants. Premature infants receiving cysteine- or tyrosine-free diets demonstrate lower plasma levels of these amino acids and impaired nitrogen retention and growth.[61]

Low plasma levels of taurine have been noted in infants receiving taurine-free parenteral solutions. Taurine is involved in neural transmission and in retinal, cardiac, and muscle function.[62] Retinal changes have been noted in infants receiving long-term taurine-free parenteral solutions.

New amino acid solutions have been developed for the neonate and preterm infant.[26] These solutions have been designed to produce plasma amino acid levels similar to those observed in enterally breast-fed infants. These solutions are efficacious in normalizing plasma amino acid levels. The clinical significance of these plasma amino acid patterns is not known.[27]

Lipid. Intravenous fat emulsions are used to meet essential fatty acid needs of preterm infants and to provide energy in a kcalorically dense, isotonic form. Preterm infants are at risk for essential fatty acid deficiency in the first week of life. A provision of 0.5 to 1.0 gm/kg/day of an IV fat emulsion will meet the essential fatty acid needs of these infants.[57,62a,63]

Preterm infants receiving intravenous lipid are at risk for adverse changes in oxygenation, pulmonary function, and displacement of bilirubin from albumin.[57] Preterm infants also have limited lipoprotein lipase activity for hydrolysis of lipid to free fatty acids, and therefore have limited tolerance to IV lipids. Lack of exogenous carnitine may contribute to impaired lipid tolerance. Carnitine facilitates transport of fatty acids across mitochondrial membranes for oxidation and utilization as energy.[64-67]

Methods of improving lipid tolerance to meet the fatty acid needs of preterm infants are the subject of ongoing research. It has been suggested that heparin may improve lipid clearance by stimulating the release of lipoprotein lipase.[57,68] Carnitine supplementation has been shown to improve lipid clearance in some preterm infants.[65] It has also been suggested that alteration in the fatty acid profile of preterm infants receiving intravenous fat emulsions may improve lipid clearance. Haumont and others[69] noted that preterm infants receiving 10% Intralipid had higher triglyceride levels, higher cholesterol levels, and a higher percentage of low-density lipoproteins compared with infants

receiving 20% Intralipid.[69] These solutions differ in the ratio of phospholipid to triglyceride. No specific recommendations, however, have yet been made related to carnitine supplementation, heparin infusion, or alterations in fatty acid composition of fat emulsions for IV use.

Vitamins and minerals. Vitamins and minerals should be added to parenteral solutions according to the guidelines established by the Committee on Clinical Practice Issues, Subcommittee on Pediatric Parenteral Nutrient Requirements[35] (Table 13-7).

Nutritional Support and Monitoring

LBW infants who are unlikely to tolerate adequate volumes of enteral feeding in the first week of life may be started on parenteral support by 48 to 72 hours of life. Infants receiving parenteral nutrition should be monitored to determine the adequacy of nutrient intake and to detect and treat complications. Preterm infants have a small blood volume and the need for monitoring should take into account the relative probability that a particular complication will occur, the potential risks of monitoring, and the likelihood that the information provided will change clinical actions. A number of monitoring schedules have been proposed for infant's receiving parenteral support.[54,70] These schedules often include electrolytes, acid-base status, serum glucose or Dextrostix, protein status (albumin and prealbumin), bone mineral status (calcium, phosphorus, and alkaline phosphatase), and liver function tests. Additional tests may be indicated in an individual infant, including white blood cell count (WBC) and culture, zinc, copper and iron, and lipid tolerance studies.

Case 1
Initial stabilization and parenteral support

A 26-week-gestation infant weighing 750 gm at birth was admitted to a neonatal intensive care unit shortly after birth. The baby developed severe hyaline membrane disease and required assisted ventilation with oxygen needs of 85% to 90%. An umbilical arterial catheter was placed to aid in ventilatory management; fluid, glucose, and electrolytes were also infused through this line.

The initial solution contained 10% dextrose; this was started at a rate of 70 ml/kg/day and was increased to 12.5% dextrose at a rate of 110 ml/kg/day by day 3 of life. Dextrostix measurements simultaneously increased from 60 to 80 mg/100 ml to 180 to 240 mg/100 ml; serum glucose measurements confirmed hyperglycemia. The dextrose infusion was subsequently reduced to 9% dextrose at a rate of 100 ml/kg/day. Blood sugar levels normalized and the glucose load was gradually increased without further difficulty.

Because the serious nature of the infant's medical condition prohibited the introduction of enteral feedings in the first week of life, and because metabolic reserves were presumed to be meager, parenteral nutrition was started on day 3 of life. At this time the infant had lost 60 gm and weighed 9% less than birth weight. The initial hyperalimentation order included (1) rate: IV + hyperalimentation = 4.2 ml/hr (IV at keep-open rate of 1.5 ml/hr and hyperalimentation at rate of 2.7 ml/hr); (2) 8% dextrose, and (3) amino acids 0.5 gm/kg/day. All electrolytes, trace elements, and minerals were added to the 250 ml bottle in quantities that provided appropriate amounts to be delivered in 96 ml/kg/day of hyperalimentation solution. Intralipid was ordered at an initial load of 0.5 gm/kg/day. Tolerance to all components of the hyperalimentation solution was routinely monitored as intake was advanced.

TRANSITION FROM PARENTERAL TO ENTERAL NUTRITION

Infants who receive TPN have relatively low digestive mass and delayed gastrointestinal growth compared with infants who receive enteral stimuli.[70] This is particularly true for infants who receive TPN for prolonged periods. Pancreatic hyposecretion, intestinal mucosal atrophy, and decreased parietal cell mass during TPN are, however, reversible on resumption of enteral feeding.[57,70]

It is desirable to initiate enteral feedings in LBW infants as early as possible. Even in small amounts, these feedings act to stimulate enzymatic development and activity, promote bile flow, and increase small intestinal villous growth. Small amounts of feeding may also contribute to maturation of peristaltic wave patterns in immature infants.[71-74] Infants who are not ready for advancement of enteral feeding but who can tolerate small, constant amounts of an appropriate type of milk benefit

from this gastrointestinal stimulation. Later, transition to total enteral nutrition may be easier for these infants.

When making the transition from parenteral to enteral nutrition, it is important to adjust both sources of nutrition to provide adequate intake for growth but avoid excessive intakes of any particular substrate. In general, when an infant is receiving optimal energy, protein, vitamins, and minerals from parenteral support, this is accomplished by slowly decreasing the volume of parenteral infusion as enteral intake increases. Intravenous fat emulsions may be decreased or discontinued when half to three fourths of the intake is derived from an appropriate enteral feeding. When an infant is tolerating 75% of total feedings from an enteral source and continued advancement to full feeds is anticipated, parenteral support may be discontinued and the remainder of the infant's fluid volume may be provided by IV dextrose until full feeds are achieved.

Case 2
Transition from parenteral to enteral support

An infant born at 28 weeks of gestation developed necrotizing enterocolitis during his fourth week of life. The necrotic damage to the small intestine necessitated surgical removal of 30 cm of bowel, encompassing the distal ileum and the ileocecal valve.

After 8 days of TPN, it was decided that enteral feeds could be introduced and cautiously advanced. An elemental infant formula (e.g., Pregestimil) was chosen to facilitate digestion and absorption of nutrients. The initial volume was 1 ml/hr fed by oral gastric gavage on a continuous drip schedule; this provided 25 ml/kg/day, given a body weight of 960 gm.

The composition and infusion rate of the parenteral nutrients remained unchanged until day 3 of enteral feedings when the oral volume was increased to 2 ml/hr. At this point, the volume of the parenteral infusion was decreased to provide a total daily volume of 150 to 160 ml/kg/day. The concentration of parenteral nutrients was adjusted to meet the goals of nutritional therapy (to provide 2.5 to 3.0 gm/kg/day of protein and at least 90 kcal/kg/day).

Enteral volume was slowly increased in small amounts to allow time for morphological and functional adaptation of the remaining small bowel and to guard against the volume-induced dumping syndrome. Full enteral feeds were not achieved until 28 days after the reintroduction of enteral feeds; at this time the infant weighed 1150 gm and was able to tolerate a continuous orogastric infusion of 8 ml/hr.

ENTERAL NUTRITION
Initiation of Enteral Feedings

The decision to begin enteral feeding is often difficult and involves many factors (see box, page 325). The degree of prematurity, history of perinatal insults, current medical condition, medical and metabolic stability, and functioning of the gastrointestinal tract all influence the success and tolerance of enteral feeding. Optimal timing of the first feeding and advancement of subsequent feedings must be individualized.

There is growing evidence that early initiation of small amounts of enteral feedings may be advantageous to preterm infants because it may stimulate the production and secretion of a

❖
FACTORS TO CONSIDER BEFORE FEEDING A PRETERM INFANT BY AN ENTERAL ROUTE

- *Perinatal*
Birth asphyxia
Apgar scores
- *Respiratory status*
Stability of ventilation
Blood gases
ABCs
- *Medical status*
Vital signs (heart rate, respiratory rate, color, temperature, blood pressure, tone)
Acute illness (sepsis)
- *Gastrointestinal tract*
Anomalies (gastroschisis, omphalocele)
Patency
Functioning (bowel tones present, passage of stool)
Risk of necrotizing enterocolitis
- *Equipment/procedures*
Umbilical artery catheter
Intubation/extubation
Others

number of gastrointestinal enzymes and hormones including **gastrin, enteroglucagon, motilin,** and **neurotensin,** which have **trophic and motility effects.**[71-73] Enteral feeding may contribute to maturation of motility patterns, improve glucose tolerance, increase bile flow, decrease hyperbilirubinemia, and improve calcium and phosphorus status.[74,75] Awareness of the potential benefits of enteral feeding, even in immature infants, has led clinicians to consider "nonnutritive feeding," which consists of feeding preterm infants small amounts to allow their gut to mature and adapt while supporting them nutritionally with parenteral infusions.

Methods of Feeding

Once it has been decided that enteral feedings will be initiated, the optimal feeding technique must be selected. Preterm infants can be fed by gavage (tube) (Figure 13-3) or by nipple (Figure 13-4).[76,77]

Techniques. Gavage feeding is the choice for infants who are unable to coordinate sucking, swallowing, and breathing. Immature suck-swallow-breathe patterns are seen in infants less than 32 to 34 weeks' gestation. Respiratory distress and insults to the central nervous system may further impair suck-swallow-breathe coordination. Enteral feeding in these infants may be by orogastric or nasogastric gavage. Nasogastric tubes are more stable in their placement but may obstruct or irritate the infant's nasal passages. (This may be a problem for infants who must breathe through their noses or for infants with respiratory disease.) Orogastric feeding is preferred for infants with these conditions, but this method is associated with bradycardia and aspiration during tube placement, particularly in infants who are developing a cough and gag reflex. Nipple feeding may be attempted in infants who are greater than 32 to 34 weeks' gestation. The transition from gavage to nipple is often a complicated and slow process. Factors that can impede successful nipple feeding are shown in Table 13-13.[78-80]

Composition of Feeding

Preterm infants can be fed human milk or formula. Selection of a milk with the following characteristics may facilitate tolerance to enteral

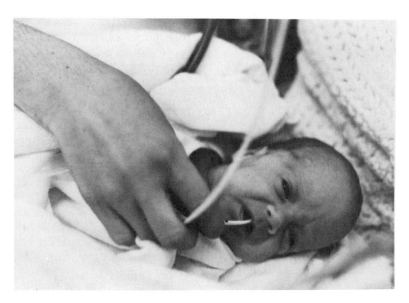

FIG. 13-3 A growing premature infant is being fed by oral gastric gavage.

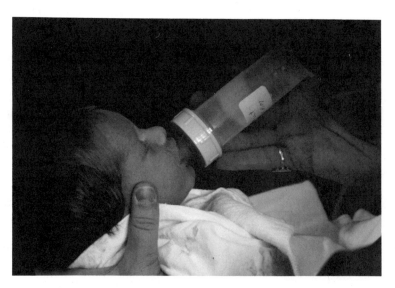

FIG. 13-4 A mother feeds her premature infant using a small, soft "premie" nipple.

TABLE 13-13 *Factors Influencing Preterm Infants' Nippling Success*

Factor	Significance
Poor coordination of suck-swallow-breathe	Risk of aspiration
	Decreased feeding efficiency
	Fatigue
Decreased or absent sucking pads	Decreased sucking strength and endurance
Decreased tone	Inability to maintain optimally flexed feeding posture
Diminished or absent gag and cough reflex	Increased risk of aspiration
Neurological and behavioral immaturity	More time is spent in sleep with short periods in quiet alert and awake states (which make feeding easier)
	Subtle cues of hunger, satiety, and distress (which alters infant-caregiver interactions)
	Difficulty maintaining an organized state (which can disrupt feedings)

Modified from Shaker CS: Nipple feeding premature infants: a different perspective, *Neonatal Network* 8:9, 1990, and Vandenberg KA: Nippling management of the sick neonate in the NICU: the disorganized feeder, *Neonatal Network* 9:9, 1990.

feeding. Criteria that promote tolerance to enteral feedings are (1) nutrient composition that is readily digestible and absorbable; (2) whey-predominant protein; (3) low renal solute load; and (4) iso-osmolality (300 mOsm/kg water). Human milk and premature formulas meet these criteria.

Human milk. Human milk has unique properties that benefit both full-term and preterm infants (see Chapter 4).[81,82] Human milk contains growth factors that exert a trophic effect on the developing intestinal epithelium. The presence of enzymes such as lipase and amylase contribute to improved digestion and absorption of fat and carbohydrate. Human milk proteins are whey predominant, and their amino acid composition favors the needs of preterm infants. Human milk also contains a number of antiinfective factors that can provide protection against infection.

When preterm infants are fed their own mother's milk, they grow more rapidly than infants fed banked breast milk (mature milk). Preterm infants fed adequate volumes of their own mothers' milk can achieve intrauterine rates of weight gain.[83] The different rates of growth observed in these infants can be attributed to the unique nutrient composition of preterm human milk. During the first month of lactation, preterm human milk contains more energy and higher amounts of protein and minerals.[83-88]

Human milk does not meet the calcium and phosphorus needs of the rapidly growing preterm infant. Decreased bone mineralization, osteopenia, and rickets can occur in these infants when human milk is fed without calcium and phosphorus supplementation.[81,88-91]

Formula. Formulas designed for full-term infants do not meet all of the nutrient needs of preterm infants. There are, however, specialized premature infant formulas that differ from standard cow's milk–based formulas for full-term infants. Table 13-14 summarizes these differences. Premature formulas support the special needs of preterm infants for growth and bone mineralization. These formulas are also well tolerated when fed in appropriate amounts.

Vitamin and mineral supplementation. Since the vitamin and mineral requirements of preterm infants are not precisely known, the guidelines established by the American Academy of Pediatrics[30] serve as references in determining supplementation needs. Premature infant formulas vary in nutrient composition, and therefore differ with respect to specific needs for vitamin and mineral supplementation. It is important to know the current nutrient content of premature formulas in order to make appropriate decisions regarding supplementation (Ta-

TABLE 13-14   *Comparison of Premature Formulas and Standard Formulas*

	Premature Formulas	Standard Formulas
	Designed and tested in preterm infants	Designed and tested in full-term infants
Energy concentration	24 or 20 kcal/oz	20 kcal/oz
Protein	Whey casein; 60:40	Whey casein; 60:40
Fat	Medium- and long-chain fats	100% long-chain fats
Carbohydrate	Lactose and glucose polymers	100% lactose
Vitamins and minerals	Fortified to meet the needs of preterm infants	Fortified to meet the needs of full-term infants
	Available with or without iron	Available with or without iron
Osmolality	Iso-osmolar	Iso-osmolar

ble 13-15). Infants fed human milk also require supplementation. Human milk fortifiers are available which provide kcalories, protein, vitamins, and minerals. The amounts of calcium and phosphorus in these products promote optimal bone mineralization in preterm infants.[92-95]

Stable growing preterm infants are likely to deplete their limited iron reserves by 2 months of age. A supplement of 2 to 4 mg/kg/day of elemental iron is recommended no later than 2 months of age for preterm infants fed either formulas or breast milk. The American Academy of Pediatrics recommends that supplementation continue until 12 to 15 months of age.[31]

Management of Enteral Feeding

The initial goal of enteral feeding is to facilitate normalization of gastrointestinal function and tolerance to the milk provided. Subsequent feedings should meet all the nutrient needs of growing infants. Human milk or premature formulas are usually fed to infants who weigh less than 2 kg. Infants greater than 2 kg may receive human milk or formulas designed for full-term infants.

Volume and Schedule

The amount of milk fed to preterm infants depends in part on their **estimated stomach capacity.** This varies with the size and postnatal age of the infant (for example, an 800 gm infant has an undistended stomach capacity of 2 to 3 ml). Pre-

term infants also have poor gastrointestinal motility, which may further limit volume tolerance. Small, frequent feedings improve tolerance to milk feedings. Initial feedings should approximate the undistended stomach capacity (for example, 1 to 2 ml in the infant < 1 kg). Feedings may be initiated as either continuous drip or bolus feedings every 2 to 3 hours. Feedings are advanced as tolerated on an individualized basis. Many VLBW infants may not tolerate increases in total daily volumes greater than 20 ml/kg/day. Rapid advancement of enteral feedings has been associated with **necrotizing enterocolitis.**

Monitoring

Tolerance to enteral feeding should be monitored daily. Indicators for feeding intolerance include gastric residuals, regurgitation, abdominal distention, changes in frequency and consistency of bowel movements, the presence of reducing substances, or occult blood in the stool. These symptoms may be associated with necrotizing enterocolitis. They may also be changes in clinical status which will impact the decision to reduce or discontinue enteral feeding.

NUTRITION ASSESSMENT
Growth

All neonates have a **growth pattern** characterized by three phases: (1) weight loss; (2) regaining of birth weight; and (3) sustained growth. Postnatal weight curves are used to as-

TABLE 13-15   *Select Nutrient Composition of Premature Formulas (Per 124 ml of 24 kcal/oz)**

	Similac Special Care	Enfamil Premature Formula	Preemie SMA
Protein			
Grams	2.71	3.0	2.4
% kcal	11	12	0.6
Fat			
Source	MCT, soy, and coconut oil	MCT, soy, and coconut oil	Coconut, oleic, oleo soy, and MCT
Grams	5.43	5.1	5.4
% kcal	47	44	48.5
Carbohydrate			
Source	Lactose, glucose polymers	Lactose, corn syrup solids	Lactose, glucose polymers
Grams	10.6	11	10.5
% kcal	42	44	41.9
Vitamins and Minerals			
Calcium (mg)	180	165	90
Phosphorus (mg)	90	83	50
Sodium (mg)	43	39	40
Vitamin A (IU)	680	1200	300
Vitamin D (IU)	150	270	60
Vitamin E (IU)	4.0	4.6	1.9
Vitamin B_{12} (μg)	0.55	0.3	0.3
Vitamin C (mg)	37	35	8.6
Folate (μg)	37	35	12.5
Estimated Renal Solute Load (ESRL)	18.3	18.7	15.8
Osmolarity			
mOsm/L	250	260	246

*For complete and current nutrient composition of formulas, consult the most recent product information.

POSTNATAL GROWTH PATTERNS OF PRETERM INFANTS

Weight loss	5%-15% of birth weight
Regain birth weight	1-2 weeks of age
Sustained growth	15 gm/kg/day weight gain and 0.5-1 cm/wk increase in length

sess weight changes in the early neonatal period and depict this pattern. Two postnatal weight charts are currently available for clinical use with preterm infants. The Dancis, O'Connell, and Holt curves are based on data collected over 40 years ago.[96] The postnatal weight curves by Shaffer and others are based on more recent data and demonstrate that infants currently lose less weight, regain birth weight sooner, and sustain a greater rate of growth (see box above).[97]

When an infant has regained birth weight and demonstrates a pattern of sustained growth, it is important to begin weekly measurements of body length and head circumference. Longitudinal reference growth curves for preterm infants are not available. Two growth curves are available that depict growth in weight, length, and head circumference for infants between 28 weeks' gestation and 1 to 2 years corrected age.[98,99] These curves were generated from data collected in the 1960s and represent a cross-sectional sample of infants less than 40 weeks' gestation and full-term infants. Although these curves do not represent optimal growth for preterm infants, they are useful in evaluating patterns of growth.

The NCHS curves for full-term infants can also be used to monitor growth after 40 weeks' gestation. When using these growth charts, age should be adjusted for prematurity until 1 to 2 years corrected age.

Laboratory Indices

Several laboratory measurements such as serum proteins (albumin, transthyretin), serum vitamins (vitamin D, retinol), and serum miner-als (calcium and phosphorus) have been used as indicators of nutritional status in children and adults. These measurements are difficult to interpret in preterm infants because reference ranges for enterally fed preterm infants are not available. Serial measurements of certain laboratory indices may be useful in some preterm infants. These infants include those at risk for protein-energy malnutrition, inadequate bone mineralization, inadequate intake, or drug-nutrient interactions. Judicious ordering of blood tests and consideration of the risk versus the benefit of taking a blood sample is advised in using laboratory indices for monitoring nutritional status.

OUTCOME

From the preceding discussion, it is apparent that it is possible to meet the metabolic and nutritional needs of premature and LBW infants in a manner sufficient to sustain life and to promote growth and development. With adequate nutritional support and advances in neonatal intensive care technology, more tiny immature infants are surviving than ever before.

During the past 10 years survival rates for infants between 750 to 1000 gm have increased from 50% to 80%; for infants with birth weights between 500 to 750 gm, survival rates have increased from 10% to 50%.[100,101] Many of these small preterm infants have experienced complicated and prolonged hospitalizations and are discharged with ongoing medical problems and neurodevelopmental concerns. Studies are attempting to determine the long-term neurodevelopmental consequences and to delineate

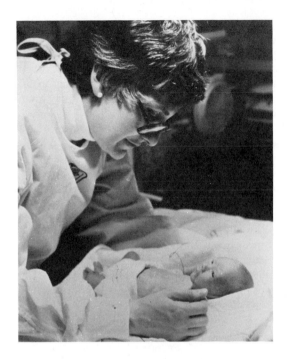

FIG. 13-5 A mother interacts with her premature infant who is 10 weeks old.

FIG. 13-6 Same child as in Figure 13-5. Here she is healthy and $2\frac{1}{2}$ years old.

appropriate cognitive expectations for these vulnerable infants as well as appropriate growth expectations.

Neurodevelopmental Outcome

Surviving LBW infants are at increased risk for neurodevelopmental problems as they grow older. These problems range from minor motor and sensory impairment to severe handicapping conditions such as visual/hearing losses and cerebral palsy.[101-104] It is unclear what factors contribute to major and minor handicapping conditions in these vulnerable infants. Statistically, the ELBW infant (< 800 gm) has the greatest risk of morbidity. Neurodevelopmental evaluation during the first year may not be predictive of long-term developmental status or academic achievement.

Ongoing follow-up is crucial for detecting those infants with neurodevelopmental concerns and employing appropriate intervention strategies to further improve outcome (Figure 13-5). It is important to recognize that many preterm infants will not be impaired (Figure 13-6). Some larger LBW infants will develop and perform academically at the same level as healthy infants born at term.[104]

Growth

Preterm infants show different growth patterns than full-term infants even when corrected for gestational age. Although larger, stable preterm infants may demonstrate **"catch-up growth"** in the first 1 to 2 years of life, VLBW and ELBW infants are unlikely to show catch-up growth in the first 3 years of life.[105-107] Small size at 1 to 3 years of age in this group does not necessarily indicate small size at school age. Many of these infants achieve weights, heights, and head circumferences by 7 to 8 years of age that are similar to those of the reference population.[108,109]

Nutritional expectations. It is common practice to view the nutrient needs of preterm infants weighing 2 to 2.5 kg to be similar to the nutrient needs of full-term infants. The RDA is often used as a reference. This practice requires validation, particularly for VLBW and ELBW infants. Recent evidence suggests that calcium and phosphorus needs may differ from

full-term infants during the first year of life. For example, bone mineralization has been reported to be lower in preterm infants fed unfortified human milk during the first year of life. Monitoring of bone mineral status may be appropriate for preterm infants throughout infancy.[110,111]

Discharge and follow-up. Preterm infants continue at nutritional risk after hospital discharge, particularly VLBW and ELBW infants and infants with ongoing medical and neurological concerns. Identification of nutritional risk, assessment of nutritional status, and education and support are part of the discharge and follow-up process for these infants. Critical times for nutritional evaluation include the immediate discharge period and key developmental stages of feeding. The latter include the in-

TABLE 13-16   Nutritional Risk Factors for Preterm Infants

Risk Factor	May Have
Infants < 6 lb or infants < 37 weeks' gestation	Less nutrient reserve than > 7.5 lb infant
	Feeding difficulties related to immaturity
Medical conditions (e.g., BPD, heart disease, short bowel syndrome, neurological impairment)	Increased nutrient needs
	Increased nutrient losses
	Feeding difficulties (impaired nippling skills, regurgitation, impaired fluid tolerance)
	Special dietary needs (fluid restriction, alteration in carbohydrates or fat due to malabsorption)
History of nutritional concerns or inadequate intake (e.g., SGA, long-term TPN, ELBW infants, documented nutritional deficits such as osteopenia)	Increased nutrient needs for catch-up growth or to correct deficits and replace losses

troduction of semisolids at about 4 to 6 months developmental age, and weaning from the bottle to the cup and to table foods at about 9 to 12 months developmental age. Assessment at these stages assists in evaluating an infant's readiness for change, in selecting appropriate foods, in reassuring parents about growth and nutrition, and in preventing growth setbacks in infants with a history of slow growth and small size.

Identification of Nutritional Risk

Infants who are at nutritional risk include those who have increased nutrient needs, increased nutrient losses, or difficulty ingesting adequate amounts of nutrients (Table 13-16). Additional physical and environmental factors can also place preterm infants at nutritional risk. Infants with ongoing nutritional concerns should be monitored more frequently.

Assessment

Periodic growth measurements, diet assessment, and feeding observation should be a part of the follow-up nutrition assessment of preterm, LBW infants. Figure 13-7 provides one set of guidelines for this purpose. Evaluation of individual growth patterns and growth velocity are useful indicators of nutritional status. Infants who remain smaller than term cohorts should have an established growth channel that parallels reference curves. Weight gains should be about 20 to 30 gm/day in the first 6 months of life but may decline to about 10 to 15 gm/day from 6 to 12 months of age. Weight to length should be proportional. Normally, the

---

GUIDELINES FOR NUTRITION ASSESSMENT FORM USE

1. Weight, length, and head circumference
   - Horizontal bars indicate target growth rate.
   - Draw bar graphs of weekly changes in growth. These can be compared in a glance with target growth rates.
2. Kcalories
   - Refer to energy intake goals.
   - Graph parenteral and enteral kcalories in 2 different colors to show proportion of energy from these sources. Height of bar graph shows weekly average energy intake in kcal/kg/day.
   - The chart at the bottom of page 1 relates energy intake to growth in weight. This chart can be used to help determine the individual energy needs of a particular infant. The horizontal bar is usually about 120 kcal/kg/day, but it can vary depending upon the individual energy intake goals for the infant.
3. Parenteral nutrition
   - Refer to IV protein and fat intake goals.
   - Graphs for protein, calcium, and phosphorus are included on this assessment because preterm infants often receive inadequate amounts of these nutrients unless careful monitoring occurs.
4. Type of milk
   - The adequacy of intake of enteral nutrients depends on the type of milk that is fed to preterm infants. Use these spaces to identify the type of milk (formula or breast milk), and comment on the adequacy of this milk for meeting the nutrient needs of preterm infants.
5. Supplements
   - Use these spaces to identify what supplements are given and whether they are appropriate. Include information about fortified breast milk (F-BrM). Use blank spaces to provide information about other supplements not mentioned here.

Continued.

GROWTH AND NUTRITION: WEEKLY AVERAGES

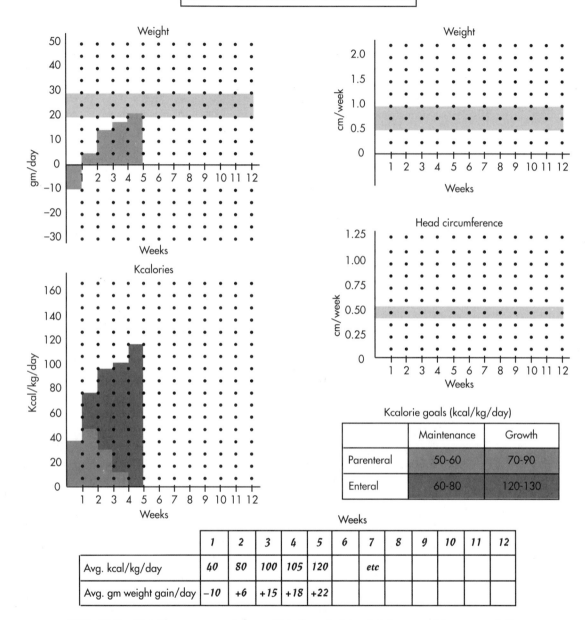

Weeks	1	2	3	4	5	6	7	8	9	10	11	12
Avg. kcal/kg/day	40	80	100	105	120		etc					
Avg. gm weight gain/day	-10	+6	+15	+18	+22							

Kcalorie goals (kcal/kg/day)

	Maintenance	Growth
Parenteral	50-60	70-90
Enteral	60-80	120-130

FIG. 13-7 Nutrition assessment form. This form is intended for use with preterm infants who are cared for in hospital settings. This assessment form was designed to meet the need for a graphic summary of growth and nutrient intake information that is collected daily, but frequently gets 'buried' under piles of flow sheets. The form will create a "picture" of nutritional status that is readily visible to dietitians, nurses, and physicians involved in making decisions regarding the nutritional support of preterm infants. Each form summarizes 12 weeks of data, and in hospitals where this form is used, it has been approved for inclusion in the infant's medical record. This form represents data from a hypothetical infant. See the Appendix for a form without data.

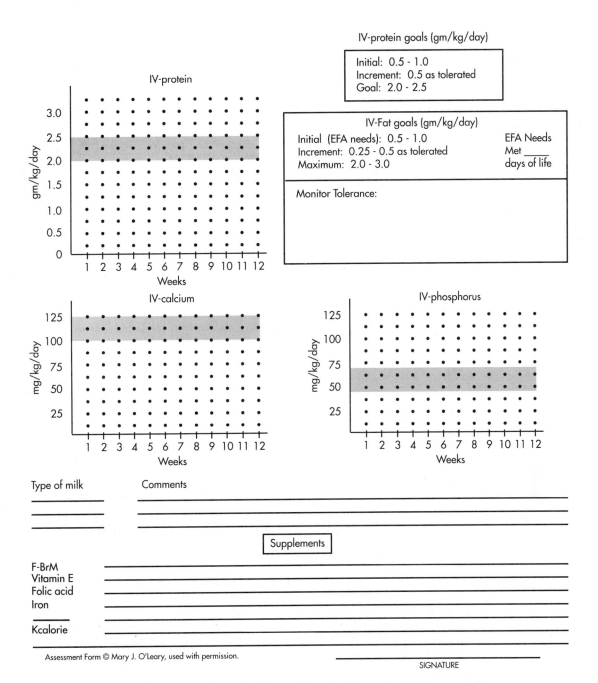

IV-protein goals (gm/kg/day)

Initial: 0.5 - 1.0
Increment: 0.5 as tolerated
Goal: 2.0 - 2.5

IV-Fat goals (gm/kg/day)

Initial (EFA needs): 0.5 - 1.0   EFA Needs
Increment: 0.25 - 0.5 as tolerated   Met _____
Maximum: 2.0 - 3.0   days of life

Monitor Tolerance:

Type of milk   Comments

Supplements

F-BrM
Vitamin E
Folic acid
Iron

Kcalorie

SIGNATURE

Assessment Form © Mary J. O'Leary, used with permission.

FIG. 13-7, cont'd For legend see opposite page.

Three Steps to Nutritional Assessment of Preterm Infants

Step 1: Assess Risk Factors

All preterm infants should be initially assessed for nutritional risk factors. Check all boxes that apply.

A. History of Nutritional Risk	B. Ongoing Nutritional Risk
☐ Prematurity (especially <32 weeks) ☐ Very low birthweight (<1,500 grams at birth) ☐ Small for gestational age (SGA) ☐ Total parenteral nutrition (TPN) >2 weeks in hospital	☐ Infant <6 lbs. at home ☐ Breast-fed preterm infant (<6 lbs.) ☐ Feeding difficulties ☐ Home TPN, tube feedings ☐ Medical problems (e.g., BPD, congenital heart disease, neurological immaturity or delay, short bowel syndrome) ☐ Osteopenia of prematurity, rickets

Step 2: Assess Growth

All infants should have regular measurements of weight, length and head circumference as part of their well-child care. Infants who have one or more <u>ongoing</u> nutritional risk factors (Step 1-B) should be measured more frequently (at least once a month).

To assess growth, plot measurements on reference curves using adjusted age for at least one year. Infants with ongoing problems may need to have their age adjusted for 2 years.

Compare individual growth patterns with reference curves to determine if growth is normal or if problems exist. Check all boxes that apply.

Normal Growth

☐ Growth proceeds steadily along growth trajectory between 5th and 95th percentiles on the reference curves.
☐ Growth is proportionate in weight, length, and head circumference.

Growth Problems

☐ Growth curves fall below the 5th percentiles for weight, length, and head circumference.
☐ Weight is not proportionate to length (underweight or overweight).
☐ Rate of growth decelerates (moves downward across growth percentiles).

Mary J. O'Leary, M.S., R.D.

Developed by the NANI Project, Sutter Memorial Hospital and University of California, Davis, Medical Center Sacramento, CA. Funded by the Maternal Child Health Branch, Department of Health Services, State of California, under contract #90-10455, 6/91

FIG. 13-8 For legend see opposite page.

Step 3: Assess Intake

All infants who have growth problems must have intake assessed. Compare the following average calorie guidelines for preterm infants with the infants kcal/lb/day calculated from the 3-day "Baby's Food Record."

under 6 lbs.: 50-55 kcal/lb/day
over 6lbs.: 45-50 kcal/lb/day

Consider individual variability as discussed in Guidelines, Step3. Check all boxes that apply to preterm infants with identified growth problems.

Calorie Intake

☐ Calorie intake *below* average guidelines for infant's weight. Increase amount and/or caloric density of feedings and monitor monthly to determine effectiveness in achieving normal growth patterns.

☐ Calorie intake *at or above* average guidelines for infant's weight. Poor growth indicates that infant may have higher than average calorie needs. Increase amount and/or caloric density of feedings and monitor growth monthly.

☐ Calorie intake apparently *too high* for this infant. Weight disproportionately greater than length. Reduce amount and/or caloric density of feedings and monitor growth monthly.

☐ Growth problem apparently not related to calorie intake. Refer to nutritionist for further assessment.

Compare formula/breastmilk and food intake reported on "Baby's Food Record: with feeding recommendations listed in Step 3 of the Guidelines. Check the box that applies.

Type of Feeding

☐ Infant receives formula/breastmilk with supplementation and baby foods (if appropriate) according to Guidelines.

☐ Infant *does not* receive formula/breastmilk with supplementation or baby foods (if appropriate) according to Guidelines.

Mary J. O'Leary, M.S., R.D.

Developed by the NANI Project, Sutter Memorial Hospital and University of California, Davis, Medical Center Sacramento, CA.
Funded by the Maternal Child Health Branch, Department of Health Services, State of California, under contract #90-10455, 6/91

FIG. 13-8, cont'd These guidelines facilitate posthospital discharge nutrition assessment of preterm infants. This stepwise assessment tool can be effectively used to facilitate coordination of services between community-based care providers and to communicate with tertiary care center consultants.

fluid intakes of preterm infants approximate 150 to 180 ml/kg/day ($2\frac{1}{3}$ to $2\frac{2}{3}$ oz/lb) throughout the first year. This approximates 105 to 120 kcal/kg/day. Energy intake may need to be adjusted on an individual basis to support optimal growth. Feeding observations, particularly during the first year, may be useful in identifying specific feeding difficulties related to immaturity (e.g., BPD or neurological impairment). Modification of feeding environment, position, schedule, or method may improve intake in some infants. A multidisciplinary observation including the fields of nursing, nutrition, and occupational or physical therapy may be necessary in individual infants with specific feeding, neurodevelopmental, or oral-motor concerns.

Figure 13-8 demonstrates a process for assessment of preterm infants at nutritional risk followed after hospital discharge. Individual infants identified as at nutritional risk may require a more in-depth evaluation, intervention, follow-up, and referral.

Education and support. Growth, developmental expectations, and early feeding experiences of preterm infants differ from term infants. Hospitalization alters the infant-caregiver feeding experience of preterm infants. These infants may have multiple feeders. Parental access to feeding may be limited. Adequate growth and feeding is often a final criterion for discharge, generating anxiety around these issues. After discharge, some infants may experience setbacks in feeding and growth. Provision of information regarding preterm feeding skills, nutritional needs of preterm infants, and growth expectations may facilitate the transition home and relieve parental anxiety. For the infant with ongoing growth and nutritional concerns, education and support may facilitate normal feeding transitions, appropriate food choices, and improved growth.

Case 3

Enteral feeding

Infant John was a 30-week gestation baby who weighed 1080 gm at birth. He was admitted to the neonatal intensive care unit with severe respiratory disease; although he was weaned from the ventilator by 4 weeks of age, he developed chronic lung disease and continued to require oxygen by hood. After $2\frac{1}{2}$ weeks of TPN through an umbilical arterial catheter, John's respiratory status was stable enough to permit the introduction of enteral feeds.

Premature formula feedings were initiated at full strength, but in small amounts, and John was gradually weaned from the hyperalimentation solution to a regimen of complete enteral nutrition by 36 weeks of gestational age. At that time he weighed 1360 gm and received 17 ml of 24 kcal/oz premature formula every 2 hours. This provided a total enteral volume of 150 ml/kg/day and a total kcaloric intake of 120 kcal/kg/day. Appropriate vitamin supplements were started, including iron supplements when John was 37 weeks of gestational age.

Daily measurements of body weight and weekly measurements of occipital frontal circumference and length were plotted on growth charts on an age-corrected basis. During the next 2 weeks, bolus feedings were increased as the infant grew to maintain a total enteral volume of 150 ml/kg/day and a kcaloric intake of 120 kcal/kg/day. However, John failed to grow at an adequate rate, and his growth attainment was low compared with the reference curves on the growth charts. John was a fussy baby with chronic lung disease, and he obviously expended considerable energy in his labored efforts to breathe. Furthermore, John received theophylline (a medication that increases basal metabolic rate).

Because of John's high energy expenditure and his extra energy needs for catch-up growth, it was decided to increase his total kcaloric intake. Volume was limited to 150 ml/kg/day, so it was decided to add medium-chain triglyceride oil and glucose polymers to the formula to achieve a total kcaloric intake of 140 kcal/kg/day. John tolerated this modification of the formula, and his rate of growth increased. John continued to be followed by regular measurements of growth changes to ensure that his energy and nutrient intake adequately met his needs for normal growth and development.

REVIEW QUESTIONS

1. List the major reasons why a premature infant is at greater nutritional risk than a full-term infant.
2. What are the major factors that determine whether a premature infant will receive parenteral or enteral feeds?
3. What are the differences between formulas designed for LBW infants and those for full-term infants?
4. Under what circumstances is human milk appropriate for the LBW infant?

5. How do the vitamin and mineral requirements of preterm infants differ from those of full-term infants?
6. How do parenteral protein and energy requirements differ for preterm infants?
7. Why is lipid intake so important for the preterm infant?
8. How do parenteral requirements for vitamins and minerals differ from the enteral requirements of preterm infants?
9. Describe the most frequent complications associated with parenteral nutrition.

SUGGESTED LEARNING ACTIVITIES

1. Review the chart of an infant in a neonatal intensive care unit who is receiving total parenteral nutrition. Describe the conditions that made total parenteral nutrition the appropriate method of feeding. Calculate the energy and nutrient intake for the past 24 hours.
2. Describe how the transition is made from total parenteral nutrition to enteral feeding in a premature infant.
3. Discuss the advantages and potential problems of human milk as the sole feeding for a premature infant.
4. Describe appropriate vitamin supplementation for the premature infant on enteral feedings.
5. Investigate the long-term prognosis for growth and development of premature and low birth weight babies.

Terms and Concepts

Provided here for your review is a listing of terms and concepts within this chapter. The definitions for terms can be found in the glossary, which begins on page 413. To aid your understanding of the terms' and concepts' application within this text, the page number designating the first mention of each term or concept within the chapter is given.

REFERENCES

1. Committee on Perinatal Health: *Toward improving the outcome of pregnancy,* New York, 1976, The National Foundation—March of Dimes.
2. Committee on Fetus and Newborn: *Guidelines for perinatal care,* Evanston, Ill, 1983, American Academy of Pediatrics; and Washington, DC, 1983, American College of Obstetricians and Gynecologists.
3. Committee on Fetus and Newborn, American Academy of Pediatrics: Level II neonatal units, *Pediatrics* 66:810, 1980.
4. Committee on Nutrition of the Mother and Preschool Child, Food and Nutrition Board: *Nutrition services in perinatal care,* Washington, DC, 1981, Assembly of Life Sciences, National Research Council.
5. Poole RL, Kerner JA, Jr: Establishing a nutrition support team for an intensive care nursery, *Nutr Supp Serv* 3:35, 1983.
6. Widdowson EM: *Growth and composition of the fetus and newborn.* In Assali NS, editor: *Biology of gestation,* vol II, New York, 1968, Academic Press.

7. Heird WC and others: Intravenous alimentation in pediatric patients, *J Pediatr* 80:351, 1972.
8. Ziegler EE: *Malnutrition in the premature infant,* Acta Paediatr Scand Suppl 374:58, 1991.
9. Doelkel RD and others: Clinical semistarvation: depression of hypoxic ventilatory response, *N Engl J Med* 295:358, 1976.
10. Chandra RK: Immunodeficiency in undernutrition and overnutrition, *Nutr Rev* 39:225, 1981.
11. Abel RM and others: Malnutrition in cardiac surgery patients, *Arch Surg* 111:45, 1976.
12. Van Aerde JEE: *Acute respiratory failure and BPD.* In Hay WW, editor: *Neonatal nutrition and metabolism,* St Louis, 1991, Mosby–Year Book.
13. Dobbing J: The later growth of the brain and its vulnerability, *Pediatrics* 53:2, 1974.
14. Rosso P, Hormazabal J, Winick M: Changes in brain weight, cholesterol phospholipid, and DNA content in marasmic children, *Am J Clin Nutr* 23:1275, 1970.
15. Grand RJ, Watkins JB, Torti FM: Development of the human gastrointestinal tract: a review, *Gastroenterology* 70:790, 1976.
16. Lebenthal E, Leung, YK: Feeding the premature and compromised infant: gastrointestinal considerations, *Pediatr Clin North Am* 35(2):215, 1988.
17. Kerner JA, Jr: *Vitamin requirements.* In Kerner JA, Jr, editor: *Manual of pediatric parenteral nutrition,* New York, 1983, John Wiley & Sons.
18. Anderson TL and others: A controlled trial of glucose versus glucose and amino acids in premature infants, *J Pediatr* 94:115, 1981.
19. Zlotkin SH, Bryan MH, Anderson GH: Intravenous nitrogen and energy intakes required to duplicate in utero nitrogen accretion in prematurely born human infants, *J Pediatr* 99:115, 1981.
20. Heird, WC, Sudhe K: *Intravenous feeding.* In Hay WW, Jr, editor: Neonatal nutrition and metabolism, St Louis, 1991, Mosby–Year Book.
21. Bronstein, M: *Energy requirement and protein energy balance in preterm and term infants.* In Hay WW, Jr, editor: *Neonatal nutrition and metabolism,* St Louis, 1991, Mosby–Year Book.
22. Sinclair J and others: Supportive management of the sick neonate: parenteral calories, water and electrolytes, *Pediatr Clin North Am* 17:863, 1970.
23. Lebenthal E, Lee PC, Heitlinger LA: Impact of development of the gastrointestinal tract on infant feedings, *J Pediatr* 102:1, 1983.
24. Raissen D: *Amino acid and protein metabolism in preterm and term infants,* In Hay WW, Jr, editor: *Neonatal nutrition and metabolism,* St Louis, 1991, Mosby–Year Book.
25. Kerner JA, Jr: *Indications for parenteral nutrition in pediatrics.* In Kerner JA, Jr, editor: *Manual of pediatric parenteral nutrition,* New York, 1983, John Wiley & Sons.
26. Heird WC and others: Pediatric parenteral amino acid mixture in low-birth-weight infants, *Pediatrics* 81:41, 1988.
27. Helms RA and others: Comparison of a pediatric versus standard amino acid formulation in preterm neonates requiring parenteral nutrition, *J Pediatr* 110:466, 1987.
28. Ziegler EE, Biga RL, Fomon SJ: *Nutritional requirements of the premature infant.* In Suskind RM, editor: *Textbook of pediatric nutrition,* New York, 1981, Raven Press.
29. Ziegler EE and others: Body composition of the reference fetus, *Growth* 40:329, 1976.
30. American Academy of Pediatrics, Committee on Nutrition: Nutritional needs of low-birth-weight infants, *Pediatrics* 75:976, 1985.
31. Gross SJ and others: Growth and biochemical response of premature infants fed human milk or modified infant formula, *N Engl J Med* 308:237, 1983.
32. Raiha NCR and others: Milk protein quantity and quality in low-birth-weight infants. I. Metabolic responses and effects on growth, *Pediatrics* 57:659, 1976.
33. Fomon SJ, Ziegler EE: Protein intake of premature infants: interpretation of data, *J Pediatr* 90:504, 1977.
34. Avery GB, Fletcher AB: *Nutrition.* In Avery GB, editor: *Neonatology,* Philadelphia, 1981, JB Lippincott.
35. Greene HL and others: Guidelines for the use of vitamins, trace elements, calcium, magnesium, and phosphorus in infants and children receiving total parenteral nutrition: report of the Subcommittee on Pediatric Parenteral Nutrient Requirements from the Committee on Clinical Practice Issues of The American Society for Clinical Nutrition, *Am J Clin Nutr* 48:1324, 1988.
36. Nutrition Advisory Group: *Guidelines for multivitamin preparation for parental use,* Chicago, 1975, American Medical Association.
37. Tsang RC: Vitamin and mineral requirements in preterm infants, New York, 1985, Marcel Dekker.

38. Kerner JA, Jr: *Fluid requirements*. In Kerner JA, Jr, editor: *Manual of pediatric parenteral nutrition*, New York, 1983, John Wiley & Sons.

39. Fanaroff M and others: Insensible water loss in low-birth-weight infants, *Pediatrics* 50:236, 1972.

40. Oh W: *Fluid and electrolyte management*. In Avery GB, editor: *Neonatology, pathophysiology, and management of the newborn*, Philadelphia, 1981, J.B. Lippincott.

41. Friis-Hansen B: Changes in body water compartments during growth, *Acta Paediatr Scand* 46 (suppl 110):1, 1957.

42. Bell EG, Oh W: Water requirement of premature newborn infants, *Acta Paediatr Scand Suppl* 305:21, 1983.

43. Hodson WA, Truog WE: *Parenteral nutrition*. In Hodson WA, Truog WA, editors: *Critical care of the newborn*, Philadelphia, 1983, WB Saunders.

44. Wu PYK, Hodgman JE: Insensible water loss in premature infants, *Pediatrics* 54:704, 1974.

45. Oh W, Karechi H: Phototherapy and insensible water loss in the newborn infant, *Am J Dis Child* 124:230, 1972.

46. Marks KA, Friedman A, Maisels MJ: A simple device for reducing insensible water loss in LBW infants, *Pediatrics* 60:223, 1977.

47. Spitzer AR, Fox WW, Delivoria-Papadopoulos M: Maximum diuresis—a factor in predicting recovery from respiratory distress syndrome and the development of bronchopulmonary dysplasia, *J Pediatr* 98:476, 1981.

48. Bell EF and others: Effect of fluid administration on the development of symptomatic patent ductus arteriosus and congestive heart failure in premature infants, *N Engl J Med* 302:598, 1980.

49. Stevenson JG: Fluid administration in the association of patent ductus arteriosus complicating distress syndrome, *J Pediatr* 90:257, 1977.

50. Goldberg RN and others: The association of rapid volume expansion and intraventricular hemorrhage in the preterm infant, *J Pediatr* 96:1060, 1980.

51. Brown ER and others: Bronchopulmonary dysplasia: possible relationship to pulmonary edema, *J Pediatr* 92:982, 1978.

52. Harkavey KL: Water and electrolyte requirements of the very-low-birth-weight infant, *Perinatal Press* 6:47, 1982.

53. Ziegler EE: Nutritional management of the premature infant, *Perinatology-Neonatology* July/Aug 11, 1985.

54. Heird WC: Total parenteral nutrition. In Lebenthal E, editor: *Textbook of gastroenterology and nutrition in infancy*, ed 2, New York, 1989, Raven Press.

55. Winters RW: An historical review of the development of criteria for intravenous amino acid requirements, Clinical Conference on Pediatric Nutrition, *Acta Chir Scand* (suppl 517):7, 1982.

56. Ziegler M and others: Route of pediatric parenteral nutrition: proposed criteria revision, *J Pediatr Surg* 15:472, 1980.

57. Lebenthal E, editor: *Total parenteral nutrition*, New York, 1986, Raven Press.

58. Binder ND and others: Insulin infusion with parenteral nutrition in extremely low birth weight infants with hyperglycemia, *J Pediatr* 114:273, 1989.

59. Collins JW and others: A controlled trial of insulin infusion and parenteral nutrition in extremely low birth weight infants with glucose intolerance, *J Pediatr* 118:921, 1991.

60. Snyderman SE: *The protein and amino acid requirements of the premature infant*. In Jonxis JHP, Visser HKA, Troelstra JA, editors: *Metabolic process in the fetus and newborn infant*, Baltimore, 1971, Williams & Wilkins.

61. Gaull GE and others: Milk protein quantity and quality in low-birth-weight infants. III. Effects on sulfur amino acids in plasma and urine, *J Pediatr* 90:356, 1977.

62. Gaull GE: Taurine in pediatric nutrition: review and update, *Pediatrics*, 83:3, 1989.

62a. Friedman Z and others: Rapid onset of essential fatty acid deficiency in the newborn, *Pediatrics* 58:640, 1976.

63. Cooke RJ, Zee PL, Yeh Y-Y: Essential fatty acid status of the premature infant during short-term fat-free parenteral nutrition, *J Pediatr Gastroenterol Nutr* 3:446, 1984.

64. Christensen ML and others: Plasma carnitine concentration and lipid metabolism in infants receiving parenteral nutrition, *J Pediatr* 115:794, 1989.

65. Melegh B: Carnitine supplementation in the premature: metabolic problems of the newborn, *Biol of Neonate* 58(suppl 1):93, 1990.

66. Schmidt-Sommerfeld E, Penn D: Carnitine and total parenteral nutrition of the neonate: metabolic problems of the newborn, *Biol of Neonate* 58(suppl 1):81, 1990.

67. Helms RA and others: Enhanced lipid utilization in infants receiving oral L-carnitine during long-term parenteral nutrition, *J Pediatr* 109:984, 1986.

68. Zaidan H and others: Lipid clearing in premature infants during continuous heparin infusion: role of circulating lipases, *Pediatr Res* 19:23, 1985.

69. Haumont D and others: Plasma lipid and plasma lipoprotein concentrations in low birth weight infants given parenteral nutrition with twenty or ten percent lipid emulsion, *J Pediatr* 115:787, 1989.

70. Kerner JA, Jr, editor: *Manual of pediatric parenteral nutrition,* New York, 1983, John Wiley & Sons.

71. Lucas A, Bloom R, Aynsley-Green A: Gut hormones and 'minimal enteral feeding,' *Acta Paediatr Scand* 75:719, 1986.

72. Aynsley-Green A: Plasma hormone concentrations during enteral and parenteral nutrition in the human newborn, *J Pediatr Gastroenterol Nutr* 2(suppl 1):S108, 1983.

73. Aynsley-Green A: Hormones and postnatal adaptation to enteral nutrition, *J Pediatr Gastroenterol Nutr* 2:418, 1983.

74. Berseth LL: Neonatal small intestinal motility: motor responses to feeding in term and preterm infants, *J Pediatr* 117:777, 1990.

75. Dunn L and others: Beneficial effects of early hypocaloric enteral feeding on neonatal gastrointestinal function: preliminary report of a randomized trial, *J Pediatr* 112:622, 1988.

76. Benda GI: Modes of feeding low-birth-weight infants, *Semin Perinatol* 3:407, 1979.

77. Hay, WW, editor: *Neonatal nutrition and metabolism,* St Louis, 1991, Mosby—Year Book.

78. Mathew OP: Science of bottle feeding, *J Pediatr* 119:511, 1991.

79. VandenBerg KA: Nippling management of the sick neonate in the NICU: the disorganized feeder, *Neonatal Network,* 9:9, 1990.

80. Shaker CS: Nipple feeding premature infants: a different perspective, *Neonatal Network,* 8:9, 1990.

81. Lebenthal E, editor: *Textbook of gastroenterology and nutrition in infancy,* ed 2, New York, 1989, Raven Press.

82. Steichen JJ, Krug-Wispe SK, Tsang RC: Breastfeeding the low birth weight preterm infant, *Clin Perinatol* 14:131, 1987.

83. Davies DP: Adequacy of expressed breast milk for early growth of preterm infants, *Arch Dis Child* 52:296, 1977.

84. Tyson JE and others: Growth, metabolic response, and development in very-low-birth-weight infants fed banked human milk or enriched formula. I. Neonatal findings, *J Pediatr* 103:95, 1983.

85. Gross SJ: Growth and biochemical response of preterm infants fed human milk or modified infant formula, *N Engl J Med* 308:237, 1983.

86. Jarvenpaa AL and others: Preterm infants fed human milk attain intrauterine weight gain, *Acta Paediatr Scand* 72:239, 1983.

87. Chessex P and others: Quality of growth in premature infants fed their own mothers' milk, *J Pediatr* 102:107, 1983.

88. Gross SJ: *Effect of gestational age on the composition of breast milk.* In Grand RJ, editor: *Pediatric nutrition,* New York, 1987, Raven Press.

89. Atkinson SA, Radde IC, Anderson GH: Macromineral balances in premature infants fed their own mothers' milk or formula, *J Pediatr* 102:99, 1983.

90. Chan GM: Human milk calcium and phosphate levels of mothers delivering term and preterm infants, *J Pediatr Gastroenterol Nutr* 1:201, 1982.

91. Rowe J and others: Hypophosphatemia and hypercalciuria in small premature infants fed human milk: evidence for inadequate dietary phosphorus, *J Pediatr* 104:112, 1984.

92. Schanler RJ, Garza C, Nichols BL: Fortified mothers milk for very-low-birth-weight infants: results of growth and nutrient balance studies, *J Pediatr* 107:437, 1985.

93. Schanler RJ, Garza C, Smith EO: Fortified mothers milk for VLBW infants: results of macromineral balance studies, *J Pediatr* 107:767, 1985.

94. Ronnholm KAR and others: Supplementation with human milk protein improves growth of small premature infants fed human milk, *Pediatrics* 77:649, 1986.

95. Carey DE and others: Growth and phosphorus metabolism in premature infants fed human milk, fortified human milk, or special premie formula, *Am J Dis Child* 141:511, 1987.

96. Dancis J, O'Connell JR, Holt LE: A grid for recording the weight of premature infants, *J Pediatr* 33:570, 1948.

97. Shaffer SG and others: Postnatal weight changes in low birth weight infants, *J Pediatr* 79:702, 1987.

98. Babson SG: Growth of low-birth-weight infants, *J Pediatr* 77:11, 1970.

99. Gairdner D, Pearson J: A growth chart for premature and other infants, *Arch Dis Child* 46:783, 1971.

100. Phelps DL and others: 28-day survival rates of 6676 neonates with birth weights of 1250 grams or less, *Pediatrics* 87:7, 1991.

101. Hoffman EL, Bennett FC: Birth weight less than 800 grams: changing outcomes and influences of gender and gestation number, *Pediatrics* 86:27, 1990.

102. Bennett FC: *Neurodevelopmental outcome of premature/low-birth-weight infants: the role of developmental intervention.* In Guthrie RD: *Neonatal intensive care,* New York, 1988, Churchill Livingstone.

103. Collin MF, Halsey CL, Anderson CL: Emerging developmental sequelae in the "normal" extremely low birth weight infant, *Pediatrics* 88:115, 1991.

104. Resnick MB and others: Educational outcome of neonatal intensive care graduates, *Pediatrics* 89:373, 1992.

105. Casey PH and others: Growth status and growth rates of a varied sample of low birth weight preterm infants: a longitudinal cohort from birth to three years of age, *J Pediatr* 119:599, 1991.

106. Keith JK and others: Growth to age 3 among very low birth weight sequelae free survivors of modern neonatal intensive care, *J Pediatr* 100:622, 1982.

107. Georgieff MK and others: Catch-up growth, muscle and fat accretion, and body proportionality of infants one year after newborn intensive care, *J Pediatr* 114:288, 1989.

108. Ernst JA and others: Growth outcome and feeding practices of the very low birth weight infant (less than 1500 grams) within the first year of life, *J Pediatr* 117:S156, 1990.

109. Ross G, Lipper EG, Auld PAM: Growth achievement of very low birth weight premature children at school age, *J Pediatr* 117:307, 1990.

110. Abrams SA and others: Bone mineralization in former very low birth weight infants fed either human milk or commercial formula: one-year follow-up observation, *J Pediatr* 114:1041, 1989.

111. Abrams SA, Schanler R, Garza C: Bone mineralization in former very low birth weight infants fed either human milk or commercial formula, *J Pediatr* 112:956, 1988.

14

Developmental Disabilities and Other Special Health Care Needs

Peggy L. Pipes
Robin Pritkin Glass

Objectives

✦✦

After studying this chapter, the student should:

✔ *Be aware of the many physical and environmental factors which affect food and nutrient intake in children with special health care needs.*

✔ *Be able to identify children at risk for nutritional problems for whom preventive intervention is appropriate.*

✔ *Have knowledge of ways to secure anthropometric indices for children with contractures.*

✔ *Recognize factors that may modify the energy needs of children with special health care needs compared with those of average children.*

✔ *Be able to screen children with motor difficulties that affect eating and who need referral to a therapist.*

✔ *Have knowledge of the many factors that must be assessed to design an intervention program for any nutritional and feeding problems that may be found in developmentally delayed children.*

Between 10% and 20% of children in the United States have special health care needs that include chronic illnesses and developmental disorders. Many of these children have more than one developmental or medical problem. A significant number have issues that result from maternal abuse of alcohol or drugs during pregnancy or from maltreatment and neglect. Children with acquired immunodeficiency syndrome (AIDS) have unique problems that must be addressed.

Most children and families will require several disciplines or programs to control or resolve nutrition concerns. Currently the development of community-based interdisciplinary teams is encouraged. Since many of the children are at risk of difficulties in achieving an adequate nutrient intake, the inclusion of a dietitian/nutritionist on the team is essential. Services should be family centered and delivered in a culturally relevant manner.

DEVELOPMENTAL DELAYS

Approximately 3% of all infants and children are developmentally delayed. Often these children also have medical conditions (such as heart disease or seizure disorders) that may increase or modify their nutrient and energy needs. In addition, psychosocial factors, developmental delays, or motor dysfunctions may create nutritional and feeding concerns.

Nutritional problems in this population range from severe undernutrition to gross obesity; activity patterns range from immobility to hyperactivity. Often a nutritional problem is caused by several etiological factors. For example, a child with failure to thrive and osteomalacia may be undernourished because of inadequate energy intake secondary to oral motor dysfunction and parent-child interactions; the osteomalacia may result from the metabolic interaction of drugs and nutrients.

Commonly reported parental and professional concerns relating to handicapped children's food and nutrient intakes include the following:

1. Slow growth in length and lack of appropriate weight gain
2. Excessive weight gain in relation to length gains
3. Obesity
4. Iron deficiency anemia
5. Refusal of the child to consume specific foods or groups of foods
6. Refusal of the child to progress in feeding behavior when developmentally ready
7. Pica
8. Bizarre feeding patterns
9. Lack of appetite
10. Excessive appetite
11. Gagging, vomiting, or rumination
12. Food allergies
13. Limited fluid intake
14. Constipation
15. Abnormal motor patterns that affect the child's ability to consume food
16. Inability or unwillingness of the child to finger feed or self-feed
17. Limited attention span at mealtime
18. Disruptive behavior at mealtime

Difficulties in weight control are often clustered in specific syndromes. Obesity is common in children with **Down syndrome, Prader-Willi syndrome, Carpenter syndrome, Cohen syndrome,** and **Laurence-Moon-Biedl syndrome.** Underweight is frequently noted in children with **Rett syndrome,** athetoid cerebral palsy, **hyperactivity,** and behavior problems.

Underweight children with limited energy intakes commonly have less than desirable intakes of several nutrients because of the limited volume of food they consume. Inadequate intakes of vitamins A, C, and D and folate are the most frequent problems.

Feeding problems and growth retardation appear to be issues most often in children with mental retardation, cerebral palsy, congenital heart disease, and deaf blindness. Children who have oral motor dysfunction and who require assisted feeding have lower nutrient and energy intakes and are shorter and leaner than children with normal oral patterns and who can feed themselves.[1,2]

NUTRITIONAL NEEDS OF THE DEVELOPMENTALLY DELAYED CHILD

Developmentally delayed children require the same nutrients as any individual. However, no dietary standards exist that are applicable to groups of developmentally delayed children. Many of these children, although not all, are growth retarded because of a genetic or biological defect. Syndromes with which growth retardation is associated include Down syndrome, Prader-Willi syndrome, **trisomy 13 and 18 syndromes, Cornelia de Lange's syndrome, Hurler syndrome, Russell's syndrome, Williams syn-**

drome, and many syndromes and conditions whose etiology remains unknown.

Early studies of the growth and nutrient intake of developmentally delayed children were conducted primarily in institutions on children with cerebral palsy. More recent studies have focused on children in the free-living population and on nutrition problems encountered in specific syndromes.

Measurements of Physically Handicapped Children

Evaluating the adequacy of a child's nutrient and energy intake includes assessment of his or her physical growth. This means the child must be accurately weighed and measured and the data plotted on growth charts (see Chapter 1). However, difficulties may be encountered in securing and interpreting the data for children who have developmental delays.

Accurate measurements of linear growth may be impossible to secure for children who have contractures or cannot stand. Roche[3] suggests using crown-rump length or sitting height. The measurements, however, cannot be considered accurate when a child's trunk or torso is affected. To estimate linear height, Manenica and others[4] have investigated the applicability of measurements of arm span for children with spina bifida, and Gleason[5] has used tibia length for boys with **Duchenne's muscular dystrophy.**

Using a control group of normal children, Manenica and others[4] found a correlation of arm span to linear height. They found that a normal arm span/height ratio of 1:1 provides a simple approximation technique. Arm span measurements are made with an anthropometer, a stainless steel detachable rod approximately 7 feet long with etched gradations to 0.1 cm and one movable sleeve. The arm span has been defined as the greatest distance between the outstretched fingers of the right and left hands with the arms and forearms extended horizontally sideways and the back pressed against a flat surface.[6] To secure this measurement, the subject stands in the erect position with arms outstretched (Figure 14-1). The fixed end of the anthropometer is held by one individual at the tip of the subject's middle finger of one hand, while another individual positions the sleeve at the tip of the middle finger of the subject's other hand. The subject is then told to stretch his or her arms, and the movable

FIG. 14-1   Arm span measured from tip of one middle finger to the other.

sleeve is adjusted to the maximum arm span.

Estimation of linear length and height using tibia length had higher standard errors because of the dynamics of relative tibial length. Although less accurate than arm span, this measurement was believed to provide useful information for individuals who have contractures in the arms and had previously been mobile.[5]

Tibia length is defined as the distance between the medial tibial epicondyle to the medial malleolus.[7] To measure tibia length, subjects are seated with their feet resting as flat on the floor as possible. The top of the right tibia is located by palpating downward from the medial condyle of the femur to the zone of articulation between the femur and the tibia. This point is marked at the closest approximation to the highest point of the medial condyle of the tibia, which is buried. The tip of the medial malleolus is easily identified and marked. The distance between these two points is measured with a sliding anthropometer (Figure 14-2). Height is estimated from the equation:

$$\text{Height (cm)} = 3.54 \times \text{tibial length} + 32.23$$

Although more data are needed on normal children to establish standards, arm span can be used to estimate linear height for children who cannot stand, and tibia length can be used for children with contractures in their arms.

Syndrome-specific growth expectations. Some classifications of handicapped children show normal growth, whereas others with **congenital** or metabolic disorders are associated with significant growth deviation. Researchers realize that the growth curves for normal children are not applicable for individuals with some handicapping conditions and that syndrome-specific reference data are needed. Growth curves have been developed for children with **dysplasia congenita, pseudoachondroplasia, Turner syndrome** (in girls), and Down syndrome.[8,9] These growth charts should be used for plotting measurements of these children. For other children who have developmental delays, monitoring the rates of gain in height and weight, weight for height percentiles, midarm circumference, and triceps fatfold measurements over time provides useful information. The professional interpreting this data should have knowledge of specific syndromes associated with growth retardation.

Energy Requirements

Culley and Middleton[10] have reported that institutionalized retarded children who are ambulatory have energy requirements similar to those of normal children, if height is used as a standard for estimating kcalorie needs. Because many of the children in their study had short stature, their kcalorie requirements were less than those of other children the same age. Only when motor dysfunction became severe enough to cause children to be nonambulatory did it reduce the kcalorie requirement per centimeter of height significantly. Pipes and Holm[11] have re-

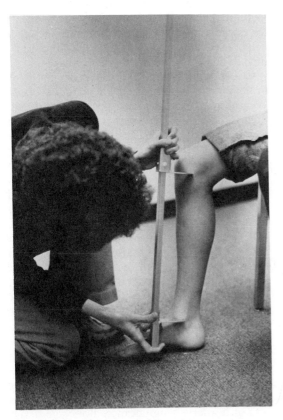

FIG. 14-2 Tibia length measurement.

ported that children with Prader-Willi syndrome have reduced energy requirements per centimeter of height as compared with energy requirements of normal children. Mertz and others,[12] on the other hand, reported that a group of emaciated children in an institution for the mentally handicapped had energy requirements in excess of those of normal children. Even though such children consumed kcalorie intakes recommended for their ages, they remained emaciated.

Children with **spasticity (hypertonia)** frequently become overweight for their heights consuming low-kcalorie intakes for their ages. One obese 16-year-old female quadriplegic with spasticity has been described who had a basal energy expenditure of a person half her body weight. The girl was confined to a wheelchair; her total energy expenditure was estimated to be 1270 to 1370 kcal/day.[13]

Children with **athetosis** (mixed pattern of too much and too little tone) consume greater numbers of kcalories than do those with spasticity and are less likely to become obese because they are able to engage in greater amounts of activity. Some children with athetosis expend energy constantly in involuntary movements. Researchers have found that basal energy expenditures of children with athetosis are similar to those of normal children and that the energy cost of activity depends on the child's capacity for muscular work. As levels of activity reach limits, activity becomes costly and uneconomical.[13]

Developmentally delayed children are often less active than their peers because of low muscle tone, immobility, or general disinterest in their environments. This inactivity limits their energy expenditures and therefore their energy requirements. Grogan and others[14] found that the mean energy intakes to maintain normal weight gain for height in children with **myelomeningocele** (which often limits ambulation) was approximately 50% of that for children without myelomeningocele. Children with cerebral palsy who have decreased levels of activity have been noted to need 10 kcal/cm of height, whereas those with normal or increased levels of activity need 15 kcal/cm of height.

Recommendations for energy intakes of developmentally delayed children must be individualized. Because physical growth of handicapped children frequently deviates from the norm, kcalories per centimeter (kcal/cm) of height may prove to be a more useful reference on which to base estimated needs than kcalories per kilogram (kcal/kg) of body weight.

Cerebral Palsy

Children with cerebral palsy have abnormal motor patterns that range from hypotonia to **hypertonia** and include spasticity and athetosis. Most studies have focused on those who have spasticity and athetosis. Body compositions of individuals with cerebral palsy may differ from those of normal children. Isaksson[15] found reduced body cell mass in children with both spasticity and athetosis caused by atrophy of skeletal muscles resulting from disease and low levels of physical activity. Reduced cell mass may reduce requirements for essential nutrients and kcalories. On the other hand, a reduced cell mass may result from a lifetime of limited nutrient and energy intakes.

Children with cerebral palsy generally grow in height and weight at rates less than average. Weight may be greater than that of normal children in children with spastic cerebral palsy and less than average in children with athetoid cerebral palsy. Oral motor involvement may be associated with growth retardation. Most health care practitioners believe that mouth area involvement is closely associated with poor food intake, and that the extent of mouth involvement is limiting on nutrient and energy intakes, and as a result slow growth is associated. Krick and Van Duyn[16] found a relationship between oral motor involvement as defined by two or more of the following: weak suck, swallow, **tongue thrust,** tongue incoordination, **tonic bite reflex,** lip retraction, hypotonia of the tongue and lips, and growth retardation. Children with cerebral palsy who had oral-motor problems were significantly thinner for their age and height than their age-matched counterparts who had cerebral palsy but no oral-motor impairment. They were also shorter, but this was of borderline significance. Bone age delays of 2 to 47 months have been reported by several investigators indicating less than expected maturation for age.[17,18]

Studies of free-living populations of children with cerebral palsy have shown acceptable intakes of nutrients other than iron.[19] Dietary intakes of less severely retarded children have been found to be markedly higher in all nutrients except vitamins A and C than intakes of the more severely delayed children. The energy value of the diets is influenced by the children's ability to self-feed. Children with motor involvements and mental retardation severe enough to interfere with their ability to feed themselves tend to consume fewer kcalories than do those who are able to self-feed.[19]

Prader-Willi Syndrome

Children with Prader-Willi syndrome have nutritional problems both in infancy and in older childhood. An absence of the long arm of chromosome 15 is found in some but not all individuals with Prader-Willi syndrome. Diagnosis is made on the basis of clinical symptoms.

Infants with the syndrome are hypotonic at birth; most have a weak suck. Failure to thrive is common in the first year. They often require tube feeding. Between 2 and 4 years of age these children become obese, unless aggressive intervention is instituted before the rapid rate of weight gain. An insatiable appetite will be noticed. Then food behaviors that include gorging, stealing, and hoarding food develop. They eat unusual food items such as raw hamburger and ornamental berries. One individual with Prader-Willi syndrome ate 12 pies at one sitting and 14 milkshakes at one time.

Most of these children gain excessive weight if permitted an energy intake recommended for normal children their age. Restriction of energy intakes to approximately two thirds of the RDA is necessary to maintain a weight gain within the growth channel. However, the ranges of appropriate intake are wide at any age. The following is one successful approach to management of weight control in children with this syndrome. Parents record (in household measures) all food offered and returned for 30 consecutive days. During this period individuals are weighed on a beam balance scale every 2 weeks.

The energy value of the food consumed is calculated. The energy value of weight lost or gained is added to or subtracted from this energy value of that consumed (using the conversion figure of 7.7 kcal/gm of weight change). The individual's energy needs per centimeter of height are estimated by dividing the height into total energy expended, and a diet plan to effect weight maintenance or loss is prescribed.[20]

Successful intervention requires control of the environment so that food is totally inaccessible to the child with Prader-Willi syndrome. Refrigerators and cupboards must be locked. Food must be removed from the table as soon as a meal is finished. The children must be supervised at school so that they do not steal others' lunches or rummage in the garbage.

Down Syndrome

Children with Down syndrome (trisomy 21) often have problems with nutrient intake. Some have conditions that require nutrition therapy or that can be prevented by anticipatory nutrition guidance. For example, there is a high incidence of cardiac anomalies among infants with Down syndrome. The child therefore may lack the endurance to ingest sufficient nutrients. Early or repeated cardiac surgery may lead to the use of supplemental tube feeding or the delayed introduction of solid foods. These children frequently have difficulty with tongue control and have tongue protrusion or a tongue thrust that impairs eating ability. Constipation secondary to hypotonia is not uncommon. Overweight has been suggested as a characteristic of children with Down syndrome from 2 to 3 years of age to adolescence. Some feel there is a constitutional but not inevitable tendency for individuals with this syndrome to be obese.

Limited intakes of nutrients may create concern. One study of 47 children with Down syndrome from ages 6 months to 6 years noted 16% to have low intakes of calcium, 14% to have low intakes of iron, and 10% to have low intakes of vitamin D and ascorbic acid.[21] Feeding problems were also identified. These children commonly refused to chew textured food when developmentally ready to do so. This resulted in the child accepting only a limited variety of foods. Social and emotional situations also resulted in feeding problems that compromised feeding and the children's nutrient intakes or developmental progress in feeding behavior or both.[21]

Early individual or group intervention has proven effective in remediating these problems. Effective programs use an interdisciplinary approach including a nutritionist, an occupational or physical therapist, and a behaviorist. Counseling and therapy should focus on developmental readiness for the transition to appropriate textures of foods, the use of food to support developmental progress, parental feelings about and interaction with their children, physical growth, maintenance of normal weight for height, and foods that supply appropriate nutrients.

Rett Syndrome

Rett syndrome, a degenerative disorder affecting only females, results in a number of food, feeding, and nutrition issues as the children grow older. The girls grow and develop normally until 6 to 9 months of age when developmental stagnation begins and the rate of head growth declines. Previously acquired skills may be lost. Stereotypical hand movements that include hand wringing, clapping, tapping, and mouthing begin. The majority of the girls grow in channels below the 5th percentile on the NCHS growth charts.[22] Many require long-term anticonvulsant therapy.

The etiology of the syndrome is unknown. There is speculation that an inborn error of carbohydrate metabolism may be the cause.[23]

Oral-motor dysfunction is often a problem of girls with Rett syndrome. Over 50% have poor lip closure and drool. Most girls with Rett syndrome learn to feed themselves, although they may go through phases when self-feeding is lost and then regained. Most girls with Rett syndrome are undernourished even though they have good appetites and consume more energy than would be expected for their age. However, some adolescents and adults have been noted to be overweight during clinical observation. Constipation is a concern of all individuals with Rett syndrome.

The range of nutrition concerns presented in girls with this syndrome mandate that therapy be individualized. Therapy is most likely to focus on increasing weight of the undernourished and on resolving constipation through dietary approaches. Because an inborn error of carbohydrate metabolism is suspected, a high-fat diet may be suggested. In some instances a ketogenic diet to control seizures may be prescribed. Texture of the food offered to these individuals often has to be modified. Most girls are able to eat soft, well-cooked food. It is often mashed with a fork, but sometimes it must be pureed. Thickening liquids may make them more acceptable. Attention should also be given to the interaction of drugs and nutrients.

Phenylketonuria

Infants born with metabolic disorders are at high risk for developmental disorders. Early detection, intervention, and surveillance are urgent. Of the many disorders identified, programs for the hyperphenylalanemias are the most comprehensive because mental retardation can be prevented if treatment is begun immediately after birth.

Currently, all states have newborn screening programs for children with **phenylketonuria (PKU)** and other disorders. Blood samples obtained by heel prick and applied to Guthrie filter paper are taken from every infant before he or she leaves the nursery. Infants who leave the hospital before 24 hours of age are screened again at 3 weeks of age.[24] Newborns with a positive screening test are tested again by both qualitative and quantitative methods. Criteria for the diagnosis of PKU are blood levels of phenylalanine consistently above 16 to 20 mg/dl, tyrosine levels less than 3 mg/dl, and the presence of O-hydroxyphenylacetic acid in the urine.

Nutrition therapy. Effective management of PKU requires special formulas, food products modified in their content of phenylalanine, and a cohesive team that includes the child, parent, nurse, social worker, psychologist, and pediatrician.[25] Goals of nutrition therapy include both the provision of an adequate energy and nutrient intake and restriction of phenylalanine to maintain appropriate blood levels (2 to 10 mg/

dl) so that normal growth and development proceed. To achieve these goals blood levels are taken frequently, and the diet is adjusted until the exact prescription for the individual child is developed.

Several low-phenylalanine or phenylalanine-free formulas supplemented with tyrosine are available. These formulas are designed to meet age-specific nutrition needs, thus the manufacturers have developed formulas for infants and toddlers (e.g., Lofenalac or Analog XP) and older children (e.g., Phenyl-Free by Mead Johnson and Maximaid by Ross). In early infancy and childhood, these special formula mixtures should provide 90% of the protein and 80% of the kcalories needed by the individual. Foods with a low-phenylalanine content are introduced when it is developmentally appropriate for the child and in amounts to maintain the desired blood levels.

Appropriate nourishment and maintenance of sufficiently low blood phenylalanine levels contribute to normal physical and cognitive development. Blood levels continue to be monitored frequently, and adjustments are made in children's phenylalanine intake to support their changing needs as they grow.

Current recommendations are to continue the diet throughout adulthood. Discontinuation of the diet at ages 4 to 6 has resulted in learning difficulties, progressively decreasing IQ, poor attention span, and behavioral difficulties. Structural changes in the white matter of the brain, which caused neurological difficulties, have been found in adolescents and young adults who have discontinued or relaxed dietary treatment and have allowed blood phenylalanine levels to rise.[26]

Pica

Pica, an eating disorder noted in some institutionalized retarded individuals but found occasionally also in the free-living population, has been shown to result in malabsorption of zinc and iron. Danford, Smith, and Huber[27] found that individuals with pica had low plasma zinc levels and low measures of iron status even though they received adequate dietary intake of minerals.

Environmental Deprivation

Children who are developmentally delayed from lack of appropriate stimuli are at risk for an inappropriate nutrient intake as well as environmental deprivation. These children frequently live in families that have limited economic resources and limited education. The parents may have poor interpersonal and parenting skills. They may abuse drugs or alcohol or both; they may have learning or developmental disabilities or both. Frequently the parents are young and single. Their children may also have experienced abuse or neglect; some may have experienced hunger, others inappropriate nutrient intake. Most families rely heavily on convenience and prepackaged foods. When food is offered, gorging or hoarding may be secondary to erratic feeding times. On the other hand, children may have familiarity with and accept only a few foods. Delayed feeding behaviors such as continued use of a bottle and eating of strained food when children are developmentally ready to consume food in a more mature manner may be noted.

When children who have experienced deprivation are identified, it is likely that a number of agencies will be involved in alleviating the cause of the environmental deprivation. Therapy will be intensive and prolonged. Surveillance will be provided, and efforts will be made to maintain children in their homes. However, in some situations foster placement is indicated. While the child is in a new environment and probably an early childhood stimulation program, efforts will be made to motivate and educate the parents to care for their children. Some parents will need help in planning food and mealtimes for their children, creating an environment for the children to learn nutritionally and socially appropriate food habits, and responding appropriately to their children's food behaviors. Efforts are usually made to return children to their natural parents. However, if they cannot be returned to a safe and nurturing environment, a permanent out-of-home placement or adoption may be planned.

Parents are often overwhelmed by the numbers of agencies and individuals involved in helping the child and family. In many instances, parents are given guidance from several individuals about what and how to feed their children. Often the advice is conflicting, and the parents then become confused and frustrated. To avoid this, a team approach is most appropriate. The nutritionist may be asked to provide education directly to the parent or other family members such as the grandparents. However, it may be more productive for the individual who is providing other services to include a nutrition and feeding plan as a part of their intervention efforts. In all instances, efforts should be made to see that the parents are instructed in only one approach on what and how to feed the children.

Socioculturally developmentally delayed school-age children have been shown to consume less protein, iron, thiamin, and kcalories than nonretarded children of the same age and sex from low-income families. Intakes of iron, calcium, and ascorbic acid were less than recommended in the developmentally delayed children.[28]

Bronchopulmonary Dysplasia

The number of children with **bronchopulmonary dysplasia (BPD)** in the community has increased in the last decade because of an increase in the survival of premature infants who have received oxygen and ventilation for the treatment of **hyaline membrane disease.** The problem may also be found in full-term infants. There may be medical problems such as heart disease secondary to BPD. Feeding difficulties and poor weight gain are also common.

Growth and development of new lung tissue can occur. The process is slow and may require continued oxygen, physiotherapy, medications, and nutritional support. It is likely that infants will remain hospitalized until they can tolerate feeds, even if they must be taken by tube.

Difficulties in achieving an adequate nutrient intake are common in these children. Most infants and children expend more than average energy in breathing. Respiratory infections also contribute to increased energy needs. Infants with BPD may expend as much as 25% to 50% more energy than normal, healthy babies. The elevated energy needs are likely to continue into childhood. There is, however, a subgroup of children with BPD who have lower than average energy needs. These include those who require mechanical ventilation, are steroid dependent, have a slow rate of linear growth, or have limited activity.[29]

Eating difficulties, such as anorexia, secondary to illness or medication may create problems in achieving an appropriate intake. Infants may have difficulty coordinating sucking, breathing, and swallowing. They may tire easily during a feed. Gastroesophageal reflux and episodes of vomiting may make feeding aversive.

Heights and weights of children with BPD should be monitored frequently, and adjustments in nutrient and energy intakes should be made on the basis of medical status, growth rate, and activity level. Fluid shifts need to be carefully evaluated. When children have difficulty meeting their energy needs, only food with high kcaloric density should be offered. Small frequent feeds should be timed so that the effects of medication, chest physical therapy, and suctioning will not have an aversive effect on food intake. Diets should include at least 7% of the kcalories from protein to avoid excess fat and carbohydrate. Children with BPD may require multiple medications that necessitate monitoring fluid and electrolyte intakes.[30]

Acquired Immunodeficiency Syndrome

Pediatrics **acquired immunodeficiency syndrome (AIDS)** was the 9th leading cause of death in children 1 to 4 years of age in 1987 and the 12th leading cause of death in children 5 to 24 years of age the same year. Of the children identified 80% had been infected in the gestational period. Evidence collected to date indicates that 25% to 35% of infants born to infected mothers will ultimately be infected. Postnatally, infants can become infected during breast-feeding. Most other cases have resulted from blood or plasma transfusions.[31]

Children with AIDS experience a number of medical problems that compromise their nutritional status and make the consumption of adequate nutrition difficult and in some cases impossible. Many live with parents who are also infected and often with low incomes. Abdominal pain, recurrent diarrhea, and failure to thrive are common in infected children. They may develop oral thrush, dysphagia, and a diminished appetite. A variety of bacterial infections determine the medical course of the children's therapy. Complications include infection, *Pneumocystis carinii* pneumonia, oral and esophageal candidiasis, herpetic gingivostomatitis, nonspecific diarrhea, and fever.[32] A pattern of developmental delays in infancy and progressive cognitive delays in older children most pronounced in fine and gross motor and speech occurs. Acquired microcephaly and cerebral atrophy become evident as the disease progresses.

School-age children become mildly to moderately retarded. There are problems with visual motor tasks. The majority have a pattern of plateaus and deceleration with a declining course.[32]

Children with AIDS experience weight loss and decreased triceps skinfold thickness and arm circumference resulting from a greater decrease in lean body mass than fat. A decrease in serum protein levels indicates protein-kcalorie malnutrition.[33]

A taskforce on nutrition support for AIDS has suggested nutrition goals for infected individuals (Table 14-1). They include the preser-

TABLE 14-1   *Plan for Nutrition Intervention in the Pediatric Patient with AIDS*

Problem	Approach
Poor oral intake	Evaluate food preferences
	High-kcalorie, nutrient-dense feedings
	Frequent snacks
	Nutritional supplements
	Multivitamin supplement
	Tube feedings—supplemental or total diet
	Parenteral nutrition
Oral lesions	Soft, nonirritating foods served cold or at room temperature
	Nonacidic juices
Infection/pneumonia	Increase kcalories and protein
	Multivitamin supplement
Receiving steroids	Sodium restriction
	Encourage foods high in potassium, calcium, and vitamin C
	Multivitamin supplement
	Folate supplement if indicated
	Avoid overconsumption
Diarrhea/malabsorption	Lactose restriction
	Elemental diet
	Slow, continuous drip tube feeding
	Parenteral nutrition
	Avoid long-term severe dietary restrictions, which cause poor intake
Abdominal distention	Elemental diet
	Parenteral nutrition
Fever	Keep patient hydrated (e.g., with popsicles, gelatin)
	Increase kcalories and protein
Developmental problems/ neurologic impairment	Utilize feeding therapist (knowledgeable speech, physical, or occupational therapist or dietitian)
	Bottle feed or spoon feed as necessary

From Bentler M: *J Am Diet Assoc* 87:488, 1987.

vation of lean body mass, provision of an adequate nutrient intake, and minimization of the symptoms of malabsorption. A kcalorically dense formula may be used for infants. Protein intakes of 1.5 times the RDA and a multiple vitamin and mineral supplement have been suggested. Frequent high-kcalorie and nutrient-dense feeding should be readily available. During diarrhea adequate potassium must be provided. When children have oral lesions, soothing foods such as ice cream, nonacidic juices, and puddings should be offered. Nasogastric feedings may be used to supplement oral intakes.[34] If oral or tube feedings cannot support an adequate nutrient intake, **total parental nutrition (TPN)** may be used. However, oral or gavage feedings should continue to maintain sucking ability, mastication, and deglutition and to promote repair of the intestinal mucosa.

Fetal Alcohol Syndrome

Fetal alcohol syndrome (FAS), the birth defect that results when the fetus is exposed to the teratogenic effects of alcohol, is the most common cause of mental retardation in the western world.[35] Also, since FAS is only the tip of the iceberg, many children exposed to alcohol in utero who do not have the syndrome may exhibit FAS.[36] It is important to recognize that the syndrome is totally preventable by abstinence from alcohol during pregnancy. Features of Fetal Alcohol Effect (FAE) include craniofacial anomalies, growth deficiency, and central nervous system effects. The children have short palpebral fissures, a hypoplastic or long philtrum, a thin upper lip, a flat midface, a short upturned nose, a small chin, eye anomalies including strabismus, and some minor anomalies of the external ear. Other anomalies that occur with less frequency include heart defects and cleft lip and palate. Auditory and vision problems and malformed and misaligned secondary teeth are also frequently noted. FAS effects include learning disabilities, language delays, and **attention deficit disorder.**

Growth deficiency in height or weight is present at birth and continues during childhood. The growth deficiency results from the prenatal insult and is not usually associated

with nutritional deficiency. In adolescence weight gain among females is so common that the short thin prepubescent phenotype may change into the obese adult. The short stature remains in both sexes into adulthood. During the preschool-age years hyperactivity, language, and motor problems become evident. During the school-age years attention and memory deficits are often noted.

Children with FAS have poor appetites secondary to their slow rate of growth. Most are finicky about the foods they will accept. Behavior problems often result from the parental concern about the child's slow growth and limited food intake compared with average children their age. Delays in the acquisition of feeding skills secondary to their delay may be of concern to parents and may exacerbate feeding problems. If the children remain in homes with alcoholic parents, they may experience erratic meal patterns, the use of much convenience foods, and occasionally deprivation of an adequate intake.

Nutrition intervention is not specific to FAS but approaches similar to these described for the environmentally deprived individual should be instituted. For children whose attention span is limited, small, frequent feedings may result in a more appropriate intake than three meals a day. During adolescence weight gain should be monitored. Counseling should focus on teaching those individuals whose rate of weight gain is excessive appropriate food intake and exercise patterns.

Children of Drug-Abusing Women

Children of mothers who abuse drugs during pregnancy are at high risk for a number of difficulties that affect physical growth, eating, and feeding. The infants are usually irritable and have a greater incidence of tremulous and hyperactive behavior and motor-impaired function than average children. Drug-exposed babies experience fetal growth retardation, lose more than average weight after birth, and take twice as long as average babies to regain birth weight. Interestingly some infants exposed to cocaine in utero become obese before growing into normal weight. Delays in the acquisition of developmental milestones are often noted. Permanent disabilities may include attention deficits, difficulties in coordination, and atypical mood patterns.[36]

Withdrawal from the drugs, typically noted between birth and 4 days of age, usually continues until 2 to 4 weeks of age. Behavior problems that may result and affect feeding include irritability, vomiting, uncoordinated suck-swallow, sneezing and nasal stuffiness, and inability to sleep. Swaddling the infant may help.[37]

Infants who are hypertonic, hyperactive, or excessive criers will have increased energy needs ranging from 150 to 250 kcal/kg/day in the neonatal period.[35] Frequent feeds of kcalorically concentrated foods are usually offered. Nasogastric feeds or TPN may be required if oral feeding is unsuccessful. The infants will require monitoring and readjustments of their energy intakes until their energy needs become similar to those of unaffected infants. Breast-feeding may be contraindicated if the mother is still using drugs. Several drugs cross into breast milk and can be detected 12 to 60 hours after use.

Problems for these children are likely to extend beyond the neonatal period. Mothers may lack parenting skills to adequately feed and care for their infants or to provide psychosocial and emotional support for optimal growth and development. Many live on limited incomes and may continue to have problems associated with addictive behavior.

Drug and Nutrient Interrelationships

Anticonvulsant drugs prescribed to control seizures increase children's needs for vitamin D and alter their folate metabolism. Evidence of vitamin D deficiency has been found in both institutionalized patients and outpatients treated with anticonvulsant drugs for longer than 6 months for control of seizures. Serum calcium levels may be normal or low; serum parathyroid hormone concentrations may be increased; serum phosphate levels may be low; and serum alkaline phosphatase levels may be elevated. Plasma 25-OHD levels have been found to be low. The degree of reduction of serum 25-OHD concentrations correlates with the relative decreases in serum calcium concentration, intestinal calcium absorption, and bone mass.[38]

Cases of rickets and osteomalacia confirmed by roentgenograms have been reported. All drugs commonly used to control seizures have been implicated. The incidence of abnormalities increases with duration of therapy. Multiple drug regimens cause the most problems. The abnormalities may result from an increase in hepatic microsomal catabolism or a biliary excretion of vitamins. The drugs may also have an inhibitory effect on calcium transport and bone metabolism. In addition, some feel that anticonvulsant drugs may affect the metabolism of vitamins D_2 and D_3 differently.[39]

Rickets and osteomalacia are most often diagnosed in nonambulatory individuals who have infrequent exposure to sunlight and receive a combination of anticonvulsant medications. Amounts of vitamin D necessary to prevent deficiency and rickets in children receiving anticonvulsant therapy appear to vary depending on the number and dosage of anticonvulsant drugs, the duration of therapy, the pattern of mobility, and the exposure to sunlight. Hahn, Shires, and Halstead[38] administered 75,000 IU vitamin D_2 per week for 6 weeks to patients maintained on phenytoin and phenobarbital. This treatment normalized the serum levels of calcium and parathyroid hormone in 7 of the 12 patients. Assessment of vitamin D status and appropriate intervention are important for children maintained on anticonvulsant therapy for more than 6 months. Such children should be monitored biochemically.

Folate. Drug-induced disturbances of folate metabolism have been found in a significant number of patients receiving anticonvulsants. Phenytoin is the drug of primary concern; however, therapy with phenobarbital, primidone, or carbamazepine is also associated with folate deficiency. Low serum folate levels accompanied by a fall in red blood cell folate and cerebrospinal folate levels have been reported in 27% to 91% of patients studied. **Megaloblastic anemia** is reported to occur in less than 1% of patients. The mechanism by which these drugs cause a fall in folate concentrations is not understood. Suggested hypotheses include the following:

1. Malabsorption of folate caused by an increased intraluminal pH effected by the drug

2. Inhibition of intestinal conjugases that split dietary polyglutamate forms of folate to the absorbable monoglutamate
3. Compromised transport of folate into the tissue
4. Depletion of folate from its use as a cofactor in some metabolic process that is increased because of the drug's ability to induce liver enzymes[40]

Administration of folate has been reported to precipitate seizures or to increase seizure frequency in some patients treated with anticonvulsants. In most patients no effect has been noted. At least eight different large controlled studies found no significant difference in seizure frequency between folate-deficient patients treated with folate and those treated with placebo.

Long-term anticonvulsant therapy may be associated with other vitamin deficiency states. Clinical evidence of cardiac beriberi and subclinical ascorbic acid deficiency has been noted in a 28-month-old black girl who allegedly was receiving a full diet in a nursing home and was receiving phenobarbital, phenytoin sodium (Dilantin), and primidone (Mysoline).[41]

Megavitamin therapy. For many years there have been claims that megadoses of vitamins and minerals will increase the intelligence of children who are developmentally delayed.[42,43] Evidence supporting these claims has been scant and unconvincing. Not much attention has been focused on this therapy. However, Harrell and others[44] reported in 1981 that 16 developmentally delayed children experienced gains in IQ with megavitamin therapy. Children with Down syndrome experienced the greatest gains. Attention was again focused on the use of nutrients. Many parents became very hopeful that help was available for their children and requested help in following the megavitamin regimen.

Replication of the Harrell study has been undertaken in several clinical settings using a double-blind control design to test the hypothesis. The studies were conducted on both school-age children and adults with Down syndrome. In no instance has the vitamin supplement increased intelligence, motor performance, or communicative abilities of the individuals involved.[45,46] However, some who offer the supplements for sale continue to offer false hope at considerable expense to families of affected children.

FEEDING THE DEVELOPMENTALLY DELAYED CHILD

Planning for feeding developmentally delayed children implies that recommendations for intakes of energy, nutrients, and textures of food, as well as expectations for the acquisition of self-feeding skills, must be individualized for each child. Some children may have oral, fine, and gross motor, language, and personal-social development that is proceeding at a less than normal rate. Others may also have physical anomalies that imply the need for special equipment to sustain sitting posture to eat and to adapt utensils to self-feed.

Many of the problems of nutrient intake in developmentally delayed children are preventable. Guidance and support for parents as they select nutritionally adequate foods for their children, and as they create an environment in which children learn to consume foods in a manner appropriate for their developmental level, are important. Parents may need instruction to understand the appropriate time at which to change the textures of food, to determine when to expect the child to self-feed, and to know the degree of messiness to expect when a child is self-feeding.

Factors That Influence Food Intake

Because of the many factors that interact to determine the food available to and accepted by developmentally delayed children, concerns about food and nutrient intake and feeding rarely result from a single cause; many factors must be considered. An understanding of those factors that contribute to problems of food intake is important in planning for feeding of such children.

Developmentally delayed children experience the same responses to parental anxiety about their food intake as any child; they too can control their parents by their acceptance or rejection of food. Most normal preschoolers reduce their intakes of milk and vegetables, go on food jags, and have brittle, unpredictable appetites. It is not unreasonable to expect developmentally delayed children to present the same food-related behavior. There may be, in addition, difficulties in feeding developmentally delayed children that are not encountered with normal children.

Developmental level. Delays in motor development may result directly or indirectly in an inappropriate nutrient intake. The development and sequence of acquisition of feeding behaviors of delayed children proceed in the same orderly predictable sequence as that of normal children. The chronological age at which the developmental stages occur, however, is not predictable, and wide ranges are seen both in the timing at which stages occur and in the ultimate developmental level of function of delayed children. Abnormal motor and behavioral patterns may interfere with the sequence of development and acquisition of feeding skills.

Parents who fail to recognize developmental readiness often fail to provide children with appropriate stimuli. If this happens, parents do not encourage their children to progress in the oral motor skills of eating and the gross and fine motor skills of self-feeding. For example, parents may offer their children strained foods when they are capable of masticating coarser foods, or they may feed their children who have the ability to learn to feed themselves.

Readiness to accept solids is demonstrated blatantly in normal children and is difficult to ignore: they reach for food and bring it to their mouths. Handicapped children may give more subtle clues, and as a result the stage is often ignored. Some parents do not realize the importance of the introduction of solids at the proper time. When these parents finally decide it is time for children to learn to eat table food, conflicts often occur between children and their parents that may appreciably reduce the children's nutrient and kcaloric intakes. The children refuse to eat at all or skillfully spit out lumps while sucking and swallowing the soft, strained foods.[47]

Parents have reported restraining their children and forcing them to accept foods with tex-

ture. For example, one mother stated that it took four adults to hold her 10-year-old child who was developmentally 4 years of age when she attempted to make the transition from strained to table food. The child eventually accepted the foods but later accepted only small amounts of soft food and lost weight.

Some children are hypersensitive in the oral area. It may be important for an occupational, physical, or speech therapist to institute a program to normalize sensation before presenting more textured foods to the child.

Children so delayed that they are unable to feed themselves depend on other people. Feeding the infant is a culturally defined maternal role, but feeding a handicapped child over a period of many years may become a tedious process that interferes with other activities several times a day. Some parents become so overwhelmed with such a schedule that they continue feeding soft foods that do not support developmental progress; others cease their efforts at feeding their children before the children consume sufficient food. Achieving self-feeding skills may appreciably increase the child's nutrient intake, self-confidence, and self-image.

Children whose delays in motor development impair their ability to learn to walk must be moved by their caregivers. The more weight the children gain, the more difficult they become to lift, move, and care for. Parents and caregivers of such children have expressed concern about the difficulties that may be created for them when children grow and gain weight; some have been known to limit inappropriately the amounts of food they feed. Obesity must be prevented, but children should have the advantage of nutrient and energy intakes that support the best possible growth and development for them. Parents may need information and counseling in methods of moving and caring for their children and in accepting their needs for increased amounts of nutrients and energy.

Abnormal oral-motor patterns and muscle tone. Children with developmental delays, particularly those who also have abnormalities in muscle tone and movement patterns, frequently also demonstrate abnormal oral-motor patterns. They may have pathological oral-motor patterns, that is, oral patterns that are never observed as part of the normal developmental sequence, or may show primitive oral patterns with the retention of primitive oral reflexes. These immature, primitive, or abnormal patterns can make the acquisition of mature feeding skills difficult. For example, a child who sucks reflexively when food is placed in the mouth cannot learn to chew until this reflexive behavior is integrated and more isolated movements of the lips, tongue, and jaw are developed.

Abnormalities in overall muscle tone can exacerbate problems in oral control. Many pathological oral patterns are seen in association with specific types of abnormal muscle tone and are frequently heightened by these tonal abnormalities. A tongue thrust may be seen as part of increased **extensor** tone throughout the body. With **extension** of a child's head, the tongue thrust can be exaggerated. Hypotonia of the body and face may lead to inadequate stability of the oral musculature. The mouth will tend to be open and lip closure will be poor. Asymmetry in the distribution of muscle tone can be observed in jaw deviation toward the more involved side during chewing or during opening of the mouth for spoon insertion. In addition to abnormalities of tone and movement, children with developmental delays may have oral-facial structural anomalies. Clefts of the lip or palate or deviations in the shape or size of oral features such as micrognathia, can significantly affect oral control. If these facial anomalies are also combined with abnormalities in muscle tone, feeding difficulties will be compounded.

Primitive oral reflexes. The full-term infant is normally born with a variety of well-established oral reflexes making the infant fully equipped to take in nourishment. The human fetus has a primitive swallow by 12.5 weeks' gestation and sucking behavior by 14 weeks' gestation,[48,49] and the fetus is sufficiently mature for functional use at roughly 36 weeks' gestation. The child with motor and developmental delays, however, may retain the primitive oral reflexes and not develop the voluntary oral motor patterns that subsume the role of the primitive reflexes. Most of these primitive oral reflexes are involved in the sucking and swallowing of liquids or pureed foods. If they are retained, the child will be unable to develop the more mature oral movements involved in chewing higher textured foods.

In a child who has feeding difficulties, evaluation of individual primitive oral reflexes may provide some insight into the nature of the feeding difficulty. Ingram,[50] however, believes that merely testing oral reflexes provides little information about the individual's feeding abilities other than the presence of basic reflex arcs. Rather, Ingram states that one needs to consider how the primitive reflexes are integrated with breathing, adaptive feeding behavior, and vocalizations to adequately assess a child's feeding problems.

Protective oral reflexes. In addition to primitive oral reflexes, several important protective reflexes remain with the child through life and are not superseded by other functions. These are the cough and **gag reflexes.** The cough reflex protects against foods or liquids entering the airway or serves to remove them should they become aspirated. It is a violent expiratory effort preceded by a preliminary inspiration; the accessory muscles of expiration are brought into action as air is noisily expelled. When related to food, the stimulus is the presence of food or liquid in the laryngeal vestibule that must be expelled so that it does not enter the airway. The gag reflex serves to keep food items or foreign bodies that are too large and could potentially cause obstruction from entering the pharynx or the esophagus. Gagging occurs when the soft palate is stroked or pressure is applied to the posterior wall of the pharynx or the posterior half of the tongue; there is an arching of the tongue, mouth opening, head extension, and facial grimacing. Intense gagging may induce a vomit response.

In normal development, the gag reflex is frequently elicited when a baby puts a toy far into the mouth. Oral play helps the child to accommodate to a variety of sensations and aids in the normal reduction in the intensity of the gag reflex. Through oral exploration, the infant experiences a variety of textures, temperatures, shapes, and sizes that may lay the groundwork for future learning. The parent of a child with feeding problems, however, often reports that the child never participated in this normal mouthing stage of development. This fact should alert the professional to a potential problem with a hyperreactive gag response. In this case, gagging may be elicited to a wide variety of food tastes, textures, or even smells that are new and unfamiliar to the child. This type of hypersensitive gagging may often be observed in children who have had a period of nonoral feeding such as gastrostomy tube feeding.

The gag reflex can also be inhibited or sensitized (increased) by physiological or psychological factors. A physiological sensitization may occur when a person is ill, dizzy, or emotionally upset. The normal reaction to these feelings is to avoid eating. If food were to be offered or forced, the reaction might well be a gag. Fear of choking resulting from a previous incident may cause a gag response at the sight of a particular food. This behavior usually receives attention from adults who frequently do not persist in offering the undesirable food. When there has been a lengthy period of nonoral feeding, the child may become unaccustomed to touch and taste within the mouth. When foods are introduced, gagging may result from lack of previous sensory experiences with foods. Children with these sorts of behavioral responses often severely restrict the variety of food textures in their diet, resulting in further sensory deprivation and increased oral sensitivity. Treatment to decrease this hypersensitive response is needed to change feeding behavior and improve nutrition. This type of treatment is discussed in the next section.

Transition from tube to oral feeding. For many infants and children with developmental delays, feeding performance is so impaired that they require supplemental or total nonoral feedings. The need for nonoral feedings can stem from severe oral-motor dysfunction that impairs the ability to take appropriate quantity or quality of nutrition (Figure 14-3), from medical conditions that limit the child's endurance for feeding, from food refusals because of hypersensitive and aversive feeding behavior, or secondary to swallowing dysfunction. Nonoral feedings can occur through a **gavage** tube (through the nose or mouth), via a gastrostomy tube, or below the stomach via duodenal or jejunal tubes. Nonoral feeding may only be needed for a short period of time but frequently

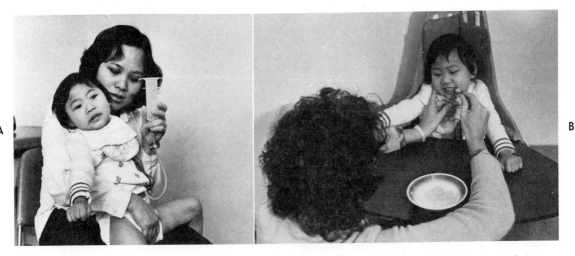

A   B

FIG. 14-3 **A,** Child with cerebral palsy being tube-fed. Note the asymmetry of arms and legs and lack of head and trunk control. **B,** In a specialized chair she has better head and trunk control and can engage in more age-appropriate feeding behaviors.

is required for lengthy periods to support overall good nutrition and appropriate growth.

Since oral/tactile hypersensitivity can result from the lack of oral experiences that occurs during tube feeding or may be the factor that resulted in the need for a tube, professionals should begin treating oral hypersensitivity at the time tube feedings are instituted and not wait until a transition off the tube is considered to deal with this problem area.[51] Frequent, pleasurable oral experiences need to be continued even though feeding may occur via the tube. This can be done through oral play and mouthing of toys, through hygiene activities like toothbrushing, and through physical contact with the face and mouth.

The association between sensations in the mouth and sensations in the stomach can be maintained by using a pacifier during tube feedings.[52] For the toddler or older child who is receiving gastrostomy feedings, the hunger-satiation cycle may be established by normalizing the volume at each gastrostomy feeding to approximate the normal mealtime schedule. Thus a gastrostomy-fed child who receives six equal-volume feedings per day might have the schedule changed to three larger gastrostomy "meals" and three smaller gastrostomy "snacks." This feeding schedule would approximate that of a normal child and would help the developmentally delayed child experience hunger and satiation while still maintaining the necessary kcaloric intake per day. It will set the stage for the transition of not using the tube.

At some point the professionals managing the child's care may feel that a transition from the tube to oral feeding is indicated. The professionals need to establish that the child is indeed ready to make the transition off the tube.[53] They need to determine that the original problem that necessitated the tube feeding has been resolved. If not, then some level of tube feeding may still be indicated. The child needs to have sufficient oral-motor control to allow food intake to occur safely and in a reasonable length of time. In addition, the professionals need to establish that the child's swallowing abilities allow for safe feeding. Not only does the child need to show readiness, but the parents and caregivers also need to be ready to participate in the process. Programs to make the transition from tube to oral feeding require a high level of parent and caregiver involvement and persistence to be successful. Their readiness and commitment to the program are crucial to ensure success.

Once readiness has been established, a treatment program can be developed. It is at this point that problems with oral and tactile hypersensitivity may become apparent when the transition from nonoral to oral feeding begins. If oral treatment has always been a part of the child's feeding plan, this oral hypersensitivity may be manageable. If the oral hypersensitivity or aversive behavior is more significant, however, a treatment program under the direction of an occupational, speech, or physical therapist is indicated. Treatment for hypersensitivity to oral and tactile stimulation is a gradual, careful program of increasing the amount and variety of oral-sensory experiences.[54] The program is carefully graded according to the child's response because overstimulation could cause negative emotional and behavioral reactions or further increases in abnormal muscle tone that might interfere with feeding to a greater extent than the original problem. The therapeutic techniques used to normalize facial and oral sensitivity therefore are varied according to the individual child's reactions and needs.

Treatment programs designed to make the transition from the use of supplemental or tube feedings generally take a slow, more gradual approach. The child who has been fed via a tube for a long period may have missed the critical or sensitive period for the introduction of solid foods.[55] Therefore the process can take months or several years to complete. Some programs, however, are designed to make this transition more quickly—in a matter of weeks.[56] These types of programs generally require an inpatient stay. They are strongly behaviorally based and have an element of force-feeding to them. Patient selection criteria for these types of programs is stringent. The decision regarding what type of transition program is appropriate for each individual child should be made in consultation with a multidisciplinary team that may be involved with the child.

Components of feeding treatment programs

Oral-motor therapy. When oral-motor dysfunction is present and is interfering with feeding, a treatment program should be developed by an occupational, speech, or physical therapist to improve oral control. These treatment programs often include facilitation or inhibition techniques to improve control of the lips, tongue, jaw, or cheeks. Hands-on support to the jaw during feeding is frequently used as a technique to improve the grading of jaw movement, improve tongue position, and increase lip control.[57] Specialized spoons, cups, or bottles may enhance oral control.

Alterations to the diet can be made to support the child's highest level of oral-motor control. This is particularly true for liquids. Thin liquids are frequently difficult or impossible for a child with oral-motor dysfunction to handle. Thickening liquids may enable the child to drink by mouth. When liquids are thickened, they may hold together in a more cohesive bolus and move through the mouth and pharynx more slowly so that the child is better able to move the liquid from the front of the mouth to the back and prepare for swallowing. Liquids can be thickened with baby rice cereal, pureed foods, or commercially available thickeners such as Thick-it.[58] If liquids are thickened, the amount of liquid consumed in the child's daily diet should be monitored carefully to ensure adequate hydration.

Positioning during feeding. The position of the child during feeding is of prime importance, since abnormal gross motor patterns can influence and impede oral control.[54] Frequently a child's feeding difficulties can be greatly improved just by changes in the child's position during meals. Normalization of the child's muscle tone through positioning may minimize abnormal oral movement patterns and increase the child's voluntary oral control. Proper positioning considers the child as a whole—the relationship of the head position to the body as well as the overall body position.

Head position is especially important for children who have oral-motor dysfunction or swallowing difficulties and do not have a normally responsive gag or cough response. The child should never be fed with the head or body tipped backwards in a position often referred to as a **"bird-feeding"** position. In this position normal swallowing and tongue control are impaired. The food bolus will slide into the pharynx without control, and the child is in danger of aspirating or choking. Acute or chronic aspiration could then lead to pneumonia or other respiratory difficulty. The head should therefore always be upright or slightly flexed forward 5 degrees to 10 degrees. The body should be upright or, if support is needed for head and trunk, within 30 degrees of vertical.

Children with feeding problems, especially those with abnormal muscle tone, are often difficult to position. It is essential that a pediatric, occupational, or physical therapist assess each child and recommend appropriate positioning. If the child has a customized, adapted seating device that is used at other times, it should also be used for feeding. Adapted positioning during mealtimes should be comfortable for both the child and the caregiver and should enable communication and interaction.[59]

Figure 14-4 demonstrates some feeding positions that may be prescribed by occupational and physical therapists. Each position incorporates basic principles of appropriate, therapeutic positioning. The head is in good alignment with the body, and the mouth is in the midline.[60] With the head aligned with the body or slightly **flexed** forward, abnormal head extension or pushing backward can be inhibited. In some children this pushing back with the head is not caused by increased extensor tone, but rather it is a compensatory behavior that reflects an inability to stabilize the head in an upright position. Whether the abnormal head position is caused by increased tone or by a lack of stability, proper head support during feeding can significantly affect oral-motor control.

The position of the arms is also related to and influences head and trunk control. When the arms and shoulders pull backward, the head tends to tilt backward and overall muscle tone increases. Therefore the shoulders and arms should be held forward and oriented toward the midline of the body. This forward position of the arms can be achieved by the manner in which the child is held near the feeder's body or

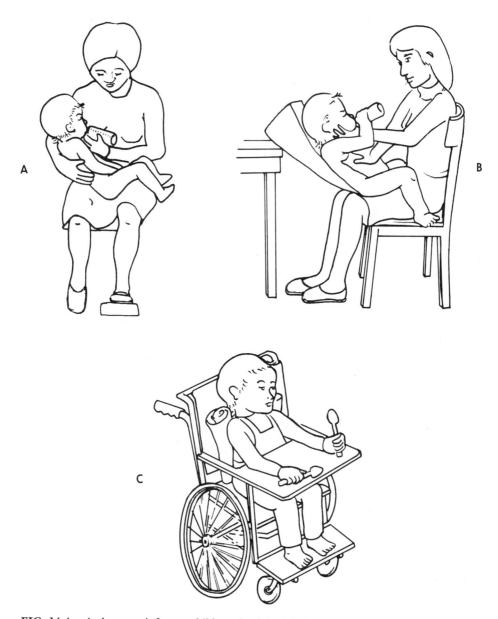

FIG. 14-4 **A,** A young infant or child can be fed while being held in one's lap. The head is in line with body, and arms are forward. With left knee raised, hip flexion can be maintained. **B,** When firmly wedged, a young child can be fed while facing the feeder. Legs are abducted and flexed, which inhibits extension. The feeder's hands are freed to assist with jaw control. **C,** Rolls can be inserted into wheelchair to provide temporary trunk support and help keep arms forward and toward midline.

by rolled towels or cushions placed behind the child's shoulders in the child's chair. Some children learn to stabilize their arms forward by grasping the far end of the wheelchair tray or supporting themselves with both elbows on the table.

Trunk stability is essential because the trunk provides the base on which to achieve good head and arm control. If the child is unable to sit independently, support should be provided by the feeder or through the use of an adapted seating device. The position of the hips and legs affects trunk control and thus influences the position of the rest of the body. Extension at the hips can increase tone throughout the body and cause extension of the head, tongue, and jaw. Stiffness or spasticity in the legs can cause the legs to pull together, narrowing the child's sitting base and impairing the postural adjustments needed for sitting balance. Lateral support to the hips may be a component of the child's seating device, or a pommel can be placed between the child's legs to widen the base of support and to provide adequate leg separation.

The hips should be flexed to a 90-degree neutral position or slightly greater. This increased hip flexion can be provided by adding a wedge to the child's chair with the larger edge under the child's knees. Often just a seatbelt firmly fastened across the hips keeps the hips in a normal neutral position and provides a better base for trunk control. Finally, good stability at the feet can be achieved with a foot rest allowing the feet to be flat and flexed at the ankle.

Proper positioning during mealtime supports the child's highest level of oral-motor control. The relationship between the child's gross motor level at rest and during eating must be considered so that excessive demands are not placed on the child's gross motor skills. For example, a child may be able to sit independently with good head control when simply sitting and watching an activity. The level of the child's head and trunk control may deteriorate, however, when a child is eating or self-feeding. Mealtime should not be the time to make the child work on better head and trunk control. Rather, sufficient support should be provided through adapted positioning to reinforce the child's motor level while fostering better oral and feeding skills.

In addition to the type of static positioning used during meals, the environment and the placement of the food or spoon can influence the child's feeding skills. If the spoon and foods are presented above eye level, the child may tilt the head backward to orient toward the food and thus reinforce an extension pattern. Presenting the food in the middle, from a low angle, encourages slight head flexion and symmetry. Likewise, placing the container or plate of food at the side may encourage the child to turn sideways and increase asymmetry. By placing the food in front of the child, a symmetrical midline position can be encouraged. The manner in which the spoon is withdrawn from the mouth can also influence head position. If the spoon is lifted up and scraped against the upper front teeth, the head will tend to tilt backward and lip control will be impaired. In addition, if the feeder simply scrapes the food off on the upper teeth or lips, the child does not have the opportunity to use lip closure.

The foregoing information should prove useful in improving the quality of food intake when therapy services are not immediately available. It is important to use a problem-solving approach that includes ideas and feedback from the child and the caregiver. Consideration of the child's and the caregiver's comfort, feelings, and opinions when making changes in positioning or feeding techniques is likely to yield a workable plan with better follow-through. Changes in motor control may be slow to develop, but the quality of the daily feeding experience and the amount of positive interaction it allows the child will have great impact on the skills that develop.

Management of Feeding

The diversity of concerns about the food and nutrient intake of handicapped children and the many factors that affect children's level of function and food acceptance imply that the skills of several disciplines may be necessary to find solutions to the concerns and to set priorities for therapy for individual children. The occupational, physical, or speech therapist will be called on to provide therapy for children with

TABLE 14-2   *Nutrition Problems of Children with Special Health Care Needs*

Problem	Children "At Risk" Include Those with:	Team Members Needed	Intervention Strategies
Feeding problem (inability or refusal to eat certain foods or textures because of neuromotor dysfunction or behavioral or psychological factors)	Oral-motor disorders Inappropriate parent-child interaction with food	Nutritionist or dietitian Pediatrician Neurodevelopmental therapist Social worker or psychologist Nurse	Proper positioning Oral-motor feeding program Define reasonable expectations and developmentally appropriate feeding skills and food Behavior management programs
Overweight and obesity	Prader-Willi Syndrome Spina bifida Down syndrome Spastic cerebral palsy Hypotonia Decreased mobility	Nutritionist or dietitian Pediatrician Social worker, psychologist, or family therapist	Define appropriate energy intake level for individual child to maintain or lose weight Increase activity Family counseling
Underweight	Athetoid cerebral palsy Oral-motor dysfunction Frequent infections Rett syndrome Attention deficit hyperactive disorder Dysfunctional parent-child interaction Parents who do not know what or how to feed	Nutritionist or dietitian Pediatrician Social worker, psychologist, or behavior therapist	Refer for appropriate therapy Promote appetite with behavior management approach Increase kcaloric density of food offered If severe, may need to consider tube feeding
Constipation	Spina bifida Spastic cerebral palsy Hypotonia	Nutritionist or dietitian Pediatrician Nurse	Increase fiber Increase liquid Regular toileting schedule Stool softener Behavior management

abnormal motor tone. The dentist will correct dental caries and malocclusions. A professional proficient in behavior modification techniques may be required to change behavior. Table 14-2 defines many of the problems an interdisciplinary team serving children with special health care needs may encounter, team members needed to address specific concerns, and possible intervention strategies. Correcting these concerns may solve nutrient intake concerns. Parents may, however, still need help in planning appropriate foods for their children.

Behaviors. Children may have inappropriate nutrient intakes and food habits because of

TABLE 14-2 *Nutrition Problems of Children with Special Health Care Needs—cont'd*

Problem	Children "At Risk" Include Those with:	Team Members Needed	Intervention Strategies
Excessive fluid loss or poor fluid intake	Spastic cerebral palsy Hypotonia Drooling Refusing fluids	Nutritionist or dietitian Behavioral therapist Oral-motor therapist	Position child correctly Oral-motor intervention Thicken fluids, if appropriate Offer foods with high water content
Drug-nutrient interactions	Children who require: Anticonvulsants Tranquilizers Stimulant medications Diuretics AZT	Pediatrician Nutritionist or dietitian	Appropriate vitamin supplements Small, frequent meals and snacks (stimulants) Follow Na, K levels (diuretics) Cool, noncitrus juices for sore mouth (AZT)
Disorders in which early intervention is essential to prevent failure to thrive, mental retardation, and death	Inborn errors of metabolism (e.g., PKU, galactosemia, glycogen storage disease, urea cycle defects)	Nutritionist or dietitian Pediatrician Nurse Social worker Psychologist	Screen at birth to identify infants who need immediate intervention Adjust intake of specific nutrients to neutralize the impact of the metabolic defect while providing adequate nourishment for growth and development

learned behavior. Children learn from the model set for them by their parents, peers, and relatives. If examples of poor food habits are set, the children will imitate them.

Disruptive and inappropriate feeding behaviors such as throwing food and utensils, stuffing the mouth before swallowing, and refusing to eat generally attract parental attention. These behaviors often compromise a child's nutrient intake. Resolution of the problems requires a structured, well-defined behavior modification program (Chapter 15). Since, as a rule, behaviors get worse before they begin to get better,

energy and nutrient intake should be monitored when the programs are implemented.

The behavior pattern and attention span of children affect their kcalorie and nutrient needs and consumption. Hypoactivity reduces energy expenditure and needs. Lack of planned activity and stimulation for such children often results in boredom, which leads to children spending their days seeking and consuming excessive amounts of food.

Hyperactive children never appear to be quiet and expend much energy in their numerous activities. The attention span of hyperactive children may be as limited at the dinner table as in other activities resulting in very small intakes of food at one time. It may be important to offer hyperactive children frequent small feedings of high nutrient content.

Constipation. Constipation is a common problem in children with developmental delays, especially in those who are hypertonic or hypotonic. The infrequent passage of feces or the passage of unduly hard, dry fecal matter results from a variety of causes, such as lack of muscle tone in the intestine or duodenal wall, excessive fatigue, anxiety, inappropriate dietary intake, or failure to establish a routine bowel pattern. When children are constipated, they usually complain of stomachache, distention, swelling of the abdomen, discomfort, or pain.

Increasing the amount of fluid and roughage in the diet may be useful for treating children who are constipated. Parents should also observe for individual food stimuli. Some children may need to limit milk intake to 1 pint/day. Prunes and prune juice are also frequently helpful.

Appetite. Central nervous system damage causes a lack of appetite in some children. These children never express hunger, and some mothers of such children have stated that setting alarm clocks helps them remember to feed their children. Children so affected are rarely pleased by any food and limit the volume of food they consume. The children's unresponsiveness gives the parents no positive reinforcement for their efforts to feed the children. This lack of positive interplay between parent and child may cause dissatisfaction in each; the parents may lose motivation to continue helping the child consume food, and the children may lose motivation to consume appropriate energy and nutrient intakes.

Damage to or developmental defects of the hypothalamus can cause insatiable appetites in children. Children so affected sometimes gorge, steal food, or eat animal food. Extreme measures, such as locking refrigerators and kitchen cupboards, have been necessary to control obesity in such children. Food-related behaviors of such children cannot be altered by behavior modification methods.

Parental Expectations

Parents need to have realistic expectations about the child's potential for physical growth. It is not possible to increase a child's height beyond his or her genetic potential; it is possible to increase a child's weight for height. Parental concern about a child's slow rate of growth may create anxiety about the volume of food the child is consuming. Counseling about expectations and growth response to food intake is important.

People who take care of the handicapped are often overindulgent, giving such children large amounts of preferred high-carbohydrate, sweet foods frequently. As with anyone, it is difficult to design a food intake pattern that provides necessary amounts of essential nutrients and maintain weight gain in growth channel if many of the foods consumed supply only carbohydrate and fat and few other nutrients. It may be important to help parents find ways to express their affection other than with food. Parents should also be aware of why they offer the foods they do.

Identifying readiness to progress. Assessing children's developmental levels of function and their readiness to progress in eating and self-feeding is necessary to define reasonable expectations for parents and caregivers. Parents often need help in accepting their children's handicaps and in recognizing their potential to progress.

Changes in food and feeding behavior should be effected when the children are developmentally 6 to 7 months of age, when they demonstrate readiness to self-feed and to use a cup. Table 14-3 defines important developmental landmarks and suggested foods appropriate for changes in feeding behavior.

Early intervention programs can aid in preventing later problems of food and nutrient intake.

Assessment of problems and suggested solutions. Efforts to prevent problems of nutrient intake are not always successful. Frequently expressed concerns about food and nutrient intake of developmentally delayed children, factors that need to be assessed, and suggested solutions are provided in Table 14-4.

TABLE 14-3   *Developmental Stages of Readiness to Progress in Feeding Behaviors*

Developmental Landmarks	Change Indicated	Examples of Appropriate Foods
Tongue laterally transfers food in the mouth Voluntary and independent movements of the tongue and lips Sitting posture can be sustained Beginning of chewing movements (up and down movements of the jaw)	Introduction of soft, mashed table food	Tuna fish; mashed potatoes; well-cooked mashed vegetables; ground meats in gravy and sauces; soft diced fruit such as bananas, peaches, pears; liverwurst; flavored yogurt
Reaches for and grasps objects with scissor grasp Brings hand to mouth	Finger-feeding (large pieces of food)	Oven-dried toast, teething biscuits, cheese sticks (food should be soluble in the mouth to prevent choking)
Voluntary release (refined digital grasp) Rotary chewing pattern	Finger-feeding (small pieces of food) Introduction of more textured food from family menu	Bits of cottage cheese, dry cereal, peas Well-cooked chopped meats and casseroles, cooked vegetables and canned fruit (not mashed), toast, potatoes, macaroni, spaghetti, peeled ripe fruit
Approximate lips to rim of the cup Understand relationship of container and contained	Introduction of cup Beginning self-feeding (messiness should be expected)	Food that when scooped will adhere to the spoon, such as applesauce, cooked cereal, mashed potatoes, cottage cheese
Increased rotary movement of the jaw Ulnar deviation of wrist develops	More skilled at cup and spoon feeding	Chopped fibrous meats such as roast and steak Raw vegetables and fruit (introduce gradually)
Walks alone Names food, expresses preferences; prefers unmixed foods Goes on food jags Appetite appears to decrease	May seek food and get food independently	Food of high nutrient value should be available Balanced food intake should be offered (child should be permitted to develop food preferences without parents being concerned that they will last forever)

TABLE 14-4 *Assessment of Concerns About Foods and Nutrients*

Symptom	Assessment	Action and Counseling Suggestions
Lack of appetite	What is child's total food and nutrient intake? Is some essential nutrient consumed in insufficient amounts? Is child receiving adequate amounts of food at other meals without having to eat large amounts? Is the food properly prepared? Is child's rate of growth normal in spite of his or her apparent lack of appetite? Is child reinforced? When he or she is eating? (appropriate) When he or she is not eating? (inappropriate) Is child receiving too many snacks? (inappropriate) Is child too weary to eat at mealtime? Is child attending to eating or is his or her attention diverted at mealtime? Is child psychologically deprived?	Counsel with parents about child's needs and help them obtain needed food Provide only between-meal snacks of high nutrient content at intervals that will not interfere with appetite at mealtime Serve very small portions Provide child with a quiet period before mealtime to prevent weariness Reinforce child's acceptance of food with social reinforcement Do not reinforce with food Eat with child to provide a model Refer the emotionally deprived child to the nurse or social worker
Refuses specific groups of foods	Is food properly prepared? Has child had previous experiences with the foods? Does child have a model (parents, teacher, peers) who eats these foods?	Continue offering very small portions of foods refused Reinforce foods accepted with foods child likes Provide a model for child by eating the foods Provide guidance in food preparation for children
Inappropriate feeding behavior Throwing Gorging Stuffing food in the mouth Will not sit at the table	What started the behavior? What follows the behavior? Is child reinforced? Is child punished? Is child ignored?	All inappropriate behaviors should be ignored even if it is necessary to remove child from feeding situation All attempts at appropriate eating should be encouraged through social reinforcement and food the child likes

Refuses to eat table food; insists on strained food	Has child had experience with table food? Has it been offered and refused? Has child eaten table food previously but refuses it currently? How is child positioned for feeding? Can he or she sit upright? Has a critical stage of development been ignored? Is child delayed so that strained foods are appropriate for his or her stage of motor development? Can child bite or chew? Is child hypersensitive in or around the mouth? Does child have a hypersensitive gag reflex? Does child have dental caries or malocclusion? Can child close the mouth? Has child been offered foods that require biting? Can child breathe through the nose?	Consult with occupational, physical, or speech therapist regarding positioning, development, and hypersensitivity Seat child in upright sitting position (using props if necessary) If child demonstrates readiness: Choose a food the child enjoys and place it between back molars (watch your fingers) Offer crunchy foods such as arrowroot biscuits, melba toast, crackers (be careful of foods that splinter, such as graham crackers)
Will not bite	Is child delayed so that only munching or sucking is appropriate? Can child lateralize the tongue? Has child been offered foods that require chewing? Is child hypersensitive or hyposensitive? Are foods offered that are too tough to chew?	Offer easy-to-bite foods such as arrowroot biscuits and melba toast Manually assist child in closing the jaw Provide social reinforcement when child takes a bite
Does not chew with a rotary motion	Can child lateralize the tongue? Has child been offered foods that require chewing?	Consult an occupational, physical, or speech therapist regarding lateralization of the tongue and sensitivity Model for child by demonstrating chewing Manually move the jaw in chewing motions Encourage chewing with social reinforcement and with foods child likes
Refuses harder-to-chew foods	Is hypertonia or hypotonia preventing development of oral motor skills? Does child have dental caries? Is child sufficiently delayed that hard-to-chew foods are inappropriate?	Consult with occupational, physical, or speech therapist about oral motor skills; stimulate area around the lips and mouth before feeding as directed Consult about dental caries

Developmentally delayed children frequently experience failure in their many efforts. It is therefore important that any plan to modify a child's food intake pattern be designed so that success is obtainable and the child and the parents are reinforced for each gain, however small. Adequate nutrition is important for every child to achieve his or her physical, mental, and emotional potential. Delayed and physically handicapped children should have the advantage of a nutrient intake that can support well-being, optimal growth, and development. Solutions to difficulties in attaining such goals may be complex and may require a multidisciplined approach.

Summary

Children who are developmentally delayed are vulnerable to the same problems of nutrient intake as other children. The incidence of feeding and nutrition problems appears to be greater than in the normal population, and they are often more severe. The causes of nutritional problems in developmentally delayed children often involve motor abnormalities or delays, infantilism, and lack of attention to critical periods of development. Therefore an interdisciplinary approach to intervention is appropriate. Specific syndromes are associated with undernutrition; others, with obesity.

REVIEW QUESTIONS

1. List common problems of nutrient intake of handicapped children.
2. What parameters not found in the average child must be considered when evaluating the adequacy of nutrient intake of a handicapped child?
3. What measure of physical growth can be used to assess the adequacy of energy and nutrient intake of children who have contractures?
4. What environmental controls are necessary to control the food intake of children with the Prader-Willi syndrome?
5. Why do children with heart and lung disease often have increased energy requirements?
6. Which nutrients must be carefully monitored if a child is taking anticonvulsant medications?
7. Why is an interdisciplinary team important in resolving problems of nutrient intake for children with special health care needs?

SUGGESTED LEARNING ACTIVITIES

1. Describe factors that must be addressed in evaluating the nutrient intake of a 3-year-old child with athetoid cerebral palsy.
2. Describe syndromes associated with both mental retardation and growth failure.
3. Define the nutritionist's role in early intervention programs for developmentally delayed children.
4. How would you respond to parents of a developmentally delayed child who were considering megavitamin therapy?
5. Determine an appropriate energy intake for a 14-month-old girl with Down syndrome.
6. Observe a school lunch program in a school for special education. What motor problems of feeding do you observe? What adaptive equipment is being used to facilitate self-feeding?
7. To experience the effect of head position on eating, try to chew or swallow semisolid foods with your head tilted backward. Try to drink with your head tilted backward.
8. To experience the effects of the position of the body on the head and on feeding ability, try to eat with your hips slid forward in the chair without your feet touching the ground.

Terms and Concepts

Provided here for your review is a listing of terms and concepts within this chapter. The definitions for terms can be found in the glossary, which begins on page 413. To aid your understanding of the terms' and concepts' application within this text, the page number designating the first mention of each term or concept within the chapter is given.

acquired immunodeficiency syndrome, 344
athetosis, 348
attention deficit hyperactivity disorder, 354
"bird-feeding," 361
bronchopulmonary displasia (BPD), 352
Carpenter syndrome, 345
Cohen syndrome, 345
congenital, 347
Cornelia de Lange's syndrome, 345
Down syndrome, 345
Duchenne's muscular dystrophy, 346
dysplasia congenita, 347
extension, 358

REFERENCES

1. Thommessen M and others: Feeding problems, height and weight in different groups of disabled children, *Acta Paediatr Scand* 80:527, 1991.
2. Thommessen M and others: Energy and nutrient intakes of disabled children: do feeding problems make a difference? *J Am Diet Assoc* 91:1522, 1991.
3. Roche AF: Growth assessment of handicapped children, *Diet Curr* 6:25, 1970.
4. Manenica K and others: *Evaluating growth and obesity in the child with myelomeningocele,* unpublished master's thesis, Seattle, 1981, University of Washington.
5. Gleason C: *Nutritional assessment of boys with Duchenne's muscular dystrophy,* unpublished master's thesis, Seattle, 1982, University of Washington.
6. Berke AR, Wilmore JH: *Evaluation and regulation of body build and composition,* Englewood Cliffs, NJ, 1974, Prentice-Hall.
7. Zorab PA, Prime FJ, Harrison A: Estimation of height from tibia length, *Lancet* 1:195, 1963.
8. Horton WA and others: Growth curves for height for diastrophic dysplasia, spondyloepiphyseal dysplasia congenita, and pseudoachondroplasia, *Am J Dis Child* 136:316, 1982.
9. Cronk CC and others: Growth charts for children with Down syndrome: 1 month to 18 years of age, *Pediatrics* 81:102, 1988.
10. Culley WJ, Middleton TO: Calorie requirements of mentally retarded children with and without motor dysfunction, *J Pediatr* 75:380, 1969.
11. Pipes P, Holm V: Weight control of children with Prader-Willi syndrome, *J Am Diet Assoc* 62:520, 1973.
12. Mertz ET and others: *Protein malnutrition in mentally retarded children.* In Food and Nutrition Board: *Meeting protein needs of infants and children,* Pub No 843, Washington, DC, 1961, National Academy of Sciences, National Research Council.
13. Eddy TP, Nicholson AL, Wheeler EF: Energy expenditures and dietary intakes in cerebral palsy, *Dev Med Child Neurol* 7:377, 1965.
14. Grogan C and others: The effect of nutrient intake and physical activity on the body composition of myelomeningocele patients as determined by K40, anthropometic measures and urinary creatinine, *Fed Proc* 36(3):1165, 1977.
15. Isaksson B: *The nutritional needs of disabled children.* In Blix G, editor: *Nutrition in preschool and school age,* symposium of the Swedish Nutrition Foundation, VII, Stockholm, 1969, Almqvist & Wiksell Forlag A.B.
16. Krick J, Van Duyn MAS: The relationship between oral motor involvement and growth: a pilot study in a pediatric population with cerebral palsy, *J Am Diet Assoc* 84:555, 1984.
17. Hammond MI, Lewis MN, Johnson EW: A nutritional study of cerebral palsied children, *J Am Diet Assoc* 49:196, 1966.
18. Leamy CM: A study of the food intake of a group of children with cerebral palsy in the Lakeville Sanitorium, *Am J Public Health* 43:1310, 1953.
19. Karle IP, Blehler RE, Ohlson MA: Nutritional status of cerebral palsied children, *J Am Diet Assoc* 38:22, 1961.
20. Pipes P: *Nutritional management of children with Prader-Willi syndrome.* In Holm V, Sulzbacher S, Pipes P: *The Prader-Willi syndrome,* Baltimore, 1980, University Park Press.
21. Pipes PL: *Nutritional aspects in individuals with Down syndrome.* In Pueschel SM, Pueschel JK,

editors: *Biomedical concerns in persons with Down syndrome,* Baltimore, 1992, Paul H. Brookes.

22. Hagberg BA: Rett syndrome: clinical peculiarities, diagnostic approach, and possible cause, *Pediatr Neurol* 5:75, 1989.

23. Rice M, Haas RH: The nutritional aspects of Rett syndrome, *J Child Neurol* 3(suppl):35, 1988.

24. Committee on Genetics, American Academy of Pediatrics: New issues in newborn screening for phenylketonuria and congenital hypothyroidism, *Pediatrics* 69:104, 1982.

25. Trahms CM: Long-term nutrition intervention model: the treatment of phenylketonuria, *Top Clin Nutr* 1:62, 1986.

26. Shaw DWW and others: MR imaging of phenylketonuria, *Am J Neuro Radiol* 12:403, 1991.

27. Danford DE, Smith JC, Huber AM: Pica and mineral status in the mentally retarded, *Am J Clin Nutr* 35:958, 1982.

28. Wilton KM, Irvine J: Nutritional intakes of socioculturally mentally retarded children vs. children of low and average socioeconomic status, *Am J Ment Defic* 8:79, 1983.

29. Adams E: *Nutrition for the young child with bronchopulmonary dysplasia (BPD),* Nutrition Focus 6 No 3, Seattle, May/June, 1991, Child Development and Mental Retardation Center, University of Washington.

30. Yeh TF and others: Metabolic rate and energy balance in infants with bronchopulmonary dysplasia, *J Pediatr* 114:448, 1989.

31. Caldwell MB, Rogers MF: Epidemiology of pediatric HIV infection, *Pediatr Clin North Am* 38:1, 1991.

32. Burroughs MH, Edelson PJ: Medical care of the HIV-infected child, *Pediatr Clin North Am* 38:45, 1991.

33. Spiegel L, Mayers A: Psychosocial aspects of AIDS in children and adolescents, *Pediatr Clin North Am* 38:153, 1991.

34. Bentler M, Stanish M: Nutrition support of the pediatric patient, *J Am Diet Assoc* 87:488, 1987.

35. Streissguth AP: *Testimony to subcommittee on children, family, drugs, and alcoholism committee on Labor and Human Resources,* Feb 5, 1991, US Senate.

36. Rice-Asaro M and others: *Nutritional concerns for children born to drug abusing women,* Seattle, July/Aug, 1990, Child Development and Mental Retardation Center, University of Washington.

37. American Academy of Pediatrics Report: Neonatal drug withdrawal, *Pediatrics* 72:895, 1983.

38. Hahn TJ, Shires R, Halstead LR: Serum dihydroxyvitamin D metabolite concentrations in patients on chronic anticonvulsant therapy: response to pharmacologic doses of vitamin D_2, *Metab Bone Dis Rel Res* 5:1, 1983.

39. Hahn TJ: Bone complications of anticonvulsants, *Drugs* 12:201, 1976.

40. Rivey MP, Schottelius DD, Berg MJ: Phenytoin-folic acid: a review, *Drug Intell Clin Pharm* 18:292, 1984.

41. Klein GL and others: Multiple vitamin deficiencies in association with chronic anticonvulsant therapy, *Pediatrics* 60:767, 1977.

42. Turkel H: *Medical amelioration of cytogenic anomalies,* Brooklyn, NY, 1971, Copen Press.

43. Williams RJ: Let's pursue nutrition to heal and prevent, *Fam Week* Apr 25, p. 4 1976.

44. Harrell RJ and others: Can nutrition supplements help mentally retarded children? *Proc Natl Acad Sci USA* 78:574, 1981.

45. Ellis NR, Tomporowski RD: Vitamin/mineral supplements and intelligence of institutionalized mentally retarded adults, *Am J Ment Defic* 88:211, 1983.

46. Bennett FC and others: Vitamin and mineral supplements in Down's syndrome, *Pediatrics* 72:707, 1983.

47. Illingworth, RS, Lister J: The critical or sensitive period with special reference to certain feeding problems in infants and children, *J Pediatr* 65:839, 1964.

48. Hooker D: Fetal reflexes and instinctual processes, *Psychosom Med* 4:199, 1942.

49. Ianniruberto A, Tajani E: Ultrasonographic study of fetal movements, *Semin Perinatol* 5:175, 1981.

50. Ingram TT: Clinical significance of infantile feeding reflexes, *Dev Med Child Neurol* 4:159, 1962.

51. Morris SE: Development of oral-motor skills in the neurologically impaired child receiving non-oral feedings, *Dysphagia* 3:135, 1989.

52. Measel CP, Anderson GC: Non-nutritive sucking during tube feedings: effect on clinical course in premature infants, *J Obstet Gynecol Neonatal Nurs* 8:265, 1979.

53. Glass RP, Lucas B: Making the transition from tube to oral feeding. *Nutr Focus* 5:6, 1990.

54. Morris SE, Klein MD: *Pre-feeding skills,* Tucson, Ariz, 1987, Therapy Skill Builders.

55. Deleted in proofs.

56. Blackman JA, Nelson CLA: Rapid introduction of oral feedings to tube-fed patients, *J Dev Behav Pediatr* 8:63, 1987.

57. Mueller H: *Facilitating feeding and prespeech.* In Pearson PH, Williams CE, editors: *Physical therapy services in the developmental disabilities,* Springfield, Ill, 1972, Charles C Thomas.
58. Feucht S: Guidelines for the use of thickening agents in foods and liquids, *Nutr Focus* 3:6, 1988.
59. Connor FP, Williamson GG, Siepp JM, editors: *Program guide for infants and toddlers with neuromotor and other developmental disabilities,* New York, 1978, Teachers College Press.
60. Mueller H: *Feeding.* In Finnie NR: *Handling the young cerebral palsied child at home,* New York, 1975, EP Dutton & Co.

15

Management of Mealtime Behaviors

Sally M. O'Neil

Objectives

++

After studying this chapter, the student should:

✔ Be aware of behavior management as a therapeutic approach to changing food patterns of children.

✔ Understand one approach to the analysis of behavior.

✔ Recognize the need to individualize reinforcers.

✔ Understand when it is appropriate to use food as a reinforcer.

✔ Be aware of methods used to teach children self-feeding.

Parent-child interactions are important determinants of children's acceptance of food and attitudes toward eating. These interactions often are responsible for difficulties that are presented to health professionals. Parents, anxious about their children's nutrient intakes, sometimes urge, nag, or pressure children to eat, and children often assume control of the feeding environment. The battle for control may become so intense that the children's nutrient intakes may be compromised. The conflict may result in a variety of problems including failure to thrive and obesity.

Parent-child interaction is a complex reciprocal process in which each response to an action can become the cause of future behaviors and in which both parents and children learn new behaviors. This interaction continuum includes parents' expressions of attitudes, values, interests, beliefs, and their caregiving behavior, as well as children's individual growth patterns, learning potential, and ability to incorporate increasingly complex experiences into their current stages of thinking and functioning. Behavior is both the cause and effect of other behaviors. All parent-child interactions both are elicited by the child and influence the child. For instance, the cries of an infant who is hungry can become the stimulus for the mother to respond by feeding the infant.

Behavior modification is a therapeutic tool that is often employed as a system of analysis and intervention for a wide variety of child development problems.[1-3] It is also commonly used as a therapeutic tool to manage weight problems (such as obesity), to extinguish socially unacceptable feeding behaviors (such as throwing food), and to increase a child's acceptance of a variety of foods or to teach self-feeding.[4,5] Sometimes nutritionists and dietitians work jointly with behaviorists in establishing and monitoring such programs. Often, nutritionists and dietitians apply behavior management concepts themselves. Concepts and methods of behavior modification are presented in this chapter.

BASIC CONCEPTS IN BEHAVIOR ASSESSMENT AND MANAGEMENT

Behaviorists have determined that behaviors are increased, maintained, or decreased by the consequences that immediately follow them.[6] These consequences can be reinforcing or punishing. Since **reinforcers** and **punishers** are defined from an individual's point of view, what may be reinforcing to one person may not be to someone else; the determination of what is reinforcing or punishing depends on the effect of a particular consequence on the behavior that preceded it. To be a reinforcer, a consequence must increase the behavior that it follows.

Reinforcers are of two types: positive and negative. Positive reinforcement is a consequence in which something desirable to the subject is added or applied to his or her environment as a result of a specific behavior. A smile, a hug, praise, food, and money are examples of positive reinforcers. Negative reinforcement, on the other hand, is a consequence in which something unpleasant is removed or terminated. For example, a person who is annoyed by loud static on the radio may turn down the volume or turn off the radio.

The silence, or absence of static, is a negative reinforcer for turning off the sound, and the person is likely to do it again if static recurs. All reinforcers must increase the behavior that they follow. The important distinction between these two concepts is that in positive reinforcement something pleasant is added as a consequence and in negative reinforcement something unpleasant is removed as a consequence.

Punishers decrease the behaviors that they follow. They are defined operationally in two ways. **Punishment** involves consequences in which something averse is added or applied, such as a spanking. **Extinction** involves those consequences in which a positive reinforcer is removed. For example, the withholding of adult attention (ignoring) during a child's temper tantrum or withholding eye contact when someone else is talking should decrease negative behaviors.

Interaction Processes Between Positive and Negative Reinforcement and Punishment

To examine positive and negative reinforcement and punishment as interactive processes, it is important to analyze the various parts of interaction. Peterson[7] has suggested that one way to do this effectively is to consider interaction in terms of A (antecedent events), B (behavior), and C (consequences). Consider the following example in which the **ABC analysis** is used. A mother takes her preschool son into a grocery store. The child immediately begins to ask for candy, then whines and cries when the mother refuses to give him any. After several minutes of loud crying and repeated looks from other shoppers, the mother gives the child a piece of candy. The child immediately stops crying. A diagrammatic analysis of this situation is presented below.

A (antecedent)	B (child's behavior)	C (consequence)
1. Enters store	2. Asks for candy	3. Mother refuses
	4. Cries and yells	5. Mother gives candy
	6. Stops crying	

In giving her child candy the mother reinforced her child for crying. Also, because he was reinforced, it is highly likely that the child will repeat this behavior during future trips to the grocery store. The mother received negative reinforcement because the crying ceased after the mother gave the child the candy. By giving candy, she terminated something that was aversive to her—the child's crying. In this interaction both mother and child were reinforced for their behaviors. The child was positively reinforced (candy was added) for crying, and the mother was negatively reinforced (crying was removed) for giving the candy. Both are likely to repeat their behaviors next time.

What if, in a similar situation, the mother decided to ignore the child? What would the mother's consequences be if ignoring stopped the crying? As before, she is negatively reinforced if she successfully stops the crying. Because the mother will be negatively reinforced for whatever she does that stops the crying, she may be reinforced for being inconsistent: giving candy one time, ignoring the child the next, and perhaps spanking another time.

It is easy for parents to become trapped in their responses to their children's behaviors and thus become unable to see those aspects of their interactions that are ineffective for both of them. It becomes important for parents to consider how they would like to respond most consistently to their child in the light of the behaviors they would like their child to learn. Parents have to consider their child's stage of development and reinforcers that fit his or her particular stage and personality. In addition, they have to be aware of the effects of the child's behavior on themselves. This is no small task, and it seems to become especially important around mealtimes. Since nutrition, socialization, and intense family interactions converge in this event, it is no wonder that so many clinical issues arise around mealtime behaviors.

Assessment of Mealtime Behaviors

Initial assessment consists of identifying the patterns of parent-child mealtime behaviors. The observation checklist (box, page 377) is a useful recording guide that pinpoints both problem behavior and desirable behavior. This tool can be used by professionals who are recording their direct observations or by parents who are recording the mealtime behaviors of themselves and their children. Behaviors can be tallied for each meal.

Once problem behaviors are identified, the most frequent eating and noneating behaviors and their consequences can be identified in ABC sequences. Parents are helped to identify those child behaviors that they wish to change as well as the appropriate eating behaviors that they wish to foster in their children. The next step is to determine appropriate consequences for all the behavior categories.

As noted earlier, parents generally behave toward their children (reinforce, punish, or ignore) in certain ways because of the reinforcement they receive from their children. For instance, they may reinforce a crying child with a cookie because they know this will stop the crying. Thus the parent is negatively reinforced for giving the child the cookie. Frequently, to help parents change the consequences they provide their children, it is necessary to look at the reinforcers parents are getting for their own behavior. One way to do this is to help them identify the subsequent child behavior step to the ABC pattern. For parents to alter their antecedent cues to the child, they must be aware of these behaviors and their part in the entire ABC pattern. The brief case studies that follow illustrate a variety of parent-child ABC patterns that relate to mealtimes.

1 Laura refuses to drink milk.

A (mother)	B (child)	C (mother)
1. Pours milk into glass	2. Starts crying	3. "Drink your milk."
	4. Cries	5. Removes milk and gives child soda
	6. Stops crying and drinks soda	

In this instance the mother was negatively reinforced. She successfully terminated the crying by giving the child soda, which, in turn, positively reinforced the child's crying when milk was presented to her.

2 Billy, a toddler, writes his own menu.

A (mother)	B (child)	C (mother)
1. Presents applesauce to Billy in highchair	2. Cries and whines, points to refrigerator	3. "What do you want?"
	4. Cries, points to cupboard	5. "Do you want a cracker?"
	6. Cries, points to refrigerator	7. "What do you want?
	8. Cries, points to refrigerator	9. "No, you can't have ice cream."
	10. Child screams	11. "OK, here is some ice cream."
	12. Stops crying	

CHILD BEHAVIORS AT MEALTIME

Meals Observed

• *Noneating behaviors*	1	2	3	4	5	6
Arguing						
Complaining						
Crying						
Hitting						
Noncomplying						
Not sitting at table						
Teasing						
Yelling						
Pouting						
Whining						
Moving hands nonpurposefully						
Talking back						
Throwing food or utensils						
Spitting						
Gagging						
Refusing certain foods						

• *Eating behaviors*	1	2	3	4	5	6
Using fingers for finger foods						
Using utensils appropriately						
Sitting at table						
Accepting variety of foods						
Socializing as appropriate						
Complying to requests						

PARENT BEHAVIORS AT MEALTIME

Meals Observed

• *Antecedents to child behaviors*	1	2	3	4	5	6
Commanding						
Requesting						
Questioning						
Prompting verbally						
Physically assisting						
Interrupting						
Positioning child appropriately						
Presenting food appropriately						
Presenting appropriate utensils						

• *Consequences of child behaviors*	1	2	3	4	5	6
Commenting positively						
Commenting negatively						
Ignoring						
Touching						
Spanking						
Yelling						
Arguing						
Laughing						
Using same tone of voice						
Talking irrelevantly						

In this situation the child keeps his mother going in circles in an effort to stop his crying. A management plan was developed with her in which she would leave the room and when the child would stop crying she would return and praise him for eating so nicely. The ABC looked like this:

A (mother)	B (child)	C (mother)
1. Presents applesauce to Billy in highchair	2. Cries, points to cupboard	3. Leaves room (can see child, but he can't see her)
	4. Slowly stops crying, starts eating applesauce	5. Returns and says "My, what a big boy!"
	6. Child laughs and keeps on eating	

3 John, a school-age child who has a hearing impairment, wanders at mealtimes.

A (parents)	B (child)	C (parents)
1. Announce dinner	2. Sits at table with parents	3. Talk to each other, ignore John
	4. Gets up and wanders around house	5. Yell, "Come back here!"
	6. Approaches dining room	7. Ignore John
	8. Wanders away from dining room	9. "Come here, John," Father goes and leads him to table
	10. John sits and looks at food	11. Ignore John

In discussing this ABC with John's parents they decided that they had been reinforced by John's absence at the table since, before that time, he had had tantrum behavior at the table. They believed that he should eat with them, but it was more comfortable to eat without him and to feed him later. A management program was developed with them in which they agreed to reinforce him for sitting at the table, using signing as well as verbal praise, and to try to include him in the general conversation. A subsequent ABC looked like this:

A (parents)	B (child)	C (parents)
1. Announce dinner	2. John sits at table, starts eating	3. Talk and sign to John
	4. Leaves table	5. Ignore John
	6. Approaches table	7. Talk and sign to John, discussing day's events
	8. Sits down, starts to eat	9. Eat, yet continue to socialize with John
	10. John talks, signs, eats, and remains seated during meal	

The importance of antecedents. Although consequences are important in maintaining behaviors, the antecedent events frequently tell a child or parent that certain behaviors will be reinforced. As discriminative stimuli, antecedents set the occasion for reinforcers. For example, when the mother in case 1 poured the milk, the child knew that if she cried at that time she would be likely to get soda instead.

Frequently, in an attempt to get control of such a situation this parent may have suggested as she poured the milk, "You have to drink milk, you will not get soda this time." However, the child cries anyway, even louder and longer than before. To terminate the crying the parent generally gives in and replaces the milk with soda. Instead of discouraging the child, the parent has only made the discriminative stimulus even stronger by adding the verbal reminder when pouring the milk.

Another example of important antecedents is demonstrated in case 4.

4 Suzi was a preschooler with a handicapping condition that caused blisters on her esophagus. She vomited often, which caused her mother great anxiety. In her anxiety, she actually inadvertently cued Suzi's behavior. Suzi, in turn, used these cues to control her mother's responses.

A (mother)	B (child)	C (mother)
Meal 1		
1. Presents food	2. Eats	3. Sits with book, does not talk to child
Meal 2		
1. Presents food	2. Gags and spits up food	3. Fusses over Suzi, cleans her up, then finishes feeding her the meal

In assessing this situation, it was found that Suzi did not vomit every meal. Yet somehow she was getting cues about when to vomit. In an attempt to further identify these cues, the mother's meal preparation was observed as part of the antecedent behavior. Surprisingly, the typical ABC pattern for vomiting and nonvomiting meals looked like this:

A (mother)	B (child)	C (mother)
Vomiting meal		
1. Preparing lunch, says, "Suzi, you have carrots today. I hope you don't vomit them."	2. Starts eating, then gags and vomits carrots	3. Attends, cleans up child, and feeds her the rest of the meal
Nonvomiting meal		
1. Preparing lunch, says "Oh good, Suzi, you have macaroni today."	2. Eating well	3. Sitting with book, ignoring Suzi

For the vomiting meal, mother was cueing Suzi to the fact that if she vomited she would get attention, be cleaned up, and be fed her lunch. For the nonvomiting meal no such cue was given, so Suzi ate her lunch as expected. These ABC patterns were discussed with the mother, and a strategy was developed in which she would not read at mealtime, would reinforce Suzi for eating by talking with her at mealtime, and would only provide antecedent verbal cues such as in the nonvomiting meal. A later ABC pattern looked like this:

A (mother)	B (child)	C (mother)
1. "Suzi, we have carrots today."	2. Eats, smiles, and talks to mother	3. Attends to Suzi by smiling and conversing

ADDITIONAL CONCEPTS IN BEHAVIOR MANAGEMENT

There is no doubt about the importance of food as an effective reinforcer for most people. Since it meets a basic biological need, it is considered to be a primary reinforcer. Secondary reinforcers such as affection, praise, and touch derive their reinforcing qualities from having been paired with food during the early infant period. Later, money becomes reinforcing when used to buy a wide variety of reinforcers such as food, shelter, clothing, and other desirable items. Food is a potential reinforcer for a wide variety of activities; it is frequently paired with or follows attendance at outings, movies, sports, and social events.

The decision to use food as a reinforcer is made after a careful assessment process in which a variety of reinforcers are tried. Reinforcers are individualized, as discussed earlier. What may be reinforcing for one individual may not be for another, depending on biophysiological factors within an individual and his or her history of experiences.

For some children social praise may be reinforcing; for others, food may be reinforcing. For still others neither social praise nor food is reinforcing, and parents must seek other kinds of reinforcement. Children who have developmental delays may not be able to use the usual things that most children find reinforcing. Because of sensory deficits or problems in neuromuscular development or because experiences have been limited, these children may need specialized reinforcers such as vibration, flickering lights, or even music. Therefore an effort must be made to determine what kind of reinforcer is effective for any given individual. In some instances food is the only reinforcer with which a child can learn appropriate behaviors. If this is the case, food should be used and other reinforcers (e.g., affection and praise) can be paired with it until they also become reinforcing for this particular individual and food no longer needs to be used. When it has been determined that food will be the most effective reinforcer for a particular child, several considerations are important. The first factor is the kind of food to use. Again, this should be individualized according to the child's tastes, and care should be taken to use food with high-nutrient value whenever possible. In many instances potato chips and candy are used when raisins or cheese might be just as effective. Any food reinforcement should be considered as part of the total nutrient and kcaloric intake for the child.

Another factor to consider is the timing of food reinforcers. If one is concerned that the child eat adequate meals, training programs that use food reinforcers should not immediately precede a meal. Likewise, if success in the training program is important, a program using food reinforcers should not directly follow a meal. Any individual may become satiated by food unless adequate time has elapsed between intervals of food intake.

Satiation can also occur when too much of the same food is given to ensure maximum effectiveness of the reinforcer. Particular foods used during a training program should not be available to the child at any other time of the day. For instance, a child may be given a dish of ice cream daily at home. If a decision is made to use a dish of ice cream in a program at school, the ice cream should no longer be available at home.

Another factor to consider when using food reinforcement is the pairing of another potential reinforcer with food. Because it is important for the child to be able to use other reinforcers, it is necessary to provide reinforcers such as praise at the same time that food is given. After it is determined that the combination of food and praise is reinforcing to the child, the food can be given less frequently, whereas praise will still be provided every time the desired behavior occurs. The food is gradually eliminated, and praise will have become a reinforcer for the child.

Consistency is also important when applying reinforcers. As children learn an increasing variety of behaviors, they learn about new and different reinforcers. Food and feeding habits may be incorporated into behavioral repertoires designed to gain adult attention. Throwing utensils or food may cause a variety of interesting adult reactions. A parent may laugh at one such incident, respond with anger at another, and at a third may feed the child in exasperation. In the effort to keep up with the child, parents may respond inconsistently, depending on their mood at the time. Consistency means that desirable behaviors generally are reinforced, whereas undesirable behaviors are not reinforced and may even be punished. The child should know what desirable behaviors are expected by his or her parents and, in turn, what consequences can be expected for certain behaviors.

Experience has indicated that reinforcers other than food are more effective for managing feeding behaviors. For instance, if a child must be on a special diet for a biological reason such as allergy, parents and professionals usually become concerned that the child may not eat adequate amounts of acceptable foods. In this instance the child receives mixed messages if he or she is reinforced with food yet perceives that the parents will not allow certain other foods. The child quickly learns that by refusing foods that are allowed he or she can gain a great deal of attention and may even receive the forbidden foods as parents become upset by the child's refusal to eat. The use of nonedible reinforcers such as outings, toys, and games following meals generally helps to refocus the parents' and child's attention to other activities.

TEACHING SELF-FEEDING BEHAVIORS

In addition to the use of reinforcement, **shaping** and **fading** techniques are useful for teaching new behaviors and skills. Both of these procedures are used by parents and professionals for teaching feeding behaviors.

Shaping is the reinforcement of successive approximations to a desired behavior. In this procedure the behavior is broken down into its component steps. The types and number of steps are determined by the task to be learned. The first step is reinforced; when that step is learned, the next step is added and the reinforcement is shifted to the second step in the chain of responses that lead to the desired behavior.

Teaching Spoon-Feeding by Shaping

1. Desired behavior: independent spoon-feeding
2. Changing steps in child responses
   a. Child looks at spoon
   b. Child moves hand toward spoon
   c. Child touches spoon
   d. Child picks up spoon
   e. Child puts spoon in dish
   f. Child scoops food
   g. Child brings food to mouth
   h. Child takes food off spoon
   i. Child returns spoon to dish
3. Reinforcement: bites of food or other reinforcers as each step is accomplished

Fading is a different procedure in that the entire behavior is used each time for reinforcement. Instead of requiring the child's responses to proceed through several steps, the trainer's cues are changed as the child's skill develops. For example, the trainer holds the child's hand around the spoon and puts the child through the motions of scooping food onto the spoon, bringing the spoon to the mouth, and returning the spoon to the dish. As the child gradually assumes independent movement, physical assistance is decreased and the trainer only provides assistance as needed to complete the task. The number and type of trainer cues needed depends on the task to be learned and the abilities of the child.

Teaching Spoon-Feeding by Fading

1. Desired behavior: independent spoon-feeding
2. Steps:
   a. Holding child's hand around spoon, scoop food, and bring arm, hand, and spoon to mouth. Allow child to take food off spoon in mouth, then (still holding child's hand around spoon) return spoon to dish.
   b. Holding child's hand around spoon,

bring it toward mouth and allow child to complete movement to mouth if possible. Assist through rest of cycle.
   c. Assist child in holding spoon and scooping food. By touching arm slightly, provide cues that assist child in completing movement to mouth. Also by touches, assist child in returning spoon to dish.
   d. Provide only as much assistance as child needs to pick up spoon, scoop food, move spoon to mouth, and return to dish.

The actual number of steps delineated for any given individual depends on the developmental level and skill that the individual possesses before using either of these procedures.

Using the Behavior You Want to Extinguish as a Reinforcer

Anytime the actual behavior can be used as a reinforcer, it becomes under your control and can be changed. Annie was a child with severe handicaps whose meals were given in liquid form in a bottle. At almost every meal she was offered food on a spoon, but when she refused it, she was given her bottle to hold for herself and was left alone. Thus, she was being continuously reinforced for refusing food on a spoon.

A plan was devised in which her bottle would be used as a reinforcer for Annie taking food in any other way. Because she was reinforced for refusing food from a spoon, it was decided to start with teaching her to drink from a cup with a cover and spout. Accordingly, every 4 to 5 swallows Annie took from the cup, she was reinforced with 4 to 5 swallows from her bottle. At first, much of the cup food was spit out, but by the second meal Annie got the idea, and she began to swallow the food from the cup.

In addition to the bottle as a reinforcer, she received positive attention for drinking from the cup. By the sixth meal, Annie was drinking her whole meal from the cup, with just a bit of food as "dessert" from the bottle.

Then it was decided to try spoon-feeding again, this time using the cup as a reinforcer. The bottle would be given only occasionally with juice. The same procedures were repeated, only this time for every mouthful of thickened food taken by spoon, a drink of milk was given from the cup.

At first the spoon with a bit of food on the end was touched onto her lips, followed by a drink from the cup. As soon as she accepted this (by the third spoonful), food on the spoon was introduced further into her mouth, until by the end of the meal she was accepting half-full spoonfuls. By the next meals she was reinforced with the cup for several spoonfuls of food.

This type of program, using one behavior to reinforce and strengthen another, was a very effective method of learning for Annie. She learned to accept a variety of soft table food, some of which she was learning to chew. She learned to hold a cup by herself, and she was beginning to learn to feed herself with a spoon.

GENERAL CONSIDERATIONS IN THE USE OF BEHAVIOR MANAGEMENT TECHNIQUES

Behavior modification is generally easy to use as a method of therapeutic intervention. The difficulties lie in the behavioral analysis, which is necessary to pinpoint specific behaviors and their consequences. Frequently, the relationships between behaviors and their consequences (particularly when two or more persons are involved) are difficult to discover, and care must be taken to delineate them with accuracy and reliability. Behavior is never simple, and it becomes increasingly complex when viewed within a framework of human interaction. Yet to try to remedy behaviors in isolation is to treat them outside the context of their everyday occurrence. This, in turn, leads to unsuccessful programs.

The preceding examples have been assessed by direct observation of mealtime behaviors, yet there are more complex situations that would preclude direct observation or that would be greatly altered by the presence of an observer. In-home videotaped recordings frequently work well for these situations. Parents are usually willing to allow several meals to be videotaped to pinpoint difficulties. These tapes are analyzed according to their ABC patterns. Important segments of tape are then played back to the parents, who frequently are able to discover the problems themselves. Frequently, this is an impetus for them to discuss their feelings and concerns about the situations and to generate alternative ways of behaving with their children. The combination of media and behavioral approaches to parent training for children with behavioral and developmental disabilities are considered to be effective means for dealing with a variety of child development issues.[8,9] Professionals must consider all the possible effects of the techniques before implementing them and should secure assistance while learning the procedures involved. Collaboration of nutritionists, nurses, and professionals from other disciplines helps continually refine observation and recording techniques and management procedures. The role of each discipline in the analysis, program design, and implementation must be well defined to make the program successful.

During nutrition and feeding evaluation, observations of parental and child behaviors by professionals from two or more disciplines help to identify more reliably the cause of a specific problem. Programs should be designed jointly with parents by one team member who is skilled in behavior management. Changes in physical growth, nutrient intake, and behavior should be monitored on an interdisciplinary basis to direct attention to both psychosocial (behavioral) and physical parameters.

Summary

Feeding and nutrition problems during childhood may result from inappropriate parent-child interactions. Behavior management programs when adequately implemented can resolve these problems. Observations of parent-child interactions give clues as to the antecedent to the behavior and the reinforcers that cause it to continue. Reinforcers used in behavior management programs must be individualized for each client. If food is used as a reinforcer, the program and nutrient intake should be carefully monitored to ensure that it does not compromise the child's nutritional status.

REVIEW QUESTIONS

1. Define positive and negative reinforcers.
2. Why are antecedents important when analyzing behavior?
3. What food behaviors are most often modified with behavior modification?
4. Why does one collect ABCs?
5. How does one teach self-feeding using behavior modification techniques to a developmentally delayed child?

SUGGESTED LEARNING ACTIVITIES

1. Observe a child eating a family meal. What cues do parents give the child to eat? Identify positive and negative reinforcers parents consciously or unconsciously use.
2. How would you identify appropriate foods and reinforcers for a child who needs a behavior management program?
3. Describe feeding problem behaviors for which a behavior management program would be appropriate.
4. Define factors that should be monitored to ensure that a child's nutritional status is not compromised when a behavioral management program is planned to change a child's feeding behavior.
5. Design a behavior management program to effect an increase in textures of food acceptable to a developmentally delayed child.

Terms and Concepts

Provided here for your review is a listing of terms and concepts within this chapter. The definitions for terms can be found in the glossary, which begins on page 413. To aid your understanding of the terms' and concepts' application within this text, the page number designating the first mention of each term or concept within the chapter is given.

ABC analysis, 375

behavior modification, 374

extinction, 375

fading, 380

punishers, 375

punishment, 375

reinforcers, 375

shaping, 380

REFERENCES

1. France KG, Hudson SM: Behavior management of infant sleep disturbance, *J Appl Behav Anal* 23(1) 91, 1990.
2. Rostain AL: Attention deficit disorders in children and adolescents: difficult diagnoses in pediatrics, *Pediatr Clin North Am* 38:3, June 1991.
3. Selinske JE, Greer RD: A functional analysis of the comprehensive application of behavior analysis to schooling, *J Appl Behav Anal* 24:107, 1991.
4. Epstein LH and others: Ten-year followup of behavioral, family-based treatment for obese children, *JAMA* 264:19, 1990.
5. Finney JW: Preventing common feeding problems in infants and young children, *Pediatr Clin North Am* 33:4, 1986.
6. Cooper JO, Heron TE, Heward WL: *Applied behavior analysis,* Columbus, Ohio, 1987, Merrill Publishing.
7. Peterson LW: Operant approach to observation and recording, *Nurs Outlook* 15:28, 1967.
8. Dauz-Williams P, Harrison-Elder J, Hill S: Media approach to family training in behavior management: two families, *Issues Comp Pediatr Nurs* 9:59, 1986.
9. Van Hasslet VB, Sisson LA, Aach SR: Parent training to increase compliance in a young multi-handicapped child, *J Behav Ther Exp Psychiatry* 18:3, 275, 1987.

Appendix

GIRLS: BIRTH TO 36 MONTHS
PHYSICAL GROWTH
NCHS PERCENTILES*

NAME_____   RECORD #_____

Ross
Growth &
Development
Program

* Adapted from: Hamill PVV, Drizd TA, Johnson CL, Reed RB, Roche AF, Moore WM: Physical growth: National Center for Health Statistics percentiles. AM J CLIN NUTR 32:607-629, 1979. Data from the Fels Longitudinal Study, Wright State University School of Medicine, Yellow Springs, Ohio.

© 1982 Ross Laboratories

MOTHER'S STATURE _____   GESTATIONAL
FATHER'S STATURE _____   AGE _____ WEEKS

DATE	AGE	LENGTH	WEIGHT	HEAD CIRC.	COMMENT
	BIRTH				

GIRLS: BIRTH TO 36 MONTHS
PHYSICAL GROWTH
NCHS PERCENTILES*

NAME _____ RECORD # _____

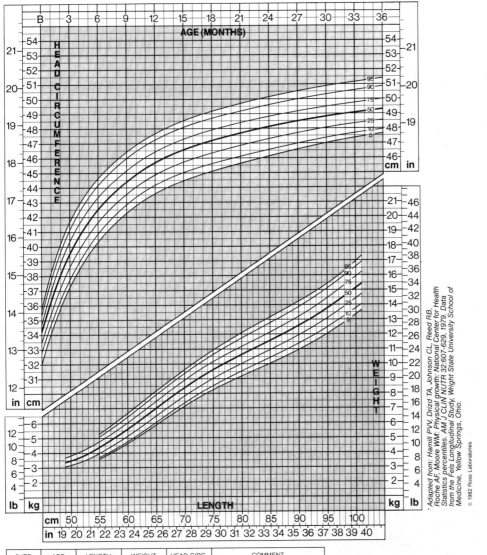

ROSS LABORATORIES
COLUMBUS, OHIO 43216
DIVISION OF ABBOTT LABORATORIES, USA

G106(0.05)/JANUARY 1986   LITHO IN USA

BOYS: BIRTH TO 36 MONTHS
PHYSICAL GROWTH
NCHS PERCENTILES*

NAME _____ RECORD # _____

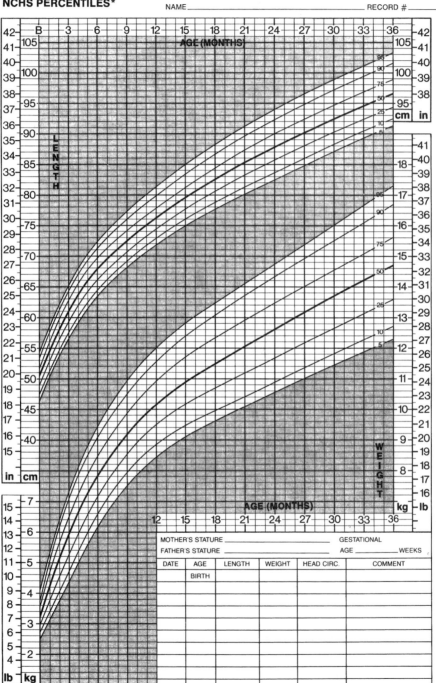

Ross
Growth &
Development
Program

*Adapted from: Hamill PVV, Drizd TA, Johnson CL, Reed RB, Roche AF, Moore WM: Physical growth: National Center for Health Statistics percentiles. AM J CLIN NUTR 32:607-629, 1979. Data from the Fels Longitudinal Study, Wright State University School of Medicine, Yellow Springs, Ohio.

© 1982 Ross Laboratories

MOTHER'S STATURE _____ GESTATIONAL
FATHER'S STATURE _____ AGE _____ WEEKS

DATE	AGE	LENGTH	WEIGHT	HEAD CIRC.	COMMENT
	BIRTH				

BOYS: BIRTH TO 36 MONTHS
PHYSICAL GROWTH
NCHS PERCENTILES*

NAME_____   RECORD #_____

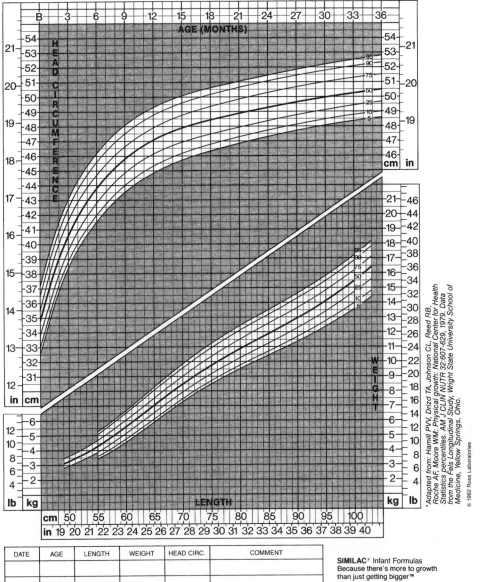

*Adapted from: Hamill PVV, Drizd TA, Johnson CL, Reed RB, Roche AF, Moore WM: Physical growth: National Center for Health Statistics percentiles. AM J CLIN NUTR 32:607-629, 1979. Data from the Fels Longitudinal Study, Wright State University School of Medicine, Yellow Springs, Ohio.

© 1982 Ross Laboratories

DATE	AGE	LENGTH	WEIGHT	HEAD CIRC.	COMMENT

SIMILACᴿ Infant Formulas
Because there's more to growth than just getting bigger™

ISOMILᴿ Soy Protein Formulas
When the baby can't take milk

ROSS LABORATORIES
COLUMBUS, OHIO 43216
DIVISION OF ABBOTT LABORATORIES, USA

G105(0.05)/APRIL 1989   LITHO IN USA

GIRLS: 2 TO 18 YEARS
PHYSICAL GROWTH
NCHS PERCENTILES*

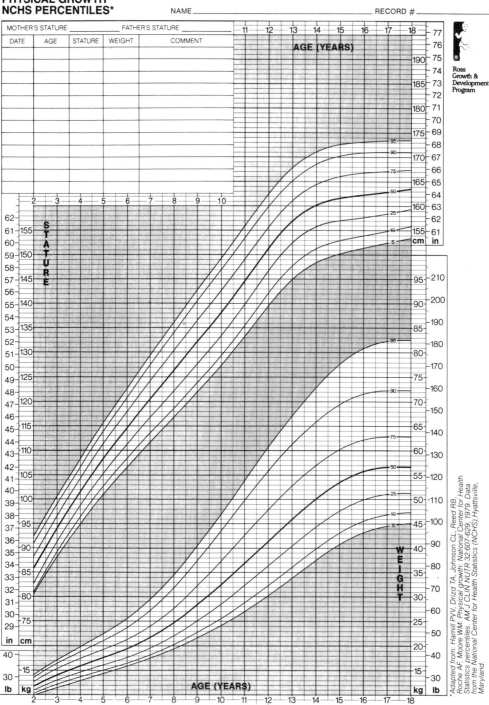

Ross
Growth &
Development
Program

GIRLS: PREPUBESCENT
PHYSICAL GROWTH
NCHS PERCENTILES*

NAME _____ RECORD # _____

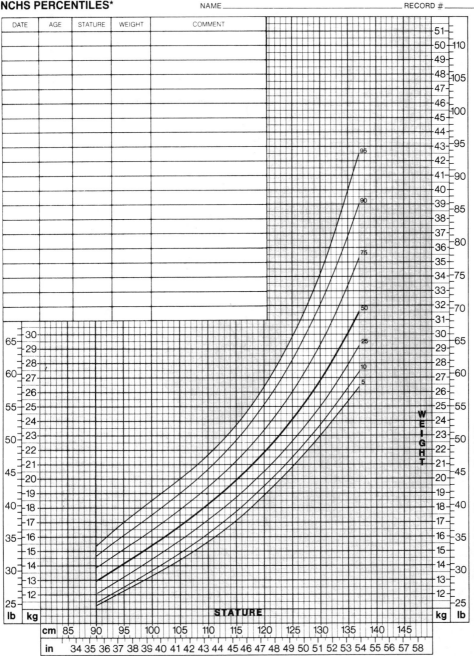

DATE	AGE	STATURE	WEIGHT	COMMENT

Adapted from: Hamill PVV, Drizd TA, Johnson CL, Reed RB, Roche AF, Moore WM: Physical growth: National Center for Health Statistics percentiles. AM J CLIN NUTR 32:607-629, 1979. Data from the National Center for Health Statistics (NCHS) Hyattsville, Maryland.

© 1982 Ross Laboratories

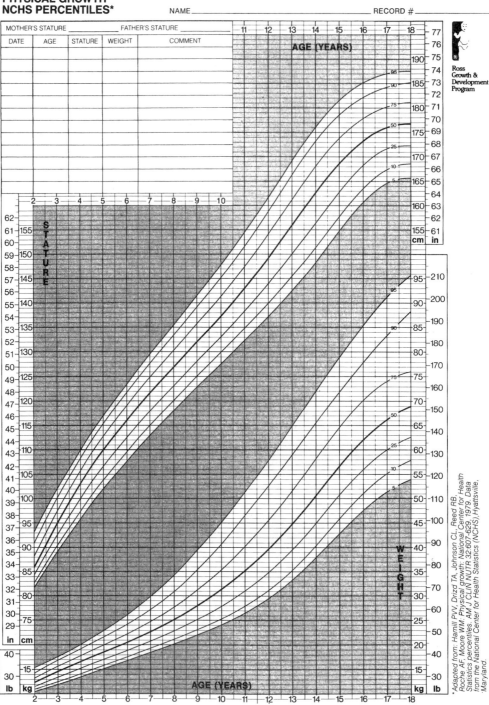

BOYS: 2 TO 18 YEARS
PHYSICAL GROWTH
NCHS PERCENTILES*

NAME _____ RECORD # _____

Ross
Growth &
Development
Program

*Adapted from: Hamill PVV, Drizd TA, Johnson CL, Reed RB, Roche AF, Moore WM. Physical growth: National Center for Health Statistics percentiles. AM J CLIN NUTR 32:607-629, 1979. Data from the National Center for Health Statistics (NCHS), Hyattsville, Maryland.

© 1982 Ross Laboratories

BOYS: PREPUBESCENT
PHYSICAL GROWTH
NCHS PERCENTILES*

NAME _____ RECORD # _____

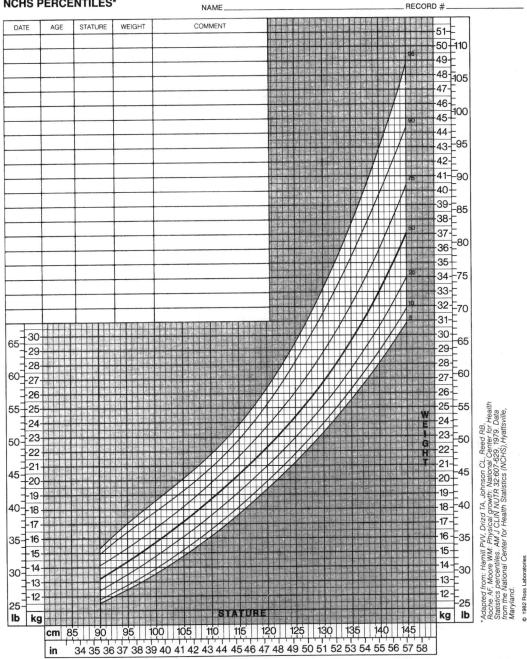

Adapted from: Hamill PVV, Drizd TA, Johnson CL, Reed RB, Roche AF, Moore WM: Physical growth: National Center for Health Statistics percentiles. AM J CLIN NUTR 32:607-629, 1979. Data from the National Center for Health Statistics (NCHS), Hyattsville, Maryland.

© 1982 Ross Laboratories

 ROSS LABORATORIES
COLUMBUS, OHIO 43216
DIVISION OF ABBOTT LABORATORIES, USA

G107(0.05)/APRIL 1989   LITHO IN USA

Ross
Growth &
Development
Program

INCREMENTAL GROWTH CHARTS—GIRLS

Growth charts such as those that display the National Center for Health Statistics (NCHS) percentiles are used for routine assessment of physical growth.[1] Occasionally, growth rate (growth velocity or increment divided by time between measurements) should be assessed, eg, when an infant or preadolescent child is found to be at an extreme percentile or when a substantial shift of percentile has occurred on an NCHS growth chart. The accompanying incremental growth charts are useful for assessing growth rates. They do not replace written records of growth data or NCHS growth charts.

These incremental growth charts have been prepared from serial data for white US children whose growth is very close to that of children from whom the NCHS percentiles were derived.[1,2] Highly standardized anthropometric methods that conform to current recommendations were used to make all measurements.[3] Weight was measured as, or corrected to, nude weight. Recumbent length and stature were measured without shoes. Appropriate use of the incremental growth charts requires that similar methods be applied. Ideally, the same person should measure a child at the beginning and end of an interval.

References:

1. Hamill PVV, Drizd TA, Johnson CL, Reed RB, Roche AF, Moore WM: Physical growth: National Center for Health Statistics percentiles. *Am J Clin Nutr* 32: 607-629, 1979.

2. Roche AF, Himes JH: Incremental growth charts. *Am J Clin Nutr* 33: 2041-2052, 1980.

3. Fomon SJ: *Nutritional Disorders of Children. Prevention, Screening, and Follow-up.* Washington, DC: DHEW Publication No. (HSA) 76-5612, 1976.

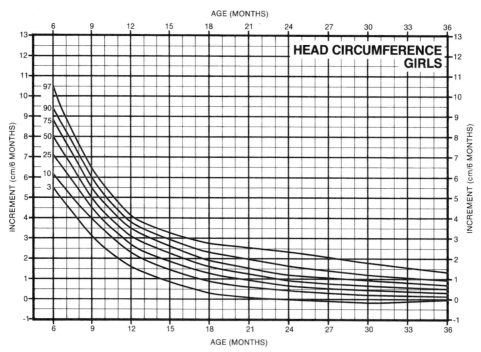

INSTRUCTIONS

1. Measure the child at the beginning and the end of a 6-month interval, if possible.

2. Subtract the initial measurement from the follow-up measurement to obtain the increment.

3. If the interval between measurements is not exactly 6 months (182 days), divide the increment by the interval in days and multiply by 182 to obtain the adjusted 6-month increment. The Table of Consecutively Numbered Days can be used to determine the interval between the measurements. If measurements are made in different years, add 365 to the day of the year for the follow-up measurement. Extrapolating increments from intervals of 3 months or less is not recommended.

4. Locate the intersection of the increment and the child's age at the **end** of the interval to determine the 6-month incremental percentile.

Interpretation: The accompanying charts permit definition of growth rate (growth velocity) relative to current reference data. Further investigation is indicated for children growing at rates markedly different from the 50th incremental percentile or for children whose incremental percentile changes rapidly.

Example 1 Girl at 5th NCHS* percentile at ages 6 and 12 months; aged 12 months at follow-up measurement.

Measurement	Length	Date	Day**
Follow-up	69.8 cm	July 16, 1981	197
Initial	61.8 cm	January 15, 1981	15
Increment =	8.0 cm	Interval =	182

Her increment is 8.0 cm/6 months.
Her increment is between the 25th and 50th percentile.
She is short but growing at a normal rate.

 * National Center for Health Statistics
 ** From Table of Consecutively Numbered Days

Example 2 Girl, aged 8 years at follow-up measurement.

Measurement	Stature	Date	Day*
Follow-up	118.0 cm	April 22, 1981	477**
Initial	116.9 cm	November 21, 1980	325
Increment =	1.1 cm	Interval =	152

Her adjusted 6-month increment is $\frac{1.1 \text{ cm}}{152} \times 182 = 1.3$ cm.

Her increment is below the 3rd percentile.
Further investigation is indicated.

 * From Table of Consecutively Numbered Days
 ** April 22 is day 112, to which 365 is added because follow-up measurement is in a different year (112 + 365 = 477).

Table of Consecutively Numbered Days

Day	JAN	FEB	MAR	APR	MAY	JUN	JUL	AUG	SEP	OCT	NOV	DEC	Day
1	1	32	60	91	121	152	182	213	244	274	305	335	1
2	2	33	61	92	122	153	183	214	245	275	306	336	2
3	3	34	62	93	123	154	184	215	246	276	307	337	3
4	4	35	63	94	124	155	185	216	247	277	308	338	4
5	5	36	64	95	125	156	186	217	248	278	309	339	5
6	6	37	65	96	126	157	187	218	249	279	310	340	6
7	7	38	66	97	127	158	188	219	250	280	311	341	7
8	8	39	67	98	128	159	189	220	251	281	312	342	8
9	9	40	68	99	129	160	190	221	252	282	313	343	9
10	10	41	69	100	130	161	191	222	253	283	314	344	10
11	11	42	70	101	131	162	192	223	254	284	315	345	11
12	12	43	71	102	132	163	193	224	255	285	316	346	12
13	13	44	72	103	133	164	194	225	256	286	317	347	13
14	14	45	73	104	134	165	195	226	257	287	318	348	14
15	15	46	74	105	135	166	196	227	258	288	319	349	15
16	16	47	75	106	136	167	197	228	259	289	320	350	16
17	17	48	76	107	137	168	198	229	260	290	321	351	17
18	18	49	77	108	138	169	199	230	261	291	322	352	18
19	19	50	78	109	139	170	200	231	262	292	323	353	19
20	20	51	79	110	140	171	201	232	263	293	324	354	20
21	21	52	80	111	141	172	202	233	264	294	325	355	21
22	22	53	81	112	142	173	203	234	265	295	326	356	22
23	23	54	82	113	143	174	204	235	266	296	327	357	23
24	24	55	83	114	144	175	205	236	267	297	328	358	24
25	25	56	84	115	145	176	206	237	268	298	329	359	25
26	26	57	85	116	146	177	207	238	269	299	330	360	26
27	27	58	86	117	147	178	208	239	270	300	331	361	27
28	28	59	87	118	148	179	209	240	271	301	332	362	28
29	29	—	88	119	149	180	210	241	272	302	333	363	29
30	30	—	89	120	150	181	211	242	273	303	334	364	30
31	31	—	90	—	151	—	212	243	—	304	—	365	31
Day	JAN	FEB	MAR	APR	MAY	JUN	JUL	AUG	SEP	OCT	NOV	DEC	Day

Continued.

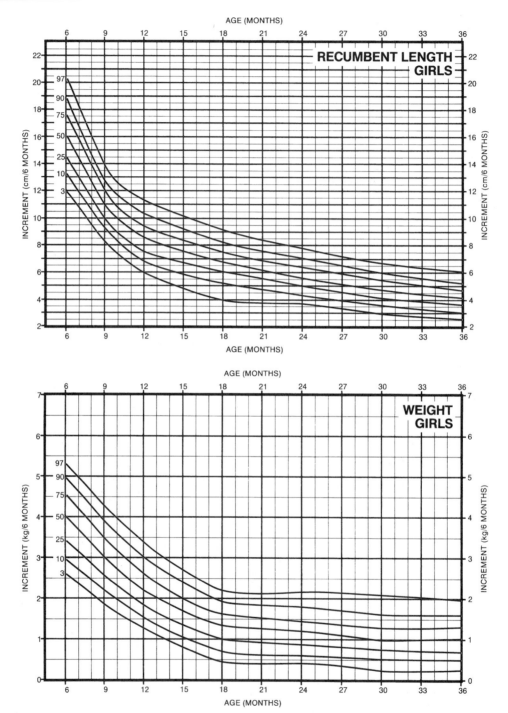

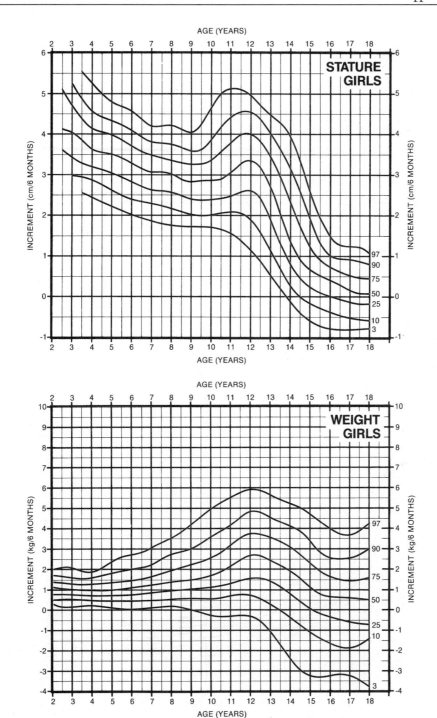

Ross
Growth &
Development
Program

INCREMENTAL GROWTH CHARTS—BOYS

Growth charts such as those that display the National Center for Health Statistics (NCHS) percentiles are used for routine assessment of physical growth.[1] Occasionally, growth rate (growth velocity or increment divided by time between measurements) should be assessed, eg, when an infant or preadolescent child is found to be at an extreme percentile or when a substantial shift of percentile has occurred on an NCHS growth chart. The accompanying incremental growth charts are useful for assessing growth rates. They do not replace written records of growth data or NCHS growth charts.

These incremental growth charts have been prepared from serial data for white US children whose growth is very close to that of children from whom the NCHS percentiles were derived.[1,2] Highly standardized anthropometric methods that conform to current recommendations were used to make all measurements.[3] Weight was measured as, or corrected to, nude weight. Recumbent length and stature were measured without shoes. Appropriate use of the incremental growth charts requires that similar methods be applied. Ideally, the same person should measure a child at the beginning and end of an interval.

References:

1. Hamill PVV, Drizd TA, Johnson CL, Reed RB, Roche AF, Moore WM: Physical growth: National Center for Health Statistics percentiles. *Am J Clin Nutr* 32: 607-629, 1979.

2. Roche AF, Himes JH: Incremental growth charts. *Am J Clin Nutr* 33: 2041-2052, 1980.

3. Fomon SJ: *Nutritional Disorders of Children. Prevention, Screening, and Follow-up.* Washington, DC: DHEW Publication No. (HSA) 76-5612, 1976.

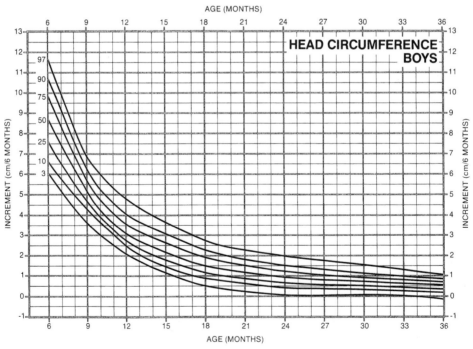

INSTRUCTIONS

1. Measure the child at the beginning and the end of a 6-month interval, if possible.

2. Subtract the initial measurement from the follow-up measurement to obtain the increment.

3. If the interval between measurements is not exactly 6 months (182 days), divide the increment by the interval in days and multiply by 182 to obtain the adjusted 6-month increment. The Table of Consecutively Numbered Days can be used to determine the interval between the measurements. If measurements are made in different years, add 365 to the day of the year for the follow-up measurement. Extrapolating increments from intervals of 3 months or less is not recommended.

4. Locate the intersection of the increment and the child's age at the **end** of the interval to determine the 6-month incremental percentile.

Interpretation: The accompanying charts permit definition of growth rate (growth velocity) relative to current reference data. Further investigation is indicated for children growing at rates markedly different from the 50th incremental percentile or for children whose incremental percentile changes rapidly.

Example 1 Boy at 5th NCHS* percentile at ages 6 and 12 months; aged 12 months at follow-up measurement.

Measurement	Length	Date	Day**
Follow-up	71.7 cm	August 10, 1981	222
Initial	63.4 cm	February 9, 1981	40
Increment =	8.3 cm	Interval =	182

His increment is 8.3 cm/6 months.
His increment is just below the 50th percentile.
He is short but growing at a normal rate.

* National Center for Health Statistics
** From Table of Consecutively Numbered Days

Example 2 Boy, aged 8 years at follow-up measurement.

Measurement	Stature	Date	Day*
Follow-up	119.1 cm	February 10, 1981	406**
Initial	118.0 cm	September 24, 1980	267
Increment =	1.1 cm	Interval =	139

His adjusted 6-month increment is $\frac{1.1 \text{ cm}}{139} \times 182 = 1.4$ cm.

His increment is below the 3rd percentile.
Further investigation is indicated.

* From Table of Consecutively Numbered Days
** February 10 is day 41, to which 365 is added because follow-up measurement is in a different year (41 – 365 = 406).

Table of Consecutively Numbered Days

Day	JAN	FEB	MAR	APR	MAY	JUN	JUL	AUG	SEP	OCT	NOV	DEC	Day
1	1	32	60	91	121	152	182	213	244	274	305	335	1
2	2	33	61	92	122	153	183	214	245	275	306	336	2
3	3	34	62	93	123	154	184	215	246	276	307	337	3
4	4	35	63	94	124	155	185	216	247	277	308	338	4
5	5	36	64	95	125	156	186	217	248	278	309	339	5
6	6	37	65	96	126	157	187	218	249	279	310	340	6
7	7	38	66	97	127	158	188	219	250	280	311	341	7
8	8	39	67	98	128	159	189	220	251	281	312	342	8
9	9	40	68	99	129	160	190	221	252	282	313	343	9
10	10	41	69	100	130	161	191	222	253	283	314	344	10
11	11	42	70	101	131	162	192	223	254	284	315	345	11
12	12	43	71	102	132	163	193	224	255	285	316	346	12
13	13	44	72	103	133	164	194	225	256	286	317	347	13
14	14	45	73	104	134	165	195	226	257	287	318	348	14
15	15	46	74	105	135	166	196	227	258	288	319	349	15
16	16	47	75	106	136	167	197	228	259	289	320	350	16
17	17	48	76	107	137	168	198	229	260	290	321	351	17
18	18	49	77	108	138	169	199	230	261	291	322	352	18
19	19	50	78	109	139	170	200	231	262	292	323	353	19
20	20	51	79	110	140	171	201	232	263	293	324	354	20
21	21	52	80	111	141	172	202	233	264	294	325	355	21
22	22	53	81	112	142	173	203	234	265	295	326	356	22
23	23	54	82	113	143	174	204	235	266	296	327	357	23
24	24	55	83	114	144	175	205	236	267	297	328	358	24
25	25	56	84	115	145	176	206	237	268	298	329	359	25
26	26	57	85	116	146	177	207	238	269	299	330	360	26
27	27	58	86	117	147	178	208	239	270	300	331	361	27
28	28	59	87	118	148	179	209	240	271	301	332	362	28
29	29	—	88	119	149	180	210	241	272	302	333	363	29
30	30	—	89	120	150	181	211	242	273	303	334	364	30
31	31	—	90	—	151	—	212	243	—	304	—	365	31
Day	JAN	FEB	MAR	APR	MAY	JUN	JUL	AUG	SEP	OCT	NOV	DEC	Day

Continued.

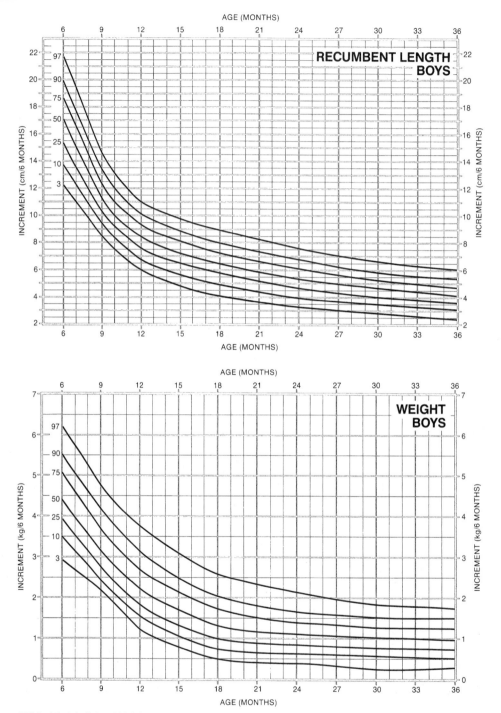

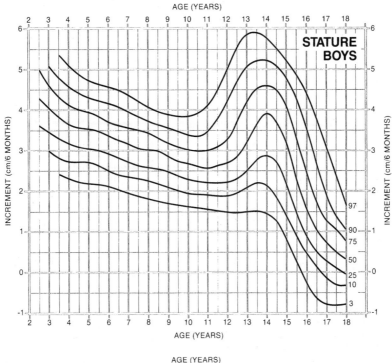

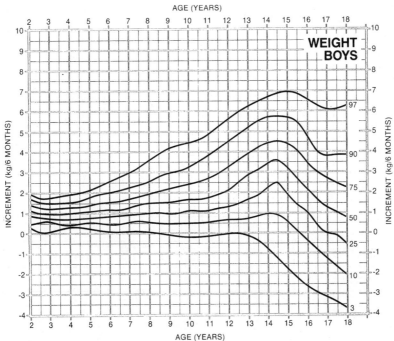

12-WEEK SUMMARY

GROWTH AND NUTRITION: WEEKLY AVERAGES

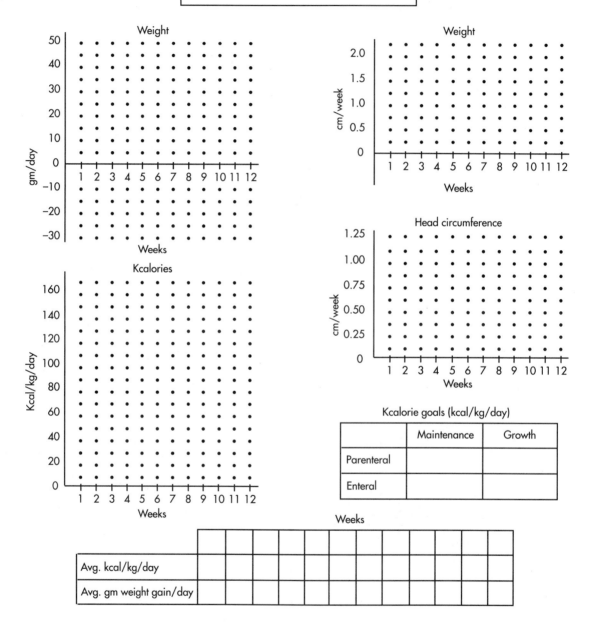

		Maintenance	Growth
Parenteral			
Enteral			

Kcalorie goals (kcal/kg/day)

Weeks

Avg. kcal/kg/day												
Avg. gm weight gain/day												

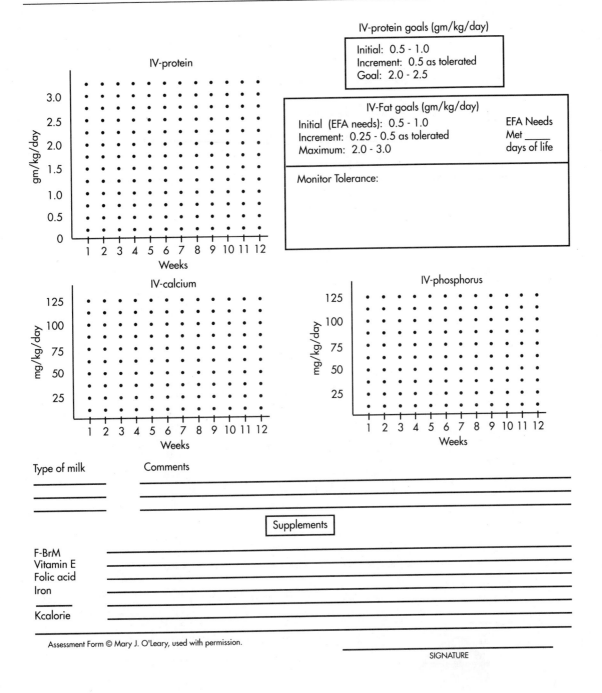

IV-protein

IV-protein goals (gm/kg/day)

Initial: 0.5 - 1.0
Increment: 0.5 as tolerated
Goal: 2.0 - 2.5

IV-Fat goals (gm/kg/day)

Initial (EFA needs): 0.5 - 1.0
Increment: 0.25 - 0.5 as tolerated
Maximum: 2.0 - 3.0

EFA Needs
Met _____
days of life

Monitor Tolerance:

IV-calcium

IV-phosphorus

Type of milk

Comments

Supplements

F-BrM
Vitamin E
Folic acid
Iron

Kcalorie

Assessment Form © Mary J. O'Leary, used with permission.

SIGNATURE

Ross
Growth &
Development
Program

Midarm Circumference and Skinfold Thickness Measurement Instructions and Percentiles

Midarm circumference and skinfold thickness measurements may be made on infants and children with an Inser-Tape™ Ross Insertion Tape and an Adipometer™ Skinfold Caliper. The measurements may be compared with age- and sex-specific percentiles prepared by the National Center for Health Statistics (NCHS) to facilitate their interpretation.[1] The NCHS data were collected on some 20,000 children between 1963 and 1974 in National Health Examination Surveys and in the first National Health and Nutrition Examination Survey (NHANES I).

The NCHS percentiles describe the distribution of these measurements for American children. The percentiles may be used as reference data but should not be considered "standards," "norms," or "ideals."[2] It is inappropriate to conclude that a measurement above or below an arbitrary percentile or value is unacceptable, because data are insufficient to validate associated risks. However, midarm circumference and skinfold measurements are useful for screening and for monitoring the progress of individual children who have been identified as having a potential or real problem of undernutrition or overnutrition.

Instructions

Measurements may be made on the right or the left side; measurements for the NCHS percentiles were made on the right side. Midarm circumference and triceps skinfold thickness are measured at the level of the midpoint between the acromion and olecranon. To locate the midpoint, use the side of the Inser-Tape labeled MIDPOINT MEASURE. With the child's arm bent at the elbow and palm up, position the tape vertically along the posterior arm so the same figure appears at the acromial process of the scapula and at the olecranon process of the ulna. The midpoint is at zero. Mark the midpoint to identify the level to measure midarm circumference and triceps skinfold thickness.

To measure midarm circumference, slip the loop of the Inser-Tape up the arm to the midpoint. With the arm hanging freely at the child's side, tighten the loop without compressing the arm. Measure to the nearest 0.1 cm.

To measure triceps skinfold thickness, grasp a fold of skin and subcutaneous tissue between the thumb and index finger about 1 cm above the midpoint, with the long axis of the skinfold parallel to the long axis of the arm. Place the jaws of the Adipometer over the skinfold at the previously marked midpoint. Holding the Adipometer in a horizontal position, apply force with the thumb and index finger until the lines on the caliper are opposite each other. After 2 or 3 seconds, read the measurement on the scale opposite the pointer to the nearest millimeter.

Subscapular skinfold thickness is measured by grasping a fold of skin and subcutaneous tissue just below the angle of the scapula and applying the jaws of the Adipometer. The child's shoulder and arm should be relaxed. The skinfold should parallel the natural cleavage lines of the skin, approximately 45° from the horizontal extending medially and upward. Apply force with the thumb and index finger until the lines on the caliper are opposite each other. After 2 or 3 seconds, read the measurement on the scale opposite the pointer to the nearest millimeter.

References

1. Johnson CL, Fulwood R, Abraham S, et al: Basic data on anthropometric measurements and angular measurements of the hip and knee joints for selected age groups, 1-74 years of age, United States, 1971-1975. *Vital and Health Statistics* Series 11, No. 219. DHHS Publication No. (PHS) 81-1669, 1981.
2. Owen GM: Measurement, recording, and assessment of skinfold thickness in childhood and adolescence: Report of a small meeting. *Am J Clin Nutr* 35:629-638, 1982.

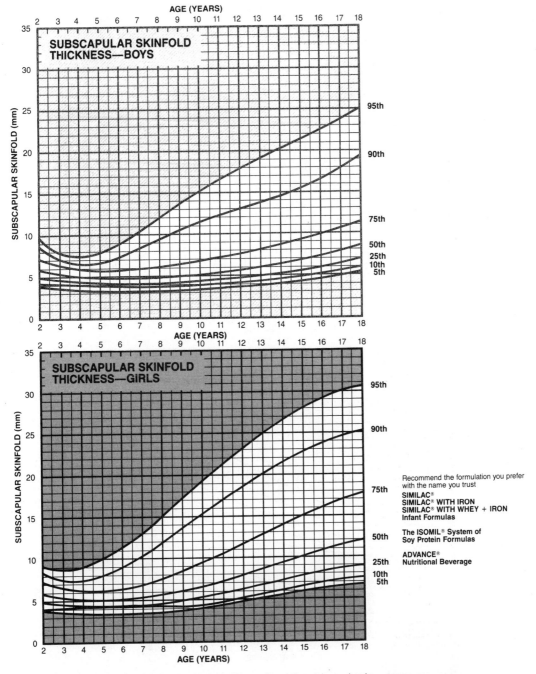

AGE (YEARS)

SUBSCAPULAR SKINFOLD THICKNESS—BOYS

SUBSCAPULAR SKINFOLD (mm)

95th
90th
75th
50th
25th
10th
5th

SUBSCAPULAR SKINFOLD THICKNESS—GIRLS

SUBSCAPULAR SKINFOLD (mm)

95th
90th
75th
50th
25th
10th
5th

AGE (YEARS)

Recommend the formulation you prefer
with the name you trust

SIMILAC®
SIMILAC® WITH IRON
SIMILAC® WITH WHEY + IRON
Infant Formulas

The **ISOMIL®** System of
Soy Protein Formulas

ADVANCE®
Nutritional Beverage

Figures adapted from Johnson CL, Fulwood R, Abraham S, et al: Basic data on anthropometric measurements and angular measurements of the hip and knee joints for selected age groups, 1-74 years of age, United States, 1971-1975. *Vital and Health Statistics* Series 11, No. 219. DHHS Publication No. (PHS) 81-1669, 1981.

© 1983 Ross Laboratories, Columbus, Ohio 43216. May be copied for individual patient use.

ROSS LABORATORIES
COLUMBUS, OHIO 43216
Division of Abbott Laboratories, USA
P552/DECEMBER 1983
LITHO IN USA

Continued.

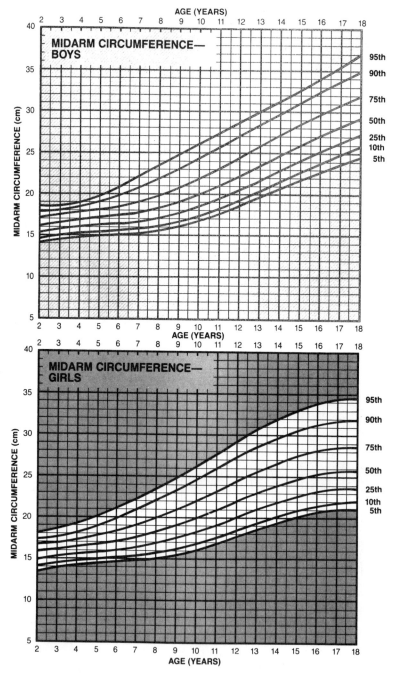

Figures adapted from Johnson CL, Fulwood R, Abraham S, et al: Basic data on anthropometric measurements and angular measurements of the hip and knee joints for selected age groups, 1-74 years of age, United States, 1971-1975. *Vital and Health Statistics* Series 11, No. 219. DHHS Publication No. (PHS) 81-1669, 1981.

© 1983 Ross Laboratories, Columbus, Ohio 43216. May be copied for individual patient use.

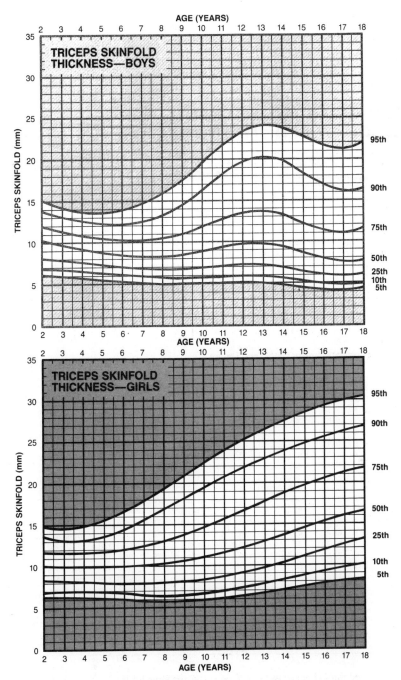

Figures adapted from Johnson CL, Fulwood R, Abraham S, et al: Basic data on anthropometric measurements and angular measurements of the hip and knee joints for selected age groups, 1-74 years of age, United States, 1971-1975. *Vital and Health Statistics* Series 11, No. 219. DHHS Publication No. (PHS) 81-1669, 1981.

© 1983 Ross Laboratories, Columbus, Ohio 43216. May be copied for individual patient use.

Ross
Growth &
Development
Program

PARENT-SPECIFIC ADJUSTMENTS FOR EVALUATION OF LENGTH AND STATURE–GIRLS AND BOYS

Recumbent length and stature (standing height) are affected by both genetic and nongenetic factors. The genetic component should be considered when concern arises that diet or disease may have retarded or accelerated growth. Adjustment of length or stature to take parental stature into account may help identify or explain the nature of a growth problem. Such adjustment may prompt diagnostic studies or suggest a genetic basis for the growth problem.

Parent-specific adjustment procedures have been developed for US children by Himes, Roche, and Thissen.* The accompanying tables of adjustments are adapted from their research. Parent-specific adjustments need not be done routinely but should be considered when a child has unusual length or stature. As a guideline for applying parent-specific adjustments, "unusual" may be defined as below the 5th percentile or above the 95th percentile in length or stature for age.

Occasionally, a child's length or stature may appear normal, but the parents (one or both) are very tall or very short. Under such circumstances, parent-specific adjustment also is appropriate. Rapid decrease or increase in a child's percentile for length or stature generally is not an indication for applying parent-specific adjustments because the cause is more likely to be nongenetic than genetic.

*Himes JH, Roche AF, Thissen D: *Parent-Specific Adjustments for Assessment of Recumbent Length and Stature.* Monographs in Paediatrics. Basel, Switzerland: S Karger, 1981, vol 13.

Table 1.   Metric Equivalents (cm) for Length and Stature

INCHES	0	¼	½	¾	INCHES	0	¼	½	¾	INCHES	0	¼	½	¾
12	30.5	31.1	31.7	32.4	36	91.4	92.1	92.7	93.3	60	152.4	153.0	153.7	154.3
13	33.0	33.7	34.3	34.9	37	94.0	94.6	95.2	95.9	61	154.9	155.6	156.2	156.8
14	35.6	36.2	36.8	37.5	38	96.5	97.2	97.8	98.4	62	157.5	158.1	158.7	159.4
15	38.1	38.7	39.4	40.0	39	99.1	99.7	100.3	101.0	63	160.0	160.7	161.3	161.9
16	40.6	41.3	41.9	42.5	40	101.6	102.2	102.9	103.5	64	162.6	163.2	163.8	164.5
17	43.2	43.8	44.4	45.1	41	104.1	104.8	105.4	106.0	65	165.1	165.7	166.4	167.0
18	45.7	46.4	47.0	47.6	42	106.7	107.3	107.9	108.6	66	167.6	168.3	168.9	169.5
19	48.3	48.9	49.5	50.2	43	109.2	109.9	110.5	111.1	67	170.2	170.8	171.4	172.1
20	50.8	51.4	52.1	52.7	44	111.8	112.4	113.0	113.7	68	172.7	173.4	174.0	174.6
21	53.3	54.0	54.6	55.2	45	114.3	114.9	115.6	116.2	69	175.3	175.9	176.5	177.2
22	55.9	56.5	57.1	57.8	46	116.8	117.5	118.1	118.7	70	177.8	178.4	179.1	179.7
23	58.4	59.1	59.7	60.3	47	119.4	120.0	120.6	121.3	71	180.3	181.0	181.6	182.2
24	61.0	61.6	62.2	62.9	48	121.9	122.6	123.2	123.8	72	182.9	183.5	184.1	184.8
25	63.5	64.1	64.8	65.4	49	124.5	125.1	125.7	126.4	73	185.4	186.1	186.7	187.3
26	66.0	66.7	67.3	67.9	50	127.0	127.6	128.3	128.9	74	188.0	188.6	189.2	189.9
27	68.6	69.2	69.8	70.5	51	129.5	130.2	130.8	131.4	75	190.5	191.1	191.8	192.4
28	71.1	71.8	72.4	73.0	52	132.1	132.7	133.3	134.0	76	193.0	193.7	194.3	194.9
29	73.7	74.3	74.9	75.6	53	134.6	135.3	135.9	136.5	77	195.6	196.2	196.8	197.5
30	76.2	76.8	77.5	78.1	54	137.2	137.8	138.4	139.1	78	198.1	198.8	199.4	200.0
31	78.7	79.4	80.0	80.6	55	139.7	140.3	141.0	141.6	79	200.7	201.3	201.9	202.6
32	81.3	81.9	82.5	83.2	56	142.2	142.9	143.5	144.1	80	203.2	203.8	204.5	205.1
33	83.8	84.5	85.1	85.7	57	144.8	145.4	146.0	146.7	81	205.7	206.4	207.0	207.6
34	86.4	87.0	87.6	88.3	58	147.3	148.0	148.6	149.2	82	208.3	208.9	209.5	210.2
35	88.9	89.5	90.2	90.8	59	149.9	150.5	151.1	151.8	83	210.8	211.5	212.1	212.7

© 1983 ROSS LABORATORIES

*The term "girl" is used throughout, however the process is the same for boys.

Table 2. Parent-Specific Adjustments (cm) for Stature of Girls From 3 to 18 Years

Age (Years)	Stature (cm)	Midparent Stature (cm)																	
		150	152	154	156	158	160	162	164	166	168	170	172	174	176	178	180	182	184
3	82.0– 83.9	6	5	4	4	3	2	1	1	1	0	−1	−1	−2	−3	−3	−4	−5	−6
	84.0– 93.9	6	6	5	4	3	3	2	1	1	0	−1	−1	−2	−3	−4	−4	−5	−6
	94.0–102.9	7	7	6	5	4	4	3	2	2	1	0	−1	−1	−2	−3	−3	−4	−5
4	92.0– 93.9	6	6	5	4	3	3	2	1	0	0	−1	−2	−3	−3	−4	−5	−6	−7
	94.0–103.9	7	6	6	5	4	3	2	2	1	0	−1	−1	−2	−3	−4	−4	−5	−6
	104.0–112.9	8	7	7	6	5	4	3	3	2	1	0	0	−1	−2	−3	−3	−4	−5
5	100.0–101.9	8	7	6	5	4	3	2	1	1	0	−1	−2	−3	−4	−5	−5	−6	−7
	102.0–111.9	8	7	6	6	5	4	3	2	1	1	0	−1	−1	−2	−3	−4	−5	−6
	112.0–120.9	9	8	7	7	6	5	4	3	2	1	1	0	−1	−2	−3	−4	−5	−6
6	106.0–109.9	9	8	7	6	5	4	3	2	1	0	−1	−2	−3	−4	−5	−6	−7	−8
	110.0–119.9	9	9	8	7	6	5	4	3	2	1	0	−1	−2	−3	−4	−5	−6	−7
	120.0–128.9	11	10	9	8	7	6	5	4	3	2	1	0	−1	−2	−3	−4	−5	−6
7	112.0–117.9	9	8	7	6	5	4	3	2	1	0	−1	−2	−3	−4	−5	−6	−7	−8
	118.0–127.9	10	9	8	7	6	5	4	3	2	1	0	−1	−2	−3	−4	−5	−6	−7
	128.0–136.9	11	10	9	8	7	6	5	4	3	2	1	0	−1	−2	−3	−4	−5	−6
8	116.0–123.9	9	8	7	6	5	4	3	2	1	0	−1	−2	−3	−4	−5	−6	−8	−9
	124.0–133.9	10	9	8	7	6	5	4	3	2	1	0	−1	−2	−3	−4	−5	−7	−8
	134.0–142.9	11	10	9	8	7	6	5	4	3	2	1	0	−1	−2	−3	−4	−6	−7
9	122.0–131.9	10	9	8	7	6	5	3	2	1	0	−1	−2	−3	−4	−5	−6	−7	−9
	132.0–141.9	11	10	9	8	7	6	4	3	2	1	0	−1	−2	−3	−4	−5	−7	−8
	142.0–150.9	12	11	10	9	8	6	5	4	3	2	1	0	−1	−2	−3	−5	−6	−7
10	126.0–127.9	10	9	7	6	5	4	3	2	1	0	−1	−2	−3	−5	−6	−7	−8	−9
	128.0–137.9	10	9	8	7	6	5	4	2	1	0	−1	−2	−3	−4	−5	−6	−7	−8
	138.0–147.9	11	10	9	8	6	5	4	3	2	1	0	−1	−2	−3	−4	−5	−7	−8
	148.0–156.9	12	10	9	8	7	6	5	4	3	2	1	0	−1	−3	−4	−5	−6	−7
11	130.0–133.9	10	9	8	6	5	4	3	2	1	0	−1	−2	−3	−4	−6	−7	−8	−9
	134.0–143.9	10	9	8	7	6	5	4	3	1	0	−1	−2	−3	−4	−5	−6	−7	−8
	144.0–153.9	11	10	9	7	6	5	4	3	2	1	0	−1	−2	−3	−5	−6	−7	−8
	154.0–162.9	11	10	9	8	7	6	5	4	3	1	0	−1	−2	−3	−4	−5	−6	−7
12	134.0–139.9	10	9	8	7	6	5	3	2	1	0	−1	−3	−4	−5	−6	−7	−8	−10
	140.0–149.9	11	10	9	7	6	5	4	3	2	0	−1	−2	−3	−4	−6	−7	−8	−9
	150.0–159.9	12	10	9	8	7	6	5	3	2	1	0	−1	−3	−4	−5	−6	−7	−8
	160.0–168.9	12	11	10	9	8	6	5	4	3	2	0	−1	−2	−3	−4	−5	−7	−8
13	140.0–145.9	10	9	8	7	6	4	3	2	1	0	−1	−3	−4	−5	−6	−7	−8	−10
	146.0–155.9	11	10	9	7	6	5	4	3	2	0	−1	−2	−3	−4	−6	−7	−8	−9
	156.0–165.9	12	10	9	8	7	6	5	3	2	1	0	−1	−3	−4	−5	−6	−7	−8
	166.0–174.9	12	11	10	9	8	6	5	4	3	2	1	−1	−2	−3	−4	−5	−7	−8
14	146.0–149.9	10	9	8	6	5	4	3	2	1	0	−1	−3	−4	−5	−6	−7	−8	−9
	150.0–159.9	11	9	8	7	6	5	4	3	1	0	−1	−2	−3	−4	−5	−7	−8	−9
	160.0–169.9	11	10	9	8	7	6	5	3	2	1	0	−1	−2	−3	−5	−6	−7	−8
	170.0–178.9	12	11	10	9	8	6	5	4	3	2	1	0	−2	−3	−4	−5	−6	−7
15	146.0–151.9	10	9	8	7	5	4	3	2	1	−1	−2	−3	−4	−5	−6	−8	−9	−10
	152.0–161.9	11	10	9	7	6	5	4	3	1	0	−1	−2	−3	−4	−6	−7	−8	−9
	162.0–171.9	12	11	10	8	7	6	5	4	2	1	0	−1	−2	−4	−5	−6	−7	−8
	172.0–180.9	13	12	11	9	8	7	6	5	3	2	1	0	−1	−3	−4	−5	−6	−7
16	146.0–151.9	11	10	8	7	6	5	3	2	1	−1	−2	−3	−4	−6	−7	−8	−10	−11
	152.0–161.9	12	10	9	8	7	5	4	3	2	0	−1	−2	−4	−5	−6	−7	−9	−10
	162.0–171.9	13	12	10	9	8	6	5	4	3	1	0	−1	−3	−4	−5	−6	−8	−9
	172.0–180.9	14	13	11	10	9	7	6	5	4	2	1	0	−2	−3	−4	−5	−7	−8
17	148.0–153.9	11	10	9	7	6	5	3	2	1	0	−2	−3	−4	−6	−7	−8	−10	−11
	154.0–163.9	12	11	10	8	7	6	4	3	2	0	−1	−2	−4	−5	−6	−8	−9	−10
	164.0–173.9	13	12	11	9	8	7	5	4	3	1	0	−1	−3	−4	−5	−6	−8	−9
	174.0–182.9	14	13	12	10	9	8	6	5	4	2	1	0	−1	−3	−4	−5	−7	−8
18	148.0–149.9	10	9	8	7	5	4	3	2	1	−1	−2	−3	−4	−6	−7	−8	−9	−10
	150.0–159.9	11	10	8	7	6	5	4	2	1	0	−1	−3	−4	−5	−6	−7	−9	−10
	160.0–169.9	12	11	9	8	7	6	4	3	2	1	0	−2	−3	−4	−5	−6	−8	−9
	170.0–178.9	13	11	10	9	8	7	5	4	3	2	1	−1	−2	−3	−4	−5	−7	−8

Continued.

Table 3.   Parent-Specific Adjustments (cm) for Stature of Boys From 3 to 18 Years

Age (Years)	Stature (cm)	Midparent Stature (cm)																	
		150	152	154	156	158	160	162	164	166	168	170	172	174	176	178	180	182	184
3	86.0– 87.9	7	6	5	5	4	3	2	1	1	0	−1	−2	−3	−3	−4	−5	−6	−7
	88.0– 97.9	8	7	6	5	4	4	3	2	1	0	−1	−1	−2	−3	−4	−5	−5	−6
	98.0–106.9	8	8	7	6	5	4	4	3	2	1	0	0	−1	−2	−3	−4	−4	−5
4	90.0– 93.9	7	6	5	4	4	3	2	1	0	−1	−1	−2	−3	−4	−5	−5	−6	−7
	94.0–103.9	8	7	6	5	4	3	3	2	1	0	−1	−1	−2	−3	−4	−5	−6	−6
	104.0–112.9	8	8	7	6	5	4	3	3	2	1	0	−1	−1	−2	−3	−4	−5	−6
5	96.0–103.9	8	7	6	5	4	3	2	1	0	0	−1	−2	−3	−4	−5	−6	−7	−8
	104.0–113.9	9	8	7	6	5	4	3	2	1	0	0	−1	−2	−3	−4	−5	−6	−7
	114.0–122.9	9	9	8	7	6	5	4	3	2	1	0	0	−1	−2	−3	−4	−5	−6
6	102.0–111.9	8	7	7	6	5	4	3	2	1	0	−1	−2	−3	−4	−5	−6	−7	−8
	112.0–121.9	9	8	7	7	6	5	4	3	2	1	0	−1	−2	−3	−4	−5	−6	−7
	122.0–130.9	10	9	8	7	6	6	5	4	3	2	1	0	−1	−2	−3	−4	−5	−6
7	108.0–117.9	9	8	7	6	5	4	3	2	1	0	−1	−2	−4	−5	−6	−7	−8	−9
	118.0–127.9	10	9	8	7	6	5	4	3	2	1	0	−1	−2	−4	−5	−6	−7	−8
	128.0–136.9	12	10	9	8	7	6	5	4	3	2	1	0	−1	−2	−4	−5	−6	−7
8	114.0–115.9	10	9	8	6	5	4	3	2	1	−1	−2	−3	−4	−5	−6	−8	−9	−10
	116.0–125.9	11	9	8	7	6	5	4	2	1	0	−1	−2	−3	−5	−6	−7	−8	−9
	126.0–135.9	12	10	9	8	7	6	5	3	2	1	0	−1	−2	−4	−5	−6	−7	−8
	136.0–144.9	13	12	10	9	8	7	6	5	3	2	1	0	−1	−2	−4	−5	−6	−7
9	120.0–121.9	11	9	8	7	6	4	3	2	1	0	−2	−3	−4	−5	−7	−8	−9	−10
	122.0–131.9	11	10	9	8	6	5	4	3	1	0	−1	−2	−3	−5	−6	−7	−8	−10
	132.0–141.9	12	11	10	9	7	6	5	4	2	1	0	−1	−2	−4	−5	−6	−7	−9
	142.0–150.9	13	12	11	10	8	7	6	5	4	2	1	0	−1	−3	−4	−5	−6	−7
10	124.0–127.9	11	10	9	7	6	5	3	2	1	−1	−2	−3	−5	−6	−7	−9	−10	−11
	128.0–137.9	12	11	10	8	7	6	4	3	2	0	−1	−2	−4	−5	−6	−8	−9	−10
	138.0–147.9	13	12	11	9	8	7	5	4	3	1	0	−1	−3	−4	−5	−7	−8	−9
	148.0–158.9	14	13	12	11	9	8	7	5	4	3	1	0	−1	−3	−4	−5	−7	−8
11	128.0–133.9	12	10	9	8	6	5	4	2	1	0	−2	−3	−5	−6	−7	−9	−10	−11
	134.0–143.9	12	11	10	8	7	6	4	3	2	0	−1	−2	−4	−5	−6	−8	−9	−10
	144.0–153.9	14	12	11	10	8	7	5	4	3	1	0	−1	−3	−4	−5	−7	−8	−9
	154.0–162.9	15	13	12	11	9	8	7	5	4	3	1	0	−2	−3	−4	−6	−7	−8
12	132.0–141.9	12	10	9	8	6	5	4	2	1	0	−2	−3	−4	−6	−7	−8	−10	−11
	142.0–151.9	13	11	10	9	7	6	5	3	2	1	−1	−2	−3	−5	−6	−7	−9	−10
	152.0–161.9	13	12	11	9	8	7	5	4	3	1	0	−1	−2	−4	−5	−6	−8	−9
	162.0–170.9	14	13	12	10	9	8	6	5	4	2	1	0	−2	−3	−4	−6	−7	−8
13	136.0–139.9	12	10	9	8	6	5	4	2	1	−1	−2	−3	−5	−6	−7	−9	−10	−12
	140.0–149.9	12	11	10	8	7	6	4	3	1	0	−1	−3	−4	−6	−7	−8	−10	−11
	150.0–159.9	13	12	10	9	8	6	5	4	2	1	−1	−2	−3	−5	−6	−7	−9	−10
	160.0–169.9	14	13	11	10	8	7	6	4	3	2	0	−1	−3	−4	−5	−7	−8	−9
	170.0–178.9	15	13	12	11	9	8	6	5	4	2	1	0	−2	−3	−5	−6	−7	−9
14	142.0–145.9	13	11	10	8	7	5	4	2	1	−1	−2	−4	−5	−7	−8	−10	−11	−13
	146.0–155.9	14	12	11	9	8	6	5	3	1	0	−2	−3	−5	−6	−8	−9	−11	−12
	156.0–165.9	15	13	11	10	8	7	5	4	2	1	−1	−2	−4	−5	−7	−8	−10	−11
	166.0–175.9	15	14	12	11	9	8	6	5	3	2	0	−1	−3	−4	−6	−7	−9	−11
	176.0–184.9	16	15	13	12	10	9	7	6	4	3	1	−1	−2	−4	−5	−7	−8	−10
15	148.0–151.9	14	13	11	9	7	6	4	2	0	−1	−3	−5	−7	−8	−10	−12	−14	−15
	152.0–161.9	15	14	12	10	8	7	5	3	1	0	−2	−4	−6	−7	−9	−11	−13	−14
	162.0–171.9	17	15	13	11	10	8	6	4	3	1	−1	−3	−4	−6	−8	−10	−11	−13
	172.0–181.9	18	16	14	13	11	9	7	6	4	2	0	−1	−3	−5	−7	−8	−10	−12
	182.0–190.9	19	17	16	14	12	10	9	7	5	3	2	0	−2	−4	−5	−7	−9	−11
16	156.0–163.9	17	15	13	11	9	7	5	3	1	−1	−3	−5	−7	−9	−11	−13	−16	−18
	164.0–173.9	19	17	15	13	10	8	6	4	2	0	−2	−4	−6	−8	−10	−12	−14	−16
	174.0–183.9	21	19	17	15	12	10	8	6	4	2	0	−2	−4	−6	−8	−10	−12	−14
	184.0–192.9	23	21	19	17	14	12	10	8	6	4	2	0	−2	−4	−6	−8	−10	−12
17	162.0–165.9	17	15	13	11	9	7	4	2	0	−2	−4	−7	−9	−11	−13	−15	−17	−20
	166.0–175.9	20	17	15	13	11	9	6	4	2	0	−2	−4	−7	−9	−11	−13	−15	−18
	176.0–185.9	22	20	18	16	13	11	9	7	5	3	0	−2	−4	−6	−8	−11	−13	−15
	186.0–194.9	25	23	20	18	16	14	12	9	7	5	3	1	−1	−4	−6	−8	−10	−12
18	160.0–165.9	18	16	13	11	9	6	4	2	0	−3	−5	−7	−10	−12	−14	−17	−19	−21
	166.0–175.9	20	18	16	13	11	9	7	4	2	0	−3	−5	−7	−10	−12	−14	−17	−19
	176.0–185.9	23	21	19	16	14	12	9	7	5	3	0	−2	−4	−7	−9	−11	−14	−16
	186.0–194.9	26	24	22	19	17	15	12	10	8	6	3	1	−1	−4	−6	−8	−11	−13

INSTRUCTIONS

1. Measure and record mother's stature.

2. Measure and record father's stature.

3. When one parent's stature cannot be measured, the measured parent's estimate of the other parent's stature (in cm) can be substituted for measured stature, and midparent stature can be calculated as in instruction 4. Alternatively, the measured parent's perception of the other parent's stature (short, medium, or tall) can be used to determine midparent stature directly from Table 4.

Table 4. **Midparent Stature (cm) When Measured Parent Reports Other Parent's Stature as Short, Medium, or Tall**

Measured Parent's Stature (cm)	When Mother Reports Father's Stature as			When Father Reports Mother's Stature as		
	Short†	Medium†	Tall†	Short‡	Medium‡	Tall‡
146	156	162	166	150	154	158
148	158	162	166	152	156	160
150	158	164	168	152	156	160
152	160	164	168	154	158	162
154	160	166	170	154	158	162
156	162	166	170	156	160	164
158	162	168	172	156	160	164
160	164	168	172	158	162	166
162	164	170	174	158	162	166
164	166	170	174	160	164	168
166	166	172	176	160	164	168
168	168	172	176	162	166	170
170	168	174	178	162	166	170
172	170	174	178	164	168	172
174	170	176	180	164	168	172
176	172	176	180	166	170	174
178	172	178	182	166	170	174
180	174	178	182	168	172	176
182	174	180	184	168	172	176
184	176	180	184	170	174	178
186	176	182	—	170	174	178
188	178	182	—	172	176	180
190	178	184	—	172	176	180
192	180	184	—	174	178	182
194	180	—	—	174	178	182
196	182	—	—	176	180	184
198	182	—	—	176	180	184

* All midparent statures are rounded to the nearest 2 cm to facilitate use of Tables 2 and 3.
† Values for father's stature used in calculations of midparent stature: short, 167.6 cm (5 ft 6 in.); medium, 176.3 cm (5 ft 9½ in.); tall, 185.4 cm (6 ft 1 in.).
‡ Values for mother's stature used in calculations of midparent stature: short, 154.9 cm (5 ft 1 in.); medium, 162.8 cm (5 ft 4 in.); tall, 170.7 cm (5 ft 7¼ in.).

4. Calculate midparent stature by adding the mother's stature and the father's stature in cm and dividing by two. Metric equivalents for stature are shown in Table 1.

5. Measure, record, and plot the girl's length (birth to 36 months) or stature (3 to 18 years) in cm on the appropriate growth chart that displays the National Center for Health Statistics (NCHS) percentiles. Metric equivalents for length and stature are shown in Table 1.

6. Calculate the girl's adjusted length or stature by using the parent-specific adjustments from Table 2 for length or from Table 3 for stature:
   a. Locate the age closest to that achieved by the girl.
   b. For that age, locate the horizontal row that includes the girl's length or stature.
   c. Locate the vertical column closest to the midparent stature for the girl's mother and father.
   d. The parent-specific adjustment (in cm) appears at the row-column intersection.
   e. Add the parent-specific adjustment to the girl's length or stature if the factor has no sign; subtract the adjustment if it has a minus sign.

7. Determine the girl's parent-specific adjusted percentile by plotting adjusted length or stature on the appropriate NCHS growth chart. Clearly label plotted measurements as being actual or adjusted values.

Interpretation: A girl at a low percentile for actual length or stature whose parents are short probably is genetically short. However, her shortness, particularly if it is extreme, may have additional contributing factors that should be considered.

If the girl's adjusted percentile is low, her growth probably has been slowed by nongenetic factors, and diagnostic studies should be considered. If the parents are tall, the girl's adjusted percentile will be lower than her actual percentile, and her shortness is more likely due to malnutrition or disease.

A girl at a high adjusted percentile for length or stature most often will be found to have accelerated maturation. Rarely, a specific disorder such as Marfan's syndrome or pituitary gigantism may be responsible for the girl's unusual length or stature.

Follow-Up: Counseling may be advisable when a girl is judged to be genetically short or tall. Additional contributing factors should be considered and growth monitored to confirm the relative stability of the girl's length or stature percentile.

Further investigation and modification of diet or specific therapy are indicated for a girl with unusual length or stature due to malnutrition or disease. Growth should be monitored to evaluate the effectiveness of dietary management or drug therapy.

Example	Girl aged 8 years, stature 46¾ in., mother's stature 68½ in., and father's stature reported as "tall."

Daughter's actual stature in cm is 118.7 (from Table 1).
Daughter's actual percentile is 10th (from NCHS growth chart).
Mother's stature in cm is 174.0 (from Table 1).
Midparent stature is 180.0 cm (from Table 4).
Adjustment is − 6 cm (from Table 3).
Daughter's adjusted stature is 118.7 cm − 6 cm = 112.7 cm.
Daughter's adjusted percentile is below the 5th (from NCHS growth chart).
Interpretation: Probably nongenetically short. Further investigation is indicated.

Example	Boy aged 8 years, stature 47¼ in., mother's stature 68½ in., and father's stature reported as "tall."

Son's actual stature in cm is 120.0 (from Table 1).
Son's actual percentile is 10th (from NCHS growth chart).
Mother's stature in cm is 174.0 (from Table 1).
Midparent stature is 180.0 cm (from Table 4).
Adjustment is − 7 cm (from Table 3).
Son's adjusted stature is 120.0 cm − 7 cm = 113.0 cm.
Son's adjusted percentile is below the 5th (from NCHS growth chart).
Interpretation: Probably nongenetically short. Further investigation is indicated.

In vivo performance confirms . . .
SIMILAC®
SIMILAC® WITH IRON
Infant Formulas
closest to mother's milk

Glossary

ABC analysis a method of analyzing interactional behavior between two individuals utilizing antecedents, the behavior being analyzed, and the consequences of that behavior

acidosis a pathological condition resulting from accumulation of acid or depletion of alkaline reserves

Acquired Immunodeficiency Syndrome a syndrome caused by the human immunodeficiency virus which causes cell dysfunction or death after the virus replicates

acrocyanosis a condition characterized by cyanotic discoloration, coldness, and sweating of the extremities

adolescence the period of maturation of a child's mind and body terminating with attainment of adulthood

affectional ties emotional attachment and degree of psychological involvement between parent and child

allergens substances that cause an altered response of cells and, as a result, allergies

allergy a hypersensitive state caused by the interaction of an allergen with an antibody

alopecia partial or complete loss of hair

alopecia totalis complete loss of hair

amenorrhea absence of menstruation

amylase an enzyme that catalyzes the hydrolysis of starch to glucose

anabolic steroids compounds derived from testosterone to promote body growth and masculinizing effects

anorexia lack of appetite for food

anorexia nervosa a disorder characterized by prolonged refusal to eat, resulting in amenorrhea, emaciation, and distorted body image

anthropometric scientific measurements of various parts of the body

appetite the natural desire or craving for food

arteriosclerosis hardening, thickening, and loss of elasticity of the arteries

aspiration inhaling

assessment a critical analysis of the status or quality of a condition

asymmetry dissimilarity in corresponding parts or organs on opposite sides of the body that are normally alike

atherosclerosis a term denoting a number of different processes resulting in patchy deposition of various materials in the intima of the arteries

athetosis a condition characterized by constant but slow and recurrent movements of the hands, feet, and other parts of the body

Attention Deficit Hyperactivity Disorder (Attentional Deficit Disorder) a clinical diagnosis in children characterized by fidgeting and squirming, easy distractibility, excessive talking, and other disruptive behaviors

basal energy needs energy expended in maintenance of basal metabolic processes or involuntary activities in the body (respiration, circulation, gastrointestinal function, muscle tone, and body temperature) and functional activities of organs

behavior modification a therapeutic tool often employed to extinguish socially unacceptable behavior

bioavailability the degree of availability of a substance to the organism

biochemical malnutrition (biochemical signs of malnutrition) abnormal levels of constituents indicative of normal nutritional state that can be attributed to excess or deficiency of nutrient intake

"bird-feeding" feeding an individual with his or her head thrown back

body image a mental picture a person has of his or her physical self

body image distortion an abnormal or untrue view of one's body size

bonding development of a close emotional tie to another individual or to a newborn infant

413

botulism food poisoning caused by the toxin produced by *Clostridium botulinum*

bronchopulmonary dysplasia a disorder characterized by hypoxia, hypercardia, and oxygen dependency: a complication of hyalinemembrane disease

bulimia nervosa an insatiable craving for food, often resulting in periods of continuous eating followed by depression and self-deprivation and purging

cachexia general ill health marked by weakness and emaciation

carotenemia the presence of high levels of carotene in the blood resulting in yellow appearance of the skin

Carpenter syndrome a syndrome of abnormalities which include obesity, mental deficiency, and abnormalities of the hands, feet, and craniofacial area

casein the principal protein of milk

catch-up growth increased growth velocity after remediation of medical or nutritional insult which precipitated growth failure

cell differentiation diversification of cells

central vs. peripheral vascular routes techniques for administering parenteral solutions to the preterm infant; the route chosen depends on the energy needs of the infant and the expected duration of parenteral support

cephalocaudal from head to toe, the sequence in which a normal developmental pattern occurs

cheilosis fissures of lips and mouth due to dietary riboflavin deficiency

chylomicron the largest and lightest of blood lipids

cineradiographic the making of motion picture record of successive images appearing on a fluoroscopic screen

clinical malnutrition (clinical signs of malnutrition) changes in skin, hair, membranes, or growth that can be attributed to an excessive or deficient intake of a nutrient or nutrients

Cohen syndrome a syndrome of abnormalities including obesity, moderate mental retardation, narrow hands and feet, lumbar lordosis, and facial abnormalities

colostrum the first milk secreted by the mammary gland after parturition

congenital existing at, and usually before birth

convenience foods foods requiring little or no preparation

Cornelia de Lange syndrome a syndrome associated with short stature, thin down-turned upper lip, and micrognathia

cultural paradox when two conflicting situations prevail in a society, such as when abundant food is available and used lavishly while at the same time slimness is highly valued

desquamation the cornified layer of the skin is shed in fine scales

developmental obesity obesity which results primarily from psychological factors in the family

Down syndrome a congenital condition caused by trisomy 21, a chromosomal abnormality; characterized by a small, anteroposteriorly flattened skull, short flat-bridged nose, epicanthus, short phalanges, widened space between the first and second digits of hands and feet, and moderate to severe mental retardation

Duchenne's muscular dystrophy a sex-linked recessive genetic disorder involving progressive degeneration of skeletal muscle and resulting weakness

dysplasia congenita a congenital condition resulting in abnormal reduction in cell size and small stature

eating disorder to have an abnormal use of food, that is, to eat too little, too much or to purge and accompanying psychological problems

enteral by way of the intestine

enteroglucagon a gastrointestinal hormone

epiphyseal closure the final calcification of the ends of the long bones causing cessation of growth

erythropoiesis the production of red blood cells

extension movement that brings the members of a limb into or toward a straight condition

extensor any muscle that extends a joint

extinction removing a positive reinforcer to decrease negative behaviors

fading a technique used to teach new behaviors in which the entire behavior must be completed before reinforcement

family-style service meal service where individuals select their portions from serving containers that are passed

fast food food items that are cooked and ready to be eaten immediately

feedback chains of response between parent and child

ferritin an iron complex found in liver, spleen, bone marrow, and reticuloendothelia cells; it is the chief storage form of iron in the body

fetal alcohol syndrome a syndrome resulting from fetal exposure to the teratogenic effects of alcohol

flexed bent or put into a state of being bent

food asphyxiation loss of consciousness from too little oxygen and too much carbon dioxide in the blood; brought about by a piece of food lodged in the throat

food idiosyncrasies individual or peculiar food habits or choices

gag reflex elevation of the soft palate and retching elicited by touching the back of the tongue or the wall of the pharynx

gastrin a hormone elaborated by the pyloric mucosa

that stimulates hydrochloric acid secretion by the parietal cells

gavage feeding by insertion of a stomach tube through the mouth and into the stomach

gestational age the age of the infant calculated from the beginning of conception, often used with low birth weight infants

gluconeogenesis the formation of glucose or glycogen from non-carbohydrate sources such as glyceral and glucogenic amino acids

glucosuria the presence of sugar in the urine

goitrogenic effect an effect of substances in some foods capable of producing goiter

Healthy People 2000: Nutrition Objectives based on Dietary Guidelines for Americans, proposes achievable goals for improved nutritional status

hematocrit the volume percentage of red blood cells in the blood

hemoglobin the oxygen-carrying pigment of the erythrocytes

heparin an anticoagulant; it inhibits coagulation by preventing conversion of prothrombin to thrombin

high density lipoproteins protein combined with lipids which carries cholesterol in the blood to the liver where it is released and excreted

hirsutism excessive body hair in a masculine distribution

hunger craving for food more pronounced than appetite

Hurler syndrome a condition described by Hurler in 1919 characterized by deceleration of growth between 6 and 18 months, gross retardation, and a number of physical malformations

hyaline membrane disease respiratory distress syndrome occurring most frequently in premature infants

hyperactivity abnormally increased activity

hyperammonemia an abnormally high level of ammonia in the blood

hyperbilirubinemia excess bilirubin in the blood that may lead to jaundice

hypercholesterolemia a condition in which blood cholesterol is above normal limits

hyperglycemia increased glucose concentration in the blood above normal limits

hyperglycinemia increased glycine concentration in the blood

hypernatremia high level of sodium in the blood

hyperplasia an abnormal increase in the number of cells composing a tissue or organ

hypertension elevation of blood pressure above normal

hypertonia a condition of excessive tone, tension, or activity

hypertrophy increase in cell size

hypocalcemia below normal levels of calcium in the blood

hypocholesterolemia a condition in which blood cholesterol is below normal limits

infectious complications difficulties in providing adequate parenteral nutrients due to infection

insensible water loss loss of water non-perceptible to the senses

ketones compounds derived from the oxidation of a secondary alcohol

kwashiorkor protein deficiency disease occurring in children

lactoovovegetarian a vegetarian who consumes dairy foods and eggs in addition to plant foods

lactovegetarian a vegetarian who consumes dairy foods in addition to plant foods

Laurence Moon-Biedl syndrome a syndrome characterized by obesity, mental retardation, polydactyly, genital hypoplasia or hypogonadism (or both), and retinitis pigmentosa

linoleic acid essential fatty acid; a polyunsaturated fatty acid with 2 double bonds and 18 carbon atoms

low density lipoproteins a plasma protein containing high levels of cholesterol that appears to damage the arteries

macrobiotic vegetarian persons who consume vegan or vegetarian diets which also involve non-animal food avoidances and extensive use of unprocessed, unrefined foods

marasmus a form of extreme undernutrition

megadose an amount of a substance, i.e., nutrients or vitamins, that vastly exceeds the typical amount

menarche the beginning of the menstrual function

metabolic acidosis a disturbance in which the acid-base status of the body shifts toward the acid side because of changes in the fixed acids and bases

metabolic complications problems arising in provision of nutrients via parenteral nutrition because of changes in metabolic response to the solution being administered

methemoglobinemia the presence of methemoglobin, a compound formed after poisoning by some substances, in the blood

microcytic abnormally small red blood cell

modified fast a provision of a small percentage of the energy and nutrients needed to maintain nourishment

morbidly obese to be so overweight that the condition interferes with health and physical function

motilin a gastrointestinal hormone

motility effects effects on motility of gastrointestinal tract

myelomeningocele a developmental defect in which

a hernial sac containing a portion of the spinal cord, its meninges, and cerebrospinal fluid protrudes from the back

narcissism an abnormal interest in oneself, especially one's body and sexual characteristics

National Cholesterol Education Program a federal program that provides guidance and education to reduce coronary heart disease in the general population, including health screening and dietary changes

National School Lunch Program a uniform federal school feeding program administered by the USDA

necrotizing enterocolitis a disease seen in infants which involves degeneration of a part of the intestinal tract

neonatal growth pattern the three phases of growth of neonates are (1) weight loss, (2) regaining of birth weight, and (3) sustained growth

neurotensin a gastrointestinal hormone

neutrophil a cell that stains easily with neutral dye

Nutrition Education Training Program a federally funded program administered by the USDA to improve nutrition education and knowledge for school children, teachers, and school feeding staff

nutritional adequacy the provision of all essential nutrients in amounts necessary for the individual

obese about 20% or more above normal weight-height ranges with a high degree of fatness

obesity a state of malnutrition in which the accumulation of depot fat is so excessive that function is disturbed

occiput the back part of the head

omphalocele hernia of the naval

oral motor skills the motor coordination of tongue, lips, mandible, cheeks, and other parameters that affect sucking, chewing, and the coordination of other skills with swallowing

osmotic diuresis increased secretion of urine due to difference in concentration gradient across a membrane wall

osteomalacia inadequate mineralization of the organic matrix of the bones resulting in skeletal deformities and fractures

osteopenia insufficiency of bone resulting from reduced production or increased breakdown of the bone

osteoporosis decreased density of bone

overweight the term applied to a person who is about 10% to 20% above desirable weight

palmar grasp grasp of objects with the palm of the hand

paraprofessional a trained aide who assists a professional person

parenteral injection of substances into the body through any route other than the alimentary tract

passive response pattern behavioral patterns that subordinate the individual's own interest to the demands of others

pharynx the muscular and membranous tube extending from the oral cavity to the esophagus

phenylketonuria inactivity or absence of phenylalanine hydroxylase in the liver; early and continuous restriction of dietary phenylalanine can prevent mental retardation

photodegradation the break-down of nutrients in a solution due to exposure to light

Piaget's theory of learning a theory of cognitive development in children based on progressive developmental stages

pica an abnormal craving to consume unusual substances such as clay, chalk, laundry starch, and dirt

pincer grasp grasp of small object with the thumb and index finger

plasma amino acid levels/patterns the amino acid concentration in plasma; often measured as an index of protein quality

plate waste food items refused or discarded from the standard menu

poverty line guidelines for family income for eligibility for federal supplemental income or food programs; these guidelines are periodically revised to reflect the economic status of the nation

Prader-Willi syndrome a syndrome characterized by small genitals, mental retardation, and obesity; affected individuals have an abnormal craving for food

prehension the act of seizing or grasping

propensity to interact the ability and desire of parent or child to give and receive communication

proprioceptive facilitation the promotion or hastening of receiving stimulations within the tissues of the body

protein energy malnutrition the generic term to cover any protein energy deficiency state; infants and children are particularly vulnerable; early symptoms include loss of appetite, easy fatigability, loss of weight, and retarded growth

prothrombin the protein in blood plasma needed for blood clotting

pseudoachondroplasia a group of disorders producing short-limb short stature, moderately severe retardation of trunk height, and normal face

puberty the period of sexual development terminating with capability to reproduce

punishers consequences applied after a behavior that decrease the behavior

punishment something aversive added or applied in response to an undesired behavior

raking grasp grasp of objects by raking with palm of the hand

reciprocity the activity of one that occurs as a direct result of stimuli from another

reflex sum total of any particular involuntary activity

reflux backward or return flow

reinforcers an individually designed consequence that increases the behavior that precedes it

renourishment to provide appropriate nourishment to an individual who is malnourished

resting metabolic rate the energy expended by a person at rest under conditions of thermal neutrality

Rett syndrome a degenerative disorder affecting only females; characterized by autistic behavior, dementia, seizures, ataxia, and loss of purposeful use of the hands

roentgenographic studies the study of x-rays

rooting a food-seeking movement which occurs in response to stimulation of the lips or cheeks; the head turns toward the stimulus and the mouth opens

Russell Silver syndrome a syndrome of malformation with short stature of prenatal onset, skeletal asymmetry, and small incurved fifth finger

School Breakfast Program a federal breakfast feeding program for school children in the U.S.

secondary sexual characteristics outward features of male or female sexuality

"secular trend" (of menarche) tendency for women to menstruate at younger ages throughout the world

sedentary inactive

self-esteem satisfaction in oneself

separation anxiety to be fearful of being independent, especially of one's parents

sepsis infection in the blood stream

set-point theory the theory that a certain body weight is physiologically normal for each person

sexual maturity the stage of development in reproductive capability toward the maximal development

shaping the reinforcement of successive approximations to a desired behavior

spasticity a state of hypertonicity or increase over normal tone in the muscles

specific dynamic action increase in metabolism as a result of extra heat production when food is digested, absorbed, and metabolized

spermarche initial semen production

"sports anemia" iron deficiency anemia associated with a high level of physical activity

staple food a primary food in the diet

stomach capacity the volume of fluid or masticated food that the stomach is able to contain at one time

sucrose table sugar; made from cane or beet sugar; it is a disaccharide consisting of glucose and fructose which is readily split into those components by intestinal sucrase

superobesity the definition of children with triceps skinfold measurements greater than or equal to the 95th percentile in the NHANES cycle 3 or 3 sample of children

suprao.bital situation above the bone cavity that contains the eyeball

tactile pertaining to the sense of touch

tactile sensitivity a state or quality of being unusually responsive to touch

tasks of adolescence goals of psychological and social development

technical complications difficulties in providing parenteral nutrition precipitated by the technique in use

tetany a syndrome characterized by muscle twitchings, cramps, and convulsions

"The Farm" a cooperative vegetarian community in Tennessee

three levels of neonatal care nurseries are classified as level I, II, or III based on care they can provide, e.g., Level I nurseries provide uncomplicated care, Level II nurseries care for normal newborns and screen and refer high-risk infants, and Level III nurseries cope with the most serious neonatal illnesses

tongue thrust moving the tongue through the lips when swallowing, normally associated with suckling in infants less than 4 months of age; an abnormal reflex in some individuals with motor coordination difficulties

tonic characterized by continuous tension

tonic bite reflex an automatic clamping of the teeth on any food, implement, or other article placed in the mouth

tonic neck pattern when the head is turned forcibly to one side the arm and leg on that side will extend while the opposite arm and leg will be flexed; described as the fencing position

total parenteral nutrition provision of all nutrients into a large central vein, usually the superior vena cava

toxicity the quality of being poisonous

toxicology the study of poisons

transferrin serum B-globulin that binds and transports iron

trisomy three of a particular chromosome

trophic effects the stimulation of cell reproduction and enlargement

Turner syndrome a syndrome resulting from chromosomal abnormalities characterized by short stature, sexual infantilism, and a webbed neck in females

vegan (pure vegetarian) a person who consumes only foods of plant origin and excludes all animal protein from the diet

vegetarian a person who consumes primarily plant foods (grains, legumes, vegetables, and fruits) and eliminates meats, poultry, and fish from the food pattern; dairy foods and eggs may be consumed

very low density lipoproteins protein in combination with fat which transports endogenous triglycerides in the blood

volvulus an intestinal obstruction caused by twisting of the bowel

weaning changing nourishment to another form other than breastfeeding

weight management to provide nourishment to maintain a person's weight at a stable and appropriate level

whey the residue of milk remaining after the curd and cream have been removed

Williams syndrome a syndrome characterized by mental retardation, unusual facies, and cardiovascular abnormalities

Index

Page numbers in *italics* indicate boxes and illustrations.
Page numbers followed by *t* indicate tables.

419